Marc Blitzstein

Also by Howard Pollack

Walter Piston
Harvard Composers: Walter Piston and His Students, from Elliott Carter
to Frederic Rzewski
John Alden Carpenter: A Chicago Composer
Aaron Copland: The Life and Work of an Uncommon Man
George Gershwin: His Life and Work

Marc Blitzstein

His Life, His Work, His World

HOWARD POLLACK

OXFORD
UNIVERSITY PRESS

OXFORD
UNIVERSITY PRESS

Oxford University Press is a department of the University of Oxford.
It furthers the University's objective of excellence in research,
scholarship, and education by publishing worldwide.

Oxford   New York
Auckland   Cape Town   Dar es Salaam   Hong Kong   Karachi
Kuala Lumpur   Madrid   Melbourne   Mexico City   Nairobi
New Delhi   Shanghai   Taipei   Toronto

With offices in
Argentina   Austria   Brazil   Chile   Czech Republic   France   Greece
Guatemala   Hungary   Italy   Japan   Poland   Portugal   Singapore
South Korea   Switzerland   Thailand   Turkey   Ukraine   Vietnam

Oxford is a registered trade mark of Oxford University Press in the UK and certain other countries.

Published in the United States of America by Oxford University Press
198 Madison Avenue, New York, NY 10016

Library of Congress Cataloging-in-Publication Data
Pollack, Howard.
Marc Blitzstein: his life, his work, his world / Howard Pollack.
p.   cm.
Includes bibliographical references and index.
ISBN 978-0-19-979159-0 (alk. paper)
1. Blitzstein, Marc. 2. Blitzstein, Marc—Criticism and interpretation.
3. Composers—United States—Biography. I. Title.
ML410.B6515P65   2012
780.92—dc23
[B]
2011028591

3 5 7 9 8 6 4 2

Printed in the United States of America
on acid-free paper

to the memory of
William W. Austin
(1920–2000)

Marc Blitzstein's life exemplifies a truism that bears restatement today: Every artist has the right to make his art out of an emotion that really moves him. Those of our composers who are moved by the immense terrain of new techniques now seemingly within their grasp would do well to remember that humanity's struggle for a fuller life may be equally valid as a moving force in the history of music.

Aaron Copland, 1967

He can draw laughter and tears as few living composers can.

Virgil Thomson, 1941

CONTENTS

Marc Blitzstein

Introduction

On April 19, 1964, a few months after Marc Blitzstein's violent death the previous January, a large audience gathered at Philharmonic Hall at Lincoln Center for a memorial concert aimed at raising funds for a Marc Blitzstein Musical Theater Award, a prize still granted every few years to a composer, lyricist, or librettist by the American Academy of Arts and Letters. This lengthy tribute, organized in large part by Leonard Bernstein, Aaron Copland, and Lillian Hellman, featured stars from the theater and opera worlds that Blitzstein had helped bridge. Betty Comden, Howard Da Silva, Will Geer, Adolph Green, Barbara Harris, Phyllis Newman, and Charles Nelson Reilly performed scenes from *The Cradle Will Rock* (for which Blitzstein had written both the libretto and the music), with Bernstein accompanying at the piano, as he had done some twenty-five years earlier when he presided over the work's Boston-area premiere as a Harvard undergraduate; an ensemble headed by Phyllis Curtin and William Wilderman performed excerpts from another of Blitzstein's operas, *Regina*, with Julius Rudel conducting and Lillian Hellman (on whose play, *The Little Foxes*, the work had been based) providing some narration; and actor José Ferrer, chanteuse Anita Ellis, and tenor Luigi Alva sang solos from dramatic works left unfinished at the time of the composer's sudden death. Blitzstein's wide range might have been evidenced still further had the concert also featured Louis Armstrong, Bobby Darin, or Ella Fitzgerald, all of whom recently had had hits with "Mack the Knife" from the composer's successful adaptation of Bertolt Brecht and Kurt Weill's *The Threepenny Opera*.

The participants and spectators who attended this event presumably had some familiarity with Blitzstein's career, including the legendary circumstances surrounding the premiere of *The Cradle Will Rock* (1937), whose telling they now heard as recorded by the composer himself. Some further would have known something about his early days as a piano prodigy in his native Philadelphia; his musical studies with Alexander Siloti and Rosario Scalero at home (1923–26) and Nadia Boulanger and Arnold Schoenberg abroad (1926–27); his association with Orson Welles, John Houseman, and the Mercury Theatre (1937–39); his collaborations with such outstanding film documentarians as Joris Ivens, Willard Van Dyke, Leo Hurwitz, Paul Strand, Garson Kanin, and Carol Reed (1937–45); his *Airborne Symphony* for soloists, chorus, and orchestra (1946), first introduced by the young Leonard Bernstein with Orson Welles as the monitor; his ballet *The Guests* (1949), which had occasioned choreographer Jerome Robbins's first work for the New York City Ballet; the slow acceptance of *Regina* (1949), whose faltering run on Broadway had prompted a group of theatrical luminaries, including Bernstein, Clifford Odets, Cole Porter, Jerome Robbins, and Tennessee Williams, to take out an advertisement in the *New York Times* urging audiences to see the work; his adaptation of *The Threepenny Opera* (1954), which by the time of its close in 1961 had broken the record for New York's longest-running musical; the sorry histories of his last completed musical dramas, *Reuben Reuben* (1955) and *Juno* (1959); and his unfinished opera on the controversial subject of Sacco and Vanzetti. Whatever their knowledge of the particulars of his life and work, for many at this benefit concert, Blitzstein represented not only a consummate master of his profession, but a model of social conscience and moral integrity all the more impressive for tackling the commercial confines of Broadway.

The Cradle Will Rock and *Regina*, the latter in recent years a star vehicle for Lauren Flanigan, Patti LuPone, Carol Neblett, and Catherine Malfitano among others, continue to be performed, as do other works by the composer, including his adaptation of *The Threepenny Opera*. And yet Blitzstein has become a much dimmer figure today than in 1964, a landmark biography by Eric Gordon (1989) and a monumental bio-bibliography by Leonard Lehrman (2005) notwithstanding. Even the art music community has been neglectful, so much so that students of American history and theater often recognize his name sooner than classical musicians and music lovers, although he was above all a composer, and a highly accomplished one at that. And so while this book addresses literary, theatrical, cultural, and political matters, and aims as well to enlarge the biographical record, it also engages sketch and manuscript study and musical analysis so as to help elucidate Blitzstein's extraordinary achievement.

Because of the relative unfamiliarity of Blitzstein's work, readers might profitably consult recordings, videos, and scores in conjunction with this book. Among recordings currently available, a core Blitzstein discography would include Leonard Bernstein's first recording of the *Airborne Symphony* (RCA Victor) and the original cast albums of *The Cradle Will Rock* (Musicraft) and *No for an Answer* (Keynote), all three of which are available on a two-CD release, *Marc Blitzstein: Musical Theatre Premières* (Pearl); a more complete recording of *The Cradle*, such as that by the Acting Company (Jay) or the Blank Theatre Company (Lockett Palmer); the New York City Opera recording of *Regina* (Columbia/Masterworks Broadway); the original cast albums of *The Threepenny Opera* (MGM/Decca) and *Juno* (Columbia/Fynsworth Alley); and *Marc Blitzstein: Zipperfly and Other Songs* (Koch), a good sampling of the composer's theater and art songs as performed by baritone William Sharp, soprano Karen Holvik, and pianist Steven Blier.

Other outstanding items in print include *Marc Blitzstein: First Life*, a release of several early piano and chamber works (Other Minds); recordings of *The Harpies* with the Gregg Smith Singers (Premier) and the Piano Concerto with pianist Michael Barrett under Lukas Foss (CRI); Bernstein's second recording of the *Airborne Symphony* (Columbia/Sony); and the Scottish Opera recording of *Regina* (London).

Some important recordings released in 78 and 33 rpm format await commercial transfer to compact disc, including the original cast recording of *I've Got the Tune* (Musicraft); *Marc Blitzstein: Songs of the Theater*, with mezzo-soprano Muriel Smith singing a few Blitzstein songs accompanied by the composer (Concert Hall); *American Composers at the Piano*, with Blitzstein performing three movements from the ballet *Show*, an early incarnation of *The Guests* (Concert Hall); *Marc Blitzstein and his Theatre Compositions*, with the composer both discussing his work and accompanying several singers on selected numbers (Westminster); Blitzstein's demo recordings for *Juno* (Box Office); and the Theater Four production of *The Cradle Will Rock* starring Jerry Orbach (MGM/CRI). Important archival recordings, including a performance of the *Orchestra Variations* by the American Composers Orchestra under Dennis Russell Davies, demo recordings and a complete taped performance of *Reuben Reuben*, and the 1964 Marc Blitzstein memorial concert discussed above, also remain commercially unavailable. However, some of this material can be accessed through libraries or online sites, as can videotaped performances of the Theater Four and Acting Company productions of *The Cradle*, broadcast on CBS and PBS in 1964 and 1986, respectively. (The earlier broadcast, which contains only excerpts, also forms part of a documentary about Blitzstein released by Creative Arts Television.)

Fortunately, all five surviving films for which Blitzstein provided the music can be readily acquired, including *Hände* and *Surf and Seaweed* (both Image Entertainment, with the score to the former played by the composer, the latter realized electronically by Eric Beheim); *The Spanish Earth* (Sling Shot, the score compiled from popular Spanish recordings by Blitzstein and Virgil Thomson); the reedit of *Valley Town* (Prelinger Archives, with the stronger original version housed at the Metropolitan Museum of Art); and *Native Land* (Kino). The scores for these pictures—the first two benchmarks in early avant-garde filmmaking, the latter three, in social documentary filmmaking—represent a particularly undervalued part of Blitzstein's legacy.

By contrast, with the principal exception of the theater and art songs found in the three-volume *Marc Blitzstein Songbook* (Boosey & Hawkes), commercially published scores remain hard to come by, although a fair number of works—including *Triple-Sec*, *The Harpies*, the Piano Concerto, the *Orchestra Variations*, *The Cradle Will Rock*, the *Airborne Symphony*, *The Guests*, and *Regina*—can be obtained through libraries or rental agencies. Moreover, the public has access to virtually the composer's entire oeuvre by way of the Marc Blitzstein Papers at the Wisconsin Center for Film and Theater Research in Madison, a collection available on microfilm through interlibrary loan.

Several names recur with such frequency in the course of this book, especially as sources, that identifying them here might be helpful as well: the composer's sister and brother-in-law Josephine (Jo) and Edward (Ed) Davis, and their children, Stephen and Christopher Davis; his wife Eva Goldbeck; his friends Berenice Skidelsky, Minna Lederman, and Mina Curtiss; his colleagues Aaron Copland, David Diamond, Leonard Bernstein, and Ned Rorem; and his biographer Eric Gordon. In order to avoid confusion, the book often refers to Blitzstein's relatives by their first rather than their last names, including Eva Goldbeck after she became Mrs. Blitzstein in early 1933 (although she continued to use Goldbeck in a professional capacity).

In quoting and citing sources, I have endeavored to retain the syntax, punctuation, and spelling of the original texts, including Blitzstein's occasional habit of not capitalizing certain proper names. Especially in the endnotes, I refer to several New York papers without necessarily mentioning their identifying city, including the [New York] *Daily Mirror, Daily News, Herald Tribune, Journal-American, Post, Sun, Times,* and *World-Telegram.* Note too that endnote numbers refer back to entire paragraphs.

As for the book's multitudinous debts, only a few can be mentioned here. The composer's nephews Stephen and Christopher Davis crucially aided my work, including providing me with a copy of their uncle's voluminous papers on microfilm. Brent Oldham and John Ellis similarly helped me gather recordings. Eric Gordon and Leonard Lehrman generously offered expert guidance, increasing all the more the enormous amount I owe them for their published work. Numerous librarians, scholars, and administrators assisted my research, especially Katie Buehner of the Music Library at the University of Houston, but including as well George Boziwick and Jonathan Hiam of the Music Division at the New York Public Library for the Performing Arts; Stephen Luttmann of the Music Library at the University of Northern Colorado; Gina Genova-Duffy of the American Composers Alliance; Mary Kiffer of the Guggenheim Memorial Foundation; Harry Miller and Dorinda Hartmann of the Wisconsin Historical Society; Kim Kowalke and Dave Stein of the Kurt Weill Foundation; and Mark Horowitz, Ray White, and others of the Music Division at the Library of Congress. John Grimmett, Meghan Hendley, Jennifer Kobuskie, Alex Lawler, Gail O'Brien Stewart, and Daniel Zajicek also provided excellent assistance. Christopher Davis, Stephen Davis, Eric Gordon, Alex Jeschke, Leonard Lehrman, Tony Sessions, and Wayne Shirley knowledgeably commented on the entire book in manuscript, and Steven Cassedy, Andrew Davis, Tim Koozin, Richard C. Norton, and other friends and colleagues helped revise sections. Editor Thomas Finnegan and indexer Sue Marchman ably helped ready the book for publication. Lastly, Edenfred in Madison, Wisconsin, graciously awarded me a brief residency, and the Kurt Weill Foundation of Music, the National Endowment of the Humanities, and the University of Houston gave financial support in the form of grants.

1

The Boy from Philadelphia

Born in Philadelphia on March 2, 1905, Marcus (Marc) Samuel Blitzstein was of Jewish-Russian descent. His paternal grandparents—Moishe (Marcus) Lionel (M. L.) Blitzstein (1846?–1897), for whom in part he was named, and Chana (Anna) Galanter (1854?–1929)—had left Odessa, Ukraine perhaps in the 1880s, and apparently made their way to the Galician town of Podwoloczyska (like Odessa, then part of the Russian empire) and onward to Southampton and Liverpool before arriving in Philadelphia in 1889. Alternately transliterated as Blitstein, Blistein, and so forth, the name Blitzstein possibly originated from the Yiddish word for "lightning stone" or "bloodstone." (Like his friend Leonard Bernstein, Marc Blitzstein used the German pronunciation of his surname, "Blitzstyne," as opposed to the more Yiddish-American "Blitzsteen.") Chana's surname, meanwhile, derived from "galanterie," that is, a dealer in leather or fancy goods.[1]

Of Marcus and Anna's eleven children, seven survived infancy: Samuel (Sam) (1879–1945), the composer's father, and his slightly younger brother Jacob (b. 1880); and the sisters Sonia (Sophie) (b. 1871), Rosalie (Rose) (b. 1873), Jenny (b. 1876), Alberta (b. 1884), and Miriam (Mary) (b. 1887), the last named born in Podwoloczyska. Alberta died at age five, before the family left England (a tragedy that allegedly precipitated their departure), while Jacob died at age eighteen in 1898 in Philadelphia, the victim of a ruptured appendix.

At the time of the family's arrival in 1889, Philadelphia, with a population of about a million, was the third largest city in the country. Historically a major port of entry for immigrants (with many, like the Blitzsteins, coming from Liverpool), the city over time laid claim to large numbers of Englishmen, Scots, Germans, Irish, and, by the end of the nineteenth century, Italians, Russians, and Poles. By 1915, immigrants accounted for around one-quarter of the total population, but the town remained nonetheless a conservative Republican stronghold and, in the words of Henry James, "settled and confirmed and content" as compared to the only somewhat larger cities of New York and Chicago.[2]

Soon after arriving in Philadelphia, the Blitzsteins settled at 431 South Fourth Street, a three-story building at the northeast corner of Lombard and South Fourth in the center of a once-genteel but long-dilapidated area of town near the Delaware River. Since the 1880s home to many Jewish immigrants from Eastern

Europe, this historic district, traditionally known as Society Hill, at the time was referred to as "the Jewish quarter" or more generally as "downtown" or the "slums." As in New York's larger but similarly congested Jewish ghetto on Manhattan's Lower East Side, the area teemed with retail stores, food markets, synagogues, sweatshops, and bathhouses.[3]

After some involvement in the tobacco business, in January 1891, Marcus and Anna established in their South Fourth row house what would become one of the quarter's preeminent institutions, M. L. Blitzstein and Company, a so-called immigrant bank. As with other such businesses, the Blitzstein company began as a storefront money and ticket-order office, exchanging and transmitting currency and selling steamship tickets on credit. Their agents even greeted newly arriving immigrants at the docks, for which the Blitzstein address, located close to the city's wharves and down the street from a Wayfarer's Home ("Hakhnosses Orkhim," also known as Abraham's Hotel), was well situated. Serving the city's Eastern European Jews—as opposed to a nearby rival, the Rosenbaum bank, which catered to German Jews, many situated further north, past Market Street—the bank further offered legal and business advice, often in Yiddish, to these "greenhorns," who occasionally took a meal or even lodging with the Blitzsteins. This background plainly affected the young composer, whose dramatic work would deal at times tangentially, at times centrally, with both immigrants and the poor. In such an environment, the young Marc naturally picked up some Russian and Yiddish, anticipating his later familiarity with Latin, French, German, Italian, and Spanish, among other languages.[4]

Although a banker, Marcus apparently had socialist convictions, which he bequeathed to both son Sam and grandson Marc. After Marcus's death in 1897, Anna—known in the family as "Babushka" ("grandmother")—assumed control of the business. Assisted by Sam, who became a naturalized citizen in 1896, and daughter Sophie's husband Constantine Borisevich Voynow, Anna expanded operations, converting the company into a bona fide bank with savings and checking accounts, although they continued to sell steamship tickets until closing their doors on December 23, 1930, and otherwise differed from "regular banking institutions," in the words of a Congressional oversight report of 1910, in that such banks "are without real capital, have little or no legal responsibility, and for the most part are entirely without legal control." In 1919, the bank opened, across the street from its old location, a new building on the northwest corner of Fourth and Lombard, an imposing limestone structure with a mezzanine inside.[5]

Anna Blitzstein was a remarkable matriarch: a Jewish woman banker at a time when the banking profession was inhospitable to both Jews and women. She became a community leader in other ways, serving intermittently as president of the aforementioned Wayfarer's Home as well as the same hotel's Old People's Home ("Moyshev Zkeynim"), which she founded in 1898. A surviving photograph registers a strongly determined countenance in contrast to her husband's milder gaze. After her death in 1929, she was accorded a public funeral at Kesher Israel, the synagogue—once home to a Universalist church—located down the street from the bank, a rare honor for a woman during these years.[6]

Anna's daughter Rose also blazed trails; as one of the city's first women obstetrician-gynecologists, she held a supervisory position in the Jewish Maternity Hospital and lived with a woman pharmacist, Fanny Slobodkin. The other girls married: Sophie, to Constantine Voynow, as mentioned; Jenny, to shirt manufacturer William Tutelman; and Mary, to Marcus Zamustin, an importer and amateur violinist, and after his death, to Charles Silverman.[7]

Meanwhile, the composer's maternal grandparents—Louis Levitsky (Levitt) (dates unknown) and Khaye (Clara) Baumfeld-Kaufman (ca. 1870–1914)— emigrated to America from their native Russia around 1878, first settling in Baltimore, but by the 1890s, in Philadelphia. They had several children, including the composer's mother Anna (1882–1970). While living in Baltimore, Louis and Clara Levitt—along with Clara's sister, Bracha (Bessie)—became drawn to the stage under the spell of the outstanding Yiddish actor Boris Thomashefsky, whom all three befriended. Bessie subsequently married Boris and became a leading Yiddish actor in her own right; in contrast, Louis Levitt's acting career, such as it was, proved only a sideline to his principal occupation as a businessman. After the Levitts moved to Philadelphia, Clara, in 1891, helped co-found the Wayfarer's Hotel, a charitable activity that surely brought her into contact with her daughter Anna's future mother-in-law, Anna Blitzstein.

Sam Blitzstein and Anna Levitt married on April 30, 1901, and had their first child, Josephine (Jo) (1902–1987), the following year. Their second and last child, Marc, was born three years later at 419 Pine Street, on the northwest intersection of Pine and South Lawrence Street (now Lawrence Court), around the corner from the bank, although as a child, he and his family resided mostly with the formidable senior Anna Blitzstein at 431 South Fourth. Marc presumably attended nearby George M. Wharton public school, where he skipped two grades. And in lieu of a formal Jewish education, he and Jo attended Sunday school at the ecumenical Ethical Culture Society, an organization with which various family members were affiliated. Never studying Hebrew (until late in life) or participating in a bar mitzvah, Blitzstein recalled that his parents viewed "all religions as delightful poetic myths."[8]

Sam was charming and gregarious, content, it seems, with the modest middle-class income afforded by the family bank, indeed, far less interested in business than in women, food, drink, and lively conversation. Like his son, who strongly resembled him in many ways, he could be delightful or exasperating, according to his friend Helen Hough: "Whenever you went out with Sam there was something bound to happen which was funny or silly or sometimes awful." Sam, who reportedly hosted Maxim Gorky on the Russian playwright's trip to Philadelphia, spent some time on the vaudeville stage, so that son Marc inherited his love for the performing arts from both sides of his family. Hough in particular recalled his "Sherlock by [Joe] Weber and [Lew] Fields" (presumably a comic sketch after Shakespeare), writing, "He [Sam] did not debase Shylock nor the man who made him. He just made it into a comi-tragedy, like Charlie Chaplin or the Irish." Even in later years, Sam would entertain his grandsons—Jo's sons Stephen and Christopher—singing the Tin Pan Alley hit "Ragtime Cowboy Joe" (1912) and other sometimes vaguely Jewish songs, occasionally accompanying himself with knives. Marc remembered too not only Sam's way with knives, but the "sound of my father's whistling—that piercing two-pitched sound which is a prolonged *ssss* instead of everybody else's *whhhh*."[9]

However, Sam's great passion was politics, as intimated by this recollection of Helen Hough:

> The only time he would interrupt himself would be to read a patch of news from a radical newspaper he always had around called the *Daily Worker*, or some thought which struck him as outrageous from the regular newspapers or some thought which struck him as particularly apt from the little tracts he always had around. At such times he would read with spelled out emphasis and inordinate attention, hold the paper close to his eyes, and pointing to the print with the hand which wasn't holding the paper. Suddenly he would look up, transfixing his audience with an intent expectant look, and he would remark extravagantly on his opinion of what he had just read. . . . He would thunder insults at the intelligence of all present who did not rise to his defense and mutter that they would see, then relapse into a morose fit from which it was impossible to dislodge him for an hour or more. Then the appearance of food or a new visitor would rouse him against his will.

Sam urged that Hough wrestle with the writings of Karl Marx, V. I. Lenin, and Wilhelm Pieck, which suggests that although his earliest political associations seemed to have been socialist—Jo remembered that she and Marc would accompany him to meetings of the Socialist Literary Society—he later became more decisively communist in orientation, an inference supported not only by his many later activities on behalf of the Soviet Union, but by a letter that his son wrote to the artist Julian Levi in early 1934 inviting the latter to a reception for his father and stepmother in which he was "getting up strictly Communist companies for them." In any case, through her interaction with Sam, Hough "learned that the most wonderful thing in life can be the successful communication of an idea from one person to another," a lesson son Marc took to heart as well.[10]

Anna remains a more indistinct figure. As the daughter of amateur actors and the niece of the celebrated Thomashefskys, she presumably shared something of Sam's interest in the theater. Indeed, a marginal comment jotted down by the composer late in life suggests that she possibly introduced him to some operatic repertoire.

At the very least, she plainly supported her son's musical education, even in hard times. Her two grandsons remembered her as compliant and sweet, and as someone closer to Jewish traditions than their grandfather Sam.[11]

Marc grew up among the extended Blitzstein family, becoming especially close to the Voynows, in particular his cousins Lionel (Leo) (b. 1900), who played piano and who died in the influenza epidemic of 1918; and Andrew (Andy) (1905–1993), who eventually became a correspondent for the *Moscow Times* and married film director Sergei Eisenstein's wife's sister. Another Voynow cousin, Vera, became an architect and the mother of Robert Fagles, whose career as an outstanding translator of Homer and Virgil echoed after a fashion Blitzstein's own achievements as a translator. Over time, Marc grew increasingly apart from his more distant relatives on both sides of his family, although his Broadway career brought him into contact with his first cousin once removed, Ted Thomas, the son of Boris and Bessie Thomashefsky (and the father of conductor Michael Tilson Thomas, who was thus a second cousin to Marc Blitzstein as they shared the same great-grandparents).

In 1912, Blitzstein's parents separated over his father's infidelity, although the divorce was not finalized until 1920, when his mother was able to prove adultery. Anna suddenly found herself in straitened circumstances and dependent on her own family for support. Following her mother's death in 1914, she took the children to live for three years with her sister Sadie and brother-in-law Herman in Venice, California, near Los Angeles, where Marc attended junior high and Santa Monica High School. During this time, Marc and Jo, although greatly upset by the separation, amused themselves by going dancing at the Santa Monica pier, seeing movies in downtown Los Angeles, and making up their own stories in which, according to Christopher Davis, "their grownup characters triumphed, grew rich, rewarded their mother for her determination, and, royally, forgave and continued to love their father who assured them of his own love in infrequent letters."[12]

In early 1917, Anna and the children returned to Philadelphia, where Marc completed junior high and attended West Philadelphia High School (1917–21). During these years, the family lived in two largely Jewish enclaves, first at 4204 Parkside Avenue and then at 1418 Broad Street. In high school, Marc took classes in English, French, Latin, drawing, various sciences, and banking procedures—perhaps with an eye to going into the family business—and participated as well in the glee club and the dramatic club. His high school friends included Lillian Apotheker, whom Eva Goldbeck described as his "childhood sweetheart," and who eventually married Walter Lowenfels, a poet Blitzstein admired. Graduating first in his class, Blitzstein gave the school valedictory address in June 1921.[13]

About this time, Marc developed an important friendship with a friend and former Cornell classmate of his young aunt Mary's, Berenice Skidelsky (1887–1984), who had moved from Philadelphia to New York to pursue a literary career.

"He [Marc] thinks I hold some key to the puzzle of life," Skidelsky wrote in her 1921 diary. In the early 1930s, Skidelsky became convinced that communism offered, as she wrote in 1936, "the one hope of mankind," a hope more or less held throughout her life, as evidenced by her journals, which make occasional references to Marc and his family (father Sam wanted to marry her in 1927). "I embrace Marxism," she wrote in 1944, "on the ground that it would liberate the self, would give it, for the first time in all history, the opportunity for fullest expression and growth." Skidelsky's views plausibly influenced Blitzstein's parallel ones. At the least, she introduced him to the poetry of James Stephens and told him "that it was more important to Be than to Do."[14]

Skidelsky proved one of the first of several intellectual, progressive, often older Jewish women with whom Blitzstein developed some of his most intimate ties, including not only his wife Eva Goldbeck, but patron Claire Reis, editor Minna Lederman, writer Mina Kirstein Curtiss, playwright Lillian Hellman, and editor and philanthropist Irene Diamond. But only his relationship with Goldbeck and perhaps Curtiss rivaled that with sister Jo, the prototype for all these other friendships. In a letter to Jo from 1929, Blitzstein spoke of their inordinate closeness as follows: "I am not shocked at your incestuous instincts; as you must know, I have known about them as long as you have—perhaps longer; a great portion of our 'rapport,' and the largest part of the reason we understand each other in a unique way is engendered by it. I have no such inclinations (I couldn't have) [an apparent reference to his homosexuality]; but I have always known that you are and probably always (ultimately) will be the most important person for me." And in early 1931, after returning to the States from Europe, he wrote to his future wife Eva Goldbeck, "Only one thing, of things I find in America, remains steadfast: Jo. We have come together beautifully; a union conditioned by her hero-worship of me, and my reluctant acceptance of it." Jo more simply described her relationship with Marc as "more like mother and son than sister and brother."[15]

As with all of Blitzstein's relationships, theirs could become turbulent. "It is our doom," he wrote to her in 1942, "to keep torturing ourselves by guilt about each other; we should simply call a truce and a halt." And she admitted that he "could be quite difficult." But their profound devotion to each other never wavered, and in the course of his life, she provided him with more material and emotional support than anyone else. Moreover, this close bond surely colored Blitzstein's creative imagination, as suggested by the sister-brother relationships that course through his dramatic work, including Intersecta and Rectangula in *Parabola and Circula*, the Mister children and Ella and Joe in *The Cradle Will Rock*, the Hubbard siblings in *Regina*, and Mary and Johnny in *Juno*.[16]

Jo and Marc remained solicitous toward both their parents as well. And if they harbored some resentment toward their mother, whom they thought overly dependent, and their father, whom they regarded as something of a wastrel, they also appreciated Anna's warmth and Sam's charm. Indeed, Marc credited his father as one of the great influences of his life, describing him as "a very sensitive, socially aware, vital and real person."[17]

Blitzstein began playing piano at an early age, although little is known about this, including when exactly he began lessons and with whom. No one else in his immediate family apparently played the piano or any instrument, although they all enjoyed music, including Jo, who in her younger days was something of a singer and over time developed a taste for such classics as Beethoven and Berlioz as well as more popular fare.

But in any event, Marc gained access to a piano early on: Berenice Skidelsky pictured him as an infant prodigy, clambering onto a piano stool at about age two-and-a-half, playing Mendelssohn's "Spring Song" and music from *The Tales of Hoffmann*, and proudly turning around to say, "Look, Aunt Mary, wif double notes!" At about the same age, he also amazed his parents by reproducing at the piano tunes he had heard his father whistle. After working with a woman teacher who discovered that he had perfect pitch, at age seven he entered the studio of Constantin von Sternberg, with whom he studied during the years 1912–14 and with whom he allegedly performed Mozart's "Coronation" Concerto.[18]

Born in St. Petersburg, von Sternberg (1852–1924) had studied with Ignaz Moscheles, Franz Liszt, Theodor Kullak, and Carl Reinecke before moving to the United States, where he settled in Philadelphia in 1890 and founded the Sternberg Conservatory of Music. According to composer George Antheil, another of his students, Sternberg offered a "severe theoretical" and "very splendid basic training." A composer in his own right, Sternberg—who, as Antheil recalled, disliked "the Debussy-Ravel school"—expressed his reverence for Bach and Beethoven in a series of lofty writings, including one essay, "National Music and the Negro," that argued for the potential of African-American folk music to white American composers. In general, his writings emphasized clarity of communication as an artistic and social ideal, with Blitzstein's famous parody of "Art for Art's Sake" in *The Cradle Will Rock* echoing Sternberg's remark, "'Art for Art's sake' is esthetic trumpery. 'Art for sensible, normal people's sake' is a far safer motto."[19]

After the family moved to California, Anna continued to nurture her son's remarkable talent as he continued private piano lessons from 1914 to 1916 with Katherine Montreville Cocke, a New England Conservatory graduate who used a pedagogical approach, the Fletcher Method, devised by Evelyn Fletcher-Copp; and then briefly in 1917 with Julian Pascal, the composer-pianist best remembered today for teaching Myra Hess. The young Marc possibly performed with an orchestra during this time, as one source reports such a performance at age nine.[20]

Returning to Philadelphia, he pursued his piano study from 1917 to 1918 under Maurits Leefson (1861–1926), a Dutch pianist who had moved to Philadelphia in 1887 and had founded his own conservatory in 1899. Marc then made his way to the Philadelphia Musical Academy, where he studied piano with the school's managing director, Dirk Hendrick Ezerman, for five years, from 1918 to 1922, that is, through his freshman year at the University of Pennsylvania.[21]

Born in Zierikzee, D. Hendrick Ezerman (1880–1928), another Dutchman, studied piano and cello at the Amsterdam Conservatory and toured extensively as a pianist before settling in Philadelphia in 1901. After his death as a result of injuries sustained in a trolley car accident, the music critic Philip Goepp wrote, "There was about the man a simplicity, a dignity, a sturdiness, a kindliness, that in their blending, wonderfully endeared him to a world of music lovers, colleagues and pupils." He also introduced Philadelphia audiences to "many unfamiliar modern works," according to his *New York Times* obituary.[22]

Blitzstein became one of the academy's star pupils, performing pieces by Chopin and Brahms at various concerts in the period 1919–21. In June 1921, he won the school's prestigious Gold Medal, and in June 1922, by this time a student at the University of Pennsylvania as well, he received the Philharmonic Society's Gold Medal, which meant a solo appearance with the Philharmonic Society Orchestra. Founded in the early nineteenth century, the Philharmonic— not to be confused with the Philadelphia Orchestra—performed at the city's Academy of Music during these years, usually under the baton of Josef Pasternack. Blitzstein duly made his debut with the orchestra under Pasternack on February 5, 1922, playing the Saint-Saëns Concerto in G minor, one of Ezerman's signature pieces.[23]

Blitzstein's performance impressed the critics. "'Ff' [fortissimo] meant 'ff' and a bit more to him," reported one paper. "His softer passages were light ripples of sound.... The pianist, a brilliant technician abounding in power and a deep poetic feeling, swept his audience with him in his interpretation. There is little of the academist about Mr. Blitzstein. He sought emotional expression and found it." "It does not shoot wide of the mark to state that he has genius . . . ," stated another review. "There were infinitely subtle shadings and nuanced tones ranging from gossamer lightness to crashing reverberations worthy of seasoned concert pianists. And through it all flowed a wonderful, innate sense of rhythm." These observations accorded with Blitzstein's own assessment of his pianism, which he contrasted with what the French call the "jeu perlé" ("pearly touch"), so appropriate to Chopin: "Me, I'm lighter and heavier than *jeu perle*; when I mean it, I sink and bang away; when I don't, you almost don't know the music is there. And yet, I have a feeling that my point of view is close to the method."[24]

Blitzstein's Saint-Saëns received an ovation from the audience, and after playing Tchaikovsky's "Troika" as an encore, he left the stage, "throwing his hands heavenward to indicate that he would play no more." He subsequently sent the rave reviews to Berenice Skidelsky, who detected a deep sadness in the accompanying letter. "He has much suffering ahead of him, no matter what his successes," she presciently noted in her journal. "Already his deepest intuitions are warning him that even in success one does not touch reality."[25]

By this time, indeed, by age fourteen, Blitzstein, who had long improvised at the piano, had begun to set his sights on becoming a composer rather than a concert pianist. "For one thing, I hated the drudgery of practicing," he later explained, adding on another occasion, "I'd have made a second-rate pianist anyway." While with Ezerman, he studied theory and composition with William Happich (1884–1950), and by the time he entered the Curtis Institute at age nineteen, he could claim several years' study of harmony, counterpoint, fugue, and formal analysis. A graduate of the Vienna Conservatory of Music, Happich—a noted conductor and violist—taught at the Philadelphia Musical Academy, where Blitzstein might have worked with him, and later at Temple University. Another of his students, J. Leon Lichtin, remembered him as "a tremendous teacher."[26]

Blitzstein's earliest known music dates from these teenage years, including the piano pieces *Waterfall* ("Barcarolle") (1918, conceived also with words as "Silver Stream"), *Andante* (1919), *Persienne* (1919), *Rondo* (1920), and Prelude in C minor (1922, apparently one of nine otherwise lost piano preludes composed that year); the string quartet, *For EmJo's "Bitter Fantasy"* (1923); and the song "Where Love Is Life" for baritone and piano (text, Duncan Campbell Scott) (1920). In 1920, he also wrote a one-movement orchestral work, the vigorous *Marche Vainqueur* ("A Festival March for Complete Orchestra," marked "Pomposo"), and in 1923, a symphonic poem for large orchestra, *Pandora* (lost). His Piano Sonata in F minor, various drafts of which survive, presumably dates from this period as well.[27]

The young composer also attempted his own setting of Louis Payen's libretto to Jules Massenet's last opera, *Cléopâtre* (1912), getting only as far, to judge from an extant sketch, as the opening chorus and part of Marc Antony's first solo, the music in the style of the original Massenet, which the Chicago Opera Association brought to Philadelphia on March 3, 1919, with soprano Mary Garden in the title role; so in all likelihood, Blitzstein, just turned fourteen, attended the opera (perhaps for his birthday), obtained the libretto, and then sought to recreate or embellish what he had heard at the Academy of Music. This would make the fragment contemporary with some of his earliest surviving pieces, a notion supported by the manuscript's child-like hand. At any rate, this parody strikingly recalls, at least in intention, Copland's youthful setting of a bit of the libretto to Pietro Mascagni's *Cavalleria rusticana*, an early and fascinating instance of numerous parallels that might be drawn between these two American composers. At the same time, Blitzstein's attraction to the glamorous Massenet versus Copland's to the rustic Mascagni suggests a contrast of temperament that foreshadows, among other things, differences between such mature works as Blitzstein's *Regina* and Copland's *The Tender Land*.[28]

As a whole, Blitzstein's youthful pieces, although rather rudimentary, display a bold adventurousness for a teenager of the time, their basically Romantic idiom enriched by some incorporation of the work of such composers as MacDowell, Debussy, and Scriabin along with American popular music, and perhaps Jewish

music as well. (In a "Musicredo" that Blitzstein "read with horror" in 1961 and
that he guessed dated from 1922, the young composer tellingly deemed jazz "a
significant and important phase of music" that "should produce those authentic
pieces of art, of which it so far evinces no slightest promise.") These early attempts
in particular show a characteristic tendency toward harmonic novelty, epitomized by the sonority that opens *Persienne*: a G-minor triad in the right hand
against an open B–F$^\sharp$ fifth in the left.[29]

Moreover, these pieces reveal an innate preoccupation with form, as suggested
by the "plans" set forth on the cover pages of some of the piano pieces, each consisting of an outline broken down into measure units. For example, he prefaced
Andante as follows: "1. Small 3 Part Primary Form (8+8+6), 2. Small 2 Part Primary Form (10 [repeated] 10 [repeated]), Return of 1., elaborated (8+8+8+6+8+6),
Coda (11)." Blitzstein presumably sketched out these plans before committing
pen to paper. Whether such an approach was Happich's, his own, or someone
else's, not only did he remain highly concerned with form, but he actually used
this very method as late as the aria "What Will It Be?" from his opera *Regina*
(1949).

In the fall of 1921, Blitzstein entered the University of Pennsylvania as a merit
scholar and spent three semesters there before taking a temporary leave of
absence, which developed into a permanent one. (His sister Jo, who spent the
1922 calendar year at the university's School of Education, perhaps not coincidentally left school at about this same time.) During these years and beyond, he
shared a room with his father at 4122 Girard, conveniently located near the Penn
campus. Meanwhile, in 1921, his mother married a local doctor, Bernard Segal,
whose former wife, Pauline, had been Sam's mistress, and whose three daughters
included Vivienne Segal, already by this time a Broadway star.

Although Penn offered a degree in music, with nearly all of its music courses
taught by Hugh Clarke, an organist-composer who had been on the faculty for
over forty-five years, Blitzstein did not enroll in any music classes during his three
semesters there. Rather, he took Latin and French and pursued other subjects,
including Indian studies (Sanskrit 6), an interest presumably related not only to
Persienne for piano, but to *Svarga*, a ballet he composed in the mid-1920s. In addition, he spent time discussing "girls, Bach, and psychoanalysis" with friends and
"timidly trying my first-legs in sex," as he told Berenice Skidelsky. An admirer of
Rupert Brooke, George Meredith, and James Stephens, he also wrote poems,
three of which he sent Skidelsky in November 1921, including one, "Poet-
Student," that began, "Demurely as a debutante/he settles him at the study desk,"
and that decades later elicited this comment scribbled in the margins: "Something
very wrong here—what a conceited brat I was!" By the following fall, Blitzstein
had become familiar as well with the sophisticated imagist Richard Aldington,
his own poems revealing a corresponding ripening, as in "Hint," a short poem
dated November 9, 1922:

It is not commonly voiced about
that people, with fire in their eyes.
dance one gleam, then flatten

We are loth to tell you
that under the peak of your sky.
(stark and brave and wild, you think it)
a cobweb feels for musty places to hang on,
clings....[30]

Blitzstein did well in all his classes except physical education, which he failed during his second semester. Although athletic and an avid swimmer, he objected to the idea of having to take a gym class, a reason given for his failure to return to school. More to the point, perhaps, he planned to start studying piano with Alexander Siloti (Ziloti) (1863–1945), who apparently advised against college if he wanted a musical career. But although he never completed college, Blitzstein read voraciously throughout his life and became exceptionally knowledgeable about a wide range of topics.[31]

Blitzstein saw Siloti about every other week during the academic year, apparently from the spring of 1923 through the spring of 1926, traveling up to the Russian's apartment in the Ansonia Hotel on Manhattan's Upper West Side for lessons. (Blitzstein took advantage of these trips by socializing with his stepsister Vivienne Segal and her theater friends and by attending such shows as Eugene O'Neill's *Welded* and *Desire Under the Elms*.) How Blitzstein discovered Siloti, who only recently had arrived in the States, remains unknown, although he might have heard him perform at the Academy of Music on January 29, 1922. In the event, Blitzstein reportedly became his first American pupil.[32]

Although Siloti taught at Juilliard from 1925 to 1942, he never achieved the fame in America that he had in Russia, in part because he made few public appearances in his later years. Born in the Ukraine, he had studied piano with Nikolay Rubinstein and theory with Tchaikovsky at the Moscow Conservatory, and then piano with Liszt in Weimar. Back in Russia, he distinguished himself as a pianist, composer, and teacher, his students including his cousin Serge Rachmaninoff. He also directed a concert series in St. Petersburg, the Siloti Concerts (1903–17), that presented new works by Debussy, Stravinsky, Prokofiev, and others, thereby rivaling the similarly adventurous Serge Koussevitzky Concerts in Moscow. He left Soviet Russia in 1919, settling in New York some two years later.

Siloti possibly taught Blitzstein in a French spiced with other languages, as he was wont to do. Benning Dexter, a student from the 1930s, recalled that Siloti began every student with "a technical routine" derived from either Beethoven's *Thirty-Two Variations* or Mendelssohn's *Variations sérieuses*, after which students could choose their own repertoire. Dexter and other students further remembered Siloti as a figure of brusque vitality and refined elegance, a dichotomy that informed his piano playing and that perhaps not accidentally characterized Blitzstein as well. The young Philadelphian in any case established a warm relationship with both Siloti and his wife Vera, who in a 1923 letter to Blitzstein referred to him as one of her husband's "disciples." And in 1927, Siloti recommended Blitzstein for a Guggenheim fellowship, writing, "I consider him a talented and accomplished pianist, and a gifted and highly educated composer as well."[33]

In reminiscences of his childhood and his early life as a musical prodigy, Blitzstein typically described himself as a brilliant and charming "brat." "I became a most insufferable brat, precocious and spoiled," he once stated. "I didn't have to work nearly hard enough for my success, and I was completely cut off from my own contemporaries and really didn't know how to get on with them at all. I really was a horror." In a fragment entitled "Me," apparently intended for a never-completed autobiography, Blitzstein traced such traits back to his first recollection, when at age three he fell into a pail of boiling starch and suffered burns on his back and buttocks:

> I remember next a sofa, placed in the dining-room beside the kitchen; a sofa on which the injured child was laid upon his belly so he could have company all during the day, and be undisputed monarch of things and people in the room. And I remember the child, inexorably eking the last drop of sympathy from parents already shattered by guilt, looking pitifully up: "Mumsie, are you sorry? Are you sorry, mumsie?"
>
> Began the relentless career of a charming, talented, self-salving brat.
>
> I was angelically beautiful; I recited from memory stories and poems read to me once; I insisted on going to school (at age four) with my sister (aged seven) as a "visitor," staying to outsmart the entire class, and to proceed to further scholastic honors, "skipping" every year or so. The accident had as one result a series of night-attacks, "spasms," accompanied by delirium and screaming; occasionally I would come to during an attack, and continue it with nice theatrical flair and plausibility.

In a 1929 letter written to his sister from France, Blitzstein again alluded to the vanity that shadowed his childhood:

> Do you remember, when we were kids, a game we used to play? I was always the beggar, who cringed in the gutter; and you were the kind rich lady, who took me in, gave me rich clothes (a portiere or a trunk cover) to wear, and fed me dark and greasy slices of banana. I don't know who invented the idea; but it was bad for me. Probably even so early it was I who demanded the game. At any rate, what is going on in me now, what

has been going on for a couple of years, is a hellish struggle between this vanity of mine—it was an inverted vanity: being coddled, petted,—the greater the objectives the more ready and enthusiastic the coddling—between this vanity and a something else, which I can perhaps badly explain, and perhaps which you can understand without my explaining. I really ran away from America, as I feel you know. One of the reasons was that I was actually beginning to enjoy the nickle-plated adulation coming my way. Had I gone in for it seriously, I should have been doomed—a neat provincial "artist" taking in the shekels, and "believing" in himself. I take no great credit in avoiding it—after all, I ran away, my exit had the precipitateness of flight. What will happen here is my own problem.

By "nickle-plated adulation," Blitzstein presumably meant his early accomplishments as a pianist rather than as a composer. As for the "game" described above, it partook of those Horatio Algeresque sensibilities that colored some children's literature of the time, but it also likely derived from the spectacle of watching legions of immigrants approach his family for loans, or possibly his own dependence on his grandmother's largesse. At all events, the game seemed to resonate in the composer's theatrical depictions of such overbearing matrons as Mrs. Mister and Madame Arbutus, and found a particularly bitter echo in the song "Penny Candy" from *No for an Answer*.[34]

In later years, Blitzstein further described his demeanor to his colleague and friend David Diamond as one of "rigid social evenness"—"That [sic] I wouldn't give to have a taste of Aaron [Copland]'s perfect poise, or your perfect violence for a bit"—but he seems himself to have vacillated between these extremes of "poise" and "violence," remaining at times something of a "brat," and gaining the reputation of an *enfant terrible* in life as much as in art. He could be obstinate, argumentative, brusque, and he often seemed agitated, biting at his fingernails or gnawing at his moustache. He had some difficulty cultivating close friendships, writing to his sister while stationed in London during the Second World War, "I've become more or less a hermit; not new for me, but here people seem to think it strange. I think you know how lonely I can get, and how restless and nearly-rude I am when the substitution of polite conversation and milling-about-among-people is offered me."[35]

Minna Lederman, a good friend for many years, admitted that in his early thirties, in the wake of *The Cradle Will Rock*, Blitzstein became "grave, mature, worldly" and in general "adult and contained." But she added, "he never, alas, quite outgrew his early irascibility. His boiling point was unpredictable. . . . no one was too surprised to see him march into the Russian Tea Room and right out again, refusing to join a composers' gathering because a 'Trotskyite' was present." He could become particularly irritable about his work, especially during stressful rehearsal periods, when he might harangue colleagues or snap at friends. Aaron Copland, a devoted colleague, described him as "complicated and difficult at times," while another friend, Irma Bauman, reflected, "Marc was not an easy person to love. But we [she and her husband Mordecai] continued to love and admire him," the Baumans even naming their son Marc after him.[36]

Friends like these "continued to love and admire" Blitzstein in part because of those traits that served him since childhood: his charm—"the word often used to describe him was courtly," remembered Lederman—and his talent, the operative word here seeming to be "gifted," as in varied recollections of friends, colleagues, and teachers, including Siloti as seen above, although conductor Lehman Engel preferred the phrase "brilliant," using the word three times in a single paragraph about the composer. And his headstrong convictions, however wearisome, generally inspired from friends deep respect.[37]

Moreover, Blitzstein was in the end a thoughtful and generous person; even when financially strapped, as was often the case, he enjoyed picking up the bill in restaurants, buying costly gifts for friends and relations, and entertaining at home with flair, making a rite out of preparing canapés and mixing martinis ("he was very precise about how many times he waved the vermouth cork over the gin," soprano Brenda Lewis recalled). Mina Curtiss, who appreciated the exotic flowers he would send to her ship at various transatlantic crossings, wrote that the fresh caviar he would bring with him on visits to her estate "involved material sacrifices that I hated to think about." Producer Carmen Capalbo similarly recalled that although often "agitated" and "touchy," he was "kind and generous," a "wonderful person." Writer Joseph Stein thought him "the sweetest man I ever met." And his aunt Mary's granddaughter, Carol Zaleski, remembered the time she accidentally broke a folding wooden chair as a child and Blitzstein "tried to cheer me up by breaking it into smaller and smaller fragments to demonstrate that it was of no concern."[38]

Between the time Blitzstein left the University of Pennsylvania in early 1923 and entered the Curtis Institute a year-and-a-half later in the fall of 1924, some important family events transpired. In 1923, the composer's stepfather Bernard Segal died. And in June of that same year, his sister married Edward (Ed) Davis (1893–1987), a previously married Philadelphia attorney nearly ten years her senior whom she had met through mutual friends at a University of Pennsylvania football game. Davis came from an Orthodox Jewish family and had even studied to become a rabbi, although he had grown agnostic, if not as completely so as his wife and her family. A quiet and judicious man who tended to vote Republican, he was more conservative in his manner and politics than the Blitzsteins as well. At the same time, he led a successful career representing unions and did not interfere with his wife's leftist political activities. He also became very fond of Marc and welcomed his extended stays over the years, whether in Philadelphia or at one of their summer homes. The Davises had two children: Stephen (b. 1925), who became a banking attorney; and writer-sculptor Christopher (Kit) (b. 1928), who described his parents' marriage as "strong, loving, lasting," and whose romans à clef, *A Kind of Darkness* (1962) and *The Sun in Mid-Career* (1975), contained intriguing portrayals of various family members, the later novel in particular offering, in the figure of Alexis Weisshorn, as knowing a depiction of his uncle Marc, especially in the context of family life, as exists. After Jo's death in 1987, Stephen and Christopher became co-owners of their uncle's estate.[39]

Meanwhile, Marc—who as an adult stood lean and good-looking at five feet seven inches tall and about 140 pounds, with flashing blue-gray eyes, receding brown hair, and, by his mid-twenties, an ever-present moustache, and who impressed friends with his immaculate grooming and snappy attire—had begun to have romantic involvements of his own. In 1924, at age nineteen, he traveled to France with the conductor Alexander (Alex) Smallens, with whom he had his first known sexual relationship. Born in St. Petersburg, Smallens (1889–1972) grew up in New York and made his name in Chicago and elsewhere before establishing himself in Philadelphia as musical director of the Philadelphia Civic Opera (1924–31)—with which he gave the first American performances of Falla's *El amor brujo* (1927) and Strauss's *Feuersnot* (1927) and *Ariadne auf Naxos* (1928)—and assistant conductor of the Philadelphia Orchestra (1927–34); he also conducted the world premieres of Virgil Thomson's *Four Saints in Three Acts* (1934) and George Gershwin's *Porgy and Bess* (1935). For a while, Blitzstein remained friendly with Smallens, who premiered the composer's opera *Triple-Sec* (which Blitzstein dedicated to him) in 1929, and who conducted the scores to his films *Valley Town* (1940) and *Night Shift* (1942) as well. In a 1931 letter to his sister, however, he faulted Smallens for a lack of understanding of his music; and in a 1961 letter to his nephew Christopher, he referred to his relationship with the conductor, who had been "mad for years," as for some time "nonexistent."[40]

Back in Europe in 1929, Blitzstein also had sexual relations—perhaps his first—with women, but that same year he declared his basic homosexuality to, among others, his sister, which he did in a series of letters from France and Austria. (Blitzstein implied to Jo that their new stepmother already knew about his homosexuality, and that Sam probably knew as well, as father and son had lived together for years "during which I was certainly no virgin"; as it turned out, Jo herself suspected his homosexual orientation.) In one such letter to his sister dated August 29, Blitzstein spoke of prior attempts to suppress "the emotional—sexual au fond—thing," writing,

> It has become imperative at last that I cut out the "balance," the "control" (I am a pretty good actor, I project well, nearly everybody thought it was the real thing), and let out what has been secret and furtive in me for so long. Shame is the largest single enemy; the sense of being sick, of living a

diseased life, is another—the social obstacle, the individual one. I have reasoned it out, this time with my mind; until now what has gone on has been an instinctive process of self-protection, with my mind playing handmaiden to my cowardice,—evolving more-or-less successful methods of diverting the issue. Now, I accept what I am; really, knowing all it involves. . . . In this light, it is absurd to assert that there are no sins; there are definitely cardinal sins—sins against oneself, against one's law. My sin is, has been, vanity of this special sort; the willingness to corrupt my nature.

In another letter to Jo dated October 29, he speculated on the origins of his sexuality: "Whether or not my homosexuality can be traced to an original and repressed feeling for you, can only be guessed at. It was more likely due to a childhood among women (including Uncle Herman), and a natural distaste for boys' activities." And in a letter written on December 24, he elaborated further by describing himself as "bisexual":

By the way (this is for information) don't get the idea that I have a repressed horror for women. I believe I should be medically classed a bisexual, since I have had sexual experience with women, and liked it. That also Europe has done for me; I decided it was silly for me not to find out everything possible about myself; and so went through a series of self-imposed experiments in Cannes, which convince me that I'm quite there. If ever the social gesture is demanded of me (and I go so far as to consider marriage for me as a possible social gesture), I can accept or reject it as I choose, without any fear of incapacity.

Asked about Blitzstein's homosexuality in 1970, Henry Murray, the noted psychiatrist who had treated the composer's wife Eva in 1936, commented, "They [the Blitzsteins] were both so multiphasic sexual, that I couldn't put either one of them in any category. They were just anything at all. Animal, vegetable, mineral. I don't know. There was nothing that was the slightest bit normal about them at all."[41]

In still another letter from 1929, Blitzstein assured his sister that he had "no intention of wearing my sexual heart on my sleeve," that he would be discreet, especially with respect to their mother, as opposed to their father, "since I feel that he already knows, and might actually be helpful." True enough, Blitzstein took pains to keep his sexual life distant from, for instance, his nephews Stephen and Christopher, who even into their late adolescence had little inkling of their uncle's homosexuality. Indeed, when the nephews learned of this, they were all the more surprised because Marc seemed to them so masculine in appearance and behavior, even more so than their own father. Some of Blitzstein's friends, like Irma Bauman, similarly had scant knowledge of that part of his life.[42]

The specifics of Blitzstein's sexual and romantic life remain to a large extent unknown. In his younger days, including his eight-year romance and marriage to Eva Goldbeck, he appears to have had sex with both men and women; after Eva's death in 1936, he seems to have been exclusively homosexual, with one lover, Bill Hewitt, telling biographer Eric Gordon that Blitzstein was versatile in his lovemaking but preferred a more dominant role.[43]

Over the course of his life, Blitzstein apparently engaged in a good deal of casual gay sex, and while at times, especially during periods of intense work, he could withdraw into almost hermetic solitude, he prowled bars and other public places for sexual partners with some frequency. As late as 1961, at age fifty-five, he wrote to David Diamond from Rome that he kept his "social life to a minimum" to allow for "a maximum work-session, and a substantial time for sex." He appears to have been attracted to "rough trade," that is, masculine working-class men possibly heterosexual-identified but who had sex with other men as an accepted form of release or perhaps for favors of one kind or another. His penchant for sexual cruising and rough trade, which, his nephew Christopher sensed, "went into Marc's covenant with creative work," led to incidents of theft, abuse, and violence, including his eventual death in Martinique at the hands of three seamen.[44]

At the same time, Blitzstein had some more long-term homosexual relationships, although aside from his early affair with Smallens, only two such are known by name: Bill Hewitt, a Southerner whom he met in 1944 while the two were stationed in England and with whom he cohabited for a few years; and Adolfo Velletri, an Italian with whom he had a brief affair while in Rome in 1961. But there seem to have been others. In 1953, for instance, he kept Mina Curtiss apprised of an apparent lover, writing, "I discover someone even more introvert and suspicious than myself; and proud, proud as all get-out. The thing is not feverish (any more); love of music and a budding deep affection are the keystones of this one. One hopes."[45]

Whether this hope included finding a lasting romantic relationship, he at least expressed on occasion the "desire" and "need" for love. "As usual, when I work as hard as now," he told Diamond in 1942, "I have a passionate and completely unrealistic desire to fall in love. Unrealistic since I wouldn't find it if I looked for it, and there's no time to look; but it would be practical in the deepest sense to have it there warm and waiting for me to drop into as I drop out of work. The day-dreaming of a drip." The following year, he wrote to Mina Curtiss from London, "The one thing missing is Love, Perfect Love. Still, I should be used to that by now. I am, and take my chances on occasional lechery." And in 1950, he informed Leonard Bernstein, "I am not in love, and I need to be; that's a perillous [sic] state."[46]

The composer's largely unrequited desire for romantic love—problematically, according to Paul Moor, a friend of his later years, with "men who could only make him miserable"—possibly bore some relation to his depressive mood swings. For although he was by nature gracious and affable, even the life of the party—"juicy in every way," commented Joan Peyser—he could as easily become moody and irritable; a soothing cigarette dangling from his lips, he sometimes drank to excess, leading some friends to conclude that he had a drinking problem. Although like many leftists of his time, he largely seems to have eschewed psychoanalysis, the Federal Bureau of Investigation reported in March 1947 that he had consulted with the noted psychiatrist Bernard Robbins and had applied for treatment with the Veterans Administration, who declared him "a rather detached withdrawn individual with marked depressive features, some of which are relative in character to present and real difficulties, the majority of which, however, are the inevitable outcomes of very severe psycho-neurotic disturbances. He has blocking in his creativeness, marked inhibitions in his inner personal contacts with some suicidal preoccupation."[47]

As seen in the dejection that followed his 1922 Philharmonic performance, Blitzstein was especially prone to depression upon the completion of some artistic project, in part because his creative work provided such great satisfaction. "I am happier than I have been in a long time," he wrote to his sister in November 1929; "and I see before me a life in which this sort of happiness is due to continue, since it is based upon the most constant thing one can hope for—beloved work. In many ways I have been, am, lucky." Blitzstein expressed this sense of solace and gratitude in his autobiographical radio opera, *I've Got the Tune* (1937), in which the protagonist, Mr. Musiker, hoping to find lyrics to a tune he has written, responds to the death of a suicide (an episode patently inspired by wife Eva's death the year before) by ruefully stating, "And I've still got the tune."[48]

Blitzstein certainly worked enormously hard. Although he enjoyed socializing over food and drink, he often worked from early morning to late afternoon, and sometimes into the night, with only brief breaks for light meals and such diversions as swimming, sun-bathing, reading, and doing crossword puzzles. Moreover, he managed to devote most of his working time to composing, although this meant reconciling himself early on "to a life in which barely adequate money is earned sporadically." Indeed, he lived much of his adult life in rather precarious financial circumstances. True, the success of *The Cradle Will Rock* brought some monetary relief in the late 1930s, and he always seemed able to afford housekeeping help; but not until the mid-1950s, thanks largely to his adaptation of *The Threepenny Opera* (1954) and its "Mack the Knife," did he attain a measure of economic security.[49]

2

Journeyman Years

In October 1924, at age nineteen, Marc (no longer Marcus) Blitzstein enrolled in Philadelphia's new Curtis Institute of Music, located on Locust Street off Rittenhouse Square. Founded as an elite arm of the city's Settlement Music School by Mary Louise Curtis Bok, the wife of editor Edward Bok (and later violinist Efrem Zimbalist), the Curtis Institute boasted such celebrated faculty as conductor Leopold Stokowski, pianist Josef Hofmann, and violinist Carl Flesch. Still a few years away from its remarkable policy of free tuition for all pupils, Curtis charged full-time students $500 for the academic year, although it awarded scholarships of various amounts, especially to those in need.[1]

Blitzstein applied to Curtis primarily in order to study composition privately with Rosario Scalero, who, upon examination, accepted him as a student. (On his application form, he gave his race as "Jewish" and his nationality as "American," but marked a line by religion, signifying none; this accorded with his family's general attitude, which although nonreligious, acknowledged its Jewish heritage.) Blitzstein worked with Scalero for two years, taking half-hour lessons the first year and forty-five-minute lessons the second. As a part-time Curtis student concurrently working with Alexander Siloti in New York, he was charged a halved tuition of $250, which, along with a $100 scholarship, reduced his total fees to $150 for the year. After his first year, he petitioned for a further reduction, explaining that studying with Siloti had cost him, with transportation expenses, $500 per year, and implying that his study schedule (four hours per day at the piano, three at his schoolwork) prevented him from making up the difference himself. Unmoved, the administration left the tuition at $150, stating, "We fail to see why you should expect to get entirely free tuition from The Curtis Institute of Music and continue at a considerable cost your private piano lessons in New York."[2]

Rosario Scalero (1870–1954) had studied violin in his native Italy and in England as well as composition with Brahms's good friend, Eusebius Mandyczewski, in Vienna. He initially made his name as a concert violinist and composer, but he devoted his later years to teaching, first in Rome, and then, after 1919, in the United States, where he taught at the Mannes School of Music and almost uninterruptedly from 1924 to 1946 at the Curtis Institute.

Scalero's early American students included not only Blitzstein but Virgil Thomson, who studied privately with him in 1923, and Samuel Barber and the Italian-born Gian Carlo Menotti, who began lessons with him at Curtis in 1924 and 1928, respectively. These four—who proved among the most successful American opera composers of their time, even if Scalero was, according to Menotti, "always very scornful of opera"—remembered him, perhaps more respectfully than fondly, as a taskmaster who revered Palestrina and Brahms; emphasized the teaching of counterpoint as opposed to harmony; had his students write masses, motets, and madrigals; and could be as devastatingly critical about his students' exercises as about their free compositions. When in 1951 Barber visited his former teacher in Italy, Scalero handed him back a "corrected" copy of his Piano Sonata (1949) saying, "You are talented—why do you write such bad music? You can do better. Go on, keep working. Goodbye." Commented Barber, "I felt just as I did twenty years ago, making a violent effort not to show the annoyance coming through every nook and cranny of my face, even though I saw the funny side." Menotti, who eventually taught at Curtis himself, spoke more admiringly of the man: "He never taught us rules; he wanted us to find out for ourselves what the rules were through the study of great music." And Blitzstein, too, held him in considerable esteem, to judge from this comment provoked by Arnold Schoenberg's arrival in the United States in 1933: "I can think of perhaps only one other teacher here, Scalero, whose intellectual passion and size make intensely vital in a course of training, what would be ordinarily lifeless for purposes of composition."[3]

The Blitzstein papers contain a series of music tablets filled with contrapuntal exercises, most of which presumably date from his two years with Scalero, although some are not clearly distinguishable from those undertaken with Nadia Boulanger during the fall and early winter of 1926–27. In any case, he progressed in a short time from writing basic two-voice to elaborate six-voice species counterpoint. He also apparently studied orchestration with Scalero as suggested by transcriptions that seem to date from this time, including arrangements for various ensembles of songs and piano pieces by Edward MacDowell ("Danse Andalouse"), Nicolas Medtner ("Invocation"), Modest Musorgsky ("Impressions de voyage en Crimée"), and Serge Rachmaninoff ("Vocalise").

In later years, for all his high regard for Scalero, Blitzstein took a somewhat wry view of some of this work, annotating a list of five melodies identified as "canti firmi used by Palestrina, Brahms, etc." with the vaguely disdainful comment, "for 3 years I did nothing but work on these themes" (his mention of three years perhaps indicating study before or after Curtis as well). In any event, Scalero regarded Blitzstein's student work highly, giving him all A's his first year and A+'s his second for "talent," "application," and "progress."[4]

While at Curtis, Blitzstein enrolled in a few other classes, including in his first year, dictation and music appreciation, and in his second, dictation/sight-singing and keyboard harmony. All his classes were at an advanced level, including Law-rence Adler's "Music Appreciation and Criticism," which required "extensive mu-sical background" and which focused on the "nationalist movement in music," and his second-year theory instruction with George Wedge, which included both dictation from Bach's French and English Suites and reading a Haydn string quar-tet at the piano. During his last semester at the conservatory, Blitzstein—along with four other invited students—further took a composition seminar taught by the popular composer-critic Deems Taylor (1885–1966) that met on Monday evenings for two hours. Blitzstein's other classes included Comparative Arts, a humanities course co-taught by distinguished scholars and critics in various dis-ciplines, and apparently German as well. But Curtis's lax record keeping during these years makes the full scope of his academic work hard to ascertain.[5]

Drafts of a few essays written by Blitzstein during this period—at least some intended for Adler's music appreciation class—survive among his papers as well. His discussion of "the attitude toward life of the Russian people" as reflected in their music discloses a wide familiarity with Russian music and literature. In an essay on George Santayana—the Spanish-American philosopher then at the height of prestige—he pondered over the author's equation of "beauty" with, in some instances, "pleasure" (a notion that Blitzstein seconded) and at other times, the "presence of something good." And in a piece on Musorgsky, in which he showed himself steeped in that composer's work and cognizant of its influence on Debussy, Ravel, and Stravinsky, he argued that the composer is Russian not so much in style as in "his deep humanity, his bitterness and introspection."[6]

Blitzstein supplemented his Curtis education by attending student and faculty recitals and professional concerts. In yet another student essay, "On Conductors," he appreciatively critiqued the work of Leopold Stokowski, Walter Damrosch, Willem Mengelberg, Fritz Reiner, and Serge Koussevitzky, singling out performances of Scriabin, Stravinsky, Gershwin, and Copland, among others, a discussion that reveals that between his regular treks to New York and the lively musical scene at home, including guest appearances by New York and Boston orchestras, he heard an im-pressive range of new orchestral music expertly performed. He naturally became especially familiar with the British-born director of the Philadelphia Orchestra, Leopold Stokowski, whose renditions of Mahler, Sibelius, Schoenberg, Stravinsky, Falla, and others had established him as one of the nation's most eloquent cham-pions of new music. During Blitzstein's two years at Curtis, Stokowski furthered this reputation with performances of Paul Hindemith's *Nusch-Nuschi Dances*, Leo Orn-stein's Second Piano Concerto, Sergey Prokofiev's *Ala and Lolli*, Karol Szymanowski's Violin Concerto, and Edgard Varèse's *Hyperprism* and *Amériques*. Blitzstein heard at least some of these works, including *Amériques*, which caused an uproar; but most memorable, it seems, was a January 30, 1925, all-Stravinsky program with the com-poser leading the orchestra in performances of his *Firebird* and *Petrushka* suites, *Fireworks*, *Scherzo fantastique*, and *The Song of the Nightingale*.[7]

On July 13, 1926, Blitzstein himself performed the Liszt Concerto in $E^{\flat}$ major, a work he surely studied with Siloti, with the Philadelphia Orchestra under the direction of Henry Hadley at the city's U.S. Sesquicentennial International Exhibition. As in 1922, one reviewer noted striking contrasts in his playing—"The poetry of power was there adjacent to the most delicate of fairy notes"—but his success was not as complete as before, with one critic faulting his "original and sincere" reading for "over-sentimentalizing" merely technical passages.[8]

While at Curtis, Blitzstein naturally came to know Samuel Barber, not only from Scalero's studio, but from Deems Taylor's 1926 composition seminar, where they were considered the two outstanding talents. But they never seem to have cultivated much of a friendship, even in later years, when Blitzstein had some cordial professional interaction with Barber's companion Gian Carlo Menotti (who did not begin his studies at Curtis until after Blitzstein had left for Europe). On the other hand, Barber proved one of the relatively few composers to contribute to the Marc Blitzstein Memorial Fund established after Blitzstein's death.[9]

Blitzstein left Philadelphia in the fall of 1926 to briefly tour Europe, including a visit to Venice with his father, and then to pursue studies with Nadia Boulanger in Paris. Of Franco-Russian descent, Boulanger (1887–1979) grew up in Paris, where she excelled as a music student under Charles-Marie Widor and Gabriel Fauré. After the death of her younger sister, composer Lili Boulanger, she renounced composition and established herself rather as an outstanding organist, conductor, and teacher. Her ability to inspire her students, foster their individuality, refine their technique, broaden their horizons, and facilitate their careers quickly became legendary, as did her Wednesday afternoon teas, at which students sang choral music, investigated new scores, and mingled with an eclectic mix of visitors, some quite celebrated. (Blitzstein described her studio as "the hangout, so to speak, of all the musical factions imaginable.") Promoting the French virtues of textural clarity and formal elegance, she held, among contemporary composers, Fauré, Ravel, and Stravinsky—all of whom she knew well—in special regard.[10]

Blitzstein presumably chose to work with Boulanger on the strength of her recently achieved reputation as the teacher of such American composers as Virgil Thomson, Aaron Copland, and Walter Piston. (Some sources report that he studied with Boulanger at Copland's suggestion, but the two men had yet to meet.) Moreover, he might have made her acquaintance when she visited Curtis to lecture on Bach in early 1925. At any rate, he studied with her for a mere four months, from October 1926 through January 1927. "I have started studying composition with Nadia Boulanger, an incredible Spartan woman," he wrote Berenice Skidelsky on October 24; "her musicianship is limitless, she is entirely charming, and she likes me."[11]

Blitzstein wrote free compositions under Boulanger's guidance while he undertook more formal projects as well. Although he did not date this latter work, various endeavors consistent with Boulanger's pedagogy and grouped together in a tablet—canons composed at various intervals; a double canonic setting of a Latin hymn ("Nocte surgentes"); a series of texted "circular canons" for four treble voices, including settings of James Branch Cabell, Paul Laurence Dunbar, Edna St. Vincent Millay, and Murasaki Shikibu, as well as passages from the Bible in English ("How doth the city," Lamentations) and French ("Dieu tout puissant," Psalm 94); choral preludes and a chorale variation for organ; transcribed madrigals by Monteverdi; and skeletal analyses of various melodies by Chopin, Massenet, Fauré, Ravel, and Honegger after a fashion not unlike that popularized by theorist Heinrich Schenker—all seem to date from this time.[12]

At one point, Boulanger queried Blitzstein about why he thought "'modern' music was so full of the cliché of the minor second, major seventh, minor ninth," a possibly veiled criticism of the young man's increasingly dissonant music. But she proved highly admiring of Blitzstein, in early 1928 penning the following letter of recommendation for him: "Having had the musical joy to have Mark [sic] Blitzstein as pupil for several months, I could not praise too highly his gifts— *Born musician*, he is especially bright minded—and gives the greatest reasons to believe he is to become a *true* great artist. What he has already accomplished is of unusual quality."[13]

Blitzstein retained a lifelong affection for Boulanger, but what he might have learned from her during their brief time together, aside ostensibly from some refinement of taste and skills, remains open to speculation. Two songs apparently composed during this period, "Gods" and "O Hymen! O Hymenee!" intimate that she helped bring him closer to Stravinsky, although especially the latter song points to the influence of Schoenberg as well. The ballet *Megalopolis*, partly composed under Boulanger's tutelage, seems likewise suggestive, given not only its Stravinskian features (including the increased presence of changing meters), but its distinctive absorption of the American vernacular, with some of its passages tellingly reappearing in such mature pieces as *The Cradle Will Rock* and *I've Got the Tune*. At the least, Boulanger would have raised no objection to his use of popular American idioms and very likely encouraged him in this direction.

While in Paris, which he thought "divine," Blitzstein also met Maurice Ravel (from whom he hoped to receive some "valuable criticism") and attended numerous concerts, plays, and presumably operas and ballets as well. In this way he became more familiar with such composers as Georges Auric, Arthur Honegger, Darius Milhaud, Francis Poulenc, Sergey Prokofiev, and his young compatriot George Antheil (1900–1959), whose piano sonatas and *Ballet mécanique* for player pianos and percussion (1925) influenced the music Blitzstein started to write (although a performance of Antheil's First Symphony and *Symphony en fa*, which he described to Berenice Skidelsky as "the tortured, strained product of a talented and vain mind, determined to be original," failed to impress him). As for Édouard Bourdet's play about an adulterous lesbian affair, *La prisonnière*, which was then causing a furor on Broadway as *The Captive*, he wrote Skidelsky, "To me, it failed on the side of sentimentality; it lacked that genuine courage which is not willing to be done until it has said its say; and presented that spurious and ambiguous courage which toys with a new and hitherto forbidden subject."[14]

On January 22, for a lecture-recital by Boulanger on Albert Roussel's *Padmâ-vatî* at the École Normale, Blitzstein furthermore joined forces with his teacher to accompany the participating singers in a two-piano reduction of the orchestral score. As of January 18, his second-piano part had yet to be transcribed, prompting him to write to fellow Boulanger student, Dorothy Smith (later, Dushkin), "Why Boulanger should have chosen me, thumping-clumsy sight-reader that I am, I can not imagine. Did you, by any chance, connive? . . . Picture me in the throes of toil until Saturday, and in the depths of despair afterwards."[15]

By this time, Blitzstein had resolved to leave Paris in order, he hoped, to study with Arnold Schoenberg, a surprising decision given Boulanger's typical regimen of several years of lessons, not to mention her conflicted feelings about the German composer (especially after his adoption of the twelve-tone method in the early 1920s). But Blitzstein had come to Boulanger unusually well-prepared and did not need as much training as, say, Roy Harris, who arrived about the same time he did and who studied with her for three years. Moreover, he had limited financial resources and was intent on "imbibing" as much "European culture" as possible. "Though I think I disagree profoundly with his [Schoenberg's] aesthetic," he wrote to Curtis's director, William Walter, "I think he will be a marvellous person to butt my musicality against." Blitzstein accordingly set out for Vienna, not realizing that the previous year Schoenberg had moved to Berlin to take a position at the Prussian Academy of Arts; but he finally found him in the German metropolis, and in mid-February, an initially doubtful Schoenberg accepted him into his master class at the academy after examining his scores. (Schoenberg expected his composition students to have attained some mastery of harmony, counterpoint, form, and orchestration, as evidenced by completed works.) Blitzstein thus became not only one of Schoenberg's first American pupils but one of the relatively few who studied with Boulanger as well.[16]

On February 10, 1927, shortly before beginning his lessons with Schoenberg, Blitzstein, even at this age the keen social observer, shared his first impressions of Berlin with Dorothy Smith, back in Paris: "Berlin is the metropolis of a country which has not yet settled down to the psychology of a republic. Everything is imperial, official; the catchword is 'verboten'. . . . *Everybody* eats, all the time. . . . Entirely different from Paris. Intense, sincere, thick, or on the other hand hysterical, turgid, graceless. Yet refreshing, and torn from rich soil." He wrote Smith too that he had been "feasting upon beautiful orchestral music," mentioning a "superb production" of Eugen d'Albert's "trivial" opera *Tiefland* (1903) and a performance by Bruno Walter of Mahler's First Symphony and "some Wagner, in grand, if a little heavy, style."[17]

To judge from transcriptions for large chamber ensemble of Debussy's "Hills of Anacapri" and Tchaikovsky's "Troika" completed in March, Blitzstein studied orchestration along with free composition with Schoenberg. Approving mention of Schoenberg's "first course" in "rigid academic counterpoint" in a lecture series given in the winter of 1928–29, "The Modern Movement in Music," suggests that he studied counterpoint with him as well. In the event, he attended Schoenberg's seminars for five months, but stopped private lessons after three, by which time tensions between him and Schoenberg "had become unbearable," as he wrote to Boulanger the following October, adding, "I had it out with him; we had a very direct and very frank discussion, which ended in a 'bust-up' so far as the private hours were concerned. I still went on with the classes, however; we were doing some interesting analysis of Mahler (sixth symphony and 'Lied von der Erde'), Schönberg (Quintet for wind instruments, which I played at the piano), Hindemith, Berg, etc."[18]

Blitzstein had felt some frustration with Schoenberg virtually from the start, writing to William Walter in March,

> I disagree with him [Schoenberg] more and more. He would make of music an inert, dead pattern, fit only for the laboratory. But he is undoubtedly one of the greatest intellectual musicians alive—and as an opposing force to test one's own quality against, he is superb. Even to have found out his theory directly from him, makes the studying with him profitable. I have an uneasy suspicion, however, that my silence will be unable to hold out much longer in the face of his insistent demands to sacrifice beauty on the altar of Scheme—and there will be an explosion.

He similarly expressed his discontent to composer-critic Marion Bauer, who published in the April 21, 1927, issue of *The Musical Leader* a portion of a letter from an unnamed "young student" who could only have been Blitzstein: "Now I am hard at work with Schoenberg. I think I disagree with him entirely. His is a totally scientific aesthetic; his principles are based upon a masterly knowledge of the machinery of Beethoven and Brahms; but he does not *hear*, he does not know the quality of the projectivity of sound."[19]

By "the altar of Scheme" and "scientific aesthetic" Blitzstein had in mind, at least in part, Schoenberg's new method developed in the 1920s of basing a work on a twelve-tone row and its permutations (which Blitzstein referred to as a "Zauberquadrat" or "magic square"), an approach, as he stated in his "Modern Movement" lectures, that resulted in pieces "in which the music elements seem to be frightfully subordinate, not to say absent altogether." (By contrast, he thought that with Milhaud, "we always get the sense that the musician is leading his theory, and is not being led by it," an observation cited by Sointu Scharenberg as underscoring a basic conflict between Schoenberg's emphasis on theoretical principles and Blitzstein's higher regard for artistic autonomy.) "I wish I could show you the yards of diagrams and schemes he made out before a note of the Quintet was written," he wrote Boulanger in his letter of October 1927; as with Schoenberg's other twelve-tone works, "the whole composition . . . is soluble into some perfectly elementary problem in algebra or calculus."[20]

Nor was this all, as he told Boulanger: "The man has no ear; as an instrumentalist he is abominable; his viola playing is excruciating, lacking even the most fundamental qualities of intonation or grace. In his lectures, he enunciated some impossible theses in aesthetics, and retracted them, usually half an hour later. His taste is, for me, highly faulty and frequently vulgar, though this is of course a completely personal reaction." Although Schoenberg would cite Benedetto Croce on the need for man to "say clearly what he thinks," he "has a terrific and losing struggle to express himself."[21]

Blitzstein objected to Schoenberg's chauvinism as well. "It is only since the war that you American composers have been cut off from your source of supply, which is Germany, and have been writing Franco-Russian music," Blitzstein remembered him as saying. "Ten years before the war you were all writing German music; and ten years from now you will all be writing German music again." Blitzstein similarly recalled a resigned Schoenberg telling him to "go ahead" and write his "Franco-Russische Hübschmusik" ("Franco-Russian pretty music"). "That I might not be interested in writing German, French, Russian, or even American music did not occur to him," remarked Blitzstein. "I found it useless to argue with him. We parted on polite but not very warmly friendly terms." (Asked about American music upon his arrival in New York in 1933, Schoenberg, after admitting little familiarity with the subject, said, "I of course know Roger Sessions' work which greatly pleases me, and some compositions by Marc Blitzstein which are excellent," indicating in fact real admiration for Blitzstein's work.)[22]

Blitzstein clashed not only with Schoenberg but with many of his mostly German students. He found a sympathetic ear, however, in Schoenberg's assistant Josef Rufer and in his Spanish classmate Roberto Gerhard, who wrote to him in 1963, "How well I do remember our Berlin days, what a couple we made, you and I, you (at that time) the anti-Schoenberguian, or the very reluctant Schoenberguian, and I, the non-conformist, or the Schoenberguian *malgré moi*. Maybe I've got it all wrong, but that's how I remember it; anyway, the two recalcitrants in the fold." Blitzstein kept in his files a slow and melancholy Catalan folk song used by Gerhard in a chamber work composed during these years, a melody that "haunted" him throughout his life.[23]

In his "Modern Movement" lectures, Blitzstein further described Schoenberg as "enormously magnetic and fascinating; a hideous little man, with fine keen eyes, kind when he knows himself surrounded by disciples, and belligerent when there is a stranger in the midst. There seems to me to be something almost pathological in his attitude toward his pupils' work." Blitzstein went so far as to condemn his teaching as "positively dangerous":

He wants his pupils not to compose; he stifles every natural spontaneous urge in them. His first course, in rigid academic counterpoint, is very good indeed; but at the point where the pupil should be able a bit to strike out for himself, Schonberg comes in with this terrible theorizing about making the work exist on its own as a perfect piece of design. He approaches every work of his pupils with a scissors, so to speak, the idea being not to listen but to cut. Of some fifty or seventy-five pupils, it is significant that only a few are still working; the others have given up in despair, convinced by the man's really immense magnetism that he is right, but feeling the whole job hopeless. I have spoken to them and worked with them; they are in the main like people caught in an evil but inextricable influence.

As exceptions Blitzstein recognized only Alban Berg and Anton Webern, the second of whom he thought—at least in 1929—Schoenberg's "most important" pupil: "his [Webern's] works are marvellous and subtle compositions, some lasting only seconds, of the strangest, most evocative pianissimos from unexpected instruments I have heard anywhere."[24]

As for Schoenberg's music, he decided that he preferred the work from the period around 1910, including the Second String Quartet, the Piano Pieces, op. 19, and especially *Pierrot lunaire*; he thought such pieces, in their own way, "perfect" and "poetic," as opposed to the composer's still earlier scores, which revealed "a surprising lack of taste," and the twelve-tone works, which simply bored him (a judgment later qualified). But even admired masterpieces like *Pierrot* elicited an ambivalent response: "We get a minute delineation of the passions, nervous reactions, climaxes and anticlimaxes of a soul, to the point where the thing begins to take on the aspect of neuasthenia [sic]."[25]

In the 1930s, Blitzstein's attitude toward Schoenberg mellowed considerably (as in the case of another Schoenberg student, Hanns Eisler, whose career paralleled Blitzstein's own in a number of respects). He assailed the neglect of Schoenberg's music—the "Schoenbergian silence is deafening," he stated in 1936—and championed *Pierrot lunaire* in particular, declaring it a "bonafide masterpiece" comparable to Joyce's *Ulysses* (even while deeming its poetry second rate and parodying the work in his 1937 radio opera *I've Got the Tune*). He further welcomed Schoenberg's arrival in the United States as "an extremely good thing for America. In particular his almost fanatical academicism is an unfamiliar and needed quality among us." Perhaps most surprisingly, in 1931, he declared the Third Quartet (1927), a recent twelve-tone work, "among Schönberg's best, least aloof music; it is noble, tender and gives off a rare sense of fullness." Indeed, near the end of his life, now viewing Schoenberg as antithetical not to Stravinsky, as in earlier years, but to John Cage, he identified sooner with Schoenberg, stating in a lecture at Brandeis in 1962, "I love many serial works."[26]

Blitzstein himself made use of serial techniques as early as 1933, which alone refuted Henry Brant's claim, in a seminal 1946 profile of the composer, "In none of Blitzstein's output is there any trace of the methods of . . . Arnold Schönberg, except occasionally for purposes of parody." But Blitzstein's debt to Schoenberg arguably went deeper than that, Peter Gradenwitz noting, for instance, that his music embodied two of Schoenberg's main compositional principles: economy of means and developing variation.[27]

During his time in Berlin, Blitzstein also importantly became familiar with the members of a "very Left Art-Group," the November Group, which he placed in the context of a long line of German avant-garde movements and which he associated with, among others, the painters George Grosz, Wassily Kandinsky, Paul Klee, and Issai Kulvianski; writer Arnold Zweig; photographer László Moholy-Nagy; and composers Hansjörg Dammert (a fellow Schoenberg student), Hans Heinz Stuckenschmidt, and Stefan Wolpe. On May 2, 1927, he attended the nineteenth evening of the November Group, at which he heard new piano sonatas by Dammert, Stuckenschmidt, and Wolpe. "They are philosophers all, and musicians second," Blitzstein stated in his "Modern Movement" lectures, although he thought Wolpe, whose sonata (1925) he described as having a "rather sharp dazzling quality," the most musical of the three. Blitzstein apparently did not find them as impressive as such other German composers as Paul Hindemith or, at least in later years, Hanns Eisler and Kurt Weill. However, he adapted Stuckenschmidt's percussive use of the piano lid for his *Piano Percussion Music* (1929) and felt greater rapport with this group than with Ernst Toch or Ernst Krenek, whose opera *Jonny spielt auf*, the sensation of 1927, he detested. Meanwhile, the work of German dancers—including Mary Wigman's monumental cycle *Die Feier*—also made a lasting impression. Clearly, certain trends among Weimar artists—long before his association with Brecht—spoke deeply to him, as they did to Antheil, who found that postwar Berlin cleansed him "of all the remaining old poesy, false-sentimentalism, and overjuicy overidyllicism."[28]

Still in his early twenties, Blitzstein spent the nearly two years from August 1927 to May 1929 mostly back in Philadelphia, where he lived with his father Sam at 1826 Spruce Street. During this time, on May 21, 1928, Sam married writer and editor Madelin (Madi) Leof (1901–1987), a girl young enough to be his daughter; indeed, Madi counted Jo, her junior by one year, as one of her best friends. Madi was the daughter of a Russian-born doctor, Morris Vladimir (Poppa) Leof (originally Lipschitz), and his common-law wife Jennie Chalfin, a schoolteacher. The Leofs were well-known locally for their socialist and feminist activities and for gatherings at their four-story residence at 322 South 16th Street—commonly known as "322"—at which one might find Eugene Debs, Emma Goldman, or Communist Party leader Earl Browder. Madi shared her father's—and new husband's—Marxist worldview, as did her sister Charlotte, who married noted physicist Robert Serber in 1933. Sam and Madi moved in with the Leofs in the early 1930s, and Helen Hough probably had that household in mind when she wrote the following:

> Each individual in the house in which Sam lived is so completely different from every other that it is always remarkable to note how perfectly all work together into the family whole. And the combined talent and good will which has been generated by the family group have been so great that they have richly overflowed to all who visited them. . . . It is a house where argument and excitement are eternal. But the respect of the individual for the group and the group for the individual are abiding.

Marc, who proudly referred to Leof as his "grandfather," himself became for many years a habitué at 322; one photograph shows Blitzstein at a party at the Leofs as late as 1949, four years after his father's death.[29]

Blitzstein presumably met through Leof (if he had not known them otherwise) such Philadelphian contemporaries as playwright Clifford Odets (1906–1963), journalist I. F. Stone (1907–1989), and eventually civil-rights attorney Leonard Boudin (1912–1989), all leading progressives of their generation. (Odets, who borrowed Sam Blitzstein's name for his 1936 monologue about a worker coming to terms with his social conscience, "I Can't Sleep," dedicated his 1949 play *The Big Knife* to Leof "with love.") But Blitzstein seems to have developed only the most casual of friendships with these three, including Odets, although they had such other mutual friends as Copland, not to mention strikingly parallel careers in the theater. As his nephew Stephen recalled, Blitzstein did not much care for Odets personally, but he at least had relatively nice words for Odets's *Night Music* (1940)—"spotty but brilliant," with characters "rich in color"—and in the late 1940s, he even considered adapting the playwright's *Awake and Sing!* as an opera.[30]

Meanwhile, in April 1929, Blitzstein's widowed mother married for a third time, joining her new husband William Levy in Pittsburgh. But the marriage lasted only a few years, after which Anna eventually retired to Ventnor, New Jersey, near Atlantic City and not far either from Brigantine, where her children regularly summered after the Second World War. During these later years, she also resumed using Blitzstein as her surname. Marc always stayed in close touch with his mother, and in the course of his life wrote her some of his most warm and sensitive letters. And when he achieved some modest wealth in the 1950s, he began to share with Jo and Ed Davis the responsibility for supporting her financially as well. Anna would survive her son by some six years.

Prior to studying abroad, Blitzstein had turned down an offer from William Walter to teach theory at Curtis, a position he hoped to secure upon his return. But by 1927, that department had been fully staffed, and so after returning home, he started teaching piano and lecturing privately. With his knowledge of the latest musical trends and his flair as a speaker and musician, his lectures—typically on contemporary music—proved particularly successful and became a principal mainstay over the next ten years.[31]

Blitzstein took a break from teaching and lecturing in the summer of 1928 to spend six weeks at the MacDowell Colony, an artist's retreat in Peterborough, New Hampshire, operated by composer Edward MacDowell's widow, Marian. During this stay, as he worked on his opera *Triple-Sec*, he befriended his future wife Eva Goldbeck and composer Douglas Moore, among others. Aaron Copland, who in April had recommended him to the MacDowell Association as "one of our most gifted young composers," arrived at the Colony himself in early August about the time of Blitzstein's departure for home.[32]

Blitzstein had first met Copland the previous fall, at which time he described him to Berenice Skidelsky as a "nice, stimulating fellow" and a "good contact," while Copland, about to give a December 16, 1927, lecture on "Youngest Americans" at the New School, sized up the twenty-two-year-old Blitzstein as follows: "Characteristics: facile; danger of memory-writing. No marked individuality yet. Much musicality and promise." In March of 1928, after Blitzstein performed his Piano Sonata in New York, the young Philadelphian wrote to a friend, "Aaron Copland and some others are for me—the 'profession' takes me more or less seriously—so I'm not quite alone," revealing—along with the already cited letter of recommendation to the MacDowell Colony—that virtually from the start of their careers, Copland rallied behind Blitzstein, as he would his entire life. "I have been meeting Aaron Copland rather frequently, and like him tremendously," Blitzstein wrote to Nadia Boulanger toward the end of the year. "He is a candid, clear and supple personality— we disagree more often than we agree, and that makes for stimulation." (One area of disagreement possibly concerned Copland's hopes for a distinctly American art music, whereas Blitzstein felt, as reported in 1933, that "American composers can best develop a national school by not seeking that result too conscientiously.")[33]

In an article published in 1929, and even more in a lecture that same year, Blitzstein made it clear that he thought Copland, although still in his twenties, one of America's finest composers, perhaps the very best, even if he lacked the talent of George Antheil or the originality of the Mexican Carlos Chávez—an assessment as prescient in its own way as his earlier noted esteem for Webern. "To say that his work has gusto, has a kind of intent and aware breeziness which sometimes becomes dark frenzy, that his harmonies are always fresh and pungent—that is, in Copland's case to utter the obvious and the superficial," he remarked. Blitzstein delved deeper to consider Copland's romantic personality, which he compared to both Mahler and Milhaud—perhaps not incidentally, two other Jewish composers. He further discerned a growth of "breadth" and "purity" in Copland's *Lento Molto* for string quartet (1928), which Blitzstein transcribed for piano in 1933. "Copland is one of the freshest and most spontaneous musical talents we possess," he concluded; "already we are secure about him; we know beforehand that whatever he produces will be mature, vital, beautiful." Copland's music not surprisingly made a considerable impact on the young Blitzstein, who remained appreciative of later scores as well—"I think of *Billy the Kid* with glow," he wrote to Mina Curtiss shortly after the ballet's New York premiere in 1939. "That was something!"—although by the time of *A Lincoln Portrait*, he expressed the wish to David Diamond that Copland "would 'get off that dime'; he's done how many works now, based on one-or-two tunes from [John] Lomax or [Stephen] Foster, and combining the fun-exaltation-melancholy spirit of middle-and-far-west?" But in the end, Blitzstein thought even this piece not only "effective," but "true as well, and deep; so why cavil?" And near the end of his life, after hearing Copland's *Connotations* (1962), he wrote to the composer, "I am all for the 'Connotations,' as a work, and as a picture of growth. It makes me happy."[34]

On April 25, 1929, Blitzstein joined Copland, along with Frederick Jacobi and Louis Gruenberg, as one of four pianists in the American stage premiere of Stravinsky's *Les Noces* conducted by Leopold Stokowski and sponsored by the New York based League of Composers. A few weeks later, he and Copland left together for Europe, where they looked forward to seeing their mutual friend Eva Goldbeck, whom both had met at the MacDowell Colony in 1928, and whom Blitzstein would marry in 1933.

Before returning to Europe, Blitzstein gave a series of ten lecture-recitals, "The Modern Movement in Music" (1928–29), at his home in Philadelphia and at East 93rd Street in New York. Beginning with a discussion of the elements of music, followed by one on "pre-modern" composers from Musorgsky through Debussy, these talks surveyed contemporary developments in Europe and America, concluding with a lecture on jazz and popular music. Although Blitzstein gave many such presentations in the course of his life and published a number of articles besides, these lectures, which for the most part survive among his papers, stand as seminal, a virtual text comparable to Copland's *Our New Music* (1941), which it resembles in tone and sensibility, although Blitzstein's scope is more varied. Nothing that Blitzstein himself published offers the range and breadth of these lectures. That he illustrated these talks by playing dozens of examples at the piano and that he did all this at the age of twenty-three make this achievement all the more astonishing.[35]

Blitzstein seems particularly up-to-date with regard to French, Russian, Italian, British, German, and American music. In the fourth lecture, on Russian and Italian composers, for example, he discusses the work of Grigory Krein, Nikolay Roslavets, Arthur Lourié, Sergey Prokofiev, Alfredo Casella, Ottorino Respighi, Mario Castelnuovo-Tedesco, Vittorio Rieti, and Gian Francesco Malipiero, while weighing in too on the music of Nikolay Myaskovsky, Serge Rachmaninoff, Nicolas Medtner, Sergey Taneyev, Boleslav Yavorsky, and Puccini (with evaluations of Scriabin and Russian émigrés Stravinsky and Nikolay Obukhov appearing in other lectures). Breezing through an assortment of lesser English composers, he says of Lord Berners (Gerald Hugh Tyrwhitt-Wilson), "All of his music delights at first hearing," as if familiar with the man's entire output; and after commenting on a host of similarly minor Germans, he apologizes for not knowing the music of Heinrich Kaminski, given its good reputation.

These lectures reflect Blitzstein's own tastes and values even as they acknowledge the indisputable importance of Schoenberg, Bartók, Stravinsky, and Hindemith. He rates content over technique and technique over style: "'Style' is only meaningful when it attaches itself inextricably to material, when it in short disappears into the very fabric," he writes with regard to the shortcomings of the American composer Emerson Whithorne. Blitzstein generally has appreciative words about all of his subjects, including Whithorne, although several composers—including Richard Strauss, Scriabin, Schoenberg, and Cyril Scott—he plainly dislikes, usually because he finds their music banal or overly emotional (although he can play their music at the piano, too, and does so). Conversely, he seems to especially admire Debussy, Bartók, Milhaud, Hindemith, Poulenc, Chávez, Copland, and above all Stravinsky, for whom he pens "a panegyric." He at least respects, for their sincerity and youthfulness, such iconoclastic "insurgents" as George Antheil, Henry Cowell, Alois Hába, Nikolay Obukhov, Leo Ornstein, Edgard Varèse, Imre Weisshaus (Paul Arma), and the forenamed members of the November Group, although he warns, "Nothing, I am afraid, wears so badly as a faded insurgent, and Ornstein is that." (Not having any Weisshaus to play, he attempts "something very unfair to the composer, and very inaccurate; I shall try to imitate what Weisshaus' music sounded like when he played it for me.")

Indeed, Blitzstein argues that "the age of experimentation is over" and the time has come, as exemplified by the recent work of Bartók, Stravinsky, and Hindemith, for the consolidation of those innovations associated with the prewar era. In a letter to Nadia Boulanger from this time, he revealed a similar frame of mind in response to her question about the prevalence of dissonant intervals in contemporary music, stating, "An art gathers new material usually by an original rejection of old formulae, a gesture of negation. At the beginning, this gesture is conscious, defiant, it lacks any other reason for existence than the very healthy one that dogma is death. In the turmoil of growth and expansion, this negation and denial loses its identity as such, and is metamorphosed into a positive entity; the fruit of the gesture remains, and is welded into the body of the old material." Blitzstein saw this evidenced, he further wrote Boulanger, in "the rejection of the old 'unities' of time, space, action in the theater, and the resultant theater of [Henri-René] Lenormand, [Eugene] O'Neill, [Franz] Werfel; the protest against rigid metre and rhyme in poetry begun by such pioneers as Whitman, Tagore."[36]

Although Blitzstein in later years became identified with Kurt Weill and Hanns Eisler, the "Modern Movement" lectures discuss only the former, and then basically simply the piece he considers Weill's "best work," *The Czar Has His Photograph Taken* (1927), as opposed to his "most successful work," *The Threepenny*

Opera (1928), which he casually dismisses as an adaptation of *The Beggar's Opera* "for Berlin Consumption." (He does not mention the *Mahagonny-Songspiel*, whose July 1927 premiere at Baden-Baden he did not attend.) Concerning *The Czar*, he writes,

> The music Weill has written around this ["uproarious" libretto by Georg Kaiser] is certainly good theater, in that it enhances the effects of suspense and action on the stage; but as music it appears to me little more than drivel . . . instead of one single musical idea for a situation, the score is made up of thousands of little fragments, all stuck together, and making a kind of mosaic pastiche out of the thing. . . . his music is essentially ugly because it is characterless; yet he is clever enough to keep the rhythms always going, they have push and go.

Blitzstein admires far more the musical theater of Satie, stating, "In the Satie music for the theater, the music has an equilibrium, an intrinsic balance, that can be as detached as the decor itself; it refuses to be, for instance, a Greek Chorus, which notices everything that goes on in the drama, and interprets it simultaneously for the audience; it is music which also refuses to be an audience to the drama, reacting to given stimuli with appropriate responses." He makes a similar observation regarding Stravinsky's *Les Noces*, which he views as partaking of this French tradition: "the music hardly ever expresses the action as it occurs." Thus, Blitzstein's own theatrical aesthetic, which in time reflected the epic theater of Brecht and his musical collaborators, would seem to have even more established roots in the stage work of Satie and Stravinsky.[37]

Considering Blitzstein's later association with socially conscious art, his lecture on music in Soviet Russia and Fascist Italy also warrants special attention. Blitzstein argues that during revolutionary periods, literature, theater, and film can rise to great heights because of their immediate usefulness:

> I, for one, don't shudder at the so-called degradation of an art being used as propaganda. It seems to me an essentially snobbish and nouveau-riche attitude of bourgeois origins, which feels that the arts must be kept holily intact from obscene life-implications, and maintained after the fashion of candles at an altar. . . . I think too much of the work of Aristophanes, Euripedes [sic], Juvenal, Voltaire, Rabelais, Swift—all superb propagandists—to view with contempt the part propaganda can play in a new art-movement—or, to put it in larger terms, the part art can play in a new life-movement.

On the other hand, music and painting, he argues, flourish in times of greater repose, with the isolation effected in the Soviet Union by the emigration of many leading musicians along with the blockades and invasions imposed by the West debilitating that country's musical life all the more. "We assume," he writes, "that as soon as it [the Soviet Union] is freer and better adjusted the great things will come," adding, "It remains to be seen whether the Soviet government, in actively supporting its artists and composers, will cramp their style any. The most ideal of government-patronage-systems has that questionable element of official-ness." As for Fascist Italy, Mussolini's "highhanded method of patronizing young composers can have but one effect, and that is to smother them." Concludes Blitzstein, "There can be no doubt that the ideal situation for the self-respective artist is such a one in which he feels himself essential to the community, and recompensed for the importance of his work accordingly, not by a patron, upon whose whim depends the money, but by a fixed fund, established nationally."

Blitzstein speaks proudly of developments at home, notwithstanding those European "parlor Bolsheviks" who denounce America and who hail Soviet Russia "as the salvation of the age." "With talents like Copland, Sessions, Chávez and Harris at work," he writes, "we need have nothing to fear, I think." Meanwhile, Blitzstein's lecture on jazz, typical for its time, really discusses jazzy popular music, with appreciative comments about Fred and Adele Astaire, George Gershwin, Richard Rodgers (after Gershwin "our most intrinsically musical jazz composer"), Irving Berlin (with his "immensely fine gift for theme"), and the French composer Jean Wiener. He also briefly touches on the blues, a genre he identifies with the "coon-shouter, the technical name for the mournful lady who wails about how she has them blues," and whose greatest exponents, he claims, traditionally have been Jewish—he mentions Sophie Tucker and Nora Bayes among others—although a group of African-American singers, including Ethel Waters and Bessie Smith, recently "have taken over the field entirely." In his opinion, jazz amalgamates Negro, Jewish, Scottish, and French elements; the blues, only Negro and Jewish ones (although he thinks "St. Louis Blues" by W. C. Handy "pure negro").

The "Modern Movement" lectures display a sharp critical apparatus, as a few additional observations help illustrate. On Ravel: "His music is the last word in aristocracy, aloofness . . . it would be almost vulgar if it got any more refined, so to speak." On Prokofiev: "His music is always making faces, grimaces—it is a defense, perhaps, built up against the temptation to write lovely music which is no longer the vogue." On Casella: "One feels that he is one of those who knows too much about what is going on in other composers' works to have a marked personality of his own." On British music: "What happened to England since the days of Purcell and Byrd is a sad tale of second-rate talents, third-rate critics, fourth-rate publics, and in general a fifth-rate musical life." On Stravinsky's *Les Noces*: "It is an epic, not of love between man and woman, but of that larger phenomenon which uses love as a vehicle for continuance—procreation, the principle of the survival of the race." And on Virgil Thomson: "He has written articles . . . —bitter articles, most of them—which are as delicate as a surgeon's knife and quite as deadly. As to his music, it is ephemeral, plainly out to shock, deliberately pretty, banal, or excruciating."

By the time of these "Modern Movement" lectures, Blitzstein's critical writings also had begun to surface in print, including a program note for a performance by Riva Hoffman and Her Dancers on April 5, 1926, and a not entirely unfavorable notice of Gershwin's *Concerto in F* for *The Review* that appeared the following January. (Decades later, Blitzstein reflected, with respect to this latter critique, "Well! not bad for 21 years of age.") And on the recommendation of Aaron Copland, he made his first contribution to America's premier magazine on contemporary music, *Modern Music*, with a review of an April 22, 1928, concert of the Philadelphia Society for Contemporary Music that included Hindemith's *Hin und Zurück*, Stravinsky's *The Soldier's Tale*, and Isadore Freed's *Vibrations*.[38]

Meanwhile, his 1929 article for *This Quarter* on Copland, Sessions, Antheil, and Chávez offered little that "The Modern Movement" did not contain in greater depth. Still, the piece highlighted Blitzstein's early aesthetic orientation, for his music from this time could be seen as straddling the work of these four composers.[39]

Early Works (1924–1929)

In the mid-1920s, Blitzstein began to write music that he considered mature enough to include in a list of works compiled in late 1928, complete with opus numbers (a practice he later dispensed with) as follows: *Svarga*, op. 1 (1924–25) (pantomime suite for chamber orchestra); *Pieces* for piano, op. 2 (1924–26) ("Pavane," "Sarabande," "Variation sur 'Au clair de la lune,'" a set also orchestrated by the composer); *Six Songs*, op. 3 (1925) (texts by Walt Whitman) ("As If a Phantom Caress'd Me," "What Weeping Face," "Joy, Shipmate, Joy!" "After the Dazzle of Day," "Shine! Shine! Shine!" and "Blow! Blow! Blow!"—the last two, apparently of a later provenance, identified as part of a larger work, *A Word Out of the Sea*); "Gods," op. 4 (1926–27), for mezzo-soprano, solo cello, and string ensemble (text by Walt Whitman); *Jigg-Saw*, op. 5 (1926–28) (ballet suite for large orchestra); *Two Songs for a Coon-Shouter*, op. 6 (1927) (texts by Walt Whitman) ("O Hymen! O Hymenee!" and "As Adam"); Sonata for piano, op. 7 (1927); Sonata for trumpet and piano, op. 8; *Percussion Music* for piano, op. 9 (1928–29) (known also as *Piano Percussion Music*); *Theater for the Cabaret*, op. 10 (1928) (opera-farce for chamber orchestra and nineteen voices, later retitled *Triple-Sec*) (libretto, Ronald Jeans); and Quintet for flute, oboe, clarinet, bassoon, and piano, op. 11.[1]

Not all of these works survive, including the trumpet sonata and piano-wind quintet, both of which Blitzstein might not even have completed, because in August 1929, he projected writing them (or rather, a trumpet sonata and a "wind-quintet," the latter to be based on mathematician Leonhard Euler's "diagrams") over the next two years. And the "Variation sur 'Au clair de la lune'" exists only as transcribed for orchestra. Other pieces from this period not listed in the above catalog but mentioned elsewhere by Blitzstein likewise do not seem to have survived, including an unidentified A. E. Housman setting (1924); "Danse Basse" and "Danse Haute" for piano (ca. 1925); and another keyboard work, *Piano Saw* (1927), a piece likely related to his coeval ballet suite, *Jigg-Saw*. Conversely, some music from these years excluded from the above catalog survives, including "Round" for piano (1924); some fragments of incidental music to productions of *Richard II* (date of production unknown) and *King Hunger* (1924); a portion of a Rupert Brooke setting, "Song" (1925) ("All Suddenly the Wind Comes Soft," completed by Leonard Lehrman in 2003); the song "The Dream Is Mine" (1925) to the composer's own words; two A. E. Housman settings (1924–25) ("From Far, From Eve and Morning" and "Into My Heart an Air"); an unidentified piece for string orchestra ("Allegretto") (ca. 1925) that possibly represents a transcription of the missing "Danse Basse" or "Danse Haute"; the ballet scores *Blessings of the Bath* (1926) and *Megalopolis/Jigg-Saw* (1926–28); the film score *Hände* (1927–28); two additional Whitman songs (1928) ("I Am He" and "Ages and Ages"); and a Whitman chorus, "Till, Of a Sudden" (1928), that, like "Shine! Shine! Shine!" and "Blow! Blow! Blow!" was to form part of the cantata, *A Word Out of the Sea*.[2]

Blitzstein secured performances for many of these works, but only *Triple-Sec*, which the German firm B. Schott's Söhne published in 1931, made its way into print (as a piano-vocal score). Nor did this publication signal any immediate change in fortune; the ensuing five years witnessed only the publication of a single song, "Jimmie's got a goil." True, with the success of *The Cradle Will Rock* (1937), the composer entered into a long association with Chappell & Company, the firm, run by brothers Max and Louis Dreyfus, that published the work of Gershwin and other leading Broadway composers. But even after this, the limited printing and distribution of Blitzstein's music hardly proved commensurate with his importance and stature.

Decades after the composer's death, Boosey & Hawkes helped to ameliorate this neglect with the publication of the *Marc Blitzstein Songbook* in three volumes (1999, 2001, 2003). Edited by Leonard Lehrman, these anthologies included many of the composer's art and theater songs, published and unpublished alike. In the case of the theater songs, Lehrman gave preference to the composer's manuscripts over the often simplified Chappell arrangements, although he freely drew on assorted manuscript and recorded versions. As for several unfinished songs included in these volumes, he completed sketched melodies and provided missing accompaniments. Melissa de Graaf, in a review of the first two songbooks, questioned some of these editorial decisions, but she thought the volumes in any case "extremely valuable" and "desperately needed," a conclusion seconded by Barry Drogin: "The wonder, for composers, performers and music lovers everywhere, is that after a drought of fifty years, these pieces are actually available to be studied and . . . performed." With the publication of these volumes, all the songs mentioned above, close to eighty years after their composition, finally won release, whereas the instrumental music from this same period remained unpublished.[3]

According to a slightly earlier list of works from June 1928, Blitzstein composed three Housman songs in 1924, but only two Housman settings, "From Far, From Eve and Morning" and "Into My Heart an Air," survive, the manuscript of the latter giving a date of 1925. He might have excluded these songs from his later catalog because he thought them less mature, more conventional, certainly slighter in importance than his opus 1, the ballet *Svarga*. Yet they hold up well and have historic interest besides, in suggesting, as do the composer's other formative works, the romantic lineage of Liszt and others. Composed while he was still a student at Curtis, they might be compared to the early songs of his classmate Samuel Barber, who wrote his own Housman setting, "With Rue My Heart Is Laden," in 1928.[4]

Blitzstein took his texts from Housman's popular 1896 collection, *A Shropshire Lad*, whose melancholy matched the tenor of the composer's own verse from these years, although he selected two poems each of which allowed for effective contrast. In "From Far," the outer sections depict the swirling forces that frame existence, whereas the slower middle section represents the living person who asks, "How I shall help you, say?" The other surviving setting, "Into My Heart," similarly if less dramatically contrasts, through the use of minor and major modes, the sadness of loss with the joys of yesteryear. The wind imagery found in both poems and reflected in the piano accompaniment helps unify the two songs.

Blitzstein completed *Svarga*, a far more ambitious effort, in April 1925, producing a revised version that July. Although the manuscript's subtitle, "Pantomime Suite," suggests some derivation from a larger stage work, the music represents a dramatic whole, although perhaps readier than most for concert presentation. In any event, the idea of writing a "pantomime suite," as opposed to a ballet score per se, indicated even this early an adventurous dramatic sensibility, with the instrumentation of six winds, three brass, cymbals, piano, and strings (minus double basses) itself forming a novel grouping.

Although the work was never produced, Blitzstein left behind not only a scenario but choreographic instructions throughout the score. The work takes place in Svarga, "land of the Sanskrit gods," and contains six scenes. The bedaggered fire god Agni conjures up a storm assisted by two wind gods, the Maruts, before collapsing of fatigue and calling for wine ("Agni"). A bewildered mortal maiden finds herself in Svarga, where she is pursued by the wine god Soma; as she makes an escape, Soma and Agni depart, drinking ("Dance of the Mortal Maiden and Soma"). The noble Indra (the god of war, although not identified here as such) drinks wine and frolics with one, then two Svarga girls, his sword "a symbol of his energy" ("Indra and the Svarga Dweller"). Indra's drinking causes nausea and pain ("Belly-Ache"). The mortal maiden returns to find an ailing Indra, who feebly flirts with her before dying ("Interlude"). All the cast gather around the deceased Indra as flowers arise from the place where his sword has fallen ("Ritual: Rising of the Plants").

One of a number of Indian-inspired contemporary Western musical works, including Holst's *Savitri* (1909), Roussel's *Padmâvatî* (1918), and settings of Rabindranath Tagore's *Gitanjali* by Milhaud (1914), John Alden Carpenter (1914), and Stefan Wolpe (1926), Blitzstein's scenario drew on elements presumably related to his study of Indian culture at the University of Pennsylvania. The score, impressively resourceful for a twenty-year-old student, looks to the East after a fashion as well, at times recalling the work of Ernest Bloch. But like the ballet story, the music essentially goes its own way. Most unexpectedly, jazz elements emerge in the course of the piece: first, jazzy syncopations in "Indra and the Svarga Dweller," and then bluesy gestures in "Belly-Ache," complete with a wink at Dvořák's "Humoresque," a classic ragtime gesture, although handled here with an unusual edge. (Blitzstein, who apparently worked on *Svarga* for a few years, transcribed "Belly-Ache" as "A 'Blues'" for solo piano in March 1924, one month after the premiere of Gershwin's *Rhapsody in Blue*.) This use of a jazz idiom announces an important impulse, broadly situating Blitzstein among the likes of Gershwin and Copland. In contrast, the stately final scene, marked "Religioso," gives an early indication of Blitzstein's penchant for solemn, uplifting endings.

Blitzstein's lifelong interest in the theater manifested itself in other ways during this period, as in the creation of incidental music for Shakespeare's *Richard II* and Leonid Andreyev's *King Hunger*. Although the circumstances surrounding the Shakespeare production remain unknown, Blitzstein wrote the *King Hunger* score for a staging by the Hedgerow Theatre, founded in 1923 by Jasper Deeter and located in Rose Valley outside of Philadelphia; his sister, who acted in some of their productions during these years, possibly helped facilitate this commission. Written in the aftermath of the failed Russian Revolution of 1905, *King Hunger* (1907) presents the conflict between the hungry masses and the moneyed aristocracy in an allegorical fashion in which the figures of Time, Death, and King Hunger appear. At the end, the people's rebellion is brutally suppressed, but the murdered rebels arise, spreading panic and terror among the aristocracy, with a frenzied King Hunger shouting at the final curtain, "Run! Run! The dead are rising!" The Hedgerow's production, designed by the young Mordecai Gorelik, opened on December 6, 1924.

Only fragments of Blitzstein's score survive, including a sentimental "Waltz" for violin and piano and a grotesque "Macabre Dance" for violin, castanets, and piano (derived from an ostensibly earlier *Fire Dance* for violin and piano). Still less survives of the *Richard II* score, although Blitzstein apparently wrote or planned a four-movement piece for cello and piano based on this material. Both commissions anticipate later preoccupations: *King Hunger*, Blitzstein's tendency toward social allegory (with the warnings that conclude *The Cradle Will Rock* and the *Airborne Symphony* specifically echoing *King Hunger*); and *Richard II*, the composer's mature music for Shakespeare.

On October 7, 1925, Blitzstein also made his Broadway debut when producers Henry W. Savage and A. H. Woods used his song "The Dream Is Mine" ("Romance") as the theme music for the short-lived show *Stolen Fruit*, an adaptation by Gladys Unger of Italian playwright Dario Niccodemi's melodrama *La maestrina* (1917).

The first known instance of a song for which the composer, using the pseudonym Marc Blistan, wrote both words and music, "The Dream Is Mine" represents for its composer a rare venture into a world akin to American operetta. Tellingly, he recycled this song for the operetta parody "Sing Hubbard" for his opera *Regina* (1949), with the original words, "The homing birds are drifting southward,/A Breath of winter haunts the sky," changed to "Regina does a lovely party./Her festive board will reward the hearty."

During this early period, Blitzstein wrote a few piano pieces as well, including "Danse Basse," "Danse Haute," "Round," "Pavane," "Sarabande," and "Variation sur 'Au clair de la lune,'" at least several of which he intended as part of a suite of *Children's Dances*, although he ultimately grouped "Pavane," "Sarabande," and "Variation" as *Pieces* for piano, op. 2. Notwithstanding a few quirky twists, these pieces—or at least those that survive—reveal, as their titles might suggest, a classical sensibility, in particular, a kinship to the neoclassical Debussy and Ravel, a connection underlined by the use of the French folk tune "Au clair de la lune" in the "Variation." Pianist Charles Naegele performed "Pavane" and "Variation" at Aeolian Hall on January 7, 1927, on which occasion the *New York Times* declared the latter piece "a harmless skit," intimating a satirical bent already in place. Meanwhile, the classical elegance of these early piano pieces—similarly encountered in the surviving *Richard II* bits—found reverberations in many of Blitzstein's later works as well.[5]

After *Svarga*, Blitzstein composed another ballet, *Blessings of the Bath* (1926), which evolved into the ballet *Megalopolis*, further arranged as a suite, *Jigg-Saw* (1926–28). In none of these guises does the music survive in its entirety, but enough exists so as to suggest that the composer completed both *Blessings of the Bath* and *Megalopolis*, or at least, with respect to the latter, the *Jigg-Saw* suite. As far as is known, the ballet was never produced or performed in any form; nor do any scenarios survive.

To judge from a table of contents found among his papers, Blitzstein conceived *Blessings of the Bath* as in eight parts: (1) "Introduction"; (2) "Belly-Dance, Scene-Change"; (3) "In the Bath"; (4) "The Frenchman"; (5) "Drying Fugue"; (6) "Pas d'action, March"; (7) "Reprise, Scene-Change"; (8a) "Blessings I"; (8b) "Blessings II"; (8c) "Alleluia." The extant score includes neither the "Drying Fugue" nor the entire eighth movement, but all this music might well have existed at one time.

On the reverse page of this table, Blitzstein drafted a similar outline with descriptive phrases that hint at his dramatic purposes: "itching march" ("Introduction"), "bathing and rubbing" ("Belly-Dance"), an "old man and attendant" ("In the Bath"), "splashing the old man" ("The Frenchman"), "with interruption by the Swimming Lady" ("Drying Fugue"), "triumphant march" ("Pas d'action"), and "bathing like the beginning" (presumably "Reprise" and the "Blessings" finale). That the pas d'action quotes both "The Star-Spangled Banner" and the anti-Prohibition drinking song, "(Nobody Knows) How Dry I Am" (a parody of the hymn "Happy Day"), provides another clue as to the composer's intentions. What Blitzstein meant by all this—including the work's ironic title—remains unclear, but given the prominence of bathhouses as centers of homosexual camaraderie, the ballet plausibly encompassed satirical social criticism informed by a gay subtext.

With its unusual instrumentation (for clarinet, trombone, and piano), dissonant ostinatos, and octatonic inflections (as in the belly dance), the ballet reveals the growing and potent influence of Stravinsky, although considering too its relatively straightforward rhythms, the work perhaps more nearly resembles Darius Milhaud. The score at the same time accommodated some of the composer's more conservative music of the period, with two of his three *Pieces* ("Variation sur 'Au clair de la lune'" and "Pavane") adapted for "The Frenchman" and "Blessings I," respectively. Perhaps Blitzstein used or intended to use the last of the *Pieces*, "Sarabande," for the missing "Blessings II."

In turn, some of *Blessings of the Bath* resurfaced not only in *Megalopolis/Jigg-Saw* but in the composer's work from the mid-1930s: the belly dance reemerged essentially unchanged as the underscoring for the military recruitment speech by Professor Mamie in *The Cradle Will Rock*; the main theme of the pas d'action (including its allusion to "The Star-Spangled Banner") similarly reappeared, although with a thinned-out accompaniment, as courtroom music in *The Cradle* (at rehearsal number 33); and a passage from "In the Bath," only slightly tweaked, became the humorous travel music for Mr. Musiker and Beetzie in *I've Got the Tune* (as found in the first three pages of the piano-vocal score). Such recycling intimates the seminal importance of Blitzstein's music from the 1920s.

While studying with Boulanger in Paris in the fall of 1926, Blitzstein apparently worked on developing *Blessings of the Bath* into a ballet for full orchestra. For this revised score, which he at some point titled *Megalopolis*, he collaborated with Abraham Lincoln (Link) Gillespie (1895–1950), a fellow Philadelphian making his reputation during these years as a writer who could outdo the latest dadaesque poet in terms of sheer inscrutability. Blitzstein possibly knew Gillespie (who frequented the Leof salon) from home, or else met him abroad, perhaps through George Antheil, who in his memoirs called Gillespie "the most extraordinary character I've ever met."[6]

According to a surviving outline, Blitzstein planned *Megalopolis* as a three-scene work, the first of which would have included much of *Blessings of the Bath*, although altered to include "Buck and Wing" and other new episodes. This outline lists key centers, tempo and dynamic markings, time signatures, and actual themes, as well as such dramatic signifiers as "hausfrowse," "whirling methodics," and "nuptial parade" that intimate Gillespie's possible authorship, but certainly his sensibility, apparently shared to some extent by Blitzstein. The third scene was even to open with an "atonal" movement complete with "buzz saws, electric fans, riveting machines, etc."

Whether he ever completed the work as such, Blitzstein prepared a suite called *Jigg-Saw* ("Ballet for Full Orchestra") that basically contains the first of the three scenes mentioned above, its five individual movements entitled "Prelude," "The Belly-Dancer and the Salvation Army," "Liberty Throws a Party," "Buck and Wing," and "Cotton-Pickers' Shuffle." The first three movements basically correspond to the introduction, belly dance, and pas d'action from *Blessings of the Bath*, although for the new idea of pitting a belly dancer against members of the Salvation Army, Blitzstein added, as an interlude, a setting of "Onward, Christian Soldiers" (the Arthur Sullivan hymn associated with the Christian temperance group) and then combined the belly dance with the hymn. The new prelude also featured far more changing meters than the earlier introduction, bringing the music yet closer to Stravinsky. "Liberty Throws a Party" seems to have involved a Thanksgiving celebration in which a Native American, bearing a turkey, and an African American, carrying a watermelon, are surrounded by Southerners who put them in cages, at one point the score stating, "The party proceeds merrily. Witch burners and Southerners dance."

As for "Buck and Wing" and "Cotton-Pickers' Shuffle," the latter of which does not seem to have survived, both titles refer to popular African-American dance styles, and in the spirit of the jazzy music it emulates, "Buck and Wing" quotes at one point the Mother Goose ditty "Rock-a-bye, Baby." As a whole, *Megalopolis/Jigg-Saw* shows Blitzstein moving more decisively in the direction of jazzy vernacular music and caustic social commentary.

Upon his return home, the composer approached his artist friend Julian Levi (1900–1982, not to be confused with the noted art dealer Julien Levy) about designing sets and costumes for the ballet, which the Philadelphia Society for Contemporary Music expressed some interest in mounting, but nothing materialized. Neither did Fritz Reiner nor any other conductor take up the suite, as Blitzstein had hoped—one of the first major disappointments of many to come. But again he salvaged what he could, including recycling some of "Buck and Wing" for *The Cradle Will Rock* as underscoring for yet another recruitment speech, this one by Professor Trixie, the music conveniently quoting the nursery song from which Blitzstein derived the title of his opera.[7]

Blitzstein's various settings of Walt Whitman for solo voice and piano (1925–28) represent perhaps his most enduring accomplishment of this early period. He wrote the first four of these songs—"As If a Phantom Caress'd Me," "What Weeping Face," "Joy, Shipmate, Joy!" and "After the Dazzle of Day"—in the spring of 1925, with soprano Elizabeth Gutman and pianist Alderson Mowbray premiering "As If a Phantom Caress'd Me" at a League of Composers concert in New York on February 13, 1927, and soprano Lisa Roma and pianist Nicolai Mednikoff debuting "What Weeping Face" in Philadelphia on April 26 of that same year. Blitzstein subsequently composed two more Whitman songs while studying with Boulanger in Paris: "Gods" (and a French version, "Dieux") in the fall of 1926 and "O Hymen! O Hymenee!" the following January. He wrote yet another Whitman song, "As Adam," in May 1927 during his time in Berlin, grouping "O Hymen! O Hymenee!" and "As Adam" as, alternately, *Two Songs for a Coon-Shouter*, as in his 1928 catalog; *Songs for a Coon-Shouter*, as in his manuscript; and *Two Coon Shouts*, as premiered at the Academy of Music Foyer under the auspices of the Philadelphia Society for Contemporary Music on March 13, 1928, by Nelson Eddy—later an operetta star, but then a popular baritone at the Civic Opera—with the composer at the piano.[8]

In the meantime, Blitzstein arranged "Gods" for voice, solo cello (or horn), and strings, which version premiered on February 15, 1928, at the Penn Athletic Club, again with one of the city's leading operatic figures, mezzo-soprano Ruth Montague, and the Philadelphia Chamber String Sinfonietta conducted by Fabien Sevitzky, nephew of conductor Serge Koussevitzky. Blitzstein wrote two final Whitman songs, "I Am He" and "Ages and Ages," in late 1928. Transposing "As Adam" a minor third lower (he also crossed out the song's Moderato tempo marking and wrote in its stead "Faster"), he grouped "O Hymen! O Hymenee!" "I Am He," "Ages and Ages," and "As Adam" (all from the *Children of Adam* portion of *Leaves of Grass*) as *Four Songs* for baritone and piano. African-American baritone Benjohn (Benjamin John) Ragsdale premiered the set as such at a Copland-Sessions concert at New York's Little Theatre on December 30, 1928, with Blitzstein again at the piano, an early instance of the composer's many collaborations with African-American artists. Sometime later, he revised the set as *Three Songs* for baritone and piano by omitting "O Hymen! O Hymenee!"

In 1928, Blitzstein also undertook a setting of the opening section of Whitman's "A Word Out of the Sea" (retitled by the poet as "Out of the Cradle Endlessly Rocking" in 1859) for soprano, contralto, small women's chorus (four sopranos and four altos), and chamber group. This unfinished cantata was to comprise five movements that ostensibly would have set the poem from its beginning to the end of "Blow! Blow! Blow!" However, Blitzstein—who recommended the poem to Berenice Skidelsky "for a renewal of the spiritual kick in the pants Whitman can always deliver"—apparently completed only three movements: "Shine! Shine! Shine!" for soprano and orchestra; "Till, Of a Sudden" for chorus and orchestra; and "Blow! Blow! Blow!" for contralto and orchestra.[9]

Blitzstein culled these sundry Whitman poems from one or another of various editions of *Leaves of Grass*, remaining faithful to the texts at hand, aside from the minor change at the end of "I Am He" from "all I meet or know" to "all I meet and know" (altered once more in the posthumous *Songbook* to "all I meet and see"). He presumably consulted the work's 1860 edition, the only one to include "What Weeping Face," and the deathbed 1891 edition, the only one to include "After the Dazzle of Day"; based on his punctuation, however, he seems to have taken most of the texts from the 1871 edition. Although this made virtually no difference in terms of actual words, it affected Blitzstein's text setting because Whitman's commas, considerably reduced in the 1891 edition, helped guide the composer's melodic writing. The phrase "waiting, content" from "Gods," for example, contains two quarter-note rests between these two words, a dramatic break in the vocal line that Blitzstein might not have conceived had he used the phrase as found in the 1891 edition: "waiting content."[10]

Blitzstein's close association with Whitman's work during these years seems telling, given the poet's association with progressive artistic and democratic ideals. David Metzer notes in particular the composer's selection of homoerotic texts, opining that these settings "represent one of the boldest celebrations of Whitman's homoeroticism by an American artist," an observation especially befitting "As If a Phantom Caress'd Me," and even more so, the *Children of Adam* songs, which directly address sex, viewed as tantalizing ("O Hymen! O Hymenee!"), aching ("I Am He"), delirious ("Ages and Ages"), and yearning ("As Adam"). In some contrast, the 1925 songs show a more general preoccupation with transcendence ("After the Dazzle of Day" and "Joy, Shipmate, Joy!") and loss ("As If a Phantom Caress'd Me" and "What Weeping Face"), themes already explored in the composer's surviving Housman settings. Indeed, the Whitman songs, along with his correspondence, suggest that Blitzstein's time in Paris and Berlin (1926–27) made him that much more forthcoming concerning sexual matters.[11]

Stylistic differences reflect these thematic ones. Whereas the shimmering 1925 songs, sounding at times like the young Alban Berg, represent a last gasp of the composer's formative postromantic phase, the later Whitman songs move more in the direction of Stravinsky and Schoenberg. (A bit of speech-song in "As If a Phantom Caress'd Me" might already have betokened the influence of Schoenberg, although in that instance, the composer employed notes in parentheses as opposed to the Schoenbergian stems with x's adopted later by Blitzstein.) Moreover, jazz elements, although discernible in "O Hymen! O Hymenee!" and "As Adam," assume greater prominence in "I Am He" and "Ages and Ages," perhaps in part reflecting the impact of Antheil and a growing awareness of Copland.[12]

Blitzstein highlighted the connection with jazz not only with such titles as *Two Coon Shouts*, but even more explicitly in a statement published on the day of the December 30, 1928, premiere of the *Four Songs*: "Some people have questioned my use of a jazz idiom with the Whitman words; it seems to me perfectly natural to couple two media whose implications are alike universal, and whose methods are alike primitive; both jazz and Whitman contain a primal and all-pervading sex urge." (Concerning this note, Sessions wrote to Copland "that that sort of thing," besides being "fifth or sixth hand," dated back to *The Masses*, a Marxist journal published in the 1910s, an observation that placed Blitzstein's work, perhaps for the first time, in the context of radical politics.) As evidenced from his 1929 lecture on jazz, Blitzstein associated "coon shouts" and "coon-shouter" not with some antiquated minstrel tradition, as commonly supposed, but rather with the contemporary blues and women blues singers, both African-American and Jewish, making the racial and gender dissonance between such contexts and Whitman's verse all the more evocative.[13]

The terms "coon-singer" and "coon shouts" also underscore the fact that the "jazz idiom" of these *Four Songs* informs not only the piano accompaniments, with their accented syncopations and rich ninth and altered chords, but the vocal lines, with their fluid shapes, grace-note and glissando ornaments, and irregular rhythms (including an 8/4 division of a 6/4 bar in "O Hymen! O Hymenee!"). Blitzstein's Whitman songs in general stand out for their dramatic but natural prosody and the way in which dissonant harmonies color the straightforward melodies, creating an evocative atmosphere for the singer's words—traits that would prove characteristic, thereby strongly intimating Whitman's influence on the composer's developing art.

The dramatic verve of these Whitman songs, with their big climaxes—performing "As Adam" and Charles Ives's "Serenity" on a 1946 lecture-recital, Blitzstein himself cited these two songs, according to a review, as exemplifying an "extrovert" and "introvert" approach to music, respectively—no doubt helped put them over to at least some early listeners. Audience members responded well to the Philadelphia world premieres of "Gods" and *Two Coon Shouts*, insisting that Nelson Eddy encore the second "coon shout." Both works also elicited some positive remarks in the local press (along with some highly negative ones), one review stating, in reference to "Gods," "The music is modern, but carries out admirably the spirit of the text," another saying of *Two Coon Shouts*, "There is elemental power and terror in them." [14]

The New York reviews of the *Four Songs* generally proved more disparaging, with a number of critics seemingly bothered by the work's overt eroticism, as suggested by such phrases as "repellent puerility" (Olin Downes), "musical obscenity" (Oscar Thompson), and "exceedingly bad taste" (Marion Bauer). By opposing Whitman's "virile and often superb verse" with Blitzstein's "vapidness" and "lack of virility," Olin Downes at least attempted to protect Whitman from any perceived debasement. By contrast, the savvy Samuel Chotzinoff, in probably the work's most appreciative review, thought Blitzstein's songs "outwardly somewhat jazzy, but inwardly no doubt aptly expressive of the poet's important message," and that Ragsdale "entered fully into the spirit of the revelation." As for the audience's response, accounts differ; Bauer claimed that they were "insulted" by the work, whereas Robert A. Simon thought "nobody seemed to be upset about the songs." In either case, this New York airing—much like the premiere of his Piano Sonata at a League of Composers concert earlier in the year—cannot be said to have furthered Blitzstein's reputation significantly, aside from confirming his skill and gusto as a pianist.[15]

Blitzstein began his short, one-movement Sonata for piano during the summer of 1927 while he was in Berlin and completed it in Philadelphia that December. The work's bold harmonic writing, barely suggesting tonal centers, and its percussive

piano writing, including a "cadenza style" coda that contains tremolos and glissandos running across the full gamut of the keyboard, show the influence of
Stravinsky and Bartók, albeit taken to certain extremes. The piece also bespeaks
its Berlin provenance, with borrowings not only from Schoenberg, but possibly
more deeply Ferruccio Busoni, a composer Blitzstein greatly admired, and a
mentor, significantly, to both Kurt Weill and Stefan Wolpe, whose own piano sonata made an impression on the young American.[16]

At the same time, Blitzstein's sonata strikes out on its own in a number of ways,
most notably in its frequent interruptions of thematic material by single-measure
rests, a feature that earned the work a certain notoriety. The piece has an unusual
larger structure as well, as it puts forth an opening fast section, a shorter slow section, and six more sections of fairly brief duration, followed by a coda. Blitzstein
separates all eight sections with pauses, which he describes in his manuscript as
"longer than a *fermato* [sic], and shorter than the pause between movements of a
suite; about the time between sections of a theme and variations." The composer
intended thus to avoid "transitions," a notion derived from such Stravinsky works
as the *Symphonies of Wind Instruments*. "Each section of the sonata exists intrinsically, *en bloc*, for itself," he explained. "The possibility of padding while waiting
for the next 'big' thing is thus eliminated. The padding is replaced by silences."
Some of these blocks reprise material from the first two sections; Blitzstein even
had traditional sonata form in mind, including "alternating developments" and
the "return of theme two in the tonic of theme one," but no clear pattern emerges,
and the effect is one of great spontaneity. As to mood, the piece alternately features a pungency and tenderness that would remain, in less stringent guises,
keynotes of his work.[17]

Blitzstein premiered the piece in New York at a League of Composers concert of
new American music on February 12, 1928, his first major New York appearance
and one vividly recalled by Minna Lederman: "Barely 23 [actually just shy of 23],
small and slight, he moved across the stage in an anxious, darting trot, carrying his
head forward. His face was pointed and foxlike, but the gray eyes held a direct challenge. . . . it was clear at once that we were meeting a very Angry Young Man. . . .
Marc was simply angry with himself, edgy, mettlesome, sharp-tongued. He looked
at everything, he listened to everything, he quarreled with everyone. Brash though
he was, he couldn't be ignored." Blitzstein repeated the piece in Philadelphia on
March 13, 1928, at the same concert on which he accompanied Nelson Eddy in the
first performance of *Two Coon Shouts*; in New York along with Stravinsky's *Piano-
Rag-Music* (1919) and Carlos Chávez's Sonatina (1924) at a March 3, 1929, concert
at the MacDowell Club at which he also discussed contemporary musical trends;
on an all-Blitzstein concert on April 16, 1933, aired by WEVD (a primarily Yid-
dish-language radio station named after the prominent socialist Eugene V. Debs);
at a Composers' Forum-Laboratory concert in New York on April 15, 1936, at
which time he declared the piece "in a sense, my opus 1"; and at yet another

all-Blitzstein concert at Tanglewood on July 25, 1958. Meanwhile, Daniel Lazarus gave the Paris premiere at the offices of the *Revue musicale* on May 22, 1928, at a concert sponsored by Lazare Saminsky, and Keith Corelli, the Boston premiere in Jordan Hall as the closing item of a remarkable February 4, 1929, program that opened with the "Emerson" movement from Ives's *Concord Sonata* and that also included pieces by Copland, Cowell, and Ruth Crawford, among others.[18]

Many of the work's early reviews, when not simply dismissing the piece as "trite," "dull," and "monotonous," whimsically compared it to squealing mice, a stone-drilling machine, and so on, with one critic—in a review whose title, "Donner und Blitzstein," featured a pun on the German phrase for "thunder and lightning" ("Donner und Blitzen")—suggesting that the work might have been called "a Sonata in One Round for two heavyweights, the contestants last night being Blitzstein himself and a Baldwin piano. It was Blitzstein's round. With a left jab that all but drove the ivory off the keys and a pummeling right hand technique, the product of Messrs. Baldwin was quickly swatted into submission." Such wise-cracking, although typical of American music criticism of this period, perhaps disguised some unease, as suggested by Blitzstein's own recollection of these per-formances: "It was a crashing, angry piece. People didn't know what it was about. It left them uncomfortable as hell. Me, too."[19]

In contrast, later commentators found such bold vigor among the piece's attrac-tions. Reviewing a performance by Beveridge Webster at New York's Carnegie Recital Hall in 1980, John Rockwell (*New York Times*), for instance, wrote that the sonata "blended Schoenberg, Stravinsky, Prokofiev and Bartok into a compactly American statement that sounded as fresh Thursday as it must have seemed 53 years ago." Albrecht Duemling (*Neue Zeitschrift für Musik*), covering the work's 1985 Ber-lin premiere by Leonard Lehrman, similarly thought the music "astonishingly fresh," while Greg Stepanich (*Palm Beach ArtsPaper*), in a review of Sarah Cahill's 2009 recording of the piece, commended the work's "aggressive athleticism." The com-poser himself remained unashamed of this "blurted out piece," asserting in 1940, "it said what I wanted to say."[20]

Like the sonata, Blitzstein's score for the short film *Hände* (1927–28) had its origins in Berlin, where the composer befriended the work's Charleston-born producer and writer, Stella Simon (1878–1973). The widow of a successful businessman, Simon studied photography with Clarence White in New York and arrived in Berlin in the fall of 1926 to take a course in filmmaking. Blitz-stein met her in 1927 possibly through his friend and her son Louis (1906–1990), a future theatrical executive then working with producer Max Reinhardt. A landmark of experimental cinema, *Hände* would be Simon's only film.[21]

Simon apparently wrote the scenario and co-directed the picture with Miklós Bándy, Hans Richter designed the abstract sets, and Leopold Kutzleb supervised the photography. Subtitled "Das Leben und die Liebe eines zärtlichen Geschlechts"

("The Life and Love of the Gentler Sex"), the film tells its story entirely through the hands and forearms of dancers Hertha Feist, Berth Cis, and Pakka Pakka: a man and a woman meet, a coquette enters the picture, all go to a party, the man betrays the woman, the woman attempts to drown herself, and the man rescues her—or so it seems, for the action invites varied interpretations. In any case, the drama moves toward crisis, disintegration, and suicide, although the final image of two hands side-by-side, suggests that the man and woman in the end have achieved equality and independence. "The film," writes Jan-Christopher Horak, "presents a 'melodrama' of female subjectivity and *angst*. It is the drama of a woman who is afraid to lose her mate to another, more desirable woman, the melodrama of a woman who is continually playing out masochistic fantasies of defeat and self-mutilation, ever fearful that she is no longer the object of man's desire. The film's narrative closure . . . inscribes woman's desire for sexual harmony, and is indicative of Simon's romantic American approach."[22]

Simon presumably provided Blitzstein with a scenario of the film in Berlin, for which he composed music for player piano and percussion (apparently lost as such). On August 31, 1927, after Blitzstein returned home, portions of the film were shown at Berlin's Neumann-Nierendorf art gallery as a work-in-progress, with music reportedly provided by pianist Else C. Kraus, who also had studied with Schoenberg. When Blitzstein finally viewed the film with Simon in New York in early 1928, he was, as he told Louis, "horribly disappointed; it seemed such a burdensome, long, unwieldy opus; monotonous, unarticulated, *German*. . . . The greatest fault seems to be the lack of any definite rhythmic scheme; after that the fact that as a *story* it doesn't quite get across . . . and as a pure abstract study it misses fire by being too long and by having whetted one's appetite *for* a story. In spite of all this, it remains an extraordinarily interesting and stimulating film."[23]

Blitzstein and Stella Simon duly edited the picture, with the composer retooling his music accordingly. The one score that survives among his papers, marked "for mechanical piano" and dated 1927–28, probably represents this revised version, most of which can be played by a single pianist, although some passages indeed require the kind of overdubbing suited to a player piano. Early viewings of the film in New York and Paris actually did not use any music at all, according to Simon, who reserved Blitzstein's score for a high-profile late-night concert sponsored by the November Group in Berlin at the Gloria-Palast on February 16, 1929, a riotous event at which the audience broke into laughter during the film, one viewer crying out "Hände weg!" ("Hands off!").[24]

The many largely negative reviews of this showing had virtually nothing to say about the music, although one reviewer who heard some mysterious sounds coming from a loudspeaker during the film thought the score by Antheil, which seems unlikely, but is telling nonetheless. Another observed that the accompanying "Blues-Musik" temporarily helped calm the crowd. Whether someone performed the music live (Stefan Wolpe, also featured on this program, could have done so) or prepared a roll of the work, no roll survived, and in 1936, after the Museum of Modern Art luckily acquired a negative of the film from the UFA studios in Berlin, Blitzstein recorded the music at the piano, dispensing with notes unplayable by a single pianist and tweaking the score in other ways as well.[25]

The score has five parts, with the first and last parts, which more or less correspond to the prologue and epilogue that frame the film, featuring the same music. These larger parts contain smaller sections that typically match breaks in the film initiated by the intertitles. Thanks in part to the clear textures and the triadic if often bitonal harmonies, the score, at turns sardonic, sensuous, and melancholy, represents one of Blitzstein's most accessible from this period, revealing, too, his talent for dramatic atmosphere. In some ways, the score emulates Antheil's *Ballet mécanique*, also associated with avant-garde film; but Blitzstein's music, embodying that same tension between the abstract and the romantic found in the film itself, has its own flavor. Meanwhile, the 1936 soundtrack recorded by RCA Victor preserves via the film medium a relatively rare document of the composer's distinctive piano playing: fleet, elegant, each rest pregnant with meaning.

Blitzstein had his first real if minor success with his "opera-farce," *Triple-Sec*. He possibly met the work's librettist, British playwright Ronald Jeans (1887–1973), in May 1927 while visiting London with Stella Simon, who had been invited by Lorenz Hart to attend the opening night of a British revue, *One Dam Thing After Another*, for which Rodgers and Hart had written the score and Jeans, the book. Earlier in the decade, Jeans, with his comic sketches, had helped pioneer the so-called intimate musical revue, an increasingly popular genre both in the West End and on Broadway that bore some resemblance to French and German cabaret. "His [Jeans's] sketches (at least eight in any production), usually gently ironic," writes James Moore, "managed the standard elements of plot and characterization, a beginning, middle, end and sometimes a moral—all in five to seven minutes, frequently capped by a startling, appropriate 'twist.'" On a trip to New York in 1928, Jeans met with Blitzstein, and the two decided to collaborate on a one-act satire of the drawing-room comedies of Eugène Scribe, Victorien Sardou, and Arthur Wing Pinero. Blitzstein thought about the work for about a month and then "dashed it off" in three weeks while at the MacDowell Colony in the summer of 1928.[26]

The authors found an original way to satirize Victorian comedy. In a prologue in front of the curtain, the Hostess—styled after speakeasy hostess Texas Guinan, famous for her greeting, "Hello, suckers"—tells an imagined cabaret audience, already tipsy on champagne, that they are to witness a "new form of entertainment" consisting of drama accompanied by food and drink: "I want you to enjoy, chicken and Tschekoff, beer and Barrie, schnitzel and Schnitzler, for one and the same price of admission."

The curtain rises on the library of Lord Rupert Silverside (tenor), a presumed bachelor soon to be married. Perkins, the maid (soprano), tells Hopkins the butler (baritone) about a lady in black who called on Silverside earlier in the day. This same Stranger (actually Silverside's wife) (mezzo-soprano) arrives, telling Hopkins, who recognizes her, that she must see Silverside. As Hopkins ushers her off stage, Silverside (tenor) returns home with his fiancée Lady Betty (soprano), and the two pass through into another room. When Hopkins and Silverside return to the library for a private conversation, there are two of each of them (with the idea that the increasingly inebriated audience has succumbed to double vision, the work's title punning the thrice-distilled orange liqueur, triple sec, with the opera's depiction of multiple vision). Hopkins (I and II) tells Silverside (I and II) that a lady awaits him, whereupon the Stranger appears, also in duplicate. The two Hopkinses leave, but when they reenter, there are three of them. The Stranger (I and II) pleads for a reconciliation with Silverside (I and II), threatening to divulge all to Lady Betty, three of whom now enter. When Betty (I, II, and III) discovers she's engaged to a married man, she faints. Silverside (I and II) calls for water, and eight Perkinses arrive, each with a glass of water. As the two Silversides, two Strangers, three Bettys, three Hopkins, and eight Perkinses sing a final chorus, the set begins to shake, the lamps go on and off, all the characters get mixed up, a green dragon with red eyes "rears its head above the turmoil," and all goes dark as the curtain falls.

The ironically portentous text sometimes gives way to clowning. "Discretion is the better part of valets," Hopkins tells Perkins, while the Stranger says, at another point, "You are surprised, Hopkins, and I am not surprised you are surprised." The work's humor broadens even more toward the end with its chaotic depiction—at the height of Prohibition, no less—of intoxicated confusion, hallucination, and blackout. Significantly, Jeans and Blitzstein conceived this cabaret-inspired farce, which targets both the well-made play and its bourgeois audience, at precisely the same time that Brecht and Weill wrote *The Threepenny Opera*, placing Blitzstein and Weill in aesthetic proximity to each other even at this early date.

Blitzstein scored the piece for nineteen singers and an orchestra of twelve, including piano four-hands and two percussionists. As with the Piano Sonata, he approached the work as a series of blocks varied in mood, although mostly insouciant or mock-solemn. The whole achieves coherence partly through its extensive use of an opening four-note gesture heard initially in the trumpet, not to mention its pervasively sardonic tone. The harmonic style features those sharp dissonances characteristic of the young Blitzstein, but here ingeniously used to create an intoxicated atmosphere, much as George Grosz or Otto Dix used modernist techniques to create their boozy portraits.

The work bears special resemblance to Hindemith's *Hin und Zurück*, which Blitzstein had reviewed in April 1928 and which might have served as a model for his own little opera. Certainly, he could have been talking about *Triple-Sec* when he said of the Hindemith, "The score is compact, rich and witty, beautifully proportioned to the trivial nonsense of the libretto. . . . It defies consistent analysis—being at various times atonal, polytonic, polytonal, even conventionally diatonic—yet it maintains a logic, however obscure, and always gives off the feeling of being completely realized. . . . Most striking in this little masterpiece is the economy of its means, the richness and variety of effect and the characteristic unity." Moreover, the relation between the motion pictures and Hindemith's opera, as perceived by Blitzstein, seems palpable here as well. About this same time, Blitzstein named Stravinsky as an important influence, and suffice it to say, the work features Stravinskian as well as Hindemithian elements.[27]

Triple-Sec premiered at Philadelphia's Bellevue-Stratford Ballroom on May 6, 1929, as the final selection of a triple bill sponsored by the Society for Contemporary Music that also included Alfredo Casella's *Pupazzetti* and the Philadelphia premiere of Schoenberg's *Pierrot lunaire* (with Blitzstein at the piano). James (Jimmy) Light directed, Louis Simon designed the costumes, and the work's dedicatee, Alexander Smallens, conducted, all three good friends of the composer's. The cast, largely recruited from the Philadelphia Civic Opera, included Ruth Montague (who had premiered "Gods") (Hostess), Ethel Niethammer (Perkins), Ralph Jusko (Hopkins), Maybelle Marston (Stranger), Albert Mahler (Lord Silverside), and Irene Williams (Lady Betty). H. T. Craven (*Philadelphia Record*) reported that "gales of laughter welcomed this novelty," although he himself thought "the satire . . . crude, its extravagance rather puerile."[28]

This particular production presented Lord Silverside as black, according to Craven, whose account misleadingly gave at least later commentators the impression that the white Albert Mahler—one of the city's leading character tenors— was black: "Librettist Ronald Jeans has made Lord Silversides [sic] a Negro. He has a love scene, all in fun, mind you, with a white lassie. This is going the Metropolitan one better, since 'Jonny,' of 'Spielt' fame [Ernst Krenek's *Jonny spielt auf*], is, in the American production, only a Caucasian blacked up like a minstrel." That the Met actually portrayed Jonny as black (even if performed by a white singer in makeup) made Craven's remarks all the more confusing, although representing a British aristocrat as opposed to a jazz musician as black plainly formed a more transgressive conceit. Indeed, the idea might have originated not with the librettist as assumed (the score gives no such indication) but with the composer, who had made similarly subversive use of racial conventions in *Two Coon Shouts* as he would years later in *Reuben Reuben*. In the event, mathematician Arnold Dresden and composer-musicologist Alfred Swan, two Swarthmore professors apparently asked to evaluate the premiere at the behest of Frank Aydelotte, the president of Swarthmore and the chairman of the Guggenheim Foundation to which Blitzstein had applied for a grant, found the opera not at all to their tastes— Swan thought it "vulgar" and "offensive"—and their reports very likely spoiled the composer's chances for a fellowship, his strong recommendations from Nadia Boulanger, Marian MacDowell, Pierre Monteux, Lazare Saminsky, and Alexander Smallens notwithstanding.[29]

Triple-Sec subsequently made its way into the third and final edition of the *Garrick Gaieties* (1930), thanks to the composer's friend Louis Simon, active in the production as costumer, writer, and stage manager. The appearance on Broadway of so bold a work constituted a stretch, even if sophisticated revues of the period like the *Gaieties* occasionally offered ambitious fare. Director Philip Loeb strategically placed the opera at the top of the second half—its best bet—and apparently removed the prologue, as some later productions would do. The program further advised the audience that the work was "a modernistic operetta which is not to be taken too seriously." Smallens rehearsed the pit orchestra, and the cast included, in the tiny role of Betty III, a young comedian, Imogene Coca, of later television fame.

The *Garrick Gaieties* opened on June 4, 1930, at the Guild Theatre, and enjoyed 158 performances, a brief return engagement, and a national tour, although at some point an older Rodgers and Hart number, "The Three Musketeers," replaced *Triple-Sec*. The critics thought Blitzstein's "blotto modernistic opera" "elaborate," "difficult," and in part "labored," but generally "successful" and in the end, "excellent music satire." Especially since some of Gershwin's innermost circle—including brother Ira, Kay Swift, Vernon Duke, and E. Y. Harburg—worked on the show, Gershwin naturally attended the production, and later told Blitzstein, as the story has been reported, that *Triple-Sec* so "entranced" him that "he used to come [to the show] just to hear it." (Gershwin and Blitzstein seem to have had some acquaintance, with Gershwin also allegedly saying to Blitzstein, at the American premiere of *Wozzeck* in Philadelphia in 1931, with regard to the Alban Berg work, "'S wonderful! Wonderful!") On the other hand, Cecil Goldbeck found Blitzstein's opera, as he told his former wife and the composer's good friend Eva Goldbeck, "boring," "pointless," and "the poorest thing on the bill."[30]

Blitzstein was himself skeptical from the start, writing to Louis Simon, "The skit is both under and over the heads of that sort of public; they will be bored by the theme, and uninterested in the only justification for it—the music." He urged, rather, that Simon use one of the popular songs he had begun to compose. Even after its successful launching, Blitzstein, in Europe at the time, took a discontented view of the matter. "As I read between the lines," he wrote to his sister, "half the applause comes from an audience who don't know what it's all about, but accept it as a spoof on grand-opera; and half is from the snobs ([Carl] Van Vechten, etc.) who are delighted to go slumming a bit, and discover a diamond in the rough, so-to-speak. However, who cares?"[31]

At the same time, he surely was delighted to sign a contract in October 1929 to have the opera published by B. Schott's Söhne, the German music firm associated with Stravinsky and Hindemith. Schott released a piano-vocal score in February 1931 with a German translation by Edwin Denby, whom Blitzstein and Copland had met in Darmstadt in September 1929. The German version even took precedence, with Denby's translation appearing above the English in the score, some stage directions given in German only, and an added German subtitle, "Die Sünde des Lord Silverside" ("The Sins of Lord Silverside"). Despite all this, no German house seems to have staged the work, which appeared during a period of national retrenchment from the adventurousness of the 1920s—one of many unfortunate timings in Blitzstein's career. During the Third Reich, Schott simply withdrew this "degenerate" opera, but republished it in the 1950s, although the original materials had been destroyed by fire during World War II.[32]

After the war, such small American companies as the After Dinner Opera (1950) and the New School Opera Workshop (1967) occasionally revived the opera, as did the Berkshire Music Festival on two occasions (1951, 1958). The critics generally deemed the work a period piece, but an amusing and flavorful one; Arthur Berger, for instance, wrote about the After Dinner production, "'Triple Sec' is as bubbling and palatable as its name. . . . It was Blitzstein's first stage effort, and it certainly predicted he would have a career in this medium."[33]

In 1941, Blitzstein himself discussed the piece with the *People's World*:

> Well, "Triple-Sec" was one of these screwy, modernist things in which, through stage devices, the audience is suppose to get drunk. It had a philosophy. I was slamming the smug people and traditions I had been brought up with. It was a philosophy of denial of their values. Actually, it was a process of clearing the field.
>
> I had been trained as a composer-pet of certain circles and I was tired of it. As for the sketch itself, if it had no results, it would have been just another arty young man bent on being a smart alec. But I see it as more than that.

And in a 1962 lecture at Brandeis University, he further reflected, "The style, I discover now, was a then fashionable mixture of Hindemith and jazz with a certain rhythmic flow characteristic, I think, of myself. It was a cold work, pretty funny, and it had some brilliance. And if it carried any philosophy at all, it was one of nihilism, a kind of surrealist nihilism."[34]

As this youthful period of Blitzstein's career neared its end, the composer, still in his early twenties, ventured another novel solo piano work, the three-movement *Percussion Music*. He completed the first movement, "Toccata," on June 3, 1928; the second movement, "Air," in February 1929; and the third movement, "Rondino," on March 12, 1929.

Commentators typically have associated the work's title with its percussive piano writing, in particular, the coda of the finale, which includes instructions for the pianist to "slap lid," "shut piano key-board [lid]," and "open piano key-board [lid]," usually in that order and always loudly—violent gestures apparently suggested by the Hans Stuckenschmidt piano sonata that Blitzstein had heard while studying in Berlin. But the working titles of the piece's three movements (as found in his 1928 catalog), "Flam," "Drag," and "Paradiddle," indicate a deeper connection with percussion, for all three words refer to snare drum techniques: "flam," to a rapid grace note that sounds almost simultaneously with the main beat (as depicted by the Scotch snaps that open the first movement); "drag," to multiple grace notes, sounding like a roll, that precede a beat (as found in the second movement's main theme); and "paradiddle," the onomatopoeic term that refers to a strong-weak-strong-strong four-note pattern (as heard at the start of the finale). The critic who thought that Blitzstein, with his Piano Sonata, seemed intent on proving "that a grand piano is a glorified bass drum" had even more reason to think of *Percussion Music* in terms of a "glorified" snare drum.[35]

The movement titles that Blitzstein ultimately decided on—"Toccata," "Air," and "Rondino"—referenced rather the work's allusions to the energetic toccatas, ornamented airs, and lighthearted rondos of the eighteenth century. The work's neoclassicism further takes shape, as compared to the sonata, through greater use of diatonic melodies and more clearly developed and unified forms. At the same time, the textures remain spiky; the endings and much else, tonally vague; and the whole—not least the slappings and slammings—fraught with tension.

That the slammings and other percussive gestures, like those of Stuckenschmidt and his friends, had a political subtext was suggested by the fact that Blitzstein scrawled the word "rebel" over a high note on the second page of the "Air," and further down, the phrase "workers of the world . . . unite" over a restatement of the movement's main theme, with the words "workers of the world" actually fitting a fragment of the melody. Blitzstein apparently jotted down these phrases at a time when he also made some slight revisions to the score; if he added these words at a time even approximate to the work's early 1929 completion, they would represent the earliest concrete link between his music and communism. Composer David T. Little in any case views the work, along with Copland's subsequent *Piano Variations* (1930), as one of the "first earnest works of political art music in the American communist/progressive tradition," citing its use of modernist dissonance and angularity as markers for revolt, a development he finds consistent with the radicalism of so-called "third period" communism (1928–35) and epitomized by Copland's reported comment from this time that he "felt that his music must be able to stand up against modern life."[36]

Blitzstein premiered *Percussion Music* at a League of Composers concert at Steinway Hall on March 17, 1929, less than a week after finishing the piece. The reviews, mostly positive, naturally commented on the use of the keyboard lid, with one notice, referring to Blitzstein as "one of our most recent terrorists of sound," stating that as the composer "studiously" slammed the lid, "A ripple of mirth spread gently over the audience and Mr. Blitzstein looked disgusted." Listeners still chuckled over the slammings some seventy years later, when

Sarah Cahill—who guessed that Blitzstein possibly had some ironic intent in all this—played the work in San Francisco on February 26, 2005, and when Leo Marcus performed it at another centennial concert about a week later on March 6 in Los Angeles. Allan Ulrich, reporting on Cahill's performance, concluded that *Percussion Music* "heralded a sophisticated musician, attuned to the emotive power of dissonance, the imitative capabilities of the traditional keyboard, a grounding in ornamentation and, in the repeated close of the keyboard cover, a taste for the dadaist flourishes of the day," while Jerry Dubins, in a review of Cahill's 2009 recording of the piece, thought the music to anticipate Pierre Boulez.[37]

‖ 4 ‖

Life with Eva, I (1929–1931)

During the period 1929–35, while in his mid- and late twenties, Blitzstein divided his time between Europe and the United States, revealing a penchant for traveling that never left him, although after settling in New York in 1935 he would not return to Europe until his military service during the war. The three years 1929–31 found him in Paris, Salzburg, Capri, Houlgate-sur-mer, Cannes, and elsewhere, including Philadelphia and New York, where he resided at 149 West 10th Street (1930–31) and then at 16 Grove Street (1931–32), both located in Greenwich Village, a bohemian neighborhood that increasingly became his home turf. In the summer of 1931, he also spent the first of what would be four residencies at Yaddo, the artists' retreat in Saratoga Springs in upstate New York run by Elizabeth Ames.

During these same three years, Blitzstein developed a romantic relationship with his future wife, writer Eva Goldbeck, who usually accompanied him on these varied peregrinations, although the two sometimes resided in separate rooms, as they would even after their marriage in March 1933. The composer proved unusually prolific during this time as well, producing the song cycle *is 5* and the opera *Parabola and Circula* in 1929; the *Romantic Piece* for orchestra, a string quartet (the "Italian"), and the ballet *Cain* in 1930; and the film score *Surf and Seaweed*, the opera *The Harpies*, and a piano concerto in 1931.

Despite such productivity, Blitzstein barely made ends meet. What few royalties and commissions he received came to little. Nor did he succeed in his attempts to obtain a Prix de Rome or a Guggenheim fellowship. Meanwhile, Goldbeck's own financial situation was precarious; she did not have the $100 to complete needed dental work in 1930. The couple's financial difficulties made such far-flung destinations as Capri, where they could live cheaply, all the more attractive. "I went to Europe to work," Blitzstein stated in 1933, "not because I believe in the superiority of European culture, but because I could live more cheaply there than in this country."[1]

Blitzstein could not expect much help from his father, who had his own financial problems. Initially, the Blitzstein bank actually weathered the stock market crash of 1929 well enough. With depositors in the thousands and a regular staff of nineteen employees, including a few of Blitzstein's cousins, the bank, under the supervision of his father and his uncle Constantine, even completed an expansion of its headquarters at Fourth and Lombard in the fall of 1930. But on December 23, 1930, following a series of other bank panics, depositors made a run for their money, forcing the Blitzstein bank to close. That very evening, the family, who themselves had lost much of their savings, gathered to cries of "Thank God Babushka's dead" in reference to Marc's grandmother, who had built up the bank and died in 1929. "Overnight, the Blitzsteins and local shopkeepers awoke to the reality of the Depression," notes historian Harry Boonin. Within days of its closing, the bank, which never reopened, declared bankruptcy, although it managed to pay back 52 percent of claimed deposits by 1937. "In view of the fact that over 50 percent of claimed deposits was repaid," observes Boonin, "a strong guiding hand might have saved the bank." Perhaps the composer's grandmother might have done so.[2]

Visiting Philadelphia in January 1931, Blitzstein gave what comfort he could to his father, who had become, he observed, "an old man through it." The composer worried too about possible criminal indictments ("the vulturous antics of lawyers sensing prey made anything seem likely," he wrote Goldbeck), and feared, moreover, that he might have to support his father financially, given that his sister Jo, who had begun to appear on local radio shows, and her husband Ed were themselves struggling to stay in their new home. But that never became necessary, thanks to Sam's wife Madi, who remained "both cheerful and useful" and who arranged the move out of 1826 Spruce and into her father's home at 322 South Sixteenth Street. There Sam lived out his days, becoming associated with the Equitable Life Assurance Company and later the National Youth Administration, and eventually involving himself as well in the Spanish Refugee Appeal, Russian War Relief, and the Philadelphia Council of American-Soviet Friendship before succumbing to a heart attack in 1945 at age sixty-five.[3]

Meanwhile, Marc supplemented his income as well as he could by writing articles and giving lectures, including "Modern Music: Latest Developments," delivered at Philadelphia's Ethical House on February 4, 1931, at which he sang the "Barbara Song" from *The Threepenny Opera* at the piano in the style of singers Carola Neher and Roma Bahn, a new German performance style, he maintained, that featured "French grace in combination with American nonchalance, two qualities often sadly lacking in German renditions heretofore." Financial aid from two patrons, Alma Wertheim and Alene Erlanger, also helped the young composer during these years.[4]

Blitzstein met Eva Goldbeck, as mentioned, at the MacDowell Colony in the summer of 1928. When she espied him for the first time, she commented, observing his walk, "Who's this fairy coming?" as fellow colonist Prentiss Taylor recalled, although Blitzstein's sexual orientation actually eluded her for some time. She and Blitzstein became friendly, and after the summer, the two remained in touch, with Goldbeck attending the December 30, 1928, premiere of Blitzstein's *Four Songs*. A freelance writer, Goldbeck primarily earned her living by reporting on French and German reviews of European pictures for Metro-Goldwyn-Mayer, for whom she continued to work after relocating to Europe in early 1929.[5]

Born August 26, 1901, in Berlin, Eva Goldbeck—Blitzstein's senior by four years—was the only child of writer Edward (Eduard) Goldbeck and singer Lina Abarbanell (1879–1963), a native Berliner of Sephardic origins. Appearing at age fourteen as Adele in *Die Fledermaus*, Abarbanell had performed light soprano opera and operetta roles in a number of European houses before making her American debut as Hansel in the Metropolitan Opera's first production of *Hansel and Gretel* in 1905. Staking out a career in America, she and her family settled in Evanston, where Edward worked for the *Chicago Tribune* until some of his viewpoints (as expressed, for instance, in a sympathetic piece on the poet Walter Heymann, a German Jew who died in battle in 1915) allegedly led to his dismissal from the paper during the First World War. Edward and Lina subsequently relocated to New York, where they lived at the Hotel Somerset, he adapting German plays, she performing in and eventually casting various shows.[6]

Eva, a striking and petite woman five feet three inches in height, with green eyes and brown hair, adored her father ("Putzi"), but in the words of her psychiatrist, "loathed and despised" her mother ("Mutzi"), whom she thought vain and self-centered. After graduating from Northwestern University summa cum laude in 1920, she briefly taught Latin in Rockville, Indiana. In early 1922, she married her second cousin Cecil Goldbeck (this made her an American citizen) and took a position at the Dial Publishing Company in New York as a circulation manager. Cecil, an aspiring novelist like Eva, "lacked very strong male attributes," according to Lewis Mumford, "particularly in relation to his career and working life." Neither had much money.[7]

In early 1924, Eva divorced Cecil (1897–1958) on the grounds of adultery, although the two remained the best of friends, with Eva writing him confessional letters, and Cecil responding with equal candor. "I imagine the reason you like only women with sex appeal," he wrote to her in 1929, for instance, "is because you are unconsciously lesbian, which may also be the reason you've never had an orgasm (You could probably give one to yourself). . . . The fact that the thought of physical intercourse with women repulses you, as you've said it does, doesn't mean that you are not unconsciously lesbian." As for his own sexuality, he insisted in 1930, "I am not homosexual," adding in 1931, "I make a point of falling in love as often as possibly, preferably with two or three girls at once as that makes it more exciting and perfectly safe." In later years, Cecil had a notable career as a book publisher with Coward-McCann.[8]

In the course of her short life, Eva produced a torrent of essays, poems, prose, translations, and journal entries, along with astonishingly long letters, frequently typed, but sometimes handwritten in, as Eric Gordon has observed, "a microscopic scrawl that often threatened to dwindle into nothingness." Writing scores of book reviews for a wide range of leading periodicals, she left among her papers an undated list (probably from the early 1920s) of "The Ten Books I Have Most Enjoyed" that provides some sense of her literary tastes at the time: *Mary Olivier: A Life* by May Sinclair; *Sons and Lovers* by D. H. Lawrence; *Crime and Punishment* by Dostoyevsky; *The Everlasting Mercy* by John Masefield; *Leaves of Grass* by Walt Whitman; *Victory* by Joseph Conrad; *Tubal Cain* by Joseph Hergesheimer; *This Side of Paradise* by F. Scott Fitzgerald; *Winesburg, Ohio* by Sherwood Anderson; and *Poems* by Christina Rossetti. (Blitzstein's own literary preferences, at least in the 1920s, ran rather to Thomas Mann, James Joyce, and T. S. Eliot.) Goldbeck managed to publish a few short stories as well, but most of her fiction—not only various stories and translations, but her three novels, the heart of her output—never found its way into print. "Either your work is of the major significance of a Proust or a Thomas Wolfe," wrote Charles Pearce of Harcourt Brace in 1935 in one of the countless rejection letters she received, "or it is doomed to oblivion."[9]

The following excerpt from the novel that occupied her at the MacDowell Colony when she met Blitzstein in 1928, *The Broken Circle*, gives some sense of her dense, opaque prose:

> She had the bland theatricality with which the most unassuming woman displays herself at her best. She was a dispassionately fond entrepreneur of herself, confident of tribute yet feigning to disclaim it, her radiance controlled to transfuse the nature of her acting, stressing her movements with a delicate and elusive precision. She was too shy and too faithfully imbued with social self-abnegation ever to glorify herself, even in playful thought; she was a little shocked at the assertive pleasure she had seen in her mirror, and was doing her best to appear unnoticeable as usual. She told herself that there was nothing about her calling for comment and, smothering an anticipatory regretfulness at being unobserved, sorrily glad resigned herself to her natural tenor.

The theme of "self-abnegation," of people so wounded and terrorized that they hoped to "appear unnoticeable," also seemed characteristic, and found, moreover, some distinct echoes in Blitzstein's work.[10]

Goldbeck maintained close friendships with a distinguished circle of mostly male writers, including Clifton Furness, Lewis Mumford, and especially Glenway Wescott and his lover, publisher Monroe Wheeler. Supporting her 1929 Guggenheim fellowship application, for which Edwin Arlington Robinson and Allen Tate also provided references, Wescott wrote,

> I have known her well for about ten years, and can testify to her substantial and very personal culture, to her courage and earnestness, to the dignity and importance of her aims.... During a period of years in New York, she worked, stubbornly, heroically indeed, by study and by experiment,

toward maturity of thought and a flexible technique, supporting herself by translation and by tedious journalistic employments of one kind and another, leading meanwhile a very retired and austere existence, and writing for her own satisfaction as much as possible. She is exceedingly scrupulous, an intolerant critic of herself.[11]

Goldbeck also had a sophisticated grasp of contemporary music, which helped spark and sustain her friendships with Blitzstein, Copland, and Israel Citkowitz. She loved Copland's music from the start, relating to her parents the following story in 1929: "Aaron had been playing me modern music, a few evenings after he got here [to the MacDowell Colony in 1928], and I had been getting more and more incensed by its brokenness, and said, 'Play me the purest thing you know,' whereupon he played the quartet [Copland's *Lento Molto*] and I leaped into a perfect whiteness of enthusiasm and after saying this and this and that found it was his." She thought that, among moderns, only Stravinsky had Copland's sort of "grand sweep." For his part, Copland clearly doted on Goldbeck. In early 1929, he and his cousin, Harold Clurman, presented her with a copy of William Carlos Williams's *A Voyage to Pagany*, inscribed, in reference to her own novel, "To Eva, about to break the circle, with love from Aaron and Harold." Later that same year, Copland wrote to her, "I often wonder how you are. And it always gives me a nice warm feeling." And in response to a 1931 letter in which she wrote, "I seem to have an inalienable and humorous affection for you," Copland responded, "I thank the lord for your inalienable and humorous affection."[12]

Goldbeck admired Blitzstein's music as well, to the point that it eventually became an overriding preoccupation of her life. At least at first, she ranked him behind Stravinsky and Copland, but she made allowance for his relative youth. Moreover, as someone who had unrivaled familiarity with the full range of his work, not to mention his intentions, she could make unusually knowing critical distinctions among not only his various accomplishments, but even the individual sections of a single piece.

In contrast, Blitzstein seemed rather distant with regard to Goldbeck's own creative efforts. Asked by Goldbeck to read a draft of *The Broken Circle* at the Mac-Dowell Colony in 1928, he handed back a largely negative critique: "Heavy, unbelievable. . . . Hifalutin verbiage—especially during conversation. N[atalie]'s and M[orton]'s capacity for gem-like formulation of their thoughts highly incredible. What in god's name is 'hypermetropic'? And can't it be done with a word less calculated to leap miles over the general texture of the page?" In their extensive surviving correspondence, he rarely acknowledged her work, although Goldbeck showed virtually no resentment or disappointment about this.[13]

When Blitzstein arrived in Paris with Copland in May 1929, Eva was at an emotional crossroads. Since her separation from Cecil, she had had an affair with writer Chard Powers Smith that ended badly, although she continued to see Smith, also in Paris, on a regular basis. (In June 1928, during their affair, Smith described Goldbeck in his diary as "feline, rapacious, brilliant, lecherous, disillusionized, hard-boiled, violent, fearless, unscrupulous, exerting a lusty pull without any endearing charm, without tenderness.") She also harbored hopes of remarrying Cecil, who visited her in early 1929, but that reunion did not go well either, Cecil subsequently writing to her, "You will always be for me the most astonishing, breath-taking, most valuable woman in life; but I cannot live happily with you and I cannot try again."[14]

Meanwhile, she and Blitzstein saw a fair amount of each other that spring, sometimes at such popular cafes as Le Dôme and Les Deux Magots. Within a week of his arrival on May 20, he informed her that he was homosexual, which left her "dumbfounded, and almost chagrined that I hadn't—I should have trusted my instinct (his walk observed the first day in Peterborough and again the other night, here) instead of all other indications." (By this time, she had known about Copland's homosexuality, although the two had never discussed the matter.) This confession only endeared Blitzstein to her the more, and by late August—after some separation, she in Juziers with Copland and Israel Citkowitz, he in Houlgate-sur-mer and Cannes—she plainly had become infatuated. "I know that if the sex were there I would be in love with Marc—perhaps I am in a way anyway," she wrote in her diary on September 7. Two days earlier, she had praised his "utter unsentimentality; his clarity and logic and physically, his laughter; and greatest of all the absolute integrity he has toward himself as toward everything else— toward himself as one of everything else—what amounts to ruthlessness toward himself. This quality, and his unique fire, are of course why he means so much to me—aside from our having such a good time together." Cecil, who thought Chard Powers Smith "a son of a bitch," was encouraging, writing in August that if Eva needed someone "to satisfy a hot box, or a succession of them. . . . couldn't it be Marc?"[15]

In the second week of September, Blitzstein and Copland toured Frankfurt, Wiesbaden, and Darmstadt together, hearing, among other things, *The Threepenny Opera* in Wiesbaden and Hindemith's *News of the Day* in Darmstadt. "For Aaron, I think (I am not sure) our week meant a growing uncertainty," he wrote Goldbeck. "From time to time we exchanged bits of information—'his type,' 'mine,' what Israel [Citkowitz] is like, why I didn't include Roy Harris in the article [for *This Quarter*]—and then, tucked in somewhere, a danger signal, such as telling the other how one acts when deeply angry. About you he is curious to the point of exasperation—why are you so wise in some things, and such a frightened little girl in others. . . . What took place, in sum, was an estrangement—one complicated by an intimate mutual knowledge" (possibly intimating some sexual relations between them, while Blitzstein's allusion to "type" referred to his preference for manly men, Copland, for boyish ones).[16]

(Whether Blitzstein first saw *The Threepenny Opera* during this 1929 trip remains a matter of some uncertainty. A chronology of activities from 1905 to 1942 presumably compiled by the composer states that he studied with Schoenberg not only in 1927, but in the summer and early autumn of 1928, during which time he heard the Brecht-Weill work "numerous times." Moreover, he often spoke in later years of having "adored" the piece since his student years, recalling further how he scandalized fellow students in a Schoenberg seminar by croaking out at the piano, "in execrable German and a composer's squeal," tunes from *The Threepenny Opera* just as the master entered the room, an incident that could not have occurred in 1927 as the Brecht-Weill work premiered on August 31, 1928. However, his correspondence fails to support the notion of a return to Berlin in 1928, but places him, rather, at the MacDowell Colony in the early summer and in Philadelphia in the late summer and autumn; nor do any other résumés mention such later work with Schoenberg, who in fact had left Berlin on an extended leave during these alleged months of study. Perhaps Blitzstein had sung something similarly provocative in class in 1927; or perhaps he visited one of Schoenberg's classes on this return 1929–30 trip and performed some music from *The Threepenny Opera* on some such occasion.)[17]

After his tour with Copland, Blitzstein spent the fall of 1929 working on his opera *Parabola and Circula* in Salzburg, which he thought "a great choice from every point of view" (including the climate and cost of living) and where Eva joined him accompanied by ex-husband Cecil. On December 1, Blitzstein told Eva that he was dedicating the new opera to her. A month earlier, he had written to Berenice Skidelsky that notwithstanding the twenty "wild and swell affairs" he had had over the preceding half-year, he was "still in love," although whether this referred to Goldbeck or to someone else remains unknown.[18]

At any rate, Blitzstein developed an intense kinship with Goldbeck, who, he wrote to his sister in November 1929, "can sometimes get more brilliance and expression out of me than any other person," describing his conversation as otherwise "dull, forgetful, commonplace." In one December diary entry, Goldbeck recounted a discussion that they had had on the theme, "What is tragedy?" including the following argument:

> Finally Marc said that comedy left the Fates out—and we agreed that tragedy was friction with the Fates, comedy their cooperation with one. Marc added that in comedy the conflict was one of process only—say conflict with circumstance. That was excellent. Like most people I suppose we instinctively felt tragedy "greater." But I said comedy would have to be considered so since it began where tragedy left off, at the end of the struggle with the Fates (only it is less dramatic).

An epistolary exchange in early 1931 about Stravinsky's *Symphony of Psalms* similarly documents their remarkable rapport: "Stravinsky's *Symphonie* is wonderful," wrote Blitzstein from New York; "[it has] the religiousness of a pagan, or a primitive (pastoral). The quick parts are done as usual with the head . . . the slow parts are at last written from the heart. It turns out to be a simple heart, breaking through, and a painful serenity that almost makes you sick." "What touched me," responded Goldbeck from Paris, "was the insistently horizontal—not rising-upward—effect of the closing section. Stravinsky's own 'respectful salutation to the Lord' seems to express it best: religious—the word you too chose—not mystical, acknowledgment more than blood-conviction, and if it is 'the heart breaking through' I thought it was in resignation, not in being-flooded." Christopher Davis wrote of his uncle and aunt, "Both were work-disciplined, Shelleyan romantics. Their currency was talk, yet she was also silent, a writer, and he worked all day then as later. Both read everything, Marc skimmingly, Eva deeply."[19]

In early 1930, Blitzstein spent about three weeks with Eva and Cecil in Berlin (where Eva's maternal grandmother resided), traveling there via Vienna, Prague, and Dresden. The composer wanted to show *Parabola and Circula* to Otto Klemperer and Bruno Walter, and to attend some concerts (including one on January 22 at which Stravinsky played his recently completed *Capriccio* for piano and orchestra) before embarking on more work in Italy.[20]

One evening in Berlin, when out with some friends, Goldbeck urged Blitzstein to attend a "fairy ball" on his own, because the cost made it prohibitive for them all to go. "I wanted to," Marc later told Cecil, "but Eva insisted I should, and you know what her personality is like—I felt I had to resist it, and not go." Such "oppressiveness" made him wary about having Goldbeck join him in Italy, something she plainly wanted to do. But in the end he relented, and by mid-February, the two had settled in the hills of Capri overlooking the Tyrrhenian Sea.[21]

Marc and Eva might have enjoyed some physical intimacy in the fall; but the two definitely had sex—or what Eva called "moonlight"—in Capri, and by early March, they had professed their love for each other. Cecil, while urging them to be discreet, was at the same time glad to hear that they were "happy and having fun." Still, given Blitzstein's basic homosexuality, the "sex business," as Goldbeck referred to it, had a disturbing element of pretense; the two even cruised men together, with Eva observing, as concerned one German who struck his fancy, "Marc was content to look at him, but isn't 'urgently' interested." Indeed, Capri had the reputation as "a sodomic capital in miniature, the Mecca of inversion," surely one of the island's inducements for Blitzstein, who discovered, however, that the Fascist government had cracked down "ruthlessly" on gay life, even if writer Norman Douglas got away with "all sorts of unpardonable things."[22]

In May, he and Goldbeck spent four days in Rome, where they saw Roger Sessions. "On the whole boring," reflected Goldbeck about their time with Sessions, although she seemed impressed with his wife Barbara. (Sessions, meanwhile, wrote Copland about Blitzstein, "I have not found him too interesting personally.") In Rome, Blitzstein and Goldbeck also heard Arturo Toscanini lead an orchestral program that included (in her words) some "very monotonous and crudely boring" Respighi as well as Brahms's Second Symphony, whose slow movement prompted these comments in Goldbeck's diary: "It is really beyond words for him [Blitzstein]. . . . It gets him not only for itself—he thinks it Brahms' greatest single movement—but for *him*self, his music." She further quoted Blitzstein as saying, "It showed me that I'm right, and that I like it. . . . I liked it as well that I didn't mind not writing like Bach for instance." This affinity for Brahms might have been related, as with Samuel Barber, to Blitzstein's early years with Scalero, but in any case, highlighted the romantic-classical tension in his own work.[23]

As Blitzstein approached the completion of his ballet *Cain* in June, he became cool toward Goldbeck, who remained "happy" nonetheless, as she explained sometime later to Cecil: "I found that just to be with the person one loves, in any conditions, is the basis of happiness and significance. . . . I found that my own work was only a pretext, that what I was 'meant' for was somebody else's work; that it more than contented me, that it fulfilled me, and that, backed up by that feeling of fulfillment, I was an average woman like any other—and perfectly happy to be one." However, after Blitzstein finished the ballet on June 19, the relationship—tested by the composer's "shame" over having completed a work he considered a "failure"—began to unravel, reaching a climax on June 25, when Marc gently told Eva, "I'm glad you came up, but I think you had better go soon," explaining that he needed to be alone. "Marc became very conscious of the fact that I loved him and he didn't love me," concluded Goldbeck, who remained in Capri for one more tense, quarrelsome month until August, when she left for Paris and he, for a vacation in Cannes on the French Riviera.[24]

In Cannes, Blitzstein stayed in close touch with Goldbeck, reporting about his interactions with composer George Antheil, then in nearby Cagnes-sur-Mer. Although Blitzstein thought his colleague's "magnetism and power" impressive, he spent one miserable day in which Antheil "failed me as composer, as person, and as spirit," including subjecting him to socialite Peggy Hopkins Joyce, whose pretentiousness and racism he found insufferable. "He [Antheil] had one good—very penetrating—criticism of my work. He said he thought it too well-made, of a technical perfection close to sterility. It's a good criticism because in the large it includes the perception of my over-intellectuality." Blitzstein also frankly wrote Copland about Antheil's readiness to "dismiss you—'dispose' of you, I imagine," adding a few remarks about the nightlife at Cannes of the sort "both you and I imagined for Capri. Very toothsome pickings—both for thee and for me."[25]

Meanwhile, Goldbeck grieved over the relationship, confessing much to Cecil, who urged her to exert some self-control. After Blitzstein arrived in Paris in late September, he and Goldbeck saw each other intermittently—"I know enough to know that I am making a mistake [concerning the relationship], but I can't seem to help it," he told her at one meeting—and this, along with reports of Boulanger's praise for his recent music, lifted her spirits. But his departure—first to Capri, then to New York—devastated her, as did some of his subsequent correspondence. "I feel with you that we have had our inning," Blitzstein wrote to her in November from Capri, to which Goldbeck responded in her journal, "Marc, not having been in love, didn't even have to struggle with his feelings. . . . Our 'inning' is over and I've lost." Blitzstein's attachment to his sister Jo, as expressed in his letters en route to New York, only added to her humiliation and sorrow.[26]

Goldbeck spent the winter of 1930–31 alternately in Paris and Juziers in abject despair; she had bouts of hysteria, drank and smoked too much, vomited, lost weight, and fantasized about the illness or death of Marc's sister ("not with desire," she wrote in her diary, "but on the contrary with panic-like fear"). Her "insanity" found its "only symbol," she thought, in the scene from the surrealist film *Un chien andalou* (1928) by Luis Buñuel and Salvador Dali, in which ants emerge from a man's hand. "Suddenly it occurred to me, ridiculously, that suicide wouldn't be difficult after all, but a relief."[27]

Blitzstein was having a rough time of it himself in New York. His family had to contend with the collapse of the Blitzstein bank; his nephew Stephen developed a serious ear infection that required a double mastoidectomy; and he was having little success either making money or securing performances of his music. In addition, he had trouble establishing a satisfactory relationship with Copland, at the time probably his closest friend: "Aaron and I are rather worse off," he wrote to Goldbeck in February, "—He will not get close—I begin to believe something in the past is responsible." The following month, he wrote Goldbeck, "I have not been happy since last August; but who has?" His anxiety climaxed in late May with suicidal thoughts when, aware of a "pain" in his genitals, "strange markings" on his penis, and "a remembrance of an evening which might have caused it," he became convinced that he had contracted syphilis, although his condition turned out to be a slight kidney ailment. "I, who want above all to write music which is least like my nature—music which grows out of peace, has no spectacularity—I seem fated by equipment and circumstance to be a nervous brilliant erratic composer," he wrote Goldbeck at this juncture.[28]

There were some bright spots. He spent "a beautiful hour" with a "really charming and affable" boxer (who did, however, walk away with his watch). He enjoyed meeting and playing *Cain* for Eva's parents Lina (who in time would become a second mother to him) and Edward, who thought his ballet score "ausserordentlich" ("extraordinary"). ("I was prepared by you for his [Edward's] erudition," Marc wrote to Eva, "and his mental aliveness, as well as the underlying futile sense.") And two months at Yaddo from late May to late July, during which time he worked on both the Piano Concerto and *The Harpies*, provided a "release" from New York.[29]

But all in all, he had a difficult half-year, which made him miss Goldbeck that much more. In the February letter in which he spoke of his frustration with Copland, he wrote to her, practically in the same breath, "O I miss you. I hate New

York," and further asked for assurance that "our friendship is *on*." He hoped that, should he win the Prix de Rome, she would accompany him to Italy, which left her confused, as she keenly felt the disparity of their affections, although she ultimately consented to go. After Rome fell through, Blitzstein still yearned to see her. "He has been thinking of you very constantly," Cecil wrote to her in June.[30]

In April, Goldbeck had some non-cancerous tumors removed from one breast, and in July, tumors removed from the other, along with a dilation and curettage because of abnormal uterine bleeding. Feeling the urgency of her condition, Blitzstein decided to leave for Paris. "The incredible has happened," wrote Goldbeck in her journal when she learned of his impending arrival.[31]

Blitzstein spent the last two weeks of August and the first week of September in Paris, where he and Goldbeck agreed that she would move to New York once she could so arrange her schedule with MGM and that they would enter into a "permanent relation" without sex, a "platonic marriage." After departing for home, Blitzstein wrote her a series of love letters, expressing such sentiments as "The thought of you, our life, has done absolutely incredible things to me," "I am boundlessly happy," and "I think you love me and need me, and I love you and need you and that the difference is one of degree, not kind." Wrote Goldbeck in her diary, "His letters are—no word joyous enough for the joy they make me feel." Jo extended her warm support for the two of them as well and suggested that they marry as soon as feasible.[32]

The proposed arrangement echoed Blitzstein's relationship with his sister, which, as stated, he had described to Goldbeck as "a union conditioned by her hero-worship of me, and my reluctant acceptance of it." Tellingly, Eva and Jo were virtually the same age, both a few years older than Marc. Apparently Blitzstein undertook this "platonic marriage"—which in fact included sexual relations—not only because it offered desired companionship, but because it served his artistic ambitions. "Now that I know for sure I have you, that we belong," he wrote to her in September, "I can pursue practical goals with keenness and no concern." As for Goldbeck, her concession to a lopsided alliance, marked by differences of "degree, if not kind," offered at least some emotional respite. Moreover, neither Cecil nor Jo voiced any reservations. On the contrary, Jo wrote Eva on September 24, "He [Blitzstein] feels so surely that you are right for each other that I know it must be so." And Eva acted so quickly that Cecil might not have had time to counsel her, although he never considered Marc's homosexuality an impediment to a successful marriage and, given Eva's mental and physical state, probably greeted the news with some relief.[33]

After she arrived in New York on October 23, 1931, Goldbeck moved into a separate room at 16 Grove Street, and the two enjoyed some blissful days together, including, in her words, a "wonderful love-coming-together" one evening. But as Blitzstein neared completion of his piano concerto in mid-November, some familiar problems resurfaced related to his tendency to withdraw when depressed. "He doesn't seem to see that, aside from my vanity and being hurt, a relationship that includes only the good moments—when one can be with almost anyone—is too superficial, that being right in the low moments is much more important," Goldbeck noted on November 15. And again, on December 30, she spoke of squabbles and the challenge living "by what another person wants, though it is the only thing I want to do." Such difficulties would continue for the rest of her short life.[34]

Concurrent with his developing relationship with Goldbeck, Blitzstein became increasingly drawn to Marxist theory and radical politics, although he never discussed this matter much either publicly or in his personal correspondence. In one of his more explicit statements—part of an interview with the *Daily Worker* in 1938, about the time he joined the Communist Party—he attributed this development to his observing

> young people thrown out into a world of topsy-turvy values—a world we never made. I soon saw that the artist, the writer, the composer suffered. . . . Then I realized that we were all striving and struggling: that I couldn't make money out of my music; that artists suffer, workers suffer, people suffer. . . . Feeling that sharp, acute discontent, I analyzed, dissected. Then began a slow social growth, and finally I saw the relationship of the world to my music. I had been composing in a vacuum. I realized that this world I never made needed change and, as an artist, I could use my music as a weapon in that struggle.[35]

Whenever this realization for "needed change" took place, some movement toward communism in the period 1928–31 could be discerned from various pieces of evidence: a Guggenheim fellowship application dated June 1928 that proposed study in Russia as well as France and Germany; a reference to accommodating a "communistic" viewpoint in his 1929 sketchbooks; a letter to his sister written en route to Paris in 1931 in which he expressed disappointment in meeting European deportees sent back "on charges other than espionage or communism"; the idea that "burst open" on the same trip for a new opera, inspired by the Sacco and Vanzetti affair, "with a background of the capitalistic machine against a radical individual," a work "that only Soviet Russia would be willing to perform" (on the return voyage some weeks later, he discussed the opera with writer and peace activist Henry Wadsworth Longfellow Dana, who offered to assist Blitzstein find a venue in Russia); and his participation at a November 7, 1931, recital in New York on the occasion of the fourteenth anniversary of the Russian Revolution at which he played "contemporary American music" and shared the stage with Martha Graham.[36]

Although the economic conditions of the 1930s surely fueled this growing interest in communism, the assumed notion that the Depression triggered Blitzstein's radicalism accordingly deserves some reconsideration. Some of the signposts mentioned above predated the Depression, while the decision to write an opera inspired by Sacco and Vanzetti further points to the 1920s as a sort of crucible, for the case transpired between 1921 and 1927. Indeed, a number of observers have singled out the Sacco and Vanzetti affair, rather than the ensuing stock market crash, as marking the beginnings of a trend toward radical politics among artists of Blitzstein's generation. In Blitzstein's case, his formative time spent in Paris and especially Berlin in the late 1920s, including some interaction with the November Group, probably helped encourage him in this direction as well.[37]

Nothing suggests, incidentally, that Goldbeck played a decisive role in this regard, as has been claimed; on the contrary, Blitzstein's radicalism, at least by 1932, had become a point of contention between the two, as suggested by this March entry in Goldbeck's journal:

> Tonight . . . began a very impassioned argument between Marc and me, about whether one should try to exercise any influence except for Communism—for temporary and individual good, such as persuading a rich man to support an artist and also begin to see something in art. Marc says no; I, yes. It is an old, but not before so pointed, difference: he emphasizes the good of all, the new order of society, Communism, and is willing to have matters until Communism get unmitigatedly worse, in fact thinks they should—which means courage on his part, since it endangers himself—and I believe in the individual care 'meanwhile' and in any society. In the end, so to the end, we agree: Communism as a soil for individuals. But the means—. . .

That July, another argument ensued as Goldbeck told Blitzstein "not to propagandize me about facts about Russia," and the composer "retaliated later by saying that I didn't feel as he does about Communism." Goldbeck even sensed that Blitzstein's interest in communism threatened to rival her own influence: "Russia always—" she wrote in her journal in September 1932, "for over a year now, anyway, in our minds as his future; in my mind as the thing after me."[38]

More to the point, Blitzstein from his earliest days had grown up in a family steeped in socialist politics, although he once intimated that he came round to his father's beliefs only after some resistance. American Jews seemed particularly disposed toward socialism and communism, especially in the early twentieth century, when they accounted for a disproportionately large percentage of radical party membership in the United States. Varied explanations for this phenomenon include longstanding Jewish involvement in European radicalism, the presence of a large Jewish working-class population, the weakened authority of religious orthodoxy in America, leftist support for immigrant and minority rights, and traditional Jewish humanistic and universalist ideals. Marx was himself of Jewish descent, and although critical of Judaism, arguably absorbed aspects of Jewish thought.[39]

Blitzstein's move toward radical politics also came at a time of increasing self-acceptance of his homosexuality, a connection particularly rife with contradictions. On the one hand, several pioneer gay activists, such as Edward Carpenter and Magnus Hirschfeld, gravitated to the radical left at least partly in response to the sexual restrictions of bourgeois mores; and socialists and communists generally proved in the vanguard with regard to the decriminalization of homosexual activity (although the Soviet Union, having repealed Russia's antisodomy statute in 1922, reinstated it in 1934). Some important American homophile liberationists of the 1950s significantly had been affiliated with the American Communist Party, including the founder of the Mattachine Society, Harry Hay, whose understanding of homosexuals as an oppressed minority derived from Stalin's theories on national minorities.[40]

On the other hand, Marx and Engels held heterosexual monogamy as a societal ideal, and over the years, many of their followers associated homosexuality with decadence and exploitation. The American Communist Party skirted the issue largely by adopting a variably tolerant stance toward homosexuality, although many homosexual communists, like Harry Hay, felt pressured to marry anyway. (Even after leaving the party in 1951, Hay defended its wariness toward homosexuality, arguing that the kind of secrecy necessitated by gay and communist activity could easily engender conflicting loyalties.)[41]

Some of these contradictions emerged in Blitzstein's earlier cited 1931 letter to his sister, a remarkable chronicle composed onboard ship over a six-day period in August on his way to see Goldbeck, the same voyage during which the Sacco and Vanzetti idea "burst open" to him. At one point, he enthused about some "peasant types," including one Yugoslav he somewhat homoerotically described as "a handsome sucker, with magnificent huge hands who has been a miner and is going back to his farm. He has that air of diffidence, sweetness, and shyness which look as though they conceal mysteries but which is nothing of the kind." At the same time, he portrayed two "fairies" onboard, one "from first class, with blondined hair and cap to match," with withering contempt. This chronicle tellingly revealed some parallel tensions regarding his Jewish identity, including repugnance toward a brutish "jew-baiter," but discomfort too with "a cheap 'tourist' crowd" of Jewish New Yorkers. Blitzstein's growing identification with society's lower classes plainly colored his developing worldview, often taking precedence over other concerns and allegiances.[42]

That the composer wrote this chronicle en route to seal his agreement with Goldbeck points to some confluence between his sociopolitical convictions and his intimate life, although precisely what remains hard to say. Perhaps he regarded his union with Goldbeck to some extent that "possible social gesture" he wrote to his sister about in 1929. But the fact remains that he and Goldbeck plainly loved and needed each other deeply.[43]

5

From *is* 5 (1929) to the Piano
Concerto (1931)

In February 1929, a few months before leaving Philadelphia again for Europe, Blitzstein set a poem from E. E. Cummings's 1925 collection of *XLI Poems*, "when life is quite through with," for voice and piano, entitling the number "Song." By this point Blitzstein already might have met the poet, possibly through Copland, who in 1927 had set a Cummings poem from a more recent volume, *is 5* (1926). Blitzstein surely came to know the poet by August 1929, at which time he claimed that Cummings (1894–1962) was writing him a libretto for a one-act opera to be called *The Termites*, a project that failed to materialize.[1]

While traveling about Europe during the latter half of 1929, Blitzstein set another four Cummings poems, all from *is 5*, and grouped them with the earlier song as follows: "after all white horses are in bed," "when life is quite through with," "mr youse needn't be so spry," "Jimmie's got a goil," and "you are like the snow." Blitzstein further appropriated Cummings's title, *is 5*, for his own work, which he dedicated to his sister, the possible inspiration for "you are like the snow" especially ("you give me/courage/so that against myself/the sharp days slobber in vain").[2]

In 1934, a small press, Cos Cob, published "Jimmie's got a goil" in an anthology of American songs compiled by Copland; in 1962, Chappell printed a slightly revised version of "when life is quite through with" as part of an otherwise new group of seven Cummings songs by Blitzstein, *From Marion's Book* (1960); and in 2003, Boosey & Hawkes released the composer's two Cummings cycles—*is 5* and *From Marion's Book*—in the third volume of the *Blitzstein Songbook* (with the revised version of "when life is quite through with" doing double duty for both cycles). Notwithstanding some inconsistencies among various source materials, Blitzstein apparently intended the first lines of the poems, including their novel lower-casings, to serve as his song titles, with the exception of the lyric "you are like the snow only," shortened to "you are like the snow."[3]

Although separated by over thirty years, Blitzstein's eleven Cummings settings constitute the bulk of his mature art songs, more than suggesting a special rapport with the poet's work. He even hoped, as mentioned, to collaborate with

Cummings on an opera, and he used the first line of a Cummings poem, "this is the garden," as the title for a choral piece composed in 1957 as well. By this point, Blitzstein must have been aware of real differences with a man who in the late 1930s privately made note of "Kweers Kikes Kumrads" as "the new KKK." Indeed, on the composer's return from the war in May 1945, he railed about Cummings to David Diamond, "threatening to expose him [Cummings] personally for protecting [the profascist poet] Ezra Pound." But apparently Blitzstein, at least in certain periods of his life, could look past such things and find much to his liking, including verse eminently congenial to musical treatment.[4]

"After all white horses are in bed" and "you are like the snow," the two numbers that frame Blitzstein's set, address the loved one; "when life is quite through with" eulogizes the deceased beloved; and "mr youse needn't be so spry" and "Jimmie's got a goil" celebrate life over artifice. Blitzstein hardly tampered with the original texts aside from repeating or omitting a phrase here and there and adding the spoken utterances "oh yes" and "yes sir" at the conclusions of "mr youse needn't be so spry" and "Jimmie's got a goil," respectively (the "yes sir" removed for the Cos Cob publication, although reinstated in the *Songbook*).

The music, which sensitively colors and shapes the verse, occasionally evokes Stravinsky, Hindemith, and Copland, along with Blitzstein's own earlier work. But overall, the cycle represents an advance in the composer's development: one hears premonitions of the Mister children (*The Cradle Will Rock*) in "Jimmie's got a goil," Leo Hubbard (*Regina*) in "mr youse needn't be so spry," and Reuben (*Reuben Reuben*) in "you are like the snow." As such, Cummings arguably helped Blitzstein hone his distinctive voice as both composer and lyricist.

Radiana Pazmor, accompanied by Edwin McArthur, premiered three of these songs—"mr youse needn't be so spry," "you are like the snow," and "Jimmie's got a goil"—at a League of Composers musicale at the Arts Centre on East 56th Street on April 6, 1930. One notice reported that "you are like the snow" possessed "moments of rare beauty," and that "mr youse needn't be so spry" and "Jimmie's got a goil" elicited "gales of laughter and enthusiasm." Another critic, who had found Blitzstein's earlier efforts, including *Percussion Music*, "formless and unimpressive," thought the cycle "charged with an electricity that makes this music glow with each bar." However, only "Jimmie's got a goil" established itself, thanks to its early publication. Even since the 2003 release of all five songs, airings of the entire cycle, including one by tenor Zachary Wilder accompanied by the author at the University of Houston on April 17, 2008, have been rare.[5]

During the fall of 1929, while in Cannes and Salzburg, Blitzstein also completed a one-act opera, *Parabola and Circula*, that he had begun earlier in the year in Philadelphia to a libretto by the little-known poet George Whitsett. On October 31, he wrote to his friend Berenice Skidelsky, "My new opera . . . has turned out a bouncing baby, much larger and heavier than I had dreamed. One hour and ten minutes already, and the end only barely in sight! I shall have to do some tall cutting, to make it fit the exigencies of Continental theaters as regards one-acters—but the procedure will be a novel one for me, so I don't complain." Finished in early November and dedicated to Goldbeck, the orchestral score for seven singers and a large orchestra, including three trombones and two harps, ran to 555 pages.[6]

Parabola and Circula takes place in the stone courtyard outside the home of the eponymous couple in an abstract land of forms. At daybreak, Rectangula (tenor) and Intersecta (soprano), the adopted son and daughter of Parabola and Circula, ready the courtyard, polishing the communal well from which the opera's others figures—Prism, Linea, and Geodesa—later come to draw water. After Parabola (baritone) and Circula (soprano) appear, singing of their perfect love, Rectangula and Intersecta cover them with flowers.

As Parabola's friend Prism (tenor) arrives, Circula exits. Haunted by doubt, Parabola asks Prism what he thinks of Circula, and Prism insinuates that love has deprived Parabola of his autonomy. As Circula's friend Linea (contralto) approaches and Prism takes his leave, Parabola asks Linea her opinion of Circula; Linea cites a few faults, including Circula's dependence on Parabola. Finally, Geodesa (bass-baritone) appears, and Parabola asks him, too, what he thinks of Circula, to which Geodesa decries the couple's romanticism as "poignantly oppressive to the modern mind." Prism returns, and he and Geodesa, happy that Parabola finally understands the foolishness of his love, assist him in throwing a black, spiky, hideous projectile that has arisen from his doubt, killing Circula. Observing the reaction of Intersecta and Rectangula to their mother's death, Parabola says, in the end, "They suffer their change well. I was worried about the children." As the curtain falls, Rectangula stands mute, while Intersecta—and in the original libretto, Linea as well—gives way to cries and lamentations.

An allegory of paradise lost, the opera's story in particular recalls that of Adam and Eve, although the libretto evokes other myths, possibly pointing to the influence of James George Frazer's study of comparative religion *The Golden Bough* (1890), a book that seems to have impressed Blitzstein as it had so many other contemporaries. At any rate, in his scenario, Whitsett summarized its moral by writing, "The higher sophistication while making it easier for doubt to enter has offered no ready means for combating it." Blitzstein further wrote in his sketchbook,

> It is a lyric delineation of destruction—the thing destroyed not so beautiful as the act, the whole first section studies banality—love, poses, doting children, a benign sun, perfect landscape gardening—a postcard beauty. This is subtly and then bluntly destroyed, the katabolism being noble, formal. . . . Parabola—essentially stupid, who bellows joyously at the beginning, and attains personal dignity only through acquiring enough courage at the end to destroy his happiness. His tragedy lies in an

unconscious need for a more human and imperfect situation, and the
lack of means to combat the doubt which is the instrument, the Franken-
stein he has not known he wished.

Looking back on the work near the end of his life, Blitzstein also stated, "Here the
human plight was met and rejected," further explaining that the characters enact
"a cruel jest on the impossibility of perfection or even satisfaction in the matter of
human relationships, especially in the matter of love." The composer presumably
collaborated on the story with Whitsett, or perhaps devised it himself and gave it
to Whitsett to poeticize, given that a draft of the scenario written in his hand survives in his notebooks; but in any event, the opera seems to cast a strong autobiographical dimension, with the incestuous Rectangula and Intersecta—he,
skeptical, she, more sanguine, both mourning over the dissolution of their parents' love—resonant of his relationship with his sister.[7]
  The highly symbolic, even surrealist libretto often approaches the arcane,
recalling Blitzstein's earlier association with Abraham Lincoln Gillespie. At one
point, Rectangula and Intersecta say, for instance, "All we erogenous flowers are
the children of your interlingual hours,/Here, under the sureness of the sky/Hide
the purity of unseen desires"; at another, Parabola tells his children, "All of the
shapes, however febrile, are attributable to your sun./In the lazy throes of night,
visibleness languishes." Reading Whitsett's novel *Jealous Mountains* in 1933,
Blitzstein thought the "turgid" prose reminiscent of *Parabola and Circula* but inferior, in that it lacked "a certain centripetal force."[8]
  Opening with a prelude in the form of a passacaglia, music that returns in the
finale, the opera largely proceeds in a through-composed manner by way of warmly
lyrical recitative, although the table of contents for the orchestral score reveals a
total of twenty discrete sections, including an "aria" for Circula; a "quasi-aria" each
for Prism and Parabola; and two dances—a ballet for men and women that accompanies the opening dialogue between Parabola and Circula, and a pas de deux that
accompanies the burial ritual. Blitzstein wanted the opening ballet to "verge
slightly on the ridiculous, with effusiveness and playfulness; if possibly, it should be
a flying ballet, with the dancers attached to wires so that they can leap and fly over
the stage" (he also spoke of this ballet as so much "sicky-sweet-Versailles-swoon-
mush"), whereas he wanted the pas de deux to be "quite serious and beautiful."[9]
  The drama inspired from Blitzstein a distinctive sound world (although one
prefigured by his Cummings songs), with room for diatonic melodies, tonal
pedal-points, triadic harmonies, straightforward dance rhythms, and a variety of
chamber-like sonorities, notwithstanding the richly scored ballet complete with
harp arpeggios. The result echoes both the classical poise of Gluck's *Orpheus and
Eurydice*, which the composer had seen in Frankfurt in September 1929 (Henry
Brant tellingly spoke of Blitzstein's work of this period as having "an austerity and
unembarrassed directness of statement suggestive of a kind of neo-Gluck") and

the latest Stravinsky, including *Oedipus rex*, *Apollo*, and *The Fairy's Kiss*, although the score sometimes comes closer to Prokofiev, as in the pas de deux.[10]

Blitzstein had mixed feelings about the opera upon its completion. "I . . . am very pleased with it in spots," he wrote Skidelsky on March 9, 1930, "and even more pleased with the direct focus it afforded me for my defects; more, for my very state as a composer. The only way I can state it is that, in my compositions, I have as yet, no face; the structure is clear and solid, the métier becoming what it should be, and the urge to get it out as strong as ever. Perhaps in my new work for orchestra (half-done) [*Romantic Piece*] I am beginning to expose features." Nadia Boulanger listened to the composer play through the entire work and found it, as he told Alexander Smallens, "'very beautiful,' 'clearly dramatic,' with some bad spots she would like to see cut out."[11]

Blitzstein hoped that, whatever its limitations, the opera might be published by Schott and championed by a conductor like Fritz Reiner, who, as the composer told Goldbeck, "fell for *Parabola and Circula*, and would like to give a performance." However, in the end, no publisher or conductor took up the work, which remains, to this day, unpublished and unperformed.[12]

Over the years, Blitzstein treated the opera and its sketches, as he wrote on the title page of the short score, "as my 'composer's trunk'—a sort of repository in which to dip for material for later works," including *No for an Answer*, the *Airborne Symphony*, *Regina*, and *Lear: A Study*, that is, some of the most important works of his career. Moreover, he adapted not simply the occasional theme or passage but sizeable chunks of the score, including whole sections for *Regina*.

Blitzstein cited such pilfering, which mark the opera as profoundly seminal, as reason enough for not wanting to have the work revived, but he plainly looked back at the piece as a whole with some aversion, citing the opera in 1940 as one of several works that he hoped would remain "in well-merited obscurity," referring to it in 1949 as "an early operatic monstrosity . . . to which I occasionally turn for needed deflation of the ego," and describing the libretto in 1962 as "grotesque and fairly impossible." At the same time, he continued to "cherish the music," as the various recyclings would suggest, and even recognized moments in the opera "where both drama and music got at the heart of a point and projected it singly."[13]

The movement toward a more accessible style continued with two instrumental works written in the spring of 1930 and dedicated, like *Parabola and Circula*, to Goldbeck: the *Romantic Piece* for orchestra, completed in March, and the String Quartet, completed in April. Blitzstein composed this music during his first idyllic months in Capri with Goldbeck, hence the nickname "Italian" eventually bestowed on the quartet.

Although in a modern idiom, both works recall at moments Beethoven and Brahms, helping to explain Blitzstein's comment after hearing Toscanini conduct the Brahms Second Symphony in May, "It showed me that I'm right, and that I like it." The title *Romantic Piece* further underscored that work's kinship with the nineteenth century. Although somewhat pallid compared to some of Blitzstein's outré scores of the 1920s, these two pieces nonetheless represent growth toward fuller maturity.[14]

Somewhat like the Piano Sonata, which it resembles formally, the *Romantic Piece* starts with an opening Allegro pesante, a Comodo transition, a Largo section, and a scherzo-like Presto section, after which the piece, subverting expectations, returns to the Comodo transition, the Largo theme, and more Presto music before concluding with the Allegro opening music and a Presto coda that closes Maestoso pesantissimo. Copland, who did not much care for the work, deemed the form "wrong," and Blitzstein duly made some changes, admitting to Goldbeck that "the first part has always seemed somewhere bad, and I find it is in a too-great length," although he doubted that his revisions would "affect his [Copland's] idea." Alexander Smallens reacted unfavorably to the piece as well. But Goldbeck, who witnessed its composition, had an opportunity to reconsider the piece, along with the ballet *Cain* (also composed in 1930), when Blitzstein played both works for her in Paris in the fall of 1930: "Both are truly great," she wrote in her journal, although she thought *Cain* "richer and more human—and also, with the Jehovah scene, which really transcends limits, and the Abel scenes in their purity—the greater." Two months later, she concluded that the *Romantic Piece* at least laid the necessary foundation for *Cain*, describing the earlier work as "the last soaring of youth above maturity; it is inhuman, abstract in that way, but already individual."[15]

Leopold Stokowski planned a premiere with the Philadelphia Orchestra for the spring of 1931, to the point of having the parts copied, but neither this nor any other performance came to light. Meanwhile, Blitzstein transcribed the first Presto section as *Scherzo* for piano, music that recalls the "Toccata" from *Percussion Music*, only more humorous. In this guise, at least a portion of the *Romantic Piece* came before the public.[16]

The four-movement "Italian" Quartet forms a sort of companion to the *Romantic Piece*, although it contains greater variety: a propulsive Allegro; a farcical Allegretto, with a sentimental Adagio middle section that slowly winds its way back to the opening burlesque; and a fleet Presto possibile that basically clears the air for the arrival of the crowning movement, a long, elegiac Lento that ends quietly on a simple major triad. Goldbeck deemed the second movement "very amusing" and the finale "beautiful" but reported that the piece only intermittently inspired Blitzstein, who, anxious to get started on *Cain*, thought the quartet "a lesser work." But for all its restraint, the music reveals real originality. The first movement, for instance, contrasts its staccato main theme with occasional appearances of a more expressive legato melody that, close to the end, reappears in diminution and stretto. The presence of two principal themes recalls traditional sonata form, but Blitzstein creates with these two ideas a highly personal design, one characteristically shorn of subsidiary themes, transitions, and developments.[17]

Blitzstein provided a copy of the score to Nadia Boulanger, who thought the string writing of this "wholly admirable" work "perfect," and who promised an airing in Paris, if possible. Performed at a February 25, 1931, recital sponsored by the Philadelphia Society for Contemporary Music at the Academy of Music (the second movement retitled "Grazioso") and then by the Modern Art Quartet at a Composers' Forum-Laboratory concert on April 15, 1936 (the first movement retitled "Moderato"), the piece apparently went unplayed for decades and eventually disappeared, with only pencil sketches surviving among the composer's effects. However, in 1980 Eric Gordon discovered the score among Boulanger's papers at Harvard, and in recent years, the work has been successfully revived, including a March 6, 2005, performance by the Tetraktys Quartet, and a 2009 recording by the Del Sol String Quartet, a release enthusiastically greeted by critics James Keller and Jerry Dubins, who noted resemblances to Virgil Thomson and Dmitri Shostakovich, respectively.[18]

While still writing the quartet, Blitzstein began work on a piece for four-voice women's chorus (SSAA) and percussion entitled Cantatina. He planned three movements—"Prelude," "Vocalise," and "Potpourri"—but he only completed, it seems, part of the first movement (also referred to as "Capriccio"). This surviving fragment uses humming and jazzy scat phrases akin to the "Do, do-die-o" passages in Triple-Sec. After an a cappella choral section, the snare drum and woodblock enter, even playing a passage on their own. The overt use of a jazz idiom—Blitzstein states in his sketches, "in jazz spirit"—distinguishes this material from most of his other music of this period.

Blitzstein apparently planned to use vowel sounds for the "Vocalise," and then, for "Potpourri," a collage of phrases in English, French, Latin, and other languages, including the old typing drill "Now is the time for all good men to come to the aid of the party" (perhaps here implying some specific political meaning), the title of Robert Lowry's popular song "Where Is My Wandering Boy Tonight?" (whose connotations for Blitzstein presumably differed from those of the Reverend Lowry), and the suggestive rhyme "amatus" and "epiglodus." Prefiguring the likes of Luciano Berio's Sinfonia (1969), such stylistic and formal adventurousness, undertaken alongside the rather traditional "Italian" Quartet, bespoke both the composer's continued daring and the wide aesthetic range of his work.

In the spring of 1930, Alexander Smallens wrote Blitzstein, encouraging him to write a ballet for a competition sponsored by the League of Composers. Blitzstein considered various ideas, including "two mythological things," before deciding on a telling of the biblical story of Cain. He put the Cantatina aside—for good, as it turned out—and spent May and June on the ballet, discussing at times the scenario with Goldbeck, to whom he dedicated the work and for whom he played each section upon completion at the piano. "He fell into the subject, or it kindled him, from the very first," wrote Goldbeck. "I had never seen anyone seized that way before." Blitzstein cut down on his swimming so as to be able to work on the piece seven hours a day, telling his sister in May, "I am writing as to eat, sleep, and drink it. It will be a wow; or at any rate the work and love going into it deserve a wow."[19]

The idea of a biblical story might have been inspired by Sergey Prokofiev's recent ballet for Diaghilev, *The Prodigal Son*, with choreography by George Balanchine and sets by Georges Rouault, which Blitzstein had seen with Goldbeck around the time of its May 1929 premiere and which he thought to feature one of Prokofiev's best scores. Gershwin and Copland explored themes related to their shared Jewish backgrounds about this time as well, as evidenced by Gershwin's hope to write an opera after S. Ansky's *The Dybbuk*, and Copland's *Vitebsk* for piano trio (1929) inspired by the same play. That Gershwin, Copland, and Blitzstein felt drawn to their Jewish heritage at just this moment, as the dizzying roar of the 1920s began to subside, suggests a sober awakening related not only to Prokofiev's *Prodigal Son* but Stravinsky's *Symphony of Psalms* (1930) and more generally the so-called "new sobriety" of the late 1920s.[20]

About thirty minutes in length, *Cain* contains two parts separated by an interlude. The first part takes place in Eden (a bit of artistic license, as the action postdates the Eden story). Abel, a "young wistful innocent," does not want to sacrifice a lamb, but Adam and Eve urge him on ("The Young Son"). Abel performs the rite, accepted by Jehovah ("Abel Offers the Lamb"). As Abel and his parents depart, Cain, "arrogant, with passion in his eyes," enters with his wife, "a humble, shrill creature" ("Cain and His Wife"). In "a haughty, proud, yet earnest ritual," Cain offers his harvested fruits to Jehovah, who rejects this offering ("Cain's Offering"). Cain's wife flees ("Cain's Wife"). Calling out Abel, Cain goes into a "blind rage" and beats Abel to death ("The Two Brothers"). A "Dialogue" ensues between Jehovah (baritone), who asks, "Where is thy brother Abel?" and Cain, who mimes his response: "I know not; am I my brother's keeper?" Jehovah sentences Cain to a vagabond existence, but places a mark on his head to shield him, saying, "Whosoever shall kill Cain shall be punished sevenfold" ("Dialogue"). Adam and Eve drive Cain and his wife out of Eden ("Imprecations and Sorrowing"), and Cain and his wife wander throughout the world ("Interlude").

The second part, representing an elaboration on the biblical story, takes place in Henoch, a "city of wantonness, blood and lust." One by one, Cain and his descendants, down to Lamech, perform a "grotesque dance, each in his own character" as a city rises in the background ("Building of the City"). A "drunken orgy" ensues ("Festival"). Lamech's daughter, Noema—"the feminine counterpart of Abel . . . , but a bit more voluptuous and knowing"—dances with small cymbals ("Dance of Noema"). Cain rushes out on stage in rags, pursued by the Stripling, who on a hunt has mistaken him for a wild beast, and who motions for the people to kill him, done so by Lamech ("Slaying of Cain"). Realizing that Cain's been murdered, the outraged crowd turns on Lamech, who flogs the Stripling to death ("Lamech and the Stripling"). Jehovah punishes Lamech with the mark of Cain, saying, "Sevenfold vengeance shall be taken for Cain; but for Lamech, seventy times sevenfold," and the people fearfully crouch. As they slowly rise, the mark of Cain appears on one and all as Jehovah cries, "Now therefore cursed shalt thou be upon the earth!" ("Finale").[21]

As part of a preface to his synopsis, Blitzstein left behind some remarks that illumine his intentions: "*Cain* is a tragic ballet. Its philosophy is that we are all killers, and that murder is our heritage. . . . Scene changes take place within the audience's views; there is no curtain until the final one. The performers are a group of solo and ensemble dancers, and one singer, Jehovah, whose voice (baritone) is heard from an amplifier placed at the top-center of the auditorium, above the audience." He also explained to Goldbeck, while composing the piece, that "its big theme is Cain against Jehovah. Jehovah wins out, but by power only; Cain is the real victor, through being the victim." This focus on man's fall and redemption typifies Blitzstein's dramatic imagination, although the work, rather uniquely, suggests the Hebraic roots of such preoccupations. Meanwhile, the ballet's novel theatrical ideas—the exchange between singer and dancer, the modernist stagecraft, the use of amplification—would prove characteristic as well.[22]

The music has a distinctive tone: serious, often brutal, with strong rhythms and severe harmonies, sometimes polymodal or polytonal, but in any case idiosyncratically chromatic, although in the background hover once again Brahms and Stravinsky. Moreover, a certain Jewish quality subtly informs the music, as in the chant-like gestures of the opening theme, the dark colorations of the "Interlude" for the wandering Cain, and the rich modal inflections of "Dance of Noema" (a more somber relative of the belly dance from *Blessings of the Bath*). At the same time, the score shows considerable variety, at turns pastoral and sweet for Abel, haughty and restless for Cain and his wife, and majestic and stern for Jehovah (the voice part dramatically notated in red ink).

Most of the score's twelve sections, whose somewhat geometrical forms recall the composer's earlier music while suggesting too the influence of film, arrive at clearly defined, often tonal resolutions, even if these sometimes involve an unexpected triad or evocative non-chordal tone. Such resolutions give the score a certain poise for all its hard-edged qualities. A few of the individual sections seem protracted and unrelentingly grim, although they might prove less so if staged, for the work has considerable dramatic atmosphere. Moreover, the ballet gains in intensity as the music moves through its thrilling climax and denouement—the slaying of Cain, the flogging of the Stripling, and the final curse—all the while interweaving a number of principal melodies.

Blitzstein scored the ballet for a large orchestra: sixteen winds, fourteen brass, two percussion, piano, and strings. At some point, he also undertook a version of the work for a smaller pit orchestra of thirty-four players, although only the first two sections and a bit of the third survive.

As discussed earlier, after completing *Cain* on June 19, the twenty-five-year-old Blitzstein grew depressed, venting his "shame" to Goldbeck, although he adopted a more measured and hopeful tone in a letter to his sister dated June 23:

> I know I have written the best thing in my career. Yet I have made a failure; no one else will know it, I do. I'm not mature enough to do a *Cain*; someday I shall be. I lack humility; one has no business to tackle a subject so overwhelmingly magnificent at my age; I get all the richness, and the scope, not the implications.
>
> Yet Cain is the work which has given me vision of works to come.
>
> I may yet be great.

Blitzstein's confidence no doubt deepened in the ensuing months as he received compliments about the music from Smallens and others. After he played the score for Boulanger in September, for instance, she paused and then said, "I think it is great," later adding, "C'est une trouvaille" ("It's a godsend"). Alfredo Casella declared the work, "'âpre' [fierce] and excellent theatre." And Copland thought the piece to represent a significant advance, "yet he is worried," Blitzstein informed Goldbeck, "about something he calls 'two esthetics' in it, a direct music and a psychological music, I gather"; the ballet further led Copland to tell Blitzstein, "you write effective music; dangerously effective." *Cain* became one of Blitzstein's relatively few early works to win Copland's emphatic endorsement; as late as 1946, participating in a symposium on neglected compositions, he cited the piece as warranting "investigation by a ballet company." On the other hand, Douglas Moore, who had admired *Triple-Sec*, found the work "disappointing," describing it in his 1932 reference for Blitzstein for a Guggenheim fellowship as "wholly lacking in charm" and "rather pretentiously ugly."[23]

In early 1931, Stokowski expressed interest in presiding over a fully staged performance the following season, possibly with choreography by Balanchine and sets by Marc Chagall. Obtaining a grant from the Juilliard School, Blitzstein had the parts copied in November, getting them to Stokowski that same month. After keeping the composer on hold—"The man *is* a bastard!" an exasperated Blitzstein wrote to his sister in December—Stokowski decided not to program the work after reading through some of it with the orchestra in early 1932. (Alexander Smallens, who attended this read-through, was reluctant to provide details, telling Blitzstein only that the first scene "sounded very thin.") Conductor-composer Howard Hanson, who launched American ballets during these years in Rochester, decided against the work as well.[24]

Meanwhile, Blitzstein managed to interest choreographer Benjamin Zemach in the work. Born in Bialystok, Zemach (1901–1997) studied with Konstantin Stanislavsky and Vsevolod Meyerhold in Moscow as a member of the Jewish theater group, the Habima, founded by his brother Naum. In late 1926, he appeared with the Habima on Broadway in a production of *The Dybbuk*, and remained in

New York, making a name for himself as a modern dancer comparable to Martha Graham. Blitzstein apparently attended Zemach's triumphant appearance with his own Jewish ballet group at the Civic Repertory Theatre on January 25, 1931, for he reviewed the dances performed on that occasion in an article for *Modern Music*, stating, "He [Zemach] has that oneness of direction of Graham's, only in her case it has to do with an individual temperament, whereas a rich full tradition supports Zemach. . . . This is one of the most important dancers we possess; it will not do to lose sight of him. He has the technic, he is alert to the spirit of the dance-as-art; and he has besides a rare humility, and a rare closeness to life."[25]

On February 5, 1931, Blitzstein wrote Goldbeck that Zemach was the dancer to play Cain: "He is the pure Cain—not tall, but powerful and rather ugly in body—muscular, a blunt eloquence. His head is divine—proud, Hebrew, and the features on the face are deeply set and etched, as if always made up. The whole tone is earthy, blunt, and barely-tamed, and rooted in the race; with a sudden elvishness or tenderness, or that wisdom so old it has gone trivial or a little rotten." Zemach choreographed and privately performed, with his company, at least portions of the ballet, with himself as Cain, Fred Berk as Abel, and Katya Delakova as Cain's wife. But his involvement with the work seems to have gone no further than that.[26]

The score went unpublished as well, aside from a short excerpt from "Abel Offers the Lamb" that appeared in the journal *This Quarter* (1931), as well as in the monograph *Contemporary American Music* (1934) by Harold Morris (who grouped Blitzstein with Cowell, Ives, Ruth Crawford, and other "Ultra-Moderns"). Blitzstein performed excerpts of the ballet at the piano at a "Manuscript Program of Contemporary Works Presented by their Composers" at Town Hall on December 1, 1935, and at the aforementioned Composers' Forum-Laboratory concert on April 15, 1936, winning appreciative comments about the music on both occasions. And in 1940, he gave some thought to revising the piece as a ballet, *The Story of Keene and Albert*, a variation on the Cain and Abel story in which a will bequeaths all to Eva and her son, Albert, and nothing to her other son, Keene. But the project never materialized, and the score not only remained unpublished, but unperformed, at least in its orchestral guise, for pianist Leonard Lehrman performed a number of movements from the ballet on two occasions in November 2005, and pianist Michael Fennelly, accompanied by baritone Peter Clark, likewise played excerpts at the American Composers Alliance's Festival of American Music on June 7, 2008. Reviewing this latter performance in the *New York Times*, Steve Smith deemed the score "mildly dissonant and rhythmically vibrant, with passages of elegant counterpoint," although he thought that the music "cried out for an orchestra."[27]

In 1931, as Blitzstein—mostly in New York, separated from Goldbeck, their relationship in abeyance—tried in vain to find outlets for some of his newly composed work, he courageously persevered, composing a film score, *Surf and Seaweed*; an opera, *The Harpies*; and a piano concerto.

Aaron Copland commissioned Blitzstein to write the score for Ralph Steiner's short film, *Surf and Seaweed*, for presentation at what would be the last Copland-Sessions concert, on March 15, 1931, at New York's Broadhurst Theatre. Copland and Roger Sessions had initiated this concert series in 1928 as a forum for young composers, especially those in their immediate orbit. Sessions, overseas for most of this time, counseled from abroad, with Copland at home in New York doing most of the work. Mary Senior Churchill largely financed the series, although Alma Wertheim also helped, as in underwriting Blitzstein's work on the Steiner film.[28]

Copland and the Cleveland-born Steiner (1899–1986) had met in the late 1920s, presumably through the Alfred Stieglitz circle with which both of them had some affiliation. Little-known at the time, Steiner would have a notable career as a photographer, but during these years, he also tried his hand at film-making, including the three experimental films shown at this 1931 concert: H_2O, *Mechanical Principles*, and *Surf and Seaweed*. Steiner even persuaded Copland to help him edit H_2O, recalling in 1978, "Not long ago I saw that film for the first time in almost forty years, and I thought that Aaron and I did not do too well in organization. I saw that Aaron, in choosing a career of composing rather than film editing, showed splendid judgment." As for *Mechanical Principles*, Steiner deemed it "in all departments, a plain mess." Still, whatever their limitations, these films represented some of the earliest known American works of their kind; and by asking Colin McPhee to compose music for H_2O and *Mechanical Principles*, and Blitzstein, *Surf and Seaweed*, Copland enhanced the importance of these films by using them to stage the sort of collaboration between avant-garde filmmakers and composers familiar enough abroad, but untried at home, a trend in which Blitzstein himself had participated with his score to Stella Simon's *Hände* (one reason Copland probably selected him for this commission). At the same time, such collaboration proved a harbinger of the more explicitly socially engaged work of the 1930s (including Steiner's 1939 documentary *The City*, with a score by Copland), so that this final Copland-Sessions concert signaled not so much an end as a transition.[29]

This "gala concert," as Blitzstein referred to it, was clearly a special event, featuring in addition two other films, both with music by Milhaud—*La P'tite lilie*, directed by the Brazilian-French Alberto Cavalcanti (Eva Goldbeck, in Paris, helped Copland acquire a copy of the film); and *Actualités*, which used a newsreel, as per Milhaud's instructions—and two orchestral works: Copland's *Music for the Theatre* and Sessions's *Black Maskers*. Members of the New York Philharmonic participated in the two orchestral pieces and presumably the film scores as well, which were performed live under the direction of Hugh Ross.[30]

On January 13, Blitzstein wrote Goldbeck, "Ralph Steiner has done a beautiful water-film. . . . I like doing it, and I like what is already done of the music." And on February 27, he added, "I have just finished the film-music, unpretentious nice music; I like it for its humbleness, and because some of it manages to be very happy." Steiner apparently thought of the work as comprising six sections and provided Blitzstein with a time breakdown that totaled the nearly thirteen-minute length of the picture. Blitzstein correspondingly divided his work into five movements—Giocoso, Moderato, Allegro vivace, Andante, and Grave—with the last movement including a sixth section intended as a coda. He also carefully indicated metronome markings throughout, and to aid synchronization further, provided pictograms in the orchestral score for flute, oboe, clarinet, bassoon/contrabassoon, trumpet, piano, and strings.[31]

Steiner's first sequence shows swirling waters; the second, waves breaking upon the shore; the third, the interaction of the surf and variously-sized stones; the fourth, single, large stones in the ocean; and the fifth, floating seaweed in murky waters, concluding once again with images of breaking waves. Blitzstein's labels for his twenty-five or so illustrated cues—"Chicken Food," for instance, for some small rocks, and "Lorelei" for some undulating seaweed that resembles hair—suggest a whimsical reading of the picture, recently described by Scott MacDonald as demonstrating "the film experience's capability to invigorate everyday sight, to alert viewers to the simple, magical visual pleasures available in nearly any circumstance." Although reflective of Steiner's imagery in terms of motivic development and, more representationally, some swirling and floating figurations, the score encompasses a variety of highly defined moods—ironic, restless, jaunty, mysterious, funereal—scarcely expected from Steiner's rather homogeneous film, and comparable, in this respect among others, with Copland's *Music for the Theatre* (1925), and even more so, that same composer's *Statements* (1932–35). Accordingly, the score can stand on its own as a concert piece, the long, lugubrious finale notwithstanding.[32]

The music has debts to Hindemith and Stravinsky, including, in the dirge-like finale, the remarkable coda to the *Symphony of Psalms*, but reveals for all that a daring profile of its own, thanks in part to the incorporation of atonal passages among the more tonal and polytonal ones (Leonard Lehrman citing in particular "Schoenbergian" manipulations of a perky, chromatic theme in the first movement). Moreover, the orchestration features an extreme leanness even compared to Copland, although richly colorful nonetheless.[33]

The sold-out event at which the film premiered proved, wrote Copland to Goldbeck, a "brilliant occasion" socially, if "hardly epoch making" artistically. "Dancers, stage directors, painters and musicians all attended the occasion to seek novelty of form, motion and design in this imaginative regrouping of the arts," reported Richard Hammond in *Modern Music*. Originally, the program planned to present the two Milhaud films, the Blitzstein film, the two McPhee films, and, after intermission, the Sessions and Copland pieces in that order; but because the projector broke down during the first of the two McPhee films—*Mechanical Principles*—the orchestra went ahead and performed the two concert works, followed by the two McPhee films after the intermission. Blitzstein, who played piano in five of the seven works, wrote Goldbeck, "It was a wild and hectic evening fruitful of not much except chaos. Everything had been rehearsed insufficiently, and went accordingly." The concert even acquired the reputation of being something of a fiasco, although it actually received fairly good notices from both Hammond and Olin Downes (*New York Times*). Hammond in particular commended Blitzstein's score for its "lean simplicity and instrumental economy," adding that the music gave "an excellent commentary on the film and was, at all times, more than mere background and not in the genre of representational music." Blitzstein himself wrote Goldbeck, "My suite is good—a minor triumph at the moment, which Aaron [Copland] persists in considering a major one. Compared to the piano concerto I am now doing, it is merely a nice work."[34]

In 2003, Eric Beheim prepared a computerized realization of the score for a release of the film on video, part of an extensive anthology issued by Image Entertainment entitled *Unseen Cinema: Early American Avant-garde Film 1893–1941*. The newly realized film score—played by the imaginary "Flotsam-Jetsam Chamber Orchestra"—took some cuts in the second and third movements, the latter cut undermining that movement's scherzo-and-trio form by radically shortening the return of the scherzo. The film and the music nevertheless managed to end together principally because the second movement was taken under tempo, which in turn led to some missynchronization, especially in the first half of the film. But the video at least provided a good semblance of this tantalizing score, which otherwise awaited a recording.[35]

About the time he completed *Parabola and Circula* in the fall of 1929, Blitzstein began work on another opera, *The Traveling Salesman* ("T.S."), a project that occupied him sporadically for over a year. In his notes, he explained that the work was to be "a fairy-tale about the rise of a young man to the Presidency of the United States. Its flavor will be that of Horatio Alger, with the premise of virtue absent. No villains, but a hero. He will attach sympathy by being timid and perplexed through the whole thing, even to the finish." The composer devised a large cast, including the Midwestern hero, Virgil Sweet; Virgil's mother Agnes; his friend Babe Kelly; his girlfriend Florrie Riegel; and three characters—Freddy Clotho, Eddy Lachesis, and Teddy Atropus [sic]—representing the three fates (their names derived from James Frazer's *The Golden Bough*). Blitzstein's plans for a large number of scenes with such typical American settings as a lunch counter, a police station, and a speakeasy foreshadowed his later stage work, and he returned to the United States in the fall of 1930 in part to soak up some local atmosphere.[36]

Meanwhile, by August 1930, the completion of *Cain* had "precipitated a whole new re-thinking" about *The Traveling Salesman*, as detailed in his notebook:

It's [sic] main theme will be success, still; but a grim success; a sort of Hardyan God, cruel, and relentless. Virgil will be nature's nobleman. . . .

It occurs to me that this theme, in one form or another, will be my theme
for a long time to come—the individual, on the one hand, the 'force' on
the other. It is not always the individual *against* the force—that is, it is
not always a pitched battle, as in *Cain*. Virgil, for instance, will be passive,
and finally wind up as the 'Darling of Success.' But there will always be
the two things at work.... What great work, by the way, lacks this theme
as the essential core?

Before abandoning the project, Blitzstein composed some of the libretto, including
lyrics for some planned "ballads," as in one "cheer-ballad" intended for Virgil's
mother ("Pack up your tears,/And sit on the rain,/Open your eyes to Sunshine!").
No music other than some sketched themes seems to have survived, although in
March 1930 he imagined that the score "will be simpler than anything I've ever
done." All told, the work represented a significant move toward the absorption of
the vernacular, including Charlie Chaplin, a figure alluded to in notes about Virgil's "eloquence."[37]

Blitzstein recognized in his approach to this piece competing "viewpoints" and
"angles," including the "communistic," the "fantastic," the "vaudeville and small-
time burlesque," and the "'classic,' 'universal.'" By "communistic," he meant art
that could be "grasped by the average intelligence" without precluding "power or
profundity," and that, moreover, "need not be 'communistic' in propaganda—it
need not 'hasten the revolution'" (suggesting, by the same token, that it could); by
"fantastic," "the feeling of a force at work," such as fate; by "vaudeville," popular
art, including "circus technique"; and by "classic," an "association with the myths
in experience." These four perspectives, juggled in the context of *The Traveling
Salesman*, became guiding precepts for his future theatrical work.

At the front of his *Traveling Salesman* notebook, Blitzstein further made some
intriguing observations of a more general nature. He spoke, for instance, of art as
arising from and returning to "a great nothing," and wrote, thinking partly of
Beethoven, "The work of art is greatest which brings us closest to a sense of measure
and content of that void, that nothing." He rejected current notions of humor, stating,
"Clearly the real humor-sense smiles, not laughs . . . the laugh paralyses, one stops, one
loses the thread." He equated "good taste" with "fashion" and "snobbishness, the great
bourgeois god," adding, "The real work of art is composed inevitably of elements
which contain both good and bad taste, the application of these latter terms changing
as eras come and pass."

In late March 1931, about the time that Blitzstein abandoned *The Traveling
Salesman*, he received a $500 commission from Claire Reis, chairman of the
League of Composers, for a ten-to-twenty-minute ballet, pantomime, or opera
"with a small cast and with only eight instruments at the maximum and one or
two pianos" to be performed by the league during its 1931–32 season. He immediately proposed to Reis (perhaps among other ideas) a ballet after Rabelais,

although a few days later, on April 1, he told Goldbeck that he had decided to write an opera in three short scenes after Ernest Hemingway's 1927 story "The Killers." "The music will be the force which has everybody—even the murderers—in its maw. Again 'the force'—it will be like doing a small *Cain* again."[38]

Blitzstein imagined a three-scene work that would replicate the larger shape of Hemingway's tale, in which two Jewish hit men from Chicago enter a Midwestern small-town luncheonette looking for a Swedish ex-boxer, Ole Anderson; an observer, Nick Adams, visits Anderson's boarding house to warn the gentle Swede, who lies in bed, passively awaiting his fate; and Nick, distraught, returns to the lunchroom, expressing his intention to leave town. Blitzstein had explored similar themes in *Parabola and Circula* and, as he mentioned to Goldbeck, *Cain*, and yet, more like *The Traveling Salesman*, this material offered—unlike those other works—the potential for local color and commentary as well.[39]

Blitzstein planned a cast of eight male characters and a small pit band of three winds, three brass, and piano. However, by the summer of 1931, Blitzstein had changed course and decided to write, for his league commission, an opera, *The Harpies*, based on an episode from *The Argonautica* by Apollonius Rhodius. He explained to Goldbeck that the thought of a work based on "The Killers" had "frightened" the league, but he also wrote to Alexander Smallens,

> What really decided me was the fact that I had promised Hemingway half of whatever I got on performances; and I couldn't afford to take the risk that that might be interpreted as half of the League's commission. I will do the "Killers" anyway, for myself; because I like the subject, and am anxious to do it. For the League I am doing (and it is already half-done) the "Harpies"—my own adaptation of a pre-Homeric legend. The only person to pay royalties to is Apollonius, who died about 180 B.C. A richly comic subject.

As it turned out, Blitzstein never completed his opera based on "The Killers," leaving behind only ten or so pages of music, sketches that contain some motives borrowed from *Surf and Seaweed*, and some jazzier material that anticipates a song from *No for an Answer*, "Expatriate," that begins, tellingly enough, "I want to be an emigré/the Hemingway." However, Blitzstein fashioned in the drugstore scene from *The Cradle Will Rock* his own story involving a thug, a counterman, and a young innocent, suggesting a role for Hemingway comparable to Whitman and Cummings in helping to shape his literary sensibilities.[40]

The episode from *The Argonautica* that Blitzstein selected concerns Phineus, an elderly oracle who has angered Zeus by irreverently divulging future events. As punishment, Zeus has blinded Phineus and plagued his final days by having the Harpies—ravenous predators, half-woman, half-bird—snatch his food from him, or else produce a stench so foul as to make what little food left him inedible. Upon the arrival of the Argonauts, two of their number, Zetes and Calais, take pity on the emaciated Phineus, and assured by the latter that they will not incur heaven's displeasure, lure the Harpies to Phineus's table and then pursue them in flight. As Zetes and Calais are about to strike the Harpies, the goddess Iris intervenes, warning them of the illegality of their intentions and promising that the Harpies will leave Phineus alone. The Argonauts provide a banquet for the ravenous Phineus, who helpfully counsels them.

From this story, Blitzstein devised a libretto for eight characters, placing all the action on the terrace of Phineus's villa in ancient Thrace. He scored the whole for forces almost identical to that planned for *The Killers*—flute, clarinet, bassoon, trumpet, horn, trombone, piano, and, for this piece, double bass—and dedicated the twenty-minute work to his mother.

Blitzstein's scenario closely follows the original story but for a few differences: Jason joins Zetes and Calais in the fight against the Harpies, here three in number and given names (Aello, Ocypete, Celaeno); the battle and Iris's intervention take place at Phineus's home and in his presence; and Iris, the Harpies, and the Argonauts together bid farewell to Phineus, who afterwards, alone, "throws himself greedily at the banquet, devouring everything before him." Blitzstein even appropriated some dialogue from R. C. Seaton's classic 1912 translation, no doubt his principal source.[41]

However, Blitzstein turned the story into a burlesque. As the curtain rises, the Harpies enter praising Zeus and torturing Phineus, who periodically exclaims, "Ow!" On hearing about Phineus's plight, Calais comments, "I *had* noticed a peculiar odor." After the climactic fight, Phineus states, "I could have foretold all this . . . and yet am powerless to help or hinder," to which Calais says, "To know all, and to be able to do nothing!" Jason adding, "It can't be good to be an oracle." And when the Harpies ask Iris if there will be someone else for them to torture, the goddess replies, "Zeus will see that ye have always plenty to do." The stage directions—Phineus "weeping hysterically" at the start of the opera, for instance, or impatiently waiting for the company to depart so that he can start to eat—enhance the sense of farce.[42]

For all its comedy, the theme of starvation certainly had serious resonance in an age of bread lines and hunger marches, and several observers over the years have interpreted the opera as an allegorical comment on the times. Eric Gordon, for instance, thought the Harpies to represent Depression conditions; Phineus, the powerless intellectual; and the Argonauts, militant action. In this sense, the story of Phineus could be seen as prefiguring those more overt Blitzstein parables about the need for artists and intellectuals to align themselves with the working class, as in *The Cradle Will Rock*, *I've Got the Tune*, and *No for an Answer*. At the same time, Gordon pointed out that *The Harpies* also parodies operatic convention, including Wagner's Valkyries, a reminder that with Blitzstein, social and artistic satire typically go hand in glove.[43]

Crafting his own libretto—his first such attempt for this, his third opera—had its advantages, including allowing Blitzstein more complete integration of word and tone. In addition, he could now exert new authority over the work's larger structure, which resembled earlier pieces, including *Triple-Sec*, in its use of discrete blocks, but which revealed a new fluency through artful tonal scaffolding and symmetrical recapitulation of materials, with those sections resembling set pieces—Phineus's recitative and aria "I beseech you, help me," his oath "Let the son of Leto be my witness," Iris's "It is not lawful, O Argonauts," and the final chorus "Farewell Phineus"—skillfully incorporated into the work's larger texture.

Blitzstein created this impressive wholeness in part through extensive use of certain basic motives, such as a four-note motto (heard at the very opening in the clarinet, with a bit of itself forming the underlying ostinato) that at a slower tempo becomes the main theme for the final chorus. The work further employs a unifying harmonic coloring involving juxtapositions of tonalities one half-step apart (as in the framing conflict between A$^\flat$ major and A minor), clashes that heighten the piece's humor.

As with *Parabola and Circula*, the work has its fair share of neoclassical gestures, sometimes employed ironically, as in the quasi-fugal passages meant to satirize Phineus's oracular abilities, and sometimes loftily, as in the same character's ethereal oath. In both respects, the work patently recalls Hindemith, and perhaps even more so, Stravinsky, not only *Oedipus*, as one might expect, but also the *Octet*, a model for the crisp and pungent instrumental writing. Still, this comic gem, lighter and more accessible than most of Blitzstein's contemporaneous scores, has its own character, the beautiful finale looking ahead to "Never Get Lost" from his 1955 opera *Reuben Reuben*.

The league paid Blitzstein his fee, but because of financial difficulties, it could not afford to mount the work. A New York company under the auspices of Henri Elkan planned to launch the opera in early 1933, and Saul Caston similarly thought to present the piece in Philadelphia in 1935, but neither production materialized. Such lack of success actually might have brought some relief to Goldbeck, who disliked the work and fretted that a production might "mean trouble" between the two of them.[44]

On May 25, 1953, the opera workshop of the Manhattan School of Music, under the direction of Hugh Ross, finally presented the opera's world premiere, with Stamford Nishimura as Phineus, on a triple bill that also included Haydn's *The Songstress* ("La canterina") and Martinů's *Comedy on the Bridge*. Howard Taubman (*New York Times*) found the work "long, even for twenty minutes" and guessed that a more professional production "would merely emphasize the thinness of the piece," but Francis Perkins (*Herald Tribune*) thought the piece "effective," and Robert Sabin (*Musical America*), "witty, skillfully written, and thoroughly entertaining."[45]

Later productions included those directed by Wakeen Ray-Riv (Joaquin La Habana Reyes) at Harvard in 1970 that featured near-nudity; and Carol Corwen at St. Bart's Playhouse in New York in 1988 that presented the piece "as a sort of metaphor for the working man who's trying to eat, and greed and capital will not let him." In addition, Gregg Smith led a concert performance of the work at the Whitney Museum in 1973 with Leonard Johnson as Phineus, and later recorded the piece for Premier Records (1991) with Thomas Bogdan in the lead role. Reviewing the Whitney performance, John Rockwell wrote that the opera "flows along a bit archly but always engagingly in a soft Stravinskian idiom" and recommended the piece in particular to college opera programs.[46]

Blitzstein, who had performed concertos by Saint-Saëns and Liszt, composed his own piano concerto in 1931, no doubt hoping that especially with himself as soloist, such a piece might finally yield a performance with one of America's great orchestras, or any orchestra for that matter. He certainly gave the work his all, creating a formidable three-movement piece lasting about half an hour, the most monumental purely instrumental work of his career.

Blitzstein spent much of 1931 working on the concerto, which he dedicated to Alene Stern Erlanger (1895–1969), the wife of textile entrepreneur Milton Erlanger. Although she made her name over time principally as a breeder and trainer of dogs, Erlanger was also a patron of the arts, and she presumably helped support Blitzstein during this difficult time, as she would some years later by commissioning him to write the score for her film short, *The Chesapeake Bay Retriever* (1936).

The concerto exploits a full range of pianistic techniques and sonorities—songful legatos, delicate staccatos, brilliant scalar and arpeggiated figures, thunderous octaves, stacked chords—although the textures remain characteristically sparse and contrapuntal for all that. With its outer movements centered around the same pitch (F), and its middle movement anchored in the dominant (C), the work honors classical tradition, but features at the same time an extended and often elusive tonal vocabulary. As for the relation of the soloist to the orchestra, Blitzstein stated, in unpublished program notes, "In general it [the concerto] follows the 19th-century model of the concerto-form, using the piano alternately as obligato and as solo instrument."[47]

The first movement (Moderato molto—Allegro) comprises, in the composer's words, a "strict sonata-form," including an exposition with a dynamic first theme (introduced by the horns) and a more lyrical second theme (introduced by the piano), a development section, and a recapitulation of both themes (although with the order of the themes reversed, an "irregularity" noted as such by the composer). Blitzstein frames this sonata structure with a rhapsodic introduction for solo piano that sets forth some principal motives, and a coda that quietly looks back to this introductory music before concluding with an exciting Presto. The music makes a less schematic impression than this suggests, in part because of the interplay among the work's thematic materials, in part because of the movement's collage-like construction. Indeed, the headlong rush of alternating thematic blocks recalls the sort of novel formal approach found in such earlier works as the Piano Sonata, although developed here on a larger scale and with increased mastery.

The poignant slow movement (Largo assai) unfolds a long singing line, its opening phrase forming its final one, with one later commentator characterizing the whole as "a very long melodic arch," although a flowing, somewhat faster middle section—its classicism once again suggesting "a kind of neo-Gluck"—provides some contrast to the bluesy songfulness of the principal strain. Still, the mood throughout remains primarily gentle and pensive, with sensitive solos for bassoon, horn, and flute. [48]

Blitzstein described the third movement (Allegro non troppo) as "a double passacaglia" in which two themes "are employed constantly, in succession and simultaneously." Whereas the first theme, introduced lickety-split by the piano, contains many notes, the second theme, which follows directly in the trumpet, puts forth, in more conventional passacaglia fashion, a measured series of eight pitches (the last two of which usually rise a semitone, but sometimes, as at the start, a whole tone). These two themes resemble one another in terms of their chromatic intervallic content, so much so that their identities sometimes merge as the piece progresses; but the first theme remains primarily associated with the pianist, the second with the orchestra. So striking a dialectical framework plausibly reflects in some fashion Blitzstein's growing Marxist orientation. In any case, this finale employs, as the composer noted, "many types of contrapuntal procedure," including augmentation, diminution, inversion, and canon, with each member of the orchestra joining the piano in a dizzying array of imitative exchanges, although the work ends quietly with a simple major triad played by the unaccompanied soloist.

The concerto overall represents a noble synthesis of Blitzstein's neoclassical and romantic leanings during this period, with a certain ardor and bravura that led Robert Dietz to describe the piece as "fundamentally neo-Romantic." But the work's romanticism, such as it is, would seem to be that of Brahms and perhaps Busoni: bold, lofty, intellectual, at times lovely but never banal. With its brittle instrumental writing, severe textures, angular forms, and ironic tone—all profoundly indebted to Stravinsky—the work speaks in any event a contemporary language akin to such compatriots as Walter Piston, Roger Sessions, and Copland, albeit with a personality of its own, one nervously restless at some points, sadly tender at others. [49]

Blitzstein tried to find a conductor for the work in the early 1930s, but Serge Koussevitzky and Leopold Stokowski showed little interest, while Fritz Reiner and Eugene Goossens offered only kind words—Reiner calling it "expertly done," and Goossens finding it "stimulating" and "refreshing." As arranged for two pianos, the piece eventually received a premiere of sorts on WEVD Radio on January 26, 1936, with Norman Cazden performing the challenging solo part and Blitzstein playing the orchestral reduction (with the young David Diamond turning pages), a rendering repeated the next evening at the New School for Social Research, and then again on April 15, 1936, at a Composers' Forum-Laboratory concert. In a review of the latter performance, composer Colin McPhee deemed the piece, as best as he could tell from this arrangement, "excellent and well constructed," if perhaps overelaborate. But this airing hardly reversed the concerto's fortunes, and the work went unplayed for decades.[50]

The piece finally found a champion in the conductor-pianist Michael Barrett, who deemed the concerto "slightly on the academic side," but "lively and urbane," a work that only could have been written by someone living in New York. On January 24, 1986, Barrett premiered the piece with Lukas Foss and the Brooklyn Philharmonic at Cooper Union, and that same week, the same artists recorded it for Composers Recordings, Inc. (CRI).[51]

As Barrett recalled, the piece went over well with both the audience and the orchestra, who "loved it," but critical response varied, especially as regarded its place in the composer's oeuvre. Peter Davis put the concerto on a rather equal footing with Blitzstein's stage works, stating, "Terse, biting, witty, melodically fresh, and with a disturbing undercurrent of melancholy, it [the concerto] is not that different, in spirit at least, from the familiar Blitzstein of *Regina*," whereas Tim Page suspected that the "strong, quirky, original" concerto would appeal more to contemporary listeners than the "shrill and naive" *Cradle Will Rock*, and Paul Moor conversely deemed the piece "a curiosity, a footnote" to the composer's "brilliantly alive" theatrical work. While these critics couched such comparisons in terms of Blitzstein's best-known theater pieces, perhaps the concerto could be placed even more profitably in the context of his contemporaneous stage work, including *The Harpies* (1931) and *The Condemned* (1932).[52]

On hearing the Barrett-Foss recording, conductor JoAnn Falletta, a champion of American music and an admirer of Blitzstein's work, recognized the concerto as a "wonderful vehicle" for the "extraordinarily vibrant" pianist Sara Davis Buechner (at the time, David Buechner), and on June 18, 1992, the two performed the work with the Hudson Valley Philharmonic at the McKenna Theatre on the campus of the New York State University at New Paltz as part of a summer festival. The performance proved, as Buechner recorded at the time, "a big success," and in later years, she attempted to interest various conductors in the piece, but to no avail. Even so, she maintained that the work deserved a place in the standard repertory, ranking the piece with Edward MacDowell's piano concertos, Samuel Barber's Piano Concerto, Leonard Bernstein's *Age of Anxiety*, and John Corigliano's Piano Concerto as "one of the very great American piano concertos."[53]

Life with Eva, II (1932–1936)

In the early months of 1932, Blitzstein, living on Grove Street in Greenwich Village, completed his *Serenade* for string quartet, which he heard premiered in late April. By then, thanks in part to some private patronage, he had saved enough money so that he and Eva Goldbeck could spend the remainder of the year in Yugoslavia, where he wrote his choral opera *The Condemned*. Starting out in Dubrovnik, which he and Goldbeck enjoyed in spite of their noisy accommodations, they spent most of their time in the nearby fishing village of Mlini, which, Blitzstein wrote his sister, "comprises 100 inhabitants, not all within fifty feet of our rooms." American dollars went far in Croatia; in Mlini, lodging and meals between them amounted to $66 per month.[1]

On his return home in late 1932 for some lecture engagements in Philadelphia and New York, Blitzstein settled into an apartment in Philadelphia at 1408 Spruce Street, where Goldbeck eventually joined him after some time on her own in Paris and New York. For the summer, they decided against the MacDowell Colony in favor of a beachfront home in the sort of small seaside town that so appealed to them, Bethany Beach, Delaware, where they arrived in late May with their new pup, a German shepherd called Very Tentative (or V.T./Very for short). Resuming his lectures in the fall of 1933, Blitzstein decided to move back to New York, and the couple, who married on March 2, 1933, briefly lived with Eva's parents before finding rooms in Greenwich Village at 17 East 9th Street (1933–34).

As in the past, Blitzstein gave both individual talks and lecture series during these years, the former including "On the Latest Aspects of Modern Music" at Columbia University on April 4, 1933; "American Music and the American Public" at the Philadelphia Art Alliance on April 21, 1933 (at which he played music by Antheil, Chávez, Copland, Harris, Ives, and Sessions, along with excerpts from his ballet *Cain*); "Debussy and the Twenty-Four Preludes" at the Brooklyn Academy of Music on October 22, 1933; and "The *Pierrot lunaire* of Arnold Schoenberg" at the Brooklyn Institute of Arts and Sciences on November 19, 1933. His lecture series, meanwhile, included the five-lecture "Form in Music," delivered at various Philadelphia and New York venues in early 1933; and the six-lecture "Esthetics of Modern Music"/"This Modern Music," presented at the Mellon Galleries in Philadelphia and at the home of Adolph Lewisohn in New

York in the winter of 1933–34 (the final session featuring a recital of contempo-
rary piano and chamber works by Blitzstein, Chávez, Copland, Hindemith,
Nicolas Nabokov, Vissarion Shebalin, and Webern, with both Blitzstein and
Copland taking part as pianists).[2]

Attending some of the lectures on "Form in Music" in Philadelphia in early
1933, Eva described them as "very good and enjoyable—even commendable. His
manner . . . couldn't be better: natural and dignified, effective and yet 'straight.'"
As in the past, when lecturing he often performed the music under discussion
at the piano, even singing the vocal parts of such works as Schoenberg's *Pierrot
lunaire* and Stravinsky's *Oedipus*. His performance of Stravinsky's *The Rite of
Spring* at a presentation about the ballet for composer Douglas Moore's class at
Columbia University, probably in 1933, made a particularly lasting impression on
Mordecai Bauman: "Impossible to do, but Marc did it." In Philadelphia at least,
the local newspapers occasionally reviewed his lectures, summarizing their
contents for the general public, with one notice speaking of Blitzstein's "usual
eloquence of expression, analytical acumen, and breadth of information."[3]

Blitzstein once described his lecture audience as comprising "dowagers, debu-
tantes and do-littlers. I was a blender of musical pills. But I made money to live
that way, and I also learned how to placate vanity—how useful it could be." Most
of these talks, which generally enjoyed private subsidy, lasted about an hour and
cost between one and two dollars, with savings, as regarded the lecture series,
upon the purchase of a complete package. Blitzstein on average made between
$50 and $125 per lecture: "Too much money (for, he says, easy work) to cast
aside—under the circumstances," noted Eva in her diary, indeed, still not enough
to provide him the kind of time he wanted for his own music. Hence, a letter that
reached him in the summer of 1933 ("just when we were down and out," as Eva
recalled) about the possibility of a residency at Dartington Hall in England proved
particularly welcome.[4]

A progressive arts, education, farming, and forestry center located near
Totnes in South Devon, Dartington was founded in 1925 by Leonard Elmhirst,
a British student of animal husbandry, and his American wife Dorothy, heiress
to the William C. Whitney fortune. (The Elmhirsts had met at Cornell
University, whose student union building Dorothy underwrote and named
after her deceased first husband, Willard Straight.) Attracting a small but
growing number of students (eighty-eight by 1932), Dartington also recruited
young artists from around the world as tutors and artists-in-residence, including
some, like painter Mark Tobey, associated with the Cornish School in Seattle.
The dance program became an especially important focus, run in its early days
by Margaret Barr, a choreographer of Anglo-American parentage who had
studied with Martha Graham and who formed a small company at Dartington
upon her arrival there in 1930, collaborating with noted British composer
Edmund Rubbra, among others.[5]

Scouting for dance composers, the Elmhirsts heard about Blitzstein through the League of Composers and arranged to meet him in the fall of 1933. "I liked him personally very much," remembered Dorothy, "and his compositions seemed to me well suited to the kind of dance productions we were giving." Moreover, the Elmhirsts' friend, architect William Lescaze, spoke highly of him. Invited to Dartington for a short trial period in the spring, Blitzstein arrived there for two weeks in March 1934 with his wife, who thought him "a huge success, musically and personally." Neither Marc nor Eva particularly cared for the school itself, including the housing facilities, but Eva thought Margaret Barr "dramatically talented and easy enough to get on with."[6]

As Barr was not yet prepared to work with him, Blitzstein agreed to return in September for a full year's stay, and he and Eva left, on a whim and with some money from the Elmhirsts, for Mallorca, settling in Cala Guya, near Cala Ratjada. "Marc is very keenly interested in working with Margaret Barr, and the prospect of their ballet seems genuinely exciting," wrote Eva to the Elmhirsts in April from their beachfront home, the "nicest" house "we have ever lived in." As Blitzstein embarked on various projects, including an unknown opera that apparently never materialized, Eva worked on her autobiographical novel *For A Life*.[7]

Meanwhile, German choreographer Kurt Jooss and his company took up residency in Dartington in April. Formerly based in Essen, Jooss, who recently had scored his greatest success with the antiwar ballet *The Green Table* (1932), had decided to leave Nazi Germany rather than purge his company of its Jewish members, including his resident composer Fritz Cohen. The Elmhirsts, happy to provide safe haven for an internationally renowned dance company, originally thought that Barr and Jooss might co-exist at Dartington, but this proved untenable, and during the summer of 1934, Barr decamped for London.

Accordingly, when Blitzstein returned to Dartington in September, he faced a new potential collaborator in Jooss—not an auspicious development, as he had published a scathing review of *The Green Table* after Jooss had brought the work to New York the previous fall. "The prize-winning ballet of Kurt Jooss is all disappointment," Blitzstein's notice began. "The thinking is muddy, and there is no dancing. . . . Jooss manages to muff all its quality by stock stampings, idiotic wavings and pointing." As for Fritz Cohen, Blitzstein admired his piano playing and "good intentions," but thought "his bagful of harmonies should be emptied."[8]

With Blitzstein and Jooss apparently unenthusiastic about working together, the Elmhirsts did not press the issue, but agreed to subsidize Blitzstein for a year with the £500 he would have received at Dartington, paid out in quarterly installments. Still entertaining the idea of a possible collaboration with Jooss, Blitzstein left with Eva for Brussels, "where," he told a Dartington contact, "living is cheap and pleasant." Indeed, in a brief travel essay composed about this time, Eva recommended the city as "a haven for Americans who used to go to Paris. It can't be their Little Bohemia, for it is bourgeois to its medieval marrow; but it makes the anaemic dollar feel like its old self again." One could make a meal of mussels and French fries for eight cents or go to a deluxe restaurant; visit the Flemish Folies-Bergère or a popular cabaret where "girls only" danced the rumba; hear Toscanini or Louis Armstrong; attend the premiere of Milhaud's latest cantata, *Pan et la Syrinx*, or a work of avant-garde theater. The city consequently offered, as Eva more privately told her mother, "a good compromise between a real whirl, which we don't want, and complete isolation, which is best when I'm at work."[9]

On November 17, this "pleasant" stay turned into a nightmare. That evening, the Blitzsteins attended a meeting of the Communist Youth of Belgium (Jeunesse Communiste Belge) that they had heard about by chance, and after listening to a "fiery two-hour speech," left with a folder full of pamphlets purchased for ten cents. As they glanced into a bakery window, two plainclothes detectives approached them and, after asking for their passports, arrested them on the pretext that they were not "en règle," that is, that they did not have domiciliation papers (which they had applied for but had not yet received). No one at police headquarters mentioned the probable cause of their arrest—their attendance at a communist meeting. Denied the use of a phone, they spent the night in jail. As Eva wrote to her mother in early December, the *New Republic* and other publications had prepared them for this outrage: "Both of us have become much more definitely conscious of 'the world we live in' in the last year, so that this really told us nothing new."[10]

The next day, they met with the chief of security, described by Blitzstein as "a bellowing bull," who ordered them to leave by train for France within hours, ignoring their requests to contact the American consul, go instead to England, or just collect their belongings. Fortunately, they had warm clothes and some money with them. Detectives accompanied them by train to the border and they arrived in Paris that evening. The following day, they reached the American consul, who in turn contacted Brussels. Blitzstein also asked Dorothy Elmhirst for help:

> Cannot some protest be made about such shameful treatment? We are not Communists, we have no political affiliations whatever. We attended the meeting in the same spirit we have gone to the Belgian theatres, the museums, etc., and out of our interest in youth-movements, the philosophy of communism, and so on. . . . What worries us most is our manuscripts (our rooms are as we left them Saturday evening), what the police will do to them, not reading English, and having no scruples.[11]

In the meantime, the Brussels police found and confiscated copies of the *New Masses* and other materials that to them justified the couple's deportation on grounds of "unwarrantable interference in Belgian politics," but they allowed an

American Express agent to ship them their other possessions, including their manuscripts. The Blitzsteins learned too that their Jewish surname likely prejudiced the Belgian authorities against them.[12]

Finding inexpensive attic rooms in a hotel near the Sorbonne (they had settled in Brussels precisely because they could not afford either London or Paris), they resumed work as best they could. By this time, Blitzstein had definitely decided against returning to Dartington, writing to Jooss from Paris, "I have come to feel more and more that the only kind of stage-work I want to do now is one of social and political import. I should be unhappy with any other sort of theme; and I should be unsatisfied even with a ballet which depicted conditions without exposing the social revolution as goal." The Blitzsteins hoped to stay in France, but they ran into visa problems, and provided with an advance from Dorothy Elmhirst, took her advice and left for New York in January.[13]

Shortly before departing Paris, Blitzstein met with Kurt Weill, who played him some of his opera-oratorio still in progress, *The Eternal Road*, conceived in response to the persecution of European Jewry. The work, which Blitzstein described to the readers of *Modern Music* as "Weill's best score, and also his most uneven," plausibly had some special resonance for him given his own recent deportation from Belgium. In any case, he offered to translate the text, but Weill, in a letter to Max Reinhardt's assistant Rudolf Kommer, sounded doubtful, knowing Blitzstein "so little" and suspecting him of being "more a music critic than a musician." In the end, producer Meyer Weisgal commissioned Ludwig Lewisohn, a notable author and Zionist, to prepare an English version of the Franz Werfel libretto.[14]

Meanwhile, the Blitzsteins debated publicizing the Brussels incident; they wanted to make people aware of their mistreatment but feared that they thereby would be branded as communists. "We are against publicity personally, but for it on principle (every case of this kind should be exposed)," Blitzstein wrote to the Elmhirsts. In the end, they pleaded with their confidantes—the Elmhirsts and immediate family members—not to say anything, at least until they were able to clear their names. "We will do the necessaries from here, when it is time," wrote Blitzstein to his sister on November 29; "since we have an entirely clear conscience there can be no harm in ultimately spreading the story. *But not now.*"[15]

Blitzstein's relationship to communism at this juncture in late 1934 seems to have been somewhat equivocal. In the course of the preceding years, he certainly had grown more Marxist in his thinking, with *The Condemned*, conceived in the summer of 1931 and composed in 1932, proving a milestone in this regard, according to Eva: not a mere accommodation, but a conscious incorporation of communism. "It satisfied (for the time being)," she wrote to her parents, "a dormant conflict of music and Communism in Marc." En route to Lake Maggiore in September 1932 to audition the opera for Albert Coates, Blitzstein heard some "first-hand data about Russian beaurocracy," especially stories about the destruction of manuscripts at the border, that "really got me," but only "for a moment": some of his sources "admit having their philosophy clouded over by bad personal experiences; some are still enthusiastic [apparently about communism]."[16]

Blitzstein's *Children's Cantata* ("Workers' Kids of the World, Unite!"), along with other evidence, suggests that by the summer of 1934 communism had become that much more important to his work. But his November 1934 deportation from Brussels might well have radicalized him further. It was, after all, in the immediate wake of Brussels that he expressed, as mentioned, his reluctance to write "a ballet which depicted conditions without exposing the social revolution as goal." It seems significant that he should seek out Weill in Paris during this time as well. Goldbeck's diary entries at the turn of the new year tellingly reference communism, for both of them, as "a light." "Since July he hasn't wanted to compose," she wrote on January 2, 1935, "yet he is full of health and energy and the new idea of Communism."[17]

At any rate, when Blitzstein temporarily repaired to the Leof-Blitzstein household at 322 South 16th Street, Philadelphia, in early 1935, his friends and family strongly advised against going public about Brussels, especially as he now hoped to get a teaching position at Curtis or Juilliard, or perhaps work for the motion pictures, radio, or a paper. He also reasoned, as he wrote to his wife, then in New York, "the point of our *not* being Communists would have to be played to the extent (and beyond it) used by that Embassy secretary in Paris. This will be so bad for our future activities that I think it's risky." He further wrote on January 22, "Most Communist activities must be carried on with less openness than I had surmised. *United Front* is the mot d'ordre, in place of the dread word. The New Theatre, Theatre Union, etc., have adopted it." And the next day, he added, "There is apparently an enormous lot of work to do [for the communist cause]; but money has to be got first . . . —all dull but necessary. Nobody seems quite sure of the dangers involved in being openly Communistic, but few take the chance who are worried about jobs."[18]

Blitzstein's insistence all this while—even privately to Eva—that he was not a communist suggests that he thought of such a designation in terms of "political affiliation," as in his letter to Dorothy Elmhirst. But if he could claim at the time of his deportation that he was simply interested in "the philosophy of communism," that distinction became all the more fuzzy in the months and years ahead. In the meantime, he at least could be called a strong supporter of communist activities and—as Ruth Fischer described her brother, composer Hanns Eisler— "a communist in a philosophical sense."[19]

In March 1935, after a brief time in Philadelphia, the Blitzsteins once more moved back to Greenwich Village, where they found, as Eva noted in her journal, two "filthy" and "noisy" rooms at 35 Morton Street; but it was at least "a place of our own." Later that year, they summered at Peaked Hill Bars on Cape Cod and spent some weeks in the Boston area for medical reasons concerning Eva, before once again returning in the fall to Greenwich Village, where they relocated to 7½ Jane Street (1935–37, Blitzstein remaining there after Eva's death in 1936).[20]

Once back in New York in early 1935, Blitzstein began regularly attending meetings of the New York Composers' Collective, which Henry Cowell and Jacob Schaefer had helped establish a few years earlier. The collective functioned as an arm of the Pierre Degeyter Club (named after the composer of the socialist anthem "The Internationale"), which in turn operated under the communist Workers' Music League (in 1936 renamed the American Music League). But whereas the Music League supported various amateur ensembles, and the Degeyter Club similarly sponsored a wide range of musical activities, the Composers' Collective more narrowly comprised a group of educated composers devoted to the creation of new music "for the workers of America which shall serve to unite and hearten them in their struggle against economic exploitation, against war and against fascism."[21]

To this end, the members of the collective met regularly to consider scores and discuss various matters, and at least several took part as well in May Day song competitions in 1934 and 1935 (the first contest won by Aaron Copland, who was only peripherally associated with the group). The collective also compiled anthologies of unison and four-part songs for workers, including the *Workers' Song Book No. 1* (1934) and *Workers' Song Book No. 2* (1935), both published by the Workers' Music League. Leading members of the collective—including, besides Schaefer, Charles Seeger (as Carl Sands), Elie Siegmeister (as L. E. Swift), Lan Adomian, and the young Earl Robinson—provided most of the songs for these collections, although the second songbook aimed for greater scope, featuring music by esteemed composers outside the group, including not only Copland, but Hanns Eisler and Stefan Wolpe from Germany and Alexander Davidenko from the Soviet Union.

These songbooks—neither of which include anything by Blitzstein—contain mostly loud march-like numbers in the minor mode, often with strong open fifths and suspended chords. As Seeger recalled, the members of the collective manipulated "ordinary fragments . . . in an unusual way" hoping "we were doing something revolutionary. Lots of compositions were in that type. They had unusual harmonic progressions in them, but usual chords. Or if there were some unusual chords, they put them in conventional patterns." Eisler, whose stirring "Forward, We've Not Forgotten" ("Solidarity Song") appeared in the second workers' songbook, became a particularly admired model.[22]

In a marked change from the first volume, the second songbook established some contact with American folk music, including arrangements of African-American songs by Siegmeister and rounds to satirical texts in Anglo-American folk styles by Seeger and Siegmeister. Whereas the collective at first had been somewhat inimical to American folk music, that changed rapidly in 1935, partly because of communist advocacy for, as Blitzstein noted, a "united front" or as more commonly called, a "people's front" or a "popular front." Still, notwithstanding Seeger's and Siegmeister's wholesale conversion to folk music in the course of 1935, and the extensive use of folk tunes in the third and last songbook associated with the collective, *Songs of the People* (1937)—which featured leftist contrafacta on such melodies as "Casey Jones," "Home on the Range," and "Polly Wolly Doodle," alongside original music by Eisler and others—the collective as a whole maintained a certain critical distance toward the use of the native vernacular, so that folk tunes, even if quoted, had to be presented in a certain way. Notes David Dunaway, the group "sought not only to raise political consciousness, but to uplift musical taste."[23]

The collective's interests spread beyond workers' songs to other genres and even more broadly, to the composer's role in society. Charles Seeger—the collective's ruling spirit—profoundly influenced the group in this regard with such publications as his 1934 article "On Proletarian Music" for *Modern Music* in which he argued for art as a social act (as a Marxist "superstructure") and urged serious composers, seen themselves as members of a propertyless class, to join with the proletariat and abet the creation of a new, classless order. Declaring virtually all traditional music (with Beethoven a prominent exception) as "bourgeois," and modernist music as "revolutionary" only in "technic" not in terms of social function, Seeger envisioned a welding of "proletarian content and the forward looking technic of contemporary music." He concluded, "Composers have three possible paths ahead of them: fascism, which means positive propaganda for the older order; isolation, which means negative propaganda for it; and proletarianism, which means propaganda for the new order." Similar ideas would inform Blitzstein's later critical writings and even animate an entire history of *Music and Society* (1938) by Siegmeister, who acknowledged a special debt to Seeger, "whose learning is both brilliant and catholic."[24]

According to the collective's 1935 by-laws, applicants needed to submit a large instrumental work or four-part chorus, making membership selective. Members further had to pay dues and attend weekly meetings. In 1935, the group totaled around twenty, including Lan Adomian, Norman Cazden, Henry Leland Clarke (as Jonathan Fairbanks), Ruth Crawford, Alex North, Jacob Schaefer, Charles Seeger, and Elie Siegmeister, with dues set at ten cents a week and meetings held at 47 East 12th Street. These gatherings often began with performances of various pieces at the piano, followed by discussion, sometimes heated, as to the music's intrinsic merit and suitability for workers, after which the group took up various matters of a practical or philosophical nature. "The discussions were quite similar to a composition course, except for the strong focus on the social revolutionary objectives," recalled Cazden.[25]

Blitzstein's association with the collective dated at least as far back as his submission, from abroad, of a setting of Alfred Hayes's poem, "Into the Streets May First," for the 1934 May Day song competition. Responded Seeger on July 18, "It was indeed a surprise and a pleasure to receive, even at so late a date, your contribution for the Mayday competition.... And I have put your name on file with the club as one whom we know 'where he stands.'" With his return to New York in March 1935, Blitzstein, briefly adopting the pseudonym M. S. Benson, became active with the group, with Eva herself contributing to the organization by writing "First of May," one of two lyrics accepted by the collective for their 1935 May Day song contest.[26]

Surviving minutes and programs of the collective document some of Blitzstein's activities with the group. At a March 22, 1935, meeting, for instance, he performed his *Scherzo* for piano, now subtitled "Bourgeois at Play" (and as such, welcomed by the collective into their approved repertoire); on May 17, he played at least parts of *The Condemned*; at a special "Symposium Meeting" on June 16, he spoke to the collective on "The Idiom of Proletarian Music," in which he criticized experimental music as "interesting music about nothing," and urged his colleagues to "absorb the past"; and on February 23, 1936, his *Sketch No. 1*, the basis for what would become *The Cradle Will Rock*, appeared on a concert sponsored by the group.[27]

The collective plainly placed great trust in Blitzstein, not only voting him secretary and member of the program committee, but selecting him to serve on the board of the *New Masses* and asking him and Seeger to represent them in meetings with the Degeyter Club. This latter responsibility required no small delicacy, as relations between the two organizations—as with comparable groups in the Soviet Union and elsewhere—were strained, in part because of the feeling, on the part of a rival composers group associated with the Degeyter Club, that the collective consisted of elite modernists, an attitude held by the influential critic Mike Gold in the *Daily Worker*. On April 27, 1935, Irwin Heilner resigned from the collective, asserting that the group offered no place for composers like himself "who write simple melodies to be sung by large groups of musically untrained workers." Blitzstein must have been somewhat sympathetic to such resentments, for on May 10 he introduced a motion that the collective join the Degeyter Club, and after its defeat, made another motion, also turned down, that both co-operatives reorganize as one large group. In the end, the collective more simply expressed their good will, requesting only that the Degeyter Club's grievances be aired in writing, not verbally.[28]

Beginning in the summer of 1935, Blitzstein spent less time with the collective—Norman Cazden often served as acting secretary for the balance of the year—but he maintained his role as gadfly, spearheading a protest in February 1936 to Lee Pattison of the Federal Music Project over the removal of a choral piece, "Biography," from an all-Siegmeister concert sponsored by the Composers' Forum-Laboratory after the project's director Ashley Pettis deemed the work "not appropriate for presentation under government auspices" (apparently because the A. B. Magil text attacked Henry Ford, Andrew Mellon, and John D. Rockefeller) and then canceled the entire concert when Siegmeister refused to proceed without the piece. Blitzstein obtained the support of Copland, Cowell, and Riegger

("A chance to show that composers sometimes stick together!" he exclaimed to Lazare Saminsky), but not Colin McPhee, Charles Seeger, or Virgil Thomson, who decided that Siegmeister intentionally had framed Pettis for personal reasons and urged Blitzstein to let the matter "drop." Blitzstein in turn admonished Thomson, "Our government is based upon, is dedicated to the principle of free speech and lack of censorship."[29]

The collective naturally welcomed the appearance of composer Hanns Eisler (1898–1962)—the "foremost composer" and "ideological leader" of the "workers' music movement of the world"—in New York in 1935. Eisler had studied, like Blitzstein, with Arnold Schoenberg, and had rejected what he considered bourgeois modernism in favor of the German workers' movement in the mid-1920s. Starting around 1930, playwright Bertolt Brecht (1898–1956) increasingly turned to Eisler as his preferred composer, collaborating with him on, among other works, the oratorio *The Measures Taken* (1930) and the musical play *The Mother* (1932). A Jewish exile from Nazi Germany, Eisler traveled to the United States for a concert and lecture tour from February to May 1935, and then again in October of that year for a short stint as teacher and lecturer at the New School for Social Research and the Downtown Music School before returning to Europe in early 1936. (In 1938, he emigrated to the United States, where he lived until deported because of his communist associations in 1948, after which he settled in Berlin.)[30]

In honor of Eisler's initial visit, the Degeyter Club helped sponsor an anti-Nazi meeting and concert at the Mecca Temple on March 2, 1935; while the collective—or more specifically, Jacob Schaefer—organized a farewell concert at the Brooklyn Academy on April 19, followed by an April 21 banquet at which the group presented Eisler with a presentation volume that included Blitzstein's "Listen Teacher" from his *Children's Cantata*. Eisler himself attended a few meetings of the collective, including a joint session with the Degeyter Club held at his instigation, and praised their attempts to forge "a new modern style based upon the latest achievements of modern music, while using it at the same time in the struggle of the workers and employees against oppression and for bread and freedom."[31]

Reacquainting himself with Blitzstein, whom he had met in Berlin in 1927, Eisler was more inclined to mention Copland, Cowell, Riegger, Seeger, and Siegmeister when discussing the outstanding talent associated with the collective, although in a Guggenheim reference for Blitzstein, he deemed *The Condemned* a "work of extraordinary quality" and called its composer "a highly cultivated musician, of great stature and knowledge" and "a critic of perception and originality." On December 1, 1935, both Eisler and Blitzstein participated in a Town Hall concert presented by the Music Guild in which the New Singers under Lan Adomian performed Marc and Eva's translation of Eisler's choral piece "On Killing" ("Über das Töten"). About this same time, Blitzstein and

Eisler each accompanied baritone Mordecai Bauman on some recordings sponsored by the Friends of the Workers' School, with Blitzstein and Bauman, along with the New Singers under Adomian, performing, in addition to "The Internationale," Eisler's "Forward, We've Not Forgotten" and "In Praise of Learning." Widely considered the finest American interpreter of this repertoire, Bauman developed a warm friendship with Blitzstein, and the two continued to collaborate in the years ahead, including performing Eisler's "In Praise of Learning" and "Song of Supply and Demand" at a *New Masses* benefit concert on February 6, 1938, and once again "Song of Supply and Demand" along with two other Eisler songs, "The Whole Loaf" and "United Front," at a "Welcome to Hanns Eisler" concert presented by the American Music League on February 27, 1938, that featured Blitzstein in a short talk on "Hanns Eisler, The Composer."[32]

In October 1935, Brecht joined Eisler in New York in order to help prepare the Theatre Union's ill-fated production of *Mother*, which opened on November 19 and closed less than a month later. As with Eisler, Blitzstein had had some acquaintance with Brecht from his time in Berlin, but V. J. Jerome, the cultural spokesman for the American Communist Party, apparently reintroduced Brecht to Blitzstein, who in turn hosted some gatherings for him. Meanwhile, Kurt Weill (1900–1950) and his companion, actress Lotte Lenya (1898–1981), arrived in New York in September 1935, and Blitzstein, who had met Weill in Paris earlier in the year as mentioned, socialized with them as well; on one occasion in November, Brecht, Weill, and Blitzstein reportedly discussed adapting *Mahagonny* for the Broadway stage, but nothing along these lines materialized.[33]

That same November, Blitzstein clipped from the *Times* an article written by Brecht, "The German Drama: Pre-Hitler," that encapsulated recent developments in the German theater associated with the playwright's work, including the rejection of Aristotelian drama in favor of what Brecht called the "epic style." The following month, Eva published in the *New Masses* her own discussion of Brechtian theater, "Principles of 'Educational' Theater," which James Lyon described in 1980 as a "lucid exposition of Brechtian dramaturgy" that "still ranks as one of the most intelligible summaries of his principles," an essay that emphasized the novel conjunction of the arts in the playwright's work: "In contrast to the fusion of the arts that has been attempted by our musical theater—most ambitiously and confusedly in Wagnerian opera—the new synthesis, [sic] is based on a 'dissociation of elements'. . . . In the epic theater all the arts are considered of equal importance and are used as independent elements; their relative importance changes as the production demands."[34]

Goldbeck furthermore translated Brecht into English, and the German playwright, who thought her "intelligent and open-minded," was impressed enough to allow her translation of the poem "How the Carpet Weavers of Kujan-Bulak Honored Lenin" to appear in the *Daily Worker* in early 1936. In the few months left her, Goldbeck explored the possibility of translating other Brecht texts as well, including *The Measures Taken* and *The Threepenny Novel*. "Except for her death in 1936," writes Lyon, "America might have known more of them [Brecht's works] earlier, and in better translations."[35]

By this time, the Composers' Collective had begun to dissolve. The departure of an increasingly disenchanted Charles Seeger for Washington in November 1935 to take a position as basically a folklorist with the Resettlement Administration represented a major loss. (Seeger hoped in vain to lure Blitzstein to Washington, promising him an annual salary of $1,800, with responsibilities ranging from recording folk music to "composing operettas upon librettos propagandising the co-operative movement.") Moreover, the group had long been riddled with dissension from within and without. But in its last year the collective managed nonetheless to sponsor a concert on February 23, 1936, to participate in an American Music League festival on May 17, to contribute to *Unison*, the league's short-lived newsletter that debuted that same month, and to help publish, as mentioned, one final songbook.[36]

In later years, Seeger, who remembered Blitzstein as one of the collective's "most brilliant members," took a critical view of the group, arguing that Eisler had integrated his native folklore in a way that they had not. "The Collective should have gotten together and made songs and sung to people," he said, thinking of such later folk singers as his son Pete. "And if the people liked one song more than another, then they'd make more songs in that style." Seeger further wrote, "The nearest we ever got to a public hearing was in Marc Blitzstein's *The Cradle Will Rock*, which was a marvelous work, but just for the leftward-minded in the city. The right wing-minded wouldn't go there in the first place, but if anybody ever got there, they would get up and get out just as quickly as they could."[37]

Henry Leland Clarke took a more upbeat appraisal of the collective, which he regarded as something "on fire with something both urgent and inspiring." As to its legacy, he commented, "Without the Composers' Collective there would have been no *Abe Lincoln Song* ["Abe Lincoln"] by Earl Robinson, and without his *Lincoln Song* there would have been no *Lincoln Portrait* by Aaron Copland. Without the Composers' Collective there would have been no *Cradle Will Rock* by Marc Blitstein [sic], and without his *Cradle Will Rock* there would have been no *West Side Story* by Leonard Bernstein."[38]

Meanwhile, Blitzstein continued to present talks, including the five-lecture "Masterworks of Modern Music" at the New School for Social Research and at private homes in Scarsdale and Hartsdale in late 1935; and the twelve-lecture "Stravinsky, Schoenberg and Their Progeny" at the New School in early 1936. By February 1936, he was lecturing every few days, sometimes two or three days in a row. Presumably, the financial hardship incurred by his wife's deteriorating health in part led him to accept so many engagements, much as it no doubt encouraged him to score the film *The Chesapeake Bay Retriever* in May 1936 for $350.

While working at the New School, Blitzstein also attended lectures there by two admired friends, Copland and Eisler, and reported on their different approaches: "Copland's lecturing, like his writing, is notable for a flat undecorated honesty. He is no felicitous phraser, he has little grace of speech, few quips; and sometimes one stops listening. Almost always something important is missed.... Eisler is blunt, forthright, what the Germans call *derb*.... listening to him one feels his authentic experience and fire."[39]

During the academic year 1935–36, Blitzstein also taught classes for the Downtown Music School, which operated under the supervision of the Communist Party. Located at 799 Broadway, the school had opened the previous spring as the Workers' Music School, a division of the Workers' School and affiliated with the Workers' Music League. One school brochure explained, "The Downtown Music School is primarily for workers. It has grown directly out of their demand for good musical education for themselves and their children. Expensive conservatories are beyond the means of workers; 'racket' schools are worse than useless; and semi-charitable schools, although they offer good musical training, operate in an atmosphere which tends to estrange the worker from his problems and those of his class." The school offered private lessons in composition, voice, and various instruments, and classes in harmony, counterpoint, orchestration, music history, and other subjects. Lessons cost one dollar each, classes, three dollars for the term. The school also maintained choruses and a children's drum, fife, and bugle corps, the sort of ensemble that Blitzstein would use in the finale to *The Cradle Will Rock*.[40]

From the start, the school included such distinguished faculty as Adomian, Seeger, and Siegmeister, the last two using their pseudonyms, Carl Sands and L. E. Swift. By the time Blitzstein and some others, including Henry Cowell and Wallingford Riegger, had joined the faculty the following semester, in the fall of 1935, the school had changed its name from the Workers' to the Downtown Music School, with Seeger and Siegmeister now identified by their real names. In the ensuing winter term, Eisler offered a featured course, "Understanding of Music," and Copland, free lessons to a young composer chosen competitively.

"Comrade" Blitzstein became deeply involved with the school over the summer of 1935, assuming various administrative functions, soliciting financial support, and selecting, with Israel Citkowitz (not on the faculty), Earl Robinson as the recipient of the Copland scholarship. He further taught composition and counterpoint in the fall of 1935 (while himself taking a course in Marxism at the affiliated Workers' School), and counterpoint and music criticism ("from a Marxian viewpoint") in the winter of 1936. Although he made little money from this idealistic enterprise, by this point, any additional income was welcome. At the same time, he drew a line at teaching at the Henry Street Settlement, not so much because of the salary of $7.50 for three hours per week (which actually matched that of the Downtown Music School), but because he would have to teach harmony, "which," he wrote to this wife, "I should have to re-study to teach, and which is boring as hell." Blitzstein remained in the years ahead affiliated with the Downtown Music School (renamed the Metropolitan Music School in 1938), including presiding at a charity bazaar for the institution on April 20, 1940.[41]

When Goldbeck joined Blitzstein in New York in late 1931, they embarked on what she called the "honeymoon stage" of their relationship. Blitzstein seemed at times ecstatic; in February 1932, Goldbeck quoted him as telling her,

> You complete me, in my life and in my work. My life as depth and direc-
> tion, in being dedicated to one thing; you complete it, in the sense that
> no life is complete alone. My work—in that you are my purest listener,
> and the cycle is finished with you in the room listening to my work. In
> both, you are my relation to the world—you are the world. But in another
> way, too, I feel you are my other self.

And in April, Goldbeck reported Blitzstein as saying, "My darling, I love you un-believably now."[42]

The two became that much more dependent on each other. When Blitzstein decided to leave Mlini in the fall of 1932 for two weeks in order to visit conductor Albert Coates at Lake Maggiore, they wept for days prior to his departure. "The thought of any time really away from her sends the shivers up and down my spine," Blitzstein wrote to his sister during this trip; he was, he explained in another letter to Jo, "more consistently unhappy, nervous, and sick without her than if we had been separated for months." When Coates suggested to Blitzstein that he come to the Soviet Union for an extended stay, the latter insisted that arrangements would have to be made for Goldbeck to accompany him there.[43]

When they had to part again in December 1932, they thought to marry in Paris, but they had not established residency there long enough to do so. Reunited in Philadelphia in early 1933, they were married at City Hall on, at Goldbeck's suggestion, March 2, Blitzstein's birthday. As they had in the past, they spent their short married life together consumed by work, without showing interest in developing much of a social life outside their marriage, particularly on the part of Goldbeck, who grew increasingly antisocial.[44]

At the same time, they continued to bicker and get on each other's nerves, prob-lems exacerbated by binge drinking, chronic poverty, and differences in their sexual orientation. As had happened with *Cain* (1930), Blitzstein's completion of such big works as *The Condemned* (1932) and the *Orchestra Variations* (1934) initiated pe-riods of special stress, with both blaming themselves as unworthy. "You are prob-ably right, I am a bastard," she wrote to him sometime during the winter of 1933–34. But they continued to harbor great affection for each other and maintained some sexual intimacy as well. "I really don't see why you stand for me; neither I suppose, do you," he wrote to her in early 1935. "But you'd better realize I love you."[45]

Even so, their marriage became markedly more strained in the course of 1934. The death of Eva's beloved father in April left her feeling, as she would reflect at year's end, "alone and helpless in the world." Moreover, although their relationship had long rested on Eva's role as muse, Blitzstein increasingly felt a need to become more socially engaged, as Goldbeck had sensed as early as the fall of 1932. "I cut the umbilical cord and you didn't even know it," he told her, in this context, in early 1935. Goldbeck remained enthusiastic about his latest work, but both realized that her influence on him was waning, and this also took its toll.[46]

As their marital difficulties worsened in the summer of 1934, so did Eva's health. Prior to this, she had continued to have problems with growths in her breasts: in April 1932, she had had cysts removed, and in May 1933, the entire nipple areas. Both operations had left Blitzstein in tears; during one of these, he jotted down some thoughts that plagued him, including this recurrent memory: "Eva like a baby of two stalking back into the hospital room, sullen; 'I want to leave this hospital. They have no toilet paper.' (This one I can't think of without weeping.)" During 1932, she also had begun to lose weight, although characteristically she worried more about her husband's weight loss than her own.[47]

While in Mallorca in mid-1934, Eva developed a range of problems, including more serious weight loss and constipation; she also stopped menstruating. She consulted a doctor in Palma, yet her weight continued to drop from about 100 to 90 pounds. At Blitzstein's urging, they went to Paris in September to see another doctor, Alexandre Bruno, who diagnosed her as anemic and who prescribed some medication. Meanwhile, Morris Leof, back in Philadelphia, diagnosed Eva's problem as "chronic overwork, overstimulation, undernourishment," and suggested that she cut down on coffee and cigarettes and adopt a diet rich in fruits, vegetables, eggs, butter, and especially milk. In early 1935, she gained back some weight; but during the summer on Cape Cod, she lost some ten pounds, and in September, weighing only about 78 pounds, she entered Boston's Baker Memorial Hospital for forced feeding, while Blitzstein, showing an optimistic face to Eva's mother, stayed at the apartment of their friend Clifton Furness in Cambridge.[48]

After her release from the hospital, as Blitzstein moved about from New York to Philadelphia to Old Greenwich in an attempt to piece together an income, he urged her to join him; "I seem to feel I can't live without you," he wrote to her in late September, "and at the same time I can't guarantee my jitters will cease when we're together." But Eva remained in Cambridge, where she tried modifying her habits (although she found cigarettes "impossible to drop") and underwent psychological treatment with Harvard's Henry Murray, who had been recommended by her good friend, the influential critic Lewis Mumford. She increasingly had begun more fully to suspect that her problems, including her "weakened will to live," had root psychological causes; upon her return to the United States in 1935, even before consulting with Murray, she

had met with the author of *Soviet Russia Fights Neurosis* (1934), psychiatrist
Frankwood Williams, who had a practice in New York. Both Williams and
Murray found, in addition to suicidal impulses, signs of narcissism and
masochism (the last possibly related, Eva surmised, to "my early desire to be a
man"), although as of October 1935, neither doctor apparently thought
analysis "necessary." With their help, she identified a variety of "difficulties"
contributing to her decline: the shock of her father's death, her troubled relations with her mother, writing problems, financial distress, overwork, noise
phobia, eating disorders, and lack of sex. At one point, she specifically
questioned whether her malnutrition "may be a sex-substi[tu]tion." "It has
occurred to me," she further wrote, "that perhaps I am boycotting myself."[49]

In early 1936, Eva's condition worsened; now down to 75 pounds, she experienced leg swellings and significant loss of energy. Her internist Adolph Granet
injected growth hormones to stimulate her appetite and suggested immediate
hospitalization for forced feeding. To avoid that, she attempted to eat more, but
had problems swallowing, and spit out everything but ice cream, crackers, and
toast. "Marc is willing to do everything, anything, he can," she wrote on March 3
to Murray, whose guidance she sought; and again, on March 29, "You are the only
'third person' to whom I have been able to talk freely and beneficially in the past
year—and the only one familiar with Marc's and my situation, and in a position to
help both of us." Marc himself wrote Murray, requesting an early April meeting,
either privately or with Eva.[50]

In April, Eva moved into an apartment in Cambridge on her own to undergo
further treatment with Murray. By this point, she apparently was considering
a separation from Blitzstein, something Mumford, who was assisting her
financially, persuaded her to postpone "until she could be settled in a new
place." Mumford also wrote Murray,

> You have probably gotten out of her all the essential data: her hatred of
> her beautiful, self-absorbed mother, her resentment against the failure to
> pay attention to her during her childhood, plus her envy of her mother's
> beauty, her introduction into the *subject* of sex by a homosexual boy, the
> fact that her first marriage, though apparently quite normal, was to a
> cousin who lacked very strong male attributes particularly in relation to
> his career and working life, etc., etc. The one thing that is possibly missing
> from the picture you could not deduce from Eva's present appearance:
> namely, that up to about seven years ago Eva was a deeply feminine girl
> in every way, with apparently an excellent, probably varied, sex life, full
> breasts, buttocks, and curves, and plenty of sexual charm. Even her face,
> which in the abstract was 'ugly,' was often beautiful. It was not until she
> met Mark [sic] that she cropped her hair and deliberately de-sexed
> herself. She took over from her father her Prussian sense of duty, which

has probably been responsible for the fact that she has ground out her soul doing hack work when she should have been developing her real creative talents: there is a chapter in her last novel in which she expressed her sense of frustration at the possibility of not getting a chance to express herself till it is too late. She has sacrificed herself to her lovers as her father apparently did toward her mother. She has never been ruthless enough in her work to cast the economic burden of her support on anyone else, as at some point the artist usually has to do in our society if he is to go on in his development.

Mumford's observations echoed earlier ones by Sigmund Freud and Pierre Janet, who maintained that sexual anxiety led anorexic women to maintain child-like bodies.[51]

All this while, Eva desperately attempted to find literary work, but met with a ceaseless barrage of rejection letters or one doomed assignment after another, including George Antheil's request that she edit a proposed book, *Music in America*, that never came to fruition; and even with Blitzstein working at full tilt, including a hectic lecture schedule, their financial worries mounted, bringing Eva added anxiety (Marc's sister Jo helped by sending her a much appreciated package of clothes). Typically, she fretted about her husband's well-being as much as her own, and on Thursday, May 7, she wrote to him,

Don't come up here next week; it isn't necessary, Murray is against it, so am I (before I get further along in the treatment—Murray says, until the end, i.e., the week after). . . . NOW; I should like you to promise me—and manage to do it—that as soon as the film [*The Chesapeake Bay Retriever*] is over (next Mon or Tues you say), or within the day or two following that, you *scrap everything* and take a complete vacation until the time you come here, or, let's say, until you feel you can't stand a vacation any more, giving it the *minimum* of several days, a week (of course I can't dictate a day more or less). By scrap everything I mean don't look for sources of money, jobs, don't do anything; simply sleep, enjoy yourself—fuck— meditate or not, do whatever is best for your nerves and to get rested. I consider this ABSOLUTELY NECESSARY not because of the past week (present week) of overwork for you, but because it comes on too of a prolonged nervous strain—the two months with me.

Eva also raised the specter of divorce, "but the important thing I believe is that we can come to no decision we can trust unless we are both able to see each other with a degree of genuine calm and 'newness.'"[52]

Murray, who saw Eva as many as three or four times a week, traced her self-starvation to her strong aversion to her mother: "It goes back to breast feeding and wanting to bite the nipple, and wouldn't take any nourishment from her mother." But although impressed with her "extraordinary insight," he found her a difficult patient and her problems "so deep-seated that nothing short of an entirely satisfactory Love or a year's analysis can be counted on to help," as he wrote Mumford. Around May 21, he admitted her to Massachusetts General Hospital, where she continued to write sometimes delusional letters and notes, including one scribbled on May 22 in which she expressed her yearning for "belief" and "trust." Blitzstein arrived in Boston about this time as well. On May 25, Murray wrote to Eva, "You displayed remarkable strength on Saturday [May 23] and proved beyond a doubt your will to live—at least your will to live when you have complete sovereignty." However, the hospital stay proved ineffective, as Murray explained to Mumford: "She went on strike and raised the roof—damned everything and everybody, refused to eat, complained about every step of the procedure."[53]

Murray considered admitting Eva to a mental institution and having her force fed, "but in her present state," he wrote Mumford, "this would drive her into a final mental fury and life would be a torment for her. Better to die." And so he decided to release her. "What is dominating her now is suicide from *spite*. She feels she isn't loved enough and, therefore, will impose the blame and guilt on others by dying." Murray felt deeply responsible, that he had made the mistake of taking on more than he could handle and that he had botched the case. "I think what she needed," reflected Mumford years later, "was to have the patience of somebody who would have listened to her, go over the life story, but he [Murray] saw it in terms of the immediate threat to her physical body and washed his hands of her." Mumford expressed his own regrets:

> I saw her from time to time, and she was getting worse, and there was a time when she could only live on champagne and brandy, like Dickens in his final days. And there she was, dying before my eyes, and I was sympathetic and did what I could for her, but didn't do the right thing. . . . Of course, this wasn't an easy problem. If I'd given every day of my life to her, I mightn't have been able to save her, but curiously one's blind, very often, to the ailments of people who are very near to one. She was an extremely fine woman.[54]

Eva died on Tuesday, May 26, 1936. Murray later recalled, consistent with his correspondence with Mumford, that that morning, someone—probably her husband—took her home, whereupon she "got out of her bed, stood up next to the bed, and fell over dead. And this was just what she wanted to do, to defy the world. No one was going to put her down. She was going to be standing up when she died. She was a noble woman in many ways. Quite a mind."[55]

After her death, Blitzstein cabled his mother-in-law, "Eva has suddenly died. Only a few hours warning. No pain. I am having cremation performed today. Will return to New York Thursday. Love be brave. Marc." Taking a cargo steamer back to New York, he released his wife's ashes off the coast of Cape Cod. Eva's death certificate gave as cause "starvation associated with a psychosis," although some doctors even then would have used the term "anorexia nervosa." She was only thirty-four years old. Eerily, some nine years earlier, in January 1927, she had had a dream foretelling her death in the form of an index card with her name and a date of September 5, 1935.[56]

Blitzstein rarely spoke publicly about Eva after her death. But she exerted a deep and lasting influence. A woman of enormous culture, including a wide knowledge of literature and film, she helped to shape his taste and ideals during a critical stage of his development, right through the beginnings of his first work of full maturity, *The Cradle Will Rock*. She remained, moreover, the love of his life—Eric Gordon reports that he always traveled with some of her effects, including a "tiny bear and other miniatures," which he would display "as a kind of shrine in any room he made his own"—and she continued to haunt his dramatic imagination, arguably appearing in one guise or other in many of his stage works, including The Suicide in *I've Got the Tune*. And more triumphantly than she could have imagined, he realized some of her literary aspirations with his adaptation of *The Threepenny Opera*.[57]

Eva's death also provided a cautionary lesson, as suggested by a 1951 letter from the composer to Mina Curtiss: "We keep thinking so constantly and destructively of ourselves! Is there no way out? Work is surely one way; but other people are another. I don't mean only meaningful people; I mean people, period. They provide a kind of nourishment nobody can do without. I know. Eva tried another way; in a sense she died of it."[58]

Following Eva's demise, Blitzstein left their dog Very in the care of Jo's family in Philadelphia. When he learned of the dog's death while stationed in London in 1944, he agreed with his nephews that the event "does put a demarcation line around a whole lot of things, and punctuates a whole section of my life." He imagined that he would not want another dog.[59]

Meanwhile, he grew increasingly close to Eva's widowed mother Lina Abarbanell, who had given up performing and had established herself rather as casting director and assistant producer on a number of Broadway shows, often in association with producer Dwight Deere Wiman. In time, she similarly assisted her son-in-law in a variety of capacities, including serving as casting director for the composer's *Regina* and *Juno*. During these later years, Blitzstein helped financially support Abarbanell, who lived out her life at the Barbizon-Plaza Hotel in increasingly impoverished circumstances, although she retained her old-world charm to the end.

Critical Writings (1931–1940)

Between 1931 and 1936, while still for the most part in his twenties, Blitzstein wrote extensively about music, more so than during any other period in his life. These writings include a number of published articles, mostly for *Modern Music*, the country's leading journal about contemporary music, but also for the French periodical, the *Revue musicale,* and the Marxist magazine, the *New Masses.* Unpublished articles and lectures survive as well, some only in outline form, but others fully written out, including a few from the lecture series "Form in Music" (1933) and "Masterworks of Modern Music" (1935). To a large extent, financial necessity dictated these varied enterprises, but Blitzstein clearly had strong opinions that he wanted to share, while living with Eva—a prolific critic—most likely provided additional stimulus.[1]

This body of work stands out not only for its extraordinary range but for its wit and erudition, including deft comparisons with painting and literature, as with the suggestion that the score to *The Rite of Spring* carry as an inscription the opening of T. S. Eliot's *The Waste Land*: "April is the cruellest month, breeding lilacs out of the dead land." It was with good reason that Aaron Copland, Ned Rorem, and others described Blitzstein as an intellectual, Rorem commenting, "Marc was an intellectual where Lenny Bernstein was not."[2]

The quality and tone of Blitzstein's criticism can be gleaned from a few examples. He writes of Copland's *Piano Variations*, "Pain is the whole keynote, and a stunning rebound from pain," of Stravinsky's tendency to move up a semitone in *Oedipus*, "The effect is always of an almost intolerable depth and darkness pierced by illumination, just as the Sophoclean tragedy is pierced through by a divine compassion," and of Arthur Honegger's film score for *Rapt*, "I think that in movie-music he [Honegger] has found his medium. It even occurs to me that he has never written much else." Discussing Charles Ives's "In the Night," whose "lovely texture of plangent sound" reminded him of Albert Roussel, he notes the composer's lack of "sufficient craft" in other works, stating, "I feel a sketched rather than an achieved intention; this may be due to his almost deliberate dependence upon the spirit of minstrelsy." And regarding Copland's lectures at the New School, he reports, "The substance of his first talk…is that the means for spreading music are today steadily increasing, while the conditions for understanding music are just as steadily decreasing; and since music in our day makes constantly larger demands upon the understanding, it turns out that practically everybody now has a chance not to understand music." In 1964, Minna Lederman, the venerable editor of *Modern Music*, declared Blitzstein and Virgil Thomson as the most "brilliant" of the many outstanding composer-critics of their time: "As a critic he was, like Thomson, adventurous and fearless. . . . His style was brisk and severe. It had bite, insight, shattering attack. . . . His use of the vernacular was selective, of slang elegant."[3]

Blitzstein could be brash to the point of disdain. He describes Dimitri Levidis's *Symphonic Poem* as "pseudo-oriental, pseudo-Scriabinic, pseudo-romantic, pseudo-everything," and Ravel's *Bolero* as nothing "but a rank musical offense." In his private ruminations, he could be that much more waspish; in an annotated list dating from the early 1930s of some thirty Soviet compositions—a list, incidentally, that reveals the encyclopedic reach of his knowledge—he describes various pieces as "salon junk," "lousy old-stuff," and "useless," with Mikhail Ippolitov-Ivanov's *Turkish Fragments* deemed "as bad as the *Caucasian* [Suite], and still exploiting the same shitty means."[4]

Even discussing music he deeply admires—the work, say, of Stravinsky or Copland—he inevitably arrives at some objection. "Stravinsky's greatness is as the greatness of C. P. E. Bach," he says of the man he thought the supreme composer of the age. "Or as that of the Florentine monodist, [Jacopo] Peri. Several of his works approach the final greatness of Mozart, or Monteverdi, or J. S. Bach. . . . But something intervenes to make them less than crucial masterpieces—some powerful flaw, subtle or obvious, spoiling part or all of a work." Apparently Blitzstein regarded Monteverdi, Bach, and Mozart—along with Palestrina, Haydn, and Beethoven, as suggested by other writings—as paragons unmatched in modern times.[5]

Although Blitzstein typically comments on individual works and artists, he shows, especially in his lectures, and in such general essays as "Popular Music—an Invasion," "Towards a New Form," and "The Case for Modern Music," a penchant for more sweeping historical perspectives involving the categorization of contemporary trends, the history of musical forms, and the relation of music to society. His innate interest in larger historical currents might well have predisposed him to Marxism, much as over time Marxism increasingly helped inform his writings on these matters.

Concerning the categorization of contemporary trends, a favored topic, the writings (including the outline of a book, *Music for Us*, intended as "a first Marxist survey of 20th-century European and American music"), although not absolutely consistent, distinguish what he regards as eleven basic movements: four before the First World War—late romanticism, impressionism, primitivism, and expressionism—and seven after the war—experimentalism, postromanticism, postimpressionism, abstractionism, neoclassicism, neoprimitivism, and popularism.[6]

Blitzstein regards late romanticism, including Scriabin, Mahler, and Richard Strauss, as essentially Wagnerism in decline, although he acknowledges the progressive aspects of especially Mahler's achievement—his linear orchestrations, his influence on Copland—and admires the Viennese composer's *Das Lied von der Erde*, if not his "Resurrection" Symphony, deemed "a hymn of the petty-bourgeois" that "takes its heritage of passion and philosophic conviction with complacent faith, not quite at first-hand."[7]

He shows far greater sympathy for the three prewar movements that in his estimation clear the path for the future: impressionism, as exemplified by Debussy and his piano preludes, but also Fauré and early Ravel; primitivism, as represented above all by Stravinsky's *The Rite of Spring*, but also Musorgsky, Busoni, Satie, and Ives; and expressionism, as epitomized by Schoenberg's *Pierrot lunaire*, but also by the young Alban Berg. All three movements signal, in various ways, a break from late romanticism, although he observes, in particular with Schoenberg, various continuities with Wagner and other romantic traditions.

Both impressionism and primitivism further share, in his opinion, an emphasis on the sonorous moment and a rejection of thematic development in favor of fragmented and static forms. Schoenberg's *Pierrot lunaire* similarly presents a startling kaleidoscope of new sounds—Blitzstein always apologized when he played the work in piano reduction—but also a world "full of nameless horrors, perverse, of terrible imaginings, a bittersweet fragrance, and a mocking, demoniac humor." However, he judges impressionism, primitivism, and expressionism as all gravely limited, with the early Stravinsky, once the shock wore off, "monotonous"; Schoenberg, rhythmically deficient and somewhat "monstrous" aesthetically; and Debussy, unable to create a successful large form: "There is that awful endless scene after Mélisande's death," he says with respect to *Pelléas et Mélisande*, "when one inwardly wishes the curtain to go down, during which they keep indefatigably arguing in gentle tones about what a shame it is she had to die, and still not such a shame, life is good, and God knows what he is doing, etc., etc., like so many medieval philosophers."[8]

Blitzstein sees the trends of the 1920s as largely consolidating these prewar developments, with the principal exception of such "experimenters" as Henry Cowell, Wallingford Riegger, and Edgard Varèse, who, he claims, "constitute the era's academists." (Varèse, he writes in a footnote, "is stuck in his tracks; his pieces have all the same goal, an endless insistence on sonority. One extraordinary bang, one marvellously special whisper—and all of Varèse is there.") Nor do, at the other end of the spectrum, Arnold Bax, Leoš Janáček, Daniel Gregory Mason, Deems Taylor, and like-minded "post-romantics" hold much appeal: "The diagnosis most obviously called for is one of arrested development." He seems only barely more approving of such "post-impressionists" as John Alden Carpenter, Charles Tomlinson Griffes, Roussel, the later Ravel, and the early Honegger, not to mention his bête noire, Ottorino Respighi. Reviewing a one-man concert devoted to Walter Piston, he speaks of postimpressionism as contributing "to the Impressionist range of fleeting-to-profound musical sense-perception a sort of worldliness, a slightly more crass, but also a more tangible, bodied and fluent accessibility," adding, "What Piston brings to Post-Impressionism is his remarkable instinct for form and order—a quality which other composers of the school, it must be admitted, lack in abundance." (In his *Music for Us* outline, he changes tack regarding Piston, whom he now groups with other "neo-classicists.")[9]

Although Blitzstein generally places the postwar music of Schoenberg and Berg in the context of the "hysteria" and "morbidity" of prewar expressionism, he implies that a newness in their postwar work brings them in range of neoclassicism, even if the classical forms of Berg's *Wozzeck* remain "for the most part *augenmusik*," that is, discernible by the eye, not the ear. Given that Blitzstein planned on using the subtitle "Abstractionist" for his chapter on the later Schoenberg for *Music for Us*, the label "abstract expressionism" might well describe what he had in mind for this postwar development, although he notes abstract elements in such prewar works by Schoenberg as *Pierrot lunaire* as well.[10]

Blitzstein shows still greater affinity with the three trends he refers to as "neo-classicism," "neo-primitivism," and "popularism." He identifies neoclassicism—a term he decries at one point as "offensive"—above all with Stravinsky's more recent work, beginning with the *Symphonies of Wind Instruments* and the *Octet*, reaching a pinnacle with *Oedipus*, and continuing on with *Apollo* and other works. Blitzstein also associates neoclassicism with various works by Harris, Hindemith, Piston, Sessions, and the twelve-tone Schoenberg ("The careers of Stravinsky and Schönberg bear an almost appalling resemblance to each other," he writes), and more generally with the virtues of simplicity, directness, and communicability implied by the catchphrase "the new sobriety."[11]

Blitzstein's defense of Stravinsky's neoclassicism—as found in "The Phenomenon of Stravinsky" (1935) and other pieces—represents one of his most important critical achievements. He challenges the idea of an inconsistent Stravinsky, finding in his neoclassical works "really a sloughing-off and gradual emergence," something "deeper and less pat than the elimination of nationalist elements in his music"; on the contrary, he thinks parts of *Oedipus* and *The Fairy's Kiss*, as well as the entire *Symphony of Psalms*, "as Russian as borscht." He even argues for the general superiority of Stravinsky's neoclassical music over his previous work, tracing a healthy development from the "juxtaposed fragments" of the early ballets to the "organic growth" of his later compositions.[12]

For Blitzstein, the neoprimitives, continuing more directly along the lines of Stravinsky's *The Rite* and *Les Noces* than the Russian composer himself, comprise two distinct groups. The first belongs to what Blitzstein terms the "machine cult," a "self-defeating product of Primitivism" associated especially with Antheil but also with certain pieces by Honegger, Mosolov, Prokofiev, and Varèse. The second group, including Falla, Bartók, and two "Jewish Primitives," Bloch and Copland, show rather a connection to folk music, with Blitzstein finding such words as "racial," "mystic," "pagan," and "orgiastic" variously applicable to their work. (Concerning Copland, he writes that "an implacable Jehovah" haunts such pieces as the *Symphonic Ode* and that a "curious combination" of "extroversion" with the "inner mystic's spirit of the Talmudic Jew" characterizes the *Piano Variations*.) Blitzstein discerns a pervasive debt to impressionism among these folkloric primitivists, and he refers at times to Bloch explicitly as a "post-impressionist" (whereas he sometimes places Copland among the popularists).[13]

For all his admiration of Bartók and Copland especially, Blitzstein responds warily to this group and to the use of folklore in general:

> Surely it is clear by now that folk-music is literary music, whether it be the tourist-going-slumming folk music of *Petrouchka* and Poulenc's boulevards, or the wish-to-join-up folk music of Bartok, the *Sacre*, and these variations [second movement of Harold Morris's Piano Concerto]. In both cases the material (quoted or imitated) acts as a literary comment which dictates the final effect. This is not to say that the use of folk-music is good or bad. . . . It is merely to point out that when someone pleads for a "national" music ("we must have an American music") or for getting "back to the soil," he is making an appeal not really for a music but for a program for music.

This perspective helps explain his disapproving reactions to William Grant Still's *Afro-American Symphony* ("The servility that lies in the willingness to debauch a true folk-lore for high-class concert-hall consumption makes the work vulgar"); the folk-like scherzo of Piston's Second Quartet ("It is neither sufficiently virile nor crude to be authentic, and its intention is too plain to make it good comment"); and Copland's *El Salón México* ("a good chance for terse musical reportage was wasted in up-to-the-minute travel-slumming music").[14]

Blitzstein similarly divides his final group—the popularists—into separate, if overlapping, subcategories: composers who use jazz and popular music (Milhaud, Krenek, Gershwin, Copland); composers of *Gebrauchsmusik* (Hindemith, Weill); and proletarian composers (the New York Composers' Collective, Eisler, Shostakovich, Davidenko). Erik Satie casts a shadow over these varied popularists, much as Debussy does over the postimpressionists, Schoenberg, the abstract expressionists, and early Stravinsky, the neoprimitivists.

Blitzstein argues that the first subgroup, with their veneration of popular music, share a certain "infantilism" in their "flight from . . . high-mindedness," and yet he shows deep admiration for the jazzy work of Milhaud, Copland, and, if less so, George Gershwin, "a popular composer, writing what is to a Stadium-full of people important concert music, and writing it to the satisfaction of Mr. Damrosch, Mr. Koussevitzky, and the committee of the I.S.C.M. [International Society for

Contemporary Music]." At the same time, he seems equally impressed that popular music itself "has resisted wonderfully the 'invasions' of serious and popular composers," stating, "Serious music might even learn a lesson from this persistently 'low' art, in the matter of discovering one's place, and respecting it."[15]

Blitzstein regards *Gebrauchsmusik* ("functional music") as "a system of popular education, through the performance of music itself—in places and upon occasions where it cannot be escaped," such as radio, the movies, and schools; comparing this movement to Luther's call for direct congregational participation, he considers this trend a German phenomenon "born of an American popularism, a Russian Sovietism, economic collapse, and a crying need for something simple." He further associates *Gebrauchsmusik* with the dramatic work of Hindemith and Weill from the late 1920s and early 1930s, including *The Threepenny Opera* (Weill-Brecht, 1928), *News of the Day* (Hindemith–Marcellus Schiffer, 1929), *Mahagonny* (Weill-Brecht, 1930), *We Build a City* (Hindemith–Robert Seitz, 1930), and *He Who Says Yes* (Weill-Brecht, 1930), the last two examples of a didactic genre developed by Brecht, the *Lehrstück* ("teaching piece"). According to Blitzstein, Brecht stands as the guiding spirit to this entire movement: "He saw the new great public more clearly, more intensely than anyone else. He saw too that you couldn't just give the new public what it wanted; for what it wanted had been conditioned by generations of capitalist exploitation and treachery. He saw the need for education through poetry, through music." In his 1935 "Masterworks" lectures, he deems Hindemith's *News of the Day*, which he had seen in Darmstadt in 1929, *Gebrauchsmusik* at perhaps its best, but elsewhere he looks with more favor on the Brecht-Weill pieces, his opinions about such things fluctuating.[16]

However, in the end, he declares *Gebrauchsmusik* a failure. "Weill is," he admits, "relaxed, popular, and appealing, technically very easy yet extremely well-written, regular in rhythm, conventional yet fresh," and *He Who Says Yes*, "an extraordinary work." Nor can he ignore the popularity of *The Threepenny Opera*. Nonetheless, he often finds the composer banal and "super-bourgeois," as though he had "miscalculated and aimed too low." "Weill's natural sweetness and softness are probably the cause of the *Dreigroschenoper*'s enormous and mistaken success," he writes (at least at this juncture). "Brecht wanted the middle class audience to shrink in horror at the rotting, callous, spineless underworld characters, saying, 'This is ourselves!' Instead, they exclaimed with joy, 'Why they all have hearts of gold—the *dear* pimps and whores!'" Meanwhile, Hindemith, although more high-minded, lacked the dramatic talent necessary to reach a large public. "When it [*Gebrauchsmusik*] was complicated, it went over their heads, and when it was familiar you could hardly tell it from commercial music except that it seemed less up to date," he concludes, thinking of Hindemith and Weill, respectively. As a fundamental problem, he notes that the movement "had a direction; but it had little content," meaning, no doubt, that it lacked the Marxist orientation of "proletarian composers." ("When we come to the music of Eisler, of Volpe

[Wolpe], the Soviet Union composers and the left wing faction in America, the picture of an artist striving to reach a public is strengthened and clarified by a directive philosophy," he states in another context.)[17]

Blitzstein begins to extol this group of "proletarian composers" only toward the end of this period under review. Some communist-inspired work by Lan Adomian and Elie Siegmeister heard in late 1933 simply leaves him cold. But in the spring of 1934, he states,

> Communist composers are developing the idea [of popularism] with cogency. Their theory meets Classicism by relegating individual tendencies to the background. They are unfortunately committed to a policy of effusive virility and stormy protest, with the result that their music, so far, is for the most part loud and fast. But they are learning, and they have authentic, purposeful intensity to support them. In certain pages of Milhaud and Poulenc also, and now and then in the music of Weill, the spirit finds true expression.

And later that same year, he commends such American composers as Adomian and Siegmeister for enlarging their activities within this general development, which he describes as "an important indication of current concerns." Subsequent writings show an even more pronounced appreciation for proletarian composers, including an enthusiastic 1935 review of the *Workers' Song Book No. 2*, which he thinks "a remarkable advance" over the first volume.[18]

Blitzstein allots special praise to Hanns Eisler, deeming two of his collaborations with Brecht, *The Measures Taken* (1930) and *The Mother* (1932), "masterworks." Not that he remains uncritical of the composer's work. He observes, for instance, the inappropriate retention of expressionist techniques in some of his music, recalling "one lamentable occasion, when a plumber's union tried manfully to get through a completely atonal, dissonant work." He similarly notes times when the composer "gets caught up within a mood of sadness and heaviness quite against the intention." (Eva, less sympathetic, described the German composer in her journal as someone "who is sometimes Romantic early 19th-century with one hand and bitter-right with the other; and that is his best, of what I heard.") But he admires Eisler's alternation of singing, speaking, and shouting in *The Measures Taken*, and his accommodation of neoclassicism in the chorus *On Killing*. Considering Eisler an inspirational leader and philosopher as well ("possibly the first instance of the real fusion of Marxist and musician"), he writes, "By his private and public discourses, his help and enthusiasm, above all, by his works, he has rendered an inestimable service to American music and to the revolution."[19]

After attending an all-Weill concert in December 1935, Blitzstein, who found the program highly uneven (he thought some of *Mahagonny* "stunning music of the faux-populaire school," whereas "J'attends un navire" from the more recent

Marie Galante "about rock-bottom in melodic cheapness"), attempted a comparison of Eisler and Weill, largely, although not entirely, to the former's advantage:

> They write the same kind of music, although their purposes are completely at variance. Both use severely simple melodies, regular two-four stepping tunes, to hum on your way out; perfect cadences, symmetrical phrase-lengths, unvaried oom-pah accompaniments. But Eisler's music for the Theatre Union's *Mother* revealed . . . that both in temperament and knowledge he is the superior. Weill is flaccid (he wants to 'entertain'); Eisler has spine and nerves (he wants to 'educate'). . . . You will find no song in Weill to touch *In Praise of Learning* for concision or tartness; on the other hand Eisler never gets the insinuating charm of the love-duet from the *Dreigroschenoper.*

(Attending this same concert, Eva characteristically left behind a more severe assessment of the music in tiny scribblings on the program, with several numbers described as "bullshit," "lousy," and "incredibly dull.") On another occasion, Blitzstein also ventured a comparison between Eisler and the Soviet composer Alexander Davidenko: "The difference in spirit between Davidenko and Eisler brings sharply into relief the distinction between workers' music in a Soviet country and elsewhere. Davidenko's militancy is joyful, unfettered; Eisler's is stubborn, hard, it bespeaks oppression and courageous resistance."[20]

In an early 1936 review of various works by Shostakovich, including *Lady Macbeth of Mtsensk*, Blitzstein further commends that composer, described as "sharp" like Stravinsky and "lyrical" like Prokofiev, but with an ease and prodigiousness that make him the embodiment of a "third generation" of modernists. Blitzstein moreover thinks Shostakovich "the happy product of a society which believes in him and backs him to the limit; and he is practically the first composer in our day to write good music which is also contagious." On February 15, 1936, apparently after this particular article went to press, the American media reported that, in fact, a few weeks prior, the Soviet Union, through its state-run newspaper *Pravda*, had strongly condemned *Lady Macbeth* for its "Leftist bourgeois tendencies." Blitzstein clipped out and pasted into his scrapbook two such articles, including one from the *Times* marked with exclamation points and a few jottings, including "keep this" and, in reference to *Pravda*'s reported complaint that one could not whistle Shostakovich "on the way home" as one could Glinka, Musorgsky, Tchaikovsky, and Rimsky, "S[hostakovich] is this baby."[21]

Among the criteria underpinning Blitzstein's criticism, formal concerns hold central importance, most obviously in the early 1930s, during which time he delivered his "Form in Music" lectures (1933) and explored novel formal ideas in his own music. Igor Markevitch's *Serenade*, he writes, "lacks chiefly a grasp of apposite form"; Henry Brant's Sonata for two pianos has a form "with too many ups and downs"; Carlos Chávez's *H.P.* contains "episodes" that "link disjointedly" and a "form" that consequently "becomes lumpy"; and Gershwin's *Second Rhapsody*, like its predecessor, shows "the same evidence of thinking from one four-measure phrase to another." Blitzstein's preference for the "organic growth" of Stravinsky's neoclassical works over the "juxtaposed fragments" of the early ballets—with the exception, say, of the Violin Concerto, which to his mind betrays "a fundamental discrepancy between the large dimensions of the instrumental means and the small suite form"—builds precisely upon this emphasis on formal matters.[22]

Relatedly, his severe attitude toward nineteenth-century music entails his perception of that repertoire as largely formless: "Hence the escape into literature, for subject and structure. Hence the retrogression to the elementary a-b-a model, or the naïvely 'complex' a-b-c-d-e-f-g-h-i-(etc. *ad inf.*)-a of the later Romantics. Hence the Leitmotif, which shall make form wherever it goes. Hence introductions which do not introduce, interludes between interludes, epilogues which sum up a content nowhere to be discovered." Along these lines, he criticizes Roy Harris's First String Quartet as follows: "Harris insists upon, *practises*, the theory that material should dictate form; and that no two types of material should employ the same form. This is pure romanticism: the classic Beethoven of the early sonatas, the Bach of the fugues, were able to contain the most widely different subjects in approximately the same form." On the other hand, he considers (although this a few years later, in 1935) Piston's preoccupation with form "almost a vice," for it "accounts for a partial smothering of the content and at times for an actual debasing of the content."[23]

Blitzstein also pays special attention to music's social meanings, as he had in his Curtis days, when he wrote about the relation of Russian music to "the attitude toward life of the Russian people," much as his absorption with form dated back to his adolescent compositions with their outlined "plans." He often discusses the "morbidity" of Schoenberg, Berg, and some Hindemith and Weill, for example, in the context of socioeconomic developments in central Europe. In his 1936 articles for the *New Masses*, such observations assume a particularly Marxist cast. For instance, he speaks dialectically of the "decadence" and "vitality" of the *belle époque* as reflecting the "inherent contradictions" that spawned, in the years just prior to the First World War, a revolutionary music rejected by a "privileged society" that "did not wish anything new to be said, or even thought or surmised. It didn't matter that many things in the new music were a faithful reflection of the society itself; or rather, it mattered a great deal." The composer of *Pierrot lunaire*, he states, "knew what he was writing; it was the truth about the dreams of humanity in a world of war and violence. The unendurable truth; the masters listened, shivered, and said 'no!'" Stravinsky's *The Rite of Spring* "dared, in a high place, among genteel surroundings, to expose lust and wantonness and bestiality to the auditors; Caliban saw himself in the mirror, and yelled for the militia."[24]

Since this upheaval, he further asserts, many composers have accommodated radical modernism in order to please this same "privileged society" and have made themselves "the tool of a vicious economic setup. The unconscious (sometimes not so unconscious) prostitution of composers in today's world is one of the sorry sights." He writes elsewhere of these composers, "They sing praises, they prop up the obscene old dowager with assuring sonnets and sonatas, they lull her with *Stabat Maters*, they goose her with gaudy ballet music." Blitzstein cites Ravel's *Bolero* and Respighi's *Pines of Rome* as prime examples, but he also implicates, as "luxury-products," Stravinsky's *Apollo*, Hindemith's *Marienleben*, Igor Markevitch's *Psaume*, and Roger Sessions's *Chorale Preludes*, not to mention the music of Henri Sauguet and Virgil Thomson (whose 1931 *Stabat Mater* he might well have had in mind with regard to the above quote). At the same time, he especially cannot simply dismiss Stravinsky, whose neoclassical works he admires enormously; and so, thinking of works like the recent Violin Concerto, he offers this argument: "In Stravinsky you can feel that the aim towards discipline and a music of order is close to the reality of his time, even prophetic. But you can also feel that his wish to divorce music from other streams of life is symptomatic of an escape from reality, and that it has played a part in the loss of stamina his new works show." Or as he more uninhibitedly tells the readers of the *New Masses*, "In a world of cataclysmic unrest and change, he [Stravinsky] appears to be saying, 'We can at least play at tiddlywinks like gentlemen.'" Blitzstein concludes, "We may look to younger and fresher talents to combine the new discipline with an ideology that more truly reflects the reality of the day."[25]

In early 1936, Blitzstein similarly writes, "It is clear to me that one conception of music in society, with us these many years, is dying of acute anachronism; and that a fresh idea, overwhelming in its implications and promise, is taking hold." This "fresh idea"—cultivated by the composers of *Gebrauchsmusik* but now more purposefully exemplified by the proletarian composers—involves music for what he variously calls "the large public," "the great new public," "the people," "all the people," "the crowd," "the mob," "the workers," "the laboring classes," "the masses," "the mass audience," or, as in the title of his projected book, simply "us." Unlike "privileged society," which Blitzstein associates with the patrons of opera companies and symphony orchestras, this more adventurous "public"—as represented by the Workers' Music League, the Associated Workers' Club, and the American League Against War and Fascism—"wants culture, it asks for art. A culture, an art that will bring a deeper knowledge of itself and of reality, that will show it a possible new reality." With capitalism moving "towards the brink," he feels on the precipice of "a cataclysmic change such as has happened only once or twice before. . . . It may mean a participation of audiences in music to a degree unheard of since the Greeks."[26]

Blitzstein's two principal concerns—the question of musical form and that of music in society—interact, for he views the social history of music in terms of the development of forms. In other words, he sees the creation of such epochal forms as the Palestrina mass, Bach fugue, Beethoven sonata, and Wagnerian music drama as reflecting changing social structures, although his surviving writings do not really develop this thesis. In any case, he became engrossed with creating forms appropriate to current conditions. At a two-day composers' conference organized by Copland during the Yaddo Music Festival in early May 1932, he told his colleagues at the opening session,

> We need a musical form that can have a wider range than the now outmoded forms of the past or the forms of any individual composer. Ideally, material should dictate form, but many types of material can go into one form. I propose that we set ourselves a task: try to arrive, arbitrarily and collectively, at some new form and set ourselves, in all humility, each to write a piece in it. The form should be loose enough to permit individuality and tight enough to be recognizable in all the pieces as the same form. We might start by analysing the concerts we have just heard to discover what qualities the compositions played have in common. . . . One objection to this idea may be that a form is arrived at through compositions rather than before they are written, and I agree with that: I think we may begin to find the new form only after the first pieces written in some arbitrarily chosen form have been written and analysed.

When asked if he had "a working hypothesis," Blitzstein responded, "Well, as an example, one might follow the sonata two-theme structure with a form using three independent themes," a form not accidentally employed by Blitzstein for his *Serenade* for string quartet premiered at this very conference, and one possibly related to the Marxist dialectic of thesis, antithesis, and synthesis. The following day, he even proposed the *Serenade* as a prototype for such a new form, which, he added, would require "a more stable sense of tonality than we have now" and which might feature an "asymmetry" that he seemed to regard as a distinctively American trait.[27]

Some of Blitzstein's colleagues, including Robert Russell Bennett and Israel Citkowitz, liked the general idea (Citkowitz noted the precedent of the creation of opera by the Florentine Camerata), whereas others were more dubious. Wallingford Riegger, for instance, asserted the importance of individuality, which prompted Blitzstein to say, "As to individualism, we'll all have to give that up anyway in twenty-five years or less. . . . I want to discover how we are all alike. . . . It would give the individual a world in which to stand. Form would be gained, culture would be gained." Copland, noting that traditional forms served such contemporaries as Roger Sessions, also proved skeptical, and reproached Blitzstein for "putting the cart before the horse" and for attempting "to do something impossible." In turn, Blitzstein argued that "content and form are inherent in each other," further defining content as "the way the material is used." "We must compose so differently we can't understand each other," exclaimed Copland at one point. This sparring climaxed with the following exchange:

> COPLAND: "I try to help American music practically—you want to help it in a way that I think doesn't apply."
> BLITZSTEIN: "Why doesn't it?"
> COPLAND: "Because we have different conceptions of form. I think of it like the four-measure phrase that just comes—god-given."
> BLITZSTEIN: "The history of music shows you're wrong."
> COPLAND: "Oh, of course one fusses with it."

But although Copland could not support Blitzstein's proposal, in later years, he at least spoke respectfully of the composer's "concern with structure."[28]

Ironically, Copland's *Piano Variations* (1930), which received its second American performance at this same 1932 Yaddo Music Festival, became for Blitzstein an archetype for just the kind of new musical form for which he advocated during this period. Blitzstein initially had judged the piece, in a review of its unsuccessful 1931 premiere, as "harmonically thin," "too long," ultimately, a miscalculation; but like many others, he revised his opinion in light of Copland's stunning repeat performance at Yaddo. Blitzstein subsequently lectured about and performed the work with some frequency, referring to it not only as Copland's "masterpiece" but as the legitimate heir to Stravinsky's *Les Noces* in terms of formal integrity: "The large-scale conception, the continuous line achieved, the success of the architecture, make it very likely that this work is in the vanguard of the day's trend." Blitzstein similarly regarded Stravinsky's *Oedipus* (1927), with its masterful pacing of narration, song, and chorus, as yet another formal landmark; perhaps he had that opera-oratorio in mind, along with the musical plays of Brecht and his collaborators, when he stated, "From music's standpoint, the history is shaping towards some new epic form which will certainly be a theatrical one." Suffice to say, Copland's *Variations* and Stravinsky's *Oedipus* became for Blitzstein two formal models of enormous personal and world importance.[29]

Blitzstein furthermore considered the amalgamation of various modernist styles and techniques a crucial complement to the creation of new forms. He typically cited Milhaud's *The Creation of the World*, with its mixture of primitivism, classicism, and popularism, as the outstanding prototype in this regard, although he also offered as other examples the *Symphony of Psalms, Wozzeck*, and, for its incorporation of primitivism and classicism, even his own Piano Sonata.[30]

Whatever his reservations about certain contemporary trends, Blitzstein maintained the continued relevance of such varied modernists as Schoenberg, Stravinsky, Hindemith, Milhaud, Berg, and Prokofiev, as in the last installment of his three-part article for the *New Masses*, "The Case for Modern Music," in which he rejects "the doctrine of 'original sin.'" Even if Schoenberg's atonal music represents a "dead-end," the "discipline and logic" of his methodology remain "terribly important, especially for those young proletarian composers who are quite sure they can get along on 'instinct' and 'intuition.'" The great modernist composers, he concludes, "were unconsciously preparing the way, beginning something whose counterparts and possibility they did not dream of, was none of their business. It is distinctly ours, who appraise them in order to use them; who digest in order to eliminate, but also to absorb." In short, Blitzstein envisioned new forms that would synthesize varied styles and techniques for a large new audience eager to better understand the world and their lives.[31]

Blitzstein's writings from 1931 to 1936 clearly set the stage for *The Cradle Will Rock*, whose short score he more or less completed in September 1936. After this, he continued to publish and lecture but never again to the extent that he had in the early 1930s. Perhaps as he reached maturity, he felt a diminished need to survey musical developments, at least in print. Or perhaps his busy life in the theater simply allowed less time for such activities.

In any case, Blitzstein published only a very few articles for the remainder of the decade. In the fall of 1936, he wrote a review of Paul Green and Kurt Weill's *Johnny Johnson*, which began with this oft-quoted mea culpa: "I have written some harsh things in the past about Kurt Weill and his music. I wish now to write a few good things. He hasn't changed, I have." In fact, Blitzstein had not changed entirely, as he still finds the score to contain "plenty of trite music"; but he now finds this aspect of Weill "curiously not bad, but good" and "in a way terribly sophisticated." He also applauds Weill's ingenious handling of speech, song, and silence: "This almost elementary, uninhibited use of music, seemingly careless, really profoundly sensitive, predicts something new for the theatre. It runs a risk of being choppy, fragmentary; but Weill makes sure there are whole islands of music, and binding passages of music, and entr'acte sections of music. There is nothing wrong with his sense of topography." At the same time, he thinks that Weill's "nostalgic, inconsolably sad music" works better in conjunction with Brecht's "hard clean sharp jabs to the chin."[32]

With "On Writing Music for the Theatre," an article from early 1938, the now-celebrated composer of *The Cradle Will Rock* initiated the first of what would become a number of general pieces about musical theater. Discussing texts, he ridicules the "aria-style" poesy employed by Louis Gruenberg in his libretto to *Green Mansions* as opposed to the more natural "song-style" lyrics by Edwin Denby for Copland's *The Second Hurricane*. He acknowledges too the achievement of Broadway lyricists Lorenz Hart, Ira Gershwin, and Cole Porter, who "have caught wonderful slices of colloquial talk into neat and racy rhyme-schemes," although he disapproves of their occasionally "sentimentalizing a sophisticated mood, as in Porter's *I've Got You Under My Skin*, where one endless line seemed to sound like 'I told myself time and again, still and all, all through the night, night and day, both of us were quite aware this affair wouldn't go so well.'" This article also draws attention to the relation of music to dramatic action, citing various missteps in Hollywood, as with Alfred Newman's film score to *Dead End*, and more effective techniques as found in films and stage works by Honegger, Eisler, Weill, and himself.[33]

Blitzstein penned some short reflections on theatrical set design later in the year—part of a symposium entitled "Scenery or No Scenery?"—that argued for the validity of both stage realism and what he calls "non-architectural staging" so long as they fit a particular work's dramatic intentions. "The interest in non-architectural staging," he concludes, "will have served one good purpose if it succeeds in purging the theatre of the idea that the scenic designer is the paramount factor in play production—a misconception that even the critics are prone to sustain. On the other hand, it would be extremely snobbish for the theatre to veer deliberately to a diet of 'scenery-less' plays."[34]

"Theatre Music" (1940), one of the composer's last pieces for *Modern Music*, further evidenced the turn away from wide-ranging critiques and lectures on contemporary art music to the occasional piece on popular musical theater, showing Blitzstein thoroughly absorbed by a wide range of Broadway offerings, although he remains quick to point out shoddy craftsmanship and banal content. Discussing Rodgers and Hart's *Too Many Girls* and Cole Porter's *DuBarry Was a Lady*, he writes,

> In the musical-comedy field, Richard Rodgers still holds his own as the freshest talent. I personally don't always go for his sedate polished tunes, with their chic melodic contours and 'smart' harmonies. But I admire his endless variety within the small frame; and I admire the exact and fruitful collaboration he has maintained with Lorenz Hart. Hart has probably the bigger gift; Rodgers is the shrewder person. . . . The marriage here of Cole Porter to Cole Porter is a shade less successful than the Rodgers-Hart combination. Porter sometimes has more zip . . . but he sometimes has less taste.

This review also occasioned yet another comparison between Eisler and Weill, with Eisler's incidental music for Clifford Odets's *Night Music* deemed "in every way a thoroughly good job," and Weill's for Elmer Rice's *Two on an Island* "pretty shabby; standard tunes seemed never so standard, harmonizations never so trite." As for the hit song "How High the Moon" (music, Morgan Lewis, lyric, Nancy Hamilton) featured in *Two for the Show* and performed "in the English manner, which is to say throaty and bored," the number left Blitzstein humming to himself, "How Long the Song?"[35]

Meanwhile, in a 1938 article for the *Daily Worker* adapted from a talk delivered at the Workers Bookshop, Blitzstein more explicitly than ever addressed the need for composers to forsake "neutrality" in favor of engagement. Referring to opposition to the Coffee-Pepper Bill, a congressional initiative to institutionalize federal support of the arts through the establishment of an independent governmental arts bureau, Blitzstein wrote, "It is therefore necessary to support every possible progressive venture—for instance, the Coffee-Pepper bill—and oppose such anti-communist, anti-progressive measures. The musician and the composer must now tell you what they feel about the struggle against reaction both in his music and in his everyday life."[36]

Similar concerns arose in a 1939 review of Copland's music appreciation text *What to Listen for in Music* for *TAC* magazine, the in-house journal for the largely communist Theatre Arts Committee. Blitzstein very much admired the book, but he would have liked to have seen "a little more relating of the ear to the rest of the human system," presumably meaning more social context; and he objected to such "slightly fussy and stuffy phrases" as "religious feeling of calm and ease" as found in the author's analysis of Beethoven's "Waldstein" Sonata.[37]

After *The Cradle*, Blitzstein's critical writings plainly shifted focus from concert music to popular theater and film. At the same time, as Minna Lederman observed, he "retained to the end an amazing intellectual concern with the advanced technique of music." Recalling in particular a concert of twelve-tone music she attended with him and Carlos Chávez in the early 1960s, she remembered "how swift Marc was in grasping the underlying concepts . . . how eager to point out the not always striking differences between the composers, the degree of success or failure in each projection. And his tremendous zest for it all. This is wonderful, wonderful, he said, a real anti-Establishment concert."[38]

8

From the *Serenade* (1932) to *The Chesapeake Bay Retriever* (1936)

For his *Serenade* for string quartet, composed during the first two months of 1932, Blitzstein set himself the unusual challenge of writing a work in three movements all in the same tempo (in this case Largo), using one main theme for the first movement, two for the second, and three for the third. Because these themes often unfold imitatively, the quartet gives the general impression of a fugue, a double fugue, and a triple fugue in succession. For some of these novel formal ideas, Blitzstein, as earlier suggested, might have been thinking of Marxist dialectics.[1]

The work goes its own way stylistically as well, with its slow, steady rhythms helping to lend the music a certain gray, dour quality, although all three movements reach, often with material presented in augmentation, some repose, especially the last movement, whose coda opens out toward the light. Moreover, each movement imparts a somewhat different mood: the first, somber; the middle, forlorn but calm; and the finale, purposeful. Within the limits of its single tempo, this larger movement toward final affirmation marks an evocative dramatic trajectory.

"I had no idea he had come to this level of maturity," Goldbeck noted in her journal in early January concerning the first movement, adding two weeks later, "It is very fine and a small bomb." When Blitzstein began work about this same time on the second movement, he told her that he had "the feeling of having entered a whole new land," which led Goldbeck to reflect, "It is no longer neo-classicism, it is—the 'classicism' of the age . . . it is not—'you should really be dead'—not the sense of a living classic, but of the future—the living substance." While at work on the quartet, Blitzstein also told her that for the first time he had "the sense of being an instrument."[2]

On March 2, 1932, his twenty-seventh birthday, Blitzstein dedicated the piece to Goldbeck with an inscription in German that quoted the conclusion of "Love Song" by Rainer Maria Rilke, lines that alluded to his "sense of being an instrument": "Yet everything which touches us, you and me,/brings us together like a bow stroke,/that from two strings draws out a single voice./Across what instrument are we stretched?/And what player holds us in his hand?/O sweet song."[3]

Copland helped arrange the official April 30, 1932, world premiere by the Hans Lange Quartet (Hans Lange, Arthur Schuller, Zoltan Kurthy, and Percy Such) at Yaddo's First Festival of Contemporary American Music, although Blitzstein had an opportunity to hear the piece tried out in Philadelphia in early April. "It's a wonderful piece!" he telephoned Goldbeck from Philadelphia, leaving her "weak in the knees (literally) with a flash of what it must mean—and envy at not having been there."[4]

At Yaddo, the *Serenade* appeared second on a Saturday evening program that also included Roy Harris's Piano Sonata, Oscar Levant's Sonatina, and after intermission, Robert Russell Bennett's *Three Chaucer Poems*, Copland's *Piano Variations* (substituted at the last minute for some pieces by George Antheil), and Nicolai Berezowsky's String Trio. Goldbeck's opinions about the recital as recorded in her diary—she thought the Harris "interesting and original but overdone," the Levant "Broadway," the Copland "magnificent," the Bennett "pleasing parlor music," and the Berezowsky "just tricks and diddles and cheap imagination"—likely accorded with Blitzstein's, but at the same time seemed consistent with her own sensibilities.[5]

After the concert, Blitzstein told Goldbeck, "I feel very quiet inside, perfectly satisfied—as though a best-beloved child had been put to rest. I need never hear it again. It filled the room, with all those people, and it filled me, and it was supposed to fill you." After this, he kissed her and wrote in her journal, "This turns out to be it—our consummation of the dream—The Serenade—Eva's, mine, ours—comes to life. There is no more to be said—we still belong to it, and yet it is out upon its own feet. Good-bye, süsses lied [sweet song]."[6]

A number of years later, Blitzstein recalled the work as follows:

> I once wrote a "Serenade for String Quartet." The three movements were marked "Largo, largo, largo," and I came in for a lot of ribbing from colleagues and critics. It was an honest attempt at making music, however. It seemed to me that the modern spirit in music had reached a point where the "spectre of boredom" became the guiding devil of composers; pieces were short, so the listeners wouldn't get bored; not only short, they changed their pace and manner and harmony and melody-styles every few bars. *This* piece wouldn't, I maintained; and fell into the same trap, only in reverse. I wrote a long piece that didn't change.

The ribbing came in part from two pianists who in the course of the festival performed a four-hand burlesque of the piece, conducted by Bernard Herrmann; one of these might well have been Oscar Levant, who in his 1940 memoir, *A Smattering of Ignorance*, described Blitzstein's all-Largo concept as "one of the greatest presumptions toward an audience that I had ever encountered in any composer.... It was like a meal consisting entirely of stained glass, with different dressing." (Blitzstein surely did not help his cause by telling Levant at Yaddo,

regarding the latter's Sonatina, "Now try to write a little *music*.") Blitzstein recip-
rocated by way of a caustic although not unappreciative review of Levant's book:
"Piece the parts together and you will have Oscar, with his lugubrious impu-
dence, his boorish charm, his self-deprecation, his gift for hero-worship, his
sizeable knowledge, and his sizeable vanity."[7]

For all these mordant public exchanges, Levant and Blitzstein remained supportive and friendly. Indeed, Levant spoke respectfully of *The Cradle Will Rock* in
his aforementioned memoir: although he thought the "pseudo-virility" of its
libretto "forced and artificial," he regarded the music as "highly ingenious and persua-
sively rhythmic" and claimed that its "astounding success" had a "provocative
influence" on American composers, as "it opened a vista of new opportunities for
them, suggesting uses for their talents that had not previously occurred to them."
Just prior to the February 17, 1942, premiere of Levant's Piano Concerto over the
air in New York, the composer insisted that Blitzstein listen to the work, which the
latter described to David Diamond as "a strange piece—full of brilliant little *trou-
vailles* on the Shostakovich-Prokofieff pattern—but so full of that wry, dry, acid and
unleavened harmony which is his heritage both from unrequited yearning and
Schonberg, that I understand fully what [Dimitri] Mitropoulos meant when he told
Oscar 'the piece is full of hate.'"[8]

As for the *Serenade*, the work actually found a few advocates, most notably Copland, who according to Goldbeck previously had "doubted" that Blitzstein "was
fully serious" and for the first time reacted to the latter's music with "wholehearted" support. Israel Citkowitz and Robert Russell Bennett, serving on a panel
at the Yaddo conference, also spoke well of the quartet, as did Randall Thompson
in a letter supporting Blitzstein for a Guggenheim fellowship (even if the work's
form "was like a slap in the face"). But the critics at Yaddo proved, if in some ways
admiring, ultimately critical. In reference to the all-Largo structure, the *New York
Tribune* stated, "The contrasts are sought in sonorities rather than tempi; interesting as a problem, its musical ideas and thought are opaque, too little varied."
And although *Modern Music*'s Alfred Meyer found in the piece "a darksome
Hebraic cast suggestive of Ernest Bloch" and "an inherent talent above the ordinary," the work's unusual form and inscrutable title led him to deem the composer
one of the festival's "misfits."[9]

"I despair of seeing an intelligent review of your quartet," wrote Copland to
Blitzstein in May, noting that the critics could not "get beyond" the all-Largo
format and adding, "The moral is: Always cajole a listener, never frighten him
away. I mean it seriously." Perhaps with this advice in mind, Blitzstein set
aside the notion, entertained in March 1932, of using the *Serenade* as a prototype for such works as an all-Moderato piano piece and an all-Presto woodwind piece, and turned his attention instead to writing a large dramatic work,
The Condemned. And at some point, Blitzstein proposed for the *Serenade*
the alternate tempo markings: Allegro moderato, Larghetto, and Andante
maestoso.[10]

The Lange Quartet brought the work to New York on April 9, 1933, and played two movements over the air some weeks later on April 23, and the Modern Art Quartet performed the first movement at an all-Blitzstein concert on April 15, 1936. In more recent years, the Del Sol String Quartet took up the work, with their recording of the piece appearing in 2009. In a favorable review of this release, James Keller, noting significant differences among the separate movements, thought the group's retention of the Largo markings "ultimately to the piece's benefit," although he welcomed the idea of an "alternate reading of the *Serenade* at the revised tempos."[11]

Blitzstein spent the remainder of 1932 mostly in Dubrovnik and Mlini, Croatia, at work on a one-act "choral opera" or "opera for four choruses," *The Condemned*, which he had conceived the previous summer and which he completed in late November. As with *The Harpies*, he wrote the libretto himself. However, in this instance, he took his inspiration not from a classic text, but rather from the case of Sacco and Vanzetti, a subject to which he would return at the end of his life for yet another opera and one that clearly played a critical role in his development as an artist of social conscience.

The case dated back to 1920, when the Brockton, Massachusetts, police arrested two young Italian immigrants, Nicola Sacco and Bartolomeo Vanzetti, in connection with an armed robbery in South Braintree, outside of Boston, that left a paymaster and his guard fatally shot. Sacco, married with one child and another on the way, worked in a shoe factory as an edge trimmer; Vanzetti, a bachelor, was a fishmonger. As followers of the anarchist Luigi Galleani, the two had become friends shortly before leaving for Mexico during the First World War to avoid possible conscription. As the government cracked down on radicals in the late teens, some Galleanists, including comrades of Sacco and Vanzetti, engaged in terrorist bombings that only encouraged further repression in an escalating cycle of fear.[12]

Both Sacco and Vanzetti—either worried about deportation, as they later asserted, or conscious of their guilt, as prosecutors would claim—lied under police questioning. On thin evidence, the government quickly tried and convicted Vanzetti for an attempted holdup the previous year, after which he and Sacco stood trial for the Braintree crimes. A Sacco-Vanzetti Defense Committee, under the leadership of Aldino Felicani, hired Fred Moore to represent the two anarchists; the state appointed District Attorney Frederick Katzmann as prosecutor; and Judge Webster Thayer presided.

The trial took place in early summer 1921, during which the court's patent hostility toward the two defendants as anarchists, foreigners, and draft-dodgers prompted outrage both at home and abroad. After the jury reached a guilty verdict, protesters took to the street, especially in Europe and Latin America, in demonstrations often organized by a broad coalition of leftists that prefigured the popular front of the 1930s.

The defense submitted various appeals, all reviewed and denied by Judge Thayer. In 1924, another attorney, William Thompson, took over the defense, but his petitions for a new trial also met with rebuff from Thayer, even after Celestino Medeiros, a convicted killer sentenced to death, confessed in 1925 that he had participated in the Braintree robbery, and that Sacco and Vanzetti had not. In the meantime, Sacco became increasingly suicidal and paranoid, while Vanzetti emerged, primarily through his letters, a thoughtful and eloquent commentator.

In 1927, as notable politicians, writers, and jurisprudents—most importantly, Harvard law professor Felix Frankfurter—denounced the trial, Alvan Fuller, the governor of Massachusetts, appointed a three-man advisory committee, headed by Harvard President A. Lawrence Lowell, to review the case. On the recommendation of this committee, the governor denied clemency, and Sacco and Vanzetti, along with Medeiros, went to the electric chair on August 23, 1927. Sacco and Vanzetti denied their guilt to the end, but not their anarchist convictions, rejecting all religious consolation and asserting that the Braintree murders ran contrary to their principles.

After decades of continued study, disagreement about the verdict remains, with most historians either maintaining the two men's probable innocence, or at least that of Vanzetti's. A principal bone of contention concerns a bullet and a shell allegedly fired from a pistol owned by Sacco. However, virtually all students of the case agree that Sacco and Vanzetti, investigated and tried against the xenophobia that swept that nation after the First World War, never received a fair trial.

The incident assumed enormous cultural weight worldwide, comparable in its divisiveness to the Dreyfus affair in France. A number of artists, appalled by the trial, vented their dismay in varied works, including Edna St. Vincent Millay's "Justice Denied in Massachusetts" (1927), Malcolm Cowley's "For St. Bartholomew's Day" (1928), Upton Sinclair's *Boston* (1928), Maxwell Anderson's *Winterset* (1935), and John Dos Passos's *The Big Money* (1936), as well as a song by Ruth Crawford (1932) and a series of paintings by Ben Shahn (1931–32). The case more generally radicalized a number of intellectuals who had pinned their hopes on the liberal establishment and who now drifted toward communism, for all its opposition to anarchism, in part because the communists offered what many believed to be the most clear-sighted response to the affair. "The intellectuals had learned that they were powerless by themselves and that they could not accomplish anything unless they made an alliance with the working class," wrote Malcolm Cowley in 1935.[13]

In contrast to Blitzstein's later opera, which he did not live to complete, *The Condemned* only references Sacco and Vanzetti obliquely, its libretto identifying its four characters simply as "The Condemned," "The Wife," "The Friend," and "The Priest." Such abstract names naturally give the work an allegorical dimension made that much more resonant by the notion of having separate choruses play and sing the individual roles: twenty-four tenors (divided I and II) and twenty-four basses (I and II) for the Condemned, thirty-two sopranos (I and II) and sixteen altos for the Wife, twenty-four basses (I and II) for the Friend, and twenty-four tenors (I and II) for the Priest. (Blitzstein had envisioned this novel

concept early on, although he originally planned, as one of the characters, a warden rather than a friend.) The whole idea, which he had sampled in *Triple-Sec* "for
farce purposes," he now used "with deadly seriousness." "My idea . . . ," he further
stated, "was to show that no one of these persons was just a single person, but was
many persons." Tellingly, he compiled among his papers a list, headed by Sacco
and Vanzetti, of some thirty revolutionary figures mostly of the previous hundred
years, but also Judah Maccabee and Socrates. (For whatever reason, he underlined only the names of Sacco and Vanzetti, Rosa Luxemburg, Karl Liebknecht,
August Blanqui, Peter Kropotkin, Mikhail Bakunin, and John Reed.)[14]

At the same time, Sacco and Vanzetti provided the key inspiration for the work,
as indicated not only by Blitzstein's determination the previous summer to compose a "variation on Sacco-Vanzetti: the morning of the execution of a man convicted falsely of murder, with a background of the capitalistic machine against a
radical individual," but by his later admission that the opera "was influenced by
the Sacco-Vanzetti executions . . . although it is not about them." (When Blitzstein
told Goldbeck that he wanted to dedicate the work to her, she suggested rather
that he dedicate it to the memory of Sacco and Vanzetti, although in the end, the
score carried no dedication at all.) Accordingly, the figure of the Condemned
could be seen as a composite of the two Italian anarchists; the Wife as Sacco's wife
Rosa; the Friend as any number of supporters, such as Felicani; and the Priest as
the prison chaplain Father Michael Murphy, whom both men spurned on the day
of their execution.[15]

In eleven scenes, the opera takes place in the "death house" on the "morning of
the execution." The Condemned arises from a dream (scene i); he urges his
hopeful Wife to remain calm (scene ii); the Friend admits to the Condemned that
they have been beaten, that the latter is to be "killed by a nation for your faith in
man," but sees in his death, martyrdom (scene iii); the Condemned tells the Priest
that he does not believe in God (scene iv); the Condemned professes his faith in
man, but grows fearful as he approaches death (scene v); repentant, the Condemned calls back the Priest, to whom he says, "Lord, I believe; help thou mine
unbelief" (Mark 9:24), and from whom he receives absolution (scene vi); the
Condemned lies exhausted (scene vii, orchestral interlude); the Condemned
once again denies God and calls for the brotherhood of man on earth (scene viii);
the Condemned and his Wife take leave of each other (scene ix); the Wife witnesses the Condemned's execution (scene x); the Wife, the Friend, and the Priest
find glory in the death of the Condemned (scene xi).

Some surviving notes about the opera, presumably written by Goldbeck, suggest that Blitzstein had—along with Shakespeare's *King Lear*—the fifteenth-
century English morality play *Everyman*, and its famous adaptation by Hugo von
Hofmannsthal, *Jedermann*, in mind while writing this opera, an inference supported by the work itself, as *The Condemned* similarly concerns a man wrestling
with moral and spiritual issues at the moment of death. Meanwhile, the choral
operatic concept, and perhaps all those drafted two-word titles found among his

sketches (including "The Martyr," "The Innocent," "The Hour," and "The Dying" as well as "The Condemned"), might have been suggested by a March 1932 press report, saved among the composer's papers, stating that Ottorino Respighi and Gabriele d'Annunzio intended their opera-in-progress, *La fiamma* ("The Flame," 1931–33), as a "choral-orchestral symphony for theatrical production."[16]

The opera's eleven scenes average a few minutes each, with the entire work lasting a little over half an hour. Within this compressed scope, the text settings range from the syllabic and homorhythmic to the polytextural and imitative, with scenes four and eight featuring solo quartets. Such varied textures not only provide musical interest, but allow Blitzstein to draw, as Carolyn West Pace suggests, unusually intricate psychological portraits, as the individual characters at times express contrasting feelings and thoughts simultaneously.[17]

The central sixth scene, in which the Condemned repents, constitutes the work's climax; after completing this particular episode, Blitzstein told Goldbeck that her impression of the music as "nightmarish, yet tight" was "exactly what he wanted to produce," adding, "I was thinking what a task I'd set myself—a scene in which everything is supposed to go crazy, done with neo-classical means." The ensuing orchestral interlude, which depicts the exhausted hero by way of simple unisons in the woodwinds, offers some respite.[18]

In terms of style and mood, the score recalls the *Serenade*, which can be seen as a sketch for this more ambitious effort. Again, the severely contrapuntal textures feature long tonal or modal melodies (according to sketches, Blitzstein thought of each scene as in a particular major or minor key), with dissonant, contradictory bass lines that occasionally converge on a triad with the upper parts at cadence points but that often do not. (In April 1932, as Blitzstein started work on the opera, Goldbeck reported in her diary that he intended to explore a "new harmonic system," one that, as best as she was able to explain, used a four-note harmony, such as a major-seventh chord, rather than the traditional three-note triad as a "basic chord.") The use of such lucid, stepwise melodies to create so dense and dissonant a harmonic palette, including the clash of two major triads a half-step apart at the end of the finale, suggests the influence of Milhaud. Strong echoes also can be heard of Stravinsky, Beethoven, and Bach, along with Renaissance music, as in the striking unaccompanied vocalise for the Wife in scene ten.[19]

Blitzstein provided fairly detailed production notes for the work:

> The stage should be a series of ramps, descending from the rear to the footlights, something like a football stadium. Three curtains, arranged along the top section of the ramps, are used to reveal and cover the characters of the Wife, the Friend, and the Priest; the character of the Condemned is discovered at the beginning of the opera, and makes the only actual exit, after Scene IX. This character has a comparative freedom of action on the stage; the other characters stay for the most part within the space allotted them by their respective curtains.

Accordingly, as the curtain rises, the forty-eight-man chorus portraying the Condemned can assume, as directed, "various attitudes denoting sleep: lying, leaning, reclining, etc." Blitzstein's stage ideas might have been inspired in part by medieval biblical pageants and, relatedly, Max Reinhardt's famed 1920 production of Hofmannsthal's *Jedermann* for the Salzburg Festival, although he plausibly had in mind the work of Soviet director Vsevolod Meyerhold as well.[20]

Goldbeck observed the piece's progress with even more than her usual fervor; she thought the libretto "hair-raising" and the music "breath-taking," with the phrase "I do not want to die" (scene iii) reducing her to tears. "I think it is the greatest music Marc has written," she wrote her parents in October, similarly stating in her journal some weeks later, "I feel that neither Marc nor any composer could write greater music." In early 1933, in the direct wake of this work, Goldbeck penned an insightful essay on Blitzstein in which she more critically noted in his music "a certain rigor which may have been a fear of too much expressiveness—a danger of the intent on objectivity" and a general lack of "lyric warmth," although at the same time, she thought that the recent choral opera revealed "the characteristic greatness of Blitzstein's music" and predicted "a great comic work in music stemming directly out of this great tragic work."[21]

While still at work on the opera, Blitzstein sent his piano reduction of the eighth scene, dated July 1, 1932, to Nadia Boulanger, who replied on July 21:

> I read with great care, great emotion the scène you sent me—I love it in itself deeply and feel that it must take the right place in the whole!
>
> I don't realise what is the proportion of the orchestra, the distance in range and some places stay uncertain—I mean I am not sure how they sound—in some chords where the voices seem not to be sustained by the orchestra, I would fear "pour la justesse" ["for their intonation"].
>
> These things are matter[s] of détail—what matters is the quality of the music, the strength of expression, the choice of means—

This supportive feedback notwithstanding, Blitzstein wrote to his sister in September,

> I hardly know much about the value of the work just now; I am fortified by the instinct that it is very good; but I have no opinions yet. What is most important is that it should combine the quality of—"impressiveness" is the only word I can think of, or "monumentality"—with the sense of moving forward. Each scene should be static enough to get over the impression of being a universal symbol—and must yet give way to the next scene, on a continuity basis.

Later that fall, he wrote to Jo again, "Each scene moves with a narrow, hemmed-in formula, doggedly regular; the harmonies mostly bleak, hollow, underdone, occasionally passionate. It is this open quality in the vertical line, and closed one in the horizontal which gives the work its special and personal quality."[22]

As with the *Serenade*, such "static" and "bleak" qualities engender a certain grimness, as presumably intended. After Copland had a chance to review the score, he declared the drama overly abstract; the harmonies unpleasing; and the work as a whole "music one has to respect rather than love." At the same time, the opera, with its inventive word setting and effective theatrical strokes (the way, for instance, the first scene moves toward its final line, "This is the day I am to be killed!" or the alternately sinister and urbane music for the Priest), demonstrates the composer's gifts as a musical dramatist, probably more so than anything he had written to date. And the eighth scene—the one he had sent to Boulanger, in which the Condemned delivers his credo, "All men are my brothers"—offers relief from the prevailing gloom.[23]

From the start, Blitzstein—far more knowledgeable about Soviet music than most Westerners, although seemingly uninformed about current antimodernist developments—imagined Russia as the only possible venue for a work whose unconventional form and revolutionary content made it too radical for a Western opera house. Learning of a Russian competition for a new opera for which his own seemed well qualified encouraged him in this direction all the more. He accordingly approached his former teacher, Alexander Siloti, about the possibility of showing the work to Albert Coates, who recently had assumed a supervisory position over several leading Soviet orchestras. Of Anglo-Russian parentage, composer-conductor Coates (1882–1953) had been educated both in Russia—where he had studied with Siloti—and England, and led an international career as an opera and symphony conductor, retreating periodically to his villa on Lake Maggiore on the Swiss-Italian border.

Siloti helped arrange for Blitzstein, still in Mlini, to meet with Coates at Lake Maggiore in late September. Blitzstein had doubts about showing Coates an unfinished score, but Goldbeck encouraged him to go: "I trust history will credit me with prophetic words at a moment of indecision!" she wrote to the composer's sister Jo. After a somewhat harrowing trip—he arrived at the villa in the midst of a lightning storm—Blitzstein spent several days with Coates and his wife Madelon and played the opera through twice for them. Coates, who was "*very* much impressed," as Madelon later told the Guggenheim Foundation, hoped to interest Meyerhold in a production and suggested that Blitzstein travel to the Soviet Union to "demonstrate" the work.[24]

After this successful interview—"the audition of a lifetime," as the composer described it—Blitzstein envisioned spending eight months in the Soviet Union with Goldbeck so that he could not only "demonstrate" the opera, but feasibly see it mounted as well. Informed by Coates about plans to establish a music school for Americans in Russia modeled after the American Conservatory at Fontainebleau, Blitzstein hoped that he could secure a job at such an institution in order to make so prolonged a stay possible or that he would receive a Guggenheim fellowship, for which he once again had applied. But plans for a Russian trip or production never materialized.[25]

Blitzstein duly pursued other venues for the music, including a possible 1935 broadcast performance with the British Broadcasting Corporation, but the BBC declined, deeming "the text and the situation . . . unsuitable for broadcasting," the music "dark and pretentious, the technique monotonous, and the length depressing." (In another internal memo, conductor Aylmer Buesst granted that the piece seemed the work of a "highly trained, serious and sincere" musician, "yet his music is so primitive, and sounds so perfectly ghastly, that one can easily doubt both his musicianship and his sincerity. I would almost like to hear it done and think the results would be intensely funny. The work is valuable only as a museum piece, and I beg that others see it before it is returned to its parent.")[26]

Buoyed by Hanns Eisler's admiration for the opera, Blitzstein also considered preparing a concert presentation of excerpts; but as nothing came of this either, he began to cannibalize the score for other pieces. He reworked some of the music from scene five for the choral lament "Make the Heart Be Stone" that follows Joe's death in *No for an Answer* (1937–40); and he recast some of scene eight as a piece for male chorus with altos, "Invitation to Bitterness" (1939), with a new text that begins "Rise. Rise. We who dream in anger" as opposed to the original "Wrong. Weak. I deny the Father." (Published by Arrow Press, "Invitation to Bitterness" appeared on a September 20, 1989, "Workers of the World" concert at New York's Merkin Hall.) Moreover, he used the scene seven interlude to fashion some of the piano accompaniment for a late E. E. Cummings song, "silent unday by silently not night," the most severe number from his Cummings cycle, *From Marion's Book* (1960).[27]

After years of enormous productivity, Blitzstein wrote relatively little in the three years from *The Condemned* to *The Cradle Will Rock*. A busy schedule of teaching and lecturing, not to mention his wife's poor health, no doubt distracted him from composition. But he seems to have reached something of an artistic impasse as well, with his music from this time showing signs of strain and indecision. Henry Brant, noting the absence in particular of a dramatic work during this period, suggested that, with *The Condemned*, he had reached "a critical stage where his developing interest in expressing a positive social viewpoint" conflicted "with the rigid, impersonal stylization of his musical and literary language."[28]

In early 1933, Blitzstein began, in Eva's words, an "easy" work for flute, cello, and piano, which by summer apparently had evolved into the by-no-means-easy *Discourse* for clarinet, cello, and piano, a piece left unfinished. Originally calling it "Ricercata," Blitzstein devised detailed schemes for this work, imagining a piece that would change tempos, avoid repetition, and unfold contrapuntally but without the use of canon or other imitative devices. True to his intentions, the surviving music maintains strict independence of voices, with even the piano part consisting largely of two or three widely separated, often dissonant lines.

Blitzstein further planned to use four themes composed of various series of notes (ninety-one, twenty, twenty-one, and twenty-three notes, respectively), along with their inversions and retrogrades (or what Blitzstein termed "retrogressions"). He concurrently charted dozens of related four-note collections of pitches as motivic material, a method alluded to by Goldbeck, as mentioned above. Although not twelve-tone per se, such techniques plainly evidenced Schoenberg's influence, and the piece significantly coincided with Blitzstein's more positive reassessment of his former teacher.

The music's radical independence of parts also recalled some music by Henry Cowell and Ruth Crawford, and the theories of their teacher Charles Seeger, who labeled such textures "heterophony." Blitzstein's close association with Seeger dated from a slightly later period, but by this point he presumably would have known Seeger's 1930 article "On Dissonant Counterpoint," in which the author argued that such heterophonic textures depended on dissonant counterpoint, for otherwise "our homophonically over-educated ears will infer chordal structures not intended and the polyphony will be lost." Dissonant counterpoint, a method developed by Seeger and Cowell in the 1910s, attracted some notable adherents in the early 1930s, not only because of Seeger's landmark article, but quite possibly because its premise of reversing the age-old relationship between musical consonance and dissonance mirrored the widespread hope that the world as a whole could be remade, a notion supported by the fact that those relatively few composers who practiced dissonant counterpoint during this period commonly took an interest in Marx and Lenin as well. Likewise, the attraction to heterophony plausibly bore some relation to the intensified concern, as among the defenders of Sacco and Vanzetti, for the rights of each individual in society. In any case, such musical ideas allowed Blitzstein to explore through less surrealistic, more formal means that sense of topsy-turviness that he had attempted to reflect in the preceding decade, even if this new development would prove something of a phase as well.[29]

Discourse, in turn, anticipated the music of Elliott Carter (b. 1908), who, however, never acknowledged the slightly older Blitzstein as a forebear, as he did both Cowell and Crawford. At the same time, Carter socialized with the Blitzsteins in the mid-1930s—he wrote to Eva in June 1935 that "the prospect of having you and Marc somewhere within the range of vision is very pleasant"—and apparently showed Blitzstein some of his music for critical comment, so conceivably he might have gained some familiarity with the latter's more avant-garde efforts from this period; but in any case, he gained a more general appreciation for the composer's work. In later years, Blitzstein occasionally continued to spend time with Carter, whom he described to David Diamond in 1942 as "a curious, serious guy, inept, and not a little touching."[30]

Meanwhile, Blitzstein abandoned *Discourse*, leaving Carter and others to pursue such directions. "My own work has struck something of a snag," he wrote to his sister in August 1933, although as late as the following summer he hoped to finish the work (transcribed and completed by Leonard Lehrman in 2004).[31]

While working on *Discourse*, Blitzstein also intended to write other chamber works, including an intricate cycle for varied forces that would take an entire evening to perform. Independently, he planned a piano sonata to be called "piano solo," and in mid-July, completed just such a work, his last major piece for the instrument. A lean-textured quasi-sonata with, in Eva's words, "a very meaty, verveful strong first movement" (Con brio), "an ornamental slow movement" (Cantabile), "a delicious little 'whimsical' third [movement]" (Scherzoso), and "a dazzling firecracker close" (Vivace), the work, in its asymmetrical rhythms and jazzy harmonies, suggests some movement toward the American vernacular, perhaps as filtered through Copland. But if more approachable than *Discourse*, *Piano Solo* (1933) rates among Blitzstein's most inaccessible pieces nonetheless. According to Eva, the music intentionally represented a further move away from thematic restatement and development toward "a counterpoint of themes having no relation to each other" that allows the themes to "wander." Such wandering engenders an elusive, improvisatory-like impression akin to literary stream of consciousness.[32]

Blitzstein premiered *Piano Solo* at Philadelphia's Mellon Galleries on February 5, 1934, in a recital on which he apparently also played, among other works, the piano part to Anton Webern's *Three Little Pieces* for cello and piano, op. 11. The Webern—repeated on account of its brevity and difficulty—provoked laughter, according to a reviewer, who reported on most of the other pieces as well, but not the *Piano Solo*, even if the one world premiere on the program and composed, no less, by a hometown boy. Blitzstein undoubtedly served the music well, but even so, the League of Composers decided in March against programming the piece on one of its concerts; Copland, who participated in the Mellon Galleries recital, thought the work "harsh and repellent," at least according to Eva, who observed that, much as the league deemed the *Serenade* "dull" rather than "profound," so they seemed to misunderstand this work, which she and Marc considered "light" and "gay"—an observation that highlights the degree to which the Blitzsteins formed a sort of world of their own.[33]

In the spring of 1934, Blitzstein began an orchestral work—at first, perhaps, a symphony—that evolved into the *Orchestra Variations*, completed in early July on Mallorca. "The first big work since the opera [*The Condemned*]," enthused Eva to her mother, "and with a beginning rather like the end of the opera: a marvelous theme, all on the heights with the depths gone through. Oddly enough, like the best of Beethoven in spirit—not so oddly, for at a certain point of course they all meet." For a final time, Blitzstein dedicated a score to Eva, his sixth major piece (or seventh if one includes *The Condemned*) dedicated to her in a five-year period. "The Orchestra Variations are yours almost more than any other work—anyway are yours in quite a special way," he wrote to her in a dedicatory love letter. "There was more of an urge to tell you each step and go over it, wrangle about it, with you."[34]

Blitzstein patently modeled the work after Copland's *Piano Variations*, which he thought seminal with regard to new formal developments; the work likewise contains a theme and twenty variations, some only a few measures long, that form an organic whole marked by separations between only certain variations. However, Blitzstein's variations vary more in length than Copland's, most notably, the central twelfth variation, a fugue that takes up about a fourth of this approximately sixteen-minute piece. All in all, the work puts forth a uniquely conceived arched design: theme, exposition (variations 1–8, which generally grow longer, faster, and more complex), slow transition (variations 9–11), fugue (variation 12), slow transition (variations 13–14), continuation and climax (variations 15–19), and coda (marked "Finale," variation 20).

Blitzstein's variation procedures, although more obscure than Copland's, similarly involve cycling through related motivic groupings. The theme itself, which unfolds in a slow three, actually comprises two simultaneous but related themes: a lofty soprano melody and a more active bass theme, one whose resemblance to the "Dies irae" chant, Eric Gordon suggests, might have been an intentional response to the recent death of Eva's father. Blitzstein handles the material deftly, with the fugue, in particular, a contrapuntal tour de force. The skillful writing for full orchestra helps enliven the form, with many of the variations featuring different combinations of instruments.[35]

For this work, Blitzstein retreated from some of the more recondite qualities of his music from the preceding two years, writing warm triads and some frankly diatonic passages, although the whole ends evocatively on a quiet, dissonant chord for strings (C–C$^{\sharp}$–E), a sonority that duplicates three of the four notes at the heart of Copland's *Variations*. The work in general suggests a turn toward something more in the American mold, thanks in part to its assimilation of Copland and perhaps such other compatriots as Roy Harris and Walter Piston. Dennis Russell Davies, who led the work's premiere in 1988, observed, "It's in the pattern of American music from the time."[36]

Even so, thought Davies, "there's no mistaking that it's Blitzstein." The work's individuality can be discerned right from the start, with its somewhat pastoral but also slightly ominous atmosphere. The work's ironic bite also strikes a distinctive note, including the raucous fourteenth variation whose satiric tone, although comparable to the "Jingo" movement from Copland's *Statements* (1932–35), already had made itself felt in, say, Blitzstein's Cummings settings from 1929. The piece, in short, has its own personality.[37]

After his return to America in 1935, Blitzstein left the music with Leopold Stokowski and subsequently learned, to his surprise, that the conductor planned to perform the work during the 1935–36 season. But as with the *Romantic Piece, Cain*, and the Piano Concerto, Stokowski ultimately shelved the music. Apparently at

the suggestion of Henry Cowell, Blitzstein also wrote conductor Nicolas Slonimsky about a possible airing in Soviet Russia, but the work went unplayed.[38]

On October 9, 1988, over fifty years after its composition, the *Variations* finally
received a premiere at Carnegie Hall by the American Composers Orchestra
under Dennis Russell Davies on a program that also included music by Kurt Weill
and Stephen Sondheim. "It's a very serious work—skillfully wrought and spare in
texture, but harmonically very accessible and actually quite delicate," Davies told
the *New York Times*. Most of the critics thought the piece "dull," "arid," "purely
academic," "entirely ordinary," and "hopelessly dated," but the audience roared its
approval, and Bill Zakariasen of the *Daily News* wrote, "Sad Blitzstein never heard
it, since it's one of his strongest works—tough yet expressive, brilliantly orchestrated and amazingly concise. Surely a piece like this would confound the nay-
sayers who dubbed Blitzstein a poor man's Kurt Weill."[39]

Around the time of the *Variations*, Blitzstein wrote and submitted a setting of
Alfred Hayes's poem "Into the Streets May First" for a May Day song competition
sponsored by the Music League and the journal, the *New Masses*. The first of May,
an ancient holiday, had become a festive rallying day for workers demanding
better conditions, in particular, an eight-hour work day—a goal finally realized
nationwide by the New Deal's Fair Labor Standards Act of 1938. Blitzstein's song
resembles Copland's winning setting, but its dissonant bass lines and idiosyncratic progressions strike an edgier profile, prompting this counsel from Charles
Seeger: "I think you would be wise to try things for the concert stage until you
come back [from Europe]. The mass song, which is to be sung by large crowds not
because it is taught to them but because they have heard it and want to sing it, has
some definitive limitations that you must know about before trying again."[40]

By the time Blitzstein received this letter of July 18, 1934, he was nearing
completion—or already had finished—another socially engaged work, the *Children's Cantata*, subtitled "Workers' Kids of the World, Unite!" He wrote the music,
and presumably the lyrics as well, quickly in July after completing the *Variations*. A
series of short numbers for child soloist, unison children's chorus, and piano, the
piece contains, according to a surviving libretto, eight movements: "Workers' Kids
of the World," "My Father's a Tailor," "Don't Cry Kids," "Speech," "Choosing a
Leader," "Writing a Letter" ("A Child Writes a Letter"), "Listen Teacher," and "Riddles," although the music to "Don't Cry Kids" and "Riddles" does not appear to have
survived, while conversely, an additional number, "March" ("March on the
Bosses"), not found in the libretto, appears among the composer's musical sketches.[41]

Blitzstein's first work to reflect explicitly his communist leanings, the *Children's Cantata* falls in the tradition of agitprop, a cultural movement associated
with the Soviet Union that aimed to incite agitation through propaganda. The
piece repeatedly calls for unity and resistance in the fight against "the bosses"
(that is, corporate power) but also teachers and preachers, with "Riddles" adding

Hitler and the U.S. Supreme Court to the list of foes, while praising "our" Lenin (this last-named number recalling Charles Seeger's song "[Lenin!] Who's That Guy?" to a lyric by H. T. Tsiang). About this same time, if not earlier, Blitzstein had begun to acquire what would become a fairly extensive library of communist-related pamphlets and books, in particular, the writings of Lenin.[42]

During or after its initial composition, Blitzstein attempted to moderate the work's militancy, perhaps in the hopes of securing a performance for the piece. He substituted new phrases for "revolution" and "revolt," replacing, for instance, "The revolution is coming!" with "The worker's hour is coming!" In addition, he revised "Riddles" so as not to include President Franklin Roosevelt with Hitler, the bosses, and the Supreme Court as an object of ridicule, as in an earlier version: "Who is it who smiles and talks on the radio/and smiles and talks on the radio/ and smiles and talks and talks and talks on the radio?/Roosevelt!" But even soft-pedaled, the piece nevertheless revealed Blitzstein's newfound determination to produce works advocating such ideals as "Equality—a decent living wage—/ Shorter hours—recreation—a decent life" (from "Speech").

Although still rather dissonant and complex, especially for a work for children, the *Cantata* relatedly betokened a pivotal move toward greater simplicity, as evidenced by its plain triads, march and walking rhythms, clear cadences, and tuneful melodies, with "Speech" incorporating the opening of "The Internationale." Blitzstein might well have had in mind the learning pieces of Brecht and his collaborators, with Carol Oja and Eric Gordon noting affinities specifically to Weill and Eisler, respectively, while connections also could be drawn to Hindemith's children's cantata *We Build a City*. The work has its "grim" moments, as Oja has observed, but a jubilant side as well, as exemplified by such numbers as "Choosing a Leader" and "Listen Teacher."[43]

In April 1935, the Composers' Collective included "Listen Teacher" in a presentation volume to Eisler, but did not program the *Cantata* on their May 12, 1935, concert as they had hoped, possibly because of difficulties in assembling a children's choir, especially one that could handle the score. Although the work as a whole never received a performance, Mordecai Bauman, accompanied by the composer, sang "A Child Writes a Letter" at an all-Blitzstein concert on April 15, 1936. (Reviewer Louis Biancolli deemed the song "vividly worded and scored.") Moreover, Blitzstein adapted "Choosing a Leader" as the chorus "Take the Book" from *No for an Answer*, and the opening lyrics of "A Child Writes a Letter" as "Emily" from the *Airborne Symphony*.[44]

In the spring of 1935, after the collective adopted Eva Goldbeck's "First of May" as one of two texts for another May Day song competition, Blitzstein once again tried his hand at a mass song with a setting of his wife's poem under the pseudonym "Hammer." The music puts forth a strong modal (specifically mixolydian) tune supported by open fifths in the accompaniment, a concession toward a more accessible language, even if the fifths often jangle dissonantly with the melody—an old instinct that dated back to the composer's youth. Indeed, for all its accommodation of popular song, the music goes its own dissonant way before concluding with a firm tonal cadence.

In June 1935, Blitzstein composed another mass song, "Strike Song," this one consisting of just an unaccompanied melody, as would be appropriate for striking workers. The melody, now entirely diatonic although still complex, suggests call-and-response, the tune dipping low for the insistent phrase, "Strike, workers, strike!" Whether striking workers ever sang this tune remains unknown; in recent years, the Solidarity Singers of the New Jersey Industrial Union Council, a street chorus that performs at picket lines and labor rallies, found the music too difficult for their purposes.[45]

Around this same time, Blitzstein also wrote or at least began a song, "Marić and Colić," protesting the imprisonment of two Serbian composers, Dragutin Čolić and Ljubica Marić: "We the musicians of America say no!" the text states. Only the Marcato tune survives, one similar to "Strike Song," although in this instance, blank staves suggest that Blitzstein intended not only an accompaniment, but an obbligato bass part.

Despite the personal significance of such music, and his deep involvement with the Composers' Collective, Blitzstein wrote very little else in the way of mass songs. He presumably felt that his gifts did not run in that direction. At the same time, his brilliantly stylized versions of mass song for theatrical presentation, as in the title songs of *The Cradle Will Rock* and *No for an Answer*, and the "tune" in *I've Got the Tune*, became an important ingredient in his dramatic work of the 1930s, as did similar evocations of such music in his later work for stage and screen. Moreover, in time he would compose two of his most important concert works for amateur chorus: the *Airborne Symphony* (1946) and *This Is the Garden* (1957).[46]

In early 1935, Blitzstein hoped to collaborate with choreographer Martha Graham, one of his Guggenheim fellowship references, and designer Isamu Noguchi on a ballet, but this dream went unfulfilled. Then in August, Copland helped arrange an offer from Ruth Page (1899–1991), the noted Chicago dancer-choreographer whose ballet company performed under the auspices of the Chicago Civic Opera, and for whom Copland recently had written a satirical ballet about the American judicial system, *Hear Ye! Hear Ye!* (1934). "Expect nothing from the choreography or the dancing," Copland warned him—nor, for that matter, much money, orchestral rehearsal time, or publicity, since for the Chicago press "'twill always be Ruth Page's ballet." On the other hand, a commissioned work, reasoned Copland, would make Chicago "Blitzstein-conscious," and "the general experience of a stage production, and contact with an orchestra and working organization is always a salutary one for a composer." Blitzstein apparently had his own ideas about Page, describing her to his wife as having "theatrical flair and ambition, but not much else." Meanwhile, Page sent Blitzstein a detailed scenario,

"American Woman," and asked in turn to see the piano score to *Cain*, explaining that "it would help give me an idea of what you do." With no such copy on hand, Blitzstein provided her with that ballet's scenario instead. In early September, a drafted contract arrived, specifying, as with Copland, a fee of $250 (not including royalties, which in Copland's case came to about $50). Page envisioned an October 1935 production with sets by Nicolai Remisoff.[47]

"American Woman" intended to show "the struggle of the individual against organized society and standardization, and the futility of the struggle. The real tragedy of the American woman is that she plunges into one thing after another in a continuous whirl of activity, in an attempt to make her life have meaning and to avoid the solidity and respectability of a patterned life." In various scenes, the young heroine tries hedonism, Hinduism, and communism before joining "the procession of standardized American womanhood."[48]

"Disgusted" with this "cheap" and "utterly traditional" scenario (he scribbled on some notes, "girl sympathetic?—a sap really"), Blitzstein would have preferred that Page simply stage *Cain*, but, as Eva explained to her mother, that earlier work had a central male character and with Page's ballets "every single solo dance and every scene are hers." Eva encouraged her husband to go forward with the ballet nonetheless and revised the scenario to his liking, but between his lack of enthusiasm for working with Page and her refusal to guarantee him $500, their planned collaboration came to naught. (Another Copland protégé, Jerome Moross, subsequently collaborated with Page not only on this protofeminist ballet, which premiered in 1937 as *An American Pattern*, but on one of her biggest hits, *Frankie and Johnny* of 1938.)[49]

In May 1936, Blitzstein, by this point in desperate financial straits, made more money than offered by Page—$350—for a much easier if less glamorous commission: scoring the short documentary film, *The Chesapeake Bay Retriever*, for Pedigreed Pictures. Written and produced by his patron Alene Erlanger and Thomas T. K. Frelinghuysen, the now-lost film showed, according to a press release, the "amazing versatility" of champion retriever Skipper Bob, who "retrieves everything from the rope and basket to the duck and pheasant, to say nothing of the fish." Photographed by Dal Clawson and narrated by John Holbrook, this short also featured another champion retriever, Sodak's Gypsy Prince. *The Chesapeake Bay Retriever* previewed on May 26, 1936, at New York's Chanin Auditorium along with *The Poodle* and *The Collie*.[50]

For the film, Blitzstein composed a jaunty and unpretentious score for violin, clarinet, bassoon, and piano, with square-cut melodies and simple triads only occasionally shadowed by some pungent dissonance or unusual progression. The work thus could easily accommodate two familiar sailor tunes, "A Life on the Ocean Wave" (music by Henry Russell) and "A-Roving" (anonymous), that no doubt provided some special humor in the context of the picture. As a whole, the music might be compared to—and might have been influenced by—Virgil Thomson's for *The Plow That Broke the Plains*, a documentary that had begun to circulate in New York during this time and that Blitzstein surely would have sought out. In any event, the importance of this slight score should not be minimized, as something of its breezy directness made its way into *The Cradle Will Rock*, composed later in the year.

On April 15, 1936, the New York Composers' Forum-Laboratory presented at the Federal Music Building on West 48th Street a retrospective of the thirty-one-year-old Blitzstein that included the Piano Sonata, the first movement of *Serenade*, three vocal excerpts from larger works ("Jimmie's got a goil" from *is 5*, "Dialogue" from *Cain*, and "A Child Writes a Letter" from the *Children's Cantata*), and the Piano Concerto, which concluded the program. Except for the *Serenade* movement, Blitzstein performed throughout, accompanying his friend Mordecai Bauman in the vocal selections, and another friend, Norman Cazden, who played the solo part in the concerto.

A division of the Works Progress Administration's Federal Music Project, the Composers' Forum-Laboratory, under the directorship of Ashley Pettis, promoted various ventures aimed at bringing new American music before the general public—principally recitals dedicated to a wide range of individual composers, including students, followed by an open forum in which attendees could ask questions and make comments. Established to provide financial relief for musicians, the Forum-Laboratory concerts compensated the participating performers but usually not the featured composers.[51]

The Blitzstein concert attracted "a large group of eager, forward-looking musicians," according to music critic Louis Biancolli, who, along with composer Colin McPhee, reported on the music with perhaps greater respect than enthusiasm. Written transcripts of many of the Forum-Laboratory's postconcert discussions survive, but apparently not of this particular one.[52]

Shortly after this recital, Copland produced his first public assessment of Blitzstein, described as "probably the best known" of the nation's "youngest composers." Observing his "definite 'flair' for composition," Copland traced three phases in Blitzstein's development: a "largely derivative" style, with Stravinsky "the all-absorbing influence"; a later, more individual period, featuring music whose "exaggeratedly laconic and abstract quality . . . militated against its even achieving performance"; and a new simplicity, heralded in some portions of *Cain* and *Surf and Seaweed*, that "may be attributed to Blitzstein's sympathy for Leftist ideology." Aside from perhaps Goldbeck, Copland knew Blitzstein's work better than anyone, and such works as the Piano Sonata (1928), *The Condemned* (1932), and the *Children's Cantata* (1934) could be marshaled to support his thesis, which seems, nonetheless, overstated.[53]

In Copland's *Our New Music*, published a few years later in 1941 (a text that privileged Blitzstein, one of only six Americans to receive a separate essay, the others being Ives, Harris, Sessions, Thomson, and the author himself), Copland could see all these early phases as more simply preliminary to *The Cradle Will*

Rock, before which Blitzstein had written "a fairly long list of concert pieces, few of which actually reached the concert hall. The reason was that not many of them came off in a way that one could thoroughly approve. Either a composition was too obviously derivative, or it tried too hard to be astonishing, or the style adopted was too rigidly abstract. It wasn't until Blitzstein began writing primarily for the stage that he really found himself."[54]

These seminal discussions by Copland helped establish that somewhat clichéd perception of a young man who "found himself" in the mid-1930s through his "sympathy for Leftist ideology" and by writing "primarily for the stage," even though by the time of *The Cradle*, Blitzstein already had written a number of ballets and operas, including some that had showed or implied leftist sympathies. Furthermore, as Copland himself intimated, nearly all of Blitzstein's more ambitious early stage and concert works simply went unstaged and unplayed, hardly grounds for a fair assessment of either their distinctiveness or their viability. Even his smaller works received only the occasional performance. That Blitzstein recycled so much of this youthful output throughout his life further suggests that he discovered his mature voice earlier than often assumed. To be sure, *The Cradle* proved a stunning accomplishment, composed in a blaze of inspiration, and in many ways significantly different from most everything he previously had written. But even this piece need not cast too large a shadow over his earlier or, for that matter, later work.

Figure 1. From left: Marc, Anna, Sam, and Jo Blitzstein, ca. 1906.

Figure 2. Marc Blitzstein, ca. 1912.

Figure 3. Marc and Jo Blitzstein, ca. 1917.

Figure 4. From left: Lina Abarbanell, Edward Goldbeck, and Eva Goldbeck, ca. 1906. Wisconsin Center for Film and Theater Research.

Figure 5. Anna Blitzstein, the composer's mother, 1922. Photo: Turgeon.

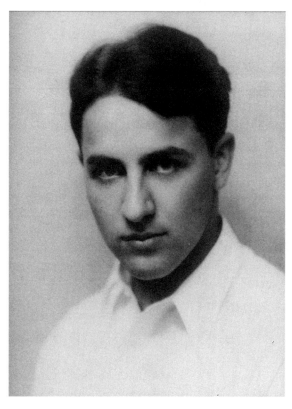

Figure 6. Marc Blitzstein, ca. 1922.

Figure 7. Marc Blitzstein in Salzburg, 1929.

Figure 8. Eva Goldbeck, early 1930s.

Figure 9. Marc and Eva Blitzstein on Cape Cod, 1935.

Figure 10. Marc Blitzstein and cast rehearsing *The Cradle Will Rock*, 1937. Federal Theatre Project Photograph Collection, Special Collections Archives, George Mason University Libraries.

Figure 11. *The Cradle Will Rock* at the Venice Theatre, with Marc Blitzstein at the piano, 1937. Billy Rose Theatre Division, New York Public Library of the Performing Arts. Photo: George Karger.

Figure 12. Hank Azaria (as Marc Blitzstein) in *Cradle Will Rock*, 1999. Photofest.

Figure 13. Julius Caesar at the Mercury Theatre, 1937. Arthur Anderson (Lucius) and Orson Welles (Brutus). Photofest.

Figure 14. Marc Blitzstein working on *Valley Town*, 1940.

Figure 15. No for an Answer,
1941. Olive Deering (Clara)
and Martin Wolfson (Nick).
Billy Rose Theatre Division,
The New York Public Library
of the Performing Arts.
Photo: Talbot.

Figure 16. Native Land, 1942. Clancy Cooper (Whitey's eulogist) and Virginia Stevens
(Whitey's widow). Photofest.

Figure 17. Marc Blitzstein, early 1940s. Photo: Talbot.

Figure 18. The U.S. Army Negro Chorus and the London Symphony Orchestra at the Royal Albert Hall, London, September 1943. Wisconsin Center for Film and Theater Research.

Figure 19. Marc Blitzstein at the BBC, London, ca. 1943.

The Cradle Will Rock, I (1936–1937)

When Louis Simon approached Blitzstein in the spring of 1930 about introducing *Triple-Sec* into the *Garrick Gaieties*, the composer proposed instead three popular songs he had written: "Looking for Love," which he thought "pretty hot as to words" and suited to a blues singer like Libby Holman, Ethel Waters, or Bessie Smith; a less "rough" song "for a boy-and-girl presentation, all about wanting love"; and a "sad inferiority-song" that he already had sent to Sterling Holloway, the musical comedy star who would later become a familiar voice for Disney. "It's all crap to me," wrote Blitzstein to Simon, "done in off moments, as relief from the real work, when my funny kind of mind has to be turning out some tune or other. I don't take any of the songs seriously or with cherishment, and I won't be at all offended if they fail to please. However, if there's anything to be made on them in the way of—what-is-it?—kudos, I'm agrible." These songs, for which Blitzstein apparently wrote both lyrics and music, coincided and perhaps arose in conjunction with his work on the aborted *Traveling Salesman* (ca. 1929–31), with the lyrics to "Looking for Love" appearing among his sketches for that work.[1]

Simon decided not to use any of these songs, of which only the words to "Looking for Love" and a bit of the "boy-and-girl" song survive, although if the "sad inferiority-song" refers, as Eric Gordon reasonably supposes, to "What's the Matter With Me?" then that particular number could be dated to around 1930, making it one of Blitzstein's first extant popular or, as he would say, "jazz" songs.[2]

"What's the Matter With Me?" in which the lovelorn singer finds his "manhood" and "virility" impaired, has a sort of Noël Coward-like smartness, with a breezy chorus whose urbane lyric sports what would become a characteristic penchant for triple rhymes: "I'm train'd in all the arts./My heart's like other hearts./I've all the essential parts./Tell me, what's the matter with me?" Holloway might well have made the song a success on stage, but the number contains so many peculiarities—including an irrepressible harmonic daring—as to defy commercial appeal.

When Blitzstein returned to the United States in 1930, he did so partly motivated by "the 'junk' idea of making a lot of money," and to that end, he continued to write popular songs, informing Goldbeck in January 1931, "Three new jazz songs are to be tried over by Ethel Merman a famous torch-singer; maybe I'll sell them." In April, he similarly told Goldbeck that he had been collaborating with her ex-husband Cecil on some songs, adding, "Nothing will come of it, since they have all been punk; but I get the feeling of doing something in the Broadway field." None of this material seems to have survived.[3]

Four years later, in the spring of 1935, during a period of artistic reassessment and heightened social awareness, Blitzstein composed two songs in a popular manner—"Send for the Militia" and "People"—that anticipated the creation the following year of *The Cradle Will Rock*, with "People" actually making its way into that work. Indeed, for all their modesty, these two songs stand as pivotal achievements in his development, revealing more fully his gifts as a composer and wordsmith for the lyric theater. Blitzstein possibly wrote both for the Broadway revue *Parade*, but only "Send for the Militia" appeared in that show, introduced by a young Eve Arden at the start of her notable stage and screen career.

Parade was conceived and written by George Sklar and Paul Peters, two playwrights associated with the current theatrical movement of "social significance" that addressed from a left-wing perspective such problems as poverty, unemployment, racism, and militarism. This trend, which would intersect profoundly with Blitzstein's career, took root on Broadway in the course of the 1920s with such plays as Maxwell Anderson and Laurence Stallings's *What Price Glory?* and John Howard Lawson's *Processional* (both 1924), and less directly with such musicals as Jerome Kern's *Show Boat* (1927) and George Gershwin's *Strike Up the Band* (1927/1930). Such developments gained further momentum in the course of the 1930s before abating with America's entry into the Second World War.

However, even at its height in the 1930s, socially engaged theater formed only a relatively small part of the Broadway scene, with such productions originating not so much with individual producers as with theatrical collectives, including the Theatre Guild (Robert E. Sherwood's *Idiot's Delight*, 1936); Workers' Laboratory Theatre/Theatre of Action (Peter Martin, George Scudder, and Charles Friedman's *The Young Go First*, 1935); Group Theatre (Clifford Odets's *Waiting for Lefty*, 1935); League of Workers' Theatres/New Theatre League (Ben Bengal's *Plant in the Sun*, 1937); Theatre Union (John Howard Lawson's *Marching Song*, 1937); the government-sponsored Federal Theatre (*Triple-A Plowed Under*, 1936, one of their Living Newspapers); Actors' Repertory Company (Irwin Shaw's *Bury the Dead*, 1936); Labor Stage (Harold Rome's *Pins and Needles*, 1937); and Mercury Theatre (Blitzstein's *The Cradle Will Rock*). Moreover, the day's socially progressive drama tended neither to exhort radical political change nor to embrace the more modernist stagecraft of Brecht, whose *Mother*, presented in somewhat diluted fashion by the Theatre Union in late 1935, baffled many spectators (although not the Blitzsteins, who recognized the piece as a masterwork). Rather, such plays generally drew on the more conservative tradition of realistic melodrama and a liberal-left perspective that, writes historian Ilka Saal, typically affirmed "the ideals of Jeffersonian democracy," thereby subsuming the American Communist Party slogan, "Communism is 20th Century Americanism."[4]

George Sklar and Paul Peters, both communists, stood on the far-left of this continuum. Sklar had co-written three of the period's landmark Marxist dramas: *Merry-Go-Round* (1932) and *Peace on Earth* (1933), both with fellow communist Albert Maltz; and *Stevedore* (1934) with Peters, who adapted Brecht's *Mother* for the Theatre Union. Sklar and Peters initially conceived *Parade* for the Theatre Union, which, however, did not have the means to produce it; turned down by the Group Theatre as well, the revue finally found a home with the Theatre Guild, which generally had had little truck with musical theater, but which, besides having produced various editions of the *Garrick Gaieties*, would launch Gershwin's *Porgy and Bess* later that season.[5]

Parade might well have been the Theatre Union's "Red Revue" that, according to Goldbeck, Copland was "working on" in early 1935. But in any event, although Copland apparently never wrote anything for *Parade* or any other "red revue," he perhaps served in some capacity as a consultant, for Sklar and Peters eventually brought on board Jerome Moross and Blitzstein, both of whom Copland recommended to choreographer Ruth Page later that same year. Moross wrote most of the score, with Will Irwin composing a few additional numbers and Blitzstein represented only by "Send for the Militia."[6]

The revue premiered in Boston at the Colonial Theatre on May 6, 1935—on opening night, Arden stopped the show with the Blitzstein number—and in New York at the Guild Theatre on May 20. Philip Loeb directed, Lee Simonson designed the sets, and the brilliant pantomimist Jimmy Savo starred. In a series of sketches, some with music, the show satirized the police, industrialists, college presidents, fascists, anticommunists, white Russians, and others (a parody of the Hearst media empire featured characters some of whose names—Mr. Capitalist, Mrs. Capitalist, Junior Capitalist—foreshadowed those of *The Cradle Will Rock*). The critics widely thought the revue overlong and dull, notwithstanding some moments of giddy humor and satiric bite. Some notices also thought the material too radical, whereas the *Daily Worker* conversely complained that the writers had watered down the revue in deference to the Theatre Guild and its patrons. Others simply did not know what to make of it. "Some of the sketches may or may not be Communist propaganda," wrote Elliot Norton (*Boston Post*). "It would appear that they are. Which is something new in a revue." Savo could not save the show, which ran for forty performances in New York—and only that long because of guild subscribers.[7]

"Send for the Militia," more sketch than song, seems the prototype of various Blitzstein numbers to come in its dramatic verve and satiric wit. In a series of five strophes, a society matron expresses interest in socialism, peace, a longshoremen's strike (a reference to the 1934 West Coast Waterfront Strike), social welfare, and birth control until distressful implications lead her, in the chorus, to overreact: "Send for the Militia, the Army, the Navy!/Quick, bring out the Boy Scouts, ev'ry Captain, ev'ry Ace!" The music employs dissonant harmonies, changing meters, and disjointed phrases (including a quote of "Columbia, the

Gem of the Ocean" nestled in the chorus), all framed by jazzy gestures and scoring, to render a portrait of a smug liberal turned, by anger and fear, into a vigilante. In her memoirs, Eve Arden described the song as "avant-garde."[8]

In contrast, "People," a militant protest song, condemns poverty, its searing anger probably militating against inclusion in *Parade* or really any Broadway revue. "Listen, here's a story," begins the verse, which concludes with a sardonic echo of musician Ted Lewis's "Is everybody happy?" The chorus bluntly opens, "Poor people starve," and concludes, "One big question inside me cries:/How many bread lines,/how many flopjoints,/hunger marches,/how many toiling ailing dying piled-up bodies,/Brother does it take to make you wise?" Blitzstein's powerful music—"Grim, hard—don't break down and whine!" serves as a tempo indication—features dark tonalities (the verse is in A minor, the chorus, C minor) and finds some middle space between Eisler's "Solidarity Song" and Jay Gorney and E. Y. Harburg's "Brother, Can You Spare a Dime?" the latter composed for the Broadway revue *Americana*. Mordecai Bauman introduced the number, with Blitzstein at the piano, at an evening of dance and drama on May 16 and 17, 1936, at the Young Men's Hebrew Association at 92nd Street, with the company, directed by Elsa Findlay, miming along.

Blitzstein seems to have made some revisions to the song for this particular performance—including changing the title from "People" to "Poor People"—but in any case continued this process by adapting the number for use in *The Cradle Will Rock*, first as "Work People" and finally as "Joe Worker," changing the focus for dramatic reasons from the plight of poor people ("Poor people starve") to their oppression by others ("Joe Worker gets gypped"). Exploring these different versions, Carol Oja notes a trend toward greater muscularity, including some added thwacks in the accompaniment that she likens to African-American work songs.[9]

On May 26, 1935, a week after *Parade* opened, Blitzstein accompanied Arden on "Send for the Militia" at a benefit for the Theatre Union before an enthusiastic audience. No doubt encouraged by the work's success, he continued to compose music in a popular vein, including three numbers written in the latter half of 1935 all probably intended for stage presentation: "Stay in My Arms," "The Way You Are," and *Sketch No. 1*. Two other works, neither of which survive in their entirety, "War Department Manual, Volume 7, Part 3" (1935) and "Gauley Bridge Tunnel" (ca. 1935), date from this general time as well, with one of the composer's résumés listing "War Department Manual" as "film music."[10]

Referring to a "new love song" (possibly "Stay in My Arms"), a "sketch number" (presumably *Sketch No. 1*), and a piece based on Albert Maltz's story "Man on a Road" (surely "Gauley Bridge Tunnel"), Eva welcomed this engagement with more popular styles, which she regarded as signaling a new period for her husband:

I think he has found the way to his medium—musically—to form his musical idiom. What we used to speak of as a "new form"—but it comes now out of the psychology, a way of speaking; it is simple, straight, straight from the heart too, "real." That word has come back! The simplicity he always wanted before—no "words" about it and absolutely communicable, to anyone, and instantaneously. (This doesn't mean that the "abstract" will be out; the two go together—the "abstract" now more "filled in"; bigger works to come.)

Blitzstein himself felt, as Eva reported, "on the threshold." As for the "sketch number," Eva wrote to her mother in late August, "if that's not a theatrical wow, I'll be something. . . . It isn't at all deep, or on the other hand very 'class-consciously' significant, but within its scope—really good 'theatre.'"[11]

More than most Blitzstein, "Stay in My Arms" and "The Way You Are" approach commercial popular song, especially "Stay in My Arms," a warmly romantic number reminiscent of Gershwin but grown sage and somber—"an amazing, touching, great song," in the words of experts David Jenness and Don Velsey. "Forget them"—the song's lover says of the day's "grasping and shrieking . . . Jacks and Jills"—"Or let them/Grow dim and hazy;/The world's gone crazy,/So stay in my arms." While recognizing the "mad existence of our time," the music also offers some repose, a duality that would have been highlighted on stage by Blitzstein's "production idea" for the number, one that in some ways reads as a metaphor for his own artistic development, at least as represented by this song: "Eccentric, modernistic, futuristic sets, costumes, dances, music, give way slowly (piece by piece) to familiar, lovely, comfortable, luxurious sights and sounds." On a still more personal level, Blitzstein surely intended the song as a balm to his increasingly ill wife. The bolero-like "The Way You Are," more Cole Porter than Gershwin, reflects another side of Blitzstein—teasing, although ultimately accepting: "I like you best the way you are."[12]

Blitzstein derived his text for "Gauley Bridge Tunnel" from Albert Maltz's short story "Man on a Road," in which the narrator picks up a hitchhiking West Virginian miner, Jack Pitckett, who asks the narrator to edit a letter to his wife explaining that he left home because he's dying of silicosis, contracted in the mines because of negligent work conditions. Blitzstein, who found the story in the *New Masses*, decided to set Pitckett's letter to music, hence such working titles for his setting as "Letter of Jack Pitckett" and "West Virginian Letter."[13]

Blitzstein considered two alternate treatments—one for baritone, unison chorus, and piano; the other just for baritone and piano. Whether he ever completed one or another version of this "scena," he subsequently used the material in later works, including one section ("Bein as our hom is a good peece frum town") as the opening chorus of *No for an Answer* ("Song of the Bat"), and a melody that accompanies the words, "i hope you will be well an keep the young one out of the mines," for the "tune" in *I've Got the Tune*, while the whole concept anticipates "Emily" from the *Airborne Symphony*.

Blitzstein adapted his text for "War Department Manual" from a section in the government's 1935 *Basic Field Manual* covering "Employment of Troops in Civil Disturbances." "Mobs develop from crowds," the singer intones to bluesy, "dreamy" music after a "grim" introduction; as the music goes into "hot" double-time, the singer continues, "When rifle fire is resorted to,/the aim should be low/So as to prevent shots going over the heads of the mob" (Blitzstein omitting the remainder of this sentence, "and injuring innocent persons that could not get away"). At one point, the composer considered using "War Department Manual" in *The Cradle Will Rock* for the faculty room scene, in which case Mr. Mister would have recited the text to President Prexy.[14]

Meanwhile, *Sketch No. 1* gave literal rise to *The Cradle*, where it reappeared, albeit revised, as that work's first scene. This sketch, which takes place on a street corner, involves four characters: Jane, a prostitute; her Pimp (a silent role); a Gent; and a Cop. Leaning against a lighted lamp post, Jane wearily sings about her life in "blues tempo" ("I'm On My Last Trip"). Her Pimp enters, and in a brief pantomime ("like an Apache-dance," a reference to a sensuous dance style of the period), he exacts money from her and leaves. To a jaunty strain "like a Nikolodean," a Gent arrives, and he and Jane haggle over a price. Overhearing their altercation, a Cop enters, demands money from the Gent, tells him to "scram," extorts more money from Jane, and, as a member of the vice squad, bribes her to have sex. Near the end of the sketch, in a second song, Jane relents, but warns, "By and by there's gonna come a wind./You better mind that wind./It's gonna blow."

Blitzstein presumably meant the sketch as a parable about capitalism, with Jane unable to negotiate a fair wage and subject to predatory conditions. However, the composer leavens this pitiful tale with wit and vigor, Jane emerging as a figure of strength and determination. The music, meanwhile, represents a pathbreaking synthesis of varied styles and moods, encompassing the blues and jazz, along with Satie, Stravinsky, Eisler, and Weill, with the composer mediating all with a distinctively sardonic touch. During the exchange between the Gent and the Cop (Gent: "Certainly not, officer!" Dick: "Aw, shut up!"), the accompaniment even alludes to a tag associated with the early Three Stooges films.

When he adapted this scene for *The Cradle*, Blitzstein made various adjustments, including deleting the character of the Pimp and his whole pantomime with Jane, renamed the Moll. Moreover, he has the Cop, renamed the Dick, ask the Moll only for sex, and has the Moll refuse his advances, which leads to her arrest, thus catapulting the story forward. Nor does the Moll warn the Dick about the coming "wind," although that idea now generates the entire opera. Leaving the scene's melodic structure largely intact, he extensively retooled and refined both the harmonies and the lyrics as well.

Sketch No. 1 appeared on a Composers' Collective concert at the New School on February 23, 1936, with Gladys Frankel, Thomas Frank, and Nat Fichtenbaum accompanied by Blitzstein at the piano. The *Daily Worker* observed some similarity to Weill and thought the piece to give "an unprecedented purpose and scope to what, nowadays, has become a way of thinking. One should look forward seriously to his [Blitzstein's] future work."[15]

In the course of 1935, Blitzstein received some financial assistance from Motty Eitingon and his second wife, Bess Tepfer Rockmore, well-heeled philanthropists and art patrons. A Russian fur dealer, Motty, a Kerenskyite, had been incarcerated briefly by the Bolsheviks before escaping to New York, where he reestablished his fur trade, a major enterprise during the interwar years, although not without its vicissitudes. During this period, Motty established close business relations with the Soviet Union and helped negotiate conflicts between fur manufacturers and the communist-controlled Fur Workers Union. He also funded young impecunious musicians. Bess, meanwhile, took a special interest in the theater, serving as an assistant stage manager for the Group Theatre's production of Weill's *Johnny Johnson*.[16]

In the fall of 1935, Blitzstein stayed with the Eitingons in Old Greenwich, Connecticut—first in a rented house, and then, with Eva, in a separate apartment on the grounds of their sprawling country home, Hillcrest. "It is not country so much as 'rich estate,'" he wrote to his wife in September about the set-up at Hillcrest, "—lawns, woods, greenhouses, etc. Just far enough away from the main house, road, and other houses." Bess, he further wrote Eva, gave him "the uneasy impression of being about to 'take charge' of us," but she seemed "honestly nice and interested in my career," if "rather silly and stupid about it too." And although Motty initially appeared "very cold about me as a musician," after hearing Blitzstein play some of his pieces at the piano (including *Cain*), "striving valiantly, actually got to like them."[17]

During the summer of 1936, soon after his wife's death, Blitzstein returned to Hillcrest, where he completed the number "Few Little English" and an initial draft of *The Cradle Will Rock*.

Blitzstein wrote "Few Little English" for Lotte Lenya, the German actress divorced from but soon to remarry Kurt Weill. Hearing her perform at an all-Weill concert several months earlier, he had written, "Lenja is too special a talent, I am afraid, for a wide American appeal; but she has magnetism and a raw lovely voice like a boy-soprano. Her stylized gestures seem strange because of her natural warmth; but in the strangeness lies the slight enigma which is her charm." Lenya indeed had difficulty establishing herself in the United States, although nearly twenty years later Blitzstein would play a decisive role in securing her American reputation.[18]

Blitzstein had had some contact with Weill and Lenya since their arrival in New York in 1935; but during the summer of 1936, he had the opportunity to get to know them better, thanks to their residence with the Group Theatre during preparations for *Johnny Johnson* in Trumbull, Connecticut, not far from Hillcrest. Blitzstein not only attended rehearsals, but also Weill's July 27 lecture "Music in the Theatre," in which the German composer took issue with "art for art's sake" and explained how he came to write "operas for actors."[19]

Completed on July 15, Blitzstein's number for Lenya, "Few Little English," tells—in three verses—how the narrator, a wily moll from Europe who takes up with a Chicago gangster, dodges her landlord, her boyfriend's business rival, and the FBI by pretending that she speaks "few little English," although in the end, the ruse fails to work: "Okay, boys, let's go," she tells the G-men. Contrasting the low-down narrative, which gets more intense as the story develops, with the disingenuous chorus, the song evidences the composer's winsome humor, as when the moll tries to elicit sympathy by telling the FBI, in minor strains, "My wallpaper's crackin'/My bed's got no backin',/Pretty curtains lackin'." David Farneth writes that the number "not only pokes fun at her [Lenya's] German accent and lack of perfect English, but also parodies Weill's music."[20]

"Few Little English" intimated that growing appreciation of Weill that took expression later in the year with Blitzstein's review of *Johnny Johnson*, as discussed earlier. Tellingly, Blitzstein approached Weill in the course of the summer about the possibility, never realized, of performing the latter's *Seven Deadly Sins* "in a small series of chamber-operas." "I should greatly appreciate the opportunity of examining the score," he wrote to Weill; "I have heard of the work only through reviews, and your own comment; and the idea seems to me very attractive." This heightened interest in Weill no doubt played its part in the creation of *The Cradle Will Rock*, an "opera for actors" that explicitly rejects "art for art's sake."[21]

For a while, "Few Little English" entered Lenya's repertoire. "I always sing the Blitzstein song," she wrote to Weill in May 1938 in reference to her nightclub act at Le Ruban Bleu, where the number proved popular with audiences. Blitzstein also cast Lenya in his radio opera *I've Got the Tune*, which aired in October 1937, and otherwise attempted to "make a lot of publicity for me," as she explained to her husband, who nonetheless came to regard Blitzstein negatively as an epigone who profited by imitating his work. "I would love to tell them to go to hell," Weill told Lenya in 1942 concerning an upcoming meeting with some Broadway producers, "but I am afraid they'll steal my ideas and some louse like Blitzstein will get the credit."[22]

At his Jane Street apartment in late 1935, Blitzstein performed *Sketch No. 1* for Bertolt Brecht, who said, as the composer recalled, "Why don't you expand this? In our society, prostitution can involve many more things than just our lily white bodies. There is prostitution for gain in so many walks of life: the artist, the preacher, the doctor, the lawyer, the newspaper editor. Why don't you pit them against this scene of literal selling." Blitzstein soon after told Minna Lederman, "I've taken up his [Brecht's] idea and am making an opera of it," and ultimately dedicated the resultant work, *The Cradle Will Rock*, to Brecht, "since it was his ideas which impressed and influenced me so deeply."[23]

Blitzstein often stated that he composed the piece, meaning the reduced score, "at white heat, as a kind of rebound from my wife's death in May" during a five-week period in what would seem to range from late July to early September. The drafted short score, marked August 10–September 2, suggests the even shorter time frame of three weeks. But given that the work's orchestration and various revisions occupied the composer at least through early 1937 (the full score bears a completion date of May 12, 1937, although orchestra rehearsals began in mid-April), the work actually took a number of months to prepare in its finished form.[24]

In the tradition of *Parade*, Blitzstein initially called each of the opera's ten scenes "sketches," even referring to the whole work as *Ten Sketches*, but he eventually settled on the more common term, "scene." Some evidence, including the work's published libretto and its planned Federal Theatre production, suggests that he originally intended for the opera to be done in one act, but most performances since the premiere have presented the work in two acts, with a break after the sixth scene, as indicated in the musical manuscripts, both published and unpublished.

The Cradle Will Rock takes place on the evening of a steel workers' union drive in Steeltown, U.S.A.

Scene one. Streetcorner. A poor, hungry prostitute, the Moll, walks the street ("I'm Checkin Home Now" or "Moll's Lament"). Overhearing the Moll and the Gent haggle over a price, a police officer, the Dick, demands money from the Gent before dismissing him. After telling the Moll about a drive that evening at union headquarters, the Dick, a member of the vice squad, pressures her for sex. She refuses ("So That's the Way"). Virgil the Cop arrives with members of the Liberty Committee in tow—the "sleek, urbane, deferential" Reverend Salvation; the "glib" Editor Daily; Yasha, a violinist; Dauber, a painter; the "timid, thin-lipped" college President Prexy; the "seedy and pompous" Professor Mamie; the "frankly tough and unacademic" football coach Professor Trixie; and the town's "'big' physician" Dr. Specialist—all of whom Virgil has mistakenly taken for union agitators and placed under arrest. Virgil and the Dick haul the Liberty Committee and the Moll to night court.

Scene two. Nightcourt. Harry Druggist, formerly the proprietor of a pharmacy but now a vagrant drunk, speaks with the unsympathetic court Clerk. The others enter. The Cop explains, "Mr. Mister sent in orders,/Arrest everybody formin a crowd./A fella started makin a speech—/I pulled in all the guys I could reach." The outraged Liberty Committee protests that Mr. Mister—who, as Harry tells the Moll, "owns steel and everything else too"—formed their group "to combat socialism, communism, radicalism, and especially unionism, and to uphold the Constitution," and that they were protesting the union drive. Meanwhile, the police have taken into custody the man making the speech (Larry Foreman) and are "givin him a little workout next door." The Clerk calls the first case, Reverend Salvation, and Harry tells the Moll that the charge against him should be "habitual prostitute since 1915."

Scene three. Mission. Looking after her husband's business interests, Mrs. Mister ("chairman of all the women's clubs in Steeltown") entices the Reverend to preach neutrality in 1915, bias against the Germans in 1916, and war in 1917 ("Reverend Salvation"/"Thou Shalt Not Kill"). Back in night court, Harry refers to the next case, Editor Daily of the Steeltown News, as "procurer, also known as pimp" to the Mister family.

Scene four. Lawn of Mr. Mister's Home. Swinging in hammocks, Junior and Sister Mister—he, "sluggish, collegiate and vacant," she, "smartly gotten-up and peevish"—relax ("Croon-Spoon"). Mr. Mister—"so much the archetype of all the Mr. Misters in the world that he resembles the type not at all; is, in fact, rather eccentric, a distinct individual"—enters with Editor Daily as Junior and Sister exit. Mr. Mister, who just that day acquired the local paper, strongarms Editor Daily to smear Larry Foreman ("Freedom of the Press"). He also asks him to find an out-of-town position on the paper for Junior, who "doesn't go so well with union trouble." Junior and Sister reenter "displaying that other aspect of boredom—they're going crazy" ("Let's Do Something!"). Editor Daily suggests that Junior become a correspondent in Hawaii ("Honolulu"). Back in night court, Harry Druggist confesses that he sold out too.

Scene five. Drugstore. Harry Druggist, "a sunny little man, somewhat vague," chats with son Steve, "an agreeable adolescent, really much smarter than his father, and a little amused by him." Bugs—"an underworld character, one step above the common thug; slicker and more presentable"—enters and reveals a plot to bomb union headquarters across the street after a Polish immigrant steel worker Gus Polock—a regular customer of Harry's—leaves the drugstore; and unless Harry implicates Gus (sure to be killed along with his wife Sadie, who's always by his side) in the explosion, Mr. Mister will clamp down on his mortgage. As Gus and Sadie enter, Bugs needs to restrain Steve with a concealed revolver ("Drugstore Scene"). The Polocks "are simple, nice people, just married, terribly in love. Sadie is fat, and Gus loves her that way. He talks with an accent, but Sadie doesn't; Gus would never have married a girl with an accent." (The libretto also implies that Sadie is in an early stage of pregnancy.) Gus tells Sadie that both management and the union want his support, and the two look forward to having a child ("Gus and Sadie Love Song"). As the Polocks leave, Steve rushes out to warn them, and all three perish in the explosion.[25]

Scene six. Hotel lobby. Yasha and Dauber meet unexpectedly in a hotel lobby and discover to their mutual disgust that they both have appointments with Mrs. Mister ("The Rich"). Mrs. Mister enters, her Pierce Arrow horns tuned, at Yasha's suggestion, to the main theme from Beethoven's *Egmont* Overture. She invites both artists for the weekend ("Ask Us Again"). Both also agree to join her husband's Liberty Committee—but without caring to know what the group's about. "Politics?" asks Yasha. "We're artists," says Dauber ("Art for Art's Sake").

Scene seven. Nightcourt. The Moll muses about current dog-eat-dog conditions ("Nickel Under the Foot"). Larry Foreman, "the hero of the piece," enters, roughed up. "He's not very good-looking—a humorous face, and an engaging manner. Confidence is there, too; not self-confidence; a kind of knowledge about the way things probably have to work out. It gives him a surprising modesty, and a young poise." An ex-foreman at the steel mill turned union organizer, Larry tells the Moll that he's been arrested for making a speech ("Leaflets!"), warns of the fate in store for the Liberty Committee ("The Cradle Will Rock"), and excitedly awaits the results of the union drive. As President Prexy and Professors Mamie and Trixie approach the Clerk, Larry suggests that their charge should be "maintaining a disorderly house."

Scene eight. Facultyroom. Planning to use college boys as his private militia, Mr. Mister has had College University expand its compulsory military training and demands that President Prexy supply a speaker to rouse the students at an upcoming rally. Prexy calls for Professors Mamie, Scoot, and Trixie. Mamie, applied science, laboratory 54, auditions with a speech full of academic clichés ("Young Gentlemen of the University"); Scoot, ethics 42, esthetics 6, logic 1 (suggesting that he's very ethical, but not very logical), reveals, to the "rage, amazement and despair" of the others, that he's a pacifistic Tolstoyan who served on Henry Ford's Peace Ship ("Then I Don't Like Military Training"); while Mamie, football coach, elementary French, strips to his waist and gives a manly pep talk ("Listen, Fellas!"). Mr. Mister invites Prexy, Mamie, and Trixie to join his Liberty Committee, "but not that Peace Ship—!"

Scene nine. Dr. Specialist's Office. Examining Mr. Mister, Dr. Specialist recommends "a long cure at Vichy this summer," and expresses his gratitude for being named chairman of the Liberty Committee, which has gained him a research appointment. When Dr. Specialist's secretary announces the arrival of Ella Hammer, whose brother, the machinist Joe Hammer, had been pushed into a ladle at the mills by hoodlums because of his union activities, Dr. Specialist tells Mr. Mister that he examined Joe and found him sober at the time of the incident. Mr. Mister threatens to have Dr. Specialist removed from the Liberty Committee unless he says that Joe was intoxicated. As Mr. Mister leaves, Ella enters. "She is no longer young; right now she is in dead earnest." Knowing that the company plans to frame Joe, Ella pleads for Dr. Specialist's support, saying that the workers' faith in Joe is at stake ("Doctor and Ella"). When reporters sent by Mr. Mister enter requesting a statement, Dr. Specialist says that he examined Joe after his injury and found him "obviously intoxicated." The reporters press for a complete story, and Ella responds with a description of the hardships of poor workers ("Joe Worker").

Scene ten. Nightcourt. Mr. Mister arrives and attempts to bribe Larry Foreman to join the Liberty Committee, whom he releases, along with Larry, by his authority; as the Liberty Committee urges Larry to accept the bribe, Harry Druggist pleads with him not to ("Nickel Under the Foot," reprise). Scorning the offer, Larry tells Mr. Mister to leave and to take the Moll with him: "Out there she doesn't cost you nothin—In jail you're liable to have to feed her!" News of a successful outcome of the union drive arrives ("The Cradle Will Rock," reprise).

Although Blitzstein patently intended the work as an allegory, as indicated by the characters' abstract names, he had real persons, places, and events in mind.

For instance, the name Steeltown pointed to Steelton, Pennsylvania, a steel mill town that had witnessed a strike by local workers in 1919. The mention of Aliquippa, another Pennsylvania steel town, suggests that Blitzstein knew about union problems there as well, including company dismissals of union activists on false charges of drunkenness—a ploy that found an echo in the opera—although a strike had not occurred there in 1933, as stated in the text, but rather lay ahead, in May 1937. (When Blitzstein revised the libretto in 1960, he set the action back to 1931 and accordingly omitted the reference to 1933.)[26]

Audiences of the time widely understood further that the opera's unnamed steel union represented the Committee (later, Congress) of Industrial Organizations (CIO), a federation of unions founded by John L. Lewis in late 1935 under the auspices of the American Federation of Labor (AFL) that aimed to unionize industrial workers, in particular, steel workers through the Steel Workers Organizing Committee (SWOC). The CIO differed from the AFL in its interest in unionizing workers within an industry, like steel, rather than a craft, like carpentry or music. Moreover, compared with the AFL, the CIO more vigorously accepted immigrants, blacks, and lesser-skilled workers among its ranks, and entertained a greater communist presence and a more militant profile as well—all of which helped lead to a formal rupture in 1938 between the two organizations (until their merger in 1955 as the AFL-CIO). Blitzstein, who consulted such publications as "Industrial Unionism" and "Organizing Methods in the Steel Industry" in conjunction with his work on the opera, followed the fortunes of the CIO with keen interest and might have decided to focus on a steel union strike because of the centrality of steel not only to the CIO's activities but to the communist movement in general.[27]

In his sketches, Blitzstein even identified Larry Foreman with John L. Lewis and considered calling him Larry Sickle, a name that, along with the work's other union organizer, Joe Hammer, had obvious communist associations. Having an immigrant, Gus Polock, represent steel workers also seems congruent with CIO sensibilities, as does Larry Foreman's vision of a broadly-based movement: "That's *Steel* marchin out in front! but one day there's gonna be/Wheat . . . and sidewalks . . . /Cows . . . and music . . . /Shops . . . houses . . . /Poems . . . bridges . . . drugstores. . . . /The people of this town are findin out what it's all about . . . /They're growin up! /And when everybody gets together/Like Steel's gettin together tonight,/Where are you then?" The opera dramatizes this communal ideal by having an offstage chorus, meant to represent "all the citizens of Steeltown," participate in the finale. (For the 1960 revival, Blitzstein slightly toned down this ending by substituting the phrase "a certain wind" for "the final wind.")[28]

The opera references other people and institutions, including the American Liberty League, an organization founded in 1934 by leading politicians and industrialists to combat New Deal legislation and thinly disguised here as the Liberty Committee, which Blitzstein further associates with the Ku Klux Klan and its affiliate, the Black Legion, a right-wing vigilante group that made headlines in the spring of 1936 with lurid reports of ritual murder and torture. For Reverend Salvation, Blitzstein possibly had in mind not only the evangelist Billy Sunday, but a more contemporary figure, Father Charles Coughlin; one working name for the character, Reverend McGuskey, along with the tag "priest," intimates as much. Sketches suggest too that newspaper tycoon William Randolph Hearst inspired the figure of Editor Daily. Blitzstein apparently modeled Mr. Mister in part after Tom Girdler, the Republic Steel Corporation executive who had managed the steel town of Aliquippa in the 1910s as a self-described "benevolent dictatorship"; but for the Misters, he also bore in mind the right-wing Du Pont family, as revealed by a draft of "Reverend Salvation" that includes the line "Make the world safe for the Du Pont family," later changed to "Make the world safe for the Mister family." And the drugstore scene evoked the notorious case of Tom Mooney, a union organizer framed for a 1916 bombing.[29]

The opera engages a still wider range of social issues. "Honolulu," for instance, lampoons, on a number of levels, imperialist fantasy. As for the faculty room scene, the advocacy, as depicted here, of compulsory military drills for college students—at the time widely associated with Nazi Germany—had become a heated issue on campuses around the country, as strongly opposed by the left as championed by the right. Mr. Mister's employment of a student militia to smash unions further bespoke big business's practice, with university support, of enlisting students as strike breakers. Long before historian Stephen Norwood related this phenomenon to anxieties over masculinity, Blitzstein explored this idea by contrasting Mamie, who makes an ineffectual speech in academic jargon against sinuous belly-dance music, with Trixie, who better meets Mr. Mister's approval by appropriating the language of hypermasculinity ("There's nuttin' like a uniform! . . . Sex Appeal! . . . Be a man!") against the strains of vaudevillian ragtime, the composer sharpening this send-up of military culture by giving Prexy, Mamie, and Trixie feminized names (Scoot is simply told to scoot, which had some basis in perfunctory faculty dismissals during this period) and by introducing a note of homoeroticism as Prexy, helping Trixie on with his sweater, says, "Enchanting, enchanting, enchanting!" The opera similarly satirizes Yasha—whose name pointed to Jascha Heifetz (who's even mentioned in "The Rich") and by extension the country's celebrated virtuosos—and Dauber as effete and preening, Eric Gordon observing a "slightly homosexual characterization to these self-styled artistes."[30]

These varied allusions reveal concerns that plainly go beyond the opera's defense of labor unions, notwithstanding its protest against such abuses as intimidation of union organizers, destruction of union property, and violence against striking workers. Indeed, the work seems less a work of agitprop, as often presumed, than a moral parable about selling out to the devil. Blitzstein himself asserted in 1938, "*The Cradle Will Rock* is about unions, but only incidentally about unions," adding in 1941, "I'm not writing music-plays of social significance. I like people and their problems. And I write plays about the vitality of people today. If they turn out to be social music-dramas, so much the better."[31]

The composer further explained in early 1938,

> What I really wanted to talk about was the middleclass. Unions, unionism as a subject, are used as a symbol of something in the way of a solution for the plight of that middleclass. I mean the intellectuals, professional, small shop-keepers, "little businessmen" in the America of today. What can they do? Where does their allegiance lie? With big business, which is ready to engulf them, buy and sell them out exactly as it does labor, exploit and discard them at will, as a sort of useful but inferior commodity?
>
> The play shows various degradations suffered by the middleclass—some of them funny, some of them less funny—and offers a possible solution: which seems to me to be the only chance for dignity, for survival in fact. The middleclass must sooner or later see that there can be allegiance only to the future, not the past; that the only sound loyalty is the concept of work, and to a principle which makes honest work at least true, good and beautiful.

Later that same year, Blitzstein similarly spoke of *The Cradle* as "a middle-class allegory for middle-class people—to shove those into progressive ranks who stood on the brink; to rescue those who were about to die by joining so-called 'liberty' committees." Most of the opera's characters indeed belong to the middle class. Larry Foreman explicitly tells the Moll, "We got a committee, too, farmers and city people, doctors, lawyers, newspapermen, even a couple of poets—and one preacher. We're middle class, we all got property—we also got our eyes open." Such concerns echoed those of the *New Masses*, which in an editorial of July 21, 1936, "Steel and the Middle Class," published as Blitzstein dug into his opera, argued, "The C.I.O. has a claim on the full support of the middle class. For this social group to remain indifferent or unsympathetic to the steel drive would be to play into the hands of the most powerful reactionary force in America."[32]

The opera's panoramic sweep moves surely and swiftly, forming a compelling whole. After the opening scene, which serves as a prologue, all the action essentially takes place in the night court, with the other scenes unfolding as flashbacks, as seen through the eyes of Harry Druggist or Larry Foreman. This highly cinematic structure might have been suggested by Clifford Odets's similarly prounion play, *Waiting for Lefty* (1935), in which the action returns to a union hall before proceeding to the next flashback. But Blitzstein's work seems at times even closer to the movies, as when Mr. Mister's "Not going to hurt," repeated at the end of the faculty room scene and accompanied by a musical fade-out, becomes the first line of the following scene.

Over and above the ingenious use of the flashbacks, the opera features an intricate, fluid, and carefully calibrated design that employs such traditional resources as recitative, song, chorus, accompanied and unaccompanied dialogue, and instrumental music, along with such novel ones as speech-song, accented recitation, and both accompanied and unaccompanied rhythmic recitation, sometimes in combination, as in the climactic ensemble, during which Larry Foreman and Mr. Mister converse while the Moll sings and the Liberty Committee and Harry Druggist utter rhythmic exclamations. ("Accented recitation" refers to passages in which slashes appear over stressed spoken syllables; and "rhythmic recitation" to passages that use unpitched, rhythmic notation with x's for noteheads.) Blitzstein adapted some of these more adventurous techniques from Eisler, in particular *The Measures Taken*, as well as from the kind of chanting found in such American plays as *Peace on Earth* and *Waiting for Lefty*, but his masterful use of such varied resources represents a unique and soaring achievement.

Discussing the work's unusual form, Blitzstein explained that he found neither the tradition of number opera, as exemplified by Mozart, Weill, and Eisler, nor that of through-composed opera, as represented by "the symphonic style of Wagner, the atmospherisms of Debussy, even the miraculous solution of Verdi," appropriate to his needs: number opera—at least as found in the contemporary musical comedy— had "subtly corrupted the method so that the alteration [sic] of dialogue and music seems oversprightly and endlessly facetious, a vehicle for girls and gags; useless for any serious purpose, or at any rate recalcitrant," while through-composed opera appeared better suited for the "exalted framework of legend" than for this sort of naturalistic drama. At first, he entertained the notion of using music only for those sections "predominantly lyric, satirical, and dramatic," but then more intuitively employed "whatever was indicated and at hand. There are recitatives, arias, revue-patters, tap-dances, suites, chorals, silly symphony, continuous, incidental commentary music, lullaby music—all pitchforked into it. There are also silences treated musically, and the music which is practically silent." "I cannot guarantee the form for a moment," he stated. "It still must prove that it works. I suspect a good deal of it is right. . . . Since it is a new form, I can only take my chances with it."[33]

Blitzstein further commented on the work's varied uses of music as follows:

> In "The Cradle" you will find all sorts of music—music to enforce a scene, music to combat a scene; music as background, music as foreground; music which is sung to, danced to, acted over, talked around; music which introduces, which connects, foreshortens, moulds, makes final. . . . Sometimes the music cooperates with the action, as when Junior's proposed trip to Honolulu is underpinned by some of the tritest Hula Hula music ever heard. Sometimes the music exposes a meaning which the words don't touch at all. . . . The use of music is casual; I have tried to make it almost impossible for an audience to be conscious of exactly when music has entered the proceedings, and when it has departed.

As an example of music that "exposes a meaning which the words don't touch at all," he cited the opera's climactic ensemble, in which the Moll's reprise of "Nickel Under the Foot" in the background signifies the dark motives behind Mr. Mister's ostensibly friendly overtures.[34]

The individual set pieces themselves display a good deal of novelty, not only in terms of their sundry combinations of sung melody and spoken word, but by way of their unusual shapes, pungent harmonies, and abrupt, interrupted, or otherwise inconclusive endings. Tellingly, perhaps the most conventional number, "Joe Worker," originated as an independent song, and even this number thwarts expectations, as the chorus balances its opening eight-measure phrase with, essentially, an extended twenty-measure phrase, a lopsided binary form of a sort also found in "Gus and Sadie Love Song."

True, a few songs approach one or the other of the day's two standard popular song designs (ABAB and AABA), but Blitzstein embellishes such forms for dramatic effect. For example, in "Croon-Spoon," a parody of Tin Pan Alley that, for obvious reasons, closely approximates popular song form (in this case, AABA), Blitzstein puts forth a main theme of seven as opposed to the customary eight measures, so that the melody falls one measure short much as the singing of Junior and Sister Mister at times goes one semitone flat; he also lengthens the bridge in conjunction with his parenthetical comment, "She [Sister Mister] can still top him." "Honolulu" carries this sort of elongation to purposefully ridiculous lengths.

Other numbers similarly go their own way. "Freedom of the Press" and "The Rich" look back to older popular song forms in concluding long verses with short choruses. "Nickel Under the Foot," after a spoken introduction underscored by the "Moll's Lament," starts with a hard-edged eighteen-measure phrase that suggests a traditional verse, followed by a mock-romantic chorus comprising three identical twenty-three-measure phrases, the nondevelopmental form serving the text's dismantling of romantic illusions.

The work's overall structure shows the influence of Soviet agitprop as filtered through the plays of the New Theatre League and the Living Newspapers of the Federal Theatre (Henry Cowell, who traveled to Russia in 1929, discerned a resemblance "in spirit" between the opera and improvisatory Soviet workers' theater circa 1930), but even more decisively, the musical theater of Brecht and his collaborators. The use of narrative and flashback techniques creates a degree of Brechtian estrangement, while the integration of music with dramatic movement points to an absorption of the Brecht-Weill concept of "gestic music." Consider the pounding chords, inspired by a courtroom gavel, that accompany the Clerk's "Order in the courtroom!" or the two-note woodblock motive that underscores Dr. Specialist's pencil taps (a gesture related to Mr. Mister's music heard earlier in the scene) and that shapes every "Yes" he utters to Ella Hammer into complete heartlessness. In "Croon-Spoon," the opening oscillating motive imitates the lazy swinging of Junior and Sister Mister in their hammocks, while the song's dissonant notes mimic their off-key singing. Early drafts of the libretto in particular include the most detailed stage directions, often showing, far beyond the hotel lobby scene, with its "vaudeville vamp" and two-man comedy shtick, the strong influence of vaudeville. In one preliminary version of the faculty room scene, for example, Blitzstein indicated dance and other movements alongside nearly every line or two of text, including chicken-step, Charleston, tap-dancing, soft-shoe, Russian leap, ballet run, bumps, Nazi salute, army salute, Boy Scout salute, and football huddle.[35]

Even the published score contains a wealth of parenthetical instructions specifying not only stage movement, but attitude, inflection, and even costume. Mrs. Mister changes her hat for the second strophe of "Reverend Salvation" into "something pretty awful and 1916," and again for the third strophe into another "new hat, all plumes"; Prexy thanks Mamie for his military recruitment speech, "Like the Madam whose first wench is discovered to be bowlegged"; and Mr. Mister, after fulminating about unions to Dr. Specialist, "grinds the cigar under his heel." Blitzstein pens particularly whimsical comments throughout "Honolulu"—practically a different one for each phrase—including, near the number's end, "Not much on geography, but with the right idea," for Sister Mister's line, "I'd be satisfied with one big Zulu." The lyrics of such songs as "Croon-Spoon," "Nickel Under the Foot," and "Joe Worker" further complement such Brechtian use of gesture by commenting on social conditions.

The opera contains, moreover, specific stylistic resemblances to Eisler and Weill, although these can be hard to differentiate, a matter complicated further by the influence of Jewish music on all three composers (which in *The Cradle* can be discerned, for example, in "Gus and Sadie Love Song," "Nickel Under the Foot," and "Joe Worker"). Blitzstein himself cited *The Cradle* as "the first example of the influence of Kurt Weill's music upon me," while Minna Lederman recalled Weill "rushing around New York" asking, regarding Blitzstein's piece, "Have you seen my new opera?" Both *The Threepenny Opera* and *The Cradle* make ironic use of hymn, waltz, march, tango, and ragtime styles, demonstrating a shared indebtedness to Stravinsky, in particular, *The Soldier's Tale*. Moreover, numbers as varied as "Reverend Salvation," "Thou Shalt Not Kill," and "Leaflets!" contain musical ideas akin to, if not suggested by, *The Threepenny Opera*.[36]

At the same time, *The Cradle* contains distinguishing features from Brecht-Weill and Brecht-Eisler. The warmth of such characters as the Moll and Harry Druggist, as John Shout notes, seems at some remove from Brecht, as does the melodramatic theatricality of the drugstore scene and the powerful catharsis provided by the deaths of Gus, Sadie, and Steve. The use of a suspenseful storyline that climaxes with the confrontation between Larry Foreman and Mr. Mister also sets the work apart from Brecht. Such confluence of the epic and the naturalistic supports Ilka Saal's contention that Blitzstein, like other American authors of political theater in the 1930s, accommodated the German playwright to more realistic native traditions, even if *The Cradle* came closer to Brecht than did most American theater of the time.[37]

The score relatedly has its own profile. Underlining the work's greater naturalism, the music occasionally turns highly descriptive, as in the dissonant counterpoint in "Thou Shalt Not Kill" that suggests the Reverend Salvation's guile, and the mock-sinister countermelody in "Leaflets!" that depicts Larry Foreman's supposed malevolence. The bluesy intimacy of the "Moll's Lament" and "Nickel Under the Foot," the clipped drive of "Freedom of the Press," and the burlesque humor of "Honolulu" or "Listen, Fellas!" strike in particular a note apart from Blitzstein's German contemporaries and closer in various ways to Gershwin, Copland, and, as Leonard Lehrman has suggested, Jerome Moross, even if, compared to these Americans, Blitzstein appears more complex in style and acerbic in tone. "Some of the tunes that he wrote [for *The Cradle*] still show the Weill or Eisler derivation," observed Copland, "but they all have their own character—satirical, tender, bitter, or pessimistic."[38]

Near the end of his life, when asked about the influence of Weill on *The Cradle*, Blitzstein emphasized such differences, once again arguing that the work's formal structure distinguished it from such number musicals as *The Threepenny Opera* and *Happy End* as well as from more through-composed works like *Mahagonny* and *Die Bürgschaft*. "My music very often slithers out of the pieces and slithers back in again," he said, adding, "I think what I most learned from Weill I had, to a degree, already learned from Satie," pointing in particular to the "reticence" of the songs Satie wrote for the chanteuse Paulette Darty. "When I use the word 'reticence,' it is simply another word for 'economy'—economy of use which is the nonsentimental use of a sentimental form."[39]

In yet another late discussion, Blitzstein, without mentioning Weill, similarly alluded to the work's individual use of popular idioms. "I think my style gelled and crystallized with that work [*The Cradle*]. It is a style which has something to do with popular material; and I don't mean popular in the sense of the fashion or fad of this year or next, but what we have come to call popular music—it's a misnomer—as against another misnomer—serious music. I think I use popular material for my actual nexus and I build around it as thoroughly serious a technical complex as I can."[40]

The opera certainly references a wide range of familiar idioms, including quotations of Bach ("Brunnquell aller Güter," adapted for "Thou Shalt Not Kill"), Beethoven (the *Egmont* Overture, cited in the hotel lobby scene), and popular American tunes (including "The Star-Spangled Banner" in the night court scenes, and "Boola Boola," "Go In and Out the Window," and "Rock-A-Bye Baby" in the faculty room scene). This broad compass serves one of the work's principal strategies, namely, the depiction of social class and attitude through musical style, including characteristic rhythm and gesture: the Moll through the blues; the Gent, jazz; the Dick, waltz; the Mister family, popular song; Reverend Salvation, chorale;

Editor Daily, vaudeville; Harry Druggist, pastorale; Gus and Sadie, Jewish melody; Yasha and Dauber, bolero, tango, and rumba; Larry Foreman, workers' march; President Prexy, college song; Mamie, belly dance; Scoot, Slavic folk music; Trixie, ragtime; and Ella Hammer, protest song. Mr. Mister's sonic world includes not only the sinister music that accompanies him in the faculty room scene, but, at least by association, the slow and chilling series of chords heard in the drugstore and Dr. Specialist scenes, music indicative of fascism, as clarified by Blitzstein's later work.

The opera's various quotations naturally hold specific connotations. "Rock-A-Bye Baby," employed sardonically in a militaristic context, suggests a certain infantilizing of university students and operates in tandem with the work's central metaphor, as expressed by its title. Meanwhile, the Bach and Beethoven allusions satirize the sort of corruption and commodification of serious music—also parodied at the top of the hotel lobby scene: "How's the concert business?" asks Dauber; "Fine; how's the painting business?" responds Yasha—that so appalled Blitzstein's contemporary, the Marxist critic Theodor Adorno.

Blitzstein made use of some of his previous music in this work as well, including the ballet *Blessings of the Bath/Megalopolis* (1926–28), which yielded the traveling music that opens scene two (including its allusion to "The Star-Spangled Banner") as well as Trixie's "Young Gentlemen" and Mamie's "Listen, Fellas!" From the unfinished *Traveling Salesman* (ca. 1929–31), he apparently derived at least parts of "Let's Do Something!" "Honolulu," "Gus and Sadie Love Song," and the signature themes for the Gent and for Larry Foreman. And as mentioned above, he revised *Sketch No. 1* (1935) as the entire first scene and "People" (1935) as "Joe Worker." David T. Little observes in addition more general stylistic continuities between *The Cradle* and the composer's earlier scores. Such borrowings and similarities further caution against exaggerating the work's indebtedness to Eisler and Weill, whom Blitzstein grew to really appreciate only in the mid-1930s.[41]

Blitzstein's snazzy and neatly rhymed lyrics—the very opposite of Louis Gruenberg's florid libretto to *Green Mansions* (1937), which he deprecated, and more akin to the work of Ira Gershwin, Cole Porter, and Lorenz Hart, which he admired—represent an important achievement in their own right. Consider, for instance, Mrs. Mister's address to Reverend Salvation in the mission scene, "The market hasn't been ideal:/We have to sell our steel/To French or English or German,/Though the latter are vermin./Father, please, in your sermon Sunday—/I rely upon you to implore that *we* stay out of the war!" with its rhymes of "ideal" and "steel," "German," "vermin," and "sermon," "Sunday" and "*we* stay," and "implore" and "the war," all the while pointedly deriding the influence of corporate power over political affairs. Indeed, although the drama occasionally grows somber, most of the lyrics tend toward the satirical, sometimes even jokey, as in Junior's comment in "Honolulu" about Hawaiian women, "I don't care if they're high born/Just as long as they're high breasted," to which Mr. Mister says, "Junior, please don't get arrested!" the whimsical rhyme of "high breasted" and "arrested" typically getting a laugh in performance. And in the course of slyly conflating the pleasures of popular music and sex in "Croon-Spoon," Blitzstein lets loose a rollicking barrage of innuendos and euphemisms ("croon till it hurts, baby," "croonin in spurts, baby," "I can, canoo, baby, spoon?" "You spoon and spoon and never get tired!" "even the poor are not immune," and so forth). However, the lyrics need the accompanying music for full effect; like many Broadway lyricists, Blitzstein typically created his verse not prior to but rather subsequent to or in conjunction with the music, with tone and word forming in any case an indissoluble whole, the sharp wit and tender poignancy of the lyrics enhancing and enhanced by the music.[42]

The opera has its own orchestral palette as well, the distinctive instrumentation calling for flute, two clarinets, alto saxophone, tenor saxophone, two trumpets, trombone, piano, accordion, strummed instruments (guitar, banjo, and Hawaiian guitar), a large percussion battery, and strings. (By very selectively having the alto or tenor saxophone double on clarinet, the score occasionally features a clarinet trio, which helps provide some of the music for the Polocks and Ella Hammer with a special pathos.) In addition, the finale specifies an optional drum, fife, and bugle corps, instructed to play ad libitum. The orchestration's refined adaptation of popular scoring reflects similar qualities in the work as a whole, while the incorporation of such sounds as telephone bell and siren matches the work's seamless integration of dialogue and music.[43]

Although commentators at the time occasionally referred to the work as an "operetta," Blitzstein objected to the term, which for him evoked "a world of Viennese waltzes and Yum Yums from the Mikado." Nor did he find the label "musical comedy" appropriate. In the published versions of the score and libretto, he designated the work "a play in music," although in some manuscripts, he called the piece "an opera," by which he meant, as he stated in 1938, a form whose music and drama had "a continuous and serious mutual relation." And when the work arrived at the New York City Opera in 1960, he flatly called the work an opera ("which it always was"), placing the piece specifically in the tradition of the *opéra comique*.[44]

Blitzstein's decision to compose the piece for singing actors constituted perhaps its least operatic feature. "Try to put a phrase like 'you keep your shirt on,' or '. . . I get arrested every week, Yes, and sometimes twice a week; Vagrancy it's called; I guess that's me,' into the mouth of any trained singer ('placed' voice, 'concert diction,' rolled r's and so on) and the difficulty of casting becomes strikingly evident. The singing actor was an obvious solution, and the style which puts over a song and which is carried by personality. 'Operatic' tone was to be avoided, theatre tone was the point." The score accordingly features relatively modest vocal lines demanding ranges of about one to one-and-a-half octaves, with the character Steve requiring a range of only a minor second. These ranges lie rather low as well, with Editor Daily the only part that contains some high notes. A few of the roles—including Virgil, Bugs, and Scoot—require no singing at all, although they emerge nevertheless as a part of the musical texture.[45]

Over time, American opera singers became better equipped at handling the work's dramatic requirements, and even in Blitzstein's lifetime, those more formal presentations of the piece that featured the full orchestra especially came to include at least some performers with classical music backgrounds. But whether productions used singing actors, operatic singers, or some combination, the work arguably remained very much an opera, even if one so inventive and vernacular as to help redefine and popularize the genre.

The Cradle Will Rock, II

When Blitzstein returned to New York in September 1936, he found the times propitious as concerned his latest opera, *The Cradle Will Rock*. Broadway—for whom he presumably intended the piece—had shown itself receptive not only to socially engaged theater but to contemporary opera in the form of Virgil Thomson's *Four Saints in Three Acts* (1934) and George Gershwin's *Porgy and Bess* (1935). Even before opening, Blitzstein's "labor opera" or "steel strike opera," as the press dubbed it, garnered an award from the New Theatre League for best play of the 1936–37 season, an honor previously bestowed on Clifford Odets's *Waiting for Lefty* (1935) and Irwin Shaw's *Bury the Dead* (1936).[1]

Signing with the William Morris Agency, with whom he would retain a lifelong association, Blitzstein auditioned the opera for several interested producers, including the Group Theatre and Herman Shumlin as well as the Actors' Repertory Company, which optioned the piece until financial hardships led them to withdraw their offer, and the Labor Stage, which as late as February 1937 considered launching the work. Meanwhile, in the fall of 1936, Blitzstein attended a Federal Theatre performance of Eugène Labiche's farce *An Italian Straw Hat*, which had been adapted as *Horse Eats Hat* by Copland's friend Edwin Denby in collaboration with the show's young director Orson Welles (1915–1985). Impressed with Welles's work, the composer found an opportunity to play his new opera for him, later recalling, "Just twenty-one but already an extravagantly brilliant and magnetic theatre man," Welles "fell in love [with *The Cradle*] straight off and made me promise that no matter who should produce it, he would do the staging." Most probably in early 1937, Welles had Blitzstein play the opera for John Houseman, who had directed the premiere of *Four Saints* and had produced *Horse Eats Hat*, and who had known Blitzstein since the early 1930s. Houseman and Welles subsequently proposed that their unit of the Federal Theatre produce the work.[2]

The Federal Theatre Project (FTP) functioned under the auspices of the Works Progress Administration (WPA), a federally financed government agency directed by Harry Hopkins and established in 1935 in order to provide work for millions of unemployed Americans as part of the New Deal. Headed by Hallie Flanagan (1890–1969), a progressive theater professor who had come to Washington from Vassar, the Federal Theatre, during its brief tenure (1935–39), launched hundreds of productions of old and new plays around the country at affordable prices, thus enriching America's theatrical life enormously, while providing modest salaries to, in any given year, about ten thousand people associated with the theater. About half of the Federal Theatre's employees lived in New York, but the plays that they produced there often toured the country.

In 1935, Flanagan appointed the Bucharest-born John Houseman (b. Jacques Haussmann, 1902–1988) co-head of the Negro Theatre Project, one of a number of specialized units within the FTP; and Houseman in turn hired Welles in the spring of 1936 to direct *Macbeth* for this unit, a successful production that initiated a celebrated association between the two. Houseman soon after left the Negro Theatre to form with Welles a new Federal Theatre unit—Project 891—aimed at presenting classic drama at the elegant 934-seat Maxine Elliott's Theatre at 39th and Broadway, a unit for whom Welles directed the Labiche farce in the fall of 1936 and Christopher Marlowe's *The Tragical History of Doctor Faustus* in early 1937. (Concerning these productions, Flanagan, who thought Houseman "our most original and imaginative mind," stated, "Since Jack [Houseman] is rather shy and Orson [Welles], to put it in Anglo-Saxon understatement, not very shy, it was difficult to tell who was responsible for what.") Deemed by actor Norman Lloyd "a perfect creative team" comparable to the equally volatile Diaghilev and Nijinsky, Houseman and Welles now hoped to follow *Faustus* with *The Cradle Will Rock*, and to have the two shows—and eventually a third—alternate short runs over the summer.[3]

Around March 1, Flanagan heard Blitzstein audition the work at Houseman's East 55th Street apartment before a small group that also included Welles and Virgil Thomson, Houseman's roommate. "It took no wizardry to see that this was not a play set to music," recalled Flanagan, "nor music illustrated by actors, but music + play equaling something new and better than either." Wrote Blitzstein to his sister, "Hallie F. is nuts about the work—but just as terrified of it."[4]

Described by Houseman as "a small, forthright, enthusiastic lady . . . who seemed to take her vast responsibilities with amazing self-confidence and sang-froid," Flanagan had reasons for concern, as the Federal Theatre Project had been singled out by conservative members of Congress as epitomizing the alleged waste and liberal bias of the entire WPA. Such tensions escalated in the course of 1937 as bloody strikes rocked the country. Reactionary forces eventually engineered the demise of the Federal Theatre in 1939, but not before, in an appearance before the House Un-American Activities Committee, Hallie Flanagan attempted to clarify, among other things, the matter of Renaissance playwright Christopher Marlowe's alleged communist associations. In such an environment, an FTP production of *The Cradle* easily could play into the hands of the Federal Theatre's enemies, so that Flanagan and her associates faced ethical dilemmas not unlike those posed by the opera itself.[5]

Flanagan and Houseman debated the issue throughout March 1937. "Flying letters of increasing temper pass between Houseman and Mrs. Flanagan—they may come to a head in a few days," Blitzstein informed his sister on March 26. But the next day, he wrote to Jo, "At last—the play is on," with rehearsals set to begin on March 29 and the opera possibly to open on May 15. Houseman later reflected that Flanagan "realized, better than her more timid colleagues, that in the storm into which the Arts Projects were headed, there was no safety in prudence and no virtue in caution."[6]

Even before Flanagan heard the work, Houseman and Welles had begun to cast the opera, snagging two rising stars: Will Geer (later Grandpa Walton on the television series *The Waltons*) for the part of Mr. Mister, and Howard Da Silva (born Howard Silverblatt, and later to originate the role of Jud Fry in *Oklahoma!*) as Larry Foreman. Other cast members included Olive (Toddy) Stanton (Moll), Guido Alexander (Dick), Bert Weston (Editor Daily), Hansford Wilson (President Prexy), Leopold Badia (Mamie), George Smithfield (Trixie), Edward Fuller (Yasha), Warren Goddard (Dauber), Frank Marvel (Dr. Specialist), John Adair (Harry Druggist), Howard Bird (Steve), Peggy Coudray (Mrs. Mister), Hiram Sherman (Junior Mister and Scoot), Dulce Fox (Sister Mister), George Fairchild (Gus and Gent), Marian Rudley (Sadie), and Blanche Collins (Ella). The dramatis personae of twenty-nine (played here by twenty-seven actors) largely conformed to the twenty-eight characters of the published score (the Federal Theatre production would not have included the Attendant, but rather two additional characters, a Maid and a third Reporter). Houseman and Welles also hired an interracial chorus of thirty-two voices, and an orchestra, as Blitzstein recalled, of thirty-two players including fourteen strings (a seeming discrepancy, based on the score, of six musicians, unless he counted members of the drum, fife, and bugle corps as well).[7]

Theodore (Ted) Thomas—a relation of Blitzstein's, and later father of conductor Michael Tilson Thomas—served as associate producer, Jean Rosenthal production manager, Abraham (Abe) Feder lighting designer, Edwin J. Schruers set and costume designer, and at Blitzstein's request, Lehman Engel conductor. Although uncredited, Clarence Yates, the African-American dancer who had worked with Houseman on previous FTP shows, helped choreograph the musical numbers. Blitzstein went on the government payroll, earning about $25 a week, the low end of Federal Theatre salaries, but seemingly on par with others in the production. On March 29, he also signed a contract giving the New Theatre League rights to serve as co-agent.[8]

During this period, Blitzstein became good friends with Welles, to the point that Houseman and Thomson, according to Welles, "were in a huff because of this marriage between Marc and myself." In later years, Welles spoke with unusual warmth about the composer:

> He was almost a saint. He was so totally and serenely convinced of the Eden which was waiting for us all on the other side of the Revolution that there was no way of talking politics to him. He didn't care who was

in the Senate, or what Mr. Roosevelt said—*he* was just the spokesman for the bourgeoisie! . . . He [Blitzstein] wasn't a finger-wagger. . . . When he came into the room the lights got brighter. . . . He was an engine, a rocket, directed in one direction which was his opera—which he almost believed had only to be performed to start the Revolution. You can't imagine how simple he was about it. They were going to hear it, and that would be it! . . . He had been "converted" and he was like one of those gray friars hopping around after St. Francis had spoken. . . . I allowed myself to be thought of as farther to the left than I was because I didn't want to lose his friendship. . . . I really did love him very much.

Welles also reported waiting for a limousine sent by his well-to-do wife Virginia and saying to Blitzstein, "You think you'll have all this after your revolution?" to which Blitzstein calmly replied, "*Everybody* will have it."[9]

Welles adapted a version of this anecdote for his final work, a 1984 unfilmed screenplay *The Cradle Will Rock*, that dealt extensively with his friendship with the composer, further described "as fine-tuned rather than highly strung. He has the attentive stillness of some birds: one of the predators—a gyrfalcon. . . . A total stranger to extravagance in any form, he is mannerly, widely educated, unaffectedly civilized, a man of natural authority and unstudied charm. If he sounds a little too good to be true, he is, almost, just that. It never occurs to him that his mere presence is a kind of rebuke to the rest of us." That Welles—who considered the Canadian comedian David Steinberg for the role of Blitzstein—would return to his early relationship with the composer for a screenplay written so late in life, and, moreover, state in its end title, "Marc Blitzstein is sorely missed. This film is dedicated to him with much affection," bespeaks the profound impression that Blitzstein made on him. "One could argue that Blitzstein not only influenced Welles," writes Jonathan Rosenbaum, "but eventually, in certain respects, came to stand for a significant part of his artistic persona—his political conscience and consciousness—over the remainder of his career."[10]

Rehearsals began in late March, but even so, Houseman and Welles ultimately decided not to hold preview performances until June 16, with a dress rehearsal the night before and an official premiere at the end of the month. This gave the company at least two-and-a-half months to work on the opera, and the orchestra, which began rehearsals around mid-April, two months to prepare their parts—the sort of luxury rarely afforded Broadway shows at the time. "We worked every moment, and sometimes we worked overtime because we loved it," recalled Hiram Sherman, the talented comedian double cast as Junior Mister and Scoot.[11]

Against the advice of Flanagan, Welles in collaboration with Schruers designed elaborate stage pictures involving, as Houseman recalled, "narrow, glass-bottomed, florescent platforms, loaded with scenery and props" that "slid smoothly past each other as the scene shifted" and that Welles remembered as "full of metal and glass and the horror of Steeltown." Welles also planned to mount loudspeakers around the house for the choral finale. Houseman described the production's overall style as falling "somewhere between realism, vaudeville and oratory."[12]

On June 2, Blitzstein wrote to his sister, "Mrs. F is getting scared all over again—I suspect the Cradle will be suppressed before it opens." Not coincidentally, escalating turmoil in the steel industry had reached a new peak three days earlier with the Memorial Day Massacre, in which the Chicago police fired into a crowd demonstrating against Republic Steel, leaving ten dead and scores wounded. Such developments made *The Cradle* more timely than Blitzstein could have imagined, and, in certain quarters, more dangerous as well. Flanagan duly brought some people from Washington to preview the opera, including one of her supervisors, Lawrence Morris, who "thought it was tremendous, that it was likely to get us into trouble, but would be worth it."[13]

However, days before the dress rehearsal, the WPA announced forthcoming cuts in their arts programs, including dismissal of about 30 percent of their New York personnel in the Federal Theatre Project and the postponement of any new plays, concerts, or art exhibitions until July 1. Officially, the government took these actions "to facilitate the reorganization of the WPA art projects," but as Flanagan wrote Blitzstein ten years later, "This was obviously censorship under a different guise. We felt that this was aimed at *The Cradle Will Rock*, which was the only big show to open. (Of course we couldn't prove this.)" Flanagan and others pleaded that an exception be made for *The Cradle*, but to no avail.[14]

Meanwhile, the Federal Theatre had sold about fourteen thousand tickets for nineteen preview performances. Many of these tickets had been purchased in blocks as benefits for various leftist organizations, who, as a means of raising funds, typically charged more than the box office prices of 25¢ (about the cost of a movie), 40¢, and 55¢. This included the Downtown Music School, with whom Blitzstein had a close association, and who bought much of the house for the June 16 opening preview.

Houseman and Welles proceeded with a full-orchestra dress rehearsal on June 15 before a large invited crowd that included playwrights George S. Kaufman and Moss Hart and Communist Party representative V. J. Jerome. The elaborate stage machinery creaked some, but the opera was "warmly received," according to the *Daily Worker*. "It seemed a success," recalled Blitzstein.[15]

In the past, Houseman and Welles had postponed other shows, but now, as the former wryly recalled, they became "demons of dependability, scrupulous to honor our public and artistic commitment," and in defiance of the Federal Theatre, decided to open on June 16 as scheduled. But if Houseman and Welles acted somewhat disingenuously, they regarded the government's actions as not only "equally fraudulent," but likely to jeopardize the project for good. "If we had not opened on June 16," stated Welles, "—we would never have been allowed to open at all: the red-baiting congressmen would have had their way."[16]

When the company arrived at the Maxine Elliott's on June 16, they found the theater padlocked and manned by WPA security guards, who allowed access within, but not the removal of anything deemed government property, including costumes, props, and music. Gathering in Houseman's makeshift basement office in the ladies' powder room with a telephone at their disposal, the production team elected to go forward with the opera at some other venue; but they faced several problems over and above the loss of scenery and costumes. First, finding an available theater at the last minute proved difficult. In addition, Actors' Equity Association refused to allow the actors of a production prepared by the Federal Theatre, many of whom had no Equity card, to appear on a commercial stage, while the musicians' union, Local 802, decided that the orchestra players, at their current salaries, could perform their parts on the stage in a concert version of the work, but not in the pit. "So there we were," recalled Blitzstein, "in the position of having a production without a theater, actors who could not appear on stage and musicians who could appear nowhere else—enough to make the stoutest enthusiast admit defeat and give up." "Marc's despair at this point was ghastly to behold . . . ," remembered Houseman. "And the unkindest cut of all came with the realization that the final, fatal blows had been dealt him by those very unions in whose defense the piece had been written," although Houseman acknowledged that Local 802, affiliated with the AFL, could hardly be expected to have sympathy for the opera's barely veiled support of the CIO, stating, "the spectacle of Larry Foreman clenching the fingers of his raised right fist was no more pleasing to an old-time craft union official than it was to a member of the reactionary Liberty League."[17]

Welles ingeniously proposed that, whatever the venue, the cast sing and speak their lines from the audience, accompanied by Blitzstein at the piano on stage. Most of the performers agreed to the idea, even though they risked losing their jobs with the WPA. With ten dollars given to her by Houseman, Jean Rosenthal found and rented a battered upright, had the instrument loaded onto a truck, and circled about with the truckers, waiting for instructions. As eight o'clock approached, a theater broker in their midst finally secured, for the price of $100 for the evening, the Venice Theatre (both formerly and later, Jolson's 59th Street Theatre), a house located on Seventh Avenue that hosted films, recitals, and other events largely targeted to the Italian-American community, including a recent May 29 presentation sponsored by a group friendly to Mussolini. Either Rosenthal's piano or a reportedly better upright otherwise obtained—accounts differ—made its way to the theater, where local firefighters helped hoist the instrument on stage.[18]

Meanwhile, many of that night's six hundred or so ticket-holders, sensing excitement, had gathered in advance of the 8:40 curtain outside the Maxine Elliott's, where Will Geer and Howard Da Silva entertained them with songs, some from the opera. As Blitzstein, Abe Feder, and Ted Thomas left by taxi, and Welles, Houseman, and writer Archibald MacLeish by private roadster, the crowd—encouraged to invite friends to the performance, as the Venice held 1,770 seats, almost twice as many as the Maxine Elliott's—proceeded uptown. Despite the watchful eyes of the WPA guards—upon collecting his mail at the Maxine Elliott's after the show opened, Da Silva had his toupée confiscated—Lehman Engel managed to smuggle out Blitzstein's conductor's score under an overcoat retrieved from home.[19]

At the Venice, Blitzstein had the front of the piano removed for better projection, and Feder set up a follow spot he either found or brought with him, injuring himself in the process. Some of the cast along with conductor Lehman Engel, according to the latter's memoir, sat in the first few rows, which had been reserved for them, but others found seats elsewhere. A tattered backdrop revealed a Neapolitan landscape, complete with Mt. Vesuvius, and an Italian flag hung over a stage box until ripped down to the cheers of the audience. Blitzstein remembered the theater "jammed to the rafters," with reporters and cameramen in the aisles and about a hundred standees. That the audience included so many friends of the Downtown Music School surely served to make these first-nighters all the more receptive.[20]

The performance finally began at about 9:45. Houseman explained the circumstances that had brought them there; Welles, positioned at a desk at the side of the stage, set the action, as he would intermittently throughout the evening; and Blitzstein, in shirt sleeves and suspenders on this mild June night, began to sing the "Moll's Lament." A few lines into the song, in one of the most riveting moments in the history of the American theater, the young, slender Olive Stanton, seated in a loge box, began to sing along, taking over the number as Feder illuminated her with his follow spot. Commented Houseman, "It must have taken almost superhuman courage for an inexperienced performer . . . to stand up before two thousand people, in an ill-placed and terribly exposed location, and start a show with a difficult song to the accompaniment of a piano that was more than fifty feet away. Add to this that she was a relief worker, wholly dependent on her weekly WPA check, and that she held no political views whatsoever." After her solo, George Fairchild as the Gent continued the scene from his place in the orchestra. "If Olive Stanton had not risen on cue in the box," remarked Hiram Sherman, "I doubt if the rest of us would have had the courage to stand up and carry on. But once that thin, incredibly clear voice came out, we all fell in line."[21]

"The audience seethed with excitement," recalled Blitzstein. "As the play progressed, they turned as at a tennis match, from one actor to another, while Feder caught as many performers as he could with his spotlight. . . . Some wonderful accidents of geography turned up. For example, Mrs. Mister was seen handing an imaginary donation from a balcony front box to the Reverend Salvation downstairs in mid-aisle." Blitzstein assumed the six or so missing parts, announced scene titles, and spoke the sound effects, saying at the end of scene five, for instance, "There is the sound of an explosion." And Hiram Sherman, already double-cast, apparently took over the part of Reverend Salvation for the missing Edward Hemmer. Occasionally, the orchestra's accordionist, also seated in the

audience, joined in, and spectators recalled hearing a piccolo and other instruments as well. "Not a hitch occurred in the continuity," recalled the composer, a
claim confirmed by *Variety*, who wrote, "It would be better reporting to say that
Blitzstein stumbled over some of his own lines or notes . . . but he didn't. He
remembered it all."[22]

The Federal Theatre planned on presenting the opera in one act, as presumably intended, but with Blitzstein "limp with exhaustion," someone announced a
fifteen-minute intermission after scene six. "The second act went like a house
afire," recalled Houseman, and the conclusion of the opera met with, in Blitzstein words, "roaring pandemonium." Not able to clear the house until midnight,
Houseman, who had rented the theater only to eleven, had to pay the Venice an
additional $20.[23]

During the interval, Archibald MacLeish, nattily attired in a white linen suit, had
gone backstage, flushed with excitement that "a new day had dawned in the theater,"
and asked to be allowed to say something at the conclusion of the performance.
Welles duly held up his hand during the standing ovation that greeted the piece and
said, "We will all now sit down and the one man left standing will be Mr. Archibald
MacLeish," at which the latter acclaimed the evening's historic importance. The tenor
of MacLeish's remarks can be inferred from his essay, "Behind the Fourth Wall"
(published in 1938 and reprinted as the "Foreword" to the work's libretto), in which
he argued that although Brecht, T. S. Eliot, and others had helped reform the contemporary theater audience—described as "both greedy and inert, both impotent and
sensual"—Blitzstein's candid and sharp "operetta" had proven most successful in this
regard. Describing the premiere at the Venice, MacLeish observed around him
"well-wishing faces: human faces such as a man may sometimes see among partisans
of the same cause or friends who hope good things for one another." In his screenplay
about this event, Welles himself described the audience response as "that mighty,
loving explosion which can be heard but once or twice in a theatre lifetime."[24]

The work's dramatic premiere made front-page news the next day around the
country, and a few sporadic notices appeared around this time as well. Having
studied the score and attended several rehearsals, Virgil Thomson (*Modern
Music*), deeming the composer's "*sens du théatre* . . . of the best, easily the equal of
[Gian Carlo] Menotti's," declared the opera a work of "passion and elegance."
Charles Dexter (*Daily Worker*), one of the few critics to review the dress rehearsal,
with sets and all, called the piece "a brilliantly conceived and executed affair,"
even though he found "the words . . . superior to the music and the production . . .
superior to both." And Wolfe Kaufman (*Variety*), apparently covering the more
impromptu premiere, stated, "It was all strangely moving and affecting. And the
music certainly was and is good."[25]

Like others closely connected with the opera, not least the composer, Flanagan
hoped that the production still might go forward under FTP auspices and planned
to arrange a meeting between Houseman and Hopkins. But on June 17, Welles

flew down to Washington accompanied by MacLeish and independently met with two of Flanagan's superiors, David Niles and Ellen Woodward. Welles asked that the production proceed at the Maxine Elliott's at least as a series of dress rehearsals, threatening that otherwise he and Houseman would seek a commercial venue, to which Niles warned, "I think if there is any other commercial performance, Mrs. Flanagan should drop it." That same evening, theater parties organized by the American Labor Party and the International Workers Order arrived at the Maxine Elliott's vainly demanding their money back.[26]

Permitted by WPA policy to take a two-week leave of absence, the twenty or so cast members who had participated in the premiere agreed to continue with the production for that duration if possible. Houseman and Welles rented the Venice for two weeks, and a diverse group of friends—including Gifford Cochran, Helen Deutsch, Bess Eitingon, Arthur Garfield Hays, Lincoln Kirstein and his sister Mina Curtiss, and Herman Shumlin—raised over $2,000 to cover expenses, including union dues, with Blitzstein himself joining the Dramatists Guild, Local 802, and Actors' Equity. The opera reopened on Friday, June 18 for two weeks, including a midnight show on June 24, with scenes broadcast on WEVD in late June and early July as well. The company also raised ticket prices to 35¢, 55¢, and $1.10, cashing in prepaid tickets at the Maxine Elliott's box office, with the production eventually breaking even.[27]

As a commercial venture with Equity actors, the cast could now appear on stage, but the company decided to recreate more or less the conditions of the June 16 premiere, with less explanation from Welles, however, and no orchestra members pitching in. "There has always been the question of how to produce a labor show so the audience can be brought to feel that it is a part of the performance," explained Houseman. "This technique seems to solve the problem and is exactly the right one for this particular piece. It will also make it possible to play the show in any sort of theatre or auditorium any place in the country." Blitzstein viewed the matter rather differently, stating in 1938, "Most people overlook the fact that in its original Federal Theatre production, *The Cradle Will Rock* had been greatly enhanced by set-constructions, lighting designs, and orchestrations. But in the form by which it finally became known, the show hardly represented a full-reading or a true theatre production. It was really only a heightened reading and, as such, had no intended relation to the theories of Brecht or any one else."[28]

The work's unconventional presentation in any event encouraged an unusual degree of audience involvement. "Mr. Blitzstein discovered the other night . . . ," reported the *New York American*, "four performers for whom he had never written parts." The *Evening Post*—which also disclosed that Blitzstein "eats peanuts continually throughout the performance"—similarly stated, "One night . . . so many volunteer actors bobbed up in the audience that the show came to a close with an entirely different ending from that evolved originally by the composer. . . . There is generally a good deal of rushing from side to side in the balcony, the better to see who's singing now, and why."[29]

After the opera closed on July 1, the company returned to the WPA "without casualties," hoping that the government might now produce the opera. "This project is and should be a people's theater," stated Blitzstein near the end of the run. But the Federal Theatre decided to "drop it," as Niles had forewarned. Welles soon after resigned from the WPA; Houseman, still not an American citizen, found himself dismissed under new WPA guidelines that forbade the hiring of aliens; and in August, the two founded a private enterprise, the Mercury Theatre, that benefited from the leftist and, in particular, communist good will forged by their affiliation with the Blitzstein opera.[30]

In retrospect, Flanagan sadly viewed the whole episode as "disastrous" to the Federal Theatre, as it bred suspicion in theater circles of government interference and censorship. But Blitzstein apparently held her somewhat responsible, and, moreover, ridiculed her, changing the name Nellie Vacuum to Hallie Vacuum in his libretto to *The Cradle* and satirizing her further in a sketch penned for the 1937 revue, *Pins and Needles*. "I never felt that it was either ethical or generous for any of you connected with the Mercury to infer that I had been on the other side," wrote Flanagan to Blitzstein in 1947, by which time the two seem to have reconciled differences. "After all, it was at my request that your show was put together on government time and money, and rehearsed for months on government time and money. It was stopped over my protest."[31]

Over the summer, the original cast regrouped for occasional performances of the work, such as one on July 10 sponsored by the CIO-affiliated Steel Workers Organizing Committee and presented at a picnic for two hundred Bethlehem Steel workers and their families. The initially befuddled audience warmed to the opera as it progressed, recognizing in Mr. Mister a figure not unlike Bethlehem Steel President Eugene Grace and cheering Larry Foreman's speeches (the steel workers seemed to enjoy best precisely those parts of the work that many critics over the years cared for least). "We all sure did like it and learnt a lot from it," stated James Ramsey, president of the local SWOC lodge. Another performance took place on July 25 in Uncasville, Connecticut.[32]

On November 27, the Mercury Theatre, which had successfully commenced operations with a production of *Julius Caesar*, began presenting *The Cradle* as well. Welles and Houseman devised what they called an "oratorio version" of the work, with Blitzstein at the piano as before, but with the principals, wearing street clothes and little or no makeup, seated on stage in two rows on a raised platform and a chorus of ten voices behind them on a second platform against a blue backdrop. This version had a few weekend airings before moving to the Windsor Theatre on January 3 in a co-production by the Mercury Theatre and Sam Grisman, who had launched the blockbuster *Tobacco Road* in 1933. On February 28, the opera returned to the Mercury Theatre, and closed on the evening of April 2 after a total of 104 performances (exclusive of pre-Windsor performances). Although the casts at the Venice and the Mercury remained essentially the same, that for the Windsor differed more noticeably, what with the inclusion of newcomers LeRoi Operti (Prexy), Jules Schmidt (Dauber), Charles Niemeyer (Reverend Salvation and Scoot), Maynard Holmes (Junior Mister), and, early in the run, Ralph MacBane (Mr. Mister). At both the Mercury and the Windsor, Blitzstein assumed the roles of the Clerk, Reporters, and Professor Mamie.[33]

In accordance with union regulations, the Windsor production was required to hire ten—later reduced to eight—musicians, who sat out each performance amusing themselves in the theater's basement. Blitzstein selected three flutists, four trumpeters, and three trombonists, citing their financial need. When told "You can't make an orchestra out of that," he purportedly replied, "That is the orchestra I want to have not play my opera!"[34]

The work continued to attract what Virgil Thomson called "the leftist front: that is to say, the right-wing socialists, the communists, some Park Avenue, a good deal of Bronx, and all those intellectual and worker groups that the Federal Theater in general and the Living Newspaper in particular have welded into about the most formidable army of ticket buyers in the world." At the same time, Blitzstein thought the Windsor audience more critical than that at the Venice: "You can almost hear them say 'What! No scenery? What kind of a show is this?' They are cold to us for the first few minutes, and you can feel it. As the play gets under way, however, their temperature rises, until we are engulfed by their enthusiasm." For Houseman, "*The Cradle* never seemed as satisfying and dynamic at the Windsor as it had in the vastness of the Venice or the intimacy of the Mercury. There was something incongruous about its austere staging and radical sentiments in the garish luxury of a renovated Broadway house."[35]

As mentioned, the opera received a few reviews early on, but the work's official premiere on December 5 and its subsequent run at the Mercury and Windsor brought out the critics in full force. To an unusual extent, the notices concentrated on the work as opposed to the production, partly of course because of the barebones staging, but also thanks to the sheer power of the opera, whose "vigor," "vitality," "gusto," and "freshness" impressed even those who found the ending contrived or the piece otherwise flawed. The opera, agreed most critics, "generates current like a dynamo" (Brooks Atkinson) and "has about it the great quality of excitement" (Richard Watts Jr.), with "songs that lift you out of your seat" (Eleanor Flexner). "Like dynamite it can't be ignored," concluded R. D. Darrell.[36]

The critics especially lauded Blitzstein's skillfully integrated words and music, even if, according to Paul Rosenfeld, the piece revealed "a brilliant dramatic talent more thoroughly than a musical one." Philip Barr thought Blitzstein's mastery of "every detail" within a large dramatic form greater than Gershwin's, and Alistair Cooke deemed this "magnificent" work, "the nearest most effective equivalent to the form of Greek tragedy." Irving Kolodin emphasized further the composer's

> surprising gift for characterization that spoke from almost every page. Without departing from a musical idiom that was intelligible to the least

sophisticated listener, Blitzstein found apt, concise musical phrases to limn such personages as Editor Daily, Mr. Mister, Junior Mister, Moll and Reverend Salvation, to make their characters apparent even without the affirmation of words. From Mozart to Strauss, the ability to characterize in music has been a distinguishing mark of every successful musical dramatist.

The reviews also concurred that the sparse production served the work well, with only a later critic like Morgan Himelstein wondering if the piece "might have had greater success if all the technical resources of the stage had been utilized."[37]

Few of these early reviews seemed to find the work's provocative content particularly troubling. On the contrary, Virgil Thomson, who described the opera as "very close to a fairy-tale," wrote, "Expounded relentlessly through a bitter beginning, a harsh, comic middle and a noble apotheosis at the end, informed with wit and passion, burning with the red flame of social hatred and glowing with the pure white light of Marxian fanaticism, the work turns out to be, curiously enough, the big charm-number of the year." Even Leonard Liebling—for whom Blitzstein's "savagely propagandistic" second act, with its frank preachment of "the overthrow of capital through violent revolution," led him to shift sympathies from "the underdog" to "the persecuted millionaire"—concluded, "There is no doubt that Blitzstein is a feeling humanist, and intends to make his play a truthful presentment of the misfortunes of the small man."[38]

At the same time, the august George Jean Nathan disparaged not only the music ("negligible") and the libretto ("for the most part commonplace"), but the work's admirers, described as "highly solvent Hollywood scenario writers, Broadway playwrights, New Republic editors, novelists, dramatic critics, and other such steady customers of the more expensive night clubs and former speakeasies." In a subsequent notice, Nathan further described the piece as "little more than the kind of thing Cole Porter might have written if, God forbid, he had gone to Columbia instead of Yale," and compared the excitement generated by the production to that of the cry of "Fire!" in a theater. The opera received a similar drubbing from Mary McCarthy in the *Partisan Review*, a bastion of the anti-Stalinist left. "What is presented is not so much the workers versus the bosses in Steeltown, U.S.A., as Mr. Blitzstein versus the ticket-holders in the Mercury Theatre," wrote McCarthy, who thought the work an open display of its composer's "sadistic impulses" and "acrid personality." Drawing analogies to such foreign phenomena as surrealist art, German expressionism, and the work of Weill, Auden, and Isherwood, she thought, moreover, that the piece violated "native sensibilities."[39]

Some of the work's most severe critics, including Nathan and in later years Samuel Lipman, plainly seemed more disturbed by the opera's reception than by the work itself. After the Sarah Lawrence campus newspaper published a feature about Blitzstein in early 1938, student editor Sybil Graham—who had witnessed the opera's supposed working-class audience hiss the villain and cheer the hero—warned that such incitement of class hostility "will eventually result in either communism or fascism," an opinion that in turn prompted a classmate to champion Blitzstein's right to express himself. Even an admirer like Copland discerned in *The Cradle* and its successor, *No for an Answer*, "a certain sectarianism that makes them come off best before a public that doesn't need to be won over to the author's point of view. This limits their circulation as works of art and therefore their effectiveness as propaganda." And in a 1947 article that identified *Porgy and Bess* and *The Cradle* as America's only two successful music dramas to date, critic Harold Clurman similarly offered as a caveat, Blitzstein's "still restricted audience."[40]

In early 1938, Random House published the work's libretto, with prefaces by MacLeish and Welles, and Chappell brought out eleven numbers from the show. In a review of the latter, Copland cautioned, "Anyone who hears this music without having first seen the drama . . . is likely to be disappointed," but added that "those who have seen the play will want to own the music; and musicians will want to study how Blitzstein turns the ordinary, banal musical language of the day into a pungent and laconic commentary on human frailty and injustice."[41]

After the opera's run ended in April 1938, Musicraft, a small, new record company, released an abbreviated version of the work on an album of seven twelve-inch records (costing a hefty $10.50), with the Windsor cast (including MacBane rather than Geer) accompanied by Blitzstein, who bridged the excerpts with commentary. This recording garnered several enthusiastic reviews, with the *New Masses* praising Milton Rein and Henry Cohen of Musicraft for having the "nerve" to record the piece. Essentially the first Broadway original cast album (a distinction often accorded the cast recording of *Oklahoma!* produced several years later), this release remains not only historically important but compelling in its own right.[42]

As Houseman foretold, the opera so denuded attracted groups with limited resources, and over time, scores of schools and small companies performed the work in some such modest guise, although often more fully staged than in its early days. Soon after its Broadway run, the piece appeared in, among other places, Brooklyn, Philadelphia, New Orleans, and Chicago, where Louis "Studs" Terkel took the role of Editor Daily in a production by the Chicago Repertory Group. The opera's success proved a considerable windfall for Blitzstein, who declared his annual income as over $7,000 on his 1938 tax returns.[43]

On May 27, 1939, Leonard Bernstein (1918–1990), then a senior at Harvard, presided over the work's Boston-area premiere at the university's Sanders Theatre, playing the score at the piano by heart. He apparently had seen scenes from the opera in early 1939 in New York at the Labor Stage "and freaked out with excitement to the point where I was determined that I was going to get it [the opera] on stage myself. I just had to do it, especially performing his [Blitzstein's] role of onstage pianist, plus scene announcer, plus taking a few minor bit parts." Supported by the Harvard Student Union and several faculty sponsors, Bernstein assembled a young cast that included his fifteen-year-old sister Shirley (appearing as Shirley Mann) as the Moll, and he co-directed the work with Arthur Szathmary, who also played Yasha.[44]

The opera provoked the ire of a local councilman, Michael Sullivan, who thought the production the work of Harvard "Reds" and urged the Cambridge chief of police "to investigate and, if necessary, prosecute the backers." But the work earned kudos in the local press from such esteemed critics as Moses Smith and Elliot Norton, even if the latter seemed alarmed at the enthusiasm with which the audience greeted a work that

> says, in effect, that the men who have been exploiting the workers had better watch out: that their day is coming. . . . It gives the professional man—the doctor, the lawyer, the artist—a matter of 10 minutes, or something like that, to get organized before the storm strikes. It's as blunt and bold as that—and as unpleasant. It does all this with simple directness and tremendous theatrical force, against a musical background that is at once unusual and unusually effective, even downright brilliant, as the whole business is brilliant.[45]

Blitzstein flew up to Boston for the dress rehearsal and the performance, and for the first time met Bernstein, who "was amazed at the slightness of this man I had imagined, through his music, to be a giant." After the dress rehearsal, the two strolled along the Charles River, the first of what would be many excursions together, although Bernstein always kept the image of this initial meeting:

> Marc lying on the banks of the Charles, talking, bequeathing to me his knowledge, insight, warmth—endlessly, with endless strength drawn, like that of Antaeus, from his contact with the earth. And gradually he became a giant again; and so he continued to be whenever he touched earth, sea, woods, snow. That was the secret of the giant who had written those special notes which seduced my soul, those thousands of special, mysterious notes that can never be forgotten.

After the performance, Blitzstein told Bernstein that the young man seemed "the spitting reincarnation" of himself ("Now *that* was an honor," stated Bernstein in 1985, "and still is to me"), and upon his return home, he further informed the Harvard undergraduate that his production "packed a thrilling wallop for me— second only to the original NY opening."[46]

The two men—both from Jewish immigrant backgrounds, both predominantly homosexual—became, in Bernstein's words, "instant and lifelong friends," especially close from the time of Blitzstein's return from Europe in the spring of 1945 to his death in early 1964. "Lenny I love," Blitzstein wrote to Mina Curtiss in 1951, "with all his neurotic compulsions and vanities. I keep seeing (and sensing when I don't see) that vein of pure gold. Of course it is deeply professional, his wild talent; but it gets personal, too." And in 1962, he stated, "We are almost telepathically close. Sometimes we compose startlingly similar music on the same day, without seeing each other." In their leisure moments, the two men enjoyed playing word games and making home movies, including a 1960 send-up of the film *Exodus* entitled "Call Me Moses" in which Bernstein played Pharaoh; his brother Burton, Moses; and Blitzstein, a sadistic Egyptian slave master. Another diversion involved singing "Blitzstein and Bernstein" to various melodies, including the Allegretto tune from Beethoven's Seventh Symphony, "to see," as Burton Bernstein recalled, "which '-stein' would come out last and thus on top." In a 1963 marginal comment in his holograph score to Bernstein's 1952 opera, *Trouble in Tahiti*, Blitzstein himself remembered one version of this game, played to the Mexican jarabe from Copland's *Billy the Kid*, in which his name came out last, adding that Bernstein "would of course reverse the order of the names in the last line." (When oral historian Vivian Perlis brought this marginalia to Bernstein's attention in 1983, he remarked, "it's cute to see that Marc would say that I 'of course' would change the order so it would come out with me. . . . well, that says something about a tangle of egos, doesn't it.")[47]

The two composers took a helpful interest in each other's work. Blitzstein counseled Bernstein about *Trouble in Tahiti* and other matters (including the notion, floated in 1952, of an opera about Eva Perón), and even wrote dummy lyrics to the tune that became "Somewhere" from *West Side Story* ("There goes what's-his-name/Unhappy what's his name./I've been wondering who's to blame?/Who's to blame? Huh?"). Blitzstein, on his part, regretted a missed opportunity to play *Reuben Reuben* for Bernstein "since there was a lot I needed decisions about." Recalled Bernstein, "We were good about telling what was wrong with each other's work." Bernstein, who premiered three of Blitzstein's most important works—*The Cradle* (in its orchestral version), the *Airborne Symphony*, and his adaptation of *The Threepenny Opera*—dedicated *Trouble in Tahiti* (1952) to Blitzstein, who in turn dedicated *Six Elizabethan Songs* (1958) to Bernstein.[48]

Their relationship further encompassed a network of friends and family, including Blitzstein's mother-in-law Lina Abarbanell (whom Bernstein found "very happy, gay, charming, affectionate," and whose name he worked into the opening scat chorus from *Trouble in Tahiti*), and Bernstein's wife Felicia (who thought Blitzstein "the most gallant gentleman," and whose impending 1951 marriage to Bernstein drew from Blitzstein, in a letter to Mina Curtiss, this response: "Good or bad, the thing has been simmering for so long a time, I am relieved; let it happen, let him hurt her, her hurt him . . . let them part or not. Hitched or unhitched, they will be through and un-itched, as Cole Porter might have written"). The Bernsteins made Blitzstein godfather to their first child, daughter Jamie (b. 1952), and named their younger children, Alexander (b. 1955) and Nina (b. 1962), after heroines (Alexandra and Nina) from two of his theater works.[49]

Blitzstein clearly respected Bernstein's work, and over the years, he arguably absorbed something of its warmth and vitality. He especially liked the *Serenade* (1954), writing to the composer, "It is just the finest work you ever wrote, and haunts me all the time." At the same time, he often expressed reservations concerning Bernstein's music, observing in a 1956 Ford Hall Forum address in Boston, for instance, how in the opening chorus of *Trouble in Tahiti*, the composer "achieves a smart satirical touch through highly-technical distortion, and a very solid musical-form, fairly extended for such deliberately facetious material. There is even a tiny reference at the opening to the Schönberg-Webern 12-tone row. It is superlatively clever and cleverness has always been Bernstein's virtue, and occasionally his pitfall." Privately, Blitzstein could be more critical. He described *Trouble in Tahiti* (1952) to friends as "lively musically," but thought the story "dreary" and the composer's lyrics "somewhat inept." And a preview performance of *Wonderful Town* (1953), destined to be "a smash hit," although not his "cup of tea," prompted these remarks to Mina Curtiss:

> Also, he [Bernstein] has been this time rather exorbitant in his demand for lenience in the matter of borrowing. I don't seriously mind when he swipes from me (he has a number, "Quiet Girl," which title I used years ago; but instead of writing *that* song, he has written another of mine: a lullaby I wrote for "No For An Answer")—but, when he calmly grabs the Brahms 2nd Piano Concerto for his "hit," called "Why-oh-why-oh-why-oh, Why-did-I ever-leave Ohio?," I gaga. (I mean gag.)

He had mixed feelings about *West Side Story* (1957) as well, although apparently more with respect to the book and the lyrics than the music.[50]

After Blitzstein's death, Bernstein, for his part, dramatized—in a way some regarded as insensitive—his friend's relative lack of commercial success, speaking of him in a memorial tribute as the author of "a long chain of beautiful work-failures. Never have I seen such glowing failures, all in a row, like falling (but not fallen) angels. You have rushed, singing but orderly, from one failure to another: another, another; always singing." In conversation with Eric Gordon, he also suggested that Blitzstein strove to be antiromantic against his natural inclinations. But in any event, he maintained great affection for Blitzstein's work, especially *The Cradle* and such songs as "Weep for Me," "Zipperfly," and "Musky and Whisky." And in 1975, he expressed deep appreciation for Blitzstein's influence "not just on me, but on American musical theater in general," which, at least in his case, he compared to Copland's importance in the field of concert music. "I was tremendously influenced by Marc in everything I wrote for the theater and even some things that weren't," he stated, mentioning the *Mass* in particular.[51]

Bernstein regarded this influence as twofold, citing first, Blitzstein's use of popular song form as a building block for the creation of extended pieces, and second, his remarkable prosody: "Marc was and still is, as far as I'm concerned, the greatest master of the setting of the American language to music." As an example, he discussed the opening of the "Moll's Lament," noting that the word "my" in the phrase "Goin up to my room" lands on an unexpected accent and a sharp dissonance: "And in that combination of wrong note and wrong accent . . . you get the whole sense of the wrongness and illiterateness and helplessness of this girl." (Composer Wallingford Riegger conversely took Blitzstein and other contemporaries to task for just such "undue stress of length given to unimportant words or syllables," saying, "It ain't natural!") Bernstein's indebtedness, as Blitzstein himself noted, extended to actual borrowings, the best-known example being "Maria," whose main theme almost certainly derived from an instrumental passage in *Regina* (with the return of the verse at the song's end also echoing one of Blitzstein's favored formal devices).[52]

Differences between Bernstein and Blitzstein naturally could be discerned along with similarities. In his 1964 text, *Music in a New Found Land*, dedicated "to Aaron Copland and to the memory of Marc Blitzstein," Wilfrid Mellers highlighted such contrasts, deeming Bernstein's "Maria" and "One Hand, One Heart" glamorized versions of such Blitzstein numbers as "What Will It Be?" and "Gus and Sadie Love Song," and stating, "Blitzstein, in 'purifying the dialect of the tribe,' creates works which are related to musical comedy but could not be mistaken for it; Bernstein, in writing a musical comedy, cannot entirely avoid capitulation to commercial values." In Mellers's estimation, Gershwin and Blitzstein, better than Menotti and Bernstein, and more like Copland, Ellington, Carter, and Cage, embodied the hope for what poet Lawrence Ferlinghetti called "a new rebirth of wonder." David Jenness and Don Velsey similarly deemed Blitzstein's songs "more personal, more authentic, than the far more successful songs of Bernstein's later (post-1950) songwriting career." On the other hand, composer Ned Rorem, comparing the relationship of Blitzstein and Bernstein to that between Thomson and Copland, wrote in 1993, "Although Lenny Bernstein would never have been quite what he was without the firm example of Marc Blitzstein, there's nothing Marc did that Lenny didn't do better."[53]

In 1941, Blitzstein prepared a five-part suite of *The Cradle Will Rock* for singers and orchestra, which premiered on March 7 at the Philadelphia Academy of Music at a benefit concert for the Committee for People's Rights commemorating the 150th anniversary of the Bill of Rights. Joseph Levine led members of the New Center of Music Chamber Orchestra, the Philadelphia Opera Company, and the New Theatre Acting Company in an "inspired performance" of this "effective" and "powerful" suite, reported Arthur Bronson in the *Philadelphia Record*. Alas, Blitzstein's hopes to have this suite recorded went unrealized.[54]

In the fall of 1947, Leonard Bernstein, now a well-known conductor and composer, presented a more ample concert reading of the work at New York City Center as the final offering of his third mini-season with the New York City Symphony, with which he had premiered Blitzstein's *Airborne Symphony* the year before. The cast featured Howard Da Silva and Will Geer in the roles they had created ten years earlier, along with Estelle Loring (Moll), Shirley Booth (Mrs. Mister), and Muriel Smith (Ella Hammer). Da Silva, who also directed, adapted the Mercury's oratorio version, although without intermission and with the small orchestra on stage. As at Harvard, Bernstein announced scenes and played the Clerk. Presented on November 24 and 25, and December 1, these performances, dedicated to the League of Composers on its twenty-fifth anniversary, played to packed houses.[55]

The widely reviewed opening night represented the work's official orchestral premiere, so several notices paid special attention to the orchestration. Virgil Thomson, who a decade earlier had found the "orchestral accompaniment . . . of a rare finesse," now opined that "the orchestra added little musically," but others agreed with Louis Biancolli that the "use of the orchestra served to point up Mr. Blitzstein's blistering technique in heightening the mood of word and action." Some further thought the opera the product of a simpler time—Cecil Smith went so far as to call it "adolescent"—but many found it effective in any case. "There it stands," concluded Olin Downes. "Regardless of theory, point of view or propaganda, it strikes home over the footlights. It has genius." A few reviews even welcomed the piece as particularly refreshing given the nation's current political climate. "In a year when the Left in general, and the labor movement in particular, is under attack," wrote Virgil Thomson, "it is important that the Left should put its best foot forward. There is no question, moreover, but that the Left's best foot is its Leftest foot." In any event, opening night brought down the house, receiving, reported the *New York Post*, "a thunderous tribute such as you hear perhaps once or twice a season."[56]

Such success helped spark interest in the work among several producers, who agreed though that an off-Broadway production by the New Theatre slated to begin previews on December 20 posed a major disincentive for reviving the piece on Broadway. After much coaxing, Blitzstein, possibly assisted by associates in communist circles (the *Times* alluded to "political friends"), persuaded the New Theatre to cancel their planned production and defer to producer Michael Myerberg, who presented the opera in his own house, the 1,075-seat Mansfield Theatre on West 47th Street (later, the Brooks Atkinson), for its second and to date last Broadway run. Directed by Da Silva, the cast resembled that for the City Center performance, including Will Geer, Estelle Loring, and Muriel Smith, although Alfred Drake (who had played Curly to Da Silva's Jud in *Oklahoma!* and who later in 1948 would star in the first production of *Kiss Me, Kate*) portrayed Larry Foreman, and Vivian Vance (best remembered as Ethel Mertz in the television series *I Love Lucy*) took on the role of Mrs. Mister. Leonard Bernstein conducted the first three performances, after which the work's musical director Howard Shanet assumed the podium. The production followed along the lines of that at City Center, with onstage orchestra and without intermission.[57]

Opening night on December 26 brought mostly favorable reviews, led by the *Times*'s Brooks Atkinson, who wrote, "the extraordinary vitality of 'The Cradle Will Rock' derives from the vigorous eloquence of the score, the sharp bite of the lyrics and the graphic simplicity of the production. . . . At the moment it is impossible to recall another musical drama so candid, so original and so fresh in stage conception." George Freedley also praised the music, writing of the orchestration in particular, "When you hear it with the full musical score rather than the original single piano, you have a chance to realize just how important a composer for the theater is Mr. Blitzstein." But some disliked the piece, with dissenting voices coming from both sides of the political spectrum: on the right, John Chapman called the piece "loud, cheap, unfair and pinko," and George Jean Nathan lambasted it as "baloney," while on the left, in an otherwise good review, O. V. Clyde criticized its "cosmopolitan air" and suggested that the work might have benefited from greater use of the "blues traditions of the unknown Negro."[58]

After twenty-one performances at the Mansfield, David Lowe brought the opera, now with an intermission, to the 1,890-seat Broadway Theatre on Broadway and West 53rd Street, where it eked out another thirteen performances before closing on February 7 for a total of thirty-four performances. Lowe tried to improve business by issuing two-for-one coupons, but ticket sales floundered nonetheless. Given the stellar cast (including Edward Bryce, who won a 1948 Theatre World Award for his performance as the Gent and Bugs) and the many fine reviews, so short a run surprised observers, who in retrospect regarded the appearance of Atkinson's notice on a Saturday a distinct disadvantage. But Blitzstein proved unpredictable that way, with the enthusiastic response of prominent critics and numerous friends rarely translating into commercial success.[59]

Beginning May 20, 1950, the Freedom House Players gave a few performances in various Miami venues; taking a leaf from the City Center and Mansfield productions, producer-director Tally Brown cast an African American, Lenora Braynon, as Ella Hammer, thereby advancing interracial theater in the South. And on June 22, 1951, the Unity Theatre presented what seems to have been the work's London premiere. Produced and directed by John Spag, the opera elicited positive reviews from a number of papers, including the London *Daily Worker*, which deemed it "a world classic," and the *Hatfield and Potters Bar Gazette*, which found it encouraging that the "exported 'American Way of Life' has critics in the States as well as abroad."[60]

In early 1960, the New York City Opera offered a short run of the work, beginning February 11, as part of an annual series of American operas established by artistic director Julius Rudel that had featured Blitzstein's *Regina* over the previous two seasons. Besides coaching the actors, the composer slightly altered the libretto (including setting the action back to 1931) and presumably prepared or at least approved the abbreviated version of Professor Mamie's solo. "I suppose certain aspects of it will seem dated, just as certain aspects of Ibsen's 'Ghosts' seem dated," he told the *Times*. "But it doesn't occur to me that one shouldn't give 'Ghosts.'" Da Silva, who directed, staged a yet more elaborate version of the original Mercury production, with sets by David Hays, costumes by Ruth Morley, choreography by Billy Parsons, and the pit orchestra led by Lehman Engel, who had last conducted the piece at the Federal Theatre dress rehearsal over twenty years earlier. In what had by now become a tradition, the conductor also played the Clerk; otherwise, the cast, which included Tammy Grimes (Moll), David Atkinson (Larry Foreman), Craig Timberlake (Mr. Mister), Ruth Kobart (Mrs. Mister), and Jane A. Johnston (Ella Hammer), sat stage rear in bleachers. Originally slated for four performances, the City Opera added an extra performance by popular demand.[61]

Although the critics widely praised the production, several found fault with the work itself, under special scrutiny because of City Opera sponsorship. Paul Henry Lang (*Herald Tribune*), for instance, dismissed the piece as "a sort of vaudeville, at times of a very low grade," some weeks later expanding on the notion of the incompatibility between the work's "representation of social conflict" and the operatic genre: "The great gestures as well as the quiet vibrations of the soul which make for true opera cannot be conjured up by social realism." The work, agreed Winthrop Sargeant (*New Yorker*), wasted the City Opera's precious resources, "and therefore ought to be left to Broadway (if Broadway wants it)." But even the more tepid reviews generally acknowledged that the piece "still packs a wallop" and admitted in any case that the audience responded with loud cheers and whistles, as documented by an archival recording of the production. "When warmer more enthusiastic responses are heard, I want to be there!" wrote producer Harold Prince "admiringly" to the composer. Blitzstein himself found that he still liked the piece, "all except the jokes," as he wrote to George Freedley, "which I find atrocious. They couldn't have been any better in 1937."[62]

Some notices, incidentally, made comparisons—mostly unflattering—to *The Threepenny Opera*, now better-known, ironically enough, thanks to Blitzstein's hit adaptation. But Harold Clurman (*Nation*), who along with Harriett Johnson (*New York Post*) and Howard Taubman (*New York Times*) penned one of the more thoroughly sympathetic reviews, observed subtle differences, describing the "particular quality" of *The Cradle* as characterized by "a certain permanent American big-city young-man cockiness, a derisive unwillingness to take any guff—political, social or casual—from anybody.... The music alternates between a note of vulgar guying and sweet, heartbroken yearning. Blitzstein is less sophisticated than his German models; more acid in anger, more tearful in hurt."[63]

Evidencing the centrality of *The Cradle* to Blitzstein's career, friends and associates staged a near-complete reading of the piece as the second half of a memorial concert in the composer's honor at Philharmonic Hall at Lincoln Center on April 19, 1964. The all-star cast featured Howard Da Silva (Larry Foreman), Will Geer (Mr. Mister), and Hiram Sherman (Reverend Salvation) of the original production along with Barbara Harris (Moll), Betty Comden (Mrs. Mister), Adolph Green (Dauber), Phyllis Newman (Sister Mister), and Charles Nelson Reilly (Junior Mister). Da Silva staged the work and Leonard Bernstein narrated and accompanied at the piano, as Blitzstein had done on the Musicraft recording. This superb performance, preserved on tape, holds many points of interest, including Bernstein's dynamic interpretation of the score, and performances by Geer and Sherman in roles long associated with them but never before recorded, all in the heightened atmosphere of public mourning for the composer, with Geer and Da Silva teasing from the work a buffo humor that suggested some continuity between on the one hand, Mr. Mister and Larry Foreman, and on the other, Don Giovanni and Leporello.

Following Blitzstein's death, productions of *The Cradle* continued to appear with some regularity, typically performed by such small companies as the Lyric Theater of New York (1978), The Acting Company (1983, 1984, 1985), Blank Theatre Company (1994, 2011), American Century Theater (1999), Jean Cocteau Repertory Theatre (2000), New Line Theatre (2001), Downtown Music Productions (2009, 2010), Theater Ten Ten (2010), and Mad Cow Theatre (2010), or by drama groups associated with colleges and universities, including Harvard (1969, 2002), UCLA (1981), Georgetown (2003), Emerson (2005), North Carolina at Chapel Hill (2005), Ohio State (2006), Whitworth (2008), Northwestern University (2009), New York University (2010), Missouri State (2010), Puget Sound (2010), the New School (2011), Vassar (2011), Syracuse University (2011), and Weber State (2012). Appearing in London at the Battersea Arts Centre Opera Festival (1997) and the Arcola Theatre (2010), the opera also made its way to the Continent, where sung in English, it received its first performances in Germany (Recklinghausen, 1984) and France (Douai, 2004).[64]

These and other productions involved a wide array of notable talent. Jerry Orbach, for example, played Larry Foreman in a 1964 production at Theater Four directed by Howard Da Silva, with Gershon Kingsley at the piano. And the Acting Company production, which toured the country before arriving at the Old Vic in London in 1985, starred Patti LuPone (as the Moll and Sister Mister) under the direction of John Houseman, who had helped launch the piece nearly fifty years earlier. "The more I rehearse the play, the more I'm convinced it's a remarkably rich work," Houseman told the *Times*. "It makes most other musicals look pale by comparison."[65]

The reviews of these varied stagings largely intimated a continued respect for the work, in particular, the music. Whatever their reservations, virtually all of the notices of the Theater Four production, for instance, emphasized the enduring appeal of the score. Reviewing the 1978 Lyric Theater revival, Andrew Porter, who saw the opera as fulfilling Carlo Goldoni's definition of comedy as "created to correct vice and to ridicule bad customs" as opposed to merely providing laughs, stated, "The opera remains undated, no mere period piece, for two reasons: the audience can still recognize the characters portrayed, in themselves or in others; and Blitzstein's music is powerfully affecting." In a review of the Acting Company production, Porter's colleague at the *New Yorker*, Edith Oliver, found that the "fresh and melodic" music "almost had me on my feet cheering along with the company," while Irving Wardle, covering the same production for the *London Times*, described the score as "theatre music *par excellence*." And discussing the Downtown Music Productions's staged concert reading, Anthony Tommasini (*New York Times*) praised Blitzstein's brash use of popular styles "while still displaying a keen ear for the modernist musical languages of his day." In contrast, after attending the Acting Company's production, Samuel Lipman, publisher of the neoconservative *New Criterion*, deemed the work "an artistic failure," mostly because of its message, but also because as opposed to Weill, the music "passes by the ears hardly noticed."[66]

In 1964, CBS Television presented excerpts of the Theater Four production on an episode of *Camera Three*, and in 1986, PBS Television aired an Acting Company performance of the work as part of its series *America's Musical Theater*. Cast albums of the Theater Four, Acting Company, and Blank Theatre Company productions also appeared, greatly enriching a discography that previously had consisted essentially of the far-from-complete original cast album and the Spoken Arts recording, *Marc Blitzstein and his Theatre Compositions* (1956), with the composer accompanying Evelyn Lear, Roddy McDowall, Jane Connell, and Alvin Epstein on two excerpts. (Producer George Avakian originally hoped that Columbia Records would record the Theater Four production with Bernstein at the piano, but when Columbia withdrew because of financial complications, MGM Records released the piece with Gershon Kingsley, a recording reissued by CRI in 1972.) All three cast albums tweaked the dialogue and cut a few musical passages, including, in the Acting Company recording, some of Professor Mamie's solo— by this time, a longstanding practice. The performers also executed the work's rhythmic recitations with variable precision, the more exact renderings proving the more effective. And finally, the pianists, faced with the challenge of reproducing the reduced score with a mere two hands, made different decisions about what to play.[67]

In the early 1980s, producer Michael Fitzgerald decided to make a film about the work's famous premiere after composer Alex North played for him Blitzstein's recorded account of the event. Fitzgerald subsequently commissioned Ring Lardner Jr., one of the more defiant members of the Hollywood Ten, to write the screenplay, and Orson Welles to direct. As Welles began work on the project in the course of 1984, he ditched Lardner's screenplay, *Rocking the Cradle*, in favor of his own, *The Cradle Will Rock*, which focused less on the work than on Welles and his relationships with others, including the composer. Unfortunately, Fitzgerald and his associates could not raise the necessary capital to produce the film.[68]

However, a picture about the opera's famous premiere written and directed by Tim Robbins, *Cradle Will Rock*, appeared in 1999. Adding various subplots, including one about Diego Rivera's Rockefeller Plaza mural *Man at the Crossroads* and another about Congressional investigations into the Federal Theatre Project, the film ingeniously mirrored the opera's theme of prostitution by way of vignettes involving a rich assortment of characters played by an illustrious cast, including Hank Azaria as a somewhat bewildered Blitzstein haunted by his deceased wife and Brecht, who serve as his muses. Even while acknowledging the era's contradictions, the film ultimately celebrated a time in which artists created a democratic groundswell for work that challenged vested political and economic interests, a perspective dramatized at the conclusion of the film with the image of a contemporary Times Square emblazoned with corporate logos.

By his own admission, Robbins "bent some facts and manipulated some dates," including having the 1934 demolition of the Rivera mural, the 1937 premiere of *The Cradle*, and the 1938 testimony of Hallie Flanagan all climactically coincide. The film also fictionalized some aspects of the *Cradle* story, such as portraying Olive Stanton (Emily Watson) not as a sophisticated and talented actress whose poetry had appeared in the *New Yorker*, but as a homeless naïf. The notion that Blitzstein's homosexuality precluded Communist Party membership seemed particularly specious, given the fact that many homosexuals joined the party, including in 1938 the composer himself. The film further took liberties with the opera, presenting snippets of various songs—with more complete versions, including Audra McDonald singing "Joe Worker," on the released soundtrack—as scored and performed in a more or less commercialized manner under the supervision of the director's brother, co-producer David Robbins, who also provided the film's original vaudeville-flavored music. (The picture's final credits in addition featured vocalist P. J. Harvey singing "Nickel Under the Foot," the music recast into a modal rock idiom.) During the reenactment of the opera's premiere, the film has Larry Foreman (John Turturro) perform "Leaflets!" without any musical accompaniment whatsoever. In attempting to make Blitzstein's opera negotiable to a contemporary movie audience, the filmmakers to some extent subverted their own message. Jason Sherman's play *It's All True*, a backstage drama about the premiere presented by the Necessary Angel Theatre Company at Toronto's Tarragon Theatre on December 31, 1998, and revised the following year, took this approach to an extreme by featuring new music by Don Horsburgh in lieu of the original score.[69]

Such nonchalance with regard to the score substantiated Michael Denning's observation that the work's "legendary" premiere often overshadowed "the musical itself," a phenomenon also related to a critical tradition, as represented recently by Joseph Swain and Ethan Mordden, that presumed that the work's interest depended more on its colorful history than on any intrinsic merit. At the same time, a number of commentators held to the work's timeless qualities. In

1964, Gerald Weales, for instance, contended that "the opera works as art in a decade in which its propaganda is no longer immediate." That same year, Howard Da Silva said on television, "There is about Marc such a passion, that he felt so deeply about his time, that he was able to glean the essence from his time, of all time." In 1969, H. Wiley Hitchcock wrote that revivals of the opera suggested "that it was not so much the message as the music that was significant in Blitzstein's art." Stated Copland in 1976, "He [Blitzstein] was passionately desirous of really giving a message to the audience, and a message that would have some kind of permanent form and that would always be true no matter what the social situation. So he was trying to both take advantage of the scene in which he was living, and also the larger frame of a work which could continue in interest through the years because of its musical quality." In 1997, Geoffrey Block concluded that, whatever its reputation as "cult musical, historical footnote, and agent of social change," *The Cradle* deserved greater recognition as "a work of musical theater art." And in 2010, Chris Hedges, examining the work in the context of a "liberal class" threatened by both its ostracisation of radical dissent and its subservience to corporate power, found its lessons all the more urgent in the early twenty-first century. Indeed, as the Occupy protests against economic injustice erupted in New York and elsewhere around the country in late 2011, the opera struck such commentators as Erin Scialabba, reviewing a Syracuse University production, as "wildly resonant."[70]

Meanwhile, the work's musical and dramatic meanings and subtleties awaited further study. A deeper appreciation of the piece plainly would benefit from more performances of the opera fully staged, including use of the original orchestration, than the relatively few it has yet received. For notwithstanding the fact that the circumstances surrounding its premiere have made for a fabled reputation, and that modest stagings of the work have proved not only useful but to some even preferable to more elaborate ones, it might be argued nonetheless that the government delivered the opera a blow from which the piece has yet to fully recover.[71]

11

From *The Spanish Earth* (1937)
to *Danton's Death* (1939)

In the 1930s, a school of progressive American motion picture documentarians arose based largely in New York, with such directors as Leo Hurwitz, Joris Ivens, Pare Lorentz, Ralph Steiner, Paul Strand, and Willard Van Dyke creating work comparable to that of Broadway's socially conscious playwrights, and such co-operatives as the Workers' Film and Photo League, Nykino, and Frontier Films fulfilling functions analogous to the day's theater collectives. Like Thomson and Copland, Blitzstein became a favored composer among these filmmakers, and in the years following *The Cradle*, having already worked with Steiner on *Surf and Seaweed* (1931), he collaborated with Ivens on *The Spanish Earth* (1937), Van Dyke on *Valley Town* (1940), and Hurwitz and Strand on *Native Land* (1942).

Before arriving in early 1936 in the United States, where he lived for some ten years before returning to Europe, the outstanding Dutch filmmaker Joris Ivens (1898–1989) spent time in the Soviet Union, where he collaborated with composer Hanns Eisler on the docudrama *Song of Heroes* (1932). After the Spanish Civil War erupted in the summer of 1936, pitting the leftist Republican government (the Loyalists), supported by Stalin, against right-wing rebels under Francisco Franco (the Nationalists), supported by Hitler and Mussolini, Ivens worked with his longtime editor Helen van Dongen on a pro-Loyalist short, *Spain and the Fight for Freedom*, based on existing newsreels; but dissatisfied with the results, he welcomed writer Archibald MacLeish's proposal that he travel to Spain to shoot his own footage for another picture about the war. Provided with a few thousand dollars raised by a sponsoring committee, Contemporary Historians, Inc., that included MacLeish, John Dos Passos, Lillian Hellman, Ernest Hemingway, Clifford Odets, Dorothy Parker, and Herman Shumlin, Ivens arrived in early 1937 in Spain, where he worked with cameraman Johnny Ferno (Fernhout) and writers Hemingway and Dos Passos. The film crew received some reimbursement for their efforts, but no salaries, with any profits from the enterprise earmarked for the Loyalist cause.[1]

Once in Spain, Ivens realized that the scenario provided him by Contemporary Historians needed a thorough overhaul, although he retained the idea of focusing on a village involved in an irrigation project along the strategically important highway connecting Madrid with Valencia, the Republic's provisional capital. Selecting the town of Fuentedueña for this purpose, Ivens followed events there and in Madrid, as well as on the front lines, exploring the interdependency between agrarian reform and military defense as embodied by Julian, a villager serving in the Republican army. Ivens so assumed sympathy for Republican Spain that neither he nor Hemingway, who wrote the film's commentary, placed the struggle in historical context, a perceived lapse that bothered even such Loyalist supporters as Hellman and Eleanor Roosevelt. "My only answer," stated Ivens, "was that a documentary film maker has to have an opinion on such vital issues as fascism or anti-fascism—he *has* to have feelings about these issues, if his work is to have any dramatic or emotional or art value."[2]

Back in New York in May, Ivens worked on the documentary with van Dongen, who helped edit the film; CBS Radio's Irving Reis, who created the sound effects; and Orson Welles, who spoke the narration. Concerning the music, Ivens consulted with Blitzstein as well as with Virgil Thomson, who recently had written the music for Pare Lorentz's documentary about soil erosion, *The Plow that Broke the Plains* (1936), and accepted their offer to compile a soundtrack from recordings of popular Spanish music, an idea no doubt particularly congenial to Thomson, whose documentary scores often employed arrangements of popular and folk tunes.

This collaboration between Blitzstein and Thomson marked a growing rapport between the two men. In previous years, both Blitzstein and his wife had spoken disparagingly about Thomson's work—Thomson even referred to Eva's review of his 1935 one-man concert at the New School as a "hatchet job"—and the two composers also had clashed over the Siegmeister-Pettis affair in early 1936, as discussed. But Thomson's developing affiliation with the political left and his appreciative response to *The Cradle* presumably helped bring them closer.[3]

Blitzstein and Thomson listened to "dozens of records," some of which Ivens had brought back from Spain, but others belonging to artist Gerald Murphy and composer Paul Bowles. Ivens simply described this repertoire as "Spanish folk music," but Thomson more precisely cited "choral numbers sung by Galician and Basque miners, woodwind *coblas* [bands] from Barcelona, and naturally lots of flamenco from Seville. Actually we used flamenco only once, for accompanying a view of the rightists; it did not seem sincere enough for dour Castilian farmers or for republican soldiers." (Thomson and Blitzstein presumably knew that Franco had co-opted flamenco as a symbol of Nationalist pride.) The film also utilized recordings of the Republican anthem "El himno de Riego," heard periodically throughout the film, and assorted military music, including the Italian Fascist marching song "Giovinezza," heard in conjunction with images of fallen Italian airmen.[4]

On one level a cost-saving measure, the use of recordings also represented an intriguing novelty in that it formed something of an aural equivalent to the director's found image. Thomson spoke of the film, in this context, as "completely documentary, since its views of Spain's patient people and high-lying farmland are accompanied throughout by the real music of that land and people. There may be other filmed narratives as authentic; I do not know them. Certainly there are few of such distinguished authorship." Although such thoroughgoing reliance on recordings naturally proved limiting, it actually helped endear the score to George Antheil, who in a review of the film wrote, "every intelligent human being is well fed up with the literal method of Hollywood underscoring." Discerning a similar approach in Shostakovich's music for the Soviet film *Alone*, Antheil thought, however, that whereas "the entire 'opposition' of the Shostakovich score is magnificently and completely articulate," in *The Spanish Earth*, the "score plays against its picture in an odd way" and "merely strings along." Still, he remained "sympathetic to the attempt."[5]

Antheil underestimated the extent to which the production team in fact coordinated image and sound. Ivens himself drew attention to Julian's homecoming, in which he strove to achieve "an overall emotional warmth" by synchronizing close-ups of Julian's various family members with different phrases of a joyful chorus, including Julian's embrace of his father at the number's climactic refrain. "Marc, Helen and I had to measure these close-ups very delicately in relation to the phases of the song and in relation to the affection one hoped to awake in the audience towards these people" (a comment that also points to Blitzstein taking a more active role than Thomson in the making of the film, as does another remark by Ivens: "We had a wonderful team with Marc, Irving and Helen working closely together"). Ivens and his collaborators similarly employed the sundry instrumental and vocal numbers, including reprises, in order to help frame larger patterns of form and mood.[6]

In her study of the soundtrack, Carol Hess noted the extensive presence above all of the *sardana*, a Catalonian circle-dance typically performed by small wind bands, and argued that, given the regional conflicts besetting Spain at the time, the predominance of Catalonian music in a picture set in Castille "subverts the utopia evoked onscreen." Since Thomson—and presumably Blitzstein—knew that the music came from different regions of Spain, they might have intended such diversity to enhance the film's theme of national unity. At any rate, the prevalence of the *sardana* might have been one reason, as Hess suggests, that the film's Spanish version used different music.[7]

After Ivens completed the documentary in June, Martha Gellhorn—Hemingway's future wife and a friend of Eleanor Roosevelt's—arranged for a July 8 screening at the White House attended by the Roosevelts, Ivens, Gellhorn, Hemingway, and the WPA's Harry Hopkins. Later that month, Ivens also showed the film at private homes and at Philharmonic Auditorium in Los Angeles before returning to New York for the official opening. Prior to this premiere, Ivens decided that the richness of Welles's voice clashed with "the actuality of the film" and had Hemingway rerecord the narration. "This sincere, direct commentary spoken simply by its nonprofessional speaker-author has since had great influence on other American and English commentaries of documentary films," claimed Ivens in his memoirs. For this rerecorded narration, after the line, "For fifty years we've wanted to irrigate," Hemingway added, in response to a suggestion from Franklin Roosevelt, "but *they* held us back."[8]

The Spanish Earth officially premiered at New York's 55th Street Playhouse on August 20, 1937. The picture received some dismissive notices but some glowing ones as well, not only from the *Daily Worker* and the *New Masses*, as might be expected, but from such mainstream organs as the *New York Herald Tribune*, who called it "the most powerful and moving documentary film ever screened," with a "brilliant musical accompaniment."[9]

In part because of its graphic images of war dead, but probably more because of its Loyalist sympathies, distribution of the film faced various obstacles, including bans in certain municipalities. The documentary nonetheless found a distributor, Prometheus Pictures, who managed to place it in hundreds of theaters around the country. It also traveled to Europe, including Great Britain, where local censors deleted references to German and Italian intervention; and France, where director Jean Renoir narrated a French translation of Hemingway's commentary. The film did not help to reverse America's policy of nonintervention as Ivens and his collaborators had hoped, but it at least raised thousands of dollars for ambulances for Republican Spain.[10]

Blitzstein continued to support in other ways the Loyalist cause, a touchstone for the people's front and one of the defining political events in the composer's life: he entertained at a December 7, 1937, fundraiser for the Medical Bureau to Aid Spanish Democracy in Philadelphia; he donated a manuscript of *The Cradle* for a March 25, 1938, auction at the Barbizon-Plaza Hotel (he similarly contributed the musical manuscript of *I've Got the Tune* for a February 20, 1939, auction at the Hotel Delmonico to assist German refugees); and he participated in two fundraisers at the Mecca Temple—a "Stars for Spain" benefit on December 11, 1938, and a revue organized for the release of international prisoners in Spain on February 25, 1939. Even after the civil war ended, he joined in another "Stars for Spain" event at the Mecca Temple on December 10, 1939; a concert for the Spanish Children's Relief Fund on May 8, 1940; premiered his opera *No for an Answer* on January 5, 1941, as a benefit for Spanish refugees incarcerated in French camps; and as late as May 11, 1947, took part in a musical salute to honor and aid Spanish exiles.

Meanwhile, although they never became intimates, Blitzstein and Thomson maintained a solid working relationship. Appointed charter members of the American Composers Alliance (ACA) soon after its founding in late 1937, they actively participated in this group—one dedicated to serving the needs of the nation's serious composers—until both men's membership with the American Society for

Composers, Authors, and Publishers (ASCAP), a performance-rights organization that Blitzstein joined in early 1939, created conflicts that necessitated their withdrawal from the alliance in the 1940s. And in 1938, they banded with Copland and conductor Lehman Engel in establishing the Arrow Press, Inc., with Engel president, Blitzstein and Thomson vice-presidents, and Copland secretary-treasurer. A nonprofit co-operative, Arrow published musical scores partly with funds raised by composers, who would receive, however, virtually all proceeds from sales and performing rights of their work. Taking over the Cos Cob catalog as well, a similar but more completely philanthropic enterprise founded in 1929 by Alma Morgenthau Wertheim, Arrow distributed scores through a sister agency, the American Music Center, established in 1939. Over the years, Arrow Press disseminated a wide range of American music, including some works by the officers themselves—at entirely their own expense—as well as important scores by Charles Ives and others.[11]

Blitzstein helped decide what the press should publish and otherwise retained his leadership position within the organization until Boosey & Hawkes purchased the Arrow–Cos Cob catalog in 1958. That he himself published nothing aside from the short choral work, "Invitation to Bitterness," under the Arrow imprimatur suggests a strong and disinterested support for American music, however much he regarded many of his colleagues as quite often on the wrong track.

Blitzstein's next dramatic work, the radio opera *I've Got the Tune* (1937), addressed this very issue of the composer's role in society. Written for the *Columbia Workshop*, an experimental CBS Radio series, this commission likely came about through the composer's association with Irving Reis, with whom he had collaborated on *The Spanish Earth* and who had founded the workshop in 1936. The composer's August 12, 1937, contract specified a half-hour "musical dramatic work . . . suitable for radio broadcasting" that employed no more than nine principals, twelve choristers, and a chamber orchestra of twenty-four pieces. (Blitzstein ultimately used seven principals and an orchestra virtually identical to the one itemized by the contract, although he added a harp and made do with one less trumpet.) The contract further specified a delivery date of October 3 and a fee of $500, with an extra $150 for each additional performance.[12]

Blitzstein completed the score at his new Greenwich Village residence at 496 Hudson Street, where he lived from 1937 to 1940. He alternately labeled the piece a "radio play with music" and a "radio song-play," the latter phrase apparently derived from the word "songspiel" as used by Brecht and Weill, but he and others often referred to the piece more simply as a "radio opera" as well.

In the 1930s, radio held a central place in American life, with tens of millions spending hours each day listening to a variety of broadcasts, including the airing of new musical compositions. Under the leadership of Davidson Taylor, CBS took a leading role with regard to the latter, initiating the Columbia Composers Commissions, which in its initial 1937 season premiered orchestral works by Copland,

Howard Hanson, Roy Harris, Walter Piston, and William Grant Still, as well as an opera by Louis Gruenberg, *Green Mansions*, that debuted on October 17, a mere week before *I've Got the Tune*. By the time interest in new serious music written specifically for radio had run its course in America in the 1950s, native composers had produced over fifty radio operas, of which Blitzstein's *I've Got the Tune* (1937) and Menotti's *The Old Maid and the Thief* (1939) proved the most durable.[13]

I've Got the Tune unfolds in five scenes as follows:

Scene one. As they walk up Broadway, composer Mr. Musiker (Otto Musiker in sketches) interviews Beetzie, a stenographer, about her references. (Beetzie's claim that her typing record of 145 words a minute is "only seven words less than the record, which was made by Billy Rose—And I guess you know who's Billy Rose!" alludes to the famous Broadway producer's early career as a champion stenographer.) Musiker wants Beetzie to accompany him on a search for the person who will provide a meaningful setting for a tune he's written ("Every Measure Note for Note"). "It sounds perfectly screwy to me," comments Beetzie as they leave for their first stop, Madame Arbutus's penthouse apartment on Park Avenue.

Scene two. Madame Arbutus from Stuttgart, a self-described "priestess of the new music, the new poetry, the new art," welcomes Mr. Musiker and Beetzie to her salon and describes her ecstatic creative process ("On Scotch and Art"). When Musiker attempts to play his melody for her, she interrupts, saying, "I have added some complications. Now it is frightful lovely, frightful beautiful," and performs her own modernist rendition of the tune ("The Moon Is a Happy Cheese Tonight"), in the midst of which she exclaims, "Ah! it is so grand to be so bored! You can afford the kind of music you cannot stand." "Let's get out of here!" Musiker tells Beetzie.

Scene three. Mr. Musiker and Beetzie hide behind some bushes in the woods and observe Captain Bristlepunkt and his followers induct a new recruit, Private Aloysius Schnook, into their secret order, the Purple Shirties. After the latter sing their anthem, a version of Musiker's tune articulated by the sounds of artillery ("How Peaceful Is Our Captain!"), they begin their initiation ceremony in which the poor Schnook—who signed up in order to retain his business clients—needs to vow death to the "mongrels" who "run the stores and banks in ev'ry town," hold down such a mongrel as the Captain whips him, and finally whip the mongrel himself ("Private Schnook"). After the Shirties reprise their anthem, they flee in terror from an approaching group of school kids.

Scene four. As Mr. Musiker suns himself on a roof with Beetzie, he prevents a Suicide from hurling herself off the building. The Suicide, less than grateful ("And So, the Last Thing Too"), sings her own morose version of Musiker's tune ("There Is a Girl I Know"), and then slips from his grasp to her death.

Scene five. Mr. Musiker and Beetzie arrive by subway to a busy corner of the city. Having traveled around the world, they recall the tune as performed as a Chinese lullaby, an Italian organ-grinder waltz, a Tin Pan Alley number ("The

Hangover Blues"), and an African war dance. Ready to return to his "ivory tower," Musiker encounters a crowd of high-schoolers celebrating Field Day and singing some familiar leftist songs ("Pie in the Sky," "Hold the Fort," and "Solidarity Forever!"). Eager to have a new tune, the kids collectively adapt Musiker's melody ("Because This Is Our Day"). "This is like a breath of fresh air!" exclaims the composer. "Here's where my tune belongs!" As the high-schoolers sing the completed anthem under the Choral Director, Beetzie joins in ("Well, can't a girl have a little fun?" she asks), and Musiker offers the crowd his tune. "Mister, you can't," a boy replies, "—it's ours already!" The work concludes with the anthem's final quatrain: "Because this is our day! We're singing songs of May! That's why we sing today! Because we'll rule tomorrow, we can sing today!"

The opera's message seems evident enough: the artist eager to overcome his isolation can find purpose by serving the people (marchers) rather than the aesthete (Madame Arbutus), the fascist (Captain Bristlepunkt), or the defeatist (The Suicide). But Blitzstein's sketches help clarify his intentions. For instance, for the final scene, he originally intended not a Field Day parade by high-schoolers at some undesignated location, but a May Day march by workers at Union Square—a traditional forum for communist rallies—which naturally would have given the opera's concluding line an even more radical resonance. Blitzstein possibly made this revision in deference to radio censors, who seemed largely untroubled by the work, aside perhaps from a line uttered by Private Schnook, "Then Mister Morgan [J. P. Morgan Jr.] must be a mongrel" (in response to Captain Bristlepunkt's statement about the mongrels on Wall Street), which the original broadcast rendered as "Then Public Utilities must be a mongrel."

Blitzstein's notes and sketches shed further light on the work. For this picaresque story of a quixotic idealist and his earthy sidekick, Blitzstein probably had in mind Don Quixote and Sancho Panza, an idea perhaps suggested by the references to Cervantes in *The Spanish Earth* (he even considered a male for the Beetzie part, as apparently he did for The Suicide—perhaps in the latter instance to deflect the obvious resemblance to Eva); but some drafts refer to Beetzie as Gracie, suggesting another prototype for Mr. Musiker and Beetzie, namely, the popular radio comedy team of George Burns and Gracie Allen. Indeed, Beetzie's lines plainly evoke Gracie Allen (after Musiker sings his tune for her and asks how she likes it, she responds, "O, I'm not a critic, Mr. Musiker, just a secretary trying to get along. Maybe if I heard somebody sing it"), while the comedienne's delivery seems to have influenced that of the original Beetzie, Shirley Booth, as well. Blitzstein's conflation of the "universal" (Quixote and Sancho) and the "vaudevillian" (Burns and Allen) along with the "fantastic" (including the sundry chance encounters) and the "communistic" (as represented by the work's moral) suggests an extension of those diverse viewpoints articulated in the context of *The Traveling Salesman.*

Sketches also reveal that for the salon scene, Blitzstein considered writing a satirical tango that would have targeted a high-society patron called Mrs. Plush modeled after Josephine Crane, who helped found the Museum of Modern Art, and who, reported Paul Bowles, reacted with willful incomprehension when Blitzstein once sang "The Rich" from *The Cradle* at one of her Fifth Avenue soirées. But the scene evolved into a satire of modernism rather by way of Madame Arbutus, whose name intimated her self-appointed role as arbiter (and whose chicken salad referenced a familiar sight at new-music receptions), and a burlesque of Schoenberg's *Pierrot lunaire*, a piece for which the composer actually had considerable admiration.[14]

The Purple Shirties plainly alluded to the Fascist black shirts and the Nazi brown shirts, with Blitzstein at some point Germanizing the Captain's name from Bristlepoint to Bristlepunkt and dubbing their latest recruit after the Yiddish-American word for a dupe, "schnook." That Blitzstein intended the term "mongrel" as a code word for Jew seems clear enough as well, even without citing sketches that mention the Captain's contempt for "the Lewish race" and "the Lew-mongrel Bommunists in our midsts!" (Such circumspection notwithstanding, this scene's psychologically devastating depiction of fascist racism and bloodlust seems remarkably bold for its time, especially for a radio opera.) Other features of the secret order, including the whipping ritual, the skull and bones insignia, and as mentioned in an early script, the robes, further recalled the Black Legion, a native racist group denounced in *The Cradle Will Rock*.

In early scenarios, Blitzstein also planned an additional scene in which Mr. Musiker, on entering the Tin Pan Alley publishing house of Finaigler, Kibitz, and McGuire, would have had some dealings with Finaigler (who in one draft confuses the names Koussevitzky and Toscanini, telling Mr. Musiker, "O, sure, I know you, they played your symphony, or your rhapsody, Koussenini? Toscavitzski? Anyway, Carnegie Hall"). According to one such outline, the publishing firm would have already "swiped his tune," hence the play on the word "finagler" (while the name Kibitz puns a Yiddish phrase that means to give meddlesome advice). In any event, the scene surely would have included yet another variation on Mr. Musiker's tune, this one involving a commercialized version of the melody (a remnant of which survived by way of a snippet of "The Hangover Blues").

Blitzstein rummaged through his composer's trunk for the work, using some ballet music from *Blessings of the Bath* for the opening travel music, and adapting a melody from "Gauley Bridge Tunnel" for Mr. Musiker's tune. (Regarding this melody, Blitzstein thought, in retrospect, that he deserved to have his "fingers smacked" for having Mr. Musiker refer to this music as "the finest tune I ever wrote.") He also considered recycling "Building of the City" from *Cain* for the Purple Shirties episode, and although he decided otherwise, the two scenes bear enough similarities to further highlight continuities in Blitzstein's development.[15]

As mentioned, the opera quotes songs popular among the left—"Pie in the Sky," "Hold the Fort," and "Solidarity Forever!"—in the final scene, all three contrafacta on traditional nineteenth-century hymns. For the most part, Blitzstein set these songs simply, with common triads, along the lines of the April 1937 recordings of such numbers by his friend Mordecai Bauman and the Manhattan Chorus (which he presumably knew). Such plainness dramatically contrasts not only with the music that accompanies the marchers' comments, "And that's an old one, another old one!" but with the climactic setting of Mr. Musiker's tune, "Because This Is Our Day," a rousing anthem reminiscent of Hanns Eisler. This anthem specifically suggests the influence of "The Song of the Peat Bog Soldiers" ("Das Moorsoldatenlied"), a number, adapted by Eisler after a protest song composed in 1933 by inmates of the Börgermoor concentration camp, that Blitzstein alluded to in his sketches for the opera and that seems to have been performed at the March 1935 Mecca Temple concert in honor of Eisler.

Over and above indicating sound effects to simulate bombs, gunfire, and sirens in the Purple Shirties scene and urban street noises elsewhere, Blitzstein tailored the work to the radio medium, writing to himself, "You can make the music do things which explain what would ordinarily take place visually." In a particularly ingenious stroke, he layered some rhythmic speech between Mr. Musiker and Beetzie in the finale with bits of choral music by the high-schoolers heard, as it were, in the distance, neatly giving the impression of a rehearsing chorus in the background (including mis-sung notes and the Director's comment, "No!"). Blitzstein further avoided "the radio problem as such: the making of intense and unmistakable visual images through purely auditory means, or through the mental image," the rationale, perhaps, behind eliminating from the fascist scene Beetzie's line, "Lookit those robes!"

Blitzstein originally wanted to cast the work's dedicatee, Orson Welles, as Mr. Musiker, but as the latter was otherwise occupied, he gave some thought to Mordecai Bauman before deciding to take the part himself—surely a rare instance of a composer performing the lead for a premiere of his own opera. He also considered his mother-in-law Lina Abarbanell for Madame Arbutus, but in the end, Adelaide Klein assumed that role. The other cast members included Shirley Booth (Beetzie), Kenneth (Kenny) Delmar (Captain Bristlepunkt), Norman Lloyd (Private Schnook), Lotte Lenya (The Suicide), and Hiram Sherman (Choral Director)—a distinguished group of actors largely at the start of their careers. Aside from Booth and Lenya, whom Blitzstein surely brought on board, all had worked under Houseman and Welles, either through Project 891 or the Mercury Theatre. Irving Reis directed, Bernard Herrmann conducted, and Davidson Vorhes engineered the sound.

The opera aired live at eight o'clock on Sunday night, October 24, from New York's WABC studio, with Orson Welles, John Houseman, and Kurt Weill in the recording booth, as Norman Lloyd recalled. The work, which barely came in at its allotted half-hour, received little advance notice; the *New York Times* did not even list this "play" as a "leading event" as they did such rival programs as a variety show with Nelson Eddy, Edgar Bergen, and Dorothy Lamour on WEAF and an orchestral concert with conductor Erno Rapee on WJZ. Nonetheless, a number of journals reviewed the broadcast, as did *Scribner's* after the work's release by Musi-craft later in the year.[16]

These notices proved excellent, with Blitzstein's inventive use of the radio medium eliciting special commendation. R. D. Darrell of the *New Masses* and Richard Gilbert in *Scribner's* even deemed the piece more impressive than any of the better-publicized CBS commissions alluded to above. For Gilbert, this involved not only the work's radiogenic qualities, but its potential to reach, in his esti-mation, a vast national radio audience, thanks to its "substance," "vitality," and "comparative simplicity." In contrast, Aaron Copland—one of those CBS com-missioned composers—penned a particularly severe review, observing similar-ities between the opera and the composer's concert work, including the same "hectic, nervous mood" and "preoccupation with form," but discerning "a synthetic quality about it [the opera] that no amount of ingenuity and talent can hide."[17]

On February 6, 1938, *I've Got the Tune* received its first staged performance at the 46th Street Theatre at a benefit concert for the Marxist periodical, the *New Masses*, that also featured the music of Copland, Hanns Eisler, Lehman Engel, Alex North, Paul Bowles, Earl Robinson, Harold Rome, Virgil Thomson, and Count Basie and his Band. Orson Welles, on hand as master of ceremonies, in all likelihood directed the work, staged as a radio show with microphones and sound effects. Performing the score at the piano as well as the role of Mr. Musiker, Blitz-stein shared the stage with Klein, Delmar, and Lloyd of the original cast along with Peggy Coudray (Beetzie), Olive Stanton (The Suicide), and Maynard Hol-mes (Choral Director). In his *New York Times* review, Howard Taubman singled out the work (along with those by Eisler and Copland), declaring the radio opera "compact, unpretentious and stirring in total effect" and "superior in these respects to *The Cradle Will Rock*." Welles subsequently presented the work at the Mercury Theatre on February 20 as part of a double bill with Ben Bengal's play about striking factory workers, *Plant in the Sun* (1937). *Variety* thought the opera, which "lacked cohesion," even less impressive on stage than on radio, but "satisfactory enough for the hysterical left audiences, who are not over critical of what is dished up to them."[18]

I've Got the Tune enjoyed occasional stage revivals over the years, including performances at the New School (1939), Carnegie Hall (1949), Provincetown Playhouse (1966), Harvard (1970), St. Bart's Playhouse (1988), and in its British premiere, the George Wood Theatre (1989). During the 2005 centennial year, Leonard Lehrman, who had directed the Harvard production, also presented at different New York venues an adapted version of the work that incorporated material derived from Blitzstein's drafts (including the line, "The moon is a bloody rag tonight," found in an early lyric for "The Moon Is a Happy Cheese Tonight" and a joke involving Beetzie's confusion of the phrase, "salon," with "saloon" and "hair salon") along with purely original interpolations. (Lehrman subsequently released a recording of the work spliced together from his Harvard and New York performances.) As with the first staged performance, these revivals typically presented the work with piano accompaniment, sometimes with added percussion. Meanwhile, the Musicraft recording of the original broadcast—full of historical interest and brilliant performances—remained long out-of-print, with no later recording with full orchestra appearing either.[19]

In mid-1936, as Blitzstein worked on *The Cradle Will Rock,* the Labor Stage, which operated a theater on West 39th Street (formerly the Princess Theatre) under the auspices of the ILGWU (International Ladies' Garment Workers' Union), began rehearsing *Pins and Needles,* a revue with songs by Harold Rome. By the time the show debuted on November 27, 1937, it featured not only Rome's songs but sketches by Arthur Arent, Emanuel Eisenberg, David Gregory, and the show's director, Charles Friedman, as well as a musical scene in the second act by Blitzstein entitled "F.T.P. [Federal Theatre Project] Plowed Under."

Under the supervision of Louis Schaffer, the Labor Stage recruited some professional talent, but featured ILGWU workers on stage, with the original cast of *Pins and Needles* consisting of forty-two mostly Jewish male and female dressmakers, cutters, and the like singing, dancing, and acting their way through songs and skits. At first, the revue appeared only on weekends, so that the actors could continue their day jobs; but as its popularity widened, the show assumed a normal Broadway schedule, with cast members given leave from their garment work. A second edition, *Pins and Needles 1939,* opened in April of that year, relocating to the larger Windsor Theatre in June; and a third edition, *New Pins and Needles,* opened in November. In the course of the run, Schaffer, to the consternation of some of the performers, began to hire professional actors partly in order to de-ethnicize a show that encountered anti-Semitism and racism on tour. Reviewing the third edition for *Modern Music,* Blitzstein himself complained that the cast had "for the most part gone pseudo-professional. . . . they are too made-up, too intent and too sly about the audience." The revue closed on Broadway June 22, 1940, with the second of its two national tours ending in May 1941. Improbably, this union show—an entertainment Virgil Thomson thought "smooth, witty and gracious" and "of a great healthiness and a great humanity"—proved by a long shot the biggest Broadway musical hit of the 1930s, earning over a million dollars for the union.[20]

Naturally pitching their material toward a union membership eager to see its values reflected on the Broadway stage, Rome and his collaborators presented satires on fascists abroad and reactionaries at home; parodies of the more serious leftist theater of Brecht and Odets; jabs at the FBI and the FTP; and more generally, light-hearted songs about working-class life. The revue further navigated around longstanding union friction between communist and anticommunist factions, as epitomized by its central love song, "One Big Union for Two," in which the merger of the AFL and the CIO served as a romantic metaphor. However, such harmoniousness began to fray especially after the 1939 Nazi-Soviet pact as the staunchly anticommunist Schaffer added Stalin to the list of villains in "Little Angels of Peace," and excised the noninterventionist song "Stay out, Sammy" as well. Two recent commentators, Michael Denning and Ilka Saal, have located still other tensions endemic to the revue, but ultimately extoll the show for triumphing over its compromises.[21]

Blitzstein's "F.T.P. Plowed Under"—whose title alluded to the Federal Theatre's Living Newspaper, "Triple-A Plowed Under"—contained a self-referential dimension along the lines of *I've Got the Tune*, although here he drew on his experiences with the Federal Theatre Project. The composer Hippity Bloomberg (played by Joe Roth) meets to discuss his play with four Federal Theatre administrators— Mrs. Clubhouse (ostensibly modeled on Hallie Flanagan), Mr. Zealous, Mr. Stallalong, and Mr. Bureaucrash—a zany and intimidated lot who blithely sign forms in the course of the sketch that turn out to be dismissal notices. At first, the administrators, who barely allow Bloomberg a word in edgewise, plan an elaborate production—"Wait!!" enthuses Mrs. Clubhouse. "Couldn't we have a revolving stage? Or I know—one of those elevator stages, so we can have flashback from the past on the second floor, and where we are is the present tense, and our hero's future is waiting to come up from down in the basement"—but after hearing about the show ("Well, it's about a boy and a girl," says Bloomberg, to which Zealous will later reply, "Ah! I was a boy and a girl myself once. I mean. . . .") decide to have, in Mrs. Clubhouse's words, "a very intimate production of—practically nothing." At the end, all that's left of Bloomberg's play is, "The curtain rises," and on hearing Bureaucrash suggest that they dispense with the curtain, the composer faints. Blackout.[22]

Blitzstein wrote both the "music and sketch" for this scene, as specified by various playbills and as corroborated further by some musical drafts found among his papers. Although the music proper does not appear to have survived, to judge from existing materials, including a script (which contains choreographed stage directions surely devised by the composer as well), the musical treatment involved both song and accompanied dialogue.

John Mason Brown (*New York Post*) thought that all the revue's skits had "something to say," but he faulted "F.T.P. Plowed Under" and "Four Little Angels of Peace" as two that went on "too long for their own good." Heywood Broun (*New York World-Telegram*) more positively singled out "F.T.P. Plowed Under" as the show's "only savage satire," even if misdirected against "a movement which worker groups ought to support in spite of its present limitations." (When Broun told Blitzstein as much, the latter replied, "You may be right.") President Roosevelt seemed particularly tickled by "F.T.P. Plowed Under," reportedly stating after a March 3, 1938, command performance at the White House of excerpts from the show, with regard to the Blitzstein skit, "I wish the Senate and House could see this one." As the show deleted and added material, "F.T.P. Plowed Under" remained on the boards for a considerable time, but was dropped for the second edition, presumably because the collapse of the Federal Theatre Project deprived the satire of its topicality.[23]

On November 13, 1937, two weeks before *Pins and Needles* opened on the Labor Stage, a pro-Soviet rally at Madison Square Garden launched a "mass play," *One-Sixth of the Earth*, for which Blitzstein wrote some music and served as musical director. Sponsored by the American Communist Party, this gala celebrated the twentieth anniversary of the October Revolution that had brought the Bolsheviks to power. Twenty thousand party and nonparty members packed the Garden, with thousands more turned away.[24]

To the cheers of those present, three thousand new party members recited an oath that concluded, "We pledge our complete devotion to the Leninist struggle for socialism, for a Soviet America." The attendees further approved a resolution praising Stalin for having "built a great Socialist society which has been a beacon light to us in our years of struggle." In his address to the crowd, Party Chairman William Z. Foster declared that the country's "people's front" did not originate in Moscow, but on the contrary constituted "a natural, native policy, with a tradition of fifty years in back of it."[25]

Performed by a company of two hundred actors and dancers, *One-Sixth of the Earth* apparently took its title (which alluded to the land mass of the Soviet Union) from Dziga Vertov's 1926 documentary of the same name. Ralph Crane, William Crockett, and Henry Stern prepared a dramatization of the history of the Soviet Union in four parts, ending with "The Struggle for World Peace." Director Howard Da Silva and choreographer Lillian Shapero stated their indebtedness to Soviet director Vsevolod Meyerhold in their attempt to "stimulate wide audience participation" (presumably unaware that the Soviet government, ironically enough, already had begun its crackdown on Meyerhold). The full extent of Blitzstein's involvement remains unknown, but he at least wrote a song for the occasion, "Moscow Metro," a lead sheet of which survives. Set to a minor mode tune reminiscent of Russian popular music, the text celebrates the construction of the Moscow Metro, which had opened in 1935 and which had become a symbol of Soviet achievement. "With our shock troops['] flags unfurled/we have challenged all the world/we have shown the doubting scoffers/how the workers build (shout!) (bang!)," states the brief middle section.[26]

However, even following this event, Blitzstein continued to sound rather noncommittal with regard to communism. After he met with some students at the Mercury Theatre on March 4, 1938, for example, the Sarah Lawrence campus newspaper reported, "Politically, Mr. Blitzstein is not a Communist, but, when asked, he replied that he agreed with many things Communism teaches. He has a great respect for it, and believes that under it art can flourish better." That said, Blitzstein plainly had been moving toward greater affiliation with the Communist Party during these years, including public support for party candidates Earl Browder and James Ford in the 1936 presidential campaign. And in the spring of 1938, he registered with the party, retaining his membership until late 1949, as he recalled in testimony before the House Committee on Un-American Activities (HUAC) in 1958.[27]

Blitzstein joined the party at the height of its accommodation of traditional American values, as seen by its tenth convention, attended by the composer, in May 1938, with its promise to uphold the country's Constitution; its homage to Washington, Jefferson, and Lincoln, and its posters of red, white, and blue; and its denunciation of "degenerates" and "advocates of terrorism and violence." Such trends reflected a party membership increasingly middle-class, including a growing number of intellectuals and artists. For a Trotskyist critic like Max Shachtman, even if such conservatism represented a smoke screen for a more radical agenda, the party leaders "are duping only themselves, as would an atheist if he planned to destroy religious prejudices with a popular mass movement recruited by arguments to support the infallibility of the Pope and the scientific basis for Genesis." Meanwhile, in a June 1938 article, the *New York Times* reported that although a thousand communist delegates informally polled unanimously answered "yes" to the question, "Do you expect to see a Socialist reorganization in the United States in your lifetime," the large majority still liked such "typically American" diversions as baseball, Hollywood movies, and the Lindy Hop.[28]

In his 1958 HUAC testimony, Blitzstein, who admitted that he had been solicited to become a party member by an unnamed person, offered the following explanation for joining: "I was part of the generation, sir, which had lived through the Depression. I was, I suppose, an idealist. I believed very much in industrial unionism. I believed in the protection of the rights of minorities, and it seemed to me at that time that the Communist Party was the organization which was doing most toward the furtherance of my ideals." Blitzstein further told the committee that at first he attended meetings about once or twice a month but later went as rarely as once or twice a year, that these meetings usually involved about seven or eight people, and that during his indigent years, he paid only about ten cents per month in dues.[29]

Over time, Blitzstein expressed his communist ideals primarily in his work but also by backing party candidates, defending jailed communists and labor leaders, supporting Loyalist Spain and the Soviet Union, and opposing fascism and anti-Semitism, including some association with the Jewish People's Committee for United Action against Fascism and Anti-Semitism and the short-lived journal *Jewish Survey.* Such involvements differed perhaps more in degree than kind from those fellow travelers who never actually joined the party itself.[30]

Probably the most provocative of these activities involved co-authoring a letter of April 2, 1938, soliciting signatures in defense of the Moscow show trials of 1936–38, which defamed and punished to the point of death dozens of Soviet military personnel and party members as traitors (trials not to be confused with the far more encompassing great purges of these same years). Blitzstein and his co-writers—authors Robert Coates and Malcolm Cowley, artist Stuart Davis, and photographer Paul Strand—drafted this solicitation letter in response to the John Dewey commission, which had declared the trials a frame-up the previous fall. Blitzstein and his friends countered that the survival of democracy in the face of fascism depended on cooperation with the Soviet government and that support for the trials "will lend even greater weight to the worldwide defense of the right of the individual to speak, write, create, and otherwise engage in cultural activity in complete freedom." Signed by nearly 150 persons of note, mostly in the arts, the statement itself, released on April 27, went even further than this by claiming that the trials "have by sheer weight of evidence established a clear presumption of the guilt of the defendants." In addition to the originating committee, the signatories included Harold Clurman, Lillian Hellman, Langston Hughes, Albert Maltz, Dorothy Parker, Wallingford Riegger, Harold Rome, Irwin Shaw, and Richard Wright.[31]

Blitzstein signed another controversial letter, this one in reaction to a manifesto released in May 1939 by a newly formed group, the Committee for Cultural Freedom, which equated the totalitarianism of the Soviet Union with that of Germany, Italy, Japan, and Spain. In reply, on August 13, an initiating committee released an open letter signed by four hundred notables, including Blitzstein, that argued that the manifesto previously cited served fascism by sowing discord between the United States and the Soviet Union, and that listed ten ways in which "Soviet socialism differs fundamentally from totalitarian fascism," including its elimination of racial prejudice, anti-Semitism, and gender inequality; its free education and medical care; and its recognition of political dictatorship as a transitional stage toward an ever-expanding democracy. In 1941, Eugene Lyons, who had drafted the antitotalitarian statement for the Committee for Cultural Freedom, ridiculed some two dozen figures, including Blitzstein, who had signed both this open letter and the letter in defense of the Moscow trials as "stooges-*cum-laude*," writing, "Not only had they condoned the blood purges in Stalin's domain, but they had attested that the quality of his oppression was unique and not to be lightly confused with the lines offered by Hitler and Mussolini."[32]

Although the defense of the Moscow trials by American communists in particular became increasingly reviled as the epitome of dogged loyalty to the Soviet state, at the time, a number of more impartial observers took similar positions. Two weeks before the letter went out soliciting support for the trials, the *New York Times*, for instance, published a report by Harold Denny from Moscow that argued for their general validity. And in his 1941 memoir, *Mission to Moscow*, former American ambassador to the Soviet Union Joseph E. Davies justified the trials as warrantable in the context of Soviet law and exigencies, and reported that the diplomatic corps widely regarded the accused as guilty of treasonable offences. Even such rather skeptical organs as the *New Republic* and the *Nation*, whatever their concerns about the trials, tended to give the Soviet government the benefit of the doubt in the interest of preserving a united people's front both at home and abroad, plainly a strong motivation for Blitzstein and many of his friends as well.[33]

In the course of 1937, reports surfaced that Blitzstein was at work on a score for the *Ziegfeld Follies*, whose most recent edition (1936) had featured songs by Vernon Duke and Ira Gershwin. That Blitzstein would even be mentioned in conjunction with this traditionally frothy series of revues suggests, even before the arrival of *Pins and Needles*, the extent to which Broadway had become attuned to leftist social satire. But in October, Leonard Lyons reported that Blitzstein had "turned down the 'Follies' job," another edition of which would not appear until 1943.[34]

However, on March 20, 1938, at a Sunday night informal at the Casa Mañana, producer Billy Rose's recently opened nightclub on Seventh Avenue and West 59th Street in what had been the Earl Carroll Theatre, Blitzstein gave an impromptu performance of a new comedy song, "Smoking Glasses," possibly intended for some such revue. In this little dramatic sketch, the singer, a haughty movie star beleaguered by fans, disguises himself with dark glasses, the chorus opening, "You see me wearing smoking glasses./So don't compare me with the masses." In his manuscript of the nearly completed song, Blitzstein scribbled a dedication "to what I wish were the remains of Mr. Gregory Ratoff" for no known reason other than the flamboyant actor-director was in some quarters regarded as "an incredible caricature of a Hollywood director." Blitzstein sang the number in other venues as well, and in 1940, Billy Rose, in a gesture interpreted as less than gallant, suggested to Blitzstein that he send a copy of the song to Rose's recently estranged wife, Fanny Brice.[35]

In tandem with his opera *No for an Answer* (1937–40), Blitzstein wrote some other cabaret songs, two of which he eventually put forth as independent numbers: "Expatriate" and "Let's Be Blue" (also known as "Who Knows?"). In the drafted program for an April 18, 1941, dinner concert, at which he apparently sang both songs along with "Smoking Glasses," Blitzstein listed all three numbers as from 1939, although as seen, at least an early version of "Smoking Glasses" dated from 1938.

A satiric song about Americans in Europe in the 1920s, the breezy "Expatriate," which survives only in fragmentary form, opens, "I want to be an emigré, the Hemingway,/and walk and talk and look the way a hero looks/in all the latest ultramodern books." (In an April 1941 diary entry, David Diamond noted Blitzstein's "dislike" for a certain Hemingway novel—ostensibly *For Whom The Bell Tolls*—and thought his friend's "caricature" of its love scenes "a scream.") "Let's Be Blue," with its intoxicating chorus, relatedly advises the anxious listener to escape from the world's problems through a variety of ways, "For who knows/Where we'd end if we once should think or feel?"[36]

Ruth Ford—a Mercury Theatre actress remembered by Paul Bowles as "beautiful and sophisticated and more generous-spirited than any woman I knew"—performed "Let's Be Blue" in 1939 and 1940 at Cabaret TAC, a New

York venue that operated under the auspices of the Theatre Arts Committee (TAC), a group founded in 1937 as the Theatre Committee to Aid Spanish Democracy but that changed its name in 1938 as its concerns widened to include other leftist causes. During its brief existence (1938–40), TAC not only sponsored its own cabaret, but staged fundraisers, established a social center, and beginning in July 1938, published a monthly entertainment magazine, *TAC*, which along with political commentary and cartoons, featured articles on literature and the arts by an impressive assortment of writers, including composers Blitzstein, Copland, Wallingford Riegger, and Paul Bowles. At its height in late 1939, TAC had a membership of about twenty-five hundred. But its strongly critical stance toward the Allies after the Nazi-Soviet pact—plainly disclosing its communist orientation—led to the organization's outcast status and eventual demise in late 1940.[37]

Modeled after Europe's political cabarets of the 1920s, Cabaret TAC launched their first show on May 5, 1938, at the Chez Firehouse nightclub, and over the next two years, sponsored events sporadically at various locations, including the American Music Hall, Labor Stage, and Manhattan Center. "The political cabaret was a feature of pre-dictator Europe, familiar to every nation," wrote Blitzstein in the first issue of *TAC*. "It's TAC's job to see that the political cabaret, at least, is a feature of at least one city in every state in the nation. America needs such productions." Many leading New York artists, including choreographers, performed for Cabaret TAC: "the roster of performers who have appeared in its revues," reported Theodore Strauss on the occasion of its first anniversary gala at the Manhattan Center on May 5, 1939, "almost reads like a Broadway Who's Who."[38]

As might be expected in light of its communist stewardship, Cabaret TAC engaged in more pointedly leftist satire than typically found on Broadway. At the same time, their offerings hardly fit the stereotype of agitprop either, but seemed intended, rather, as sophisticated and edifying entertainment for the communist denizens of New York's theater world and their friends.

Blitzstein appears to have been particularly active with TAC in early 1939, during which time he published in *TAC* magazine a book review of Copland's *What to Listen for in Music* as well as a poem or perhaps a song lyric, "Wish," in which he imagines fascist despots quarantined on some faraway place. He also performed with Cabaret TAC, presenting the fascist scene from *I've Got the Tune* as "Fun in the Woods" (the *Times* thought it "a weak and pretentious satire on hooded organizations") and participating in a favored TAC skit, "It Can't Happen Here," with lyrics and music by John Murray.[39]

About this same time, Blitzstein devised a sketch, "What's Left?" in which some imagined Tin Pan Alley lyricists, eyeing the success of leftist popular music, decide to write "red lyrics" to well-known tunes, including "Danny Boy," Ignacy Paderewski's *Minuet in G*, Anton Rubinstein's *Melody in F*, Schubert's *Moment Musical* (probably no. 3 in F minor), and Rimsky's "Song of India." In "Danny

Boy," the singer, addressing the wearer of a non-union undergarment, concludes, "I only hope those buttons on your union suit/Like to the cork upon the bottled soda—pop." Blitzstein presumably intended the sketch, with its characteristic mix of bawdy humor and leftist sentiment—here, like "F.T.P. Plowed Under," a sort of irreverent in-joke—for a venue like *Pins and Needles* or Cabaret TAC.[40]

Following *The Cradle Will Rock*, John Houseman and Orson Welles commissioned Blitzstein to provide music for Shakespeare's *Julius Caesar*, the debut production of their Mercury Theatre, a Broadway repertory company established during the summer of 1937 after the two men had left the Federal Theatre. Houseman produced the play on a modest budget, and Welles not only directed but took the role of Brutus, with other cast members including George Coulouris (Antony), Martin Gabel (Cassius), Joseph Holland (Caesar), and in a memorable cameo, Norman Lloyd (Cinna the poet).[41]

Welles drastically shortened the play into a one-acter lasting about ninety minutes, editing the work to emphasize the role of Brutus and his relationship with Cassius (he omitted the figure of Octavius completely). He further reconceived the work as a contemporary parable, with Caesar and Antony as fascists, the mob as vigilantes, Cassius as a wayward revolutionary, and Brutus, according to a press release, as "the classical picture of the eternal, impotent, ineffectual liberal . . . the fellow who thinks the times are out of joint, but who is really out of joint with his time. He's the bourgeois intellectual." Welles enhanced this concept by lighting the stage to suggest Nazi pageantry; setting the whole on a bare stage, with the rear wall painted blood-red; and costuming Caesar and Antony in fascist regalia, the mob as gangsters, and Brutus in a blue serge suit.[42]

Welles could evoke only so many parallels between the play and current events before the analogy collapsed. But enough of these held to drive home the director's intended moral—"that not assassination, but education of the masses, permanently removes dictatorship"—and make the production an intensely timely experience for a Broadway audience. The episode in which the mob murders Cinna, who merely shares a name with one of the assassins, proved particularly riveting; for as Lloyd explained, the scene "symbolized what was happening in the world, if your name was Greenburg—and even if you weren't Jewish."[43]

Blitzstein seemed a logical choice for the music, not only because of his particular gifts and interests, but because his name could be counted on to help attract that leftist front that had rallied behind *The Cradle* and that Welles and Houseman now hoped might support their new company. The composer received $200 for his score, a small percentage of the box office gross, and an additional $50 a week when the show went on the road in early 1938.

Scoring the work for a four-person ensemble (the minimum union requirement) consisting of trumpet, French horn, Hammond organ, and percussion, Blitzstein composed about twenty-eight cues, most only a few measures in length—short duets for trumpet and horn, a few notes for chimes or snare drum, thick clusters in the lower depths of the organ—that helped smooth transitions from one scene to another, with several of these cues distinctively evocative of military fanfares and flourishes. In a review of this score, Elliott Carter credited the composer with writing "incidental sound effects that have great dramatic value but could not be played away from the shows they are written for."[44]

In fact, the overture, evocative of the sort of marches popular in fascist Italy and Germany, but distorted through bitonal harmonies and robotic rhythms, resurfaced in the composer's *Airborne Symphony* (1946) as a monotone chant that begins, "Adolf Hitler/We believe in thee/Without thee/We would be alone." In the Mercury production, Caesar interrupted this overture with the play's opening line, "Bid every noise be still!" a moment Blitzstein cited as one instance in which stage music "comes down for a closeup, and takes over, as when it gets written into the plot."[45]

Blitzstein's "Orpheus with His Lute," the score's one song, also enjoyed a life of its own. Welles interpolated the text from *Henry VIII* (III, i) for that moment in the play when Lucius sings to a disillusioned Brutus outside Philippi, Shakespeare having merely written "Music, and a Song." Blitzstein's tender setting, reminiscent of lute song, performed an important function by encapsulating Brutus's tragedy and offering, in Houseman's words, "a last moment of peace before the final, inevitable catastrophe." The fifteen-year-old radio actor Arthur Anderson, described by Houseman as "gangling, with a long neck and prominent Adam's apple, curly hair and a nice smile," sang the number accompanying himself on a ukulele disguised as a lute.[46]

During the rehearsal period, Welles reached an impasse with the Cinna episode and turned the scene over to Blitzstein, who devised an extended passage for the mob in rhythmic speech composed of such phrases as "Kill!" "Slay!" and "Tear him!" a set piece reminiscent of the finale from *The Cradle* but even more elaborate. Blitzstein rehearsed the actors as such with a metronome, but the scene, as Houseman recalled, began to resemble a parody of Martha Graham, perhaps because Norman Lloyd "was unable or unwilling to adjust his highly personal style of playing to these arbitrarily imposed, external rhythms." Still, Welles's final version of the scene incorporated to great effect some of Blitzstein's rhythmic ideas.[47]

The Tragedy of Julius Caesar opened on November 11, 1937, at the Comedy Theatre—renamed the Mercury—on West 41st Street in New York. The production met with enthusiastic critical response, *Variety* reporting that six out of eight reviews were raves. Music critics naturally paid special attention to the score, including Elliott Carter, who reported, "The wonderful roars of the Hammond organ, the sardonic Fascist march are not easily forgotten; they play their roles with great cogency." Virgil Thomson thought the score "first-class" as well: "This is a kind of musical composition at which only first-class composers are any good, because the ability to say something exact in two bars is, if not the summit of musical art, at least its base and fundament."[48]

Houseman also paid tribute to the music in his memoirs, admiring the way, with limited instrumentation, the composer

> managed to achieve amazingly varied effects—from the distant bugles of a sleeping camp to the blaring brass and deep, massive, rhythmic beat which instantly evoked the pounding march of Hitler's storm troopers that we were hearing with increasing frequency over the radio and in the newsreels. Added to this was the ominous rumble of the electric organ on certain base [sic] stops which set the whole theatre trembling and the deep booming of a huge, old-fashioned thunder drum which had been especially constructed years before, for the American production of *Chu Chin Chow*.

Blitzstein occasionally played the rumbling organ part himself, although the show's music director appears to have been I. L. Epstein.[49]

On January 24, 1938, the triumphant production moved to the larger National Theatre, where it rotated with other Mercury shows, closing on May 28 after 157 performances. In the course of the year, the Mercury company also recorded the play a few times, including a release of excerpts from the stage production (recorded in March 1938); a longer Mercury Text Records release (recorded in June and July); and an abbreviated version with narration for the radio program *Mercury Theatre on the Air* (September 11). Whereas the Mercury Text recording contains no music, both the recorded stage excerpts and the radio broadcast, a rehearsal of which survives, feature a few cues from the original score (the former for organ and percussion, the latter for brass and percussion). The radio run-through holds greater interest in this respect, for it has more music, including a performance of "Orpheus" by Anderson (cut, as the latter recalled, for the actual broadcast). In 1938, Chappell published the song as "Orpheus (Lucius' Song)," the music transposed down a semitone and the tempo changed from "Dreamily, but with beat" to "Adagio."[50]

After *Julius Caesar*, Blitzstein's close association with the Mercury Theatre continued that fall with their relaunching of *The Cradle*. In early 1938, the Mercury also considered asking him to provide the music for a planned production of John Webster's *The Duchess of Malfi*, although in the end they selected instead Virgil Thomson, who "won," as Thomson recalled, "by taking Orson [Welles] and his wife to a blowout at Sardi's." (As it happened, the Mercury shelved the production after a few rehearsals, citing "widespread concern for the precarious international situation" as well as budgetary constraints.) However, Welles subsequently commissioned Blitzstein to compose the music for another of his Mercury Text Records, *Twelfth Night* (ca. 1601–02), recorded in June

1938. Produced in conjunction with published editions of the plays by Welles and Roger Hill, *The Mercury Shakespeare*, these Mercury Text recordings—the others included *Julius Caesar* (with no music, as mentioned), *The Merchant of Venice* (music, Elliott Carter), and *Macbeth* (music, Bernard Herrmann)—were released in 1939, except for *Macbeth*, which appeared the following year. The *Twelfth Night* album, thought by Michael Anderegg "the most elaborate and unusual" of the group, opened with an imaginary conversation between Shakespeare and Richard Burbage, an idea possibly derived from Blitzstein's *I've Got the Tune*. The cast included Welles (narrator and Malvolio), George Coulouris (Duke Orsino), Will Geer (Sir Andrew Aguecheek), and Eustace Wyatt (Sir Toby Belch).[51]

Blitzstein composed no instrumental cues, but rather set only those lines from the play intended to be sung, notably, the three songs written for Feste the fool and performed here with lute accompaniment by LeRoi Operti: "Come Away, Death" (moved from Act II to the top of the play so as to introduce Duke Orsino's "If music be the food of love, play on"); "O Mistress Mine" (originally in II, iii, though here, in II, i); and the concluding number, "When That I Was and a Little Tiny Boy." In addition, Blitzstein provided tunes for those fragments sung by Belch and Aguecheek (in Welles's II, i) and by Feste (in Welles's IV, ii). Whereas Blitzstein's music for *Julius Caesar* suggested some conflation of the ancient and the modern, for this endeavor he evoked rather the Elizabethan period, the melancholy "Come Away, Death" recalling John Dowland, the sprightly "O Mistress Mine" and "When That I Was" leaning more in the direction of Thomas Morley, although the lute harmonies have their own distinctive flavor.[52]

About this same time, Blitzstein served Welles further by assuming a bit part in a slapstick silent film—actually, three separate film sequences—in the style of Mack Sennett intended to introduce each of the three acts of the Mercury Theatre's production of William Gillette's farce *Too Much Johnson* (1894). The film, which starred Joseph Cotten and Arlene Francis, had Blitzstein performing duties as an extra, as it did a young switchboard operator for the Mercury Theatre, Judith Tuvim, soon to be known as actress Judy Holliday. "I played 1) a stevedore 2) a masculine sympathizer in a suffragette parade 3) a passenger waving goodby from a steamer, and 4) a man on the dock waving back goodby to 3)," wrote Blitzstein to Copland. In a photo spread devoted to the film, *Stage* magazine reproduced a few stills that included Blitzstein, whom they described as "an excellent comedian" and "the most energetic of the extras." Welles never completed the final edit, in part because of financial difficulties, although not before Blitzstein offered to provide a live piano accompaniment for the film if needed. The show opened without benefit of motion picture on August 16, 1938, at Connecticut's Stony Creek Theatre, where it ran for two weeks. As for the film, the only known print perished by fire in 1971.[53]

Finding *Too Much Johnson* "trivial, tedious and underrehearsed," Houseman persuaded Welles to open their "critical second season" not with the Gillette—which ultimately never made it to Broadway at all—but with *Danton's Death* (1834–35) by the revolutionary German playwright Georg Büchner (1813–1837). For the music, they once again commissioned Blitzstein, whose contract specified a small percentage of the gross receipts.[54]

Set in 1794, the Büchner play dramatizes the conflict between two leaders of the French Revolution: Georges-Jacques Danton, portrayed sympathetically as an epicure grown weary of revolutionary violence, and Maximilien Robespierre, who appeases the mob by preaching purity and who, aided by Saint-Just, manages to send Danton and several of his associates to their deaths. Only recently published for the first time in English by Geoffrey Dunlop (1927), the text posed challenges because of its highly episodic structure, but Houseman and Welles thought it "a play of keen political and human insights—one that seemed to offer us scope for creative and experimental production and, at the same time, reflected significant aspects of the modern scene." Houseman and Welles surely noted parallels with *Julius Caesar*, with Brutus and Cassius roughly comparable to Danton and Robespierre. Although Max Reinhardt had had a triumph with his elaborate production of the play (presented in German as *Danton's Tod*) on Broadway in 1927, Houseman and Welles decided to treat the work not as spectacle but rather as "a 'drama of lonely souls and the mob,' with the mob ever-present but rarely visible."[55]

Blitzstein's music, scored for voices, clarinet, trumpet, percussion, and piano/harpsichord, featured two original songs: a neoclassical air associated with the rarified world of Danton, "Ode to Reason" for voice, clarinet, and harpsichord (or "spinet," as Blitzstein writes); and a folkish number associated with the rowdy mob, "Christina" for solo man, solo woman, chorus, clarinet, trumpet, percussion, and piano. Blitzstein composed not only the music but the lyrics for both songs, the former in the style of revolutionary hymns of the period, the latter freely adapted from Büchner's text.[56]

Blitzstein also arranged three famous tunes associated with the Revolution—"Ah! ça ira" ("Ah! It'll Do"), "La Carmagnole" (a reference to the costume worn by provincial militants), and "La Marseillaise" ("The Song of Marseille" by Rouget de Lisle)—for chorus, tweaking their melodies and words (and giving early proof of his excellence as a translator, as evidenced by his version of "La Marseillaise," which begins, "Arise ye children of the nation!/The day of glory is at hand!/See the tyrant's foul bloody banners!/Lifted brazenly in our land!"). In addition, he wrote some instrumental cues, including most notably a little "spinet-piece" for harpsichord in the style of Mozart.[57]

Welles trimmed the play into an uninterrupted ninety-minute act and, unable to afford a big cast, gave the impression of an "ever-present" mob through the use of hundreds of Halloween masks stacked in rows on a curved backdrop created by set designer Stephen Jay Tichacek. Blitzstein assumed responsibility for training the chorus and seemed, Houseman recalled, "the only completely content and confident person in the organization"—that is until some ten days before the scheduled previews, when he anxiously informed Houseman and Welles that the Mercury's extensive communist base had deep concerns about the play and there was talk of boycotting and even picketing the production. Indeed, on October 20, the *Daily Worker* stated point blank, "Orson Welles stands to lose a great many of his most ardent admirers in the theater if his present version of 'Danton's Death' ever reaches Broadway," arguing that the show distorted the history of the French Revolution and pleading that Welles either revise the script or drop the play entirely.[58]

It appears that the communist establishment feared that, given the escalating rift between Stalinists and Trotskyists, viewers would interpret the play's conflict between Danton and Robespierre (a hero in communist circles) as reflecting that between Trotsky and Stalin, with the arrest and execution of Danton and his friends analogous to Stalin's recent purges—all of which might debilitate support for the Soviet regime. This seems not to have been the Mercury's intention; indeed, Blitzstein apparently considered this a shallow reading of the play. But concerned about the fate of the production, he arranged for Houseman and Welles to meet with the Communist Party's cultural commissar, V. J. Jerome. Houseman and Welles subsequently made some adjustments to appease Jerome—but only enough to forestall a boycott, not to procure party endorsement. "When we needed them desperately after our mixed notices in the capitalist press," Houseman wryly recalled, "they did nothing to help us survive."[59]

The show opened on November 2, 1938, with a cast headed by Martin Gabel (Danton), Vladimir Sokoloff (Robespierre), and Welles (Saint-Just), with Adelyn Colla-Negri singing "Ode to Reason," and Joseph Cotten and Mary Wickes the soloists in "Christina." The critics generally agreed that the production had many impressive features, including the incidental music: Brooks Atkinson stated that Blitzstein's "raffish songs" conveyed "the mindless treachery of the mob," while John Gutman noted that the "discrepancy" between the "modernity" of the songs and the "'period' style" of the instrumental music created "a kind of ironic high-lighting." But ultimately the critics deemed the evening largely drab, with Gutman suggesting that the show might have "gained by a more ample score." In attempting to placate communist opinion, Houseman and Welles seem to have downplayed sympathy for Danton, thereby confusing viewers. Houseman also wished that Welles had directed the actors more carefully and taken the role of Danton himself. At all events, lack of support from the popular front, whose theater parties previously had gone far in keeping the Mercury Theatre afloat, no doubt constituted a deathblow to the production. Even with the publicity generated by Welles's notorious "War of the Worlds" radio broadcast on October 30, the show folded after a mere twenty-one performances.[60]

The failure of *Danton's Death* marked the end of the Mercury Theatre on stage, and within a year, Houseman and Welles had begun to establish themselves in

Hollywood. Blitzstein presumably could have followed suit; but unlike Welles's other preferred composer, Bernard Herrmann, he showed little inclination in that direction, his involvement with film remaining more in the domain of New York's progressive documentarians.

Still, Blitzstein and Welles crossed paths at a critical juncture in their lives, and the influence that they had on each other extended beyond their time together in the 1930s, as suggested by Welles's *Citizen Kane* (1941), a picture that seemed to have a debt to Blitzstein not only in its tone and content but even in its pacing. Moreover, Blitzstein would continue to collaborate on some important projects in the years ahead with both Welles and Houseman, although independently, as the two directors went their separate ways after producing Richard Wright's *Native Son* on Broadway in 1941.

Although his Mercury Theatre scores largely fell into obscurity, in 1947, Blitzstein recorded both "Orpheus" and "Ode to Reason" with the African-American mezzo-soprano Muriel Smith on an album for the Concert Hall label entitled *Marc Blitzstein: Songs of the Theater*. During these years, Blitzstein worked closely with Smith, who had originated the role of Carmen Jones and who also portrayed Ella Hammer in the 1947 City Center revival of *The Cradle Will Rock* under Leonard Bernstein. For the two Mercury Theatre songs, he prepared the strings of the piano to simulate the sounds of a lute and a harpsichord, respectively, an example of his adapting avant-garde resources—in this case, the prepared piano associated with John Cage—to suit his own purposes.

Some of the *Julius Caesar* music also resurfaced in a 2009 film directed by Richard Linklater, *Me and Orson Welles*, adapted from the 2003 Robert Kaplow novel of the same name. Loosely based on Arthur Anderson's experiences playing Lucius in the Mercury production, the film climaxed with a reenactment of the show's premiere, including the young Anderson, renamed Richard Samuels (played by Zac Efron), singing an abridged version of "Orpheus with His Lute." The film also included some of Blitzstein's other cues in their original instrumentation, while music director Michael McEvoy wrote several others in Blitzstein's style, including the music for the finale. Aside from having his name seen in passing on a playbill, the movie made no reference to Blitzstein, but rather gave the impression that Welles virtually created the score himself in collaboration with music director I. L. Epstein (played by McEvoy). But the retained fragments from the original score gave some indication of Blitzstein's real power as a composer of incidental music, helping to explain his favored status with the Mercury Theatre.[61]

12

No for an Answer (1937–1940)

In his application for a 1937 Guggenheim fellowship dated October 30, 1936, a good half-year before *The Cradle* opened, Blitzstein proposed writing another "theatre work" described as follows: "The subject will be the joint and separate adventures of a young middle-class American brother and sister in their attempt to find their places in terms of time and country and society. . . . At the end they will both have reached a social consciousness; one will have lost himself in the process, the other will have slowly come to self-realization and organic growth." He further imagined that the drama would make integral use of music in a way related to "the old-style vaudeville song-and-dance turn" and Walt Disney's series of animated shorts, *Silly Symphonies* (as could be said of *The Cradle* as well). The notion of having as protagonists a brother and sister presumably drew in part on his relationship with his sister Jo, while the theme of "social consciousness," already explored in *The Cradle*, would remain a mainstay of the composer's dramatic imagination.[1]

The following October, in yet another failed Guggenheim application, the composer further described this new work, entitled *No for an Answer*, as a character study "with emphasis on the struggle of young people today to make an adjustment between what they have been taught and what they have learned." And about two months later, the *New York Herald Tribune* announced that he was about six weeks shy of completing this three-act "militant operetta" whose "theme" was that "youth will not take No for an Answer." However, the *Times* reported in February 1938 that although Blitzstein had been at work on this stage piece about a boy and a girl in a "Philadelphia Quaker environment" since the previous July, he had come only so far as to outline the libretto, with eight songs "planned if not actually written."[2]

In the ensuing months and years, as he traveled to and from New York, Philadelphia, St. Thomas, Saranac Lake, and Yaddo, as well as to the home of his friend Mina Curtiss in Ashfield, Massachusetts, and his sister's summer place in Ventnor, New Jersey, Blitzstein continually revised the work, producing one draft that lasted two hours and "neglected the entire plot" and another that he felt "was indispensable in the way of story and structure, and emerged as a six-hour opera; a fact I could only view with simple horror, being no Eugene O'Neill." In the course of "grimly cutting" the piece, including deleting all references to a Philadelphia Quaker background, Blitzstein produced "exercise scenes" that helped him better understand his characters so that he could "add the precisely right touches to existing scenes." In the process, he left behind a mountain of notes and sketches, many painstakingly dated, establishing a working method that would characterize his most ambitious undertakings to follow.[3]

Tracking the work's progress, the *Times* stated in August 1938 that the now two-act "operetta" would "have a sort of Greek chorus, consisting, playfully enough, of Greek waiters." Given that the completed opera, to use the composer's term, involved a workers' chorus that included Greek Americans, the piece's storyline by this point must have come into greater focus, including the theme of labor conditions in the hotel industry, a matter that had attracted national attention through various strikes and union drives around the country in late 1937 especially. The *Times* mentioned a delivery date of January 1939, but Blitzstein did not finish the work—or at least, a preliminary four-act version (to which a surviving four-act libretto most likely corresponds)—until the end of that year, after which he spent still more months shaping the piece into its final two-act form. Accordingly, although the composer spoke of the opera as taking two years to write, three years or more would seem more accurate, notwithstanding the fact that he discarded much of what he wrote along the way. Nor did he ever orchestrate the piece, which would have required several more months at the least.[4]

During this period, especially in the course of 1939, Blitzstein cemented what would become enduring friendships with Mina Curtiss and David Diamond. The sister of noted impresario Lincoln Kirstein, with whom she had a troubled relationship, Curtiss (1896–1985) grew up in Rochester and Boston, where her father became a partner in Filene's department store; a member of the English faculty at Smith, in 1926 she married, outside her Jewish faith, Henry Curtiss, who died the following year. In the mid-1930s, she temporarily left teaching in order to work for the Mercury Theatre, thereby coming into contact with Blitzstein, whose renegade *Cradle Will Rock* production she and brother Lincoln helped underwrite. After the war, she devoted more time to her writing, most notably, a study of *Bizet and His World* (1958) dedicated to Blitzstein.

Over the years, Blitzstein often retreated to the Curtiss estate, Chapelbrook, in Ashfield in northwestern Massachusetts. "The place is delicious," he wrote to David Diamond in 1939, "an old low farmhouse beautifully and carefully done over a period of twelve years by three different sets of people, each instantly understanding the idea and the mode, and each endowed with miraculous taste and imagination." Blitzstein would stay in the four-room converted blacksmith shop set off from the house, often taking an afternoon swim in a pool on the grounds, no matter the weather. In the evenings, he often assisted Curtiss on her writing, to the point that she considered him co-author of the Bizet book. After one stay in 1948, he thanked Curtiss for her "inestimable belief and confidence in me—I've met nothing like since Nadia Boulanger twenty years ago." Indeed, in a

1949 letter to John Houseman, Curtiss showed keen enthusiasm for Blitzstein's work, praising *Regina*'s "revolutionary" melodic flow and its witty characterizations, although she felt that his "strong political beliefs" hampered him as an artist. In a tribute to the composer written after his death, Curtiss further wrote, "As a personality, Marc embodied much of his Russian heritage. Some times he was a brooding or violent character out of Dostoevsky. Some times he was as high-spirited and frivolous as one of Turgenev's gamblers at Baden-Baden." She considered him an "irreplaceable friend," and, as she told Houseman, a consolation for her failed relationship with her brother Lincoln.[5]

Aside from perhaps Leonard Bernstein, Blitzstein developed no more intimate composer friend than David Diamond (1915–2005), a student of Roger Sessions and Nadia Boulanger ten years his junior. Blitzstein and Diamond had met in the mid-1930s, but they grew particularly close while at Yaddo during the summer of 1939. In conversation with Eric Gordon, Diamond fondly remembered that summer as one in which he and Blitzstein swapped stories about their homosexual exploits and visited black bars where they could dance together unmolested, but his diaries reveal tensions never entirely overcome, for Diamond's religious sympathies, his dismay over the Nazi-Soviet pact, and his association with such Trotskyists as writer Delmore Schwartz, combined with both men's volatility, sporadically led to vehement arguments. (Blitzstein felt that the Nazi-Soviet pact had been "grossly misinterpreted," according to Diamond, who added in his unpublished memoir that Blitzstein believed that Stalin had signed the pact in order to wrest nuclear secrets from the Nazis so as to be able to build an atomic bomb "before Hitler could use it to conquer the world.") "I'm not too talky now with Marc," wrote Diamond in his September journal, "—he's such a fake about using politics and violent temper to cover up his homosexuality et al." However, within two weeks, things seemed back on track: "Marc is loosening up and seems to not care whether people know he is homosexual—that's a relief."[6]

Recalling this summer at Yaddo in his memoir, Diamond further noted Blitzstein's desire to improve society "by imposition and, if necessary, force," and reflected,

> He [Blitzstein] seemed without defects. The equilibrium of behaviour was, in appearances, perfect. But the truth was otherwise. His feelings were shallow. He was delusive. His good looks were marvelous masks behind which was an equally masked intelligence functioning superficially and bordering on near indifference. Some found this attractive, even charming. When, one night, I said to him that I found his detachment a hindrance to understanding him, he replied, "Don't fret. When I'm most 'cool' is when I'm hottest."[7]

Moreover, at least for Diamond, sexual rivalry posed a potential irritation, given their attraction to a similar "type." Indeed, back in New York in 1941, a joke by Blitzstein about having a "threesome" with Diamond and a new boyfriend prompted an aggrieved journal entry: "Marc revolted me. . . . Marc's frustrated intellectuality, his sexual hintings and probings. . . . Bad talk, bad arguments, bad everything—." And after a tense dinner in 1945 with Blitzstein and the latter's boyfriend Bill Hewitt, Diamond asked himself, "Is it that I'm envious?" At any rate, Diamond's feelings about Blitzstein continued to fluctuate wildly; sometimes he thought him pugnacious, sophistic, and smug, at other times, amusing and enchanting, "like a pussy-cat."[8]

Diamond's irascibility in turn could exasperate Blitzstein. Answering an accusatory missive in late 1939, the latter wrote, "I don't know what all the shouting is about," and in response to more accusations in June 1941,

> Perhaps it's characteristic of you that it seemed I did the attacking, and you the defending. . . . As to the "political discussion," there wasn't any. You did all the talking; at a certain point, I got really drunk . . . and insulted you. That was wrong, of course I apologize, of course you're "worth it." But I do wish you had less the feeling that you were being wooed politically by something or somebody; if you don't come around to it, it will be your loss. That doesn't mean that I won't do everything in my power to help you. Your charge that you had begged and begged for help in the past, and that I had been adamant or worse—well we can count that up to the gin or the imagination.

As late as 1957 Blitzstein scolded Diamond, then living in Italy, "You must not try to run my life for me, even were we not at so great a distance from each other."[9]

However, all this bickering seemed like mere interludes between friendly rounds of drinks and meals, and in any case no serious breach ever developed; on the contrary, the two remained devoted friends, with Blitzstein helping to secure Diamond a Chapelbrook grant and Diamond traveling from Florence to Rome with Blitzstein in 1960 to help him find a flat there. "I'll tell you a little secret aboit [sic] you and me, and why I feel you're so worth holding on to," Blitzstein told Diamond in 1943. "It's because, while we practically disagree about everything political, I know you're passionately concerned about it, even tortured. You're not running away, as so many—even the 'master' [Stravinsky], I fear, are doing." And after visiting Diamond in Florence in 1959, he wrote to him, "It is hard to tell you how bursting I am with affection and gratitude. . . . thanks for showing me how life can be lived." "Sweet, kind Marc," Diamond noted in his diary in 1956 after his mother died and Blitzstein called to offer him the use of his New York apartment. "He is a good friend. And becomes more so each year. And I had *such* doubts about him. But they were based on *his* doubts about *me*." Blitzstein's death in 1964 left Diamond "numb with agony."[10]

As creators primarily of theater and concert music, respectively, Blitzstein and Diamond seemed somewhat distant with respect to each other's work, although whatever reservations Diamond might have had about the content and orchestration of Blitzstein's music, he acknowledged the "power and tenderness" of *The Cradle*, the "effective" accessibility of the *Airborne Symphony*, and the deftly calibrated "headlong flow" of *Regina*, whose libretto proved more helpful to his own operatic attempts than those by Musorgsky and Boito.[11]

For his part, Blitzstein left behind little record of his thoughts concerning Diamond's music, although some advice offered in early 1943 suggested a criticism of sorts: "Don't write pieces which have 'beauty' and 'line' and 'superb craftsmanship' as their reason for existence. They are all indispensable to a good work; and yet *communicating* with your listener is the real thing. You are talking, saying something; say it then, content." And after the premiere of Diamond's Eighth Symphony in the fall of 1961, its composer recorded in his journal that Blitzstein had said to him, "The fascinating thing about your symphony is its elusiveness. Its mastery and scope is taken for granted; but not being able to put the finger on it is what fascinates me. It's a remarkable piece."[12]

While at work on *No for an Answer,* Blitzstein kept both Curtiss and Diamond abreast of his progress. "Even my sex-life has gone completely by the board in behalf of 'No for an Answer,'" he told Curtiss in July 1939, "—and if there is any more varied, strange and elaborate sex-life in these United States than at Saratoga just before and during season, I'd like to know about it!" And in late August, he wrote Diamond, "I have slashed and cut and molded; the work is getting streamlined and all the good things are coming up like emerging lilies. I think it will be a wonderful work." (He also told Diamond, away from Yaddo at the time, about the "very gay" party he threw for the stripper Gypsy Rose Lee earlier in the month at his studio, the same Acosta Nichols Stone Tower where Copland had completed his *Piano Variations* in 1930 and where he himself had stayed in 1931.) Much of the discarded material concerned background material about the two protagonists—Paul and Clara Chase, a married couple who apparently had evolved from the original brother-sister idea—that largely disappeared, including the presence of an older homosexual friend of Paul's, Evelyn Stuart Cook ("Cookie"), a "tante" (literally aunt in several languages but also international slang for a gay man) modeled after writer Allan Ross Macdougall and composer Virgil Thomson, and described as "utterly aware and wise about everybody else. No morality, no evasion or blindness. Relentless, convictionless, honest, clear about everything except values."[13]

In an article for the *Times* published on the day of the work's official premiere— January 5, 1941—Blitzstein addressed the opera's long gestation period by explaining that after he had completed *The Cradle*, which he described as "a stage cartoon, a two-dimension allegory, involving categorical types of people . . . in a static one-act situation," he wondered if its form could be "adapted to a real story about real people? Could I develop characters with rich human relationships, which might even change through the course of the action? . . . In short: could music act as the base of a contemporary realistic play?" About this same time, he further described the earlier *Cradle* as "peopled by symbols of people I hated, not real characters. The new show is my first experiment with real people, human beings. And they're all people I love."[14]

Most of the work's characters, although not Paul and Clara, belong to the Diogenes Club, a workers' social club serving the largely seasonal employees in the town of Crest Lake, a summer resort in the eastern United States. (The libretto points even more specifically to ski country, and Blitzstein particularly might have had in mind Saranac Lake, where he wrote some of the work.) The Diogenes Club meets in the backroom of a remote roadside luncheonette run by a good-natured Greek immigrant, Nick Kyriakos. (Most of the action takes place in either the club-room or at Nick's lunch counter—occasionally both at once—and the work's principal mise-en-scène, as conceived by Blitzstein, shows these two rooms separated by a wall, with a door allowing entry from one space to another.) [15]

Nick has established the club to help meet the recreational and organizational needs of local workers, especially during the off-season, when many of the members lack employment; the action takes place at just such a time, in mid-September, after the summer season. In addition to Nick, the club members include Cutch, who holds a part-time job as a soda-jerk; Bulge, the group's jokester; Emanuel, who assists Nick at the lunch counter, and his girlfriend, Gertie Phorylles; Gina Tonieri, who is expecting a baby and whose husband is looking for work in Florida; Mery, the young mother of an infant child; Francie, who works in a laundry; and friends Alex and Steve. Nick, Emanuel, Gertie, Alex, and Steve are identified, either in the libretto or in sketches, as Greek; Gina would seem to be Italian. (Blitzstein might have derived Gina's surname from Emil and Mary Tonieri, the caretakers at the MacDowell Colony.) Although some club members speak with a pronounced foreign accent, most seem longtime American residents or native born.

The other principals include Paul Chase, an intellectual who had been a campus radical while at Princeton; his wife Clara, sister of Congressman Felix Carver, owner of Carver Aluminum and the head of the local Resort Association; Jimmy and Bobbie, two vaudevillians stranded at a local nightclub, the Pillbox Bar; Nick's son and Francie's boyfriend, Joe Kyriakos, now working with Jewish labor attorney Max Kraus as a union organizer; and Mike Stretto, a young ruffian.

The opera's action, divided into twenty scenes for its first performance in 1941, takes place, according to the premiere playbill, "in and around the Diogenes Social Club at Crest Lake, a summer resort in the eastern United States. The time is mid-September, 1939, after the summer season is over."

Act I. Scene one. The Diogenes Social Club and Nick's Lunchcounter. Friday evening. Cutch rehearses the club's chorus in didactic songs (vocalise, "Song of the Bat," and "Take the Book").

Scene two. The Counter. Paul Chase, the club's well-heeled advisor, and something of a lush, arrives for a club meeting with his wife Clara and introduces her to

Nick Kyriakos. Aware that there have been labor problems in town, Clara suggests that Nick speak to her brother, Congressman Felix Carver.

Scene three. The Club. After the rehearsal ends ("Take the Book"), the club members hold a meeting. Emanuel reports that some local vigilantes who want the club closed, the Monktowners, recently beat up Alex and Steve as a warning ("I Wish to Report"). About to give her own report, Gina instead reproaches Mery for having a child when she's so young and poor ("They Report That the World's Full of Fools"); after Gina hastily exits, Mery follows her. Alex reads a letter from his unemployed brother, who wants to come to Crest Lake; Bulge expresses dismay at the prospect of another job seeker, but the club members hope for better days ("One Day There Will Be Work for Us All"). Accusing Felix Carver and the Resort Association of enlisting the Monktowners, Cutch despairs, but Nick urges the group to campaign for their rights and recruit new members, while Paul breaks the news that the Resort Association plans to turn Crest Lake into a winter resort once they have the labor situation under control, hence the Association's interest in shutting down the club, and the reason, too, why Nick has sent for his son Joe, a union organizer ("I Have Listened"). As excitement grips the club members, Joe Kyriakos and his friend, Jewish attorney Max Kraus, arrive from Georgia, where they have been working to organize unions; but before adjourning the meeting, the club agrees to Nick's proposal that they invite Alex's brother to join them ("Take the Book").

Scene four. Pillbox Bar. Later the same night. Clara questions Paul about his involvement with the Diogenes Club, but Paul defends his and the group's sincerity, ordering plain orange juice as a token of his sobriety ("Secret Singing").

Scene five. The Club and the Counter. Saturday afternoon. Alex and Steve hold a debate about capitalism; the club members tease Bulge; Emanuel, behind the lunch counter, nauseates Cutch with talk about rotten hamburgers; and Joe discloses his intention to start unionizing local workers. As the club members pronounce the debate between Alex and Steve a draw, the Monktowners throw a projectile into the clubroom with a note attached, "Your last warning. This is it. Close your joint—or else."

Scene six. Pillbox Bar. Saturday night. Joe, Francie, and Max meet Paul and Clara for drinks. In awe of Joe and Max, Paul asks them about their jail time in Georgia. Joe, who uses the pseudonym Joe Dorgan, explains that he and Max were arrested as "outside agitators," noting that only union organizers, not other experts, get tagged as such. As Max observes a knife in Paul's hand—the latter has ordered a sandwich— he breaks down; Joe explains that Max was incarcerated with the insane for ten days in Georgia, and that when Joe complained about this, he was met with anti-Semitic invective ("Outside Agitator"). After Clara leaves to drive the others home, Paul asks the nightclub entertainers Jimmy and Bobby to perform two "escapist" numbers, one "Broadway hot-cha" ("Dimples"), the other "Broadway torch" ("Fraught").

Scene seven. The Counter. Sunday afternoon. Clara stops by the luncheonette to suggest in vain that Nick sever relations with Paul ("I Was Just Driving By").

Scene eight. The Club. Francie muses on various topics—including the trustworthiness of Paul—as Joe lovingly repeats her name; the two passionately embrace ("Francie").

Scene nine. The Counter. Clara wonders whether Paul might find himself through his involvement with the club ("I Must Be Out of My Mind"). A customer enters and plants a bottle of liquor behind the counter, followed by a policeman who, discovering the bottle, asks Nick for his liquor license; when Nick cannot produce one, the cop padlocks the luncheonette and arrests Alex and three other men.

Scene ten. The Club. Monday morning. Outraged by this police frame-up, the club members plan on silently picketing the town courthouse. Clara offers to serve as a witness and Paul prepares to join the demonstration ("Did They Think They Could Get Away With That?" and "No for an Answer!").

Act II. Scene one. The Club. Monday, early evening. Bulge, watching the club on the day of the demonstration, recalls for Clara the time, on a dare from Alex, he panhandled a rich woman ("Penny Candy"). Drenched from a long walk in the rain, Cutch, Emanuel, and Steve appear and relate the events earlier in the day.

Scene two. Courthouse steps. (Flashback to the afternoon.) During the protest, Paul, somewhat intoxicated, baits the police until the other protestors force him from the picket line. Paul leaves.

Scene three. Pillbox Bar. Monday evening. A remorseful Paul befriends a young tough, Mike Stretto, who's a stooge for the Resort Association. Mike talks about himself ("I Ain't the Scared Kind, See?") and impresses Paul as "the real thing" ("Where Is the Solace?").

Scene four. The Club. Monday night. The club members continue their tale to Clara, explaining that because Paul had the keys to their car, they had to walk home in the rain. Joe, Francie, Nick, and Max enter and report further that the police presented as evidence a bomb allegedly intended for Carver Aluminum found on club premises and that the judge tried and convicted Alex and the others without their even appearing. Appalled that such judicial impropriety could take place in America, Clara offers to testify that the police never entered the clubroom proper and that they left only with Alex's dumbbells. She and Joe depart to find Paul.

Scene five. Pillbox Bar. Paul, "very high, carrying on, for the people in the bar," publicly names Joe Kyriakos/Dorgan as the leader of the demonstration and vents his despair, describing his recent experience as a "Walpurgisnacht" ("Escape by Flight" for offstage chorus/"Weep for Me" for Paul). Clara and Joe arrive and take Paul home.

Scene six. Paul's Bedroom. Later that night. As Paul sleeps, Clara reflects on the challenges posed by maturity ("In the Clear").

Scene seven. The Counter. Thursday evening. Mery sings a lullaby to her baby ("Baby, Don't You Cry"). Clara enters, telling Francie that she and Paul are about to leave on a trip. Francie informs her that Alex and the others have been released from jail on a stay of execution prepared by Max. Clara declines Francie's invitation to attend a birthday party being held for Joe in the clubroom and withdraws. Mery continues her lullaby ("Baby, Don't You Cry," reprise).

Scene eight. The Club. At the birthday party, Bulge pays tribute to Joe ("The Purest Kind of a Guy") as does Nick, who's concerned about protecting his son's anonymity ("A Happy Birthday to You Know Who!" a reworking of Emanuel's first-act hamburger song). Mike surreptitiously enters. Paul and Clara rush in to warn the club members about the approach of Monktowners. Mike signals the vigilantes, who taunt Joe from outside. Caught, Mike defends himself by saying that Paul revealed Joe's identity at the Pillbox Bar the other evening. Clara hopes to divert the rioters so that Joe might escape, but an arriving officer takes him into "protective custody" and leads him outside, where the Monktowners shoot him. As the vigilantes tear-gas the club, all flee.

Scene nine. A Filling Station. A short distance from the club, Clara stops her car in order to telephone her brother. Disillusioned and ashamed, Paul leaves on his own. Clara deduces that Felix has been complicit in Joe's murder. Anxiously searching for a phone, Alex tells Clara that the Monktowners have set fire to the club.

Scene ten. Road by the Club. The club members mourn Joe's death ("Make the Heart Be Stone"). Clara arrives, offering encouragement and help, and explaining that the promise of her country to the "little people" needs to become "real again." Nick makes plans for the club to soldier on, and urges them to try to salvage their mimeograph machine: "Gertie, Steve, mimeograph machine is our voice. We no let them take away our voice" ("No for an Answer!" and vocalise, reprise).

The opera's complex twenty-scene structure moves with a fluidity reminiscent of film, especially the first half of the second act, with its flashback interruptions set alternately on the courthouse steps and at the Pillbox Bar. The four-act version, as represented by a surviving libretto with twenty-five separate scenes, some extremely short (one, with Clara's face in a pool of light, lasts less than a minute), others broken down into as many as six subsidiary scenes, seems even more cinematic. This four-act script conforms to the above scenario fairly closely, but as Blitzstein streamlined the work to a twenty-three-scene script and then a twenty-two-scene vocal score, condensed still further to twenty scenes for the premiere, as outlined above, he cut a considerable amount of material, including a discussion between Clara and Joe that intimates some romantic attraction between them, and an interlude, intended to represent sexual decadence, in which a boy and a girl pick up Mike for a three-way tryst.

Although these cuts arguably improved the opera, some clarifying information disappeared as a result, such as the fact that Crest Lake sits some miles from the resort town of Monktown, explaining the name Monktowners, and that Joe had been run out of town and told not to return, thus the need for secrecy. Moreover, in the more preliminary versions, Paul (who's an aspiring writer just passing through) befriends Mike (identified as Mike Tonieri, Gina's son) much earlier in the drama, allowing a more ample context for their relationship. At the same time, as the composer tightened the story, he found room to intensify some of its antiwar sentiments in apparent response to the outbreak of hostilities in Europe.

Blitzstein had special difficulty deciding which of the four cabaret numbers intended for the work to include and where to place them. In the four-act script, they appear in the Walpurgis Night scene in close succession as various manifestations of escapism: a blues parody, "Let's Be Blue," sung by Paul to Mike; a Tin Pan Alley parody, "Dimples," sung by Jimmy; a Cole Porter parody, "Fraught," sung by Bobbie; and a Hemingway parody, "Expatriate," sung by Paul and a Girl. For the two-act script, he omitted "Let's Be Blue"; moved "Dimples" and "Fraught" to the first act; and left "Expatriate" in the second act as a number for Johnny and Bobbie—a solution found in the completed vocal score as well, except for "Expatriate," which in the end he cut and which does not survive in completed form. Blitzstein also removed the bitter "Outside Agitator" for the opera's 1941 premiere, but not from the score itself or for the work's 1960 revival.[16]

The opera patently reflects the ideals of the American League for Peace and Democracy (1936–40, originally the American League Against War and Fascism, founded 1933), a communist front organization with which Blitzstein had some affiliation. Tellingly, its original cast planned to sing excerpts from the work at a rally at Triborough Stadium on Randall's Island sponsored by the league's successor, the American Peace Mobilization (1940–41), on April 5, 1941, a rained-out event that also would have included performances by Paul Robeson and various choruses and folk dances "symbolizing the international solidarity of all peoples." The American League had two major planks as suggested by its name: first, the promotion of peace abroad, including opposition to financial transactions with aggressor nations and support for collective international security (which distinguished them from right-wing isolationists); and second, the protection of democracy at home, including the struggle against anti-Semitism and racism and the support of measures friendly to labor unions and refugees from fascist countries.[17]

The theme of peace subtly weaves its way throughout the opera, beginning with the opening didactic chorus in which the Bat—the worker—learns not to join either the Beasts or the Birds lest he be "torn to pieces—by both sides." Joe and Max explicitly warn Nick against American involvement in a European war, predicting that workers will otherwise lose their recent gains "in the name of patriotism" (I, v). Elsewhere the opera similarly refers to war as a diversionary tactic, comparable to alcohol and sex, as in the offstage chorus "Escape by Flight." Such antimilitarism informed *The Cradle* as well, but here it implied support for the Nazi-Soviet pact of August 1939 and neutrality toward Great Britain, a stance that reflected a specifically communist position as opposed to the pro-Allies sentiments held elsewhere among the temporarily factionalized popular front.

However, the opera takes for its main theme the survival of democracy at home in the face of domestic fascism. Speaking of the work shortly before its premiere, Blitzstein stated,

> The theme is what happens to basic democratic principles in time of stress—what happens to the little people, in whose behalf the democratic principles exist, in times of stress. . . . I am glad that, at last, people are realizing the true proportions of the menace of fascism. But a great many are giving lip service to the idea of preserving democracy here and using it to fight fascism abroad who aren't nearly vigilant enough about spotting fascism and fighting it right around them. . . . As we were late in thinking in terms of a collective security of nations to stop Hitler, so now we are late in fighting the Hitler infection right here. And the infection may have spread to a degree undreamed of. . . . Until we have attained our own future, a blazing and beautiful democracy at home, we will fight abroad only at the risk of losing our democracy at home.

Although the composer had addressed domestic fascism before, this new work presented a fuller and more harrowing treatment of such threats, with Joe's narrative of abuse at the hands of the Georgia police—who call him a "sheenie" and tell him, "But you're an Outside Agitator!/So you must be jew, you're either jew—/and if you ain't, it's just the same—/you're under jewish power!"—mincing no words.[18]

The opera frames this fight against fascism in the context of nonviolent resistance. Significantly, in early drafts, Blitzstein referred to the workers' group as the Spartacus Club, but possibly felt that the association between the Roman rebel Spartacus and communist revolt, as in Germany's Spartacus League, placed too great an emphasis on violence; the figure of Diogenes, the virtuous Greek philosopher who railed against social corruption, not only seemed more befitting this mostly Greek workers' association, but better suited the drama's tenor. "Clara does not conduct or promote a bloody overthrow of an existing society," notes Paul Talley, "rather she joins a group which implements a gradual change by altering public opinion, by interpreting existing laws, and by lobbying for legal changes in society's laws." Many American communists of the time, as evidenced by the party's 1938 national convention platform, favored just such nonviolent methods, which echoed at least a strain in Marx's thinking as expressed in "The Possibility of Non-Violent Revolution" (1872).[19]

As in *The Cradle* and *I've Got the Tune*, the drama hinges on moral choices confronting educated citizens, here represented by Paul and Clara Chase. In early sketches, Blitzstein imagined them as friends Don and Clara, both about twenty years old and living together, although he eventually portrayed them as a married couple, with the story revolving around the dissolution of their marriage as Paul moves from advocacy to disengagement, and Clara, conversely, from skepticism to commitment. Indeed, Blitzstein considered their marriage as central to the story in ways not necessarily apparent from the finished work. "The whole play can center about their love—hers for him . . . ," he wrote in one sketch, "her faith in him is unbounded and gets systematically beaten down by his inadequacy. (Leora in *Arrowsmith*). He takes her faith and love, feeds on it, his vanity needs it." Blitzstein drew here not only on Sinclair Lewis's 1925 novel *Arrowsmith*, but likely on the dynamics between himself and both his sister Jo and his wife Eva. As with Larry Foreman in *The Cradle*, Clara further plays a special role in establishing that connection between popular democracy and national traditions as promulgated by the people's front during this period: "I have even more at stake than you!" she tells the club members in the last scene, "My roots are here, deep!"[20]

Blitzstein meant Paul, by contrast, to represent "the lost youth of our time," a brilliant but self-destructive romantic who seeks release by way of intoxicants, the "Escape by Flight" chorus suggesting his use of cocaine and marijuana—Blitzstein himself had some first-hand experience with at least the latter drug—as well as alcohol (at one point the composer even referred to "Weep for Me" as part of a "Marijuana Scene"); and for whom the workers' cause becomes yet another escape. (In his sketches, Blitzstein noted such other "escapes" as Moral Re-Armament, Trotskyism, anarchism, spirituality, mysticism, expatriation, perversion, and suicide.) This theme struck a note congruent with contemporary communist tracts, including Earl Browder's critique of elitist revolutionaries as found in *The People's Front* (1938)—which the composer read closely—and V. J. Jerome's appraisal of intellectual fellow travelers in *The Intellectuals and the War* (1940). Eric Gordon mentions, too, a connection to "that whole tradition of Russian novels by Turgenev and others that feature bourgeois youth going out to the countryside or to the working class and throwing themselves into the revolutionary movement, usually with disastrous results."[21]

At the same time, Blitzstein regarded Paul's attempt at social engagement as essentially positive, writing, "Somewhere spike the feeling that Paul's thing was just a phase of youth (the 'revolutionary'), that he could have 'come out of it' like other 'wild oats' to a 'useful life.' Show that the one hopeful thing was the 'revolutionary' direction." As the libretto stands, his fate remains uncertain, although some handwritten annotations suggest that he leaves for Washington to see Felix while Clara stays behind. In any case, the figure of Paul became the principal sticking point with many people who otherwise loved the piece, not only critics, but friends like Minna Lederman, who in early 1940 wrote to the composer, "I kept wondering too what he [Paul] stood for, just what kind of symbol, how much meaning or importance was intended." On the other hand, Virgil Thomson especially appreciated the characterization of Paul and also Mike: "Few operas have more than one or two real people in them. *No for an Answer* has at least two, the rich boy and the little tough, the spy."[22]

As models for Paul, Blitzstein cited in his notes such figures as writers E. E. Cummings and Klaus Mann, actor-director James Light, and "the early [F. Scott]

Fitzgerald heroes," suggesting the opera's "lost" generation to be his own; indeed, the character seems to have had a strong autobiographical dimension from the start. But as he worked on the piece, he possibly also took into consideration such slightly younger friends as composer-writer Paul Bowles and filmmaker-writer Harry Dunham (both b. 1910), two artists very close to each other and both briefly members of the Communist Party. Like the fictional Paul Chase, Harry Dunham attended Princeton, while Dunham's future wife Marian Chase perhaps even suggested Paul's last name, much as Bowles possibly provided his first. That Blitzstein might have modeled his operatic protagonist in part after Bowles and Dunham seems that much more plausible given that he considered their mentor, Virgil Thomson, as a prototype for Cookie, Paul Chase's "duenna" in early drafts.[23]

As with *The Cradle*, *No for an Answer* employs a striking diversity of vocal techniques, including recitative, song, vocalise, speech-song, accented recitation, and rhythmic recitation, as well as spoken dialogue, both accompanied and unaccompanied. At times, as in the scene for Clara and Nick in the first act, Blitzstein further explores a special type of accompanied recitation that—in contrast to speech-song (with its pitched notes marked with x's), rhythmic recitation (with its unpitched notes marked with x's), and accented recitation (with its slashes over accented spoken syllables)—involves music that mirrors the rhythm and inflection of spoken dialogue but with no more coordination than the grouping of words within bar lines, a rather free combination of speech and music that might be called "measured recitation."

The opera's third scene—insightfully described in an early review of the work by James Morison as "really one long 'number,' carefully, almost like a mosaic, pieced together"—reveals a particularly intricate handling of these varied techniques in order to create a large, compelling form. The scene starts with a return to the chorus rehearsal that opens the opera. Some accompanied dialogue ensues, followed by Emanuel's heart-rending "I Wish to Report," which compactly uses song, speech-song, accented recitation, and at its end measured recitation—techniques that combine to impart a heightened sense of verisimilitude. After some spoken dialogue, the score explodes with Gina's furious solo, "They Report That the World's Full of Fools," one of the score's relatively few bona fide numbers, but with a dramatic conclusion that uses accented recitation and speech-song, thus avoiding the closure of a sung ending. Alex reads his brother's letter accompanied by instrumental underscoring and choral humming, followed by the gem-like chorus "One Day There Will Be Work for Us All." Cutch's outburst, "That's What We Have Been Hearing," exclusively features recitation with instrumental punctuations, but forms a little solo nonetheless, including a firm tonal conclusion. The large section that follows, "I Have Listened," begins with Nick's speech modestly accompanied by a single melody in the accompaniment, but effectively builds through choral humming, choral interjections, accented recitation, song, and speech-song to Joe's climactic arrival, Nick's call for order, and a brief reprise of "Take the Book." So

novel and imaginative an approach to text setting, further dramatized by the conflict between G major and G minor that undergirds the scene, enriches the drama
enormously.[24]

Blitzstein makes similar although less elaborate use of such techniques to
delineate other dramatic units, including the Saturday afternoon scene at the
club, which, aside from some brief dialogue at the very end, constitutes a sort of
rondo-scherzo, with alternating musical sections portraying Alex and Steve's
debate (accented recitation), Bulge's mock plaint (song), Emanuel's discussion of
hamburgers (song), and Joe and Max's conversation with Nick (accented recitation). The rondo form not only enlivens the scene's humor, but helps give the impression of various activities going on at the same time—all violently interrupted
by the projectile thrown into the club at the rondo's conclusion. In liner notes to a
1941 recording of excerpts from the work, Blitzstein might well have had this
scene in mind when he stated that the opera featured, in addition to "continuous
music-for-action, as in Verdi or Charpentier" and "'numbers' as in Mozart or Kurt
Weill," "scenes using special instrumental forms, as in Berg's 'Wozzeck.'"[25]

Notwithstanding the presence of such "numbers," the work contains hardly
any self-contained set pieces, certainly far fewer than *The Cradle*, which had
eleven songs published by Chappell to this opera's none (although reviewing the
work's premiere in the *New Yorker*, Robert A. Simon thought that Blitzstein "could
remodel several of his airs into out-and-out song hits if he cared to"). Except for
"Dimples" and "Fraught" (which actually combine to make one number), "Penny
Candy," "The Purest Kind of a Guy," and "A Happy Birthday to You Know
Who!"—all of which are performances of one kind or another—the songs tend to
trail off, end ambiguously, or conclude—as do even some of these performed
numbers—with spoken words, thereby subverting the kind of ending a sung note
might provide. To take a particularly dramatic example of this last strategy, as the
soulful "Weep for Me" (whose lyric originated as an idea for a torch song)
approaches a cadence at the phrase, "Maybe I'll weep for," rather than concluding
on the expected word, "you," Paul shouts at Bobbie, against a flurry of clashing
triads, "Take your goddam feet off my lap!" which essentially brings the number
to an end. Even "In the Clear," a real set piece, ends subtly as the melody settles on
a soft, dissonant note, followed by a hushed cadence.[26]

In an article for the *Herald Tribune* published soon after the work's 1941 premiere, Blitzstein spoke about how writing his own libretto facilitated the work's
"close-woven texture of words and music, of ideas and treatment," citing this as
"the one real advantage of collaborating with one's self." For although he recognized that having a collaborator would help save time and energy—"I am a musician, addicted to the theater, not a playwright"—he could not find one "who has
either the patience or the inner strength to put up with me." He concluded, "If I
must go on doing both book and music, perhaps I should resign myself to easy
plots. And if another complex story occurs to me, maybe I shall be able to forget

that I don't write words first, or music first, but both in a discontinuous and muddy stream; and maybe I will make another telephone call to Playwright No. 2, or Poet No. 1, and ask for another chance." In 1956, Blitzstein further expounded on the difficulty of saying what came first, the words or music, in writing such works as this one, describing his "operational method" as follows:

> I first chart the outline and general idea of a scene or a song or a musical dialogue, lightly, as though it were a rough freehand drawing. Then a tune will perhaps suggest itself and suggest the right words to go with it, and the words when found will in turn evoke the next musical phrase, or even the shape of the whole musical form. This is by no means an easy method because when you are doing a large-scale work, you have to examine and reexamine a single hunk to make sure it is not only right in itself but is right for and has the proper relation to the entire work. It is my way and I don't apologize for it. There are advantages and disadvantages in being your own librettist. The main disadvantage is that you lack the fresh perspective of another mind working with you, and you have to dig up that perspective within yourself, be two people as it were in constant alternating battle and agreement. The advantage, I suppose, is that there is a chance the final marriage of words and music will be close-knit and inextricable and will give off a sense of naturalness, even necessity, a sense that it all had to be this way and no other.[27]

Blitzstein's words for this opera indeed combine with the music to "give off a sense of naturalness." "Weep for Me," with its evocation of intoxicated rambling, seems particularly arresting in this regard, as do the two numbers for the youngest and least sophisticated characters: Mike's "I Ain't the Scared Kind, See?" and Mery's "Baby, Don't You Cry." The words for Mike's number hardly resemble a typical stage lyric—"I ain't the scared kind, see?/I don't get scared./I got my nerve. I got my two fists—/And I'll get by./When I was in New York, I got scared"— much as the accompanying prose-like music stretches the conventions of popular song. Mery's lullaby sounds similarly spontaneous; Gina even teases, "Mery—no other words, only 'baby, don't you cry'?" to which Mery playfully responds, "Oh yes. Then it goes, 'Baby, baby, don't you cry.' It seems to work," the music emphasizing the extra "baby." For Michael Tilson Thomas, this lullaby epitomized Blitzstein's "sort of artless approach to vocal expression. . . . It is almost tuneless, a shapeless melody of very few notes, but it has immense power, because Marc has somehow captured what a woman who can't sing, but wants to comfort her baby, would sing." At the same time, the opera displays a cultivated hand throughout, with such numbers as the mock-pathetic "Penny Candy" allowing scope for clever lyrics and rhymes: "Ah madam, I will spare you my tale of woe—/You'd sorrow so, your heart would break./There was my darling mother, who cursed and drank/ One night she sank down in that lake./The lake by her window, and she in bed,/by liquor maimed./She musta fell out and fell in, she's dead,/And still unclaimed./For ten years we haven't found the body."[28]

To some extent, *No for an Answer* made contact with Blitzstein's earlier music, literally so in its recycling of some of "Gauley Bridge Tunnel" for "Song of the Bat," the *Children's Cantata* for "Take the Book," and *The Condemned* for "Make the Heart Be Stone," but more generally in its adaptation of stylistic characteristics that dated back to the 1920s, again refuting the notion of a complete break from longstanding habits and traits. That the composer used the same shorthand for Paul and Clara—"P & C"—as for the eponymous couple in *Parabola and Circula* intimated dramatic continuities as well. But the work reveals growth in both range and individuality. Some of the music for Joe and Bulge recalls American folk song, which during these years had become increasingly associated with left-wing political protest. Other numbers relatedly suggest Greek or Jewish music. In contrast, the nightclub music at the Pillbox Bar evokes the world of Cabaret TAC (one early critic even described "Fraught" as "a raw and rousing take-off in the TAC style on the Cole Porter idea of the hot song in the key of Mink-flat"), so much so that the opera can be seen as absorbing the American political cabaret of the late 1930s much as Brecht and Weill incorporated German cabaret in their Weimar works. Still such other numbers as "Francie," "I Ain't the Scared Kind, See?" and "In the Clear" sound like nothing else. "With *No for an Answer* Blitzstein finally found his own musical style," Copland stated in 1941. "You can recognize it in the short, clipped musical sentences, the uneven phrase lengths, the nervous energy, the unerring sense of design."[29]

Beginning in 1938, the press occasionally mentioned both the Mercury Theatre and Billy Rose as possible producers of the opera, but nothing along these lines materialized. In early 1940, Jed Harris also expressed interest, telling Blitzstein, improbably enough, that he would be willing to discuss a deal if the composer would turn the work into a comedy. Meanwhile, Blitzstein performed excerpts from the piece privately at Muriel Draper's fashionably bohemian salon on January 30, 1940, and publicly at a New Theatre League benefit on February 11, with the *Times* reporting that some individuals who had liked what they heard planned to raise the $30,000 necessary to mount the opera, including a small pit orchestra of about a dozen musicians, the following season. The composer also performed selections later in the month at an Arrow Press benefit, and then, on May 8, at an American Music Festival concert at the Mecca Temple for the Spanish Children's Relief Fund, sharing the stage with folk singers Woody Guthrie and Huddie Ledbetter, jazz pianist Jelly Roll Morton, and composers Paul Creston, Morton Gould, Earl Robinson, and Elie Siegmeister. Archibald MacLeish and librarian Harold Spivacke had scheduled Blitzstein to deliver a lecture-recital about the piece at the Library of Congress for January 6 earlier in the year as well, but that event was canceled at the last minute, suggesting perhaps the specter of government censorship.[30]

By November 1940, a committee headed by James Proctor that also included Bennett Cerf, John Hammond Jr., Lillian Hellman, Lincoln Kirstein, Arthur Kober, and Herman Shumlin had raised enough money to subsidize three staged performances of the opera at the Mecca Temple (later, New York City Center). Originally scheduled for December, these performances took place on the first three Sunday nights of the new year, with the premiere on January 5, 1941, designated a benefit for Spanish refugees sponsored by the American Rescue Ship Mission, Helen Keller, honorary national chairman (although Keller soon after severed ties from the Mission, then under attack as a communist front). Brooks Atkinson deemed the low ticket prices especially important during this time of political crisis: "There ought to be some food for bitter thought in the fact that a left-wing play is the only new production this year that has been able to crack the box-office barriers and let the people in without robbing them first." Concessions from the Dramatists Guild and Actors' Equity, along with good will from cast and crew, helped make such low prices possible, with Blitzstein further keeping down costs by dispensing with a pit orchestra and accompanying the performers at the piano himself.[31]

William Watts directed, Maxine Geiser designed the costumes, Trude Rittman prepared the chorus, and Norman Cazden served as rehearsal accompanist. Presented without scenery, the show featured a cast of twenty-seven, including Lloyd Gough (Paul Chase), Olive Deering (Clara Chase), Martin Wolfson (Nick Kyriakos), Robert Simon (Joe Kyriakos), Alfred Ryder (Max Kraus), Norma Green (Francie), Curt Conway (Bulge), Hester Sondergaard (Gina Tonieri), Charles Polacheck (Cutch), Ben Ross (Emanuel), Eda Reis (Gertie Phorylles), Charles Mendick (Alex), Martin Ritt (Steve), Ellen Merrill (Mery), Coby Ruskin (Jimmy), Carol Channing (Bobby), and Bert Conway (Mike Stretto), with an additional seventeen in the chorus.[32]

In early 1939, the press had reported two possible Broadway stars, Burgess Meredith and Katherine Locke, for the leads; but with the principal exception of Wolfson, the cast ultimately featured—partly, no doubt, for financial reasons— journeyman actors like Deering and her brother Alfred Ryder. Indeed, Carol Channing, a recent Bennington graduate, had never acted on the New York stage before; the William Morris agency simply sent her to audition for Blitzstein, who apparently cast the show himself. "Marc treated me as if I were dear and tender," recalled Channing. "I was so grateful I talked, sang, and danced for him everybody that I had seen on Broadway, mostly because he seemed delighted with my renditions and I enjoyed making him happy." Once cast, she asked him, regarding her big number "Fraught," if she could make parts of its sound like Ethel Merman, Gertrude Lawrence, Beatrice Lillie, and Sophie Tucker, to which he replied, "Absolutely! That's why I want you to do this song."[33]

A number of cast members had close communist affiliations, including Gough, Wolfson, and Sondergaard (all of whom would feel the sting of the blacklist after the war, as would such relatives of the cast as Gough's wife Karen Morley, Olive Deering's husband Leo Penn, and Sondergaard's more famous sister Gale); but in testimony before the House Un-American Activities Committee, Blitzstein stated that any employment of communists on his part "would always depend on whether they were the people with the most talent for the job." Channing, who found herself participating in various leftist events with Blitzstein and other company members, took, incidentally, a droll view of later accusations of un-Americanism against her colleagues: "Most of the company seemed to be Russian Jews whose parents were still celebrating having a congressman to write to and not being executed for it. They couldn't stop writing to him they were so happy to be Americans."[34]

On opening night, a heckler in the balcony caused a commotion by cheering the opera's villains, but the near-capacity audience quieted him down by crying, "Throw him out!" Carol Channing stopped the show with "Fraught," marking an auspicious start to an exceptional career, and the entire company received thunderous cheers and ovations at the work's end.[35]

Most reviewers, including Brooks Atkinson (*New York Times*) and Virgil Thomson (*Herald Tribune*), thought the opera thrilling, some caveats about the libretto notwithstanding. The critics applauded Blitzstein's integration of word and tone, which reminded Samuel Barlow (*Modern Music*) of Wagner, as well as the work's novel form, which Lou Cooper (*New Masses*) compared to the song plays of Mozart, Weber, Weill, and Eisler, but developed "to an infinitely higher stage." "America at last has an opera composer . . . ," wrote Ira Wolfert (*Cleveland Plain Dealer*). "The piece uses music to tell a story and uses story to make its music tell." Alluding to his review of *Porgy* ("Gershwin does not even know what an opera is"), Thomson stated, "Marc Blitzstein knows what an opera really is," a week later adding, "He can draw laughter and tears as few living composers can." In light of the fact that the critics thought such cast members as Gough not quite up to the work's vocal demands, especially in the cavernous Mecca Temple, such enthusiasm seems all the more impressive. Nor did the reviews make much allowance for the bare-bones production. "With an orchestra and sets to heighten the illusion," wrote Nina Naguid (*Musical Leader*), an exception, "Mr. Blitzstein's work would be a knockout."[36]

The critics naturally identified the work's perspective as left-wing, sometimes even communist—Brooks Atkinson described the piece as "leaning so far to the left that it is practically horizontal"—but they generally found it more "rounded" and "personal" than *The Cradle*, however inferior in other ways. "If Robespierre's dogmatic frock coat is faintly evident in Blitzstein's wardrobe," wrote Samuel Barlow, "the music is entirely undogmatic and flexible." A few critics nevertheless ventured Marxist interpretations of the action, with both

Ralph Warner (*Daily Worker*) and James Morison (*New Masses*) similarly reading the meeting scene (I, iii) as reflecting the processes by which, to quote the former, "the workers, slowly groping for class consciousness, discover self-reliance, learn the first steps in proletarian democracy." Warner even evoked Soviet Russia, writing, "Blitzstein knows that the people are gay in their hearts, that this world, when, as in the Soviet Union, the people control its natural resources and organize its economy, is filled with lusty, happy, healthy men and women, devoid of pessimism because they are devoid of fear"—this even though the work made no mention of the Soviet Union whatsoever.[37]

Two days after the premiere, New York License Commissioner Paul Moss, who attended the Sunday night opening, informed the Mecca Temple that they would have to obtain a license in order to proceed with a second performance, but then refused their application, stating that they needed three separate certificates from various city departments and that the whole process would probably take about three months. Moss specifically expressed concern that because the Temple had not screwed the chairs to the floor, they could be overturned in the event of a panic. However, Blitzstein quickly denounced Moss's order as flagrant censorship—the Temple, after all, had been staging works in this condition for years, including a series of operas produced by Alfredo Salmaggi the previous season—and stating, "I have no intention of submitting quietly to what I consider is censorship of a cultural endeavor," announced that the second performance would take place as planned. Moss in turn threatened to call out the police and fire brigade. As the company prepared to stage a protest at city hall, and the Mecca Temple better secured its seats, distinguished leaders in the theatrical community—including Brock Pemberton, Antoinette Perry, and Virgil Thomson—urged that the two remaining performances be given. Moss finally relented by issuing a temporary permit. During this tense ordeal, Orson Welles, battling censorship problems in Hollywood over the release of *Citizen Kane*, reportedly wired Blitzstein, "You tell me about your troubles, and I'll tell you about mine."[38]

The sponsoring committee presented the second performance of the opera also as a benefit, this one for another communist front, the International Labor Defense, on behalf of a group of Oklahomans convicted of either Communist Party membership or disseminating subversive literature. Sentenced to ten years in jail and a $5,000 fine and released on bail, one of the defendants, Alan Shaw, secretary of the Oklahoma Communist Party, addressed the Mecca Temple audience himself during intermission. (In 1943, the Oklahoma Criminal Court of Appeals reversed these convictions.)[39]

Encouraged by the opera's excellent critical and popular reception—including a total attendance of about ten thousand and receipts of about $9,000 for the three performances—Blitzstein and his friends began a grass-roots campaign to collect donations for a regular production aimed to begin in April at the Venice Theatre, where *The Cradle* had premiered in 1937. Hoping to raise $17,000 for an initial two-week run at full union scale, they attempted to find 170 backers to invest $100 each, producing a brochure that included a detailed breakdown of the show's costs along with excerpted reviews by leading critics and personal testimonials from singers Lawrence Tibbett ("I find it a joy to herald a major work of music and speech in our own idiom, and our own language, and about our own people") and Paul Robeson ("For me, 'No for an Answer' is the most significant achievement in opera in our time") as well as composer Aaron Copland ("The result is a moving and exciting drama that should be seen by everyone").[40]

Blitzstein and his associates also tried soliciting organizations to purchase booklets of twenty-five tickets each, suggesting that they sell them at one dollar apiece (though worth $1.50 at the box office), in the hopes of finding ten thousand buyers and thereby raising $10,000. "Commercial Broadway won't touch it because it is a people's opera . . ." explained yet another brochure. "This is the first time in the history of the commercial theatre that the audience is asked to become the backer of a Broadway show—*a show which will be produced if you purchase that single ticket in advance*." Blitzstein had some success securing pledges—the American Youth Theatre helped by staging a benefit revue on March 23 at Carnegie Chamber Music Hall—but on April 14, about a week after he performed selections from the opera at an April 6 benefit for the Washington Committee to Aid Agricultural Workers, the *Times* announced that a production had been postponed until fall.[41]

About this same time, Keynote Records, a mostly folk and jazz label founded the previous year by Eric Bernay, released a recording of excerpts of the opera on five discs for $4.75. (Decca Records reportedly made some earlier pressings, but concerned that the hero's name, Joe, alluded to Joseph Stalin, decided, over Blitzstein's protestations, to forgo the project.) This 1941 Keynote release featured the same cast as the premiere, with the exception of Michael Loring (Joe), who substituted for Robert Simon. Although the excerpts lost much of their impact out of context, the album drew a warm response from Harold Taubman, who, however, wanted more of the work's choral music, and more muted praise from Colin McPhee, who preferred the solo numbers, saying that the "belligerent buttresses of the choruses" failed to touch him "any more than does a sermon by a Presbyterian minister." Random House announced the publication of the libretto, which the communist-sponsored League of American Writers voted best play of the year at their June 1941 Fourth American Writers' Congress (which Blitzstein attended, joining its call to "resist the drive toward war and reaction," "protect persecuted writers," and "restore WPA projects," among other goals); but no such printing ever came to light.[42]

On April 18, 1941, ostensibly as a fundraiser for the opera, Blitzstein sang some of his cabaret songs at a two-dollar-per-plate after-theater supper and program in his honor sponsored by Lee J. Cobb, Gene Kelly, John Hammond, Lincoln Kirstein, and Paul Robeson at New York's Piccadilly Hotel. Then, on June 19, he flew to Hollywood to raise more money for the production, to which end he gave four public performances of the work sponsored by various leftist organizations as well as private auditions at the homes of screenwriter Dalton Trumbo, the author of the antiwar novel *Johnny Got His Gun* (1939), and Elaine Barrie, the ex-wife of actor John Barrymore. "Hollywood seems to be a bit more of everything than I had imagined," wrote Blitzstein to David Diamond on a postcard that showed a blossoming orange tree framed by snow-capped mountains, "—more reality, and more fake. Not only fabulous,—but interesting." On his return East, Blitzstein again wrote Diamond, "I fear it [Hollywood]—it has a corroding and rotten influence on so many—even good people. Others thrive, and turn industrious. Where would I be? I think the answer really would depend on my having work there that I loved."[43]

This Hollywood trip proved a success, with the opera winning the support of a number of notables, including Orson Welles, who "went overboard" and resolved to make a picture with the composer. Then, on October 5, the *Times* reported that production plans had been abandoned at least temporarily and that money was being returned. In a subsequent letter to the paper's editor, Blitzstein explained that he and his associates actually had met their newly estimated goal of raising $20,000, in large part due to small contributors who "prove that a real culture in this country, from the ground up, is no myth," but that a decision had been made against staging the work,

> because we feel that the red-hot urgency of today's war news has relegated all other social themes to a comparatively secondary role. During this emergency we believe the stress should be on plays reflecting the growing unity of all anti-Fascist forces; and particularly we feel that the energies of the people should be concentrated on such plays. But "No for an Answer" is presumably a work of art, not a pamphlet; and the validity of its content holds, if not its immediacy. And so we are authorizing an experimental production of the opera in Philadelphia, which we will use as a kind of testing ground for the work.

Although unmentioned by Blitzstein, the German invasion of the Soviet Union on June 22—just as the composer left for Hollywood to pitch his opera—no doubt prompted this striking turnabout, with the phrase "unity of all anti-Fascist forces" signaling a return to popular front solidarity, challenged in the opera not only by its antiwar sentiments but by the depiction of Paul as an undependable liberal. "The tide of the war and the world is so gigantically absorbing that nothing can happen to me personally right now that matters a damn," Blitzstein tellingly wrote to Diamond in July. "What a moment! The real fight at last—and just as I was beginning to despair of ever being alive to see it!" As a sign of the changing times, Blitzstein entertained from the piano at a "Stars for China Today" concert at Town Hall on November 8, 1941, sponsored by the American Friends of the Chinese People, a communist front organization that supported China in its fight against Japan.[44]

Meanwhile, no Philadelphia production of *No for an Answer* materialized either; again, the perceived need for national unity seems to have dampened local interest in launching the opera at this time. A revival of the work had to wait until April 18 and 25, 1960, when Charles Schwartz, the director of the Composers' Showcase, presented a concert version of excerpts from the opera staged by Bernard Gersten at Circle In The Square in Greenwich Village, with Blitzstein narrating, Joseph Liebling at the piano, and a cast that included Martin Wolfson in the role that he had originated nearly twenty years earlier. ("He was almost too nice for Peachum," wrote Philip Barr to the composer in reference to Wolfson's intervening work in *The Threepenny Opera*. "—Nick is his great part.") As with the 1960 City Opera production of *The Cradle*, Blitzstein moved the action back to 1931, perhaps to erase the taint of any association with appeasement toward the fascist menace abroad.[45]

The critics liked the performances but proved exceedingly mixed about the piece itself. Lester Trimble (*Herald Tribune*) and Leonard Altman (*The Villager*) thought it compelling ("Do not walk for tickets—run!" wrote Altman); Howard Taubman (*New York Times*) and Nancy Siff (*Village Voice*) found it dated and contrived; while John Freeman (*Opera News*) criticized the drama as "naive" and "doctrinaire," but praised the score's "vigor" and "candor," describing the music as "mostly Gershwinized (i.e., proletarianized) Stravinsky sprinkled with Weill and splashed with backwash from *Les Six*."[46]

Over the years, some individual songs from the opera came before the public as well. In the months following America's entry into the Second World War, for instance, the outstanding African-American bass Paul Robeson (1898–1976) recorded "The Purest Kind of a Guy"—at a much slower tempo than had Curt Conway and the composer—on his debut song album *Songs of Free Men* (1942), a compilation of eight songs from Germany, Russia, Spain, and the United States that formed, in Robeson's words, "a very important part of my concert programs, expressing much of what I deeply feel and believe," and that, moreover, "have that folk quality and show in no uncertain way the common humanity of man. Beyond this, they issue from the present common struggle for a decent world, a struggle in which the artist must also play his part." Robeson presumably appreciated, among other things, the song's modal complexion and its racially accepting lyric ("Black or white or tan ain't the reason why/I will know that man's the purest kind of a guy"). Given that Robeson performed the song as a public tribute in 1941 to William Z. Foster on the occasion of the latter's sixtieth birthday, and in 1949 to Eugene Dennis, about to serve jail time for contempt of Congress, he also plainly saw this paean to the opera's hero as pertinent to his own regard for certain high-ranking members of the American Communist Party.[47]

In 1947, People's Songs, an organization aimed at creating, in the words of its director Pete Seeger, a "singing labor movement," published "The Purest Kind of a Guy" in its July–August *Bulletin*. Printing the song's melody and lyric with no other accompaniment but chord symbols, the editors explained that although the number had "long been one of our favorite songs," they did not have the space to print it in its entirety with full accompaniment (although readers could send in a dollar and receive the complete song in photostat). *Sing Out! The Folk Song Magazine*, a successor to the *Bulletin*, also published the song with chord symbols in 1978 as a tribute to Paul Robeson, with the comment that the number "stands out as if it were a portrait of Robeson himself." Some thirty years later, at a 2010 New York Festival of Song recital entitled "Manning the Canon: Songs of Gay Life," bass Matt Boehler opened the evening with this same song, its text now perceived as registering gay—as opposed to communist—overtones.[48]

Other numbers from the opera occasionally surfaced as well. Blitzstein recorded "In the Clear" (with Muriel Smith) in 1947 and "Penny Candy" (with Joshua Shelley) and "Francie" (with Evelyn Lear and George Gaynes) in 1956; Charlotte Rae, "Fraught" in 1955 (with the end of the song's Cole Porteresque cadenza, possibly in collaboration with Blitzstein, changed from "you positively go to my bedroom!" to "you positively go, down the hall and turn to the left, if I'm a little late, start without me"); William Sharp, "In the Clear" and "Penny Candy" in 1991; and Dawn Upshaw, "In the Clear" in 1994.[49]

Critical reactions similarly appeared from time to time. In early 1963, composer Douglas Moore told Blitzstein that he remembered the original production of *No for an Answer* as offering him, along with *Regina*, "my best moments in the whole catalogue of American opera." (This admiration seems to have been mutual: a mere week earlier, in an attempt to interest his friend Tennessee Williams in allowing Moore to adapt *The Rose Tattoo* as an opera, Blitzstein had described Moore as "a rip-snorting good theatre composer, skillful and lyrically at home, who sets naturally and passionately what he feels. He works easily with a text, with or without a collaborator; he neither pulls the reins stiffly in behalf of his ego, nor gives in when the work and its new-medium demands are at stake.")[50]

The British critic-composer Wilfrid Mellers likewise remained fond of the opera. An avowed admirer of Blitzstein since 1941, when he declared *The Cradle* "the first convincing answer I've seen to the problem of reinstating the composer as an active member of society," he quickly came to regard *No for an Answer* as the more significant achievement, more "homogeneous" and "elliptical," as he wrote in 1942, with the "authentic American language" of its choruses "as remote from anything normally implied in an aggressive musical nationalism as could well be imagined." In 1944, he further ventured a comparison between the work and British composer Michael Tippett's oratorio *A Child of Our Time* (1939–41). And in 1964, describing the work as a "tragedy with satirical implications" (as opposed to *The Cradle*, "a satirical piece with tragic undertones"), he suggested that its "wonderfully sensitive treatment of speech inflection" revealed "the roots of some features of jazz in American dialect."[51]

In 1965, Paul Talley also praised the opera, despite its "diffused" and "confusing" libretto, whereas in 1985, John Shout rendered a far more severe assessment, although his claim that "audiences, then as well as now" have had trouble tolerating the piece's "overbearing" emphasis on "communal harmony" suggested a limited knowledge of both the work and its reception. David Kushner, in 1993, simply concluded that the opera's title formed "the essential verdict on the work as a whole, since it has not been resuscitated in thirty years."[52]

A 2001 revival of the opera by San Francisco's American Conservatory Theater (A.C.T.) proved this latter judgment premature. Staged by Carey Perloff, the production had as its musical director Peter Maleitzke, who led the relatively small student cast of twenty from the piano. Conductor Michael Tilson Thomas, who recalled hearing some of the original cast members sing portions of the work at his parents' home, served as artistic advisor and helped Maleitzke create a working edition of the score that involved a number of cuts, but some interpolations as well, including the reinstatement of "Expatriate" (as completed by Leonard Lehrman). In order to give more opportunities to some of the cast—and compensate for vocal weaknesses among them—Perloff and Maleitzke also redistributed some of the parts, with a few songs presented as ensemble rather than solo numbers.[53]

A.C.T. workshopped the opera in the fall of 2000 and presented it for a two-week run the following season. Reviewing the October 26, 2001, premiere, Robert Hurwitt (*San Francisco Chronicle*) thought the production "a series of revelations both of musical riches and of some talented young actors," singling out the choral numbers as "outstanding and curiously complex." Even a rough videotape of the production evidenced the opera's enduring power (according to Maleitzke, Tilson Thomas wept at some points in the action).[54]

This revival notwithstanding, the general dearth of interest in so strong a work presumably involved not only its provocative content, but on a more practical level, the absence of a published vocal score as well as an orchestral score of any kind. The lack of a recording of the complete opera could not have helped either, although AEI Records reissued the original cast album of selections on a long-playing record in 1982, and Pavilion Records on CD in 1998.

Some of this neglect also involved unfortunate timing, for had Blitzstein managed to find a producer early on, the opera might have established itself as a classic of its day, comparable to John Steinbeck's *The Grapes of Wrath* (1939), with which it shares many notable features. A full-scale launching at least would have allowed him to orchestrate the work. But the struggle against the Axis powers took precedence over such considerations, and letting four years of work go by the wayside, Blitzstein moved on to newly pressing needs.

13

From *Valley Town* (1940) to *Labor for Victory* (1942)

After six attempts to obtain a Guggenheim fellowship—"I think I must hold a record of some sort of persistence!" he wrote the foundation's Henry Allen Moe in the fall of 1939—Blitzstein finally received one for "creative work in musical composition, especially for the musical stage" in the spring of 1940. Whereas in his earliest Guggenheim applications he primarily had enlisted the support of musicians, including composers Copland, Robert Russell Bennett, Hanns Eisler, Roy Harris, Douglas Moore, and Randall Thompson, after *The Cradle*, in addition to musicians, he increasingly named as references theater professionals and writers, including for the 1938 competition, Benno Schneider, Lee Simonson, and Herman Shumlin; in 1939, Philip Barry (who, according to the *New York Post*, hoped that Blitzstein might write the incidental music for one of his plays), John Dos Passos (who stated in his confidential report, "Besides workmanlike skill I think his work shows occasional traces of genuine musical invention [nonexistent among 'serious' musicians in this country] that might portend great things"), and Archibald MacLeish; and in 1940, Brooks Atkinson, Lillian Hellman, Lincoln Kirstein, Elmer Rice, and once again MacLeish. That in this last batch of reports Copland (one of his most faithful sponsors) deemed Blitzstein the most important American composer working in musical theater and Lincoln Kirstein even more sweepingly, "the most important man working in the theatre today in this country," presumably helped his case considerably.[1]

The twelve-month, $2,000 award, which he successfully renewed the following year, allowed Blitzstein not only to continue revising *No for an Answer*, but to pursue other projects, such as composing music for the film documentary *Valley Town*, which occupied him especially in April and May 1940, and for which he received from the filmmakers a fee of $1,000. In May, he asked that the Guggenheim Foundation further assist his research by providing him with "some sort of pass to attend frequently exhibitions and performances" at the New York World's Fair, stating that such shows as *Railroads on Parade* and *American Jubilee* "would, I think, repay fairly careful study." The foundation kindly took up the matter with the New York World

Fair Corporation, which although sympathetic, had no mechanism for granting such a request.[2]

Directed by Willard Van Dyke, *Valley Town: A Study of Machines and Men*
(1940) was co-produced by Documentary Film Productions, formed in 1939
by Van Dyke and Herbert Kerkow, and the Educational Film Institute of New
York University, founded in 1939 under the sponsorship of the Alfred P. Sloan
Foundation. Sloan, president of General Motors, considered film documentary
an important tool in fulfilling his foundation's stated mission of promoting "a
wider knowledge of basic economic truths generally accepted by authorities of
recognized standing and as demonstrated by experience." He accordingly
appointed as director of the Film Institute the Harvard-educated economist
Spencer Pollard, who in turn hired three leading documentarians—John
Ferno, Joris Ivens, and Willard Van Dyke—to make short films about some
current economic problems.[3]

Born in Colorado, Van Dyke (1906–1986) had studied photography with
Edward Weston in California before moving in 1935 to New York, where he abandoned still photography for documentary film, joining the film collectives Nykino
(1935–37) and its successor Frontier Films (1937–42), and serving as Pare
Lorentz's cameraman for *The River* (1937). Dissatisfied with his subordinate position at Frontier under Leo Hurwitz and Paul Strand, and disconcerted by the
group's close association with the Communist Party, Van Dyke and another
Frontier staff member, Ralph Steiner, formed a rival company in 1938; their initial
venture, *The City* (1939), created for the New York World's Fair, established Van
Dyke's reputation as a director (and provided as well Aaron Copland with his first
credit as a film composer).

With *Valley Town* (1940), Van Dyke began to direct on his own, eventually
making dozens of what he called "social documentaries," a genre he defined as "a
film in which the elements of dramatic conflict represent social or political forces
rather than individual ones." Inspired by the work of the Soviet Aleksandr
Dovzhenko and the British John Grierson as well as by Pare Lorentz, he further
contended, much like Joris Ivens, that the social documentarian had a "responsibility to express his attitude" and "take a position in relation to the things in which
he believes."[4]

Valley Town, stated Van Dyke soon after its completion, "was to be an experimental film dealing with the relationship of machinery to men. It was to show
how machines created jobs under a certain set of conditions, and how they displaced men from their jobs under other conditions." Working with the institute's director Spencer Pollard, Van Dyke selected as a case study New Castle, a
Pennsylvania steel town that recently had experienced the closing of two hand-
mills that could no longer compete with more automated strip mills, leaving
over half the town's population of about fifty thousand unemployed. After
spending time visiting with the townspeople, Van Dyke and Pollard created a

scenario that outlined the dire current situation, flashed back to more prosperous times, explored the impact on the town caused by the introduction of new automated machinery elsewhere, and offered some cautionary lessons.[5]

Like other American documentarians of this period, Van Dyke crafted the film in ways that approached fiction filmmaking. He had a character based on the town's mayor serve as narrator, like the Stage Manager in Thornton Wilder's *Our Town* (1938). He also simulated the history of New Castle with footage from other locales, including holiday shoppers in nearby Lancaster in order to portray the town's bygone prosperity. Furthermore, he staged, at least to some extent, the central domestic drama about an unemployed worker and his family. "A good documentary," said Van Dyke, "has all of the elements of suspense, conflict, climax, and resolution that a story film has, but it pits man against natural or social forces instead of involving him in personal situations. Thus instead of 'boy meets girl, boy loses girl, boy gets girl' our plot was 'man gets job, man loses job, this is how man may get job again.' Not a single individual, but a whole group of men."[6]

Assisted by Herbert Kerkow, Van Dyke engaged cameraman Roger Barlow, stillman Bob Churchill, and film editor Irving Lerner, who viewed the rushes in New York and sent daily reports back to the director on location. Meanwhile, Pollard co-authored the narrative with Frontier Films's leading scriptwriter Ben Maddow, who used his familiar pseudonym David Wolff. The hiring of Maddow, like that of Lerner, indicated that despite his break with Hurwitz and Strand, Van Dyke had nothing against working with communists or fellow travelers per se, including Marc Blitzstein, whom he hired for the score at Lerner's suggestion and, as he also claimed, because he loved *No for an Answer*. In later years, both Lerner and Maddow had estimable careers in Hollywood, notwithstanding setbacks occasioned by anticommunist bias.[7]

Impressed with Copland's work on *The City*, Van Dyke made music an even more integral part of this film. Most strikingly, rather than use a simple voice-over to simulate the thoughts of an unemployed worker on his way home as originally planned, he yielded to Blitzstein's suggestion that the composer himself pen the voice-over, and, like those measured recitations in *No for an Answer*, coordinate it with music in order to create a set piece; and, moreover, that he compose another musical soliloquy for the man's wife, although one that moved from measured recitation to actual song (and that also wound up involving, as an interlude, some further recitation for the man). "We worked closely this way—the director, the editor, and the composer—conceiving sections musically the whole time," recalled Van Dyke, who also singled out the sequence showing men at work in a hand-mill: "It was shot as a ballet, edited as a ballet, and scored as a ballet."[8]

Working with the young Canadian-born Henry Brant (1913–2008), who had assisted Copland on the puppet show *From Sorcery to Science* the previous year, Blitzstein scored the piece for flute, clarinet, saxophone, trumpet, trombone, percussion, piano, and strings. The composer's longtime friend Alexander Smallens conducted, and Ray Collins, a Mercury Theatre player soon to appear as Jim W. Gettys in *Citizen Kane*, recorded the narration, with other professionals providing the musical soliloquies and dubbing a few spoken lines as well—all in keeping with the film's mixture of real and fictive elements.

The picture unfolds a series of discrete episodes, each containing a well-shaped musical movement featuring the credits ("Title Music"), the town ("Abandoned Factory—Graves—Roof-tops"), the start of a workday ("Morning Music"), a hand-mill ("Steel Rolling Mill"), the locomotive as a symbol of prosperity ("Trains"), economic collapse ("Depression"), a strip mill ("Machine Rollers"), an unemployed worker and his family ("Russell Alley—Blues"), and the destruction of an old mill and final thoughts ("After Stacks—The Mayor—Finale"). These nine episodes form a larger three-part design that corresponds to Van Dyke's description of the film as "man gets job, man loses job, this is how man may get job again." The music highlights this larger trajectory by putting forth, after a dramatic prologue, a lively first part, a bleak second part, and a hopeful finale that reprises the title music, thereby creating a frame for the whole, with more thoroughgoing unity achieved by way of some key motives throughout.[9]

For his depictions of assorted machinery, Blitzstein employed those mechanistic gestures long a part of his musical vocabulary, although in order to dramatize the film's dialectical attitude toward technology, he provided the sequences for the hand-mill and the trains with an appealing lilt and that for the automated strip mill with a more robotic quality. These latter passages sound at times like Prokofiev or Copland, whereas other sections sooner recall Eisler or Weill—with Eric Gordon even deeming the "Blues" (also known as "How Long?") "one of the most Weillian songs of Blitzstein's entire output." The score has its own character nonetheless, especially the "Russell Alley—Blues" sequence, whose static tonal motion helps register a particularly dark despair.[10]

Created by Van Dyke a year apart, *Valley Town* and *The City* throw into special relief likenesses and differences between their two composers. Blitzstein might even have had Copland's title music in mind for his own, as both scores begin with declamatory lines articulated by accented harmonies; but whereas Copland's theme flows easily in a baritone register, Blitzstein's moves nervously, with syncopations and changing meters, high above; and whereas Copland writes closely spaced parallel triads supported by mildly dissonant bass lines, Blitzstein favors more angular, dissonant harmonies. Overall, Copland emits greater restraint and warmth. Part of this involves his greater inclination to curtail a certain complexity in working with the film medium, as opposed to Blitzstein, who more aggressively imposes himself, shaping the film into a virtual concert suite and virtually taking over in the "Russell Alley—Blues" sequence.

Valley Town premiered on May 14, 1940, at a Steel Workers Organizing Committee convention in Chicago, but soon after, the Educational Film Institute recalled all three of its completed films and suspended production on others. In a

July 1940 issue of *Film News*, the institute, presumably reflecting the apprehensions of the Sloan Foundation, stated that the new wartime economy necessitated a more constructive approach to economic problems.[11]

The institute subsequently released a reedited version of *Valley Town*, overhauling in particular the final sequence, which had chastised industry for failing to provide dismissed workers with adequate notice and severance pay, expressed dismay that it might take years for the unemployed to find work, and urged more responsible policies, stating, "Let's not forget the people!" In contrast, the new ending, set against the background of a rejuvenated war economy (although the war in fact brought New Castle only limited economic relief), replaced images of unemployed workers with those of want ads and bustling factories, and observed government and industry working together to retrain the unemployed, concluding, "Let's keep their skills as modern as the new machines!" A fair amount of the score wound up on the cutting room floor, not only much of the finale, but the opening "Abandoned Factory—Graves" segment (apparently cut so as not to situate the town in a depressed present, although omitting the gravestone sequence also undermined Van Dyke's intention to reveal the town's ethnic diversity) and the end of the "Blues" (with the wife's prediction that her husband will leave her). The institute also redubbed the entire narration with an actor less nuanced than Ray Collins, who remained credited nonetheless.[12]

These revisions not only distorted the documentary's very essence, leading to a less coherent narrative, but damaged the integrity of so carefully a designed film and score. Van Dyke, who reluctantly participated in the revisions, later recalled, "It hurt because, among other things, Marc Blitzstein, whom I liked very much, was absolutely furious at me and felt that I had really sold a piece of work down the river and I was a whore." The director himself felt "traumatized" by the incident, which apparently played some part in his inability to ever again produce work of the stature of *Valley Town*, arguably his greatest achievement, and his personal favorite among his films, although not, in his opinion, a "successful artistic whole."[13]

On January 12, 1941, the League of Composers sponsored an evening of "Music and Film" at the Museum of Modern Art that featured an excerpt from *Valley Town* along with clips of documentaries composed by Copland, Thomson, Roy Harris, and Douglas Moore and an entire documentary with music by Paul Bowles. Such an event, deemed "a rousing success" by Howard Taubman in the *New York Times*, highlighted the extent to which some of the country's finest composers collaborated with film documentarians during these years, casting light on one reason the documentaries of this period remain among the best ever produced in America.[14]

The limited critical response to *Valley Town*, both as a film and a film score, has centered for the most part on the innovative "Russell Alley—Blues" episode. In the film's early days, Paul Bowles opined that the "Blues," for all its near sentimentality, "managed to remain dramatically effective," whereas B. H. Haggin thought the entire sequence typical of its composer's tendency to write "novel" and "daring" music shorn of "significance" or "power." In more recent years, James Blue and William Alexander, like Bowles, found the scene compelling, whereas Richard Barsam, more like Haggin, deemed it "more successful as an experiment in narrative style than as communication." However, the score contains much of interest throughout, as a concert suite might demonstrate, and deserves more attention as a whole, although a fair and full assessment requires consideration of the original cut housed at the Museum of Modern Art.[15]

Following his work on *Valley Town*, Blitzstein scored the documentary *Native Land* (1942) for Frontier Films. Founded in 1937 by Leo Hurwitz (1909–1991) and Paul Strand (1890–1976), this nonprofit company aspired to create progressive fiction and nonfiction pictures with gifts and loans from individuals rather than through commercial investments or government subsidies, and to distribute such films independently to theaters in working-class neighborhoods. The Frontier staff boasted an impressive array of cinematic talent and attracted a prestigious advisory board that included writers John Dos Passos, Lillian Hellman, and Archibald MacLeish, and composers Carlos Chávez and Aaron Copland.

Over eighty minutes in length, *Native Land* became the organization's longest and most ambitious undertaking. Originally conceived as *Labor Spy* in 1937 but not completed until early 1942, the documentary took over four years to produce. Van Dyke filmed some early sequences, but Hurwitz and Strand, both of whom had assisted Pare Lorentz on the ground-breaking documentary *The Plow That Broke the Plains* (1936), took over direction, a factor that apparently played some part in Van Dyke's defection from the group. In 1938, Ben Maddow prepared a feature-length script, and Frontier, with only $7,000 on hand and a projected budget of $40,000, began the time-consuming process of soliciting donations from individuals and organizations, which often involved screenings of partly completed rushes. Because many involved in the film worked for minimal or even no salary, including narrator Paul Robeson, who donated his fee to the company, Frontier managed to hold down expenses. Even so, the film cost around $70,000 to produce.[16]

The need to raise capital only partly explains the film's lengthy genesis. The filmmakers encountered several mishaps, including traveling to Maine for footage of a stormy coast, only to find the waters calm, necessitating a return there months later. Moreover, Strand, an outstanding photographer who did most of the camerawork, and Hurwitz, a visionary director who edited much of the film, labored over the smallest details. Robeson similarly held up production by taking weeks to rehearse his narration. Concludes William Alexander, "Whatever the amount of time taken and whatever the degree of perfectionism, however, the completed work made it all worthwhile: *Native Land* remains a beautifully made and perennially timely film, as the enthusiastic audience reaction to its rerelease during the Watergate era testifies."[17]

The film took as its main frame of reference the findings of the La Follette Civil Liberties Committee, especially as filtered through Leo Huberman's *The Labor Spy Racket* (1937), whose opening chapter about a company mole apparently became the basis for the extended staged drama at the film's center. Established in 1936 under the chairmanship of Wisconsin Republican Senator Robert M. La Follette Jr., the Civil Liberties Committee exposed criminal attempts by some corporations to undermine union activities, including the hiring of labor spies and armed vigilantes. Hurwitz, Strand, and Maddow, all of whom worked on the shooting script (although only the last named wrote the commentary), ultimately placed such abuses in the larger context of the country's historic struggle for civil rights, as announced at the start of the film: "Since the founding of our country the American people have had to fight for their freedom in every generation. *Native Land* is a document of America's struggle for liberty in recent years." Seen largely in terms of the fight between unions and a shadowy fascist conspiracy, the film at its end describes this "struggle" as consisting of every American's right to "a job, a home, adequate food and medical care, the right to bargain collectively, to act for the greatest good for the greatest number, the right to live at peace unmolested, threatening no one."[18]

Hurwitz recalled that, in order to achieve dramatic growth and elicit audience empathy, he and his collaborators alternated episodes of triumph with those of defeat in dialectical fashion as "part of one developing process, towards a radical social transformation." The triumphal sections—the portrayals, for instance, of union activities and the La Follette investigations—tend to contain documentary footage accompanied by narration, whereas the defeats take the form of staged vignettes with amateur and professional actors, several of whom would become familiar screen presences, including Houseley Stevenson Sr. (as a white share-cropper), Howard Da Silva (as a union informant), and John Marlieb (as a thug). These interspersed vignettes depict antiunion actions against a Michigan farmer, a Cleveland union organizer, Arkansas sharecroppers, and a Memphis grocer, among others. The documentary concludes with a funeral eulogy by the best friend of a Chicago striker killed in the Memorial Day Massacre of 1937 followed by a return to the mood of the opening sequence and finally a reiteration of the eulogist saying, "We don't forget that, never." Commented Paul Strand on the occasion of the picture's release, "It is certainly an anti-Fascist preachment, but we don't think it preaches; rather, we hope, it conveys an inspirational message."[19]

The prominence of the staged episodes—the labor spy sequence alone lasts about twenty minutes—brings the picture close to what later became known as docudrama, reflecting Frontier's early stated hope—never realized—of creating feature fiction films. Hurwitz and Strand themselves described the work as a "dramatic documentary." Perhaps the most factual of these vignettes reenacts the November 30, 1935, torture of three Tampa socialists (leading to the death of one, Joseph Shoemaker) by the Ku Klux Klan, while the sequence depicting the gunning down of two Arkansas sharecroppers—its representation of interracial solidarity constituting one of the film's most progressive gestures, along with the use of an African-American narrator as the voice of America—referenced rampant violence against the interracial Southern Tenant Farmers' Union (founded 1934). Whatever difficulties the filmmakers had shaping these diverse parts into a coherent whole, so sweeping a panorama helped give the film a breadth comparable to the novels of John Dos Passos.[20]

Blitzstein agreed to write the film score in 1940 for a fee of $500, and he worked on what he referred to as the "Civil Liberties Film" or "Strand's Film" intermittently throughout 1940 and 1941. During the early stages, he composed for the picture two songs, "Dusty Sun" and "American Day," apparently with bass Paul Robeson in mind, as suggested not only by their low ranges (eventually lowered still further, probably at the suggestion of Robeson himself) and their evocation of African-American spirituals, but by the indication "Paul (& chorus?)" scribbled at the top of a preliminary sketch to "Dusty Sun." He also wrote a choral piece, "Inheritance of Freedom," for the opening sequence, but unlike the songs, this chorus never made it into the final cut.

Blitzstein rifled through his composer's trunk for this sprawling score, considering and sometimes using melodies that dated back to the blues theme from *Svarga* (for the union cruise ship party). The opening harmonies of "Dusty Sun," to cite another example, derived from an idea, "Negro revival (Yiddish synagogue?)," apparently drafted for *The Traveling Salesman*, which seems to have been the source as well for the lovely "alla Napolitano" tune that accompanies the chambermaid (played by Amelia Romano) in the Cleveland scene.

In the end, assisted by Henry Brant, he produced a 280-page orchestral score for a small number of winds and brass, percussion, piano, and strings divided into fifteen movements: "Prelude," "The Fathers," "Pastureland," "Mulberry Street," "Dusty Sun/American Day," "Adding Machines," "Hold the Fort and Street Sadness," "Parade," "Grocery Store," "Street-Fight," "Hooded Legion," "People and Things," "Memorial Day," "Stills," and "Funeral and Finale" (with "Adding Machines" and "Stills" apparently not making the final edit). The title "Mulberry Street" alludes to the main thoroughfare in Manhattan's Little Italy, although in the film, the scene takes place in Cleveland.

Blitzstein's music, recorded under the baton of Lehman Engel in early 1942, enhances the film considerably, providing much of the picture's distinctive tone: tense, grim, militant, occasionally light-hearted—but only as a prelude for some turn of the screw. The music truly soars during the staged vignettes, as might be expected from their similarity to Blitzstein's own dramatic work, with resemblances so strong as to suggest the possibility that *The Cradle Will Rock* might have influenced the picture's construction, although both these works share common ancestry in the Living Newspapers of the FTP. In contrast, the music for the documentary portions seems less effective, with the overlaid narration making some of the score sound overwritten. Yet even in these sections, the music enlivens the picture considerably.

Moreover, the score affords a sense of cohesion to the disjointed narrative. Among other strategies, Blitzstein sometimes sustains the musical thread from one segment to another, not only to achieve continuity but to help make a point. For instance, he develops a "malinconico" theme stated at the end of the labor spy episode as the documentary presents brief glimpses of dismissed workers across the country, which not only helps connect the labor spy episode with the resumption of the story, but underlines the way a single betrayal can infect an entire society. Blitzstein uses other unifying themes, including a work theme heard as the Michigan farmer plows his field, and an American dream theme, heard even earlier in the film at the words "And so we proclaimed a new world," a stirring anthem-like melody later associated with unions, thereby conflating the American dream with unions as does the film itself. More generally, much of the film's material derives from the opening title music—the high soprano melody ostensibly signifying triumph, the low bass, defeat—a trenchant embodiment of the film's dialectical intentions in musical form.

As he did in *Valley Town*, Blitzstein incorporated vocal music into the larger musical texture, here performed, however, by the narrator, not by any of the dramatis personae. The somber "Dusty Sun," accompanied by humming chorus, appears in the tragic sequence about the Arkansas sharecroppers; the delightful "American Day" follows in conjunction with the jaunty portrayal of workday routine across the country, thereby providing some relief. Blitzstein reinforces the complementary relationship of these two songs not only through their shared suggestions of African-American spirituals, including pentatonic inflections, but through related harmonic accompaniments: alternating minor triads a whole tone apart in "Dusty Sun" and major harmonies a whole tone apart in "American Day."

For the end of the long section initiated by "American Day," Blitzstein also wrote a brief vocal line that was to accompany a climactic statement of the American dream theme; but as with the choral "Inheritance of Freedom," this music never made it into the film. On the other hand, the directors accommodated the unusual idea of coordinating the Cleveland chambermaid's singing with the sequence's orchestral accompaniment, a bold blurring of that typically hard line in film between source and background music. And the final funeral oration unfolds in the manner of one of the composer's shaped recitations, reminiscent of the unemployed worker's soliloquy in *Valley Town* and similarly compelling.

All in all, the score helped redress two weaknesses in the film: its fragmented narrative and its want of a certain "depth of love for humanity" that commentator William Alexander found missing from Frontier's films generally. Tellingly, the film's coldest sequence, the labor spy episode, features hardly any music aside from some diegetic sounds: snatches of a toy piano and ukulele; the Brahms lullaby hummed by the union president's wife to her child; and, heard in the entertainment room of the union hall, two 1941 prounion recordings by the Almanac Singers, "Get Thee Behind Me, Satan" (Lee Hays, Millard Lampell, and Pete Seeger) and "Which Side Are You On?" (Florence Reece), both of which comment ironically on the action. (Blitzstein arranged the slightly tweaked version of the Brahms lullaby and apparently composed—and perhaps performed—the toy piano music himself.) This episode's dearth of background music arguably heightens its realism, but at some cost, as revealed when the score returns with a sole clarinet playing the union anthem "Hold the Fort," followed by the melancholy music mentioned above. In any event, this labor spy sequence highlights the composer's contribution elsewhere in the film.[21]

By the time Hurwitz and Strand received the answer print of the picture on December 8, 1941, the day after the attack on Pearl Harbor, they realized that the film, with its emphasis on domestic conflict, hardly suited the country's mood. Accordingly, they devised an epilogue in early 1942 that stated that the struggles depicted in the picture had strengthened the nation and that "only absolute victory over Hitler and Japan can safeguard our democratic gains and preserve the independence of America."[22]

On May 10, 1942, the day before the film's official premiere, the "American Day" episode was shown at a benefit concert, "Music at Work," for Russian War Relief that Blitzstein himself produced and for which he served, in the words of the *Daily News*, as the "engaging master-of-ceremonies." (Founded in 1941, Russian War Relief raised, through private donations, millions of dollars for medical supplies, clothing, and other items for the war-worn Soviet Union.) Blitzstein explained the program's rationale as follows: "In a time of war, everybody, everything must do a job. Music no less than machine-guns has a part to play, and can be a weapon in the battle for a free world. . . . There is only one measure, one standard: the effectiveness of the job done." Held on Broadway at the Alvin Theatre, the concert accordingly revealed Blitzstein's sense of a job well-done in the areas of folk music (Earl Robinson and Woody Guthrie), music of "the united nations" (Milhaud and Walton), Broadway music (Rodgers, Berlin, Gershwin, Porter, and Kern), radio music (Earl Robinson), film music (his own *Native Land*), ballet music (Theodore Chanler), theater music (Harold Rome), concert music (Copland), and swing music (Teddy Wilson's band). In addition, the program opened with an overture by British composer Stanley Bate—an arrangement of two Red Army songs, "Cavalry of the Steppes" and "Tachanka"—played at two pianos by Bate and Blitzstein. The event received positive notices, with Virgil Thomson's remarks about *Native Land*—"good music . . . marred by overloud recording and the accompaniment of a none too interesting spoken commentary"—presaging his subsequent review of the film.[23]

Blitzstein had struck a populist note akin to this event some months earlier, even before Pearl Harbor, in a December 3, 1941, letter to the *New York Times* submitted in response to a November 24 letter by pianist Artur Schnabel and composer Roger Sessions that in essence asked why "music for entertainment" should be heard in places reserved for "music of and for experience." "Just who decides, please," asked Blitzstein, "that Ravel's 'Bolero' is an 'experience' and may therefore join the anointed in Carnegie Hall, while Cole Porter's 'Begin the Biguine' [sic] must not crash the gate, being merely 'entertainment'?" He further pointed to the challenge of categorizing Rossini, Bizet, Offenbach, Johann Strauss, and Negro spirituals, finding the separation of what gives "pleasure" and even "fun" from what is "serious" and "good"—the subject of his old Curtis essay about Santayana—an "old Puritan notion." "The precise value of what is called 'music of experience' is that it yields greater and more lasting entertainment than other music . . . ," continued Blitzstein. "By attempting to revive and stress the worn-out conceptions of 'serious' and 'popular' music the Messrs. Schnabel and Sessions are aiming at a greater split. Luckily the trend is against them."[24]

Native Land finally opened, with strong endorsements by Lillian Hellman, Thomas Mann, and Lewis Milestone, among others, at New York's World Theatre on West 49th Street on May 11, 1942, in a premiere sponsored by the Newspaper Guild of New York for the benefit of the guild's War Relief Fund. A few film critics disagreed as to the timeliness of the work: Archer Winston (*New York Post*) argued that the picture had "missed the boat by five months at least," whereas Ralph Ellison (*New Masses*) thought its lessons as applicable as ever. But nearly all recognized the film as a first-rate achievement. "Manifestly, this is one of the most powerful and disturbing documentary films ever made," wrote Bosley Crowther in the *Times*.[25]

Viewers and critics alike further appreciated Blitzstein's score, including Pete Seeger, who penned a warmly congratulatory note to the composer, and Léon Kochnitzky, who wrote in *Modern Music*, "Blitzstein's dramatic instinct and abundant talent never fail an instant throughout this film. He has composed a magnificent work which merits painstaking analysis and deep study—more than one viewing makes possible. I was struck by the originality of his musical thought, which, without resorting to modern rhetoric, achieves poignant and grandiose effect." At the same time, Virgil Thomson, although he liked the film and its "excellent" score, argued that the directors had failed to use the music convincingly: "Sneaking little bits of musical comment in and out at the interstices of a literary text has never, in my experience, added anything of value to the understanding of that text."[26]

After playing for several months to "capacity audiences" in New York, *Native Land* arrived in Chicago, which had hitherto banned the film, perhaps because of its treatment of the Memorial Day Massacre. Wauhillau La Hay of the *Chicago Sun* suspected that not everyone would like the work, although she herself thought it "a beautifully filmed documentary." The picture also won honorable mention as best documentary of 1942 by the National Board of Review of Motion Pictures. But in the end, the film fared poorly, in part because the Communist Party refused to help in its distribution, arguing that the times called for, above all, national unity. Hurwitz even met with Party Chairman William Z. Foster to discuss the matter—"I wasn't able to quote Mao on the question of independence and initiative in the united front," Hurwitz later recalled, "but that's the basic argument I made"—but Foster counseled patience, saying, "the class struggle will be back." After investing so much in this one picture, however, Frontier Films could not afford the luxury of patience and simply folded. As for Blitzstein, the film represented yet another casualty, like *No for an Answer* and *Valley Town*, caught in the transition from peacetime to wartime.[27]

After the war, the composer adapted some of the film's cues for concert purposes. On May 17, 1946, at an American Academy and National Institute of Arts and Letters Ceremonial at which Blitzstein received a $1,000 award from the academy, Howard Hanson and the New York Philharmonic performed three movements from the score: "Mulberry Street," "Hooded Legion," and "Parade"; and some weeks later, at a July 10 concert at Lewisohn Stadium, the Philharmonic's open-air venue, Laszlo Halasz led the same orchestra in the premiere of an eight-movement orchestral suite (also without voice) consisting of "The Fathers," "Mulberry Street," "Dusty Sun/American Day," "Parade," "Hooded Legion," "Memorial Day," "Parade," "Funeral," and "Finale." Reviewing this latter outing, critics agreed that the music worked in concert form, with John Briggs (*New York Post*) admiring the work's "bittersweet harshness" and Louis Biancolli (*New York World-Telegram*), its "crisp, fiery idiom." Blitzstein also prepared a shorter, "definitive" five-movement suite with some movements apparently retitled ("Statue of Liberty" ["The Fathers"], "Mulberry Street," "American Day," "Chase" ["Hooded Legion"], and "Funeral and Finale") for another Philharmonic concert at Lewisohn Stadium, this one in 1958, but conductor Samuel Matlovsky decided not to perform the work after inclement weather led to reschedulings of various programs. Meanwhile, the song "Dusty Sun" independently received some performances and even a 1946 recording by baritone Walter Scheff, accompanied by Leonard Bernstein, that filled out RCA's 1947 release of Blitzstein's *Airborne Symphony*.[28]

In early 1942, Blitzstein worked on a very different sort of picture, a planned ten-minute film, *Night Shift*, commissioned by the Office for Emergency Management, a government agency that helped coordinate the country's national defense program. The film's director, Garson (Gar) Kanin (1912–1999), who had known Blitzstein since the mid-1930s, had made some successful screwball comedies for RKO before joining the military in 1941. (His wartime credits eventually included two 1942 shorts, *Fellow Americans* and *Ring of Steel*, and an ambitious 1945 documentary co-directed with Carol Reed about the Allied invasion of Nazi-occupied

Europe, *The True Glory*, with which Blitzstein also became involved.) Never completed, *Night Shift* was intended to build public support for Washington's policy of total war mobilization, specifically, round-the-clock operation of defense plants, articles about which Blitzstein saved among his papers.

The composer provided not only the text and music of this short "film-opera" but even the shooting script, moving a step closer toward that full integration of word, tone, and image attempted in his earlier pictures. This shooting script contains two columns running side-by-side, one indicating "what is sung and spoken," the other, "insofar as possible, what is seen." In this latter column, Blitzstein knowingly specified such camera techniques as pan, medium, full, and long shots, and long lap dissolves, with one nighttime factory sequence described as follows: "The camera slowly dollies along an aisle between two rows of machines, stopping now and then as if to examine one of the machines more carefully, and sometimes angling so as better to see a certain part. This whole camera movement must be executed slowly and delicately. The impression of moving on tiptoe so as not to waken the sleeping machines." The filmmakers apparently would have tailored the visuals to a prerecorded soundtrack, something of a novelty for a documentary, although Blitzstein, who already had encouraged Ivens and Van Dyke in this direction, noted resemblances to "the Disney-technique," even if he hoped for "very different results" (adding in a letter to David Diamond, "Not that I want to get at all snooty about Disney, whose *Donald Duck* for the Treasury [*The New Spirit*] I found enchanting").[29]

Blitzstein scored the short for two soloists, chorus, and small orchestra. The filmmakers at one point imagined Ginger Rogers and Bing Crosby for the principal roles, but they eventually retained two other stars, Kate Smith and Danny Kaye, who recorded the music under Alexander Smallens in a New York studio, and who both thought it "a great pleasure" to work with the composer. In May, Blitzstein referred to *Night Shift* as if a completed work, which in a sense it was, but in the course of the spring, Kanin abandoned shooting after receiving orders from Washington to drop the project "for reasons never made clear," according to Eric Gordon, who interviewed the director about the matter.[30]

Although the film's visuals and soundtrack seem to have disappeared, a script and score survive, the narration featuring two off-camera commentators, a savvy Gal and a less knowing Guy. After the opening titles, the Gal and the Guy view a factory sitting idle late at night, prompting the Guy to sing a lullaby to the machines ("Sleep On, Machines"). The story proceeds to scenes from the front that illustrate the need for more military supplies and then to vignettes about factory employees working the night shift (against a variety of bugle calls that dramatize the notion that workers represent a fighting force in their own right). The piece ends climactically with a montage of factories working at full tilt, accompanied by a song performed by the Gal, the Guy, and the chorus ("Turn the Night into Day").

The work leavens the seriousness of its theme with humor, with the Guy and the Gal somewhat reminiscent of Mr. Musiker and Beetzie from *I've Got the Tune*, another learning piece intended for a broad audience. During the opening titles, after the chorus sings "Directed by Garson Kanin," the Guy comments, "That's nice," whereas after they sing "Written by Marc Blitzstein," the Guy remarks, "Never heard of him." The Guy represents the common man, the Gal, the voice of freedom; in an early draft, Blitzstein named the two characters Jasper (American slang for a naïve guy) and Liberty.

The score, which Blitzstein dedicated to Kanin, combines speech, song, accented recitation, and rhythmic recitation within a thoroughly unified musical texture, with the culminating final number, "Turn the Night into Day," arising naturally out of preceding materials. This rousing march-like finale, published by Chappell, recalls Gershwin and perhaps Eisler too, but the music has—as in the stark dissonance on the word "war"—a vigor and bite of its own, as does the film-opera as a whole, in contrast to the typically shopworn propaganda soundtracks of the day.

Henry Brant once again helped to orchestrate the score. As someone who also had worked on *Valley Town* and *Native Land*, Brant developed a particularly expert knowledge of Blitzstein as an orchestrator, as evident from his 1946 article on the composer:

> The arranger cannot be allowed to have his way with a Blitzstein song, since the meticulously contrived harmonic-contrapuntal background carries so much dramatic responsibility. Each note must be clearly and literally articulated. It is perhaps for this reason that much of Blitzstein's scoring features a thin, neutral orchestral texture, bare of flashy colors or lush timbres, and favoring drab instrumental shades almost to the point of conventionality. However, in the rare cases where he requires tone-qualities evoking a special atmosphere, Blitzstein shows no lack of orchestral invention and considerable resourcefulness in handling a few instruments.[31]

Night Shift gave Blitzstein a taste of that dream he expressed in late 1940 of writing music for films that would "have a more exact and continuous relation to the visual image and to dialogue," even if such aspirations went unrealized in this instance. "I don't insist that real songs be written into every film," Blitzstein further stated, "nor that all movies become film-operas; but it seems to me that the aimless setting of mood through music, always coming from a point apparently four miles away from the scene of action, is 1) no solution and 2) a bore. Either you don't hear it at all, which is silly, or you do, which is worse; since as now manufactured, it tends to get in the hair of the things you see and the words you hear. I think we must have a music written at least as carefully as dialogue." As for *Night Shift*, in early 1943, among his notes for the *Airborne Symphony*, he commented, "The one thing about

Night Shift which was wrong, was that it was too tight, as usual—too much happened in too little time. . . . Relax on this one."[32]

In October 1940, the *New York Sun* announced that Blitzstein was working on a second piano concerto as well as on an opera, *Nine Days Wonder*, whose title suggests some connection to Great Britain's general strike of 1926 (known as the "nine days wonder") that pitted workers against the government. And in June 1941, the *Times* mentioned two operas in the works, *The Happy Family* and *New York Opera*, both projected for the following year, the latter a commission by the League of Composers that would have presented a panoramic look at New Yorkers, with a sixteen-piece jazz band and four violins in the pit. But Blitzstein became increasingly preoccupied by projects like *Night Shift* that directly served the Allied cause; and in May 1942, the *Times* reported that the *New York Opera*, although promised for that spring, would have to wait until the following season. When Blitzstein left for military service in London in the fall of 1942, he arranged to have the sketches for that work sent to him, but the material was lost in transit; and although he attempted to resurrect some of it from memory, he never completed the piece. "I should have finished the *New York Opera* before we got into the war," he wrote to the league's chairman, Claire Reis.[33]

In the meantime, in the spring of 1942, he began to host and write a weekly radio show, *Russia Is Singing*, one of few such shows (including also *Russia Dances* with Walter Terry) launched as part of a drive to raise $6 million for Russian War Relief. Four scripts, dating from May 25 through June 15, survive among the composer's papers, but the program apparently premiered on May 18, suggesting at least five episodes. The show aired on Monday evenings alternately for fifteen or thirty minutes on the Hearst New York station, WINS.

These programs largely presented a variety of folk and popular songs with short introductions by Blitzstein. The show's title actually proved something of a misnomer, for in addition to Russian music, including the theme song, Konstantin Listov's "Tachanka," the show featured Cossack, Georgian, Jewish, Mingrelian, Romani, Tartar, Ukrainian, and Uzbek music as well. (One episode also featured the Russian operetta star Claudia Novikova singing "Ah! quel dîner" from *La Périchole*, an indication of Blitzstein's increasing interest in Offenbach.) Blitzstein specifically hoped to impress on his listeners that what went by the name Russia involved dozens of diverse "nationalities," although unified in sundry ways: "All of them are musical, whether they play on a balalaika or a doira, when they sing in Russian or in Gypsy or in the language of Uzbedistan [sic]. Now all of them are marching off to the front, singing." Perhaps he viewed the Soviet Union as a prototype for an even more encompassing union of nations. In any case, the programming of so many obscure recordings—some of which apparently only recently arrived from the Soviet Union—documented once again the thoroughness with which he approached topics that engaged his interest.

Blitzstein further strove to counter ethnic stereotypes, pointing out, for example, that although Cossacks had oppressed Jews and other minorities under the Czar, in recent years, they had fought in a cavalry unit led by the celebrated Jewish Major-General Lev Dovator. He took particular pleasure in noting that the Soviet film *Red Tanks* had been produced before the German invasion of the Soviet Union, thus revealing that "Soviet hatred of Fascism and the Fascists and the Soviet's knowledge of its enemy were no sudden trumped up thing" (adding in notes to himself, "rib those who played the Soviet-Reich alliance"). In the course of the programs, he also drew comparisons with which Americans presumably could relate: the Ukrainian bandura "sounds a little like a mandolin to our ears"; a particular Russian singer "does a kind of speaking performance not unlike the style of Marlene Dietrich"; the Russian composer Isaak Dunayevsky "occupies a place in Russian music similar to that of Irving Berlin or George M. Cohan here. He is beloved for a popular, easy musical approach and for his knowledge and sense of what goes on in the peoples' hearts."

All told, the radio show revealed Blitzstein in an unusually expansive, even exhilarated mood. He hopes that his audience will listen to the music not only "as a thing in itself," but for what lies "behind the notes," stating, "we should listen to what it tells us of the battles going on, the unbelievable courage and gallantry of the Red Army fighters and of the whole Soviet peoples; of their calm and prepara-tion even in the midst of ruin; of their thoughtful and brilliant use of victories to force through even greater victories; of their capacity for the big throw, to go all the way, the whole hog." He thinks Prokofiev's *Alexander Nevsky* "one of the most brilliant scores ever made for a film" and "one of the first movies to recognize the value of music as an integrated element in the whole emotional scheme and design." He calls Lev Knipper's "Meadowland" (sung here by the Red Army Chorus) "one of the most stunning songs this century has brought forth." And regarding an Uzbek number, he confesses to having "a special place in my heart for the local color of this kind of piece."

Earlier in the year, Blitzstein similarly had written an enthusiastic review about John and Alan Lomax's *Our Singing Country: A Second Volume of American Ballads and Folk Songs* (1941), edited by Ruth Crawford Seeger. This collection, he comments, "is wonderful in most of the ways similar books are disappointing, exasperating, or even appalling. . . . Scholarship, human warmth and remarkable taste have joined hands to make a collection which, together with Volume I, rates with Bartok and Kodaly. . . . These tunes spring from the page in the same way they leapt from the throat," a welcome change from what the author wryly calls "folked-up arrangements." The "astounding" holler, "Mamma, Mamma, Make me a Garment" ["Make Me a Garment"], has that "wild fresh juice" that repre-sents "what we have all been talking about, when we said that the 'folk art' must stimulate and fertilize the 'fine art,'" although he warns the "fine art" composer against going "completely overboard, to the degree that he wants to stop writing music," perhaps a comment made with Ruth Crawford partly in mind. He also makes "a quick last-minute case for *town* folklore, not as against, but as supplementary to *rural* folklore: the gutter, the honkytonk, and even the boulevards sometimes give out with a musical richness quite up to the level of the farmers' and miners' and cowboys' inspirations," adding, "I am directing this at the reader, not at the Lomaxes," who included a penitentiary blues that left Blitzstein "utterly sent." (In a note of appreciation for this review, John Lomax wrote to Blitzstein, "Few people in Texas will ever read your discriminating and pungent sentences, but I'll hoard them in my heart.")[34]

Blitzstein's scripts for *Russia Is Singing* and his review of *Our Singing Country*, much like his "Music at Work" concert and some aspects of *No for an Answer* and *Native Land*, suggest the early 1940s as a turning point for the composer in terms not only of an increasingly populist outlook, but relatedly, a more wholehearted embrace of various kinds of folk music. As such, he approached attitudes held for several years by some musical friends on the left, although his special attachment to Soviet and African-American music represented a point of difference from, say, Thomson or Copland, who seemed more attracted to Anglo-American and Latin-American folklore.

Blitzstein also expressed his deep feelings for the Soviet Union with the song "Ballad of Sevastopol," composed in July 1942. A strategically important Soviet naval base in the Crimea, Sevastopol had surrendered early that month after withstanding months of German bombing. Blitzstein's intent in writing this song remains unknown, and only its somber melody line survives as such. But he later effectively used this music in the "Ballad of the Cities" movement from the *Airborne Symphony*, changing the cry, "Sevastopol/Sevastopol," to "Are you coming? We can hold out."

In addition to *Russia Is Singing*, Blitzstein became involved with another weekly radio show, *Labor for Victory*, which premiered in the spring of 1942 and ran for the duration of the war. These fifteen-minute shows, hosted on alternate weeks by the AFL and the CIO, and broadcast in cooperation with NBC on Saturday nights, addressed the war effort from a worker's perspective, with the CIO segments somewhat more militant in content. By providing a national forum for organized labor, this series constituted a landmark in American broadcasting history.[35]

The details regarding Blitzstein's affiliation with *Labor for Victory* remain unknown, but his papers include scripts of various authorship for four programs (aired on June 20, June 27, August 1, and August 15) and his own scores for three programs (aired on June 20, July 4, and August 1), along with a script "Freedom Grows" (aired June 26) for a similar radio show, *Win the War*. Aside from the June 27 program, the CIO as opposed to the AFL sponsored all these broadcasts, including the "Freedom Grows" episode, underscoring Blitzstein's closer ties with that organization. The programs cited above covered a range of topics: the argument for having the tax burden of the war fall on corporations and wealthy individuals rather than workers (June 20, by Robert Richards and Peter Lyon); the argument for black participation in the war despite racism at home (June 26, unattributed); profiles of machinists in the defense industry (June 27, unattributed); the importance of unions to the war effort (July 4, by Lyon); the role of white-collar workers in the same struggle (August 1, by Lyon and Morris Watson); and the value of CIO war relief (August 15, by Millard Lampell).[36]

The three scores found among Blitzstein's papers—referred to as "C.I.O. Tax Broadcast," "C.I.O. Bullet Broadcast"/"The Bullet That's Going to Kill Hitler," and "C.I.O. July 4 Broadcast"—resemble the composer's film documentary soundtracks, only shorter in length, involving from five to nine cues. Scored for chamber orchestra, they all open with a signature theme reminiscent of the music for *Night Shift*. Two of the three scores contain songs, with "Tax Broadcast" interweaving two numbers, both sung by the narrator (José Ferrer): "I Had a Dream," in parlando style; and "Twenty-five Thousand Dollars a Year," in slow waltztime. "Bullet Broadcast" similarly features a song, "The Quiet Girl," sung by a switchboard operator at a union party and then reprised at the program's very end. In music marked "slow, torchy," the singer states that she "used to be a quiet girl" but now wants to give out "with one big yen," explaining, in a fast chorus, "Because I wanna make the bullet that gets Hitler!/I wanna make the bullet that gets Hitler!/Oh, let me make the bullet that gets Hitler!/And then I'll be a quiet girl again." (She later learns—the moral of the show—that she and other office workers are already helping to make that bullet.) A tribute to unions, the "July 4 Broadcast" has no vocal music, but like *Native Land*, which it recalls in its fervor, develops the union song "Hold the Fort." Overall, these scores show an accommodation of folk song and bugle calls, with "Twenty-five Thousand Dollars a Year" and some other sections redolent of Copland, but with a character of their own.[37]

"The Quiet Girl" subsequently found its way into the "Lunchtime Follies," a revue sponsored by the American Theatre Wing War Service that performed for tens of thousands of workers in defense plants, often during the lunch hour, but sometimes between shifts. An event at Madison Square Garden honoring the nineteenth anniversary of Lenin's death featured the song as well. Published as a single melody with additional words during the war in the collection *Sing America*, the song appeared fully in print in 2001 as part of the second volume of the *Blitzstein Songbook*.[38]

In July 1942, the *Times* reported that Blitzstein also agreed to provide some music for another war-minded revue, *Let Freedom Sing*, for the American Youth Theatre; but the composer soon after joined the army, and the show, which opened on October 5, featured only his Cole Porter parody, "Fraught," from *No for an Answer*. After eight performances at the Longacre Theatre, the mostly Harold Rome revue, starring Mitzi Green, toured the boroughs on the so-called subway circuit. By this time, Blitzstein had relocated to London with the United States Eighth Army Air Force.

14

To London and Back (1942–1945)

In the course of 1942, Blitzstein resolved to join the military, hoping to serve as close to the action as possible. To this end, he had his classification changed from III-A (deferred because of dependents, namely, his mother) to I-A (available for service), and obtained character references from no fewer than ten government officials and artists, including John Houseman, Garson Kanin, and Virgil Thomson. David Diamond regarded his friend's intentions as "ominous," but Blitzstein, on receiving orders to proceed to Bolling Field Air Base in Washington in late August, assured him, "This is exactly what I want, need for realization: the chance to do my own work, fused into the stream of the most terrific events of our time, and right at the field of operation. Not ominous, my boy: thrilling."[1]

Jo Davis made arrangements to have her brother's belongings shipped from his Manhattan apartment at 327 West 57th Street, where he had moved from his Hudson Street apartment in late 1940, to her Philadelphia home at 6436 Overbrook Avenue; and on August 24, Blitzstein prepared a codicil naming Jo his beneficiary and granting her power of attorney. Two days after his August 27 arrival in Washington, he entered the Eighth Army Air Force as an entertainment specialist with the rank of private. "Here, and every inch a soldier," he slyly wrote to Leonard Bernstein on the back of a postcard of the phallic Washington Monument.[2]

In the years just prior to his enlistment, Blitzstein continued to lend his name to various procommunist causes, including protests in defense of the Veterans of the Abraham Lincoln Brigade, communist officials Earl Browder and Sam Darcy, labor leader Harry Bridges, and City College professor Morris Schappes. Although the FBI under the directorship of J. Edgar Hoover had been tracking some of these activities since 1940, declaring him a "communist" and considering him "for custodial detention in the event of a national emergency," this obviously did not prevent his admission into the military, whatever reservations the government had about communist recruits. Rather, the FBI placed a moratorium on his file until he returned to civilian life in 1945.[3]

Assigned to director William Wyler's film unit attached to the Eighth Army Air Force, the thirty-seven-year-old Blitzstein prepared to go overseas. Headquartered in London, the so-called Mighty Eighth, America's largest air battalion, employed at its height about 200,000 personnel. In tandem with other units, including those of Britain's Royal Air Force, the Eighth bombed targets on the continent in order to weaken the enemy's military-industrial infrastructure, helping to prepare and later facilitate the Normandy landings of June 6, 1944. The strength of the Eighth Air Force rested largely on their B-17 Flying Fortresses, large four-engine airplanes that carried a crew of ten.

By the time Blitzstein arrived in Washington, Wyler (1902–1981) already had left for London, but he presumably had had a hand in securing the composer's assignment, as he had been told to assemble a film crew. However well Wyler knew Blitzstein or his work, the director would have heard good things about him from his frequent writer Lillian Hellman, and perhaps more to the point, his principal writer in London, Jerome Chodorov (1911–2004), a friend of Blitzstein's who shared his political views and who had co-written *My Sister Eileen*, a hit both on stage (1940) and screen (1942). Waiting to be sent abroad, Blitzstein described his commission to Mina Curtiss as "the most thrilling assignment I can imagine—planning movies and soundtracks with William Wyler," and he began hatching movie ideas. "I think he'll be impressed," he wrote to his sister.[4]

Sailing for Britain in late September on a ship crammed with thousands of servicemen, Blitzstein contracted ptomaine poisoning, making the trip all the more miserable. But he grew increasingly close to the other enlisted men; whereas he had told his sister in late August that he was "living with the boys, but not one of them," he wrote to his family after landing in early October, "I am really beginning to know the guys inside out. I find confirmation of all my hopes and beliefs. In short, I find I am for the people; I have added to my faith in men a realistic knowledge of them. Give these soldiers I have been with a purpose and they will match any one, any where, for tenacity, courage, good humor—and, incidentally, barrack-room wit. I'm having a fine time."[5]

Billeted in a cold-water flat with three other soldiers in the Mayfair area of London near Hyde Park, Blitzstein spent the fall working on film scenarios at Claridge's Hotel with Chodorov and writing songs at his publisher Chappell's British branch, owned and operated by Louis Dreyfus. On November 5, he described his daily routine to nephew Stephen as "a dazing mess of unconnected experiences: billets and barracks and mess . . . work and the theatre, typing and ballet, walks through the streets-in-blackout, drill, new acquaintances, pubs, drives to the Ministry to see unreleased films, more work—this doesn't begin to tell it!"[6]

As Wyler struggled to obtain needed equipment, Blitzstein and Chodorov worked on a movie about a particular B-17 and its crew, *Phyllis Was a Fortress*, one of a number of projects of this type that eventually yielded Wyler's celebrated documentary, *The Memphis Belle* (1944). In early December, the head of the Eighth Air Force, General Ira C. Eaker, expanded Wyler's mission and appointed as the unit's commanding officer Lieutenant Colonel Beirne Lay Jr. (1909–1982), a Yale-educated pilot and writer, who after the war would co-write both the novel and film *Twelve O'Clock High* (1947/1949). Lay arranged for Wyler's team to visit important installations, and Blitzstein duly spent a few days in early December inspecting bombing stations and taking notes "for the big epic Wyler will do," including observations of the troops, whom, he wrote to his family, he found "better-looking than the city-variety or headquarters variety. . . . No shit here about removing your cap when you eat, or having your shoes shined and brass-buttons polished; the place is designed for business, and all the faces reflect it." On December 9, he finally met Lay, "who," he wrote, "turns out to be a stunning looker and an eager but cool-headed but [sic] swell guy."[7]

In mid-December, with Wyler and some of his crew occupied, Lay loaned Blitzstein out to the Army Special Service Division under Captain Edward Duryea Dowling, in which capacity the composer and Chodorov (the latter soon to be transferred back to the States) wrote some material for *Four Jills in a Jeep*, a show featuring Kay Francis, Carole Landis, Mitzi Mayfair, and Martha Raye then on a five-month tour of England, Ireland, and North Africa. And in January, he wrote commentary for an unidentified short film by the accomplished director Major Anatole Litvak, who considered Blitzstein "an artist of distinguished and exceptional talents."[8]

In December, Lay had told Blitzstein that having him in the military at his current rank resembled "having Toscanini as a private" and that he would have to have this "crime . . . rectified." So encouraged, Blitzstein suggested to Lay that he write "a big concert work on the subject of the air-force." Lay liked the idea, but he thought that the proposal would stand a better chance had Blitzstein a higher rank, so he arranged for his promotion to corporal, which came through in late January. No doubt swayed by the endorsements of Wyler and Lay as well as noted newspaperman Lieutenant Tex McCrary, then a public relations officer for the air force, General Eaker approved the commission in February and released Blitzstein from his duties so that he could devote himself full-time to the work, the *Airborne Symphony*.[9]

By this time, Blitzstein had met, through Chodorov, a distinguished pathologist and cancer researcher at Guy's Hospital, Peter Gorer (1907–1961), who placed at the composer's disposal his "lovely old-fashioned home," the Elms, with its rock garden and grand piano, in Highgate, outside of London. With a daily stipend of four dollars for food and lodging, Blitzstein now officially took up residence with Gorer and his fiancée Gertrude, a German refugee, he informed his mother, "full of intuition as to my needs and domestic comforts, and sensitive to my convictions and purpose." "Marc was the envy of all," recalled his army buddy, writer James Dugan. "We made legends of the corporal who never turned out at revelle [sic], never ate army chow, performed no drill, saluted no one, marched nowhere, shot at nothing, and spent his days in a manor house parlor placarded do not disturb, gazing idly over a mile of heath displayed through the open french doors, and just played himself tunes on the pie-anna." After the Gorers married on August 18, the impending arrival of Peter's mother made it necessary for Blitzstein to vacate this "small Paradise," and in late September he moved into a small furnished flat in London. But even after he left the Elms, he maintained close ties with the Gorers, whom he described to his sister in October 1943 as "my real find in the way of people in this wartime country."[10]

Meanwhile, in late August, Blitzstein interrupted work on the *Airborne Symphony* in order to help prepare the two-hundred-voice U.S. Army Negro Chorus, a singing group from the segregated African-American engineer aviation battalions, for an appearance with the London Symphony Orchestra in a recital of American vocal and symphonic music on September 28 and 29 at the Royal Albert Hall, some of which would be broadcast both in Britain and back home. The military high command reasoned that these concerts, underwritten by Lord Beaverbrook's popular *Daily Express*, might help improve relations, beset by racial prejudice, between African-American GIs and white servicemen and civilians.[11]

Blitzstein accepted the commission after hearing the men—"They sing like angels, with the most incredible spontaneous harmony and rhythm; mostly spirituals, some work songs, a lot I never knew before"—and took up quarters among them, "a lone white among 500 Negro troops." "I feel more like what is fondly called a 'People's Artist' than ever in my life," he wrote to Jo on August 31. He especially came to appreciate the musicalized speech of the men, citing a few examples in an article for the *New York Times*, including one soldier who playfully crowded his way into a mess line singing, "Buddy, roll. Get out of my way. You much too young to die." As for the upcoming concert, its importance, he told his sister, transcended the betterment of Anglo-American relations: it upheld "the first tenet of Anti-Fascism—the shame of racial antagonism."[12]

Blitzstein coached the men in various spirituals and Earl Robinson's *Ballad for Americans,* and served as stage manager as well. He later recalled that the chorus called him "Maestro" or "Corp'l Marc," although a yearbook edited by the group's director, Sergeant Alexander Jordan, states that most of the men referred to him as "Blitz" because "that is the impression he gave us whenever we were off key or made a sour note. He also had an uncanny ability to go among our group of 200 men and put his finger on the man who needed help or correction." One newspaper account of a rehearsal reported Blitzstein shouting at the chorus, "No! Top heavy. In that part, you've got to travel like an airplane."[13]

Stationed in East Anglia, the chorus members apparently rehearsed six nights a week, but usually at separate encampments at Diss and Eye, an encumbrance imposed on the group, according to Blitzstein, by hostile officers wanting to sabotage the project. But Blitzstein persevered, catching the beginning of the rehearsal in one town before rushing off in a jeep, "usually during an air-raid," for the last hour in the other. He also insisted that the men be given a two-day leave just prior to the concert and transportation to London on trucks with covers.[14]

The Royal Albert Hall concerts brought Blitzstein into close contact with Sergeant Hugo Weisgall (1912–1997), a Czech-born American who had studied composition with Roger Sessions and Rosario Scalero and conducting with Fritz Reiner, and who was scheduled to conduct some of the program. Blitzstein praised Weisgall's "mastery of the baton" to David Diamond, although he wrote to his sister, "There are a lot of things wrong with his smugness, both as a person and musician." Weisgall recalled, in an interview with Eric Gordon, that following a performance of his *American Comedy 1943* for orchestra, which he had premiered at a Proms concert on July 29, Blitzstein had told him, "Now that's the kind of music you should write instead of the shit you do," a remark that forty years later (after Weisgall had established his own career as an opera composer) still carried a sting.[15]

Many military and diplomatic dignitaries joined the sold-out crowd of some five thousand—deemed by Blitzstein "the most distinguished audience seen in London in years"—who attended the opening night concert at the Royal Albert Hall on September 28, 1943, with the evening's proceeds earmarked for British war charities. Sergeant Jordan and Private James McDaniel led the chorus in various spirituals; Weisgall led the London Symphony in orchestral works by Samuel Coleridge-Taylor and John Powell, along with the premiere of *Freedom Morning*, a piece Blitzstein had written specifically for the occasion; Private Kenneth Cantril—a white participant—sang the solo part in *Ballad for Americans*; the celebrated black tenor Roland Hayes, brought over from the States, performed selections by Bach and Thomas Arne and joined the chorus in "Joshua fit de Battle of Jericho" (the words updated so that "My name is Poor Pilgrim,/To Canaan I am bound" became "Yes, we are Allied soldiers,/To Berlin we are bound"); and all joined for the singing of the American and British national anthems. The enthusiastic reception heard throughout the evening peaked with the encore, a rendition by the chorus of "Go Down, Moses," which elicited from the audience at the words "Let my people go!" as Blitzstein recalled, "the biggest collective sob and demonstration." After the concert, General Jacob L. Devers went backstage to congratulate the men, as General John C. H. Lee would do the following evening, a concert free to service personnel that also met with success.[16]

Blitzstein subsequently noted in the *New York Times*, "All my belief in the American Negro as an integral and vital part of growing American culture—musical, artistic, civic, human and social—has been strengthened," although he added in the *New Masses*, "Okay, the American Negro is to that London audience anyway a man of sensitiveness, culture, talent. And these boys now go back to their jobs and their ghetto-dom and their officers and the well-known treatment. And I go back to my bomber bases and the *Airborne*." Actually, he first spent a week in early October touring military bases with Roland Hayes and a reduced chorus of twenty-four singers; he had a good time, but eager to return to his commissioned piece, he declined the offer to accompany the full chorus and the Royal Air Force Symphony on a three-city tour of Manchester, Edinburgh, and Glasgow in mid-October.[17]

Resuming work on the symphony, Blitzstein also spent some time in late October on a short film produced jointly by the American Office of War Information and the British Ministry of Information, *Welcome to Britain*. Co-directed by Irving Reis, with whom Blitzstein had collaborated on *The Spanish Earth* and *I've Got the Tune*, and the esteemed British director Anthony Asquith, this documentary featured Burgess Meredith as a private charged with educating American servicemen about British customs, with comedians Bob Hope and Beatrice Lillie briefly spotlighted in special segments. Blitzstein, although uncredited, apparently worked on the score with the British film composer William Alwyn (1905–1985), of whom he saw a good deal during his time in London, and whose "excellent movie scores" he admired, including *World of Plenty*, which, he told Diamond, had "some adventurous devices, some of which flop, but some of which make fine sense." (To Copland, he described Alwyn himself as "nice but a little dull.") In a V-mail to home dated November 1, Blitzstein took credit for "the American part" of the film score (which presumably involved supervising the popular music heard in the restaurant and canteen scenes), and described the film as "a cute job; it should be better, but it'll do."[18]

By this time, Blitzstein had a new commanding officer, Captain John (Jock) Hay Whitney (1904–1982, and a member of the wealthy and influential Whitney family), who oversaw Blitzstein's promotion to sergeant in early November and allowed him to continue work on the *Airborne*. On November 25, 1943, the composer successfully auditioned the "virtually finished" piece for Whitney and assorted military brass, after which he and Burgess (Buzz) Meredith, who also attended, celebrated with Jamaican rum.[19]

Blitzstein now set himself the considerable task of orchestrating the symphony, only partially scored at this point. However, more distractions followed before he more or less finished the piece in April 1944 (so late that the military decided against launching the work after all): he composed some title music for French and Italian newsreels, and performed, on March 26, the solo part to Gershwin's *Rhapsody in Blue* at the Adelphi Theatre with Weisgall and the London Philharmonic Orchestra on an all-American program ("something I don't quite approve," he wrote home; "it's as though American music were being quarantined and isolated from the rest") that also included works by Bloch, Copland, Piston, and Sessions. (Blitzstein by his own admission gave a "theatrical performance" of the *Rhapsody*, playing it, as one GI told him, "like a hep-jazz-pianist"; wrote Blitzstein to his sister, "It's the way I feel it should be done; there's been too much salon-izing of the work over here.")[20]

Moreover, in January 1944, with Whitney and McCrary off to Italy, Blitzstein became music director for the American Broadcasting Station in Europe (ABSIE), an arm of the Office of War Information (OWI). Similar in purpose to the Voice of America, ABSIE first aired on April 30, 1944, about five weeks before D-Day, with the express intention of preparing Nazi-occupied Europe about the upcoming invasion, warning in particular against premature resistance. Eventually acquiring a staff of five and other support personnel, Blitzstein worked at this job alongside playwright Robert Sherwood, the director of the Overseas Branch of the OWI, as well as such CBS luminaries as William Paley and Davidson Taylor. Among other activities, he collected hundreds of discs, planned an assortment of programs, and supervised recordings of popular American songs in foreign languages by such singers as Dinah Shore and Bing Crosby. "Luckily I'm also involved with Mendelssohn, Shostakovich, Beethoven, Copland and Blitzstein (who *is* that man?) so that I'm not utterly sunk in the Rat Race of pop stuff," he wrote home. For the station's initial broadcast on April 30, he chose to open with some Stephen Foster played by Andre Kostelanetz and His Orchestra, followed by Beethoven's Seventh Symphony conducted by Toscanini—"just the right combination of serious and communicative tone."[21]

On June 2, four days before D-Day, Blitzstein programmed what he considered "surely the finest piece of music in my collection," Verdi's *Hymn of the Nations* as arranged and conducted by Toscanini, with tenor soloist Jan Peerce ("sounding exactly like Caruso in his palmiest days"), the Westminster Choir, and the NBC Symphony Orchestra. Blitzstein initially had heard this arrangement—in which Toscanini had appended "The Internationale" and "The Star-Spangled Banner" to the British, French, and Italian national anthems as found in the original Verdi—earlier in the year at a private showing of the OWI film, *Arturo Toscanini: Hymn of the Nations* (1944, directed by Alexander Hammid); and thrilled by the performance, had arranged for the soundtrack to be pressed into a record for broadcast use. The music proved a sensation, Blitzstein even asserting after the war, "I say without fear of contradiction that the Toscanini sound track provided the most potent single musical weapon of World War II." (He also thought the soundtrack's "accurate, sensitive, proportioned" engineering to represent "the first step" toward "what a real musical film can be like.")[22]

All this while, Blitzstein occasionally turned up on radio himself, including participating on a quiz show for the Armed Forces Network and intermittently appearing on the BBC. In June 1943, for instance, he presented a talk for the BBC about contemporary American music in which he identified "the chance for a free and growing world culture" as "one of the big things we're fighting for," and further deemed "relative simplicity and communicability" as "perhaps the most important single tendency" in American music. At the same time, he emphasized the country's diverse musical scene as represented by the "hard-bitten" Copland, the "sparkling" Walter Piston, the "strong" Roy Harris, the "guttural" Carlos Chávez, the "severe" Roger Sessions, the "enchanting" Virgil Thomson, the "swaggering" George Gershwin, and "that wonder of wonders, Charles Ives, the single real 'original' I think American music has produced" (revealingly selecting those figures—with the significant addition of Gershwin— featured by Copland in his 1941 text on modern music). Over that same summer, also for the BBC, he performed excerpts from his work and on a separate occasion joined Margaret Mead and others in the transatlantic show *Answering You*, his job to discuss British theater and music with columnist Ed Sullivan in New York. ("The most important thing I can think of, Ed," he said regarding differences between British and American tastes, "is that the British people 1] do not like fantasy as we know it, and 2] don't care an awful lot about youth as we know it.") And in June 1944, he interviewed Stephen Thomas and Philip Bate for another BBC show, *Television Was Fun*, about music and television, a new medium that the composer had seen in the United States but not in England.[23]

After taking a short working vacation in Scotland and Ireland in August 1944, Blitzstein left the OWI to become composer and music director for a major film about the Allied invasion, simply referred to at this point as the Anglo-American Film Project, co-directed by Captain Garson Kanin and British filmmaker Carol Reed (1906–1976) under the auspices of the Supreme Headquarters Allied Expeditionary Force (SHAEF) commanded by General Dwight D. Eisenhower. "It looks like a thrilling job," wrote Blitzstein to his father. In September, he moved into a large new office, equipped with a piano and moviola, at 27 Grosvenor Square, and began examining takes at Pinewood Studios and sketching and recording music for what would become the epic war documentary, *The True Glory*.[24]

Blitzstein previously had collaborated with his friend Garson Kanin on *Night Shift* (1942) and had become an admirer of both Reed and his work as well. He regarded Reed's educational film for inductees, *The New Lot* (1943), a better movie than Noël Coward and David Lean's *In Which We Serve* (1942), even if both pictures remained "awfully wary about naming the enemy, or the cause; and stick too much to the actual camaraderie of the men, their pluck, their team-work." He also liked *The Way Ahead*, Reed's feature-length 1944 expansion of *The New Lot*. "Carol [Reed] is a fine sensitive guy, with a marvelous way of dealing with the people under him," he wrote to his sister soon after embarking on this new assignment.[25]

In connection with the film, Blitzstein spent five weeks in late 1944, from the end of October to early December, in France with Claude Dauphin (1903–1978), who was to collect film and anecdotes related to the French Resistance while Blitzstein researched its music. A French actor described by Blitzstein as the Clark Gable of France and "a swell and sensitive guy," Dauphin had participated in the Resistance himself, as had his wife, actress Rosine Deréan, at the time interned in a German prisoner-of-war camp. Arriving in recently liberated Paris, Blitzstein found the town "more beautiful than I remembered it" (he had last seen the city in 1934), but also a "sick city," the population "circumspect, frightened, or downright hostile." While waiting for a jeep and equipment, he visited Jean Cocteau, who told him not to expect to find songs among the Resistance, explaining that it was a "mouvement silencieux" ("silent movement").[26]

Blitzstein and Dauphin made three excursions into the countryside, where they discovered "the real Resistance—now open, clear and vigorous." On their first outing, they traveled to the Rhône-Alpes, near the Swiss border, where they retrieved film from a guerrilla unit, the Maquis, in Annemasse, and where Blitzstein transcribed songs of Russian soldiers in Grenoble and the French Forces of the Interior (FFI) in Lyons. Returning to Paris for supplies, Blitzstein met with conductor Roger Désormière, an active figure in the cultural resistance who now provided the "low-down" on some important French musicians during the occupation, summarized by Blitzstein as "[Alfred] Cortot, [Arthur] Honegger, bad; [Georges] Auric, [Francis] Poulenc, [Manuel] Rosenthal, [Charles] Muench, okay; [Henri] Sauguet, [Olivier] Messiaen, apolitical, talented, unoffending."[27]

Blitzstein and Dauphin's second trip took them further north, closer to the German front and to danger. As they once again obtained some film, this time in Luxeuil, Blitzstein also recorded songs in Mélisey and Lure, and more music of the FFI in the village of Brouville: "When I sing back what I have written," he recalled, "they applaud wildly, with gasps of amazement." Back in Paris, he attended, at the suggestion of the OWI, a lavish reception in honor of two recent winners of the Prix de Rome, an event that left him "not quite nauseated, but sufficiently." On their third and last sojourn, Blitzstein and Dauphin traveled to Normandy, including Lisieux, Saint-Lô, and Caen, where they met the Resistance leader Henriette Bayeux (known locally as Marraine) and heard yet more songs. Indeed, before departing France, Blitzstein could not resist the urge to call Cocteau to say that, the latter's protestations to the contrary, he had managed to collect eighteen Resistance songs. "It seems to me I have seen war, peace (very relative), joy, heartbreak, resistance, collaboration, birth, life and death of men and ideas," he wrote to his family about his five weeks in France, which he further described as "one of the big experiences of my life."[28]

Before Blitzstein left for France, he agreed, at the suggestion of the French-American writer Lewis Galantière, head of the French division of the OWI, to organize an American Music Festival in Paris for the spring of 1945; and while in France, he apparently secured Désormière's cooperation in this effort. By late November, he had planned out a series of five concerts, all to be broadcast on radio, featuring orchestral music by Americans (including works by Copland, Diamond, Harris, Piston, Schuman, and Thomson, along with his own *Freedom Morning*); orchestral music by refugees in the United States (including recent works by Fitelberg, Hindemith, Martinů, Milhaud, Rieti, Schoenberg, Stravinsky, Toch, and Weill); chamber music; film music; and jazz (originally Glenn Miller, but after the band leader's disappearance en route from London to Paris in December, Duke Ellington). However, because so much work remained to be done on the invasion film, Blitzstein could not continue as festival director, and in February 1945, he suggested that Copland—whose tastes resembled his own—assume this post. As late as March, Blitzstein nevertheless intended to stay involved with the festival, but the OWI, nearing its termination, eventually abandoned the idea because of a lack of congressional funding.[29]

Blitzstein had hoped to complete his score for the invasion documentary first by early February, then by late March—"It's got to be the best music I ever wrote. It will be," he wrote to his mother on February 14—but progress on the film proceeded more slowly than he expected, largely because Kanin and Reed, in order to keep abreast of events, constantly reedited their work, which in turn necessitated, as Blitzstein wrote home, "the changing of the score, and inevitable frustrations for me." Another difficulty concerned some disagreement over the music between Kanin, who defended it, and Reed, who thought it "too Russian, too revolutionary," too much like Shostakovich. In any event, Blitzstein had to discard large chunks of the score, cuts he subsequently arranged into a suite called *Sound Track*, which Weisgall reportedly performed in Brussels in mid-April.[30]

In late April, before the completion of the film, Blitzstein received a request from his stepmother Madi that he return home to see his father Sam, gravely ill with heart trouble, and Kanin intervened to help secure him a furlough. Concerned about his father, and exhausted from nearly three years of unstinting service, he left for France on April 26, but unable to catch a flight, returned to England on April 28 to await a boat home. The next day, his sister telegrammed him, "Papa died this morning. Come home. Sorry darling we did not realize end so near."[31]

Blitzstein more than ever felt the need to return home—"It's bad now to be among strangers, no one who knew him," he wrote to his family on May 5—but he had to wait a few weeks before he could gain passage. "Aside from the grief," he wrote, "now he is gone there is a most intolerable sense of guilt: I neglected him, I saw him too little, I wrote too seldom," a rather harsh self-indictment considering the many times he wrote to his father in the course of the war. "I only hope he knew about the join up with the Russians before he died," he added. Blitzstein finally found transportation home, arriving in New York in late May.[32]

While stationed in Europe, Blitzstein wrote dozens of V-mails, not only to his father, but to his mother, his sister Jo, and, less often, his nephews Stephen and Christopher, his mother-in-law Lina Abarbanell, and such friends as Copland, Diamond, and Mina Curtiss. This correspondence provides, besides much of the chronicle outlined above, some record of Blitzstein's personal life during his time abroad, including his frame of mind, which characteristically wavered a good deal. In several letters, especially to his sister Jo, he expressed guilt over the privations of the fighting men and the "relative triviality" of his work, referring self-deprecatingly to the *Airborne* as the "Chairborne." But on the whole, he seemed fortified by his years in the service, which probably represented overall one of the happier times of his life.[33]

Part of this satisfaction derived from his sense of engagement in a great moral struggle, a fight not only against fascism, but for the common man, part of a struggle, in his estimation, that had predated the war and that would continue afterwards. "I think it turns out that the war we have been fighting for many years longer than this one is still the war to be fought," he wrote Jo in October 1944. All diplomatic and military cooperation between the Western democracies and the Soviet Union especially delighted him, whether the declarations made at the Moscow, Tehran, and Yalta conferences, the opening of a second front against the Germans, or the bombing of Dresden—later deemed one of the most controversial of all Allied Air Forces undertakings—in conjunction with Soviet ground advances. "I'm rooting now for that moment when the East and the West drives will meet, and we shake hands," he wrote to his sister, also in October 1944. "Boy, what a moment!"[34]

Accordingly, he wished that the average soldier had a "deeper and more unanimous conviction about the whole effort," although he appreciated the awareness of America's black servicemen: "They know what they're doing in this war—and, what is more, why!" In his private correspondence, he similarly criticized actors Laurence Olivier and Vivien Leigh for treating the war as "just a thing to talk and read about (for the moment)," and disparaged such conscientious objectors as composers Benjamin Britten and Michael Tippett. Following political events back home, he found common ground with Wendell Willkie (whose switch to the Republican Party he had trouble understanding), celebrated Roosevelt's reelection and mourned his death, and lambasted America's "bigwigs" and Truman's "Tory inclinations," expecting, after the war, a "great reactionary wave" in the United States and a "new birth" in formerly occupied Europe, although he had no intentions of remaining abroad: "America is my country it seems; which is one reason I get so exasperated with it," he stated in early 1944.[35]

Blitzstein characteristically expressed special concern with issues of social justice. He decried the disparity between rich and poor in wartime London, an inequity that likewise disturbed him when he arrived in liberated Paris in late 1944. (Between low pay and wartime rations, he himself felt deprived during his time in the military and happily welcomed the shirts, garters, mufflers, socks, toilet water, cigarettes, sweets, and other items sent to him from home.) And while sensitive to the "unpleasanter side" of the liberation of France—in particular, revenge against fifth columnists—he brooded over the easy treatment of many Vichy collaborators. "In Grenoble," he wrote home, "there was no monkey-business about trials and being let off; two days after liberation, people were taken out and shot or hanged; some innocents got it, no doubt; but *all* the collabs got it too." He himself harbored a sense of "vengeance," as many aspects of the war had left him "blood-angry." At one point, he even stated, in regard to reactionary politicians at home, "When the time comes for trying war criminals, I'm wondering if we don't have a few of our own?" And telling his mother in late April 1945 about "the sickening news of the Buchenwald, Belsen, Ordruf [sic] concentration-camps—which we all knew, and wouldn't face or believe," he added, "What the holy hell are we to do with such people?"[36]

As with *The True Glory*, which included some horrifying footage of the liberation of Bergen-Belsen, this last correspondence did not identify any of the concentration camp inmates as Jews; nor did Blitzstein otherwise seem to address the plight of Europe's Jews in his extensive correspondence during these years, although he remained quick to confront local anti-Semitism. He had little to say about communism either, although a report of a visit to Marx's gravesite with the noted British writer, broadcaster, and socialist, J. B. Priestley, and supportive remarks about the provisional postoccupation governments of Yugoslavia and Poland intimated his communist sympathies. Indeed, after the war Blitzstein related how he defended to Henriette Bayeux the communists among the French Resistance: "They wanted to have their identity made clear among you; they would pool their efforts, but not their existence."[37]

During his time abroad, Blitzstein also made the time to attend a fair number of concerts, plays, ballets, films, and revues. Thanks in part to clippings sent to him by journalist Leonard Lyons, he kept up with cultural events at home as well. In the fall of 1943, for instance, he expressed his desire to see both Kurt Weill's *One Touch of Venus* and Richard Rodgers's *Oklahoma!* and cheered his friend Leonard Bernstein's "smash debut" on November 14, 1943, with the New York Philharmonic.[38]

Of the British composers he socialized with while abroad, he especially liked Wilfrid Mellers and Alan Bush, both of whom greatly admired his own work. Mellers became something of a guide to the local musical scene, introducing him, for instance, to a symphony of Edmund Rubbra's, which Blitzstein found "dull, highly monotonous," as he told Copland. To his readers back home, he also made short shrift of William Walton's 1922 *Façade* (a piece grown "faded and limp"), Richard Addinsell's *Warsaw Concerto* from the 1941 film *Dangerous Moonlight* ("a gaudy bit of pretentious writing"), and British music in general, which he tended to find either "sternly dogmatic or deliberately trivial." At the same time, he spoke well of fellow communist Bush's work, including his incidental music to Patrick Hamilton's play *The Duke in Darkness* (1943).[39]

In early 1944, Blitzstein further made the acquaintance of two of Britain's leading senior composers, Arnold Bax and Ralph Vaughan Williams, the second of whom he warmly described as "a charming, delicious old man, remarkably patrician and human at the same time. He delighted me; something that hasn't happened in a long time." But he thought Vaughan Williams's documentary film score to *Coastal Command* (1942) "too insistent," and Bax's for *Malta G.C.* (1942) simply "wretched."[40]

Among the younger generation, Blitzstein recognized the distinction of Benjamin Britten and Michael Tippett, whose Second String Quartet (1942) he heard at the Royal Pump Room in Leamington Spa on September 11, 1944, at an Anglo-American concert that also included Blitzstein at the piano in excerpts from *The Cradle* and *No for an Answer*. He previously had met Britten, as he had

Alan Bush, in New York; the notices for the 1941 premiere of Britten's *Paul Bunyan* at Columbia University even surmised Blitzstein's influence on that work, although Britten never revealed more than a vague familiarity with Blitzstein's music, and the opera in question charts in any case its own distinctive course. Meeting him once again in London, Britten asked if Blitzstein would read the libretto to his new opera (presumably *Peter Grimes*), but then disappeared; Blitzstein, who thought Britten "super-kind," guessed that he had frightened him away by threatening to ask at their next meeting how he reconciled his pacifism with his propaganda work for the BBC. Still, as of April 1944, he regarded Britten's *Serenade* (1943) the best new British music he had heard, describing it to Copland, not entirely approvingly, as "glacially perfect—with a ratio formulistic theatricality instead of actual intensity."[41]

Blitzstein also expressed to Copland his admiration for Tippett's First Piano Sonata (1938, rev. 1942), which he thought "English to the core, without being out of V[aughan] Williams or the professional nationals, yet with real flavor, and quite of our times," and which he liked more than the composer's Second String Quartet (1942), not to mention his "conventional, dreary, tired and defeatist" oratorio *A Child of Our Time* (1944). But Blitzstein found his attraction to the sonata "partially embarrassing, since Tippett himself is anti-war, and a general nuisance all ways but musically," and in the end deemed the composer's gifts of secondary concern: "The serviceability of talent is what matters now."[42]

On the lighter side, Blitzstein enjoyed a number of musical revues on the West End, especially those produced by Robert Nesbitt, but he found no British show comparable to Cole Porter's *DuBarry Was a Lady* (1939) and *Let's Face It!* (1941), both also playing in London, saying, "They [the British] don't know how to get hot, or how to get Viennese-sweet." And after catching a performance of Irving Berlin's *This Is the Army* (1942), which featured a new number for local consumption, "My British Buddy," he wrote to his mother, "The way that man turns out tunes!"[43]

Given his current preoccupations, Blitzstein naturally paid special attention to film, his correspondence and occasional articles reporting on such varied works as *Thunder Rock* (he preferred this 1942 film version to the original Robert Ardrey play); *In Which We Serve* ("skillful," but "cold," as to be expected from Noël Coward: "It is class-angled with a vengeance, its author being a very conscious, if not entirely kosher member of British aristocracy," with a score in Coward's "purpler, or Bitter-Sweet manner, with regretfully snatched memories of lesser Elgar"); *Edge of Darkness* (which he liked); *Mission to Moscow* ("All in all, probably the first signs of a new direction for Hollywood"); *The North Star* (criticizing the "stonily formal dialogue" and "perfect close-ups," he thought Copland's music "OK, but undistinguished," and Ira Gershwin's lyrics "frankly off the beam in style, though good in subject-matter"); *Double Indemnity* ("the best movie we've had here recently," although "sordid and slick"); and the Carol Reed films discussed above. In January 1943 he also "had a glimpse" of Leni Riefenstahl's film about the fifth Nazi Party Congress, *Triumph of the Will* (1934), writing to his mother, "a more stupefying horrible picture of a cannibal-race glutting itself with barbaric mediaeval cultism I never hope to see." While in France in 1944, he further screened two Jean Cocteau films made during the occupation: *Carmen* (1942), whose opportunistic incorporation of Wagner's *Tristan und Isolde* at its climax he decried, and *L'éternal retour* (1943), whose Auric score he deemed "pretty good," although he thought that both films suffered "from too palpable a solicitousness of the approval of the Nazi Ministry of Propaganda, calculated to be its chief audience."[44]

Blitzstein furthermore attended several ballets at Sadler's Wells choreographed and danced by the Australian-born Robert Helpmann, sometimes partnered with Margot Fonteyn. The composer described Helpmann as looking like Martha Graham in drag and ridiculed the dancer's reported wisecrack, told in his "airy-fairy and effeminate" style, about performing for the troops: "There we were, buttering up the workers, just as though we liked them!" (Blitzstein similarly lampooned the "queer as a bedbug" hotel proprietor in the Rhône-Alpes who developed a crush on an American sergeant.) But he developed an unusually high regard for Helpmann's work, both on the ballet and popular stage, and thought his "stunning version" of Milton's *Comus*, in which the choreographer both spoke lines and danced to music by Purcell arranged by Constant Lambert, "thrilling."[45]

As for his "social life," Blitzstein described that to Copland as "confined to a few cronies, journalists, photogs, painters and writers—and a few well-spaced excursions on the quest." These "cronies" included Corporal James (Jimmy) Dugan, former film critic for the *New Masses*, and William (Bill) White, the husband of agent William Morris's daughter Ruth. (Blitzstein described the Whites to his sister as "so much the outside-of-family people I think most of.") He also enjoyed hobnobbing with photographer Lee Miller ("a great and lovely gal"), actor Burgess Meredith, directors George Stevens and Humphrey Jennings, publisher Ralph Ingersoll, and playwrights William Saroyan ("decenter and sweeter than his stuff would lead one to believe," and a writer whose work occasionally "shoots out sparks of something deep, human, and true"), Irwin Shaw (whose new drama, *The Assassin*, he thought the author's best work to date, adding, "It isn't sound all the way, but it has enough truthfulness, and enough excitement to give it quite a punch"), and S. N. Behrman (with whom he "got on surprisingly well").[46]

Naturally mindful of the censors, Blitzstein alluded to his sexual life obliquely, as in his reference above to "excursions on the quest." In that same missive, he also wrote, "I won't describe [my post] in terms of beauty, comforts, attentions and diversions, since you wouldn't believe me anyway," while in another V-mail to Copland, he remarked, "I like these people, these English, I like the way they behave. I was put in charge of one sector during one of them [an air raid] and I got a little taste. I wouldn't be surprised if I got a whole mouthful." And with shades of his postcard to Bernstein of the Washington Monument, he mailed

David Diamond a postcard of a French bridge tower, and another of Sir Thomas Bodley, founder of the Bodleian Library, gripping the hilt of his sword as if it were his penis.[47]

Blitzstein apparently frequented some gay-friendly pubs and cruised such popular homosexual hunting grounds as Piccadilly and Hyde Park, which, he wrote to Diamond, "have to be experienced to be believed." The blackout facilitated sexual activity in general during the war, as Blitzstein hinted to his readers in the *New Masses*: "wartime nightlife in the blackout is like—and brother, it's like nothing that's printable." Explained the composer to his sister, "There is no time for indirection, fancy plays. You look at someone, and it's 'You for me? I'm for you.' Then you get drunk, or you don't; then you go to bed, or you don't. If you do, or if you don't, it's immensely unimportant."[48]

In the fall of 1944, shortly before leaving for France, Blitzstein befriended a twenty-four-year-old radio-gunner he had met in a pub, Technical Sergeant William (Bill) B. Hewitt (1920–1990). Blond, blue-eyed, and handsome, Hewitt, who had grown up in North Carolina and Virginia, was a great reader and music-lover with a keen interest in leftist politics, and "melted" Blitzstein "completely" by telling him that his baggage in France, where he was stationed, contained a recording of *The Cradle Will Rock*. "A good kid; I'm touched," he wrote to his father and stepmother. Hewitt had girlfriends in London, including Luellen (Lou) Bowles (1914–2002), an army corporal with the Red Cross whom he would later marry; but he apparently was bisexual or at least heteroflexible, and he and Blitzstein became involved romantically.[49]

On his return in December from France, where he had seen Hewitt in Paris, Blitzstein temporarily lost touch with his "close buddy," which made him apprehensive and depressed. But he learned with relief in early 1945 that Hewitt, having finished his tour, was to return home. On January 7, he wrote to his sister, "I want you to know him; in the first place, he is as close to me as anyone I've met here; also, his ideas are like ours, from a world point of view; although you may have to worm this out of him, if he goes shy on you. I'm hoping he'll open up, since on the surface he's just another guy. But full of charms and tricks, as you'll discover." And in late February, he further told Jo, "For some reason, which I haven't as yet doped out, he's the warmest personal contact I've made in years. I think it has something to do with the ways in which he's mixed up, plus the instincts he has for being a really fine human being."[50]

After spending some time in a regional army hospital for assorted problems, Hewitt received a medical discharge. "I've done my best for a long time in the army, had my share of combat, have hated all the obvious aspects of both, have begrudged the years I've wasted," he wrote to Blitzstein on April 20. "It logically follows that I should be happy now that these things are over. But I'm not!" He subsequently traveled to Philadelphia to meet Jo, who thought him a "darling guy," and found himself with Marc's family on the occasion of Sam's death.[51]

Upon arriving home, Blitzstein met with Hewitt in New York and then made his way to his sister's place in Philadelphia. With the war in Europe ending and the music for the invasion film—released in August as *The True Glory*—now in the hands of William Alwyn and Alan Rawsthorne, there seemed no need for him to return to Europe, and he proceeded to Fort Dix for his separation from the military on June 26, receiving an honorable discharge and a Good Conduct Medal.[52]

After Sam's death, the Philadelphia Council of American-Soviet Friendship set up a memorial fund in his name aimed at sponsoring a variety of events with the express intention of promoting "world peace and equitable cooperation" through friendship between the United States and the Soviet Union. His son offered this eulogy at the end of his chronicle about his war experiences for the *New Masses*: "Goodbye, Sam; you did a job for us all, you brought up a generation of youngsters to a sense of the future. I rebelled as your own son, until it suddenly occurred to me how right you were. I, who went to war, and about whom you spent sleepless nights wondering and worrying: I, it turns out, lost you."[53]

From *Freedom Morning* (1943) to the *Airborne Symphony* (1946)

Of Blitzstein's many projects undertaken during his years in service, his two major efforts, *Freedom Morning* and the *Airborne Symphony*, survive, but little else. One finds scant evidence, for instance, of his extensive work on *The True Glory* apart from a few transcriptions of Resistance songs, including a piano setting of *Le monde libre* ("The Free World," 1944), although some of his music possibly made its way into the documentary, including a sequence depicting workers in a factory that sounds more like Blitzstein than his successor on the film, William Alwyn. Nor does much apparently survive of Blitzstein's more workaday efforts during these years, aside from a few sketches for the scrapped documentary *Phyllis Was a Fortress* and some material for *Four Jills in a Jeep*, including a propaganda speech for Kay Francis and music for Mitzi Mayfair.

Blitzstein's papers also include fragments of two independent numbers composed during his time in the military: "Lovely to Get Back to Love" and "War Song"—the former to his own lyric, the latter, a setting of a Dorothy Parker poem published in the *New Yorker* in early 1944. According to Eric Gordon, Blitzstein wrote "Lovely to Get Back to Love" at the suggestion of Garson Kanin, who thought that a successful popular song might ease the composer's financial difficulties. (In his London notebooks, Blitzstein compiled a list of "things to sell, should the going go tough," including a wallet and a large briefcase.) But after auditioning the number before appreciative friends, Blitzstein chose not to pursue publication, saying, "I don't want my name on a song like that." His reason for undertaking the Parker poem remains more cryptic—it had been a long time since he had set anyone else's words—but like "Lovely to Get Back to Love," the text concerns a soldier's need for love; not the dream of a return to the beloved back home, "all the grief swept away," as in his own lyric, but the beloved's permission for the soldier to lie with another while away so long as "When in sleep you turn to her,/Call her by my name." That Blitzstein appears to have worked on both songs around late 1944 or early 1945, during his separation from Bill Hewitt, seems suggestive. In any case, basically only their melodies survive, and their completions by Leonard Lehrman can best be regarded as joint efforts.[1]

Some of Blitzstein's wartime music presumably got mislaid, as happened temporarily with the *Airborne Symphony*. However, after his return home, he at least reconstructed some pieces, including "I Love Lechery," originally composed around late 1943 for the Canadian-born comedian Beatrice Lillie, but which survives, likely revised, in a manuscript entitled "Modest Maid" and dated July 1945. (In late 1943, Lillie participated in a short with which Blitzstein also had some association, *Welcome to Britain*, a project that perhaps occasioned their meeting.) This comedy number follows along the lines of the composer's "Quiet Girl" in that the verse coyly introduces the female protagonist as "modest," only for an assertive chorus to reveal, not as in the earlier song that she hopes to "make the bullet that gets Hitler," but that she wants to run "stark naked" in a park "steaming and screaming for lechery," explaining, "You take archery—if you're arch./You take butchery—if you're butch./Temper witchery with wit, make with bitchery a bit./When it's leching, I'm bound to admit I've come round to/Just having the time of my life." And like "The Quiet Girl," the song has a slow coda in which the singer resumes her demure demeanor, here saying, "So behold me bonneted and cloaked./Never kissed, caressed, betrothed nor yoked./And all I ask is to be mauled and pumped and kicked and choked" (a mode of humor Blitzstein previously had sampled in "Fraught" with its line, "I plan to paw you and beat you, and taste you and eat you"). One of Blitzstein's campiest flings—in 1960, he wrote to Ned Rorem, with respect to Poulenc's opera *La voix humaine*, "A comic 'camp' is bearable; a serious 'camp' is utterly phony"—the song, which ranges from mock gentility to exuberant ribaldry, all in the British manner, plainly drew on the composer's own penchant for sexual adventure.[2]

Although nicely suited to Beatrice Lillie, especially in the context of her work as an entertainer for the troops, she reportedly never performed the song, possibly because, as singer Charlotte Rae seemed to intimate, it had been banned in London by the Lord Chamberlain (who in the event no doubt would have frowned at the line, "But don't call a constable/For this mad one has had one"). Broadway actress Paula Laurence signed a contract for rights to the song in September 1945, and possibly sang the number sometime around then, perhaps at the twelve-hour "Bizarre Bazaar" benefit for the Association of Theatrical Agents and Managers in which she participated in November of that year. However, the first known performances remain those of Charlotte Rae, who had originated the role of Mrs. Peachum in Blitzstein's adaptation of *The Threepenny Opera*, and who performed the song in the mid-1950s as part of a nightclub act at New York's popular Blue Angel (singing the number in a nun's habit) and on her debut recording, *Songs I Taught My Mother* (1955). Blitzstein slightly toned down the lyric for Rae, including rewriting the masochistic coda, although he retained its bawdy humor with a pun on the word "allayed," a revision that also sported some characteristically tricky internal rhyming: "And wondering how to get this agitated maid allayed!" Singled out for special commendation in a review of the Rae release by *Playboy*, this "Marc Blitzstein plum" enjoyed later airings by cabaret and opera singers alike, including Christine Ebersole, Lauren Flanigan, and Helene Williams.[3]

Another song set down in July 1945, "The New Suit" (better known as "Zipperfly"), in which the singer, accustomed to hand-me-downs—Leonard Bernstein typically described him as a fourteen-year-old African-American shoeshine boy—imagines owning a snazzy new suit, apparently dated further back to the abandoned *New York Opera*, a work that occupied Blitzstein in 1941 and early 1942, but whose sketches got lost in transit to London. The text supports the notion of an early forties provenance, as the outfit described in the song, with its "modified peg cuffs," "high waist effect," and "zipperfly," appears to be a zoot suit, a style popular especially with African Americans just prior to the war, but banned by the government's War Production Board in 1942 because of its extravagant use of material. At the same time, Blitzstein might well have revised the song by the time he actually notated the music and lyric in 1945.[4]

The song, which presumably reflected Blitzstein's own pleasure in wearing stylish clothes, has two verses and two choruses. With its modal harmonies and scat lyrics, the verse suggests a sort of incantation, setting the stage for the actual prayer detailed in the bluesy chorus, in which the singer's fervent wish for a new suit alternately assumes humorous, seductive, and poignant overtones.

On a visit to Tanglewood in the summer of 1946, Blitzstein sang "Zipperfly" and other numbers at a party attended by some students, including Ned Rorem, who years later recalled, "With his wheezy larynx he [Blitzstein] could put over his own songs because of a fearless, horny conviction that I've never heard elsewhere. . . . Harmony churned, counterpoint spoke, the rhythm was catchy and the color luminous, the tunes came across—all precisely because they spewed from Marc's own body." Leonard Bernstein occasionally sang "Zipperfly" himself, as preserved in a private recording dating from around 1965, a television rendering in 1976 (commenting afterwards, "Is that marvelous?"), and even a large public performance at Alice Tully Hall in 1985. "I call it a masterpiece," he stated on that last occasion, "because it's the very essence in its crazy, deeply quirky way of Marc's proletarian soul, of his commonality with the suffering of the human race."[5]

Baritone William Sharp, whose performance of "Zipperfly" helped win him the 1987 International American Music Competition for Vocalists, also championed the song, with the title of his acclaimed 1991 Blitzstein recording with soprano Karen Holvik and pianist Steven Blier, *Zipperfly and Other Songs*, according the song special prominence. Meanwhile, commentary about the number emphasized possible Jewish connections: Eric Gordon, for instance, thought that the music sounded "suspiciously Chasidic," while Jack Gottlieb, who noted parallels to Gershwin's "It Ain't Necessarily So," similarly noted, "The verse opens with a patois ['Racka moochy wicky wacky and a woo, haggedy goo'] that might pass to the uninitiated for ersatz Hebrew and continues in a monotone *davenen* [praying] style."[6]

Blitzstein wrote *Freedom Morning*, a ten-minute work for orchestra, in the early fall of 1943 while helping to prepare the Army Negro Chorus for their concerts at the Royal Albert Hall on September 28 and 29, at which time the piece received its first performances by the London Symphony Orchestra under Hugo Weisgall. Blitzstein composed the piece in a tin-roofed Nissen hut that also served the segregated black units as church and recreation hall, and although ordinarily "crotchety" about needing quiet working conditions, he found himself working "steadily" among dozens of African-American soldiers "crawling over me, relaxing, working, snoring (a foot from my ear), booming out their own tunes, peering over my shoulder as I wrote and played." Once, after auditioning some of the work at the piano for the soldiers, Blitzstein tore up a page of music after hearing a soldier remark, "That ain't me. That's Russian or Chinese." Another time, while Blitzstein was playing one of the score's jazzy passages, a soldier took out a pair of drumsticks and began tapping out his own rhythms, which the composer then incorporated into his score. More generally, the music, Blitzstein later wrote, "was influenced by the ease and flow of the men themselves, and the contagion of their spirit. This was their piece I was writing, and here they were." He dedicated the composition—publicized as "the first orchestral work by a GI written and performed in a theater of operations during the war"—to the United States Army Negro Troops.[7]

The work draws extensively on two Negro spirituals: "My Lord Says He's Gwineter Rain Down Fire" and "My Lord, What a Mornin'" ("When the Stars Begin to Fall"). Both songs, which share an opening motive of two repeated notes, concern retribution, suggesting some programmatic protest against slave masters and Nazi despots alike, with the image "rain down fire" no doubt striking Blitzstein as particularly appropriate in light of the air force's bombing campaign. Yet another melody, something like a bugle call announced by the trumpet early in the work, helps establish the wartime atmosphere. As has been suggested, Blitzstein possibly wrote this trumpet theme in response to *Rhapsodie nègre* (1918) by Virginian composer John Powell, whose set of dance arrangements, *Natchez-on-the-Hill* (1932), also appeared on the Royal Albert Hall program, as did *The Bamboula* (1911) by the mulatto British composer Samuel Coleridge-Taylor. As for the work's title, Blitzstein might have had in mind the communist Yiddish newspaper published in New York, *Morgen Frayhayt* ("Morning Freedom"), thereby underscoring Jewish and African-American connections suggested by the spirituals themselves.[8]

Scored for full orchestra, the piece opens with a hushed, somewhat melancholy section that introduces the trumpet melody, an idea likely suggested, Powell aside, by the line "You will hear the trumpet sound" from "My Lord, What a Mornin'." A setting of "My Lord Says" ensues, with an impassioned development that builds to a climactic restatement of the tune. The work's middle section, whose material derives from the trumpet theme, features jazzy music (referred to by Blitzstein as the work's "boogie section" and by early program notes as its "swing sequences") that frames a more blues-like interlude. The work eventually winds its way back to the opening preludial music, followed by a delicate arrangement of "My Lord, What a Mornin'" scored largely for winds and brass, and a brief coda that includes a reminiscence of the trumpet theme, now broadened in such a way as to suggest some kinship with "When the Saints Go Marching In," one of the numbers performed by the Army Negro Chorus at the Royal Albert Hall.[9]

In its unpretentious, somewhat pastoral profile, the work perhaps absorbed something from all the British music Blitzstein had been hearing, but the music surely gleaned more from Copland, including the Piano Concerto and *Quiet City*, two pieces selected by Blitzstein for the aborted 1945 American Music Festival. At the same time, the piece stakes its own ground, with the "boogie" music in particular foreshadowing the work of Leonard Bernstein. Moreover, the relation of the spiritual to jazz as explored here would resurface as a central dramatic idea in Blitzstein's opera *Regina*.

Freedom Morning opened the Royal Albert Hall program on September 28, whereas it appeared near the end of the concert the following night. The piece received "rousing applause," as the Negro Chorus recalled, but the British press, awed by the chorus and impressed with Earl Robinson's *Ballad for Americans*, also on the program, had virtually nothing to say about the work. However, a good review by the American composer Gail Kubik eventually appeared in the pages of *Modern Music*: "*Freedom Song* [sic] is an effective, vigorous piece. . . . It is remarkably successful in sounding just like the Blitzstein of the stage works, and yet, though immensely dramatic, it is convincing as a piece of absolute music." Weisgall subsequently performed the piece in various British locales, including Oxford, where, wrote Blitzstein to Copland, it "wowed 'em." The work even made its way to Stockholm, prompting Blitzstein to write to his sister, "I'm hoping some blasted Nazi gets to hear it, and hates it as much as a Nazi should; that would be a fine tribute."[10]

Back home, the Philadelphia Orchestra, under the baton of associate conductor Saul Caston, gave the work's American premiere at the Philadelphia Academy on April 14, 1944. The orchestra commemorated the occasion by commissioning an oil painting, also entitled *Freedom Morning*, from noted black artist Claude Clark; displayed in the lobby of the academy, the painting depicted African Americans from various walks of life, with a chained clenched fist in the background and a rising sun shattering the chains. An ailing Caston presided over an abbreviated version of the score, with about three minutes cut, nearly a third of the piece. Later that year, on August 4, Alexander Smallens gave the New York premiere with the Philharmonic at Lewisohn Stadium. Blitzstein, in London, heard both performances—the Philadelphia premiere over shortwave radio, the New York performance via a recording pressed from a broadcast.

Aside from a positive notice by Edwin Schloss, who liked the work's "crusading vitality," most of the Philadelphia and New York reviews proved tepid at best, including those by Vincent Persichetti and Paul Bowles, who after observing Copland's influence, commented, "But there is none of Copland's architectural sense present, nor does it evince stylistic integrity." None of the critics seemed cognizant of the work's racial intentions, a matter fairly obvious to the Royal Albert Hall audience. Receiving several reviews in the mail, Blitzstein remarked, "I am properly abashed at all the mean things the boys have to say. Curiously, I seem to be oblivious as well."[11]

Blitzstein himself criticized all these early performances, British and American alike. He wrote to his sister that the London Symphony Orchestra "messed . . . up" the jazzy sections. Finding Caston's cuts "frightful," he imagined that if he had been in Philadelphia, or Caston had been less ill, "I or he could have taken the boogie section in hand, and made it right with the men." And he complained that Smallens took the slower passages "too slow." At the same time, he thought that the "wonderful sound" of the Philadelphia and New York orchestras "partly" compensated for these shortcomings.[12]

In 1946, composer Henry Brant offered an upbeat assessment of the piece as "music of strong and direct American folk character, kept in a deliberately bold and simple harmonic context, with a hefty and spacious orchestration." And the following year, Weisgall recorded the work with the Prague Radio Symphony Orchestra on the Supraphon label, historically a valuable document, although he too took some cuts that compromised the music's form. More performances, in particular uncut ones, would help illuminate the success of the work's architecture and the depth of its vision.[13]

The *Airborne Symphony* for speaker, tenor, baritone, male chorus, and orchestra represents not only Blitzstein's principal undertaking during the war years but the most ambitious concert work of his entire career. His correspondence from London helps flesh out the work's genesis as outlined in the previous chapter. In December 1942, with his film unit otherwise occupied, Blitzstein suggested to his commanding officer, Beirne Lay, that he compose "a big concert work on the subject of the air-force," a proposal approved, after his promotion to corporal in late January, by the military, which temporarily relieved him of other duties. Within hours of hearing the news on February 16, he wrote to his family:

> I submitted a plan to do a big lyric and dramatic symphony, to be called "The Airborne"—for orchestra, chorus, speaker, singing and acting-solos. A concert-work, but one adaptable for radio—or even film production. Four movements and a prelude. To take about an hour in performance; to be exploited in a big way (translations in Russian for Moscow performance, Spanish for Mexico and S. America, French for the underground movt.), with initial London performance radiating repeats everywhere else. A big throw, and to be treated as such.

Blitzstein's old Curtis classmate, Samuel Barber, also in uniform, proposed some months later to write his own symphony about the air force, his Second Symphony (1943–44), a development possibly suggested by word of Blitzstein's activities overseas.[14]

Blitzstein aimed to complete the work in about six months and repaired to the home of his friend Peter Gorer in Highgate to fulfill his commission. But in August, he wrote to his sister that he still "had a lot to do on the work" and had received an extension. "It's been a tough job," he explained to Copland in July, "particularly the text part, which had to be a combination of down-to-earth with something really heroic, almost exalted. And the war is the war, so there can be no soft-soaping."[15]

After spending September composing *Freedom Morning* and coaching the Army Negro Chorus, Blitzstein moved into a London flat equipped with a small piano supplied by his publisher Louis Dreyfus and resumed work on the *Airborne*, now under the supervision of his new boss, John Hay Whitney. As discussed, he successfully auditioned the "virtually finished" piece for several officers on November 25 and subsequently devoted himself to completing the work's orchestration, writing Copland on April 17, 1944, that he had "finished" his "ballad-symphony." About the same time, an article quoted him as saying, "It's a terrific assignment, and I've poured my heart into it. . . . I wrote it for those kids you see walking along the streets here wearing their jaunty wings. And if they like it . . . why I'll consider it a job well done." Blitzstein further told Copland that his "ballad symphony" would "probably be done shortly," but with attention focused on the invasion, a wartime performance never materialized.[16]

When Blitzstein returned home in the spring of 1945, he thought he had packed up the symphony (or at least the three-quarters or seven-eighths of the work he alternately claimed to have had completed, his letter to Copland notwithstanding), but discovered that he had left the score behind and had brought with him rather a parcel of sketches. He subsequently asked Garson Kanin to forward him the manuscript along with other personal effects, but after months of waiting for the music to arrive, he presumed the score lost. However, between his sketches and his recollection of the work, he managed to audition the piece that fall for Bernstein, who encouraged him to reconstruct the work for performance with the New York Symphony later that season.[17]

After overcoming several attacks of "nausea" at the thought of rewriting this mammoth wartime commission, Blitzstein retreated with his friend Bill Hewitt to the guest cottage on the grounds of Motty and Bess Eitingon's estate, Hillcrest, in Greenwich, Connecticut, where in the summer of 1936 he had written *The Cradle Will Rock*, and where he would now spend the winter of 1945–46 recreating the *Airborne Symphony*. In February, while at Hillcrest, he also wrote the song "Chez Eitingon," which he dedicated to Bess and Motty "in the vain hope of telling them what I feel about their letting me finish the 'Airborne.'" In "rhumba tempo," the song depicts Blitzstein's life at Hillcrest ("Oh, my little moustache I've been biting on./While my symphony I've been writing"), with a whimsical ending that repeats the same phrase over and again to depict the hectic activities of his hosts, their staff, and their many houseguests, including Bess "getting tight," Motty "phoning long-distance," and Arthur "wondering how many the hell more for dinner." The song, as Eric Gordon notes, recalls Yasha and Dauber's rumba from *The Cradle* ("Ask Us Again"), but this parody assumes a far more indulgent tone toward both artist and patron.[18]

About a month before the symphony's scheduled April 1 premiere, a trunk filled with Blitzstein's possessions, including the missing *Airborne* music, finally arrived in Boston. Blitzstein found to his "amazement" that "the new score was precisely at the same point at which the original had been when I had left Europe!" He also discovered that he had remembered a good deal of it accurately but that the second version was about ten minutes shorter and "a heck of a lot better." Blitzstein dated his completed manuscript, "London, 1943–44/orchestration— Connecticut, 1945–46," and dedicated the score to the men of the Eighth United States Air Force.[19]

From the start, Blitzstein imagined a chorus drawn from American military personnel, although he originally intended a four-voice mixed chorus and only later decided on a two-voice chorus of tenors and basses, which he further thought might be composed equally of white and black singers, including members of the Army Negro Chorus with whom he had worked in September 1943. Similarly, he initially projected an unspecified number of actors and vocal soloists, but he later settled on two soloists (tenor and baritone), vocal quartet (two tenors and two basses), and two narrators, eventually reduced to one "monitor," so-called "because nearly all the lines are couched in the imperative mode." While entertaining the idea of two speakers, he proposed using Burgess Meredith and Jimmy Stewart, or in lieu of one of these, the British actor John Mills. For the baritone soloist, he mentioned such white singers as Kenneth Cantril, Bruce Boyce, and Frank Tavaglione; but he wanted a "negro voice" for the tenor solo "because of what it might lend," he explained, "to the quality of the 'Ballad of History and Mythology.'"[20]

Blitzstein scored the work for full orchestra, with the added novelty of a wind machine, used at the climax of the "Kitty Hawk" movement. Early on, he considered supplementing the winds with a quartet of saxophones, an idea he ultimately dropped. He also imagined at first some motion picture accompaniment to the work, and although he decided against this notion as well, he had film technique somewhat in mind while writing the piece, as evident from such spoken directives as "Iris in" (in "Ballad of Hurry-Up") and "Iris out" (in "Recitative"). Finally, he envisioned the services of one of Britain's professional orchestras under the direction of Adrian Boult, Constant Lambert, Malcolm Sargent, or Hugo Weisgall.

A work of striking originality, the *Airborne Symphony* defies categorization. As early as December 1943, the composer referred to the projected work, already entitled "The Airborne," as a "lyric symphony," a phrase that anticipated his frequent use of the term "ballad symphony," as in his correspondence to Copland; but he also considered calling the piece a "dramatic cantata," "oratorio," "dramatic suite," and "tone poem." In his program notes to the premiere, he likened his use of the term "symphony" to Liszt's *Faust Symphony* and Stravinsky's *Symphony of Psalms*, presumably thinking in part of their use of chorus. He might have cited, too, the precedent of Beethoven's Ninth Symphony; indeed, when Bernstein revived the piece in the fall of 1946, Blitzstein wrote to his sister, "the chorus sounds better than last year, and the orchestra plays the piece as though it were Beethoven."[21]

Blitzstein was also particularly mindful of Dmitri Shostakovich's *Leningrad Symphony* (1941), a large four-movement work that quickly established itself as a symbol of Russian resistance against Nazi aggression, in particular Germany's long and brutal but ultimately failed siege of Leningrad (1941–44). Tellingly, in late November 1942, about a week before Blitzstein conceived of writing "a great concert number" of his own, he attended a performance of the symphony's first movement at the Royal Albert Hall conducted by Henry Wood (who had presented the work's London premiere the previous June). Wrote Blitzstein to his family, "It sounded really wonderful, and convinced me more than ever that the piece is not meant for radio; you really have to watch that crescendo and climax to be sent. We all got sent, practically catapulted out of the hall." (By contrast, King Kastchei's music from Stravinsky's *Firebird* on the same program seemed, as he wrote in a published review, "the merest Halloweenery.") In making the case for his own symphony, Blitzstein even alluded to the *Leningrad*, saying, "Music was on the map as a positive weapon in winning the war," an argument that presumably helped secure him this commission.[22]

While at work on the *Airborne*, Blitzstein gave some thought to other pieces, including Honegger's *King David*, presumably on account of its choral writing, and Copland's *A Lincoln Portrait*, connections to which might have been more evident had Blitzstein used, as he considered doing, President Roosevelt's words. The example of *Das Lied von der Erde*, which he considered "by far the best Mahler—almost the only one I can take whole-heartedly," and which he heard "superbly" performed by Adrian Boult and the London Philharmonic in November 1942, also hovered in the background in terms not only of the *Airborne*'s hybrid symphonic structure but its pungent orchestration. Finally, he regarded the "scherzo" of Beethoven's String Quartet, op. 131 (presumably movements five and six), with its "long pattern that repeats towards the end, gaining excitement, before Grave," as a prototype for the form of the movement "Threat and Approach"—a connection that hints at Beethoven's larger influence on Blitzstein's novel formal procedures.[23]

Describing the *Airborne* as "a large symphonic work, dealing with the history of human flight," Blitzstein characteristically arrived at the precise ordering of the individual movements only after juggling numerous outlines; but he early settled on the work's basic trajectory from the history of aviation, to the threatening and destructive uses of air power, to the successful repulsion of such threats and the establishment of freedom. Eventually, this notion coalesced into a spacious three-part design containing twelve separate movements, with movements one through four exploring aviation history, movements five through eight, the threat, and movements nine through twelve, defense and victory. In his notes, Blitzstein encapsulated this structure—which bore resemblance to a traditional fast-slow-fast format—as "Air Age, Air Threat, Air Force."[24]

Part one begins with the movement "Theory of Flight" (monitor and chorus; Moderato), in which, according to his notes, Blitzstein hoped to capture "the mechanism of an ode, or poem, or invocation, or paean." As the monitor muses on the dream of flight, the chorus, softly at first, but growing stronger in the course of this short introductory movement, sings in the background "To be airborne," developing the work's principal musical motive, put forth by the horns at the very start of the piece. Through syncopation and other means, this prelude contains an almost picturesquely floating quality, although its contrapuntal elegance recalls Stravinsky, an important influence throughout the piece.

The second movement, "Ballad of History and Mythology" (solo tenor and chorus; Allegro giocoso [non troppo]), presents, in a jocular, folksy idiom, a recitation of various attempts at flight, including those by such legendary figures as Etana, Phaëton, and Icarus, and such historical figures as Archytas of Tarentum and Leonardo da Vinci. The chorus periodically comments, "Wings on the brain," a refrain, somewhat redolent of Renaissance music, purposefully skewered harmonically (and ironically marked "poco lamentoso") to give a sense of these visionary dreamers, eventually reaching the punch line, "They all went flat on their nose."

A reiteration of the phrase "To be airborne" serves as a transition to the poem, recited against tremolos in the strings, that initiates the third movement, "Kitty Hawk" (monitor; Molto Moderato [quasi recitativo]), a mostly instrumental reflection on Wilbur and Orville Wright's famous 1903 flight, which figures as the culmination of the preceding historical overview. Blitzstein, who based this section on themes from the opening movement, regarded this music as something of a "fanfare," though clearly a rather suspenseful one. A climactic celebration of "The Airborne" (chorus; Molto Allegro), including a jubilant reprise of the "Wings on the brain" refrain, brings the first part to an end.

The second part opens with "The Enemy" (monitor and chorus; Giusto [Pesante sempre]), a depiction of primarily the German but also the Italian and Japanese foe. Drawing largely on Robert Brady's *The Spirit and Structure of German Fascism*, this section quotes various statements by Nazis, recited by the chorus in a mechanical monotone and accompanied by a lumbering march in the orchestra. The movement probably owes something to Leni Riefenstahl's *Triumph of the Will*, which Blitzstein arranged to view while at work on the piece, while the music derives from his score to the Mercury Theatre's 1937 production of *Julius Caesar,* itself influenced by the Nuremberg rallies. "The music here," Blitzstein stated, "is what I call 'idiot music'—very martial, very bare, very Teutonic in orchestration, lots of brass." At times, the orchestra interrupts the chanting with strident, expressionless music suggestive of a demented and possessed mentality; while at one remarkable moment, the chanting gives way simply to an unaccompanied ratchet, which continues the monotonous rhythm on its own.[25]

The sixth movement, "Threat and Approach" (orchestra alone; Vivo [non troppo Allegro]), the section probably closest to Shostakovich, depicts the fear and mayhem associated with the war, with a concluding slow section that provides eloquent commentary. The "Ballad of the Cities" (monitor, solo tenor and baritone, chorus; Grave) urges several beleaguered cities—Guernica, Warsaw, Manila (originally Coventry), Rotterdam, London, Malta, Leningrad—to "hold out." A reworking of the "Ballad of Sevastopol" (1942), sung here by the tenor and baritone soloists, forms the centerpiece of this movement as well as its coda, with the fortissimo cry "hold out" sung by the chorus at the movement's climax, providing one of the most thrilling moments of the entire piece. The movement concludes with a recitation of the victimized cities in reversed order against the sung mandate in the chorus to "call the names."

Blitzstein early conceived the eighth movement, "Morning Poem" (monitor, without accompaniment), as an interlude that would depict "the sheer love of flying, the exuberance" by way of "a pilot, either bored or weary or impatient or unhappy" who "seeks relief by taking a plane in the air." However, after writing some underscoring, he decided to dispense with musical accompaniment and present the text as a spoken poem, one of the work's most unusual conceits. He also eventually identified the pilot as British, no doubt to acknowledge British participation in the war effort, as opposed to the subsequent movements, which focus on America's soldiery.

Part three opens with "Air Force. Ballad of Hurry-Up" (monitor, solo tenor, quartet, chorus; Allegro), an exuberant portrayal of the "brash young funny noble" Americans in the air force, including their need to stay prepared ("old Tannoy may be calling you next" sing the vocal quartet, an allusion to the British public-address system used on American bases); their need to don elaborate gear in action, including the "electrically heated bunny rabbit suit," "fleece-lined boots," and "O.D. gloves" that provided some warmth in their unheated planes; and their frustration at having missions called off (the recitation of the stripping down after a "scrubbed" mission—"Take off your thick electric gloves.... And last but not least your long-handled drawers"—registering some humorously erotic overtones). This movement features a particularly colloquial text, often with music to match, from the vocal quartet's "Hello, fellas, Hi-ya?" (its barbershop textures suggesting the men's camaraderie) to spoken interjections that include three acronyms popular with servicemen: "Snafu" ("situation normal: all fucked up"), "Tarfu" ("things are really fucked up"), and "Fubar" ("fucked up beyond all recognition").

The gentle and lightly scored tenth movement, "Night Music. Ballad of the Bombardier" (solo baritone; Andante), which bears intriguing resemblances to Copland's *Letter from Home* for radio (1944), originated as two separate pieces, with "Night Music" describing a nineteen-year-old bombardier writing a letter home at night and the "Ballad" depicting the boy's actual thoughts as he writes to his girlfriend Emily; but Blitzstein eventually combined them to form a single movement, with a brief reprise of "Night Music" at the end. Whereas "Night Music" recalls the slow ballads of the big-band era, "Ballad of the Bombardier" has a more folk-like quality, with its simple block chords played by the solo piano (later supplemented by a few other instruments). "Keep this [the 'Ballad'] from being mawkish by someone else doing the singing," wrote Blitzstein in his sketches, helping to explain his decision to have the same soloist render the movement's entire lyric.[26]

As with "Ballad of the Bombardier," Blitzstein thought the eleventh movement as consisting of two distinct parts, to the point of labeling them "11a" and "11b": "Recitative" (monitor, solo tenor and baritone; Comodo) and "Chorus of the Rendezvous" (monitor, solo tenor and baritone, chorus; Allegro con fuoco). He apparently added the brief "Recitative," which evokes the start of an air force mission, at a later stage in order to help prepare the "Chorus of the Rendezvous," a vigorous military chorus that calls for the nations of the world "to bomb a tyrant's smile, and from his throat his insane 'heil.'" The reiterated cry, "Open up that second front!" (in some drafts, "Liberation on the march"), much like the notion of a "rendezvous," referred to the desire of the Soviets and their friends for a ground force in the West that would help relieve the Red Army. The strictly unison writing for chorus and the straightforward rondo form help to reinforce the music's strong resolve.

The final apotheosis, "The Open Sky" (monitor, solo tenor and baritone, chorus; Maestoso), starts with sounds of victory, the *a cappella* chorus singing "Glory, glory!" Comments the monitor, "One threat is down. Thankfulness, not without grief." An instrumental section featuring a solo string quartet follows, expressing this notion of "thankfulness" and "grief," with the monitor eventually stating, "Watch this victory.... Not without warning—to the Airborne." Some music from the fourth movement ("The Airborne") leads to a solemn hymn, "Open Sky," celebrating freedom and progress. The movement then recapitulates more music from the fourth movement, including the "Wings on the brain" and "To the Airborne" motives, as well as the eleventh-movement "Recitative" ("The planes! The planes!"), before arriving at a climactic restatement of the "Open Sky" hymn. As the chorus joyously repeats the word "Sky!" (finally arriving at the work's principal tonal center, D, though on a stunning added-sixth chord without the root note, making the sonority seem that much more skyward), the monitor repeatedly cries, "Warning!"

"Most symphonies, you know, end on a single note, maybe triumph, maybe tragedy," commented Blitzstein about this remarkably evocative ending shortly before the work's premiere. "But a symphony about our times cannot have that luxury—you cannot do that and be honest with yourself. . . . So the *Airborne* ends in conflict. . . . In his warning he [the monitor] is asking how mature, how good we can be in handling the gifts of the human spirit." Since Blitzstein completed the work after his return home, he very well might have conceived this ending with, among other things, the atomic bombings of Hiroshima and Nagasaki in mind. The symphony in this sense can be considered, although primarily a wartime composition, a postwar work as well.[27]

Blitzstein drafted or contemplated additional movements, one of which, "Grease Monkey and Gunner," survives virtually in its entirely, and tells the story, in rather folkish music, of two Kentucky servicemen, Eddie, a grease monkey, and his buddy Jake (or Joe), a gunner, both killed in the war. Blitzstein planned on placing "Grease Monkey and Gunner" or some such movement aimed at expressing feelings of vengeance as a preparation for "Chorus of the Rendezvous," but ultimately decided against the idea.

With regard to the "style" of his libretto, Blitzstein determined that he would aim for "something between what I have already done and a Taggard-Auden attack," referring to poets Genevieve Taggard and W. H. Auden (about whom he reportedly once quipped, after hearing the British-American poet expound on his religious beliefs sometime in the 1950s, "Wystan [Auden] doesn't love God; he's attracted to him"). Blitzstein, who while in London copied out the final stanza of Stephen Spender's poem "I Think Continually of Those Who Were Truly Great," probably had that poet's work in mind as well. The composer apparently regarded Taggard, Auden, and Spender—all leftist poets working more or less in the tradition of Whitman (whose influence can be discerned on Blitzstein's text as well)—as models for the "heroic, almost exalted" style he hoped to achieve. However, early listeners noted connections sooner to the snappy oratory of the popular left-wing American radio writer Norman Corwin, as in his famous V-E Day broadcast (with music by Bernard Herrmann): "Listen. To win is great. To learn from winning greater. But to put the lessons learned from winning hard to work, that is the neatest trick of all." (In the fall of 1942, Blitzstein had cocktails with Corwin and told him that his time in the service "had given him the richest experience of his life.") In any case, the composer worked laboriously on the libretto, constantly rewriting the text.[28]

As for the music, he adapted a fair amount of earlier material. In addition to the march from *Julius Caesar* and the "Ballad of Sevastopol," he culled music from such early scores as *Parabola and Circula* (1929) as well as from more recent efforts, including a song from the abandoned *New York Opera* for "Ballad of the Bombardier" and a "second front number" for at least part of "Chorus of the Rendezvous." He might also have made use of some of the "air-force songs" that occupied him in the fall of 1942 for, say, "Ballad of Hurry-Up."[29]

The twenty-seven-year-old Leonard Bernstein led the first performances of "Symphony: 'The Airborne'" (as the work appeared on early programs) as the grand finale of his first season with the New York City Symphony on April 1 and 2, 1946, at City Center. These two performances featured Orson Welles, monitor; Charles Holland, tenor; Walter Scheff, baritone; and the male members of the Collegiate Chorale, Robert Shaw, director. (In 1949, Blitzstein described Holland, an African-American singer as specified by the score, to Koussevitzky as "one of the great promising lyric tenors of our day" who "because of his race ... has not yet met with the success he so richly deserves," and arranged for the young man to audition for the conductor.)[30]

The premiere of the *Airborne* proved one of the great popular successes of Blitzstein's career. "Rarely has the performance of a new composition been greeted with such enthusiasm in New York," observed *Musical America*, while *Newsweek* reported that the symphony "swept the audience along to a frenzied ovation." The critics by and large shared this exhilaration, referring to the work as "remarkable," "significant," "a wonderful exciting experience," "a monumental masterpiece," "terrific music-theater," in short, one of the most "rousing" and "exciting" musical events of the season. Accordingly, *Time* magazine's comment, "Consensus of the critics: as a symphony, *The Airborne* hardly got off the ground," seemed inaccurate, to say the least.[31]

At the same time, several critics strongly qualified their praise. Virgil Thomson, for example, deemed the work "masterful if not entirely satisfactory," writing, "Actually it says little that is not already a commonplace of the sentimental press, and its folksy language is both facile and affected. With such a text it was inevitable that any musical setting designed to throw the words into high relief should have difficulty rising above the banality of these." A small minority more caustically criticized the work as vulgar or dated, with Blitzstein regarding such negative responses virtually as a badge of honor, as indicated by the congratulatory note he wrote Orson Welles following these debut performances: "The wrong people, as before, hate us both, have already evidenced their hatred; and that makes us both happy. The voice would have been something by itself. But the spirit! Thanks, baby."[32]

Two of the most insightful reviews—by composer Wallingford Riegger and critic-director Harold Clurman—emphasized the work's potential as a prototype for some desired mediation between high and low art. "He has found a common denominator between the 'highbrow' and 'lowbrow' ... and with unerring good taste has avoided any impression of incongruity," wrote Riegger in something of a rave. "Should this piece prove ephemeral," stated Clurman more cautiously, "it is still important as a pioneer piece for those ultimate syntheses which will one day come, perhaps through another generation of artists. There is an aliveness here certainly which didn't obtain in the more 'dignified' academic American music of yesteryear." Clurman further regarded the piece as helpful in preparing audiences for works requiring more "effort and patience," such as those by Roger Sessions.[33]

Although these reviews tended to give short shrift to most of the performers—even, surprisingly, to so famous a star as Orson Welles—they widely acknowledged Bernstein's contribution to the work's success. "Rarely have we seen a man so completely immersed in another man's work," noted *Musical America*. "He knew every cue, every subtlety of phrase, every nuance of timing as though he had written the score himself." The piece ostensibly left a mark on Bernstein's own work, including his *Kaddish Symphony* (1963) and *Mass* (1971).[34]

Some early listeners seemed more responsive to the work's relevance than did the professional critics. After the premiere, for instance, May Schamberg (the mother-in-law of noted attorney Edwin Lukas) wrote to the composer, "May its warning reach the proper ears and save us from destruction," while composer-arranger Trude Rittman, with whom Blitzstein had worked on *No for an Answer*, told him, "The impact of your inspired, eloquent work in these times of horrible fears and unspeakable sadness is tremendous." And the ending's cry of "warning" inspired Lee Hays to write "The Hammer Song" ("If I Had a Hammer"), later set to music by Pete Seeger, a fellow member of the Weavers, and eventually made famous by another singing group, Peter, Paul and Mary. "Since no song is entirely original," explained Hays, "I borrowed his [Blitzstein's] one word 'warning' and expanded on it and came up with the idea of singing out danger, and warning, and love."[35]

On May 26, 1946, Bernstein performed the piece over the air with the NBC Symphony Orchestra, Blitzstein narrating, prompting another round of largely positive reviews and letters, including one from composer Bernard Rogers, who wrote Blitzstein, "It is a perfectly swell piece: powerful, moving, with a wallop." Bernstein gave two more performances of the work with the New York Symphony the following season on October 28 and 29, again with Holland, Scheff, and the Collegiate Chorale, but with Robert Shaw as the monitor. On October 30, these same artists recorded the symphony for RCA Victor, who released the work on its Recordrama label in the late spring of 1947 on seven twelve-inch 78 rpm discs, with some cuts authorized by the composer (and with the fourteenth side comprising "Dusty Sun"). On the occasion of this release, Blitzstein observed, "while the 'Airborne' has had success over the air, there has been nothing like the impact the work apparently has as done in a concert-hall. I believe this has something to do with the sight of singers, conductor, narrator and instrumentalists making their attacks and entrances, and contributing a kinesthetic value which has its distinct communicative elements."[36]

The symphony did not receive, as sometimes claimed, the New York Music Critics Circle Award for the 1945–46 season—that honor went to Samuel Barber's Violin Concerto. But in November, the Newspaper Guild of New York announced Blitzstein as the winner of its Page One Award in the "serious music" category apparently on the strength of the piece. Canvassing the guild's twenty-eight awards, including one to Henry Wallace in the public affairs category, a member of that organization publicly accused the awards committee of "communist bias," but John McManus, the guild's president, rejected that charge as "patently absurd."[37]

The following year, the work's libretto appeared, misleadingly enough, in an anthology of *Radio's Best Plays* (1947) that also featured works by Stephen Vincent Benét, Archibald MacLeish, and Arthur Miller as well as Joseph Liss, who edited the volume, and Norman Corwin, who penned a preface. But the music remained unpublished, aside from "Night Music. Ballad of the Bombardier" (which Chappell released as "Emily: Ballad of the Bombardier" for voice and piano) and "Ballad of Hurry-Up" (which Chappell published in an octavo edition for four-voice men's chorus and piano). The former achieved some popularity as an independent number, often as "Emily," as in the case of a performance by the chanteuse Hildegarde on a July 3, 1946, radio program that also featured some scripted conversation with the composer.[38]

For all its initial success, the work enjoyed relatively few performances following Bernstein's. On November 30, 1947, Jacques Singer and the Vancouver Symphony gave the work's Canadian premiere with actor Juan Root and the University of British Columbia Chorus. And on December 17 and 18, 1953, in honor of the fiftieth anniversary of powered flight, Victor Alessandro led performances of the piece in San Antonio with actor Zachary Scott and the Chorus of Lackland Air Cadets. Earlier that same year, on May 4, 1953, Skitch Henderson, himself an air force veteran, launched the New York Pops orchestra with a performance of the work at Carnegie Hall featuring actor Tyrone Power and the combined forces of the Lehigh University Glee Club and the U.S. Air Force Singing Sergeants. In later years, Henderson recalled with good humor the ordeal of that particular event—Blitzstein berating the performers in rehearsal, the American Legion picketing a work by a suspected communist whose call for "a second front" made it treasonous in their eyes, the disappointingly small audience—but he nonetheless remained devoted to the piece, programming "Emily" at a Carnegie Hall concert in honor of his eightieth birthday in 1998, and scheduling the entire work for a 2005 concert, also in Carnegie Hall (conducted by Rob Fisher, who stepped in for Henderson at the last minute after the latter's death on November 1).[39]

In October 1966, as part of a survey of twentieth-century symphonies, Leonard Bernstein gave four performances of the work on a New York Philharmonic subscription concert that also included, on the program's first half, Schoenberg's *Chamber Symphony No. 2* and *A Survivor from Warsaw*. Featuring Robert Hooks (monitor), Andrea Velis (tenor), David Watson (baritone), and the Choral Art Society, the performance won sympathetic reviews, including one by Irving Kolodin that suggested that the music might be profitably "woven" into a film or other medium that would "visually evoke the events it depicts." Bernstein soon after recorded the piece for Columbia Masterworks with the same artists, except that Orson Welles assumed the speaking role. Containing small cuts similar to those of his 1947 recording, this second Bernstein release—not issued until 1976—seemed less impassioned than the earlier one, but benefited from a superior orchestra, with Welles's participation naturally affording special interest.[40]

Still later performances of the piece included the May 4, 1986, European premiere, with John Mauceri leading the London Symphony Orchestra, actor Terence Stamp, and the Richard Hickox Singers; an Avery Fisher Hall airing on April 30, 1995, with Leon Botstein conducting the American Symphony Orchestra, actor James Earl Jones, and the New York City Gay Men's Chorus; and the aforementioned November 11, 2005, performance, with Rob Fisher presiding over the New York Pops orchestra, actor William Hurt, and the Purdue Varsity Glee Club.

Over time, critics tended more and more to disparage the work, although few so savagely as Donal Henahan in a *New York Times* article prompted by the release of Bernstein's second recording in 1976: "it drapes itself clumsily over some of the worst poesy ever committed to paper," wrote Henahan of the symphony, which he compared to such relics as "a can of Spam," and which he thought emblematic of an entire generation of "infected" composers, including Copland, Barber, and Schuman, who, whatever their differences, shared "a way of approaching music that may be called public" (this last intended as a reproach). In the 1990s, Ned Rorem similarly belittled the piece as "patriotic smarm ... a *Reader's Digest* tribute to our air force, preachy, collegiate, unbuttressed, as Copland's corny *Lincoln Portrait* is buttressed, by a less-than-trite musical background." Others seemed, in comparison, merely condescending, such as Bernard Holland, who in a review of the Botstein performance described the work as "closer to Norman Rockwell than to Beethoven's Ninth," and Robert Cushman, who in liner notes to a re-release of Bernstein's 1947 recording deemed the piece "picture-postcard art." In his 2009 survey of the American symphony, Nicholas Tawa more sympathetically found the music "amazingly affecting and potent," but the work ultimately "imprisoned by its text." Only occasionally did a wholehearted endorsement of the piece surface, as in a 2005 review of Bernstein's second recording (reissued on CD in 2000) by Steve Schwartz: "Blitzstein's cleaving passionately to the truth as he saw it and—let's face it—his artistry ultimately reduce the complaints to mere carping."[41]

These critiques often disclosed certain misconceptions about the work. For instance, Blitzstein did not write the piece so much in order to "rally the folks back home" as to be performed and heard by military personnel in the field of operations. And if he wanted to amuse the "kids" in the air force with "Ballad of History and Mythology" and "Ballad of Hurry-Up," or tug at their heartstrings with "Morning Poem" and "Ballad of the Bombardier," he also meant the *Airborne* as a sort of learning piece. Relatedly, criticism of the symphony as "jingoistic" hardly squared with a work that contained a song of mourning and hope for besieged cities around the world, a poem of comfort for a British pilot, and a call for international solidarity against fascism. Moreover, the allusions to *Reader's Digest* and Norman Rockwell underrated a work of considerable sophistication; Wallingford Riegger and Harold Clurman seemed more perspicacious when they spoke of the work as a synthesis of high and low.[42]

Finally, much journalistic commentary, whether or not it referenced "the boundless optimism of the postwar years," critically ignored the work's characteristic engagement with life's moral dilemmas. "You know what a man is:/He yearns, he destroys./He kills, he builds," states the monitor at the start of the symphony's second part, words that stand at the piece's core and a sentiment memorably embodied in the work's final moments, with its cries of "warning" against a triumphant "sky," reminding us of the need for vigilance even after the greatest victories.[43]

16

From *Goloopchik* (1945) to *The Guests* (1949)

After the war, Blitzstein lived with Bill Hewitt for about two years. They spent the summer of 1945 at the home Jo and Ed Davis had purchased the previous year in Pennsylvania's Brandywine Valley at Chadds Ford, residing below the main house in a stone spring cottage that they painted pink and black. In the fall of 1945, they took an apartment at 134 West 4th Street and spent part of that winter at the estate of Motty and Bess Eitingon in Greenwich, Connecticut, where Blitzstein completed the *Airborne Symphony*. In 1946, the two moved into a modest studio apartment at 4 East 12th Street that would serve Blitzstein as home for the rest of his life, and that was equipped with a galley kitchen, bath, terrace, and large multipurpose room where the composer kept his bed, piano, and work-table. He and Hewitt summered in 1946 at the guest cottage of Mina Curtiss in Ashfield, Massachusetts, and in 1947 at the country house of writer Donald Ogden Stewart and his wife Ella Winter Stewart in Upper Jay in New York's Adirondack Mountains, near the home of artist and writer Rockwell Kent—a social circle bound by communist sympathies.

Blitzstein and Hewitt presumably maintained some romantic involvement throughout this time, although they were never monogamous: Blitzstein continued to cruise trysting places, while Hewitt maintained his relationship with Luellen Bowles, whom he apparently impregnated, prompting a strongly worded letter to Blitzstein that read in part, "I must go to thrash it out with her under these circumstances. I shall take her to a doctor and get rid of her condition after I talk sense into her, then I'll be back pronto. . . . I'll do the right thing by myself, and certainly for her, too, in the long run, which AIN'T marriage."[1]

Whereas Hewitt's brother Edmund pursued an acting career—he would make his Broadway debut as Professor Mamie in the 1947 revival of *The Cradle Will Rock*—Bill's own ambitions involved writing novels and poems, but such aspirations came to naught. In the fall of 1946 he took a job as a cutter in Motty Eitingon's fur business, but that did not last long either. When Hewitt returned with Blitzstein to New York in the fall of 1947, he moved out on his own, presumably to give more privacy to the composer, who had periods of wanting "to be alone." For a short while, Hewitt roomed with Blitzstein's nephew Christopher Davis, who recalled, "He [Hewitt] had a tough-guy, sweet-guy manner, was solemn about fun, about drinking, and, like Marc, about 'honorable behavior'— fair play, decency, tolerance. On the other hand, he was a sexual opportunist and, in that sense, a user of people." David Diamond similarly observed Hewitt's flirtatiousness with Bernstein and himself with some dismay.[2]

Blitzstein and Hewitt remained friendly for a while, but then saw each other with increasing irregularity. After a rare visit from Hewitt in 1952, Blitzstein told Curtiss,

> I believe I did the right things; was casual, chattered away, listened with half an ear. He still has the capacity to get somewhat under my skin, with his outright plea for friendship, his "need" for me, the "confidence" I inspire in him, etc. It was more boring than usual. He is still a tormented soul, and somewhere valuable—but I can't bother anymore to locate the value. He seemed less sick than the day you were here, not sick at all, really. . . . But it is all finished; and we parted amicably, and lightly, with no plans for a re-meeting.

Hewitt seems to have largely disappeared after this encounter, and the Davis family, to their surprise, did not even hear from him after Blitzstein's death in 1964.[3]

Meanwhile, Hewitt followed Luellen Bowles, whom he married in 1949, to Harrisonburg, Virginia, where she taught physical education at Madison College from 1947 to 1957. The two eventually settled in Suffolk County, New York. When Eric Gordon interviewed them in the 1980s, Hewitt remembered Blitzstein as sexually reckless, whereas Luellen recalled a caring man who visited her when she fell ill. These recollections fitted Gordon's own impressions of Hewitt as "cantankerous" and "bitter," and Luellen as "humble, long-suffering, forgiving, gracious, understanding." Hewitt, who lived a reclusive life, regarded his wartime service as among the highlights of his life, and both he and Luellen were buried in Calverton National Cemetery, near their Long Island home.[4]

In July 1945, about a month after Blitzstein's release from the military, as a sign of things to come, the U.S. House's Military Affairs Committee publicized a list of sixteen veteran army officers with communist backgrounds, including the composer, described as "one of the foremost activists in communist ranks in the United States." The War Department promptly defended the named veterans, who also included writer Dashiell Hammett, as loyal, but some news reports sensationalized the item regardless.[5]

Undeterred, Blitzstein remained socially and politically engaged. He endorsed the reelection of Harlem's African-American Communist city councilmember Benjamin J. Davis in the fall of 1945; sponsored New York's May Day parade of 1946, the first since 1941 (and a tradition, increasingly dwarfed by competing

Loyalty Day parades, that continued until the city banned May Day parades in 1953); spoke at a rally against racial discrimination in the theater on June 4, 1946; performed at a banquet in Philadelphia honoring radical labor leader Ella Reeve "Mother" Bloor on June 22, 1947; and signed, in the fall of the same year, a petition denouncing the Hollywood blacklist.[6]

Above all, he promoted friendly relations with the Soviet Union, widely seen on the left not only as the prerequisite for maintaining world peace but as a safeguard against the spread of fascism at home. To this end, he became particularly involved with the National Council of American-Soviet Friendship, participating with Copland, Koussevitzky, Elie Siegmeister, and African-American conductor Dean Dixon (with remarks by Olin Downes read in absentia) on a panel discussion held by the group's music committee at the First Conference on American-Soviet Cooperation on November 18, 1945. The *Times* reported Siegmeister's claim that "Soviet composers are among the richest men in the Soviet Union," part of an idealized view of Russian musical life common enough among American communists and fellow travelers. Whereas most panelists spoke in terms of exchanging serious music between the two superpowers, Blitzstein proposed sharing more popular music, including translating popular songs into one another's language (specified as Russian and "American, not English").[7]

Blitzstein stayed an active member of this committee, which at Koussevitzky's behest reorganized in February 1946 as the American-Soviet Music Society. In the course of its approximately two-year existence, the society lobbied for a music copyright treaty between the two nations; held a benefit recital featuring pianist Alexander Brailowsky in May 1946; hosted a reception on June 6 for visiting Russians, including writer Ilya Ehrenburg, to whom Blitzstein presented a recording of Prokofiev's *Alexander Nevsky* conducted by Eugene Ormandy; sponsored an October 5 concert of two Ukrainian singers; published the one and only issue of the *American-Soviet Music Review* in the fall of 1946; commissioned in early 1947 two Americans (Burrill Phillips and Quincy Porter) and two Russians (Lev Knipper and Alexander Mosolov) to write chamber works based on folk tunes from each other's countries; and held another panel discussion, "Music and Musicians in the Soviet Union," featuring Norman Corwin, on January 24, 1947. In addition, the society mounted its own concerts, mostly in the first half of 1947, of contemporary Soviet and American music (nearly always including some Blitzstein) at such venues as Town Hall, Times Hall, and City Center. However, toward the end of the year, Koussevitzky, presumably in response to growing anti-Sovietism at home, resigned as chairman of the society, which reportedly gave its last concert on December 5, 1947.[8]

Blitzstein personally supervised one of the society's more elaborate concerts, "Theatre Music of Two Lands," a mélange of dance, theater, and film presented on May 12, 1947, that included most of the fourth tableau (scenes i–iii) from Prokofiev's recent opera, *Betrothal in a Monastery* (1946, libretto by Prokofiev's wife Mira

Mendelson, and on this occasion referred to by its alternate title, *The Duenna*), in an English version created by Blitzstein from a literal translation of the original text; the premiere of a Jerome Robbins ballet, *Summer Day*, featuring more Prokofiev; and the whole of Walt Disney's animated cartoon *Mickey's Grand Opera*, along with a smattering of other American and Soviet film excerpts. Alfred Drake narrated. The good reviews included praise for Blitzstein's translation of the Prokofiev opera, an achievement, described by Miles Kastendieck (*New York Journal-American*) as "a four-star advertisement for more opera in English when handled so expertly," that proved a further step toward the composer's adaptation of *The Threepenny Opera*.[9]

Blitzstein's admiration for Prokofiev, as intimated by this concert, took more explicit expression in a 1946 review for *Soviet Russia Today* of Israel Nestyev's biography of the Russian composer, in which Blitzstein found support for Nestyev's thesis that Prokofiev had blossomed since his return to the Soviet Union not only by a consideration of his more recent scores as opposed to his older ones, but by the "sorry sight of still-expatriated Russian composers" who continue to write "their piddling academic or destructive pieces." He only faulted Nestyev for not better appreciating those early-twentieth-century modernists who had liberated Western music from Wagner's "stranglehold." Blitzstein had been making such arguments for some time, but rarely accompanied by so exalted a picture of the Soviet Union, a nation that had provided Prokofiev, "a master at the height of his resources," with "the most forward-looking social basis of his day and age," as opposed to all other places, which permitted only conformity to "superstructures of a reactionary and decaying set of values," struggle and protest against such "values," or the "heralding" of "the possibilities of a new upsurge and a new society."[10]

Around this time, prompted by an October 10, 1948, article in the *Times* by William Saroyan, Blitzstein also penned a private note in which he stated,

> Let's try to lick this problem of "freedom"—as it applies, for example, to art. (Soviet Union, and its "lack"—our vaunted "liberty.") Saroyan . . . says the point of view doesn't matter—you can write a good play, that pleases, with the view that people are shits, that life is meaningless. But S forgets, or is ignorant, that only in a debilitated system, where values are missing or con-tradictory, could this happen; the public, hungry for some, *any*, standard, will accept what appears to be first-rate in style and presentation—and will take the content along with the form. This will never make for good art— the whole itinrary [sic] of an art on this basis is too hit-and-miss, there can be no digging for roots, no continuity. "Meaninglessness of life" is not the absence of a point of view—it is a very immoral actual point of view— immoral because it is dedicated to death, decadence, fruitlessness, and in the deepest sense, misery.[11]

By this time, Blitzstein had thrown his support behind the presidential nominee of the Progressive Party, Henry Wallace, who had been endorsed by the Communist Party as well. The composer joined the National Wallace for President Committee, attended fundraisers, and provided material for a revue, *Show-Time for Wallace*, that premiered on April 5, 1948. "If only, in this stinking moment of history," he wrote Mina Curtiss on April 17, "he [Wallace] can be surrounded by enough strength and wisdom, the world may yet not be lost— for a decade, we now say, asking little."[12]

Two weeks later, on May 2, news broke that Moscow's *Literaturnaya Gazeta* had published a letter from thirty-two American writers, painters, and musicians that allegedly placed them "squarely on the side of the Soviet Union in opposition to current United States leadership and policies," the signers including Blitzstein, novelists Nelson Algren and Howard Fast, screenwriter Alvah Bessie, artist Philip Evergood, and sociologist Max Weber. Although somewhat distorted by the press, this letter, which was published also in the May issue of *Masses & Mainstream*, and which had originated as a response to a plea from Soviet writers for America's "leaders of culture, to raise your voice against the new dangers of fascism, against the incendiaries of war" purportedly emanating from the Truman administration, indeed had expressed disapproval of many aspects of American life without any recognition of the harsh realities of Soviet life: "We know how differently artists are looked upon in your country, which surrounds them with the love of millions of people and provides them with the means to carry out their social responsibility." (This although the Soviet authorities had issued a decree the previous February castigating, among others, Prokofiev and Shostakovich, an action condoned by pianist-composer Norman Cazden in the April issue of *Masses & Mainstream*.) "I am waiting for repercussion; maybe yes, maybe no," wrote Blitzstein to Curtiss on May 5. "I feel personally secure inside, and never more the really patriotic American. And I have no taste for martyrdom."[13]

In yet another letter, this one published on May 24 in the *Times*, the same thirty-two signatories unapologetically reiterated some of their concerns, including American support of reactionary foreign regimes and capitalist pressure to censure certain types of art, now adding government suppression of free speech as represented by the Mundt-Nixon Bill, which, had it been ratified, would have restricted communists from working for the federal government, and which Blitzstein also protested in the form of a joint letter to Washington from the Civil Rights Congress, dated May 7, and signed by one hundred notables.[14]

In the aftermath of Wallace's crushing defeat in November 1948, Blitzstein further joined scores of eminent Americans in sponsoring the Cultural and Scientific Conference for World Peace held the weekend of March 25–27 at New York's Waldorf-Astoria. Presented under the auspices of the National Council of the Arts, Sciences, and Professions, the conference featured delegates from around the world, most noteworthy among them Dmitri Shostakovich, who not only spoke throughout the weekend but performed at the conference's concluding rally at Madison Square Garden on the evening of March 27. As was widely anticipated, many speakers denounced the Truman administration as the greatest obstacle to world peace, which prompted, in the course of a tumultuous weekend, dissension among the conferees, a rival meeting of anticommunist liberals, and staged protests on the streets of New York.[15]

Blitzstein apparently had the opportunity to socialize with Shostakovich over drinks and was slated to chair a reception for the Russian composer in Philadelphia, part of a planned tour of several American cities canceled at the last minute by the State Department. "I can't quite make out whether the govt is more afraid of Shostakovich and the others finding out about what the rest of America is like," wrote Blitzstein to Bill Hewitt, "or of us finding out what they are like—but fear certainly plays the biggest part."[16]

Blitzstein also probably attended the conference's Sunday morning arts panel, chaired by Arthur Miller, which featured presentations by Odets, Shostakovich, Copland, and Philip Evergood. In his prepared talk and perhaps even more so in his responses to questions from the audience, Shostakovich reportedly disconcerted the capacity crowd of about eight hundred by his criticism of the "formalism" and "cosmopolitanism" as found not only in Stravinsky and other Western composers, but in some of his own work and that of Prokofiev. Copland subsequently disassociated himself "from such an attitude absolutely," saying that it possibly made "some sense" as coming from a Soviet citizen, but made "no sense over here." In fact, Blitzstein's own statements during these years resembled to some extent those expressed by Shostakovich, although he maintained a high regard for the modernist masters and warned against throwing out the baby with the bath water.[17]

Partly because of its utter deference to Moscow and its escalating crusade against "cosmopolitanism," "white chauvinism," and other perceived heresies, Blitzstein quit the American Communist Party in 1949, but this signaled no anticommunist turn. On the contrary, having protested the imprisonment of three communists for contempt of court in June 1949, he signed an April 1950 petition to the Supreme Court to hear the appeals of members of the Hollywood Ten and a February 1951 petition to Attorney General J. Howard McGrath on behalf of dozens of individuals similarly indicted.[18]

True, after 1951, he avoided public stands concerning political matters, but this surely could be attributed largely to anticommunist harassment, as exemplified by the 1950 release of *Red Channels: The Report of Communist Influence in Radio and Television*. Published by American Business Consultants, *Red Channels* aimed to deter artists and others involved in the broadcasting industry "from naively lending their names to Communist organizations or causes in the future" by selectively (and not always accurately) listing 151 individuals along with their alleged connections to groups deemed fronts for the Communist Party.[19]

Deriving much of their information from government sources, some restricted, *Red Channels* targeted primarily actors and writers but implicated seven composers as well, namely, Blitzstein, Bernstein, Copland, Morton Gould, Lyn Murray, Earl Robinson, and Harold Rome. Why the editors chose the persons they did remains something of a mystery—in Blitzstein's case, he had had no real involvement with radio since the war—but this widely disseminated publication proved at any rate a public relations disaster for those cited, even if they merely had a single suspected affiliation (as opposed to Blitzstein, who had virtually as many entries as anyone). Fortunately, Blitzstein worked primarily in an arena, the New York theater, fairly immune to anticommunist blacklisting, thanks in good measure to the antiblacklist policies of Actors' Equity. Still, *Red Channels* and similar publications took something of a toll on Blitzstein's career, as evidenced by the American Legion's picketing of his *Airborne Symphony* in 1953, not to mention the chilling effect such publications had on open artistic expression. "There is no blacklisting on Broadway," asserted E. Y. Harburg in the 1950s. "Still, I couldn't do 'Finian's Rainbow' again, because of its content."[20]

Meanwhile, the FBI reopened its file on Blitzstein after his honorable discharge in the fall of 1946 and, compiling its own list of the composer's known leftist ties, devised in 1949 a security index card for him, meaning, at least from the bureau's perspective, arrest and detention in case of a national security emergency. The FBI further labeled him a "concealed Communist," defined as a person "who does not hold himself out as a Communist and who would deny membership in the Party." But unable to unearth any evidence of support for the Communist Party or its front organizations after 1950, the bureau in 1955 canceled his index card—for the time being.[21]

In his few lectures and writings from the late 1940s, Blitzstein often approvingly commented on the "amalgam" of the "serious" and the "popular" in American music that had developed since he had left for overseas, leaving him feeling "a little like Rip Van Winkle," although he acknowledged that Kern, Gershwin, Copland, Weill, Eisler, and his own *Cradle Will Rock* had helped to lay the groundwork for this phenomenon. Regarding this trend as "a really integral, basic thing, coming from both the top and the bottom," as opposed to, say, Dvořák's *New World Symphony*, which employed popular music "as an exotic touch," or conversely, the work of Paul Whiteman, which added "a Ravel orchestration to an originally shoddy tune," he cited as examples concert pieces by Jerome Moross, Morton Gould, and Leonard Bernstein, but mostly such Broadway shows as *Oklahoma!*, *Song of Norway*, *On the Town*, *Carousel*, *Carmen Jones*, *Bloomer Girl*, *Street Scene*, *Finian's Rainbow*, and *Brigadoon*. He considered this latter body of work as pointing the way "toward a lyric theatre" on the model of the *opéra comique* in France, although still limited both in its general avoidance of serious themes and its restricted musical forms. In this respect, he found *Carmen Jones*, Oscar Hammerstein's adaptation of Bizet's *Carmen* for the Broadway stage, particularly heartening, even performing "Stan' Up and Fight" (the "Toreador Song" as reconceived for an African-American boxer) at a lecture-recital at Philadelphia's Ethical Culture Auditorium on October 22, 1946. (This lecture-recital, incidentally, provoked divergent responses: the

Philadelphia Record thought it "necessary to point out that a tendency to pontificate was in evidence, and that the listener felt that any disagreement on his part with Blitzstein's statements would be regarded by the speaker as a violation of fact and of the laws of reason," whereas the *Philadelphia Evening Bulletin* stated more sympathetically, "His opinions were offered with charm, sincerity and an unassailable assurance.")[22]

Such advocacy for work that combined serious and popular elements recalled contemporary statements by Prokofiev, underlining the connection during these years between Blitzstein's critical writings and not only his high regard for that Russian composer, but his pro-Soviet worldview in general. He even stated in one talk, citing Khachaturian, Prokofiev, Shostakovich, and Ivan Dzerzhinsky, "I think the same kind of amalgam, with the scales tipped in favor of the serious composer, has been going on in the Soviet Union."[23]

Staying at his sister's country home in the Brandywine Valley in the summer of 1945, Blitzstein worked on a Broadway musical of his own, *Goloopchik*, composing much of the score in July and August. The *Times* reported in late August that William Friedberg and Marian Ainslee were to write the book, that Jerome Robbins had expressed interest in doing the choreography, and that press representative James Proctor, who had chaired the production committee for *No for an Answer*, was coordinating the effort. The composer eventually prepared a rather full two-act piano-vocal score, but the show (its title the Russian diminutive for dove used as a term of endearment) never got off the ground.[24]

Blitzstein derived the idea for this romantic comedy from a James Aldridge article he had read in late 1942 in the military's newspaper, *Stars and Stripes*, "about four American sergeants, inspecting American-made trucks for the Russians in the eastern wilds: how they got along, how they learn Russian, admire our Allies, who apparently adore them, and are ready to stake them against all comers. A humdinger." However, no scenario for the musical survives and knowledge of its story depends on whatever can be parsed from the vocal score and a few additional lyrics. The plot would seem to involve two American soldiers, Bud and Chester, and three Russian sisters: Tanya, Nina, and Ludmila. Chester ("Chick") and Tanya fall in love. Nina has a Russian boyfriend, Marko, also a soldier. Another character, Sasha, triggers the first-act climax, and a dramatic reenactment of the historic April 1945 meeting at the Elbe River between American and Soviet troops caps the second act.

For the show, Blitzstein not only composed at least eight original numbers ("Home for a Hero," "Conversation Piece," "Chick Song," "Tree Back Home in Kansas," "So-o-o-o Beautiful," "Three Sisters Who Did," "Tanya," "And With That Clasp of Hands"), but, presumably inspired by the adaptations of Bizet and Grieg in *Carmen Jones* and *Song of Norway*, respectively, decided to arrange and lyricize some existing Russian popular and concert music as well. He listed all this material, much of which survives (including the eight original songs), in a table of contents as follows:

Overture ("Meeting on the Elbe," "Chick Song," "So-o-o-o Beautiful"). Act I, scene one: "(Making a) Home for a Hero," marked "Quasi Marcia" and "Bubbling, with Warmth," in which the Russian villagers anticipate returning soldiers; "Conversation Piece," a waltz-like number in which Tanya, Nina, and Ludmila voice their individual desires; "Chick Song," in which the villagers explain the Russian diminutive, "chick," to Bud and Chester; "(There's a) Tree Back Home in Kansas," which alternately reflects on the American and Russian landscape; "Red Army Songs" (lyricized by Blitzstein); "Drinking Scene" (lyricized versions of Musorgsky's "Hopak" and various traditional songs).

Scene two: "Quintet: Road Song" (a lyricized version of Vladimir Zakharov's popular song hit "Strolling Home"), part of a "Meadow Scene" that also includes a pas de deux for Nina and Marko. Scene three: "So-o-o-o Beautiful," which depicts its singer—perhaps Bud—as free-spirited; "Little Meal on a Tray," a romantic duet for Chester and Tanya (a lyricized version of Tchaikovsky's "Amid the Din of the Ball," op. 38, no. 3); "Three Sisters Who Did," a comedy song in which presumably one or more of the three sisters contrast Chekhov's world (in a "gypsy-sentimental slow verse," to quote Blitzstein's sketches) with the new Russia (in a "hot" chorus); "Home for a Hero" (reprise); "Sasha!" (a lyricized chorus from Musorgsky's *Khovanshchina*).

Entr'acte ("Tanya"). Act II: "Road Song" (reprise); "Mamasha Goose," described as "the song of a child in Russia attempting to entertain two American soldiers," presumably Bud and Chester (lyricized folk tunes, including one popularized by Maximilian Steinberg); "Tanya," a love song for Chester; "Sasha's Journey" (lyricized versions of music from Khachaturian's *Gayane* and Borodin's *Prince Igor*, as well as Valery Zhelobinsky's Study, op. 19, no. 2, and various popular melodies); "Meeting on the Elbe," a depiction of the American-Soviet military linkup (Varenka Tsereteli's "Suliko," a Georgian number reputed to be a favorite of Stalin's, in Russian translation; Alonzo Elliott's "There's a Long, Long Trail" or Irving Berlin's "White Christmas"; and an anthem of the composer's own devising, "And With That Clasp of Hands").[25]

Blitzstein composed another number for *Goloopchik* not listed in this table of contents, namely, "Song of the D.P." (also called "Displaced"/"D.P."), the title of which refers to the common shorthand for a "displaced person." According to liner notes to Blitzstein's recording with Muriel Smith, the number, which was "inspired by some of the composer's experiences in the Army," represents "the song of a displaced woman, seized by the Nazis, who has been repatriated to Russia." Cast in two brief choruses, the singer recalls the destruction of her home and then her experience in a labor camp, concluding with the plea, "Make me find the joy of work again," a seeming allusion to the cynical Nazi slogan, "Arbeit Macht Frei" ("Work Makes You Free").[26]

Several of the show's original songs, like "Mamasha Goose" ("Mary had a little *ovyetchka./*Its fleece was white *kak snyegg*") and the "Chick Song," evoke Russian folk idioms, whereas others are more urbane, including "Three Sisters Who Did," which recalls the likes of the Andrews Sisters. In still further contrast, "Meeting on the Elbe" conveys some of the solemn grandeur of *Freedom Morning*, and the "Song of the D.P." imparts a pathos strongly reminiscent of Musorgsky, while the pas de deux has a nervous, peculiar quality characteristic of the much younger Blitzstein—indeed, he derived the music from his "Macabre Dance," a number prepared over twenty years earlier for a production of Andreyev's *King Hunger* (whose Russian setting might have drawn him back to this score). All these varied numbers contain striking harmonic turns, but the score as a whole represents the composer at his most ingratiating.

Blitzstein sang and played excerpts from this "musical in progress" at the Philadelphia Council of American-Soviet Friendship's inauguration of the Samuel Blitzstein Memorial Fund on December 7, 1945, and then at a concert of modern American music sponsored by the American Society for Russian Relief on May 2, 1946, a performance that apparently included "Mamasha Goose" and that elicited positive remarks in both the *New Yorker*, which thought that the music promised "an entertaining work," and the *Times*, which wrote, "judging from the cleverness of the composer's own text for the songs presented and the snappy character of their music, the work should prove a big success when it reaches the stage." For the Russian Relief concert, Blitzstein collaborated with Muriel Smith, who further performed "Song of the D.P." and "Mamasha Goose" with pianist Leon Pommers on a May 27, 1946, concert of the American-Soviet Music Society and "Orpheus" (from *Julius Caesar*) and "Mamasha Goose" with pianist Stuart Ross at a Town Hall concert on December 12, 1947. The composer himself accompanied Smith on "Song of the D.P." and "Mamasha Goose" at a January 18, 1948, all-Blitzstein concert at Severance Hall sponsored by the Cleveland chapter of Progressive Citizens of America and organized by Mordecai Bauman, with Smith and Blitzstein recording these same two numbers shortly thereafter as well.[27]

As for the show itself, the prospects of launching a Broadway charmer about American-Soviet friendship no doubt became increasingly quixotic given the political climate, and Blitzstein simply put the score in his trunk, as he had so many others. In 1949, the year he cast Jane Pickens for the title role in *Regina*, he retooled the main theme of "Tanya" as signature music, "Lovely Song," for her radio show. In addition, he adapted "Home for a Hero" as "Miracle Song" for *Reuben Reuben* (1955) and "Song of the D.P." as "Who Will Close the Door?" for *Idiots First* (unfinished).

Four songs from *Goloopchik* also appeared in the *Blitzstein Songbook*, with editor Leonard Lehrman using a portion of the "Chick Song" (retitled "The Russian Language") as an introduction to "Mamasha Goose," the latter based largely on Blitzstein's recorded version with Muriel Smith. Lehrman also fused "Tanya" and "Lovely Song" into one number, "Lovely Song," arranged for duet, with additional lyrics of his own. The published version of "Song of the D.P." remained more faithful to its fair copy source, including the use of the title found on the manuscript, "Displaced," as opposed to that appearing on programs.[28]

Blitzstein's interest in folk music took other manifestations during these years. He devised, for instance, a simple but piquant setting of the American folk song "On Top of Old Smoky" for *The People's Songbook* (1948), edited by Waldemar Hille; and he performed something entitled "Dublin Street Song" (arranged by the composer, 1941) with Muriel Smith at the all-Blitzstein concert in early 1948—a number hard to identify as the music does not seem to have survived but that nonetheless presaged Blitzstein's arrangements of Irish folk music in *Juno* (1959).[29]

In October 1946, Blitzstein accepted a fee of $750 to provide original music and "classical compositions" for use in his friend Lillian Hellman's new play, *Another Part of the Forest*. A prequel to Hellman's *The Little Foxes* (1939), this family drama also takes place in a small Alabama town and concerns the Hubbard family, but it is set twenty years earlier, in 1880.[30]

Blitzstein's primary job apparently involved preparing two compositions for the second-act musicale, in which Marcus Hubbard, a well-to-do entrepreneur and amateur violinist, plays chamber music with two hired professionals, violinist Gilbert Jugger and cellist Harold Penniman. For the piece purportedly written by Marcus and described by the fawning Penniman as "close to Buxtehude—or, the Netherland contrapuntalists," Blitzstein arranged and expanded the hymn "Urbs Beata Jerusalem," which had "haunted" him, as he wrote in his notes, since age twelve when he discovered the melody in a textbook. For the second piece, about which Hellman had told him that its length would "have to coincide with the action on stage" and that it probably would be "a trio of Bach's or Mozart's," Blitzstein ultimately selected an unidentified divertimento by Mozart's father Leopold, as referenced by Hellman in the published version of the play. In addition, Blitzstein apparently wrote a cue for the "few notes on the piano" played by Marcus's wife Lavinia in the second act, but nothing else seems known about the score.[31]

Starring Patricia Neal in her first Broadway role (Regina), Percy Waram (Marcus), and Mildred Dunnock (Lavinia), the play opened at the Fulton Theatre on November 20, 1946, with Hellman making her directorial debut. The mixed reviews generally regarded the well-crafted play as a "lurid" melodrama, although a later commentator, Katherine Lederer, thought it more "an ironic, detached comedy." None of the notices reported on the music.[32]

In September 1946, Blitzstein also signed a contract with Cheryl Crawford, co-founder and managing director of the American Repertory Theatre, to write incidental music for a production of G. B. Shaw's *Androcles and the Lion*, the terms specifying $500 with an additional $12.50 for every performance after the twentieth. Blitzstein quickly drafted a list of thirteen cues, and, a bit behind schedule, completed the short score on November 30 and the full score for oboe/English horn, clarinet, trumpet, trombone, percussion, and piano/ Hammond organ on December 8.[33]

Loosely based on an ancient Roman fable about the slave Androcles and his domesticated lion, Shaw's 1912 play, although set in ancient Rome, essentially satirizes contemporary British society. In the prologue, the gentle Androcles, a persecuted Christian, removes a thorn from the paw of a lion encountered in the wild, and the two dance a waltz. In the two acts that follow, Androcles and several other Christians face death in the coliseum, but impressed with the strength of one of these Christians, the Roman Emperor frees them all except at first for Androcles, who tames the lion as before, thereby winning his liberty as well. Shaw more than implies an analogy between, on the one hand, pagan Rome and perse- cuted Christians, and on the other, imperial Britain and radical freethinkers. Crawford and Blitzstein no doubt recognized the play's relevance in light of America's increasing vilification of the political left.[34]

Blitzstein's score opens with a short Vivo overture, with the bright and perky soprano melody articulated by declamatory chords below, much like a comic ver- sion of the title music to *Valley Town*. As with that earlier work, Blitzstein innova- tively has Androcles sing some of his lines during his initial confrontation with the lion, part of an extended cue that includes their waltz, music reprised for their sec- ond dance as well. The score features two principal unifying themes: a slinky, mys- terious motive for the lion; and "Onward, Christian Soldiers" for the Christians, as specified by the play, in which the Captain forbids his captors to sing any hymn but this one providing they change the lyric to "Throw Them To The Lions," an idea adopted by Blitzstein, who ends the first act with the chorus singing just these words to Arthur Sullivan's tune. The second act features some martial strains rem- iniscent of the composer's score to *Julius Caesar*, while the slapstick finale occa- sions a number of tiny cues of only a few measures each for various business between lines of dialogue. The work ends with a return to the Vivo opening.

Premiering on December 19 with Sean O'Casey's *A Pound on Demand* as a curtain raiser, the production, which starred Ernest Truex as Androcles, received excellent reviews, including the music, which was deemed "evocative and appro- priate" and "admirably economical, properly highlighting the proceedings with- out undue background distraction." At year's end, Robert Garland of the *Journal-American* even singled out the play's "satiric music" for a New Year's toast. On the other hand, Brooks Atkinson in the *Times* criticized Blitzstein for "musical flourishes" that "blast the dialogue off the stage," a puzzling response given not only the other critiques but the score's careful separation of music and speech, unless perhaps the tricky timing faltered on opening night.[35]

After his return home in 1945, Blitzstein enjoyed a performance of *On the Town*, the Broadway musical by his friend Leonard Bernstein freely derived from the latter's ballet for choreographer Jerome Robbins, *Fancy Free* (both 1944).

Robbins (1918–1998) originally had hoped to collaborate with Blitzstein on that particular ballet; but with the composer stationed abroad, he needed to consider other options, and eventually choose, with historic results, the relatively untried Bernstein.[36]

Both registered communists at the time, Robbins and Blitzstein now resolved to work together. As mentioned, Robbins considered staging *Goloopchik* but quit that show, according to Blitzstein, because of his dissatisfaction with its pas de deux. However, by the fall of 1946, Robbins and Blitzstein had begun work on a dance variously called *Show Window, Saturday Show, June Bride*, and so forth, but eventually just *Show*. They perhaps hoped to have the work produced by the Original Ballet Russe, to judge from references to the company's impresario Sol Hurok.[37]

Given the heightened interest in civil rights during this period, Robbins proposed the timely premise of having, as Blitzstein noted among his papers, an assembly of black and white dancers "don masks, so we don't know which is which; and then a *passionate pas de deux*—and we don't know who is who—the point being it doesn't matter." Blitzstein liked the idea, which might have been suggested in part by the masked ball in Prokofiev's ballet *Romeo and Juliet*, and he went to work on the ballet during the fall and winter of 1946–47.[38]

Although he and Robbins eventually abandoned the work in this particular guise, before doing so, Blitzstein completed a good deal of the short score to more or less the following scenario. Set in the show window of a large New York department store, the ballet takes place on a summer Saturday afternoon. Following the prelude, the general manager explains that men and women selected from the store's various departments will mask themselves and model the latest fashions before the public, with the winning pair, chosen by a panel of three judges, to receive assorted prizes. The contestants enter and register, and the judges select three masked girls and boys to dance with each other ("Grand March"). The first couple do a "frisky" and "gay" jitterbug ("Variation I"); the second, a "sensual" and "sleazy" parody of Hollywood schmaltz ("Variation II"); and the third, a "beautiful" and "wistful" dance ("Variation III"/"Pas de deux"). The judges select the Hollywoodish second couple ("The Award"). A reception follows and the contestants remove their masks ("Three-Four Dance"). When the third couple— he, black; she, white—discover each other through their stylized gestures and reunite, the assembly scorns them, and, at least in one version, she bursts into tears, and he angrily throws a punch cup into the audience ("Finale").

The ballet's prevailing tone veers toward the elegiac, framed by satire and burlesque, all characteristic of Blitzstein, although marked here by a charm and grace particularly reminiscent of his work circa 1930, with "Variation III" actually adapted from the pas de deux from *Parabola and Circula* (1929). The preludial music, which reappears in the pas de deux and the finale, seems to embody the drama by way of counterpoint that moves symbolically in contrary motion and that occasionally converges on a sort of signature harmony, a sour major-minor sonority that would seem to reflect not only the story's tensions, but even more specifically, given the chord's relation to the blues scale, its particular racial concerns. Stylistically, much of the score, including the "Three-Four Dance," a tour de force of syncopation, intimate Blitzstein's enduring admiration for Copland and newer appreciation for Bernstein, with some of the more lyrical passages more closely resembling Prokofiev.

Blitzstein characteristically experimented with the ballet genre, incorporating both the spoken and sung word, including the general manager's speech and a song that accompanies "Variation II," the latter a campy spoof of Hollywood romanticism—Blitzstein specifically had in mind the likes of *Laura* (1944, music by David Raksin)—meant to contrast with the interracial couple's genuine affection.

In early 1947, after Blitzstein had completed about forty pages of the piano score, Robbins proposed a more abstract approach, prompting the composer to write an aggrieved note on January 31 that seems like a draft for some confrontational letter or meeting. "Suppose you had choreographed one-half, and I took the score from under you?" he asked, adding, "really it seems you want this to be 'balletic' because you've done '*enough* jazz' pieces and want to move on to 'art.'" After citing other instances of Robbins's capriciousness, including his walking out of *Goloopchik* and changing composers (from Bowles to Bernstein) for *Facsimile*, Blitzstein concluded, "I want to do this—with you or without you. I *don't* want to do an abstraction of it—considering the amount I already have worked out."[39]

How they proceeded at this juncture remains unclear, although Blitzstein worked on the scenario as late as February 1947 and described the work to Mordecai Bauman that May as a "new ballet" that he had "just completed with Jerry Robbins." He also recorded three of the movements—"Variation III," "Three-Four Dance," and "Finale"—on the limited-edition anthology *American Composers at the Piano* (1947) recorded by the Concert Hall Society. In late 1947, Ray Lev, the outstanding female pianist soon to be targeted as a communist sympathizer, similarly performed two movements from the ballet—"Prelude and Three-Four Dance"—on recitals at Carnegie Hall and Washington Irving High School. And at the 1948 all-Blitzstein recital in Cleveland, the composer performed a slightly modified four-movement Piano Suite from *Show* consisting of "Prelude," "Nocturne," "Three-Four Dance," and "Finale," the "Nocturne" apparently of more recent vintage.

According to a promotional article for this latter concert, Blitzstein, who spoke of Robbins, Bernstein, and himself as a "tight little triumvirate," had interrupted work on the ballet in order to come to Cleveland, suggesting that he and Robbins had never dropped the project, or not for long, a notion that finds further support by the inclusion of "Nocturne," whose Chopinesque elegance might have been intended to satisfy Robbins's desire for greater abstraction, although this particular movement never made its way into the ballet's final incarnation as *The Guests*.[40]

In 1948, Robbins approached Lincoln Kirstein, general director of the newly named New York City Ballet, about creating a dance for the company, and the two agreed to mount some version of the Blitzstein work in progress. This would be Robbins's first piece for the New York City Ballet, and the commission came as a surprise to the dancers, conditioned as they were by the classicism of the company's artistic director George Balanchine. But Kirstein recognized that Robbins's work would neatly complement Balanchine's own. Moreover, he and especially his sister Mina had been admiring friends of Blitzstein's for some time. In any event, Kirstein, who offered Blitzstein $500 plus $25 for each performance, scheduled the ballet for the 1949 winter season (the company having separate fall and winter seasons).[41]

A few days before the premiere, Blitzstein described the collaborative process with Robbins as moving from theme to storyline to musical sketch ("which both of us considered, kicked around, flayed alive until it was right") to finished score to dance rehearsal, which sometimes led to additional steps and more music. "It is a wonderful and rather perilous experience working with someone with the drive, imagination and genius of young Robbins," added Blitzstein. "Everything, every aspect of one's craft, is constantly on trial; the composer too has to be on his toes."[42]

The completed ballet derived from the earlier *Show* in many respects, not least its theme of social discrimination, but in the end, Blitzstein capitulated to Robbins's request—all the more encouraged by the aesthetics of the City Ballet— that they "do an abstraction of it." Although the choreography does not survive, the action once again can be deduced from surviving materials, including a published scenario by Balanchine. In an abstract setting suggestive of a formal ball, the Host (also called the Discriminator in earlier versions) herds ten dancers, their foreheads marked by a star that signifies their superior status, and another group of six dancers without the distinguishing marks, into two groups whose paths cross, but who do not interact, with the smaller group showing deference to the larger group. "He [the Host] leads the party on without nervousness," states the scenario, "aware that the two groups have lived amicably side by side for a long time and cannot possibly achieve closer contact. Both sides of the party feel this almost naturally, the girls dancing only with partners from their group, gathering together and speaking together, but never paying attention to what the other side might be doing" ("Prelude and Welcome" and "Three-Four Dance").[43]

The Host invites the larger group to put on masks and engage in a competition ("The Host"), although as the game proceeds, a girl and a boy from the smaller group don discarded masks and join in ("Parade"). Still masked, the girl and boy selected as winners dance separately ("Variation I" and "Variation II") and then together "with a soft, relaxed ease as if they had been dancing together all their lives. The boy steps forward slightly and reaches out his hand, pointing the way to some distant happiness. The girl imitates this gesture" ("Pas de deux"). As the couple unmask and the boy alone reveals a forehead mark, the Host and the assembly drag them apart, but the two "defy convention and meet. The boy lifts the girl high and carries her away into the distance. The astonished guests look at each other in horror. The curtain falls" ("Three-Four Reprise" and "Finale").[44]

The idea of forehead tattoos might very well have originated with Blitzstein, given his use of such markings for his ballet *Cain* (1930), although here they signify racial difference. As to the use of masks, some jottings of uncertain authorship among Robbins's papers, although possibly written by Blitzstein, state, "They are the market-place, the supposed anonymity and equality of all comers (applicants for jobs, university-entrance, immigration, etc.). Everyone puts them on naturally when they are not at home, when they go out into the social world." Thus, the dance competition represents that struggle for social and material success reserved for a privileged group.[45]

As before, Robbins and Blitzstein considered various endings for the ballet. At one point, they imagined the spurned couple on stage, with a few members of each group slowly joining them, an idea that, like the ballet as a whole, strongly prefigured the Robbins-Bernstein musical *West Side Story* (1957). The ending that they eventually decided on, with the couple rejecting the community, more closely resembled Blitzstein's coeval opera *Regina*. The creators, in any case, did not want the work to be perceived as "negative," some extant notes stating, "there is plenty of evidence of surge and resistance to discrimination; this work is actual proof; things look up; maybe the pattern of bias and prejudice isn't fully broken down in this piece—but at least there is a clear attempt made, with tiny slow gains."[46]

Blitzstein adapted, revised, and expanded the older *Show* score, with the music's principal moods remaining those of tender melancholy and sassy humor, and with "Three-Four Dance" and "Variation I" emerging particularly intact. By contrast, he added some ironic "pomposo" music for the "Prelude and Welcome" and the "Host" movements, and rewrote "Parade," "Variation II," and "Three-Four Reprise" as well, although "Variation II" retained something of the overripe romanticism of its predecessor. The two finales also proved largely different, most noticeably their endings, with the new finale concluding not loudly and angrily as before but softly, with a quiet pedal supporting a hushed extended harmony, not unlike the close of *Appalachian Spring*. As for the revised pas de deux, Blitzstein began the number, like the earlier "Variation III," with music from the prelude, but for its big tune, he replaced the melody borrowed from *Parabola and Circula* with the discarded main theme from *Show*'s finale. That the two principals now solo, in "Variation I" and especially "Variation II," to music previously meant as satirical constitutes a certain dramatic incongruity, although this perhaps works to the advantage of the developing drama; for after establishing, by way of their solos, the male lead as carefree and the female lead as romantic, the two can now be seen as maturing in the course of their duet.

In order to meet a deadline, Blitzstein asked Henry Brant to assist on the orchestration for a modest-sized orchestra that included harp, piano doubling on celesta, and a substantial percussion battery. Given the shortness of time, the City Ballet agreed to pay around $1,600 for the orchestration as well as all copying and related costs, with the stipulation that should the work be published, the publisher would reimburse them half this amount. Blitzstein dedicated the ballet to Kirstein, to whom he telegrammed on opening night, "Thank you for the chance to work with you. You are the one man to make a lyric theatre in America. Please let me be in on it."[47]

Robbins cast Maria Tallchief and Nicholas Magallanes as the lovers and Francisco Mancion as the Host. Balanchine, Tallchief's husband at the time, not only attended some rehearsals of the work, whose theme he sardonically referred to as "the cluded—the included and the excluded," but shopped for masks and in general exhibited a degree of involvement that Robbins found "enormously aiding, helpful, trying to make it work for you, interested, and devoted." In her memoirs, Tallchief remembered the music as "rather jazzy," the choreography "lyrical and lovely," the ballet as a whole "intriguing," with a solo ("Variation II") she found "especially beautiful" and a pas de deux that had her "in the air most of the time," leaving Magallanes "often exhausted." The ballet might well have held special meaning for Tallchief, whose father was Native American and whose mother was of Scottish-Irish descent.[48]

Called *Incident* during the rehearsal period, *The Guests* debuted at New York City Center on January 20, 1949, on a triple bill sandwiched between two recent works by Balanchine, *Symphonie Concertante* and *Orpheus*. The cast wore rehearsal clothes, one reviewer guessing that the men's attire of black tights and white socks alluded to the racial conflicts undergirding the story. Jean Rosenthal provided the lighting for a minimal set that included a backdrop of black and blue panels, and Leon Barzin led the orchestra.[49]

The ballet received a warm ovation from the first-night audience, and the critics generally liked the work as well, especially the pas de deux, thought by Walter Terry (*Herald Tribune*) "a miracle of beauty." At the same time, some of the notices criticized the choreography as uneven and unclear, a perceived lapse exacerbated by the lack of any discussion of the work in the program. Terry further discerned a mismatch between the "definitiveness" of the music and the "abstract nature" of the choreography; nor was he "convinced" by the "acidulous" signature harmony in the opening bars that contained, he surmised, some "social commentary." Doris Hering (*Dance Magazine*) also critiqued Mancion's performance—he "stood around like a haughty but handsome butler" when the role called for "a sort of masculine Mrs. Vanderbilt"—and opined that the whole could benefit from some more formal costuming.[50]

Still, the reviews generally considered the ballet to represent Robbins and Blitzstein at their best, with several singling out the latter's contribution as "much the better of the ballet collaboration" and "ideally suited to Robbins's style." The critics also often noted connections between the score and jazz, with

Robert Sylvester (*Daily News*) writing, "When Blitzstein resolutely turns from melody, as he always insists on doing, he can turn out some of the strangest boiler factory sounds this side of bebop." Cecil Smith (*Musical America*), who contrary to Sylvester thought the score "continually melodious," described its "whole vocabulary" as "spontaneously and intrinsically American, as if by instinct rather than by design."[51]

In the most extensive review of the score, composer Henry Cowell (*Musical Quarterly*) argued that the music continued in the tradition not of Stravinsky's neoclassical pieces, with their "severity of form and content," but along the lines of the Russian's earlier ballets with their "incisive rhythms and striking sound combinations," a judgment perhaps swayed by Cowell's own biases, but in any event preliminary to his main argument:

> After forty years it is hard to make unresolved dissonance seem exciting or wicked, but Blitzstein's harmonies sound both wicked and zestful. They engender completely lively movements in the dancers, who are offered changes of pace induced not so much by frequent tempo changes as by irregular figures within the frame of a sustained meter, by changes of meter, and by a variety of figures within a single tempo. There is almost no polyphony, which clutters up ballet music and dulls rhythmic spontaneity. But Blitzstein's simple melodies are skilfully built into a real melodic structure.

Noting the composer's incorporation of "popular styles," Cowell further wrote, "the popular element is served for the most part with a wonderfully acrid dressing, and to hear it was a pleasure and surprise," although he cited as a lapse of taste the "saccharine" love theme, which he described as "filled with the popular glucose of Broadway."[52]

Blitzstein offered his own opinions about the ballet in a letter to Mina Curtiss dated February 20:

> The ballet was fine from my point of view—I mean I think I did a good, direct, even beautiful job on the music. Jerry Robbins' visual plan was fine but cloudy, not direct, and not *structural*; he muffed the climax, through his prudish avoidance or his own "immaturity" (a totally inadequate word), and concentrated on the *pas de deux*, a truly grand conception and execution. But a *pas de deux* isn't enough, you will grant; it was the crown of a work not sufficiently garbed, like the Emperor's new clothes which didn't exist.[53]

Blitzstein subsequently prepared a concert suite for publication, but Chappell proved unwilling to assume in particular the orchestration fee stipulated by the composer's contract with the New York City Ballet. "He [my publisher] sees no reason (and I feel he is being equitable in the matter) for him to pay for an emergency which was solely Ballet Society's last January, when the score was needed in such a hurry that Henry Brant had to be called in," wrote Blitzstein to Kirstein in June 1949. The City Ballet offered some slight accommodation, but, at least as of late August, declined to waive the clause entirely. Whether this contretemps ultimately undermined publication of the suite, the work went unpublished. The incident might also have hurt Blitzstein's relationship with Kirstein, who treated the composer highhandedly in later years.[54]

Meanwhile, in the fall of 1949, Robbins reshaped the ballet, and when the New York City Ballet revived it that November, with Tallchief and Magallanes again as the lovers, but with Robbins himself taking the part of the Host, the work—which now also featured a one-line synopsis in the program: "A ballet in one scene concerning the patterns of adjustment and conflict between two groups, one larger than the other"—won raves. "Mr. Robbins has since erased or smoothed out the rough spots," reported Terry, "and in the present staging, 'The Guests' emerges as a major work in the field of contemporary ballet." John Martin, who had written a rather tepid review of the premiere for the *Times*, similarly wrote, "The theme is the same, the choreographic scheme and the production are the same, but what emerges now is a taut and brilliant theatre work with a style all its own," and further observed that the music "has both bite and beauty, and manages to convey with a curious poignance the awareness of a sick society." When the company revived the ballet again in February 1950, during their fourth season, with Tanaquil LeClercq now paired with Magallanes, critics Terry and Martin seemed that much more taken with the piece, the latter writing, "It is an increasingly impressive ballet, not only for what it has to say on the subject of intolerance, or even for the uniquely formalized method it employs to say it, but also for the many passages of admirably sensitive invention in its actual choreography."[55]

During their London tour in the summer of 1950, the company gave the ballet's European premiere at Covent Garden on August 1, with Tallchief and Magallanes as principals. The work, including the music, received good notices in the British press by such experts as Cyril Beaumont, Richard Buckle, and L. J. H. Bradley, who thought the pas de deux "as beautiful and expressive as anything the Americans have given us," and the music, more "immediately appealing" than Bernstein's *Age of Anxiety*, with "attractive dissonances which help to produce an atmosphere of tension and mystery." By contrast, *The Scotsman* likened the score to "Soviet music at its worst combined with American music at its worst," and Benjamin Britten, attending a performance, privately deemed the music "very ungifted."[56]

The City Ballet presented the work in their 1950 fall season, again with Tallchief, and in their 1951 winter season with Nora Kaye. And in 1956, the company announced a revival with Tallchief and Magallanes, but Robbins, deep into rehearsals for a new work, *The Concert*, apparently felt overstretched, and Balanchine at the last moment created *Allegro Brillante* for the pair in its stead. The 1951 performances of the ballet would remain its last.[57]

That the company should drop *The Guests* permanently from its repertory, especially after its early success, seems somewhat surprising, although Kirstein apparently disliked the work, to judge from a letter he received from Blitzstein in August 1950, in which the composer wrote, "if you had wanted to be a part of the first talks planning it, I should have welcomed your contribution.... If now you're deçu [disappointed] with the piece, you'll know better next time, and you'll mix in, early. If there should be a next time." And Balanchine seemed ambivalent about the ballet as well.[58]

Other factors also might have played a part. In early 1951, as the City Ballet gave their last performances of the piece, Robbins, worried about the repercussions of his communist affiliations and fearful of exposure as a homosexual as well, began supplying information to federal agents, a process that climaxed with a May 5, 1953, appearance before the House Un-American Activities Committee in which he named a good many names, although not Blitzstein's. Two days later, Blitzstein wrote Mina Curtiss, "Of course I had known about Robbins for two years. As a matter of fact, you and I talked about it; but it was too miserably revolting to want to believe." Whatever their relationship prior, Blitzstein now essentially severed his association with "the worm Robbins," a move that, aside from straining at times his friendship with Leonard Bernstein, could not have encouraged revivals of *The Guests*, the planned one for 1956 notwithstanding.[59]

The matter seems to go still deeper. In a rather exhaustive list of his "principal productions" cited during his testimony before HUAC, Robbins pointedly omitted any mention of *The Guests*, a work that could have caused some potential embarrassment in light of Blitzstein's reputation, not to mention the ballet's implied critique of racial discrimination. Urged by one of the committee members to be "very vigorous and positive in promoting Americanism in contrast to Communism," Robbins might well have had second thoughts about staging *The Guests* again.[60]

Nevertheless, the legacy of *The Guests* continued in other ways. Although Robbins denied that the dance had any connection to *West Side Story*, it could hardly be mere coincidence, as Deborah Jowitt points out, that in early January 1949, during rehearsals of the ballet, the choreographer called Bernstein, as the latter reported, "with a noble idea: a modern version of *Romeo and Juliet* set in [the] slums." Even more specifically, Robbins adapted one of the rejected stagings for the end of the Blitzstein ballet for the Bernstein musical, as mentioned above.[61]

In addition, although Blitzstein's plans to fashion a concert suite never materialized, pianist Bennett Lerner recorded, on an album of American music (1986), three movements from *The Guests* ("Variation II," "Pas de Deux," and "Three-Four Dance") as a kind of suite. In conjunction with this release,

Lerner also edited "Variation II" for publication, essentially the only music from *The Guests* published to date, although he included copies of all three movements in his 2001 doctoral thesis. In 1990, as part of a Juilliard Focus! Festival devoted to "The World of Arnold Schoenberg," pianist Carol Kechulius performed the same three movements in manuscript on a concert featuring the music of Schoenberg and his students. And on November 2, 2005, Leonard Lehrman premiered his own suite of seven movements from the ballet at the Bryant Library in Roslyn, New York.[62]

Meanwhile, the choreography disappeared with virtually no trace but whatever commentators observed in the press along with some stills and a few scattered annotations in Robbins's hand—a significant loss for American dance, and one perhaps partly attributable to anticommunist anxiety. Had the planned City Ballet revival materialized in 1956, the dance probably would have survived. But by the time Robbins asked Maria Tallchief about the ballet near the end of his life, indeed, at their final meeting, she could only vaguely recall the work. Commented Tallchief, "I thought later he was very disappointed that I hadn't remembered."[63]

Regina, I (1946–1949)

In May 1946, Blitzstein accepted a $1,000 commission from the Koussevitzky Music Foundation for "a musical drama or opera suitable for performance at Tanglewood," the summer home of the Boston Symphony. The terms specified that Blitzstein inscribe his score, "For the Koussevitzky Music Foundation dedicated to the memory of Natalie Koussevitzky," and deposit his completed manuscript with the foundation, which Serge Koussevitzky, the conductor of the Boston Symphony, had established in 1942 in memory of his second wife. Having already commissioned Benjamin Britten's *Peter Grimes* (1945) as well as orchestral works from a number of internationally renowned composers, the foundation hoped to premiere the piece at the Berkshire Music Center in the summer of 1947. However, Blitzstein would not complete the work, *Regina*, until 1949, when it debuted on October 9, not at Tanglewood, but in New Haven in preparation for runs in Boston and New York.[1]

Blitzstein based *Regina* on Lillian Hellman's acclaimed play *The Little Foxes* (1939), which had premiered on Broadway in a production directed by Herman Shumlin and starring Tallulah Bankhead (Regina) and Frank Conroy (Horace). The film version (1941), produced by Samuel Goldwyn and directed by William Wyler, with Bette Davis (Regina) and Herbert Marshall (Horace) heading a cast that otherwise featured a number of actors from the Broadway production, with a screenplay largely by Hellman herself, enjoyed similar success, with its many Academy Award nominations including that for best original dramatic score, composed by Meredith Willson of later *Music Man* fame.

Born into a Jewish Southern family, Hellman (1905–1984) grew up in New Orleans and New York. Her mother's family, which had established their mercantile and banking operations in the town of Demopolis, Alabama, provided a model for the play's scheming Hubbards, while her childhood nurse Sophronia helped inspire her portrayal of one of the story's African-American characters, Addie.[2]

Hellman's prequel to the play, *Another Part of the Forest* (1946), which Blitzstein, having composed the music for its Broadway premiere, knew intimately, provides some helpful background regarding both *The Little Foxes* and *Regina*. Neglectful of his wife Lavinia, cruel to his sons Ben and Oscar, and incestuously attentive to his daughter Regina, the family patriarch Marcus Hubbard has alienated the local townspeople of Bowden, Alabama, through his profiteering from the Civil War. After wresting from his mother the dark secret that Marcus's wartime activities led to a local massacre of Confederate soldiers, Ben blackmails his father in order to take control of the family and permits his mother to leave home to pursue her dream of caring for African-American children; but he prevents Regina from eloping with her impoverished albeit aristocratic lover John Bagtry, and Oscar from leaving town with his prostitute girlfriend. Rather, he intends to extend the family wealth by having Regina wed Horace Giddens, and Oscar marry John's cousin Birdie Bagtry, heir to a run-down plantation, Lionnet.

The Little Foxes takes place in the same Alabama town twenty years later, in 1900, with Ben, Oscar, and Regina now middle-aged, and their parents presumably deceased. The action unfolds in the home of banker Horace Giddens ("a tall man of about forty-five. He has been good-looking, but now his face is tired and ill") and his wife Regina ("a handsome woman of forty"), whose servants, Addie ("a tall, nice-looking Negro woman of about forty-five") and Cal ("a middle-aged Negro"), help care for their home and their daughter Alexandra ("a very pretty, rather delicate-looking girl of seventeen"). Ben, a bachelor ("fifty-five, with a large jovial face"), lives nearby, as does Oscar ("a man in his late forties"), his wife Birdie ("a woman of about forty, with a pretty, well-bred, faded face"), and their son Leo ("a young man of twenty, with a weak kind of good looks").[3]

Ben and Oscar, proprietors of Hubbard Sons, Mercantile, having acquired cotton fields through Birdie's inheritance, now aspire to build cotton mills in town in partnership with a wealthy Chicago businessman, William Marshall. In order to meet the terms of the agreement, they promise Marshall a capital investment of $225,000 as well as free water power (obtained through government bribery), cheap wages (by playing on racial antagonisms), and labor repression (presumably by preventing workers from organizing). To keep the business in the family, the brothers, who each have $75,000 to invest, hope to obtain a like amount from Horace, who has spent the last five months at the Johns Hopkins Hospital in Baltimore for heart problems.

As the play opens, the gracious and manipulative Regina entertains Marshall at home, joined by Ben, Oscar, Birdie, Leo, and Alexandra. Having reached an agreement with the Hubbard brothers, Marshall departs for home, expecting the necessary contracts and capital within two weeks. Regina, who dreams of a glamorous life in Chicago, assures her brothers that she can secure the needed money from her husband, but holds out for 40 percent of the business; Ben acquiesces by reducing Oscar's share, assuaging the latter by pointing out that Leo, should he marry Alexandra, will inherit not only his, Ben's, estate but the entire family fortune. Regina agrees to consider such a match, and orders Alexandra to Baltimore to lure her father home. Birdie privately warns Alexandra about the marriage plans; overhearing his wife, Oscar slaps Birdie, who cries out, telling her startled niece that she only twisted her ankle.[4]

Act II opens a week later as Horace, confined to a wheelchair, returns home with Alexandra. In his troubled reunion with his wife, resentments simmer, including the fact that Regina for many years has shunned sexual relations with Horace, who has availed himself of prostitutes. Horace, hoping that his wife genuinely has missed him, soon realizes her true reason for wanting him home and refuses to go in on the deal, explaining to her that he plans to die in his "own way" without participating in her family's further exploitation of the town. Meanwhile, Leo, an employee at Horace's bank, tells his father about $88,000 worth of bonds in his uncle's safe deposit box, and Ben and Oscar encourage Leo to steal the bonds, which they plan to give Marshall as collateral and then return within three months, assuming that Horace will not look at the box anytime soon. When Regina learns, to her surprise, that the deal is going forward without her, she vents her anger on her husband in front of an anguished Alexandra, telling him, "I hope you die soon. I'll be waiting for you to die."[5]

The third act takes place two weeks later. On a rainy afternoon, Addie prepares cake and wine for Horace, Alexandra, and Birdie, who confesses that the Hubbards' cruelty has driven her to drink and warns Alexandra against a fate like her own. As Alexandra walks Birdie home, Horace tells Addie to take his daughter away after his death with $1,700 he has stashed away in a drawer. Some days earlier, Horace, wanting to change his will, had requested his safe-deposit box and discovered his bonds missing; he now informs Regina that Leo stole the bonds for Ben and Oscar, but says that as long as he lives, he will regard the theft as a loan. As Regina tells Horace of her longstanding contempt for him, he suffers an attack and reaches for his medicine bottle, which breaks; when Regina refrains from fetching his other bottle upstairs, he struggles to get it himself, but collapses on the staircase. Only at this point does Regina call for help.

After Ben, Oscar, and Leo arrive, Regina informs them that while the stricken Horace lives they are safe, but warns that if he dies, she will expect 75 percent of the business in return for the stolen bonds. At the news of Horace's death, Regina, in front of a bereft Alexandra, blackmails her brothers into accepting her terms. After Ben, Oscar, and Leo withdraw, Alexandra announces her determination to leave home and fight the corruption represented by the Hubbards. When Regina asks Alexandra if she would like to sleep in her room that night, she replies, "Are you afraid, Mama?"[6]

The play contains a clear social subtext. The aristocratic Birdie represents an agrarian world in decline, the rapacious Hubbard siblings, a capitalist one on the rise, with the year 1900 symbolic of this transition. "The century's turning, the world is open," Ben tells Regina, "Open for people like you and me. Ready for us, waiting for us." Such historical framing recalled Marxist dialectics, as in this passage from the *Communist Manifesto*: "The bourgeoisie, wherever it has got the upper hand, has put an end to all feudal, patriarchal, idyllic relations. . . . for exploitation, veiled by religious and political illusions, it [the bourgeoisie] has substituted naked, shameless, direct, brutal exploitation.... and has reduced the family relation to a mere money relation." Along these lines, Hellman contrasts Birdie's family's paternal attitude toward their underlings with the Hubbards' exploitation of poor people through low wages, exorbitant interest, and outright thievery, and their wasteful appropriation of the land, one that prohibits destitute people from hunting animals for food, but allows Oscar to do so for sport.[7]

Horace, "a shrewd trader" who has built a successful bank, to some extent shares Birdie's nostalgia for a bygone time, keeping sentimental tokens, including a piece of an old violin he used to play, in his safe deposit box. Like Birdie, too, he shows awareness and sensitivity with respect to social injustice, as does Addie, who gives voice to the indignant working class: "Well, there are people who eat the earth and eat all the people on it like in the Bible with the locusts. Then there are people who stand around and watch them eat it. Sometimes I think it ain't right to stand and watch them do it." Alexandra recalls these words at the end of the play when she tells her mother, "Well, tell him [Ben] for me, Mama, I'm not going to stand around and watch you do it. Tell him I'll be fighting as hard as he'll be fighting some place where people don't just stand around and watch"—an echo that underlines Addie's importance in helping to educate Alexandra.[8]

Although generally faithful to the play, Wyler's 1941 film version somewhat diluted the script, omitting references, for instance, to Regina's frigidity and Horace's philandering, and introducing some love interest in the form of a freethinking journalist named David Hewitt (played by Richard Carlson) who assumes the role of Alexandra's principal mentor and who accompanies her flight from home. The film also spread out beyond the confines of the theatrical medium, sometimes in ways that anticipated the opera, including the addition of an opening sequence that shows Alexandra and Addie in the town's African-American quarter and a later episode that depicts a reception hosted by Regina, scenes that probably influenced the construction and even the musical language of the opera, as Elise Kirk suggests.[9]

Previous to this project, Blitzstein had only occasionally used a literary source for his stage work, including his 1931 League of Composers commission, for which he started to musicalize Hemingway's "The Killers" and wound up adapting a passage from The Argonautica as The Harpies, titles that intimate some commonality with The Little Foxes. But with his Koussevitzky Foundation commission in hand, he began scouring possible literary vehicles, telling the Herald Tribune, "I wanted to do something that had sweep and big drama. I wanted it to be colloquial, with no poetry for the singers to worry about. I loathe poetry in musical drama except in the fantastic. And I wanted a work which was a classic without being Shakespeare or that sort of thing." Privately, he noted some literary works that he considered and his reasons for rejecting them: D. H. Lawrence's Sons and Lovers (too much "plot-detail"), Eugene O'Neill's Anna Christie (an "atmosphere" that "choked up the essence"), G. B. Shaw's Saint Joan (presumed problems with rights), and Clifford Odets's Awake and Sing! ("too cosy"). By contrast, he could envision how *The Little Foxes* might be amenable to operatic transformation: "I found spots for spectacle, action, 'laughs,' almost none of which were in the play proper." Moreover, it had "greed and glamor."[10]

Publicly, Blitzstein further discussed the appeal of *The Little Foxes*, which he thought "the greatest play written in America," as follows: "It has the stride of Greek tragedy. Regina is devoid of human kindness and is utterly selfish. She's the epitome of a whole type in America and in the end of the play her scheming and conniving reach a peak that draw together all the dramatic threads." Three aspects of the play especially attracted him: Birdie's confession, Horace's death, and the small talk among the Hubbard siblings.[11]

The other literary works that interested Blitzstein, as mentioned above, shed further light on the appeal of the Hellman play, as all of them save *Saint Joan* feature complex, often oppressive relationships between parents, particularly mothers, and young adult children set against a demeaning capitalist culture; and even *Saint Joan* pits a young woman against authority. Tellingly, his previous opera, *No for an Answer* (1937–40), similarly had charted a coming-of-age story in which a young heroine breaks with her corrupt family in favor of those less privileged than herself.

The resemblance between Regina, loosely modeled after Hellman's grandmother, and his own grandmother, a towering matriarch who operated the family banking business after the death of her husband, might have resonated with Blitzstein as well. The play's concern with racism certainly would have. On a more practical level, Blitzstein had every reason to suppose the playwright's cooperation, as the two had been friends at least since the mid-1930s, when they took part in shared leftist causes, including collaborating on the documentary *The Spanish Earth* (1937). Moreover, Hellman admired the composer, describing him as "a man of unusual talent" in support of his 1940 Guggenheim application. Indeed, Hellman, who had turned down other composers interested in *The Little Foxes*, not only gave Blitzstein permission to adapt the script, but she proved generally supportive, providing him, for instance, with some of her prodigious research for the play. She remained "worried" nonetheless, as Blitzstein recalled: "She said, 'If you want to do it, go ahead. But God knows how it will turn out. It's an unpleasant play and if you give it music it will reinforce the emotional underlay and make it more unpleasant.'" Not that she gave Blitzstein carte blanche. On the contrary, a contract between the two dated July 7, 1947, mandated that he submit his completed score to her for revisions and final approval before any production could go forward. This contract also specified that the playwright receive one-third of all royalties and proceeds to the composer's two-thirds, and that printed matter related to the opera include the phrase, "Based on *The Little Foxes* by Lillian Hellman," in a font size no smaller than that used for the producer's name.[12]

Blitzstein worked on the opera from the spring of 1946 to its fall 1949 premiere, leaving behind hundreds of pages of notes and sketches as well as drafts of several scripts. In April 1948, he wrote to Mina Curtiss about the particularly arduous challenge of proportioning the piece, which required him to write a whole scene "down to the last harrowing detail, before I know it's wrong, not in itself, but in relation to the whole: too emphatic, too 'shaped,' too inconsequential." He further told her that Lincoln Kirstein, her brother, had "berated" him "for destroying a lot of stuff."[13]

As early as November 1947, Blitzstein auditioned the piece for Hellman as well as for producer Cheryl Crawford and director Elia (Gadg) Kazan, both of whom had been associated with the Group Theatre and recently had founded the Actor's Studio. In the years ahead, the composer continued to consult with both Hellman and Crawford, as well as with Robert (Bobby) Lewis and eventually Maurice Abravanel, the stage and musical directors, respectively, of the work's first production. Hellman's written critiques tended to focus on added phrases deemed incongruous with regard to place, time, or character, and in most instances Blitzstein deferred to her strongly worded admonitions: "Regina must never, never, never answer the question 'Are you afraid, Mama?'" she wrote to him in June 1949 in response to one script that ended with Regina saying, "Me? Afraid? Ha!" (However, he sometimes held his ground; he retained, for example, Regina's use of the word "Southland" after Hellman complained that the phrase was a Northern expression, arguing, at least to himself, that Regina employs the word here "for Marshall's sake.") At the same time, Hellman consistently reproached Blitzstein for staying too close to her text, and like Crawford, she urged him to flesh out the play with more set numbers. "One of the faults of *The Little Foxes* is that the author's viewpoint is sometimes overstated," she wrote to him in September 1948. "Therefore I think any further underlining, in any form, is wrong." She had other objections, as discussed below, but proved in the end encouraging, writing in the same September missive, after a long list of criticisms, "that it [the opera] is a job of true stature and bigness and that I am grateful for it beyond words I have to tell you. Please do not be disturbed. Please be happy and very proud of yourself," the kind of praise Blitzstein regarded as "soft-soap to take the acid out of the criticism."[14]

Blitzstein completed a rough draft of the opera on August 28, 1948, and dated his finished short score and a closely corresponding orchestral score, 1946–48. However, he continued to revise the opera into the following year, so that the completed work really represented over three years of work, from mid-1946 to at least mid-1949. He subsequently cut a good deal of this original version for the work's Broadway premiere in late 1949, and made further revisions for the New York City Opera revivals of 1953 and 1958. He thus produced over time four versions of the work, all of which contain five scenes (or, beginning with the Broadway premiere, a prologue and four scenes) that traverse a similar dramatic arc, but that differ in their details. The libretto and piano-vocal score published by Chappell in 1953 and 1954, respectively, correspond to neither the original nor the Broadway version, but rather to that prepared for City Opera in 1953, whereas the first commercial recording (1959) preserves the significantly revamped 1958 City Opera mounting.

Making things more complicated, after the composer's death, John Mauceri and Tommy Krasker devised yet another version, a "reconstruction" of the opera that drew on the original score and some early discarded sketches as well as on later revisions; this so-called Scottish Opera version provided the basis for a new score (1991), recording (1992), and libretto (2003). None of these five versions can be considered definitive. The discussion that follows refers to the original, pre-Broadway score of mid-1947 (itself somewhat variable) unless otherwise indicated.[15]

Blitzstein hewed closely to the play's action and language, although he often reworded and reordered Hellman's dialogue in the interest of greater flow and musical projection. (To this end, he culled individual lines of each of the play's principal characters on separate sheets of paper, with Regina's entries running to 131 items.) Placing the action in Bowden, Alabama, and specifying the time as the spring of 1900, he at first devised a three-act libretto, with each act having two scenes. Of these six scenes, only the first, set on the veranda of the Giddenses' home, contains entirely new material. Otherwise, they correspond to the Hellman play as follows: the second scene, set in the Giddenses' living room, to Act I; the third, set in the living room, to most of Act II; the fourth, an interpolated party scene, set in the Giddenses' ballroom and veranda, to the rest of Act II; the fifth, set in the living room, to most of Act III; and the sixth, set on the veranda, to the end of Act III. However, Blitzstein eventually decided against a separate sixth scene, and chose instead to incorporate some ideas from that finale into the fifth scene for a five-scene format in three acts.

At the same time, realizing that the play lacked the "spectacle," "humor," and "romance" found in the "typical musical," the composer elaborated the basic story in numerous ways. As in the film version, he considered creating a boyfriend for Alexandra, and although he ultimately decided against this idea, he nevertheless introduced a romantic note by way of an aria for Alexandra about her romantic expectations, "What Will It Be?" Moreover, drawing on Regina's youthful infatuation with John Bagtry as depicted in *Another Part of the Forest*, he staged an encounter between the two, "Regina's Waltz," in the party scene, although he recognized that the number offered more "glamor" than "romance"; indeed, it exposed Regina's utter heartlessness.[16]

Meanwhile, Blitzstein added the party scene—unlike the Wyler film, more a reception for Marshall than for Horace—as a principal means of injecting spectacle and humor into the opera. This scene immediately establishes a mood of high satire as Regina, against the strains of the piano trio she's hired from Mobile for the occasion, cattily comments on the arriving guests, including an employee from the bank, Manders, and one from the store, Joe Horns. (Hellman disapproved of the presence of such plebeian guests, imagining a "tonier" crowd at a Giddens party.) As the scene progresses, various opportunities for choral singing, dance, and comedy naturally arise.[17]

This interpolated scene necessitated some of the opera's few changes in plot: Oscar does not leave for Chicago with the stolen bonds but instead delivers them to Marshall during the party; Marshall, not Ben, surprises Regina with the news that all's been settled; and Regina turns on her husband not just in front of Alexandra and Addie, but in the presence of the entire ensemble. "I'll be waiting for you to die," exclaims Regina against a wild gallop performed by the chorus, with her final pronouncement, "I'll be waiting," sung before the stunned assembly without any accompaniment whatsoever, followed by a silent curtain, a marvelous coup de théâtre.

Blitzstein further decided to have the opera feature a black Dixieland band, not only in this party scene but throughout the work to the point that Dixieland jazz, described by Blitzstein as "the first voice of protest of the colored people in a secular way against the eternal 'small-gypping,'" became, for the composer, a theme even "more important" than the "indignation" felt by the "good-willed characters." Indeed, whereas racism had hovered in the background of Hellman's play, Blitzstein resolved to bring this subtext to the fore, with some new forms of African-American music providing impetus to Alexandra's rebellion and solace to Birdie's suffering.[18]

Blitzstein accordingly plunged into a study of Dixieland, that is, classic New Orleans jazz. His papers suggest that he consulted the writings of jazz historian Rudi Blesh; listened to recordings by Bunk Johnson, King Oliver, and the Zenith Brass Band; studied Dixieland warhorses like "The Darktown Strutters' Ball" and "High Society"; and attended two clubs that featured this type of music—Jimmy Ryan's on West 52nd Street and Eddie Condon's on West 3rd, not far from his New York apartment on East 12th. Blitzstein in particular made note of the white trombonist Georg Brunis, who had been a member of the New Orleans Rhythm Kings and who performed with small combos at the forenamed clubs; known for his comic antics, Brunis maintained classic tradition by parading with his group onto the street and back into the club's ladies' room. In his own theatricalized use of a Dixieland band, Blitzstein retained both the processional and ironic qualities associated with the genre.[19]

The opera establishes the importance of Dixieland jazz at once by way of an entirely original opening scene, initially set in the town's African-American quarter, but later on the veranda of the Giddenses' home. The curtain rises to reveal the family's butler, Cal, serving Alexandra a late-morning breakfast, and its cook, Addie, cleaning house. As Addie and then Cal and Alexandra join in a spiritual ("The Angel Band"), an eight-year-old boy, Ezra ("Chinkypin," and described by Blitzstein as "a delicious morsel of a kid, who can't keep his feet still; an excellent jigger, with a natural marvelous rhythm, all spindly legs, and with a little brown head like the Chinkypin [sic] nut, for which he has been nicknamed"), begins to dance. Chinkypin's older brother Jabez (Jazz), a young man, "simple, without guile," who has returned from Storyville, New Orleans, "enamored of the new ragtime music," passes by with a band he has formed with fellow field hands, including himself (trumpet), Rucker (clarinet), Sebastian (trombone), Lias (banjo), and Adam (washboard/drums). (Blitzstein first envisioned Jazz as a guitarist—he specifically had in mind the African-American guitarist-activist Josh White—but possibly thinking of Buddy Bolden and other bandleaders of the period, made Jazz a trumpeter in the end.) Addie denounces the music as improper, but Alexandra finds it "wonderful," as does Cal. Blitzstein initially planned on including, after the band's opening ragtime chorus, a song for Jazz, "Naught's a Naught," that opens with the couplet "Naught's a naught, figger's a figger./All for the white man, and none for the nigger," and that contains lines about the white boss getting the black man's "gun" and "squirrel" that echoed the play's dismay over conditions that prevent poor people from hunting (with Blitzstein's mention of the boss getting the man's "gir-rul" providing an added edge). Although the composer eventually decided to use the song largely as instrumental accompaniment to dialogue, at the scene's climax, Cal sings the opening couplet, the expected word "nigger" cut short by Regina's sudden intrusion ("Alexandra!" "Hello, Mama." "What is that racket going on down there?"). Still, some knowledge of the whole song, which survives among the composer's sketches (and appears in the Scottish Opera version), helps to clarify Addie's disdainful reaction to the jazz band, and more generally, the role of jazz in this opera as an expression of social protest.[20]

In early drafts, Addie, asked by Jazz about the kind of music she does like, sings some of "The Angel Band," to which Jazz responds, "That is the same song. We just ragging it. Angel Band? That's our piece. We the Angel Band"; and as Addie, Cal, and Alexandra reprise the spiritual, the newly named Angel Band, proving Jazz's point, accompanies the tune with its own music. Over time, Blitzstein cut much of this exchange as well, but maintained the modally pungent juxtaposition of "The Angel Band" and "Naught's a Naught," thereby still suggesting connections between the spiritual and jazz, not only in musical terms, but in poetic ones as well, for the words of Blitzstein's spiritual, with its dream of inclusion ("And eat what they eat"), addresses in its own way the issues of poverty and discrimination more sardonically raised in the jazz number ("All for the white man"). As such, this juxtaposition gives added resonance to Regina's interruption of this "racket" that needs to cease in deference to the arrival of a wealthy Chicago businessman.[21]

At Alexandra's urging, Regina allows the Angel Band to perform at the party, but only on the veranda (as opposed to a piano trio, ensconced indoors), and then only because she learns from Marshall that such bands are "quite the fashion in Chicago." The band's featured party number, "Chinkypin," with vocals by Jazz, contains three alternating strains: bluesy, improvisatory-sounding riffs on snatches of overheard conversation by Regina's guests; the earthy "I Got a Gal on down New Orleans Way," rendered both with and without words; and the whimsical "Little Chinkypin (apeeking,/Peeking inda winda)," addressed to Chinkypin, who, attracted to the festivities, turns up dancing to the music. An ironic commentary on the pretentious and decadent townsfolk, "Chinkypin" establishes contact with Blitzstein's contemporaneous ballet *Show/The Guests* in its evocation of racial outsiders "peeking" into the privileged world of insiders. "You is getting educated tonight," sings Jazz to Chinkypin.

At the end of this number, Lias carries off Chinkypin, who has fallen asleep in a nook, and the other band members retire as well, except for Jazz, who, witnessing Leo's harsh words to his mother, stays to comfort Birdie with the blues song "Night" ("Blues"). "Jazz sees her, wants to comfort her," writes Blitzstein in an early synopsis; "but his gestures are stopped in mid-air by that oppressive sense of the impassable gulf between them. . . . Birdie listens, realizes this is an attempt to reach her; she is touched, but also frozen by the color- and class-line." Birdie joins Jazz toward the end of the song, and afterwards asks him about the number, to which he responds, "Made it up, ma'am. . . . Blues, I call it." Perhaps because this scene already contained a big number for Jazz, or because the work's original cast featured William Warfield as Cal, Blitzstein later decided to have Cal, not Jazz, sing the song to Birdie, omitting the exchange about the blues. He also dispensed with Birdie's obbligato line, making the number a solo rather than a duet. During tryouts, he shifted gears again, entrusting the song to Addie, which not only nullified the scene's transgressive bonding, but introduced a note of incongruity, given that the opera associates Jazz and even Cal but not Addie with jazzier forms of music; at the same time, the song's deep compassion seems consistent with Addie's character.

The Angel Band returns twice more in the course of the opera, both times in the final scene as the players accompany an offstage chorus in the spiritual "Certainly, Lord" with Jazz providing the call and the others responding. These moments carry forward that conflation of jazz and the spiritual explored in the opening scene. In the first instance, the spiritual comes at the end of the quartet for Horace, Alexander, Birdie, and Addie, "Consider the Rain," thereby providing a racial subtext to the number's progressive sentiments. At the opera's end, the same spiritual, here preceded by a brief reprise of the band's ragtime music, serves a similar purpose as Alexandra prepares to leave home.

The use of "Certainly, Lord" derived from the aborted sixth scene, in which the play's climactic confrontation between Regina and Alexandra takes place on the veranda the day of Horace's funeral, two days after his death, a scene that would have thrown the importance of jazz into still greater relief. As the procession returns (Regina, feigning a headache, has stayed home), the Angel Band begins to play spirituals in "lugubrious tempo, but are unable to resist whipping it up into jazz-tempo." (Blitzstein mentions by name "When the Saints Go Marching In" in addition to "Certainly, Lord," both of which he knew well from his work with the Army Negro Chorus in London.) In one draft, Regina tells Alexandra, "Make them stop that music! It's indecent! It's indecent!" to which the latter responds, "Go on, play. What's the matter Mama, are you afraid? Are you afraid?" as the band continues to play "more and more optimistic, breaking through, swelling, until curtain." Whereas in the play, Alexandra's determination to fight the

Hubbards frames her question, "Are you afraid?" here, the focus shifts to African-American music as an expression of resistance and triumph. Even after Blitzstein decided to incorporate such ideas into the fifth scene, he still imagined Regina expressing some objection to the music. But in the end, he made his point by letting the music, which now can be heard as a spontaneous response to Horace's death, speak for itself.

Jazz and the Angel Band thus appear a total of four times: twice on stage (scenes i and iv) and twice off stage (scene v). Blitzstein wanted the performers portraying the Angel Band to play their music themselves whether on stage or off, and accordingly he omitted the trumpet part when Jazz sings or speaks. Sometimes the band plays without orchestral accompaniment, although often the composer judiciously adds strings or other colors to enhance the sonority, in either case lending a piquant flavor to the score.

Many of Hellman's more forceful criticisms concerned just this preoccupation with African-American music. "The whole jazz-vs.-spiritual has been done before, and has no point," she said with respect to the opening scene, which she thought "unnecessary." She objected to the "Blues" as well, which she deemed sentimental: "The good-good blacks vs. the bad-bad whites is already overdone in the original." Blitzstein possibly abbreviated the first scene and made other changes in deference to such opinions, but he retained the role of African-American music as an important theme.[22]

The piano trio from Mobile represents, in contrast, privileged white society. Led by the violinist, Maestro (although a separate figure in the first production), this onstage ensemble sets the stage for the party scene by way of a trio that broadly parodies nineteenth-century salon music, with exaggerated arpeggios, trills, and chromatic scales decorating a stale harmonic rhetoric, all meant to evoke the "sleazy grandiloquent 'chamber-style' (really hotel-lobby style) of imitation Liszt-[Sigismond] Thalberg-Gottschalk." The finished score even states, with regard to this trio, "in the style of Louis Moreau Gottschalk," an apt allusion given that composer's New Orleans origins. For the music's principal strain— subsequently used as the main theme for the chorus "Sing Hubbard"—Blitzstein recycled a song in an operetta-like vein, "The Dream Is Mine," that he had composed for the 1925 Broadway melodrama *Stolen Fruit*, so that he appears to be satirizing himself as much as Gottschalk.

In the course of this party scene, the Maestro announces three dances, first in German or French, then in plain American, yet another joke: "Russicher Polka. Grande Polka de Salon. Polka," "Grande Valse de Concert. Waltz," and "Le Galop. Gallop." The trio performs these dances accompanied by the full orchestra, with the "Polka" purely instrumental, the "Waltz" doubling as an aria for Regina, and the "Gallop" a number for the entire ensemble that provides the background for Regina's quarrel with Ben and her venomous taunt of Horace. (In a footnote to the "Gallop," Blitzstein writes, "Regina and Ben's lines are heard only as a sound of altercation, under the music, dancing and singing," until Regina's "Come back here, you," at which point "the spoken words *are clear and understood*.") All this salon music serves as a foil to the Dixieland music on the veranda and similarly provides social commentary on the action.

Blitzstein characteristically conceived the opera largely as a series of discrete musical blocks, usually separated by spoken dialogue, that typically incorporate one or two set pieces. Adopting titles used by Blitzstein in his sketches as well as his published score, these blocks can be described as follows, with the set pieces or the like indicated in parenthesis.

Scene one: "The Veranda" ("The Angel Band" for Addie, Cal, and Alexandra).

Scene two: "Introduction and Birdie" ("Music, Music" for Birdie); "Small Talk" ("Birdie There" for Ben, "Gallantry" for Regina); "Big Rich"; "The Marshall Deal" ("I Don't Know" for Regina, "My, My" for Ben); "Away!" for Regina (introduced by "You Are to Say"); "The Best Thing of All" for Regina; "Birdie and Zan" ("What Will It Be?" for Alexandra).

Scene three: "Regina, Leo, Oscar" ("Right Nice" for Leo, "Little Ole Box" for Oscar and Leo); "Horace's Entrance" ("The Same Old Room" for Horace); "Greetings"; "Horace and Regina" ("Look at Me" for Regina, also known as "Summer Day"); "The Business" ("Thirty Years I Tried" for Ben, later cut); "Scene Change."

Scene four: "Polka"; "Sing Hubbard" for chorus; "Chinkypin" for Jazz; "Night" for Jazz and Birdie (subsequently "Blues" for Cal, still later for Addie); "Regina's Waltz" for Regina; "Introduction and Gallop."

Scene five: "Rain Quartet" (including "Consider the Rain") for Alexandra, Birdie, Addie, and Horace (along with "Certainly, Lord" for Jazz and the chorus); "Birdie's Aria" for Birdie; "Horace's Last" ("I'm Sick of You" for Horace, "Regina's Aria" for Regina); "Melodrama" ("Greedy Girl" for Ben); "Horace's Death" ("I Ask Myself" for Ben); "Finale."

In addition, Blitzstein devised a few numbers, like "Naught's a Naught," that never made it into the score as such. These included a more extended version of "Right Nice" for Leo; "Schottische," an instrumental dance number intended to precede "Chinkypin"; and "Lullaby," a song of comfort for Addie to sing to Birdie after "Birdie's Aria," its main theme ("Husha, husha baby") salvaged for Addie's wordless keening after Horace's death.

Blitzstein wrote "The Best Thing of All," which helped satisfy his longstanding desire to write something for Regina that would have "real singing impact" and "be a sock," late in the compositional process, apparently in Boston during the pre-Broadway tour and reportedly in response to the request of the first Regina, Jane Pickens, for a number that would garner applause. At first, Blitzstein seems to have substituted the song for "Away!" setting up the number by having Regina explain to Ben her devious rationale for sending Alexandra to Baltimore alone in order to fetch Horace home ("Men are so fussy about young girls traveling alone. Aren't they?"), and then launching into the aria in reply to Ben's "I never thought of that. How do you do it, Regina?" However, for the 1953 City Opera production, he reinstated "Away!" as a prelude to "The Best Thing of All," the latter now prepared by Regina's line, "It's getting late. Why don't you all go home?" and the stage direction, "Turns savagely to Ben."[23]

Most of the blocks listed above have their own overarching key center and arrive at some kind of tonal repose before moving on to the next block, as in the composer's previous dramatic work. But here he needed to superimpose such blocks on a more through-composed narrative, a challenge he faced with enormous ingenuity, including shaping the various blocks and set pieces so that they often begin and end seamlessly, with the set pieces carefully imbedded into the larger structure. For example, Horace's quasi-aria, "The Same Old Room," in B♭ major, ends quietly on a subdominant harmony, after which music from the opening of the scene resumes as accompaniment to spoken dialogue, with the entire block concluding some measures later by settling on a luminous harmony that suggests a tonal resolution without actually including the tonic note. The transition that follows arrives in a distant B minor, with an F♯ in the bass, helping to prepare the next block, "Greetings," in G major. To take another example, "Regina's Aria," in C minor, ends on a tonic major triad, but inconclusively, with the fifth degree, G, both in the upper and lower parts; only when Regina calls "Addie!" does the music, now at a furious clip, resolve to C, with the final cadence occurring some twenty measures later as Alexandra enters and an accented fortissimo C appears in the bass accompanied by its leading tone, which then takes over, helping to provide the transition to the next block, "Melodrama." In short, Blitzstein skillfully elides his various segments, with only "Music, Music," "What Will It Be?" "The Best Thing of All," the "Rain Quartet," "Birdie's Aria," and the party numbers featuring endings firm enough to elicit applause.

Blitzstein creates a good deal of continuity in other ways as well, including reprising several numbers, although done in such a way as to subtly amplify a certain dramatic development, as in the return of Regina's seductively scheming music ("You Are to Say") as she attempts to beguile Horace ("You know I wanted to come"). Moreover, the score features some signature themes and other unifying devices, including the ominous opening music that resurfaces at Horace's mention of Regina's frigidity in the third scene and as the basis of "Regina's Aria" in the fifth. This theme's distinctive three-note harmony, slightly altered and changed from minor to major, further serves as Ben's chuckling motive, first stated as an accompaniment to his signature theme, which in turn generates the ensemble "Big Rich." Such cross-references saturate the work, often in ways that ironically underscore the drama.

As with his evocation of Dixieland band and salon music, Blitzstein utilizes other period styles to help situate the characters in their time and place as well as to delineate them individually. Regina's music (for mezzo-soprano), for instance, tends toward a *fin de siècle* sensuality, what the composer called "a sickly neo-classic, over-sweet perfection." However, this surface glamor barely disguises her vulgarity, petulance, disdain, and greed, until she finally removes her mask to reveal her essential depravity in "Regina's Aria."

Ben (baritone), Oscar (baritone), and Leo (tenor) more consistently provide comic relief, their tunes, often gigue-like, tending toward the vaudevillian, again with turn-of-the-century overtones, but with edgy harmonies that point to Ben's callousness, Oscar's cunning, and Leo's fatuousness. At times, Ben and Oscar's darker sides emerge as well, as in the slashing minor triads that accompany Oscar's attacks on his wife, and the stentorian turn to minor that accompanies Ben's reprimand to his siblings, "My, My."

Birdie (soprano), Alexandra (soprano), Addie (contralto), and Horace (bass) have music that tends to be more open and straightforward, more limpid and diatonic, than that for the Hubbards, although Blitzstein distinguishes them musically as well. Horace's music in particular registers enormous nobility, even in moments suggesting physical and spiritual fatigue, and his anthem "Consider the Rain," with its forceful first-inversion harmonies and its incorporation of the lines about the "people" who "eat all the earth"—spoken by Addie in the Hellman play, but sung here as part of the "Rain Quartet," first by Horace alone, and then together with Birdie and Addie, accompanied by a soaring vocalise for Alexandra, who sings these words only at the opera's very end—provides a memorable credo for the opera as a whole, recalling the ideals of the popular front, as Klaus-Dieter Gross notes. (The anthem's basic metaphor, not found in the Hellman play, might have been suggested by Harold Arlen and E. Y. Harburg's "Right as the Rain" from *Bloomer Girl*, another of whose numbers, "I Got a Song," provided a model for "Chinkypin," whereas the opera's prologue seems rather to remember Magnolia's introduction to the blues in Kern and Hammerstein's *Show Boat*.)[24]

Birdie's music has greater delicacy and nervousness than Horace's, but also strength and humor, nourished by her memories of better times at Lionnet and her present devotion to Alexandra. Especially in her opening aria, her music makes contact with bel canto opera, neatly co-opting coloratura figuration within the dramatic narrative, and offering yet another dimension to the work's preoccupation with the social meanings of musical style, here suggesting the lovely but antiquated qualities of bel canto opera in contrast to the vulgarity of the Hubbards' music.

Alexandra's music seems like a fresher and purer version of Birdie's, underlining their similarities and differences. "There is, in L[illian Hellman]'s implication, a tie-up between the dying aristocracy and the not-yet-born people-consciousness," noted Blitzstein in early sketches, "with the rising industrial middle-class as enemy of both. Accept this, and build on it." At the same time, Alexandra has inherited something of her mother's determination as evidenced by her final melody, "Say it, Mama. Say it. Oh, say it. And see what happens. Away. I'm going away" (the text a passage adapted from some lines uttered earlier in the play's corresponding scene, but effectively foregrounded here in order to dramatize Alexandra's growth and resolve). Meanwhile, the African-American characters draw on jazz and folk traditions, with Addie's music coloring her wisdom and warmth, Jazz's, his wit and vitality.[25]

In composing the work, Blitzstein resolved "to see how much accompanied melody, easy melody (but not Broadway-Rodgers-Arlen style) you can get into the thing . . . for Christ's sake, eschew the damned detailed complex 'musicianly' moments," and he achieved such aims especially with such numbers as "What Will It Be?" and "The Best Thing of All," which he described, in a reference to *Carmen*, as his "toreador number." But at the same time, the opera shows the influence especially of the neoclassical Stravinsky, as in the prelude, which presumably evolved from Blitzstein's early intention to write an overture "in strict form, maybe chaconne—or passacaglia—but *harsh in harmonic treatment*," and whose formal elegance and harmonic bite characterize the score as a whole. The work's neoclassicism can also be discerned not only in its larger form, but in other details, such as its use of motoric rhythms, including the suggestion of trains in "Away!" and mills in Ben's "Birdie There"; and its allusions to bel canto opera's mad heroines in "Birdie's Aria" and its imperious queens in Regina's final commands to her brothers—music Leonard Bernstein referred to as "noble Handelian recitative."[26]

Significantly, for a number of scenes, including "Birdie and Zan," "My, My," "Melodrama," and "Horace's Death," Blitzstein recycled large sections of music, virtually verbatim, from *Parabola and Circula* (1929), a work strongly influenced by Stravinsky. Also tellingly, he scribbled in his notes for the opera the thought, "Copland—deceptively neo-classic—really still descriptive," as perhaps to suggest a difference between them. The prominence of neoclassical elements in the opera possibly involved the work's period setting, or its perceived relation to Greek tragedy, or its call for operatic singers as opposed to singing actors—the first such instance since his work from the early 1930s. In this last context, Anne Bill Foradori notes, "There is hardly a character in *Regina* who does not have sustained, difficult singing. Vocal ranges are extensive, tessituras are high, and many characters, especially Birdie and Jazz[,] must have a good command of coloratura and vocal flexibility."[27]

Much as the work traverses the tuneful and neoclassical, its dramatic content balances the naturalistic—as evident in its depiction of Horace's racing heartbeat or its directive for the sound of rain at the start of the last act—with more Brechtian ideas, including "Small Talk," in which four "sudden ensembles" (Blitzstein's phrase) comment on the action, and "Sing Hubbard," in which the townspeople satirize both themselves and their hosts in the accents of a turn-of-the-century operetta chorus ("Hooray, hooray, hooray, hooray,/Who took away that little tray?"). In "Regina's Waltz," such incongruity teeters on the absurd: "the music is suave and sensuous," notes the composer, "but the words are a frank and brutal below-the-belt blow at the man." Although such gestures in part reflected the play's ironic qualities,

Hellman, like a number of later critics, felt some discrepancy between her own style and Blitzstein's, and she objected in particular to the "sudden ensembles," threatening that she would not "let 'anybody' mess up her work like that," as Blitzstein summarized a June 1949 telephone conversation with her. But once again, he prevailed.[28]

Blitzstein scored the opera for four winds (basically flute, oboe, clarinet, and bassoon, although with considerable doublings), four brass (two horns, trumpet, and trombone), strings, piano, harp, and percussion, along with the five-piece Angel Band (the pit orchestra supplying at least the pianist for the onstage piano trio). Overall, the work eschews full sonorities in favor of shifting chamber-like ones, often to help limn the individual characters. Only some of the party music, most notably "Sing Hubbard," features, for parodistic purposes, a more conventional orchestration.

Not until he had virtually completed the work did Blitzstein seem to have decided on its title, announced by the *New York Times* on August 19, 1949. At the outset, he considered two titles, "Take Us the Foxes" and "Spoil the Vines," both drawn from the play's biblical inscription and central metaphor: "Take us the foxes, the little foxes, that spoil the vines." But over the years, he compiled dozens of other titles, some drawn from John Bunyan's *The Pilgrim's Progress* (1678), recalling his interest in the morality play *Everyman* in the context of *The Condemned*. Many of these titles, including "A Lady of Elegance," "The Siren," and "A Bitch in the House," as well as the Bunyan-inspired "Madam Wanton" and "Madam Bubble," alluded to Regina, but he ultimately settled more simply on her first name, itself metaphorical, as "regina" means "queen" in Latin and Italian.[29]

Regina thus joined a long list of such eponymous operatic sirens and hellions as Poppea, Alcina, Carmen, Salome, Turandot, and Lulu, although her clearest prototype might be the Queen of the Night or perhaps Lady Macbeth. She remains, in any case, strikingly repugnant even in the context of this motley group, for she shows little attachment to anything other than money and power. Wrote Cheryl Crawford to the composer about a year before the opera opened on Broadway, "You have lifted this piece into the evil of Lucifer, way beyond the evil of the characters and the story." True, some performers and commentators, especially in recent years, have viewed Regina more sympathetically as a product of her times and circumstances. But for Blitzstein, who ended one draft with her saying, "Me? Afraid? Ha!" Regina surely embodies unrepentant malice, even if he paints her with an ironic brush. At the same time, he gives both Alexandra and the story's African Americans, with their hope in a "new day coming," the final word, so that the opera, very much like the *Airborne Symphony*, "ends with conflict."[30]

Figure 20. Bill Hewitt and Marc Blitzstein, New York, October 1945. Wisconsin Center for Film and Theater Research.

Figure 21. Marc Blitzstein, 1946. Photo: Barney Stein.

Figure 22. Leonard Bernstein and Marc Blitzstein readying the *Airborne Symphony,* 1946.

Figure 23. The American-Soviet Music Society, ca. 1947. From left: Mordecai Bauman, Morton Gould, Betty Bean, Serge Koussevitzky, Elie Siegmeister, Margaret Grant, Aaron Copland, and Marc Blitzstein. Photo: Alton Taube.

Figure 24. From left: Christopher, Jo, Ed, and Stephen Davis, Philadelphia, 1948. Photo: John Condax.

Figure 25. The Guests at New York City Center, January 1949. Front, from left: Nicholas Magallanes, Maria Tallchief, Jerome Robbins, and Marc Blitzstein. Robbins Dance Division, New York Public Library for the Performing Arts. Photo: Fred Fehl.

Figure 26. Regina, 1949. Robert Lewis, Cheryl Crawford, Marc Blitzstein, Jane Pickens, and Clinton Wilder. Wisconsin Center for Film and Theater Research.

Figure 27. Regina, 1949. Top: George Lipton (Ben) and David Thomas (Oscar). Middle: Jane Pickens (Regina), William Wilderman (Horace), and Brenda Lewis (Birdie). Bottom: Priscilla Gillette (Alexandra) and Russell Nype (Leo). Wisconsin Center for Film and Theater Research.

Figure 28. Regina at the 46th Street Theatre, 1949. Philip Hepburn (Chinkypin) and the Angel Band. Billy Rose Theatre Division, New York Public Library. Photo: George Karger.

Figure 29. Marc Blitzstein, 1952.
Photo: Marion Morehouse.

Figure 30. The Threepenny Opera, February 1954. Marc Blitzstein, Stanley Chase,
Lotte Lenya, and Carmen Capalbo. Courtesy of the Weill-Lenya Research Center,
Kurt Weill Foundation for Music, New York.

Figure 31. The Threepenny Opera at the Theater De Lys, 1955. Scott Merrill (Macheath) and Lotte Lenya (Jenny). Wisconsin Center for Film and Theater Research. Photo: Avery Willard.

Figure 32. Reuben Reuben at the Shubert Theatre (Boston), October 1955. Evelyn Lear (Nina), George Gaynes (Bart), Kaye Ballard (Countess), and Eddie Albert (Reuben). Billy Rose Theatre Division, New York Public Library. Photo: Bob Golby.

Figure 33. *Juno*, 1959. Joseph Stein, Marc Blitzstein, Shirley Booth, and Melvyn Douglas. Wisconsin Center for Film and Theater Research. Photo: Talbot.

Figure 34. *Juno* at the Winter Garden Theatre, March 1959. Front, from left: Jack MacGowran (Joxer), Melvyn Douglas (Boyle), Shirley Booth (Juno), Jean Stapleton (Mrs. Madigan), Earl Hammond (Charlie), and Monte Amundsen (Mary). Billy Rose Theatre Division, New York Public Library. Photo: Fred Fehl.

Figure 35. Mina Curtiss, date unknown. Inscribed, "In memory of a forgettable day and an unforgettable lunch. Love, Mina."

Figure 36. Front, second and third from left: Bartolomeo Vanzetti and Nicola Sacco arriving at the court house in Dedham, Massachusetts, to receive sentencing, April 9, 1927. Photofest.

Figure 37. Marc Blitzstein,
Rome, March 1961. Photo:
Janet McDevitt.

Figure 38. Marc Blitzstein, 1963. Photo: Mottke Weissman.

Regina, II

Following her successful 1941 revival of *Porgy and Bess,* producer Cheryl Crawford (1902–1986) became increasingly involved with musical theater, producing Kurt Weill's *One Touch of Venus* in 1943 and Frederick Loewe's *Brigadoon* in 1947. Having worked with Blitzstein on *Androcles and the Lion,* before leaving for London in February 1948, she now optioned *Regina,* whose "power and originality" impressed her. Koussevitzky and Copland hoped nonetheless that Blitzstein might supervise completed scenes at Tanglewood during the summer of 1948, but the composer thought it best, as he told Mina Curtiss, to "lie low, and spring it as a full-blown affair, with the best equipment vocally and theatrically that the NY scene can offer" (although he accompanied three singers in excerpts from the opera at a dinner in honor of Koussevitzky at the Waldorf-Astoria on May 10, 1949, several months before the work opened in New Haven).[1]

Signing a contract with Crawford dated October 1, 1948, Blitzstein at one point thought that the British music publisher Boosey & Hawkes might publish and handle the work—he apparently had had an opportunity to play the piece for Ralph Hawkes, who liked it—but in May 1949, he entered once more into an agreement with Chappell, who provided a $2,500 advance against royalties. By this time, he had been holding backers' auditions, writing to Mina Curtiss, "The only thing worth anything that has come out of the auditions is the excited (and exciting) reaction of the listeners. Not being an Ivory-Tower artist, I am power-fully affected by the smallest or largest response, although rarely in the exact way indicated by such response." Crawford raised about $140,000 for the production and enlisted a young investor, Clinton Wilder, as associate producer.[2]

In his wish lists of potential collaborators, Blitzstein included such top-flight talent as directors John Huston and Joshua Logan, conductors Leonard Bernstein and Fritz Reiner, choreographers George Balanchine and Agnes de Mille, set designer Jo Mielziner, and, for the roles of Regina and Ben, mezzo-soprano Risë Stevens and baritone Lawrence Tibbett. In the end, the production featured no such superstars but a first-rate company nonetheless. Robert Lewis, the actor-director who had staged *Brigadoon,* directed; Maurice Abravanel, a European refugee known for his supervision of Kurt Weill's shows, assumed the musical direction; Anna Sokolow, a former member of the Martha Graham company, choreographed the dances; and the skilled team of Horace Armistead, Aline Bernstein, and Charles Elson designed the sets, costumes, and lighting, respectively.

Casting director Lina Abarbanell helped her son-in-law assemble fine performers as well. Several principals—notably soprano Brenda Lewis (Birdie), the German-born William Wilderman (Horace), and William Warfield (Cal)—had solid operatic credentials. Lewis had sung the Marschallin with the Philadelphia Opera and Salome with the New York City Opera, and Wilderman had performed widely as a Verdi bass with the touring San Carlo Opera Company. Less well-known, as suggested by his acceptance of so minor a part as Cal, William Warfield—later a celebrated Porgy—was underutilized here, especially after New Haven, when "Blues," his "charming little aria," was reassigned to the Addie, Lillyn Brown. "As long as I was going along grinning, 'Yes sir, no ma'am,' it was fine," he later recalled. "But let it seem that a black man might actually have the power of consolation over a white woman, and that was too much." Crawford and Lewis seem to have been more concerned that the song simply slowed an already overlong first act (as the Broadway version combined the first two acts into a single one) and cut the number entirely before opening in New York. In any case, Warfield harbored no "rancor" over this incident; on the contrary, he remembered the production fondly as providing him the opportunity to witness "the collaborative role a performer can play," and to get to know Crawford, who played "an important part in my own career."[3]

The other cast members largely had worked rather in musical comedy and operetta, including George Lipton (Ben), finishing a long engagement as Pawnee Bill in *Annie Get Your Gun* (1946); David Thomas (Oscar), the Harry Druggist in the 1947 revival of *The Cradle Will Rock*; Priscilla Gillette (Alexandra), who had replaced Marion Bell as Fiona MacLaren during the run of *Brigadoon*; Russell Nype (Leo), a future star making his Broadway debut; and Philip Hepburn (Chinkypin), an eight-year-old hoofer who had danced in *Finian's Rainbow* (1947). Lillyn Brown (Addie) had more of a background in vaudeville, although she later played Hattie in the 1952 revival of *Kiss Me, Kate*. As for singer-trumpeter William Dillard (Jazz), although he had appeared in *Carmen Jones* (1943) and other shows, he came primarily from the world of jazz, as did the other members of the Angel Band: banjoist Bernard Addison (Lias), clarinetist William (Buster) Bailey (Rucker), drummer Rudy Nichols (Adam), and trombonist Benny Morton (Sebastian); indeed, the band's many associations with such figures as King Oliver and Jelly Roll Morton assured their performance considerable authenticity.

The selection of Jane Pickens as Regina proved the most unexpected bit of casting. A native of Macon, Georgia, Pickens initially made her mark in the early 1930s as part of a singing trio, the Pickens Sisters; later in the decade, after that group dissolved, she continued on her own as a nightclub singer and radio personality, and did some stage work as well, including headlining a 1942 revival of Vincent Youmans's *Hit the Deck* at New Jersey's Maplewood Theatre, which presumably brought her into contact with Crawford. (When Tallulah Bankhead, who had originated the role of Regina, heard that Pickens had been chosen to star in the opera, she told Robert Lewis, "Darling, I didn't even like her when she was one of the Andrews Sisters.") But Pickens had studied at Curtis and Juilliard, and, harboring more serious ambitions, jumped at the chance to audition for Regina, a part she won, despite her relative lack of stage experience, thanks to her vocal talent, statuesque beauty, and Southern background, not to mention the difficulty of enticing a diva like Risë Stevens to perform on Broadway for eight perfor- mances a week.[4]

Furthermore, Pickens had a certain coldness that, while impeding her nightclub career, served her well as the frigid Regina. "I feel more wicked and cruel every performance," she enthused after the opera opened in Boston. "It's wonderful!" At the same time, Blitzstein and Robert Lewis seem to have "settled" for Pickens. Brenda Lewis even attributed her performance as the fatal flaw in the production: "she looked gorgeous and could act imperious and truly the Southern Belle, but she was no Regina. She just didn't have that kind of power onstage. . . . When you have an unbelievable central character, it eviscerates the opera." Robert Lewis recalled that Pickens, a Christian Scientist, resisted "appearing unsympathetic on the stage" and that he had to "toughen" her up "without her feeling she was playing a bad girl." Indeed, Pickens reportedly told a later Regina, Maralin Niska, that she did not con- sider the character fiendish, but rather victimized by her brothers, a misreading, Lewis contended, of both the work and his direction. Even so, many observers found Pickens compelling in the role, including David Diamond, who thought her acting and singing "superb."[5]

In anticipation of an October premiere, Pickens gave up her $1,500 per week salary at NBC Radio in July in order to prepare her part. Rehearsals proper started the first week of September. An opera enthusiast, but a severe critic of operatic acting, Lewis took the cast through three stages: first, rehearsing all their lines, including song lyrics, without music; second, having them speak and act in synchronicity with the music; and finally letting them sing their parts. "By that time," he recalled, "they were so secure as actors that they could not have thrown up their hands to sing a high note if they had wanted to." Not only did this re- hearsal strategy suppress empty gestures, but it improved communication of the text. "I always suspected that the difficulty of understanding sung English had to do, not with diction alone, but with the lack of clear thinking," Lewis later wrote. "If you know what the actor's *objective* is, it goes a long way toward understanding what he's saying—in any language." Brenda Lewis, who thought director Lewis a man with "an impeccable ear and impeccable taste," also remembered how he helped the cast make those transitions from speech to song demanded by the score by having them raise the pitch of their speaking voices to a level in proximity to where they needed to begin singing. Whatever the critics thought of the opera, all lauded the production for its sheer theatricality, Brooks Atkinson noting that the singers "act with complete understanding of the characters they are playing and with ability to project and move and express points of view," and Thomas Dash informing readers, "It will be a delight to hear an opera and understand it simultaneously."[6]

The opera arrived in New Haven's Shubert Theatre for its October 6 world premiere with a cast, including the onstage band and piano trio, of thirty-four, along with twelve dancers and a pit orchestra of some twenty-four players. Crawford compressed the work, as she had the three-act *Porgy and Bess*, into two acts, with the first four scenes making up the first act, the fifth scene, the second. Given that the Crawford production lasted about two-and-a-half hours with intermission, and that the original score contained about three hours of music, Blitzstein ostensibly cut about forty-five minutes worth of material, including, at least by the time the work reached New York, "Blues" and "Regina's Waltz," while substituting "The Best Thing of All" for "Away!" as discussed earlier.[7]

After what *Variety* called "an exceptionally smooth premiere," the production moved to Boston's Colonial Theatre, where it opened on October 11, a debut handicapped by Pickens having a cold, but resoundingly greeted nonetheless with cheers and numerous curtain calls. Following four paid previews at the Music Box Theater on Broadway, the opera, which came into New York with the first scene retitled "prologue," met with a similarly enthusiastic reception upon its Broadway debut at the plush 1,429-seat 46th Street Theatre (later, the Richard Rodgers) on, appropriately enough, Halloween night. (Opening night charged a top ticket price of $7.20, but otherwise $6.00 for evening performances and $3.80 for matinees.) The "Rain Quartet" and "Birdie's Aria" stopped the show, as they would in many future performances of the work.[8]

Avoiding the word "opera" as so much box-office poison, Crawford advertised the piece as a "musical drama," the term used by the composer on the title page of his manuscript scores. Blitzstein also had considered but then rejected "play with music" as too "arty," and "music drama" as too Wagnerian. Nor did he follow in the footsteps of those Broadway composers who used such terms as "musical play," "dramatic musical," and "musical tragedy," but rather Gian Carlo Menotti, whose "musical dramas," *The Telephone* and *The Medium*, successfully ran as a double bill on Broadway in 1947.[9]

On the eve of the work's New York premiere, Leonard Bernstein, who had been "privileged to observe its [the work's] progress from time to time," published a preview piece in the *Times* that addressed this very issue of nomenclature. Although at one point he referred to the work as "Blitzstein's newest and most ambitious music-play," he noted the limitations of all such terms, including "opera" and "musical drama"; ultimately describing the work as a "true song—a long, flexible, pragmatic, dramatic song," he opined that "this apparently unimportant semantic discussion" underscored the emergence of a vital form of native opera.[10]

The matter had practical implications as well, as Actors' Equity, which covered musicals, used a lower pay scale than the American Guild of Musical Artists, which handled operas. After attending the Music Box previews, representatives from both unions deemed the piece a "musical" rather than an "opera," perhaps partially in deference to Crawford, who naturally wanted to hold down costs. Blitzstein, possibly with an eye to such considerations, proved elusive, telling one interlocutor, "I think this really is an opera rather than a musical play," and another, "I call it drama in music. . . . But whatever its name, it's a fusion." But the critics on the whole agreed that, to quote Brooks Atkinson, opera was "the proper word," even if "operas are rarely if ever performed with so much skill and cohesion—the narrative gathering pace and sharpness as it hurries on to the dramatic climaxes." Tellingly, one commentator reported that, in Boston at least, a few people every performance would "demand their money back on the ground that 'Regina' had been misrepresented to them as a musical which, for various reasons, they contended it was not." In connection with the work's 1953 revival by the New York City Opera, Blitzstein largely settled the matter by calling the piece, as in his published libretto and vocal score, an "opera."[11]

In New Haven, Boston, and New York, *Regina* received, for the most part, glowing notices. "At last—maybe I can make a buck," Blitzstein told Leonard Lyons after seeing the New York reviews. Virtually everyone thought Robert Lewis's direction masterful, Anna Sokolow's choreography charming, Horace Armistead's revolving set effectively gloomy, Aline Bernstein's costumes bold and colorful, Charles Elson's lighting atmospheric, and Maurice Abravanel's conducting expert. Brenda Lewis, Priscilla Gillette, Philip Hepburn, and other cast members earned kudos as well, and if a few critics found Pickens less venomous than Bankhead— "The difference is that Tallulah made Regina into a capital 'B' while Jane's interpretation must be in lower case," reported *The Billboard*—she too won acclaim for her "stunning" performance, Brooks Atkinson writing, "Jane Pickens acts and sings with the ferocity of a poisonous snake."[12]

The work itself occasioned greater disagreement, although most reviews tended to be highly laudatory, with L. A. Sloper (*Christian Science Monitor*) describing the piece as "the best I have heard in the field of theater-opera," William Hawkins (*New York World-Telegram*), "the most exciting musical theater I know since 'Rosenkavalier,'" and Jack Gaver (*Columbus Citizen*), "as thrilling a theater entertainment as the season is likely to provide." Except for a handful of critics who simply detested the piece, such as L. G. Gaffney (*Boston Reporter*), who heard only "a squeak here, a squack there," and Irving Hoffman (*Hollywood Reporter*), who left after the first act of this "musicalamity," explaining, "I couldn't take it— and neither could you," even the more negative notices thought the work an "interesting experiment," a phrase that appeared with striking frequency.[13]

In evaluating the opera, many critics focused on its relation to the Hellman play, a questionable criterion, according to Brenda Lewis, who argued that, by the same token, such operas as *The Marriage of Figaro, Tosca*, and *Salome* should be judged against their literary sources; but such tendencies seemed understandable enough given that mostly drama critics as opposed to music critics reviewed the work and that the original stage production remained fresh in recent memory. Some argued that the music enhanced Hellman's script—"Without the composer's complementary setting, the nasty Alabama Hubbards are no more than talky pre-Tennessee Williams samples of Southern Discomfort at its most discomforting," wrote Robert Garland (*New York Journal-American*)—but not a few, including such influential voices as Brooks Atkinson (*New York Times*), Howard Barnes (*Herald Tribune*), and John Mason Brown (*Saturday Review*), contended that the opera, on the contrary, diluted the play, prompting this response from Thomas Dash (*Women's Wear Daily*): "How can anyone say that Blitzstein's music does not add dimension to 'The Little Foxes'? Not only does the score add stature and grandeur but through the alchemy of dramatic action, characterization and tone painting 'Regina' emerges as a new and vigorous work of art—a work of masterly integration by composer, actors, singers, stage designer and director."[14]

A number of critics cited Ben's "Greedy Girl" to make their point one way or the other. For some, this "master stroke of understatement" made Ben "twice as contemptible as bluff could make him," whereas others thought that his "strange hurdy-gurdy" music worked against character. This latter camp seemed bothered generally by what Barnard Rubin (*Daily Worker*) called the opera's "undertone of burlesque," although apparently not Hellman, who after attending the premiere, stated, "I like it very much. It's very impressive. I had a very fine evening. . . . I almost meant 'The Little Foxes' to be a kind of dramatic comedy."[15]

Similarly, some reviewers thought the Angel Band intrusive, whereas others commended their presence, including *Times* music critic Howard Taubman, who, in an article published shortly before the opera closed, argued that the jazz episodes as well as the salon dances "broadened the background" and "brought the atmosphere of the outside world into contrast with the inbred tensions of the Hubbards." Blitzstein's general treatment of racial themes, although largely ignored by the mainstream press, became a point of contention with the *Daily Worker*'s Barnard Rubin, who found the treatment of the Angel Band "patronizing" and who bemoaned the omission of certain lines from the original play that exposed the Hubbards' racism. (Blitzstein in fact had adapted some of these passages, but they had been cut, only to reappear in the Scottish Opera version.) On the whole, however, Rubin wrote a highly complimentary notice— "Blitzstein's mastery of the form adds new riches to the content"—and the suggestion that the composer left the Communist Party in 1949 because of this review seems doubtful.[16]

Although Virgil Thomson (*Herald Tribune*) might have been expected to better appreciate Blitzstein's score than most, in fact, he penned one of the more critical reviews, declaring the work "not very musical, though it is unquestionably very,

very, very, very theater." Among the work's deficiencies, Thomson mentioned its "explosive, obstreperous, and strident" sound, its recitatives at odds with the play's conversational tone, and its subordination of the orchestra to the vocal line, all of which contributed to the work's "hysterical quality." (Drama critic George Jean Nathan apparently borrowed the adjectives "obstreperous" and "hysterical" for his even harsher review.) Thomson reiterated his provocative stance a few weeks later, declaring the piece, a "play *with* music."[17]

Other composer colleagues seemed more impressed with the work. In a 1950 appraisal of musical theater trends, Rodgers and Hammerstein—their shows, ironically, often cited as preferred models by those critical of *Regina*—pronounced Blitzstein's "superb and expressive" score "a landmark in our development." Composer-lyricist Frank Loesser (1910–1969) attended the opera several times (he told Blitzstein on one such occasion, "I'm studying") and eventually penned an eloquent tribute that echoed Bernstein's preview article:

> Blitzstein has made a sort of giant song of the entire piece—consciously and deftly. Yet along with his astounding craftsmanship, he has poured in all his sense of the emotional, his instinct for finding and coloring those exclamation points in human drama (tragic or comic) at which the speaking voice can no longer contain itself and emerges as music. With the same profound talent for the dramatic, his orchestral writing delivers not only an accompaniment to what is happening on stage, but the very feel and smell of it.

Loesser's biggest hit, *Guys and Dolls* (1950), arguably absorbed some things from *Regina*, but his masterpiece, *The Most Happy Fella* (1956), plainly assimilated the Blitzstein opera, with lessons gleaned from *The Cradle* and perhaps *Reuben Reuben* as well.[18]

Aaron Copland, for his part, regarded *Regina* as "one of Blitzstein's best works and one of the significant 20th-century American operas," even if he felt the work marred by its fidelity to the Hellman play and—perhaps thinking, like so many others, of Ben's music in the final scene—the "jarring effect" of styles derived from musical comedy in "scenes of high seriousness." "The Promise of Living" from Copland's *The Tender Land* (1954) seemed to remember "Consider the Rain." Bernstein, who also admired the opera, virtually plagiarized a theme at the top of the dinner party scene for "Maria" from *West Side Story* (1957), although by this time the relation between him and Blitzstein had become so symbiotic as to make it difficult to pinpoint influence, with "Galop" from *Fancy Free* (1944) looking ahead to *Regina*'s second-act finale, which in turn anticipated "Auto-da-fé" from *Candide* (1956).[19]

On November 13, 1949, soon after the work's New York premiere, the CBS Television show *Tonight on Broadway* presented scenes from the opera adapted by

Robert Sylvester, narrated by Cedric Hardwicke, and produced and directed by Martin Gosch. *Variety* recommended the broadcast as "a highly dramatic session," although "probably too emotionally sustained for relaxing Sunday evening entertainment."[20]

Early in the opera's run, trade newspapers predicted an audience for *Regina* less like that for a Rodgers and Hammerstein musical than that for the aforementioned Menotti double bill, which chalked up 212 performances on Broadway. But *Regina* closed on December 17 after only 56 performances (toward the end, conductor Emanuel Balaban taking over for Abravanel). For all its many rave notices, the tepid reviews by Atkinson in the *Times* and both Barnes and Thomson in the *Herald Tribune* presumably hurt sales. (The *Times* music critic, Howard Taubman, thought *Regina* "one of the best operas ever written in America," but his review probably appeared too late to help much.) Moreover, the work's demanding score, surmised William Warfield, probably led to bad "word-of-mouth." "It was far too powerful for people to accept," remembered Brenda Lewis, while Douglas Watt mentioned also the conspicuous lack of "a love story." Finally, the production had a more costly operating budget than, say, the Menotti double bill, which featured a much smaller cast in a smaller theater.[21]

Some in the theater community reacted to news of the opera's impending closure with dismay and indignation. On December 13, twelve distinguished figures—Leonard Bernstein, Jerome Chodorov, Moss Hart, George Jessel, Michael Kidd, Clifford Odets, Cole Porter, Jerome Robbins, Harold Rome, Michael Todd, Tennessee Williams, and Dwight Deere Wiman—placed an advertisement in the *Times*, stating, "In our opinion, 'Regina' is an exciting new musical production which ought to be seen by the public at large. We are voluntarily paying for this advertisement in the hope that it will stimulate a greater public attention for this fine work." Fans of the opera began to appear in front of the 46th Street Theatre with such pickets as "Regina Has Been Stabbed—Save Her." Sensing the emergence of a "*Regina* underground," Crawford stored the costumes and scenery for later use in a horse barn on property owned by associate producer Clinton Wilder. She also took comfort from a letter she received after the opera closed from dance critic John Martin, who wrote in part,

I have seen a great many theatres in a great many languages over the past forty years or so, but I have rarely been so completely shattered by a performance. What Blitzstein has done is to give us a theatre of our own with heroic dimensions for perhaps the first time. I have never heard music made so integral an element in the total art of the theatre, so boldly used to heighten and create theatrical values. His figures emerge in larger-than-life proportions in a situation that, for all its specific localization, takes on universal compulsions. It is difficult not to make some comparisons with those suspect creatures, the old Greeks.[22]

Had the recently established Tony Awards at this point made it a practice to announce nominations as well as winners, *Regina* presumably would have garnered a number of these, its brief run notwithstanding. As it was, Aline Bernstein won a Tony for best costumes and Maurice Abravanel, best conductor and musical director, making *Regina* the only musical theater piece to win a 1950 Tony besides *South Pacific*, which swept that year's awards, including best score to Richard Rodgers. Moreover, Jane Pickens, presumably on the strength of *Regina*, received an award from New York University for "superb achievements in the entertainment and musical fields" in late 1949, and Priscilla Gillette won a Theatre World Award for an outstanding Broadway debut in 1950.[23]

Chappell announced the forthcoming publication of the score, but in the meantime published only six slightly simplified numbers from the opera: "The Best Thing of All," "What Will It Be?" "Look at Me" (also published as "Summer Day"), "Chinkypin," "Blues," and "Greedy Girl." Unable to secure a commercial recording, Blitzstein arranged for the Carnegie Hall Recording Company to make an acetate disc of five excerpts from the opera—"The Best Thing of All," "What Will It Be?" the "Rain Quartet," "Birdie's Aria," and "Finale"—with the original cast, the composer at the piano. Capturing the singing and in some instances the speaking of many of the principals, this historic 1949 recording also preserves something of Blitzstein's rhythmically flexible approach to the score.

On April 13, 1950, Brenda Lewis, accompanied by Blitzstein, sang Birdie's two arias in concert, along with the composer's "Orpheus with His Lute," at the Philadelphia Academy of Music. More momentously, on June 1, 1952, Maurice Levine, at the time conductor of the Broadway revival of Gershwin's *Of Thee I Sing*, led a Sunday night staged concert reading at the 92nd Street YMHA (Young Men's Hebrew Association) in Manhattan. Blitzstein arranged about eighty minutes of music from the opera that featured most of the larger set pieces, including some that had been cut for the Broadway production. Hellman wrote and recited a narration that bridged gaps in the story, and Robert Lewis supervised the stage action, arranging seats for the cast members in a semicircle, flanked by the orchestra on stage right, and Hellman, stage left.[24]

Performing without fee, the cast featured such veterans of the Broadway cast as Pickens, Lewis, Gillette, Wilderman, Thomas, Nype, and Dillard, but also Randolph Symonette (Ben), Clarisse Crawford (Addie), and Joseph James (Cal), who sang "Blues." Levine also recruited members of the chorus and orchestra from the *Of Thee I Sing* production. An expectant audience of about nine hundred crowded into the Y's Kaufmann Auditorium for the performance, presented in two acts with a break in the middle of the party scene, following "Sing Hubbard." Thousands of others had to be turned away, as Robert Lewis recalled.[25]

The performance took on added drama in light of Hellman's recent appearance on May 21 before the House Un-American Activities Committee, which had rejected her offer to testify only about herself, leaving her no choice, she felt, but to take the Fifth Amendment, which meant a possible jail sentence for contempt. (The breaking press accounts on May 22 included a quote from her letter to the committee that became legendary: "I cannot and will not cut my conscience to fit this year's fashion.") Subpoenaed months earlier, Hellman for some time had been hesitant about appearing at the *Regina* concert so soon after her House appearance, but she avoided discussing the matter with Blitzstein until May 10, when she met with him at the Russian Tea Room and suggested that Leonard Bernstein read the narration in her stead. "I should have told him before," she recalled, "but even though I love Marc, and we have been close friends, there are times I don't like to listen to him. I expected a lecture, I didn't know what kind, but a lecture." Blitzstein responded by telling Hellman, "No. We can't call you off, and you can't call yourself off. We'd all look like cowards." When Hellman expressed fear that she might be hissed, Blitzstein won her over by saying, "I don't think they will hiss you, and if they do, I won't have it. I'll just come out and say that I don't want my music played before such people, and we'll give them their money back and send them home." Recalled Hellman, "I laughed because I could hear him doing it, enjoying it." As it happened, when Hellman started to walk across the stage, she received a standing ovation, stopping her so dead in her tracks that the audience began to laugh. "I wanted very much to cry," remembered Hellman, who after settling in an armchair commented, "This seat is a lot more comfortable than the one I've been sitting in lately." For this audience, the opera's concluding cry, "Is a new day a-coming? Certainly, Lord," no doubt assumed special meanings.[26]

This outing at the Y met with a very warm reception, the capacity crowd "loudly vocal in its enthusiasm." Virtually every review—now written largely by music, not drama, critics—praised the work. Douglas Watt (*Daily News*) pronounced the opera "a masterpiece," and Arthur Bronson (*Variety*) urged a mounting by the New York City Opera, who answered the call, scheduling three performances of the work for their spring 1953 season. More of a community theater than the rival Metropolitan Opera, the City Opera performed in a smaller house (the 2,750-seat City Center) and showcased more American talent, including more native opera, especially since Joseph Rosenstock became general director in 1952. Operating with a smaller budget as well, the company fortunately was able to rent the original Armistead sets and Bernstein costumes that Crawford prudently had stored. Robert Lewis once again directed, although the company also tapped their own favored personnel, including conductor Julius Rudel, lighting director Jean Rosenthal, and choreographer John Butler. The cast included Brenda Lewis (now in the part of Regina), William Wilderman (Horace), Priscilla Gillette (Alexandra), and William Dillard (Jazz) from the Broadway production along with Ellen Faull (Birdie), Leon Lishner (Ben), Emile Renan (Oscar), Michael Pollock (Leo), and Lucretia West (Addie).[27]

Consulting with Robert Lewis, Blitzstein overhauled the work to make it more operatic: he fully set some of the spoken or half-sung lines, eliminated other portions of the dialogue, and raised some of the vocal lines, going so far as to recast the part of Regina from a straight mezzo to one with an extended range that allowed a brighter, higher tessitura, including a thrilling high C rather than a high G at the end of the party scene. He also reinstated "Away!" "Blues," and "Regina's Waltz," restored the three-act structure, and dispensed with the character of Chinkypin, but rather had Jazz sing "Chinkypin" to a "small Chinkypin statue," that is, a black jockey hitching post. (Robert Lewis and Aline Bernstein, strapped for funds, talked the owner of the "21" Club, its entrance decorated with such posts, into lending them one.)[28]

Opening on April 2, the City Opera production drew bravos from the audience and, as with the 1952 concert presentation, a more hospitable reception in the press—again now mostly in the hands of music critics—than in 1949. "Lillian Hellman may someday best be remembered as the librettist of 'Regina,'" stated Douglas Watt in stark contrast to some earlier reviews. Such praise appeared overseas with a notice in the British journal *Music Review* by Richard RePass, who opined that this "stunning work . . . left little room for doubt that Blitzstein is the most important native opera composer in American to-day." Recalling Virgil Thomson's critical review of the Broadway premiere, David Diamond wrote in his diary, "I hope Virgil gets ulcers out of envy! What a satisfaction it must be for Marc now, after the depression Virgil's first review caused him. And of course V.T. did not come to review the opera this time. Smarty-pants! He'll get *his* some day."[29]

Apparently pleased with the work's reception, Blitzstein stated, regarding its adoption by the City Opera, "This is where it belongs. This is the ideal place for it." He also particularly liked Lewis's performance, writing Mina Curtiss, "it is so *great* to have at last a Regina with humor! She has everything else, too, in superabundance; it is only necessary to trim her fury and energy." However, a subsequent production at the Cleveland Play House in May with Adele Khoury as Regina elicited a more mixed response, as did an underrehearsed return engagement at the City Opera in October with a new Alexandra (Dorothy MacNeil) and Birdie (Willabelle Underwood).[30]

About this same time, Bernstein, who in late 1953 became the first American to conduct at La Scala, attempted to interest that company's artistic directors Antonio Ghiringhelli and Victor de Sabata in launching the opera's European premiere. Aware of Bernstein's exertions on his behalf, Blitzstein wrote Ghiringhelli, "I should be most proud to have my work performed in the world's greatest opera house," and sent him the newly published piano-vocal score. Assuming that the opera would have to be presented in Italian, he also hired Natalia Murray to start translating the text, showing her version of "The Best Thing of All" ("Il vero gran ben") to Gian Carlo Menotti, who thought the translation "fair" rather than "excellent," observing that all the masculine endings gave the Italian "a slightly archaic flavor." Both Ghiringhelli and de Sabata liked the music and, by late 1954, intimated a production for the following season.[31]

When Bernstein returned to La Scala in early 1955, Blitzstein anxiously awaited word, and after weeks of silence, he wrote Bernstein, "What is it you want me to do, crawl?" an outburst for which he later apologized. Bernstein assured Blitzstein that Ghiringhelli seemed well-disposed toward a production, but that de Sabata had concerns about, first, the difficulty of rendering "the 'tough' quality" of the text into Italian, and second, the use of spoken dialogue. Blitzstein duly offered to musicalize all the spoken dialogue and further agreed to Bernstein's unusual suggestion that the African-American characters sing in English, the rest of the cast in Italian.[32]

However, de Sabata soon after informed Blitzstein that the company would not produce the opera after all, for as much as he admired the music, once he had studied the libretto, he decided that the work "does not combine with, La Scala's atmosphere, tradition, public, stage's magnitude, taste and phisiognomy [sic]" and asked Blitzstein for another work that Bernstein might perform. "Furious and disgusted," Bernstein, after telling Blitzstein that Menotti, like de Sabata, felt that the opera would be "a dangerous work for the Scala public," commented, "Screw them, I say, and do it anyway." Blitzstein in turn wrote Bernstein about his surprise that de Sabata should find such themes as "money-as-the-root-of evil" problematic—"Where has he learned about opera-texts?"—and reported Hellman's assessment that the Italians "just don't go for satire. A straight emotional bath and a minimum of creative indignation is apparently the desideratum."[33]

Beginning on April 17, 1958, *Regina* returned to City Center for three performances as part of a spring season, underwritten by a $105,000 grant from the Ford Foundation, that showcased ten contemporary American operas. Brenda Lewis (Regina) and Emile Renan (Oscar) recreated their roles, and Aline Bernstein came out of retirement to redesign the costumes, but otherwise, the production essentially employed new personnel, with staging—at Blitzstein's suggestion, as Rudel recalled—by Herman Shumlin (Blitzstein by this time had fallen out with Robert Lewis over *Reuben Reuben*); scenery by Howard Bay, who, like Shumlin, had collaborated on the original production of *The Little Foxes*; choreography by Robert Joffrey; and a cast that also included Joshua Hecht (Horace), Elisabeth Carron (Birdie), Helen Strine (Alexandra), George Irving (Ben), Carol Brice (Addie), and Loren Driscoll (Leo), all under the baton of Samuel Krachmalnick, who had premiered Blitzstein's *Reuben Reuben* in 1955. The reviews praised Lewis's searing performance and Shumlin and Krachmalnick's forceful direction, but they proved mixed about the work itself.[34]

For this 1958 revival, Blitzstein excised not only Chinkypin, as in 1953, but Jazz and all references to the Angel Band. Retaining the band's music from the prologue, he wrote a new accompanying lyric extolling "spring mornings" for Alexandra, so that the Dixieland idiom appears an expression of her youthful vitality and perhaps incipient nonconformity rather than one of African-American protest. Blitzstein retained the two offstage appearances of "Certainly, Lord" in the last act, but without Alexandra's explanation, "It's Jazz and the Angel Band!" The "Chinkypin" number he simply cut, bringing the total performance time to about two hours.

Few critics noticed the missing Angel Band, aside from Howard Taubman (*New York Times*), who regretted the absence of "some wonderful jazz color," and Harriett Johnson (*New York Post*), who thought that a new dramatic tautness compensated for the loss. Taubman attributed the revision to "budgetary exigencies," later reporting that Blitzstein felt the jazz band "a self-indulgence he could dispense with." But as Eric Gordon suggests, the decision probably rested with Shumlin, who had had little experience with musical theater and felt uncomfortable directing the Angel Band, and who for some time, moreover, had been associated with Hellman, who always had regarded the Angel Band as at best superfluous. Significantly, Hellman credited Shumlin's interpretation of the opera, which she regarded the "best" yet, as helping her to "fully" appreciate the work. (Claire Reis, the former chairman of the League of Composers, similarly thought the production "magnificent—*far* better than the last one.") Rudel, who like Taubman missed the Angel Band, marveled that Blitzstein, who had been so "punctilious" about his work, agreed to these cuts. However, the changing times might have cast a pall over what the *Daily Worker* years earlier had regarded as the quaintness of the Dixieland band, notwithstanding composer Robert Russell Bennett's conviction, stated in a 1959 letter to the composer, that "some of your raggy bits will sound much more distinguished than they do now to our age exposed to pop music."[35]

Whether Blitzstein initiated or merely acquiesced to some of these revisions, the 1958 version acquired some authority with a long-playing three-record cast album released the following year, a recording made possible by a grant from the Koussevitzky Music Foundation and contributions by individual donors. Brenda Lewis recalled that Columbia Records set aside a single block of time for the recording, and that on April 27, 1958, the company arrived at the recording studio after a performance and recorded the work from about midnight to five in the early morning hours of April 28. Except for Lewis's unaccompanied "I'll be waiting," which she and Blitzstein recorded after the session proper ("I knocked out high C's until we were sure we had one that was right and would fit"), the cast performed the work without any retakes. "What you hear in the *Regina* recording is hot off the griddle," commented Lewis. "It was do or die. We were totally abandoned to the work and energy of the drama."[36]

In a review of this release, Eric Salzman (*New York Times*) thought that although the work lost some of its effectiveness shorn from the stage, the recording showcased the opera's "musical highpoints." The recording also occasioned a reevaluation by Virgil Thomson (*Saturday Review*), who now attributed the work's "musical-verbal line," with its wide skips and subservient orchestral accompaniment, to the influence of Weill and Puccini; he also showed greater appreciation of its Brechtian aims: "It [the opera] holds the attention, moreover, by musical means, even though the interest created by music is used consistently for throwing the weight of attention toward the moral understanding of the play away from emotional identification with anybody in it." The 2010 rerelease of this recording on CD similarly met with high praise by critics and bloggers, who bemoaned, however, the lack of an accompanying text, with Eric Myers (*Opera News*) writing, "That's a shame, because Blitzstein did not simply set Hellman's play to music—he was a poet who adapted it into a true libretto."[37]

In April 1959, the opera returned to City Center with mostly the same cast, and then, over the summer, received its West Coast premiere by the San Jose Opera Association (conducted by Fred Coradetti, with Meg Broughton as Regina) as well as a performance by the Santa Fe Opera Company (conducted by Margaret Hillis, with Elaine Bonazzi in the title role). That same summer, armed with the City Opera recording, Blitzstein met with singers and directors overseas in the hope of securing a European production of the work. Soprano Inge Borkh and mezzo-soprano Regina Resnik expressed their desire to sing Regina in Berlin and London, respectively, while the piece also sparked the interest of Gerhart von Westerman, intendant of the Berlin Philharmonic. In the course of the 1950s, others similarly considered presenting the work abroad, including Peter Diamand, head of the Holland Festival; Anne Guerrieri, manager of the Teatro Club in Rome; and Friedelind Wagner, the German composer's antifascist granddaughter and a friend of Lina Abarbanell's. But no European production materialized in Blitzstein's lifetime; nor did plans go forward, as the composer hoped, for an MGM Records release of a twenty-five-minute *Regina* suite.[38]

As one of Blitzstein's better-known works, *Regina* shared center stage with *The Cradle Will Rock* at a memorial concert at Philharmonic Hall on April 19, 1964, that featured a performance of scenes with a connective narration written and spoken by Lillian Hellman, as in 1952, although containing far less music. Veterans from past productions, including a member of the original cast, William Wilderman (Horace), joined Phyllis Curtin (Regina) and others in this memorial presentation under the expert leadership of conductor Julius Rudel, which prompted whoops of cheers from the audience, but which left critics Harold Schonberg (*New York Times*) and Alan Rich (*Herald Tribune*) unenthused.[39]

In the years immediately following the composer's death, productions of the opera remained few and far between, but then increased to the point that, by the twenty-first century, the work had emerged as one of America's most frequently performed native operas. These later mountings included those by the Michigan Opera Theatre (1977: Joan Diener-Marre, Regina; John Yaffé, conductor); Houston Grand Opera (1980: Maralin Niska, John DeMain); Chicago Opera Theater (1982: Judith Erickson, Steven Larsen); Kansas City Lyric (1982: Eileen

Schauler, Russell Patterson); Long Wharf Theater (1988: Rosalind Elias and Kristen Hurst-Hyde alternating in an extended run, Murry Sidlin); Opera Theater of Pittsburgh (1990: Joyce Campana, Murry Sidlin); Boston Lyric Opera (1991: Katherine Terrell, Stephen Lord); Scottish Opera (the European premiere, at the Theatre Royal, Glasgow, May 16, 1991: Katherine Terrell, John Mauceri); New York City Opera (1992: Leigh Munro, Laurie Anne Hunter); Opera Pacific (1996: Carol Neblett, John Mauceri); Bronx Opera (2000: Sarah Hersh, Michael Spierman); Florida Grand Opera (2001: Lauren Flanigan, Stewart Robertson); Lyric Opera of Chicago (2003: Catherine Malfitano, John Mauceri); Kennedy Center (semi-staged, 2005: Patti LuPone, Steven Mercurio); Bard Summerscape (2005: Lauren Flanigan, Leon Botstein); Pacific Opera Victoria (the Canadian premiere, at the Royal Theatre, Victoria, April 17, 2008: Kimberly Barber, Timothy Vernon); Long Leaf Opera (2008 Christine Weidinger, Benjamin Keaton); and Utah Opera (2009: Deanne Meek, Keith Lockhart). The piece even became a favorite with such companies as the Chautauqua Opera, which produced it twice (1982, 1997), as did the Des Moines Metro Opera (1994, 2008). In his preview of the 1992 City Opera revival, Jamie James deemed this "highly charged, musically inventive" work, although not "a repertory staple," a "strong candidate" for the "great American opera."[40]

The 1991 Scottish Opera production unveiled a revamped version of the opera by conductor John Mauceri and producer Tommy Krasker, which led to a new score by Tams-Witmark (1991), recording by Decca/London (1992), and libretto by the Lyric Opera of Chicago (2003). Mauceri (b. 1945), while directing the Yale Symphony in the late 1970s, spearheaded this project in consultation with Leonard Bernstein, who told him, alluding to the cuts taken in the opera over the years, "I swore an oath on Marc's grave that I would fix *Regina*." (Bernstein never conducted the opera himself, although Irene Diamond thought him "the only person who could give it the kind of electricity and power it could have," and in 1972—after hearing Marilyn Horne sing Carmen at the Met under his baton—suggested that he bring *Regina* to that house with Horne, whom she thought would make "a great Regina.") In 1980, Bernstein's manager Harry Kraut wrote to Lillian Hellman, asking her permission for Bernstein to revise the opera "with a view toward restructuring its treatment of the Hubbard family in the context of race relations in the South, hoping thereby to make *Regina* a more successful opera." Hellman gave her consent, although she had serious doubts about turning the piece into a work about "race relations," and insisted on approving all changes, as stipulated in her original agreement with Blitzstein. "Unhappily, I think for all of us, I did not enforce that rule with Blitzstein," wrote Hellman to Kraut, "and some major mistakes were made because I didn't."[41]

Mauceri and a former student of his at Yale, Tommy Krasker, completed their revised edition shortly before Bernstein's death in 1990, expanding on the 1954 published score by adding material from the original score and even rough drafts, although they took some cuts of their own. Many of the reinsertions indeed broadened "the context of race relations in the South," made that much more unequivocal by the interpolation of "Naught's a Naught," which had not even made it into the original score. Mauceri and Krasker made other, more idiosyncratic alterations, including repositioning "What Will It Be?" omitting the "I Got a Gal" refrains from "Chinkypin," and, at least for the Decca recording, replacing the final measures with a longer tag found among the composer's papers. Hellman's death in 1984 obviously made the condition of her approval moot.[42]

Mauceri recorded this new version during the Glasgow run, employing the same orchestra and chorus but featuring mostly different principals, including Katherine Ciesinski (joining the cast at short notice) as Regina, Samuel Ramey as Horace, Sheri Greenawald as Birdie, and Angelina Réaux as Alexandra. The British critics attending the Glasgow premiere seemed skeptical about this new version, including Wilfrid Mellers, who suspected the reinstated cuts "a mistake," whereas American commentators reviewing the recording seemed more agreeably disposed: Patrick Smith, for instance, found that the added material helped to give the work "a more cohesive musical envelope," while David Anderson declared the longer prologue "superior not only musically but dramatically," although he questioned the restored passages in the party scene.[43]

The Scottish Opera version in no way established itself as the standard performing edition. On the contrary, subsequent productions of the opera tended to stay closer to the 1953 or 1958 versions, although sometimes with borrowings from the 1991 score. Moreover, opera companies introduced changes of their own, tweaking the vocal and instrumental parts, reshuffling the order of numbers, reinserting some of Hellman's dialogue not used by Blitzstein, and adding original material (including the interpolation, "I'll die in my own way, in my own time," stated by Horace just prior to Regina's "I'll be waiting"). John Mauceri himself presided over a 2003 Lyric Opera production that, citing concerns about perpetuating racial stereotypes, deleted not only the Angel Band but the entire prologue.[44]

Critics rarely knew the work and its history well enough to comment on particular performing versions. Indeed, Bernard Holland's *New York Times* review of the highly abbreviated Lyric Opera production appeared under the header, "'Regina,' With Music Restored." Commentators remained in any case widely divided about the merits of the work whatever the version. Some reviews criticized the opera on racial grounds, with Edward Rothstein (*Times*), in his review of the 1992 City Opera revival, finding the work problematically nostalgic for "the antebellum South." On the other hand, the 2005 Bard production elicited strong endorsements from Anne Midgette (*Times*), who found that the opera's "minstrel-show elements," whatever else, served the opera's "dramatic pacing," which she thought "quite sound"; and Joseph Horowitz (*Times Literary Supplement*), who rated the piece second only to *Porgy and Bess* in the history of American opera—"If he [Blitzstein] lacks Gershwin's human depth and melodic genius, 'Regina' surpasses 'Porgy' in ease and unity of construction"—and urged a production at the Met.[45]

British critic Wilfrid Mellers also commended the work, arguing that, although the negativity of Hellman's play disturbed the "equilibrium between power and compassion" that Blitzstein had achieved in *The Cradle* and *No for an Answer*, the emphasis given to the African-American characters in the opera helped redress this imbalance. Mellers further lauded the work's incorporation of popular elements: "Blitzstein's great achievement is that he has imbued techniques borrowed from the commercial world with the power to hit back—to stand for, rather than against, the human spirit. His embryonic awareness of emerging life, in his 'low and steady' mood, is the real America, beneath the push and go, the America that is still waiting to be born." Brenda Lewis similarly spoke of the opera's "visceral quality" as, although comparable to Verdi, recast in terms of the American experience: "It [*Regina*] is a story about the foremost capitalist society in the world; it is firmly rooted in American history and in the progress of this country. Our power struggles are not for bits of territory or kingships or principalities; they are for money. Marc translated that into music and created an opera about our society and culture that is completely American."[46]

The difficulties, both in terms of production and appreciation of the opera, remain considerable. Selecting a suitable performing edition and mastering a complex score seem only the beginning. The work needs highly accomplished performers as well as strong stage and musical direction alike. Finding an effective tone seems especially challenging, notwithstanding such clues as the "sudden ensembles" that, although limited to one scene, help establish the opera's larger ironic framework. Consideration of the opera in the context of Brechtian theater, including Blitzstein's earlier work, could assist in this regard. Given the work's enduring appeal, such efforts appear all the more worthwhile.

The Threepenny Opera (1950–1954) and Other Adaptations

Blitzstein's longtime interest in translating and adapting texts culminated with his version of *The Threepenny Opera* in the 1950s, but took other manifestations during these later years as well. In early 1950, for instance, when Leonard Bernstein, who had composed songs and incidental music for a Broadway production of *Peter Pan* starring Jean Arthur and Boris Karloff, left for Europe during the show's final rehearsals, Blitzstein served as his "deputy," revising some lyrics to "Dream With Me," "Who Am I?" and "Neverland" and in general supervising the score as needed, for which he received $200 out of Bernstein's royalties. "At this moment, two days before the first preview," he told Bernstein, "the production seems generically right (if you like *Peter Pan* at all), but specifically right almost nowhere." Bernstein wrote back apparently expressing unhappiness about some particulars, to which Blitzstein responded, "Don't be upset about the small amount, $200; I really didn't do much, just about enough to disturb you."[1]

That same summer, the show's co-producer, Peter Lawrence, contacted Blitzstein, away on a working vacation in Bermuda, to ask if he would both adapt and direct Benjamin Britten's children's theater piece, *Let's Make an Opera!* (1949), for Broadway. Ostensibly hoping to repeat the success of *Peter Pan*, in the midst of a solid run, Lawrence decided to bring the Britten opera—another British work with a nursery setting—to New York in collaboration with assistant producer Herbert Berger and the Show-of-the-Month Club, a ticket-selling operation run by the wife-and-husband team of Sylvia Siegler and Lou Cooper (the latter a songwriter who had produced *The Cradle* and *I've Got the Tune* with his Flatbush Players in the late 1930s).

Subtitled "an entertainment for young people," *Let's Make an Opera!* (libretto, Eric Crozier) consists of a two-act play followed by a one-act opera. In the first act, a group of youngsters agree to assist a composer in writing an opera based on a tale set in Iken Hall, Suffolk, in 1810 about an eight-year-old chimney sweep, Sam, who is ingeniously smuggled back home on his first day of work by the children of the manor house. In the second act, the youngsters rehearse the opera, as does the audience, called on to serve as the chorus and learn four songs. The final act consists of the finished opera, "The Little Sweep," with the cast of four adults and seven juveniles assuming various parts, accompanied by the audience and a small ensemble led by a conductor who also participates in the action.

After examining the score, which he deemed, for all its modesty, the "best opera Britten has written," Blitzstein agreed to Lawrence's terms of $3,000 plus a small percentage of the box office gross. He presumably appreciated the work's protest against child labor and its Brechtian stagecraft, but in any event, he found the prospect of stage directing intriguing:

> Up to now, I have not wanted to direct any play, feeling that with my own shows I was far too close to them to have the objectivity essential for good stage direction, and with other men's work that I didn't know enough about what they wanted to convey. Gradually it came over me, however, that perhaps I could direct, for with my own musicals . . . I actually had worked so closely with the director that I had unconsciously absorbed the understanding to stage a show independently.[2]

Blitzstein prepared a two-act version of the work, condensing the play portion into a single act in three scenes, reduced even further to two scenes by the time the work arrived on Broadway. Moreover, although he retained the Iken Hall setting for the "Little Sweep" opera, he provided an American setting for the play, which involved rewriting a considerable amount of the dialogue, including substituting native expressions for British ones, all in accordance with the wishes of Britten (who, "scared that the work will appear very whimsy & old-world," wanted the play portion "adapted to the local atmosphere"). In addition, Blitzstein more circumspectly revised some of the lyrics of the opera itself in order to avoid some racial overtones (including renaming Black Bob, "Big Bob"), or to clarify some unfamiliar phrases (writing "soap-suds," for instance, in place of "soap-balls").[3]

Let's Make an Opera—sans exclamation mark—opened at New Haven's Shubert Theatre on November 22, Boston's Wilbur Theatre on November 27, and New York's intimate John Golden Theatre on December 13. Ralph Alswang created the scenery and lighting, Aline Bernstein designed the costumes, and Lina Abarbanell served as casting director. Norman Del Mar, who had created the pivotal role of the conductor for the Aldeburgh world premiere, came stateside for the production; the other cast members included Randolph Symonette (Big Bob), Elizabeth Wysor (Miss Baggott, later replaced by Rosalind Nadell), Rawn Spearman (Clem, in this version African-American and no longer Big Bob's son, but his apprentice), and Jo Sullivan (Juliet, the oldest of the children), whom Blitzstein later would cast as Polly Peachum in *The Threepenny Opera* and who fondly remembered him as a diplomatic director sensitive to the needs of singing actors. While in production, Blitzstein had to contend with a series of financial crises as well as attempts by the producers to install a co-director. "It was frightful, nightmar-ish, even hilarious," he wrote to Mina Curtiss after the New York opening; "how I kept my head I don't know."[4]

The critics generally responded positively to the Boston premiere, happily enhanced by the presence in the audience of cast members from Cole Porter's latest show, *Out of This World*, also in tryouts. "It is gentle and it is good," reported L. G. Gaffney (*Boston Daily Record*). But reviewing the earlier New Haven debut, *Variety* expressed doubts that Broadway audiences would spend a top ticket price of $4.20 for an "unpretentious" work for "the juvenile trade" that had no star and that was "little more than an elaborated community sing." Indeed, although the production received several good New York notices, having the audience sing—something Thomas Dash (*Women's Wear Daily*) thought more congenial to the British than to Americans— became a liability on Broadway. Although Blitzstein claimed that the premiere audience on the whole had been "wildly enthusiastic," Richard Watts Jr. (*New York Post*) sensed that the "sheepish and bewildered" first-nighters sang "out of a stern sense of duty, but with few indications of ease or pleasure." "It takes all the exuberant let's get together folk spirit of Norman Del Mar to get such non-professionals as Brooks Atkinson to pretend that he is a turtle dove and sing 'prr-ooo!'" teased Howard Barnes of the *Herald Tribune* in reference to his *Times* colleague, who in his own review complained that the songs were "too Brittenesque for Gotham's guys and dolls." The producers hoped that as family fare the work would gain traction going into the holiday season, but the show closed after only five performances—"the saddest death of the season," lamented John Chapman (*Sunday News*), who wrote that the audience "would not accept its very simple charms" and that the producers had erred by inviting the drama, rather than music, critics.[5]

The notices at least praised Blitzstein's direction for its "zest" and "know-how." "I have done an honorable, even imaginative job, with something less than slight material," the composer wrote Mina Curtiss about a work he publicly had deemed Britten's "best." Publisher Leslie Boosey himself approved of the production, informing Britten, "I must say I thought it was very good, quite equal to anything that has been done in England. It did not run for the simple reason that a Broadway audience is far too hard-boiled for a work of that kind." Del Mar, who came to like Blitzstein "so much," similarly wrote Britten, "It has been a good experience even though the outcome was disappointing."[6]

Meanwhile, Blitzstein struggled to collect his fee of $3,000. Over two years later, in early 1952, Lawrence, who had gone bankrupt, and the Show-of-the-Month Club still owed him $900, money he never seems to have recovered. Fortunately, a more successful adaptation loomed ahead.

In the late 1940s, Blitzstein began translating some lyrics from *The Threepenny Opera*, the 1928 German hit with a libretto by Bertolt Brecht (adapted from Elisabeth Hauptmann's translation of John Gay's popular ballad opera of 1728, *The Beggar's Opera*, along with some borrowings from Rudyard Kipling and the fifteenth-century criminal-poet François Villon) and music by Kurt Weill (including one song adapted from the Gay opera). Blitzstein first encountered this caustic Weimar satire of bourgeois mores while in Germany in the late 1920s; and whatever qualms he had about the opera early on, in his mature view, as expressed nearly a decade after his adaptation of the work had been success-fully launched off Broadway in 1954, the piece was "a miracle, a phenomenon, a shining landmark in the history of the international musical theatre," its lyrics "biting and beautiful," its "corniness . . . quite deliberate," its score marked by "wry ironical-sweet tunes, troubled searching tunes, tunes gasping and agonized or blatant and cock-sure," and its opening number, "Mack the Knife" (also known as the "Moritat," from the original German title, the word meaning "murder ballad"), "one of the great songs of the century. Insistent, unavoid-able, it has a relaxed grandeur, a terrifying simplicity."[7]

Blitzstein himself seemed unsure about his initial reasons for adapting these texts; when he called Weill in January 1950 to tell him about his translation of one of the work's songs, "Pirate Jenny," he said, "Call it an exercise, Kurt, or call it an act of love. I don't know which." Blitzstein had been performing numbers from the show in German for some twenty years, and given his intensified interest in translating vocal texts, partly a result of his radio work in London during the war, he apparently now relished the idea of performing them in English. Indeed, he seems to have made the January phone call to Weill in preparation for an up-coming May 17 lecture, "The New Lyric Theatre," at Brandeis University, at which he sang one stanza of "Pirate Jenny" in German and another in English. At any rate, when he showed some of his *Threepenny* lyrics to producer Cheryl Crawford and conductor Maurice Abravanel during the production of *Regina* in 1949, they encouraged him to tackle the entire opera, a notion for which his success trans-lating some scenes from Prokofiev's *Betrothal in a Monastery* might have provided additional impetus.[8]

A need for a workable English version of *The Threepenny Opera* certainly existed, for with its extensive spoken portions, the work could not otherwise hold the boards in English-speaking countries. Gifford Cochran and Jerrold Krimsky had launched their own English version on Broadway in 1933, but that lasted only twelve performances. Several other translations followed, including one by Britishers Desmond Vesey and Eric Bentley authorized by Brecht and published in 1949; but none met with Weill's express approval for stage presentation, in-cluding the Vesey-Bentley, which he thought, according to his wife Lotte Lenya, "stilted, flavorless, the lyrics unsingable, the score quite distorted."[9]

When Blitzstein telephoned Weill in 1950, the latter requested that he sing his English version of "Pirate Jenny" over the phone and asked Lenya to listen in on an extension line. Blitzstein later paraphrased Weill's reaction as follows: "I think you've hit it. After all these years. . . . Marc, do it all, why don't you? The whole opera. I wish you could read the half-dozen 'versions' and 'translations' people have sent me: pfui! You do it. You're the one for it." This warmly collegial account jars somewhat with what's known about their relationship; for if Blitzstein deeply respected Weill as an important pioneer, telegramming his best wishes to the composer on the opening nights of *Street Scene* (1947) and *Lost in the Stars* (1949), as he had *Johnny Johnson* (1936) some ten years earlier, Weill maintained his distance, his dislike of Blitzstein as an imitator of his own work recently exacerbated by the decision of his preferred conductor, Maurice Abravanel, to direct *Regina* rather than *Lost in the Stars*. Weill and Lenya earlier had heard about Blitzstein's translations from Abravanel, who remembered them saying, "Don't mention that name. We don't want anything to do with him." But perhaps hearing "Pirate Jenny" over the phone made all the difference. In any case, Cheryl Crawford helped arrange a meeting between the two composers, later claiming that Weill was so impressed with Blitzstein's lyrics that he "gave Marc the rights to translate the entire work."[10]

Before Blitzstein made much headway with his translations, Weill died of a heart attack at age fifty on April 3. Haunted by one of the numbers from the work, "Solomon Song," on the way home from Weill's funeral, Blitzstein resolved to adapt the entire show. "I have sunk my teeth into a translation of the whole of the *Dreigroschenoper* as a sort of memorial to Kurt," he wrote Leonard Bernstein on April 16. "Folks (Cheryl, Lee Strasberg, Gadg [Elia] Kazan, etc.) are wildly enthusiastic at the seven songs already completed, and it may turn out to be a production." Less than three months later, on July 4, he informed Mina Curtiss from Bermuda, "The whole of the Threepenny-Opera adaptation is done, from Overture to Finale, plus text; and I think I have licked it. A little polishing of lines and lyrics should do it."[11]

Blitzstein at first changed the work's setting from nineteenth-century London to San Francisco of 1890, then Philadelphia of 1910, and, by the time of the script's March 15, 1951, copyright date, New York of 1870, with the mayor's inauguration substituting for the Queen's coronation (as in the adaptation's debut at Brandeis, although he reverted to a London setting in advance of the New York premiere). But on the whole, he prepared a roughly faithful translation of Brecht's revised three-act libretto (1931), including two songs cut from the original score and never before staged, "Ballad of Dependency" and "Solomon Song" (Blitzstein later wrote that had he known about Lucy's song, "Fight About the Property," he would have added that "strong and expletive" number as well), and an expanded gallows speech for the hero, Captain Macheath (also known as "Mack the Knife"), that highlighted the more "explicitly Marxist" nature of Brecht's 1931 text (although Blitzstein hesitated over the line "What is the murder of a man to the employment of a man?" which led him to experiment with variations on "What is an act of vice beside being made Vice-President/Viceroy?" and to offer as yet another alternative, "What is the killing of a man, compared to the subjection of a man?").[12]

Blitzstein consulted Brecht's texts and Weill's piano-vocal and orchestral scores as well as the Villon poems that had provided the basis for some of the lyrics. He also seems to have sought out Kipling's "Mary, Pity Women!" the source for "Polly's Song," and absorbed something from the Vesey-Bentley translation. At the same time, he took considerable liberties with the text in order to create a singable and idiomatic libretto. In the opening stanza of the "Ballad of Mack the Knife," for instance, he added two similar-sounding adjectives ("pretty"/"pearly") and reordered the third line so that the word "jackknife" could coincide with the melody's highest note and the name "Macheath" could provide an additional rhyme ("teeth, dear" and "[Mac]heath, dear"), all the while molding the lyric so as to neatly fit the shape of the melody: "Oh the shark has pretty teeth, dear/And he shows them pearly white./Just a jackknife has Macheath, dear/And he keeps it out of sight" (as compared to Vesey-Bentley's "And the shark, he has his teeth and/In his face they glisten white./And MacHeath, he has his jack-knife/But he keeps it out of sight").[13]

Blitzstein's rather free approach allowed him to exercise his own wit, as in Macheath's reminiscence of his life with his prostitute girlfriend: "A sailor would appear; I got out of bed,/Went out and had a beer, he crawled in instead./And when he paid his bill, back in bed I'd climb,/And say: 'Good-night, my friend, thank you, any time'" ("Tango Ballad"). As in his own music, the humor of such passages involved not just the text, but the interaction of word and tone, other examples including the sighing two-note phrase on the word "blues" ("Instead-Of Song"), the vertical leaps between each syllable of "perpendicular" ("Barbara Song"), and, like perfectly timed punch lines, the long breaks in "So not much fun/had Solomon" and "He [Julius Caesar] screamed en route:/Et tu, you brute!" ("Solomon Song").

For similar reasons, Blitzstein also tinkered with the book, sometimes drawing on the kinds of vaudevillian traditions that had long animated his own work as well as Brecht's. When on the morning of his presumed execution Macheath asks his jailor for the time, Blitzstein originally had the jailor answer, "Where's your eyes?" a near-literal translation of Brecht's "Haben sie keine Augen?" but later changed this to "You got a date?" and eventually "You got an appointment?"

Especially in later years, commentators criticized Blitzstein for diluting Brecht, an impression in part fostered by the expurgated lyrics used for the score's 1954 recording. Granted, at the point where Lucy and Polly call each other "a pile of drek" ("Dreckhaufen") in the "Jealousy Duet," Blitzstein at first opted for Lucy to produce a "fart-sound" (or as he wrote in another script, a "Bronx cheer") and tell Polly to "get lost," and then decided to have Lucy simply say to her rival, "Go peddle your wares somewhere else!"—a tart enough line, especially as rendered by Beatrice Arthur in the original production, but hardly as scatological as Brecht or even the earlier Blitzstein. But overall, Blitzstein flinched neither from the text's profanities—his own makes use of such words as "bastard," "bitch," "crap," and "slut"—nor its bawdiness, even if handled subtly, as Blitzstein emphasized in a 1956 letter to director Sam Wanamaker that touched on his translation of the "Ballad of Dependency":

> When I set out to do it in English, I thought hard, and came up with a series of side-swipes on the lascivious terms and images. I borrowed one notion from Verlaine: the poem that starts "Ces amours qu'on appelle anormales," using sounds that play and pun on the ideas (cf. "qu'on" ["that one"]—"con" ["cunt"]). I'm dead sure I don't have to point out "tool," "charges forth," "conniving cock," "meets," "feels his Old Dependency," "planted in illusion," "lush authority," "lying," "Is Death not stiff enough . . .", etc., etc. But I do it anyway. This means the performance must be sly, clearly exposed, but not overstressed.

Lotte Lenya for one thought Blitzstein's adaptation faithful to Brecht's intentions, calling it "a masterpiece, because his [Blitzstein's] changes are hardly noticeable. Everyone thinks the translation is muted, but I think it's just a matter of language. The German language has a harder sound than English, and you can't get away from that. . . . Brecht is never vulgar. Never, ever."[14]

Indeed, Lenya quickly became a strong advocate for Blitzstein's version, which in 1954 she described to Weill's publisher, Alfred Kalmus of Universal Edition, as "above all, wonderfully *singable*, probably because Marc himself is a composer, and theatrically most effective, because Marc has had long experience in the theatre." Having heard about Blitzstein's adaptation, Eric Bentley himself supposed this the one to be brought before "the American public" (under, he hoped, his direction), as he wrote the composer in November 1951, adding that Brecht, who had moved to East Berlin in 1949, was "well-disposed to you and would only wish to read your script to be finally convinced." In 1952, Blitzstein received official authorization from Brecht, who in 1955 declared his adaptation "brilliant" ("grossartig").[15]

Early that same year, the New York City Opera announced plans to present Blitzstein's adaptation of Weill's "The Beggar Opera" (a misnomer that intimated the work's relative obscurity in America at the time) in the spring, a decision publicly deplored by the Viennese-born music critic Kurt List (an "arch-worm" in Blitzstein's opinion), who thought the opera "a piece of anti-capitalist propaganda which exalts anarchical gangsterism and prostitution over democratic law and order" (in turn prompting Dwight Macdonald to denounce List's commentary as comparable to Soviet censorship). Meanwhile, on February 7, the City Opera, citing budgetary concerns, declared a postponement of the opera until the fall, leaving the impression that the company had buckled under anticommunist pressures. However, Blitzstein, who most wanted Jed Harris to direct the work ("though he is bound to be a large headache") or as lesser alternatives José

Ferrer or Harold Clurman, assured friends that he himself had prompted the cancellation once it became apparent that the company "couldn't get the right director in time for him to feel that he could do a good job in so short a period."[16]

Soon after, Blitzstein, offered a $500 honorarium and expenses, agreed to devise and narrate a concert version of his *Threepenny* adaptation as part of a four-day Creative Arts Festival at Brandeis University organized by Leonard Bernstein and scheduled for commencement week. Presented on the climactic Saturday night concert on June 14 at the university's new open-air Adolph Ullman Amphitheatre, the opera took up the first half of the program, followed after intermission by performances of Pierre Schaeffer and Pierre Henry's ground-breaking electronic composition, *Symphony for a Man Alone* (1950), and Stravinsky's *Les Noces*, both choreographed by Merce Cunningham. The performers in the Weill included Lotte Lenya as Macheath's lover Jenny, a role she had originated over twenty years earlier; David Brooks, the recent star of *Bloomer Girl* and *Brigadoon*, as Macheath; David Thomas, who had appeared in *The Cradle* and *Regina*, as Macheath's nemesis Jonathan Jeremiah Peachum; Mary Kreste as Mrs. Celia Peachum (her "Ballad of Dependency" cut for whatever reason); Jo Sullivan, who had played Juliet under Blitzstein's direction in *Let's Make an Opera*, as Peachum's daughter Polly; George Matthews as both the Street Singer and Macheath's war buddy, Police Commissioner Tiger Brown; cabaret singer Anita Ellis as Polly's rival Lucy; and the Brandeis University Glee Club, prepared by composer Irving Fine, as the chorus. Presiding over a small ensemble that closely approximated Weill's original instrumentation, Bernstein led all with enormous verve.[17]

The audience responded enthusiastically to this debut, with both Blitzstein's lyrics and narration—including his reference to Mr. Peachum as "the pioneer of the organized charity-racket"—eliciting laughter. Harold Rogers of the *Christian Science Monitor* reported, moreover, that the German refugees in attendance, including publisher Hans Heinsheimer, felt the work "so true to Bert Brecht's German original that we were hearing essentially the same piece that had taken Germany by storm 24 years ago." Such a welcoming reception prompted a flurry of interest from New York producers and Blitzstein entered into ultimately fruitless discussions with, once again, the City Opera as well as with friends Billy Rose, who wanted the composer to make unacceptable changes, and Cheryl Crawford, who "couldn't shake the memory of *Threepenny's* earlier failure" and "got cold feet." Plans for a Decca recording of the score with John Raitt as Macheath and Burgess Meredith as Tiger Brown collapsed as well.[18]

Finally, in late 1953, Blitzstein and Lenya agreed to let two young producers, Carmen Capalbo (1925–2010) and Stanley Chase (b. 1928), launch the opera in the 299-seat Theater de Lys (later, the Lucille Lortel), a movie house on Christopher Street in Greenwich Village that recently had been converted into a theater. Meeting with Blitzstein and Lenya at the former's apartment, Capalbo won them over with assurances that he would honor Brecht's and Weill's intentions, even singing some of the numbers, to Blitzstein's accompaniment, in the style of the work's 1930 Telefunken recording. For his part, Blitzstein made a strong impression on the two producers, as Chase later recalled:

> He was a tremendous person in my opinion,—primarily as a human being, second as a writer, third as a musician. In any event, he was just a terrific force, and he played for us that first day a number of the various songs. I really got chills. We actually got chills. Marc played this song and that one, and he always had a cigarette dangling from his mouth. He had this little—this upright piano, and he was just alive with Weill.[19]

Blitzstein and Lenya also liked the intimacy of the proposed venue, notwithstanding the challenge, especially in those days, of attracting critics and audiences to a locale so far from Broadway. Having contracted a short-term lease at the theater beginning January, Capalbo and Chase obtained a two-month grace period and successfully raised $10,000—though the production came in at just under $9,000—by way of small investments from friends, who hoped to make back their money by the end of a planned twelve-week run.[20]

By this point, Blitzstein had revised his text considerably. Dissatisfied with the New York setting, he decided to set the action in nineteenth-century London after all, specifically, the time just before and during the 1838 coronation of Queen Victoria. He accordingly purged his script of such American slang as "squirt," "tootsies," and "punkface." Such changes affected the book more than the lyrics, which generally retained a rather transatlantic flavor throughout this entire process. Indeed, when in 1956 director Sam Wanamaker asked the composer to make some revisions in deference to the work's British launching, Blitzstein balked at the suggestion that he change, in "Barbara Song," the refrain "Sorry" to, as in the original, "No" ("Nein"), not only because he had rhymed the first syllable of "Sorry" with such words as "cigar," "perpendicular," and "far," and because the word allowed a greater "variety of line-readings" than "no," but because "I should have thought the word [sorry] specifically English rather than American."[21]

As in the Brandeis version, Blitzstein redistributed a few songs, taking away both "Pirate Jenny" and "Barbara Song" from Polly, and giving the former to the Jenny, Lotte Lenya, who had sung the number both on the Telefunken recording and in G. W. Pabst's film version (1931), and the latter to the Lucy, Anita Ellis. This naturally gave Jenny and Lucy a larger musical presence, although at the expense of minimizing Polly's role and undermining the signifying reference of "Barbara Song" in the opera's finale. Whatever the propriety of these changes, the decision especially to have Lenya sing "Pirate Jenny" proved shrewd, as she brought down the house at Brandeis with her eerie rendition of the song, as she would proceed to do for years at the Theater de Lys and elsewhere.

Blitzstein further reshuffled some numbers, placing "Pirate Jenny" in the brothel sequence, as at Brandeis, and now "Barbara Song" in the second-act jailhouse scene. To compensate for taking two numbers from Polly, he adapted, at Lenya's suggestion, the bittersweet "Bilbao Song" from Brecht and Weill's *Happy End* (1929) as "The Bide-a-Wee in Soho" for the character to sing in the first-act wedding scene in lieu of "Pirate Jenny." (In 1952, he also began preparing various drafts of "Surabaya Johnny," also from *Happy End*, a project that occupied him as late as 1959.) Blitzstein similarly helped fill the hole left by repositioning "Barbara Song" by moving Mrs. Peachum's "Ballad of Dependency" from the second to the first act, its last stanza from the third to the second act.

Blitzstein continued to tweak the lyrics as well. In deference to Capalbo's concern that the phrase "May heavy hammers hit their faces" might suggest a communist subtext, he changed "hammers" to the even more gruesome "hatchets." He also continually toyed with "Mack the Knife," originally providing nine stanzas, like Brecht, plus a reprise of the opening stanza, his own idea; then nine stanzas including the reprise; and finally, seven stanzas including the reprise, with others offered as optional. The stanzas themselves changed as well, with Blitzstein, realizing that the names of Macheath's four girlfriends could be made to fit the song's opening phrase, writing a new quatrain that had no basis in Brecht: "Sukey Tawdry, Jenny Diver,/Polly Peachum, Lucy Brown—/Oh, the line forms on the right, dear,/Now that Mackie's back in town" (in this instance, deciding that the British "queue" would not do as well as the American "line").

Blitzstein and Lenya agreed to let Capalbo direct the opera, his limited experience notwithstanding. Saul Bolasni (who remembered Blitzstein as "a very peculiar man—rather colorful and flamboyant") designed the costumes, William Pitkin, the sets. The production called for twenty-one actors (with the same actor doubling Filch and the Messenger), including four gangmembers, four prostitutes, and two cops, supplemented by a small chorus of beggars (typically comprised of understudies and smaller roles). After considerable coaxing, Capalbo and Blitzstein, along with Lenya's new husband, George Davis—to whom the composer dedicated his adaptation "with enormous gratitude"—convinced the fifty-five-year-old actress, self-conscious about her age, to assume the role of Jenny. Otherwise, the cast largely consisted of relatively young and unknown actors willing to work, like Lenya herself, for five dollars a week during the rehearsal period and a base of twenty-five dollars after the show opened.[22]

Of the original cast, aside from Lenya, only Jo Sullivan (Polly) had participated in the Brandeis performance. The other cast members included Scott Merrill (Macheath), Leon Lishner (Peachum), Charlotte Rae (Mrs. Peachum), George Tyne (Tiger Brown), Beatrice Arthur (Lucy), Gerald Price (Street Singer), and John Astin (Readymoney Matt). Merrill, whose primary experience had been as a Broadway dancer, surmised that Blitzstein "wasn't so keen on my doing the role," and the composer indeed wondered whether Merrill could handle the part's vocal and acting demands, although at the same time, he described him as "*very* interesting. . . . Sinister, good-looking animal-sex face—body not solid, but electric." Of this original cast, Arthur and Astin later became especially well-known through their work on such television sitcoms as *Maude* and *The Addams Family*, respectively.[23]

Samuel (Sandy) Matlovsky, the musical director, coached the singers, as did Blitzstein, meeting privately with the principals at his apartment. Blitzstein transposed Lenya's part lower in order to better accommodate her tessitura, as he had at Brandeis, and similarly provided Merrill with several lower notes in "Love Song" better suited to his voice. Beatrice Arthur simply took most of her part down a full octave, as on occasion Merrill did as well. Blitzstein's version also differed from the original in having the gang members join in on the final refrain of the "Army Song," the Messenger recite rather than sing his lines, and, as in the Telefunken recording and the Pabst film, the Street Singer conclude the whole with some additional stanzas of "Mack the Knife," an ending that reestablished a dark, cynical tone after the ironic sublimity of the final chorale.[24]

As at Brandeis, Blitzstein remained essentially faithful to Weill's dazzling orchestration, with its complex doublings of reeds, brass, keyboards, plucked strings (including prominent use of banjo), and percussion, although he redistributed the scoring for eight rather than seven players; dispensed with flute, bassoon, cello, and double bass; and retooled a few doublings. He also chose not to use the original orchestration for "Ballad of Dependency," but instead to score the number for solo piano and, at the very end, trombone. Situated at the side of the orchestra in full view of the audience, the band included such accomplished players as clarinetist Charles Russo, who admired the precision of Matlovsky's conducting.[25]

Influenced by the French troupe led by Madeleine Renaud and Jean-Louis Barrault, whose 1952 American tour he had helped manage, Capalbo experimented with some epic theater techniques over and above the prescribed use of titles, including having the actors address the audience and staging the Messenger's entrance from the rear of the house. The style of the whole combined aspects of Victorian London and Weimar Berlin—Sullivan sang "The Bide-a-Wee in Soho," another showstopper, à la Marlene Dietrich—filtered through a contemporary American sensibility, without any attempt to simulate British accents. Capalbo and Lenya also encouraged Merrill, concerned about appearing effeminate on stage, on the contrary to "camp it up" and have "fun with the part," which he increasingly did over time.[26]

During the rehearsal period, Blitzstein, in what Capalbo referred to as "bursts of enthusiasm," would yell things to the actors, to the point that the director had to ask him to stay home. Still, Capalbo contrasted the composer, who "tended to lay back," with Lenya, who could be petulant with any number of people involved in the production, including Blitzstein. On one occasion, as Capalbo recalled, after a friend of Blitzstein's gave a poor audition for the musical directorship, Lenya "ripped into him [Blitzstein] for about twenty minutes" while he sat quietly, occasionally saying, "All right, Lenya, all right." Capalbo and Chase suspected that "what she was really scared of was that Marc Blitzstein was going to get credit for all this," a suspicion confirmed when the *New York Times* published an article on January 2, 1954, entitled, "Blitzstein Work Due Here March 2," prompting accusatory phone calls from her to both Capalbo and Blitzstein. Abravanel similarly recalled some resentment on Lenya's part toward Blitzstein, who, however, never lost his great affection for her, according to Capalbo: "He was very protective of her, as though she were his mother, and was respectful of her as Kurt's widow."[27]

As suggested by the *Times* article, Lenya had cause for concern, in that for many New York theater-goers at the time, Blitzstein's name meant as much as if not more than Weill's, let alone Brecht's. Indeed, although the production advertised the work as "Kurt Weill's *The Threepenny Opera*," the program books featured Weill's and Blitzstein's names in the same-sized type, the posters, nearly so, with Brecht's name appearing in smaller fonts. The marquee of the Theater de Lys even announced the names "Weill" and "Blitzstein" in equal size above "Threepenny Opera." However Brecht felt about all this, at least he successfully negotiated 40 percent royalties for himself, with another 5 percent for Elisabeth Hauptmann, leaving Lenya and Blitzstein to split the remaining 55 percent.

After the first of two scheduled previews leading up to the March 10 premiere, Capalbo convinced a reluctant Blitzstein to cut about forty-five minutes of material so that the opera could come in at about two hours and forty minutes. Blitzstein already had removed Lucy and Polly's bedroom scene, but now he made many additional excisions; most of these concerned the spoken dialogue, although according to his notes, he also shortened a few of the musical numbers. A call for some brisker tempos helped speed things along as well.[28]

Widely reviewed, the March 10 premiere (not, as earlier advertised, March 2, the birthday of both Blitzstein and Weill) met largely with excellent notices. Although Robert Coleman (*Daily Mirror*) disapproved of the play's "slick jibes at industrialists, ministers, police officials and even the Bible," many others noted the work's continued appeal, including Harold Clurman (*Nation*), who wrote, "The state of mind is one of social impotence so close to despair that it expresses itself through a kind of jaded mockery which mingles a snarl with tears.... We do not live in such a time ... but it makes the mood irresistibly present and, strangely enough, induces us to take it to our hearts with a kind of pained affection."[29]

A number of commentators especially commended Blitzstein's contribution, perhaps no one more so than Virgil Thomson: "Marc Blitzstein's translation of the Brecht text is, to my guess, the finest thing of its kind in existence. He has got the spirit of the play and rendered its [sic] powerfully, colloquially, compactly. And his English versions of the songs are so apt prosodically, fit their music so perfectly that one can scarcely believe them to be translations at all." Later in the year, Brandeis composer Arthur Berger similarly held up Blitzstein's work as exemplary, as did, in 1960, opera composer Jack Beeson, who thought the translation "the equal of the excellent German original by Brecht."[30]

On the other hand, although William Becker (*Hudson Review*) thought the adaptation in many ways "superior" to the more "faithful" Vesey-Bentley version, he faulted Blitzstein for distorting the flavor of the original, identifying his "prime mistake" as "attempting to make the words too witty in themselves, and picking a slick and frivolous form of Broadway wit to be guided by." Bentley criticized the translation along similar lines—according to Lenya, he did so "cautiously in print, and viciously in private"—but years later, admitting that he had been "excessively snotty" about the 1954 production, took a more liberal view of the matter, recognizing that Blitzstein's approach, described as "very free, leave out what's not easy or politic to leave in, make it a good Blitzstein lyric," had its own viability. "Blitzstein and I used to quarrel," he added. "There was sibling rivalry, and both the brothers wanted to own Dad (B[ertolt]B[recht]). But we agreed on a fundamental point . . . that the place to translate Brecht songs is at the piano. The translator has to sing them—with their accompaniment."[31]

On April 24, about a month after the show opened, Blitzstein offered his own assessment to David Diamond: "'The Threepenny Opera' is a nondescript production of a masterpiece; and the masterpiece comes through. My part (in translating and making it available) satisfied me, and is covered with public glory." But as he told the readers of *Saturday Review*, he remained aware of the limitations posed by any translation: "I regard my rôle as that of a relayer, a middle-man; I have simply made negotiable to our American audiences an opera I have adored since my Berlin student-days. . . . All translations—all, I say—are bound to be failures; one must be content to settle for that which fails least," sentiments repeated to journalist Meryle Secrest on the occasion of the adaptation's arrival at Arena Stage in Washington, D.C., on May 14, 1963, in what Blitzstein deemed a "superb" production directed by Alan Schneider, with whom he established a friendship.[32]

The Theater de Lys production at first attracted in large part German refugees—Marlene Dietrich reportedly attended opening night—but good reviews, including somewhat delayed ones by Atkinson and Thomson, and inexpensive ticket prices, including a top of $3.60, helped draw more diverse audiences. According to the terms of their contract, Capalbo and Chase had to vacate the theater at the end of their three-month lease, but by the time the production closed on May 30 after ninety-six performances, they had recouped their initial investment.[33]

In the course of this limited engagement, Martin Wolfson—who had created the role of Nick Kyriakos in *No for an Answer*—replaced Leon Lishner as Peachum, and Mildred Cook, Charlotte Rae as Mrs. Peachum. This cast change enabled Blitzstein to restore some of Peachum's speeches, for as the composer explained to Sam Wanamaker, Lishner was more of a singer than an actor "and with not much in the way of direction, most of his long speeches went for nothing."[34]

In late April, Wolfson also joined the original cast in recording the work for MGM Records. (Lenya had felt wary about approaching one of the bigger companies like Columbia or RCA Victor.) Blitzstein trimmed some of the score to fit a single long-playing disc and sanitized his lyrics under eleventh-hour pressure from MGM executives. In several instances, this simply involved substituting a word like "damned" or "ass" with something less offending, although concerns over references to rape, prostitution, premarital sex, and illegitimate pregnancy meant overhauling a few numbers more extensively, such as replacing two stanzas from "Mack the Knife" (including the one about the assaulted little Susie that concludes "Wonder what got into her?") with alternative quatrains. The revisions for "Tango Ballad" similarly involved rewriting not only occasional lines ("I covered her, and she took care of me," for instance, became "I cared for her, and she took care of me") but whole stanzas. One of the earliest recordings of an off-Broadway show, the album received high marks by the critics and eventually sold hundreds of thousands of copies.[35]

During the run of the show, Blitzstein accompanied Lenya on "Mack the Knife" and himself sang the "Solomon Song" at the piano on *Polly and Jerry*, a television show hosted by Polly Bergen and her husband Jerry Courtland. Discussing the "Solomon Song," the composer marveled at how "the melody seems to skip right past the lyric," telling his listeners, "watch how the lyric stops and the melody goes right on."[36]

After the production closed at the end of May, Capalbo and Chase, eschewing offers from Broadway producers, placed the costumes and sets in storage and waited—a year and a half, as it turned out—for the Theater de Lys once again to become available. In the interim, Blitzstein and Lenya sanctioned a few regional productions, including one opening March 29, 1955, by Cleveland's Karamu Lyric Theater directed by Benno Frank and Helmuth Wolfes that featured the African-American soprano Zelma George as Mrs. Peachum; and another by the Lowell House Music Society, opening a month later on April 28 under the music directorship of Howard Mayer Brown, that involved such other Harvard student musicologists as Frank D'Accone, Laurence Berman, and Colin Slim, along with student composer John Perkins, and that more faithfully presented the full play and original orchestration. Meanwhile, Brooks Atkinson sustained local interest by periodically exhorting the Theater de Lys—especially when panning some new show there—to "bring back *The Threepenny Opera*."[37]

The production finally returned to the de Lys, once more under the direction of Capalbo and Matlovsky, on September 20, 1955, this time in partnership with Lucille Lortel (whose husband Louis Schweitzer had purchased the theater). The Bolasni costumes and Pitkin sets came out of storage, Peggy Clark provided lighting, and Lenya, Merrill, Sullivan, and Arthur recreated their roles, now joined by Tige Andrews (Street Singer), Frederic Downs (Mr. Peachum),

Jane Connell (Mrs. Peachum), and Richard Verney (Tiger Brown). The salaries went up, as did ticket prices. The production received excellent notices, in some ways even better than before, and Lewis Funke of the *Times* accurately predicted a long run.[38]

After the show reopened, Edmond Pauker and John Krimsky, who early in the piece's history had acquired the English production rights, filed suit against Capalbo, Chase, Lortel, Schweitzer, Blitzstein, and Lenya (officially Karoline Weill-Davis), asking that the court block performances of the work at once, an injunction not granted on account of the hardship this would bring to the actors. The matter was eventually settled out of court, with Pauker and Krimsky obtaining a cash settlement of a few thousand dollars and a small percentage of royalties, one that cut further into Blitzstein's relatively modest income from the show.[39]

In early 1956, Blitzstein's adaptation arrived in England, playing one week at the Theatre Royal in Brighton before opening at the Royal Court in London on February 9. Produced by Oscar Lewenstein, Wolf Mankowitz, and Helen Arnold, and directed by actor-director Sam Wanamaker, this production featured Bill Owen (Macheath), Maria Remusat (Jenny), Eric Pohlmann (Peachum), and Georgia Brown (Lucy). Caspar Neher, who had worked on the original Berlin production, created the sets, and composer-conductor Berthold Goldschmidt led the pit band.

Busy at home with a production of *King Lear*, Blitzstein could not travel to England to help ready the show, and so Lewenstein and Wanamaker consulted him by mail about the libretto and other matters. Ultimately, the script changes largely involved either expurgating a few bawdy lines or Anglicizing a few expressions, such as "kick-up-the-arse" for "kick-in-the-pants" and "beefsteak tartare" (as in the Brecht original) for "hamburgers *raw*," Wanamaker explaining, "Hamburgers are a very definite American specialty." Blitzstein had concerns about the choice of musical director, telling Wanamaker, "Although I know and admire Goldschmidt, I worry that he will be influenced by the original German production or records, in the matter of style, particularly *tempi* of the numbers. *Our* recording makes them all slightly too fast; but the Germans are inordinately slow and dragging." He recommended instead Norman del Mar, but Wanamaker told him that the latter "hates the score," and in the end he hired Goldschmidt, with whom he agreed that the "too brash" approach found on the MGM recording "would need to be toned down for a British audience."[40]

The Royal Court production, which transferred to the Aldwych Theatre in March, received largely good notices, including one from Kenneth Tynan, who described it as "loyally Brechtian," although in contrast to the American reviews, virtually none took note of Blitzstein, whose name carried little weight abroad. In the end, the production, as at home, helped popularize the work, viewed as that much more foreign in light of the country's familiarity with *The Beggar's Opera*; one review even referred to Peachum—played by the Austrian-born Eric Pohlmann—as "unambiguously a German Jew in his humor, his reflections and his reactions," while another referred to Blitzstein's translation as "American-Jewish."[41]

Meanwhile, some jazz and popular artists had begun to record "Mack the Knife," in large part thanks to the cast album's bowdlerized lyrics, without which vocal renditions presumably would have been banned from radio and television playtime. Columbia Records's George Avakian, a friend of Lenya's, played a seminal role in this regard. First, he hired bandleader Turk Murphy to score a song chart for Louis Armstrong and his All Stars. He then presided over two sessions: one on September 22, 1955, with Murphy's band that produced a purely instrumental track as well as separate vocal versions by Murphy in English and Lenya in German; and another on September 28 with Louis Armstrong and his All Stars that similarly yielded an instrumental version as well as a vocal solo by Armstrong and a duet for Armstrong and Lenya. (At Avakian's suggestion, Armstrong substituted, for comic effect, "drooping [down]" for "dropping [down]," and "Lotte Lenya" for "Polly Peachum.") At about this same time, MGM Records's Ed Cole had pianist Dick Hyman's trio (with guitar and bass) record the number as well, with Hyman whistling the tune and playing a prepared piano. By the end of the year, both a Columbia release of the song spliced together from Armstrong's vocal and instrumental versions and MGM's version with the Hyman trio had climbed to the top of the charts.[42]

Although not the first jazz release of the song as sometimes claimed—clarinetist Sidney Bechet had recorded "La complainte de Mackie" in France in early 1954—the Armstrong and Hyman renditions triggered within a few years a number of other covers variously known as "Mack the Knife," "Moritat," and "The Theme from The Threepenny Opera," including instrumental recordings by Bill Haley and the Comets, Richard Hayman (with Jan August), Tito Puente, Sonny Rollins, Billy Vaughan, and Lawrence Welk, and similarly varied vocal releases by Rosemary Clooney, Bing Crosby, Bobby Darin, Ella Fitzgerald, Mary Ford (with Les Paul), Peggy Lee, and Anita O'Day. Sammy Davis Jr. also recorded the number for a 1963 dubbed English release of a German film version of the work that for the most part used Eric Bentley's translation.

The recording by Bobby Darin, which sold millions of copies, enjoyed special success, earning the young singer a 1959 Grammy Award for "record of the year" and Blitzstein an All-American Award from Radio-Television Daily for "the song hit of the year." Like Armstrong, Darin substituted Lotte Lenya's name for Polly Peachum, but more extensively played with the text, inserting the word "babe" now and then, exclaiming "eeek!" after "oozing life," and concluding with a repeat of the sixth stanza rather than a reprise of the first. Bringing the song's sexual subtext to the fore, Darin's hip version influenced future interpretations, as did Richard Wess's accompanying arrangement, which involved modulations up a semitone beginning with the third stanza, thereby glamorizing the variation structure underpinning Weill's original score.

Fitzgerald's recording also won a Grammy, this one, the 1960 award for best vocal single in the popular music category. Performed live in Berlin, Fitzgerald prefaced her rendition by saying "We hope we remember all the words," and in fact, in the course of the song, she largely began to improvise lyrics, including the following: "Oh Bobby Darin and Louis Armstrong,/They made a record, oh but they did./And now Ella, Ella and her fellas,/We're making a wreck, what a wreck of 'Mack the Knife.'" Such interpolation of names, which harkened back not only to Armstrong's and Darin's mention of Lotte Lenya, but Blitzstein's recitation of Macheath's girlfriends, marked later performances as well, including a 1994 duet by Frank Sinatra and Jimmy Buffett in which the former sang that Armstrong and Darin performed the music "with so much feeling,/That old blue eyes, he ain't going to add anything new," to which Buffett responded, "Oh yes you do!"

Blitzstein found the song's many renditions "more or less acceptable," although he thought performers "often weighed down by a self-consciousness amounting to awe." In 1958, he singled out Armstrong's release and Turk Murphy's less successful instrumental version as "having caught, in American terms of course, the sardonic insouciance asked for." Even earlier, in late 1955, he recommended that Sam Wanamaker, in casting the Street Singer for the London production, listen to Armstrong's "fabulous" recording: "It brings us absolutely into the world of the work—American in style, of course, so that an English equivalent should be found." And in 1962, he praised Bobby Darin's "sensational rendering," adding, "I am partial to Louis Armstrong's gravely [sic] version myself; also to Ella Fitzgerald's darling goofy one, with all my careful lyrics handsomely messed up." The "Tango Ballad" (recorded by Hyman as "Three-Penny Tango") and "Bilbao Song" (as mentioned, originally from *Happy End*) also found their way into the popular repertoire, the latter particularly indebted to singer Andy Williams's 1961 hit version of the song to newly devised lyrics by Johnny Mercer.[43]

The popularity of "Mack the Knife" appalled the likes of John Lewis Carver, who in the anticommunist scandal sheet *Top Secret* warned his American readers that "the knife in that song is really a dagger with which Brecht is stabbing them in the back." But the song's continued success only invigorated the show's popularity and helped draw tourists and college students to the Theater de Lys. In 1956, Lenya won a Tony Award for featured actress in a musical; Merrill, a Tony nomination for featured actor in a musical; and Capalbo and Chase, a special Tony for "a distinguished off-Broadway production." On March 16, 1958, in honor of the show's thousandth performance, NBC presented excerpts on its *Wide Wide World* television show featuring some new members of the cast, including the Macheath, Jerry Orbach, who had understudied for the production since 1955 (and who stayed with the show until 1959). And on July 31, 1958, Matlovsky unveiled a concert version of the opera with Lenya and the New York Philharmonic at Lewisohn Stadium before a crowd of about 9,500.[44]

On February 4, 1961, *The Threepenny Opera* gave its 2,249th performance, topping the record set by *Oklahoma!* as the longest-running musical in American history (even if seen by far fewer people, given the capacity of the Theater de Lys). The show finally closed on December 17 of that same year, after 2,611 performances (or, if one counts the initial 1954 run, 2,707). By this point, the production had been seen by an estimated 750,000 people, had made more than $3 million, and had proved a fertile training ground for up-and-coming actors, over 700 of whom had taken part in the show, including besides Beatrice Arthur, John Astin, and Jerry Orbach, such other future stars as Edward Asner (Peachum), Estelle Parsons (Mrs. Peachum), and Jerry Stiller (Crookfinger Jake). (Two performers, William Duell, the Filch/Messenger, and Marion Selee, the Molly, stayed with the show for its entire off-Broadway run.) None of the accomplished actresses playing Jenny could quite rival Lenya, but some thought the original Street Singer, Gerald Price— whom Blitzstein might have wanted as the male lead from the start—a particularly fine Macheath.[45]

In 1960, the show traveled with Matlovsky to the West Coast for successful engagements at the Marines' Memorial Theatre in San Francisco, where it earned some good reviews despite a miscast Anna Sten as Jenny, and at the Music Box Theatre in Los Angeles, where Lenya replaced Sten. And in September 1961, after a short run at the Paper Mill Playhouse in Millburn, New Jersey, the production, now with Merrill as Macheath and Gypsy Rose Lee as Jenny, kicked off a planned thirty-five week tour of sixteen cities that, however, survived a mere two weeks in Toronto: "Anybody who wants to see Gypsy Rose Lee is not interested in *Threepenny Opera*," commented Merrill. "And anybody who wants to see *Threepenny Opera* doesn't want to see a stripper." After the show closed off Broadway in late 1961, Blitzstein's adaptation, represented at first by the Tams-Witmark Music Library, and after 1984 by the Rodgers & Hammerstein Theatre Library, became a staple of amateur and stock companies around the country.[46]

Although Blitzstein never published either a libretto or a piano-vocal score of his adaptation as he had hoped—in 1956, Brecht's son Stefan refused the rights, citing his recently deceased father's objections to having this particular translation published, although according to Capalbo, Stefan himself disliked the idea of so free an adaptation in print—some of his lyrics appeared in the form of sheet music. Between royalties from stage productions, record and sheet music sales, and radio and television playtime, the composer made far more money from this "labor of love" than from any other enterprise of his career. At first, the proceeds amounted to several thousand dollars per year, but by the early sixties, with the success of "Mack the Knife," his royalties generated enough income for him to start purchasing securities, although his financial situation still remained tenuous from year to year. He would have earned even more money had he obtained publishing royalty rights for instrumental performances of "Mack the Knife" in particular, but he at least managed to obtain some share of such profits through the American

Society of Composers, Authors, and Publishers (ASCAP), successfully arguing that since his lyric for "Mack the Knife," by way of Armstrong's recording, launched the success of the song, he deserved some recompense for instrumental versions.[47]

In discussing the huge American popularity of *The Threepenny Opera* and its "Mack the Knife," some observers placed its appeal in the context of an antiestablishment backlash against McCarthyism. Others pointed to a more general appreciation of the work's dark view of man. Capalbo, for instance, recalled those tourists from the hinterland who would comment after seeing the show, "It's the truth," while Will Friedwald reported that Armstrong reacted to Gerald Price's recording of "Mack the Knife" by saying, "Oh, man! This cat is exactly the type of character that I knew multiplied so many times in New Orleans. A real bad guy who charms absolutely everybody," a response comparable to Pearl Bailey's reading of the same song on a January 24, 1960, episode of the *Dinah Shore Show*. In 1962, Blitzstein offered his own thoughts: "I wonder if the racy scenes, the nonchalant amorality of the characters (blithely treacherous to one another one minute after a display of virginal innocence) are not at least partly responsible. The college-student crowds kept coming and enjoying and quoting; the sophisticates refused to be left out; the music-lovers wilted with pleasure at Weill's sweetness of tune and acidity of harmonic invention." Blitzstein modestly left unmentioned his own decisive contribution, as did many commentators.[48]

In time, other English versions appeared, including those prepared by Ralph Manheim and John Willett (1976, with Raul Julia as Macheath), Robert MacDonald (1986, with Tim Curry), Michael Feingold (1989, with Sting), Robert MacDonald and Jeremy Sams (1994, with Tom Hollander), and Wallace Shawn (2006, with Alan Cumming). Moreover, although a 1989 film version with Raul Julia used Blitzstein's lyrics as a template, director Menahem Golan and musical director Dov Seltzer thoroughly revamped them. The relative merits of these various versions were debated. Such experts as Kim Kowalke, who still regarded Blitzstein's adaptation as "the best," even if burdened by "all the baggage of tradition," better understood the shortcomings of some of these later translations than those who assumed that the edgier the version, the more authentically Brechtian. Blitzstein's surely was the most lyrical of all such adaptations, and remained in wide use even into the twenty-first century. As for "Mack the Knife," a 1985 release by Sting established a vogue for the Manheim-Willett translation as seen from subsequent recordings by Lyle Lovett (1994) and Nick Cave (1995); but Blitzstein's memorable version remained the standard English one among jazz and cabaret singers, both at home and abroad.[49]

About the same time that Blitzstein met with Billy Rose in late 1952 to discuss *The Threepenny Opera*, the latter announced plans to present European operas in English beginning the following fall at the Ziegfeld Theatre, which he then owned and operated; and in this context, he proposed that Blitzstein adapt some familiar opera, suggesting about fifteen titles, but not *Carmen*, whose adaptation by Oscar Hammerstein he already had presented on Broadway as *Carmen Jones*. "I don't know," wrote Blitzstein to Mina Curtiss; "maybe 'Traviata'; that would be a reach!" After deciding that the available English versions of *La Traviata* lacked "passion" and "wit," and getting Rose to agree to his terms, Blitzstein began adapting the Verdi opera using the working title, *The Wayward*.[50]

As Verdi and his librettist Francesco Maria Piave originally intended, Blitzstein set the opera in Paris circa 1850, about the time of the composition of the opera and the novel by Alexandre Dumas fils on which it was based—an atmosphere Blitzstein described as one of "decadent glamor," with "women, flowers, perfume, drink, gaming, love and l'amour and underclothes." The project occupied him intermittently for a few years, as suggested by *Threepenny Opera* playbills that stated for some time that the composer was "at work on a translation of Verdi's 'La Traviata' and various short operas of Offenbach." When John Gutman, assistant manager of the Metropolitan Opera, inquired after the translation in November 1954 on behalf of "a very important and financially valid producer outside of New York," Blitzstein assured him that he had completed the first act and about half of the second, and that he had sketched out the rest.[51]

Indeed, a completed first act survives among the composer's papers, both in typescript and as written above the melody line in a published vocal score featuring both the original Italian and an English version by Natalia Macfarren (1899). A few translated passages from Acts II and III likewise survive, including drafts of Violetta's third-act aria, "Addio del passato." The marked contrast between Macfarren's translation and Blitzstein's own can be measured by comparing virtually any few lines of text, Macfarren's "Mysterious power, guiding the fate of mortals,/Sorrow, sorrow and sweetness,/Sorrow and sweetness, of this poor earth" from Alfredo's "Un di felice," for instance, with Blitzstein's "What is this clamor, what is it in my heart?/This torment, torment and sweetness,/Torment and sweetness, here in my heart?" For the first-act "Drinking Song," Blitzstein simply dispensed with the original text and created a new lyric inspired by the British proverb "a cat may look at a king." He went so far as to prepare a fair copy score of this number for soprano, tenor, and chorus, perhaps for demonstration or even possibly publishing purposes (and as such the piece received a premiere by the Oceanside Chorale under Leonard Lehrman on June 4, 2005). But for whatever reason, he never seems to have completed his translation of the opera as a whole.[52]

As for the "short operas of Offenbach," as early as October 1952, also in connection with Rose, Blitzstein began planning a free adaptation of the French composer's one-act opéra bouffe, *L'île de Tulipatan* (1868), as *Tulip Island*. The original text by Henri Chivot and Alfred Duru concerns a romance between a young male royal, Hermosa, raised as a girl, and a girl, Alexis, raised as a boy. Blitzstein reconceived the plot in various ways, in one instance sketching out a romance, along the lines of Julian Thompson's satirical hit *The Warrior's Husband*

(1932, adapted by Rodgers and Hart as *By Jupiter,* 1942), about an effete man, shipwrecked on a remote Polynesian island, and a masculine hunter-princess; as the story progresses, he becomes "quite virile," and she, "quite feminine."[53]

However far Blitzstein progressed with this adaptation, he left behind versions of three numbers published in 1955 as *Three Offenbach Songs:* "Canary Song (Couplets De [sic] Colibri)," "Hermosa's Song (Couplets Du Canard)," and "Duettino." Drawing on Offenbach's "Couplets d'Hermosa" for its text, but "Couplets du Canard" for its music, "Hermosa's Song" satirizes Hermosa's tomboyish nature, while the more faithfully adapted "Canary Song" for Alexis mocks that character's sentimentality. In the "Duettino," another loose adaptation, the two characters deliriously celebrate each other: "He: You're convex. She: You're concave. Both: That is just what I crave. She: You are blond. He: You're brunet. Both: Can it get better yet?"

Blitzstein dedicated *Three Offenbach Songs* to the noted Russian-American mezzo-soprano Jennie Tourel, whose premiere of the work at a Town Hall recital on March 5, 1955, delighted the critics. Composer Ned Rorem also liked the work, in 1979 recommending these "madly clever translations of Offenbach's songs" to his friend, singer Judy Collins. But although Blitzstein included some slight provision for "Duettino" when performed as a solo as at the premiere, the set essentially constitutes a sort of minidrama for two.[54]

In the context of these Verdi and Offenbach projects, mention might be made too of Blitzstein's translation of Georges Bizet's satirical lyricizing of a waltz by the British bandmaster composer Daniel Godfrey (1831–1903), a translation presumably undertaken in the early 1950s as an assist to his friend Mina Curtiss, then at work on her Bizet biography (1958). "Gounod, Meyerbeer, Berlioz and [Ernest] Reyer/Are all dust compared to thee!/Mozart and Weber, Schumann and Wagner/Have expired!/Come, let them be buried!" reads in part this literal translation by Blitzstein, who plausibly identified with Bizet's send-up of the once popular Godfrey.[55]

Following the success of *The Threepenny Opera,* Capalbo and Chase, in collaboration with Lotte Lenya, hoped next to launch Brecht and Weill's three-act opera *The Rise and Fall of the City of Mahagonny* (1930) in an English adaptation by Blitzstein. Even without a cash advance or the promise of a production, Blitzstein— "driven," as he wrote in 1958, "by vanity or imagination, but mostly by an almost unconscious, almost irresistible hunger to plumb the depths of a great and unique modern opera"—began work on the project.[56]

Preceded by the shorter *Mahagonny-Songspiel* of 1927, *The Rise and Fall of the City of Mahagonny* scathingly satirizes the modern capitalist metropolis. After years of toil in Alaska, four lumberjacks—including the work's hero, Jimmy Mahoney—arrive in Mahagonny, a city founded by three outlaws led by the unscrupulous Leocadia Begbick. (Blitzstein, who referred to the city of Mahagonny as having "for verbal image Miami," filed a 1958 *Life* magazine photo-spread of

Miami and Palm Beach by Henri Cartier-Bresson among his *Mahagonny* materials.) Mahoney rebels against the vapid decadence of the city and loses all his money, a capital offense in this materialistic pleasure dome. After Mahoney's execution, the city succumbs to chaos and dissolution.[57]

Although Blitzstein denied that the work "influenced my youth" as had *The Threepenny Opera*, the opera might well have left its mark as early as *Regina* (1949), which, as Eric Gordon notes, contains a parody of bourgeois salon music similar to one found in *Mahagonny*, while Regina herself, although a creation of Lillian Hellman, bears a likeness to Begbick. In any case, Blitzstein came to admire, as he wrote in 1958, the "personal tenderness, solemnity, and ribald garish poetry" of the work's libretto and the "great elegance" of its music: "If I seem to be grabbing for superlatives," he concluded, "bear with me; I am completely gone on the subject of 'Mahagonny.'"[58]

In 1955, probably late in the year, Blitzstein prepared a literal translation of Brecht's twenty-scene version of the work; and the following summer, while in Brigantine, New Jersey, with sister Jo and brother-in-law Ed (who in 1953 had converted the garage apartment close to their oceanside home into a "dream-studio" for him), he worked on adapting this script to Weill's twenty-one-scene piano-vocal score of 1929 (including the "Benares Song" later omitted by Brecht). Blitzstein renamed the eponymous town Magnet City, a phrase that echoed the sound and rhythm of Mahagonny (with its accented first syllable), but that also played on Begwick's reference to a "City of Nets" ("Netzestadt") and evoked further the town's magnetic appeal to men with gold. Blitzstein accordingly considered such working titles for the opera as "The Birth and Death of Magnet City" and "A City Called Magnet." He also revised the names of the characters, including creating a list of three-syllable Anglo-Irish names for the hero, such as Ackerman, Dockerty, and Flanagan, that could substitute for Mahoney, given a first-syllable stress by Brecht and Weill.[59]

During the summer of 1956, Capalbo and Chase traveled to Brigantine to hear Blitzstein audition a "rough draft" of his adaptation. "We were thrilled with it," recalled Capalbo, who entered into negotiations with Brecht's American son Stefan in order to obtain rights for a New York production. In February 1958, Stefan assured the William Morris agency that he and his mother, actress Helene Weigel, now executors of the Brecht estate, were "anxious" that Capalbo, Chase, and Blitzstein "do a production of Mohogonny [sic]," and Blitzstein wrote to Stefan about a possible early fall opening, although by this point he still only had drafted some of the scenes and songs.[60]

In March 1959, Stefan Brecht asked Blitzstein for some of these sketches so that he and his mother could "get a somewhat clearer picture of the situation." Then in May, Stefan told Blitzstein that his mother was "worried" about his "position and intentions," prompting the composer to write Weigel, in Stefan's presence, "Heaven knows there are enough beasts in the American business-jungle; I like to feel that I am not a part of that wolf-pack." In early July, on his first trip to Europe since the war, he had the chance to speak directly with Weigel, meeting with her in Berlin on several occasions. After saying his farewells, Blitzstein, who liked Weigel "enormously," recorded in his diary, "We have got on," and on his return home resumed work on the opera.[61]

That September, Blitzstein published a review of John Willett's book *The Theatre of Bertolt Brecht*, elucidating the playwright's theories, thereby continuing the efforts of his wife Eva some twenty years earlier:

> This concept [epic theater] is daringly anti-Aristotelian: it rejects atmospheric or emotional persuasion, audience-involvement, audience-catharsis; it demands floodlit exploration, unsentimental demonstration, audience estrangement, final audience realization. Set forth as a concept, this may seem forbiddingly cold; but so intense is the Brechtian energy, so varied the ingenuity, so deep the insight and compassion, and so unerring the sense of "spass" or human comedy, that in actual reading (and certainly in a good performance) the plays take on qualities of an intellectual circus.[62]

What happened next regarding *Mahagonny* remains unclear. According to Capalbo, who thought Stefan Brecht "an absolute tyrant," the latter refused to back Blitzstein's adaptation. Perhaps he thought Blitzstein's treatment too free. In any case, in 1960, Lenya, feeling the need to maintain good relations with Stefan, proposed to Capalbo that he use instead a recent unpublished translation by W. H. Auden and Chester Kallman, whose adaptation of Brecht and Weill's *Seven Deadly Sins* for a Balanchine staging (1958) featuring Lenya with the New York City Ballet had proved successful. However, feelings of disloyalty toward Blitzstein aside, Capalbo rejected this suggestion, finding the Auden-Kallman script "interesting . . . from the literary point of view," but problematic "theatrically. . . . I sang all those songs . . . and you'd have to stuff those words into a shoehorn." Some understanding for Capalbo's preference for Blitzstein's "thrilling" adaptation over Auden and Kallman's can be gleaned from a comparison of their translation of the "Havana Song," in which the prostitute Jenny, like Blitzstein's Moll in *The Cradle*, haggles over a price with a client; whereas Auden and Kallman dispense with any rhymes aside from the homophones "to" and "two," Blitzstein echoes Brecht's musicality through rhymed couplets, at the same time catching the poet's colloquial flavor, translating, for instance, "und sonst nichts" ("and that's it") as "I hope to die": "Think it over please, John Jacob Smith./Think it over please, you know what thirty dollars buy./Ten pair of stockings, I hope to die./I come from Havana;/And my mother was white as you are./How often did she say:/'Don't throw your life away./For just a couple dollar bills, as I once did,/Or you'll end up like me, and God forbid.'/Think it over please, John Jacob Smith . . . /Think it over please . . . /John Jacob Smith."[63]

At one point, Stefan Brecht, impressed with Jule Styne's *Gypsy* (1959), suggested that the show's lyricist, Stephen Sondheim, adapt the opera, and Capalbo duly attempted to interest the latter in the idea, but Sondheim felt the assignment beyond his capabilities. Meanwhile, Blitzstein continued to work on the piece at least as late as 1962. Whether he intended to complete his adaptation remains unknown, but in any event, he left behind only a fragmentary script. After his death in 1964, the interested parties at last settled on librettist Arnold Weinstein, whose version, which premiered off Broadway in 1970, closed after eight performances, despite a rave by Clive Barnes in the *Times*.[64]

In tandem with his *Mahagonny* adaptation, Blitzstein also translated Brecht's *Mother Courage and Her Children: A Chronicle of the Thirty Years' War* (1939), sometimes working on both projects virtually simultaneously. A biting indictment of war, the play concerns an itinerant peddler, Mother Courage, and her three young adult children—Eilif, Swiss Cheese (or in Blitzstein's version Holey-Cheese), and Kattrin—all three of whom are killed in the course of the action. Brecht completed the play in the early days of the Second World War, its pacifism in tune with communist support for the Nazi-Soviet pact, but out of step with the general mood in the West, helping to explain its early fitful history. But by the 1950s, with fears of nuclear conflict widespread, audiences seemed better prepared to appreciate the work, which received its American premiere in San Francisco in 1956 in a version by Eric Bentley. Blitzstein told David Diamond in October 1957 that he long had wanted to adapt the play, which he "loved," but "the problem was how to set modern Augsburger dialect, on a 17th-century Polish-Swedish subject, into some kind of English style which would be both obedient and effective," a nut he apparently cracked to his satisfaction, completing a literal translation in 1956 and a more polished "authorized" version the following year.[65]

One alluring aspect of the play for Blitzstein surely involved the prominence of song lyrics throughout—a total of no fewer than nine (twelve including reprises), most notably set to music by Paul Dessau in the late 1940s as featured in the work's legendary 1949 production by the Berliner Ensemble. Planning to use Dessau's music, which he described to Diamond as "not sensationally good, but it will work theatrically," Blitzstein entitled these nine numbers as follows: "Courage's Song," "Song of the Old Crone and the Rookie," "The Song of Fraternizing," "Hearsay Song" ("Song of the Hours"), "Song of the Big Surrender," "Soldier Song," "Song of the Great Souls" (in essence the "Solomon Song," which Blitzstein had reinstated into *The Threepenny Opera*), "Song of Shelter," and "Lullaby." Blitzstein also adapted another song, "Peter the Pipe," composed by Brecht and Dessau in 1951 especially for Ernst Busch, who had played the Cook in the Berliner Ensemble production; and a few stanzas of the Lutheran hymn "A Mighty Fortress is Our God," which Busch had interpolated into this latter production as well.[66]

Blitzstein examined Brecht's revised text published by Suhrkamp (1950) and Eric Bentley's translation published by Doubleday (1955), which he thought "as usual, dreadful, although generally accurate," as well as published and recorded versions of Dessau's music, including the full score for seven instruments and recorded excerpts by the Berliner Ensemble (in German) and Germaine Montero (in French). He also communicated directly with Dessau (1894–1979), who like Brecht and Eisler had settled in East Germany, and who had become Brecht's principal musical collaborator. Blitzstein might well have met Dessau during the latter's years of exile in New York during the war; but in any case, the Jewish-German composer now counseled Blitzstein not to include the "Peter the Pipe" song unless he could find a Cook as "excellent" as Ernst Busch, adding that the actor playing Eilif needed to be "a good dancer" as well as "a little bit musical."[67]

In November 1957, the translation completed or almost so, Blitzstein signed a contract with Stuart Scheftel for a production of the play that would star Scheftel's wife Geraldine Fitzgerald under the direction of Orson Welles (who recently had worked with Blitzstein and Fitzgerald on a City Center production of *King Lear*). "If Orson Welles ever gets off his neurotic ass, we are ready to produce," wrote Blitzstein to Diamond in March 1958. But the production "struck a snag" of some sort. Later in 1958, Blitzstein also sent copies of the script overseas to director Tony Richardson, who told him, "I would love to direct it," and to fellow translator John Willett, who offered to recommend the translation to Brecht's British publisher, Methuen, as "the best available" even if "the songs remain a problem." Nothing came of these prospects either, although Blitzstein eventually received a reader's report from Methuen with various suggestions.[68]

Then in March 1959, the *Times* announced that producer Roger L. Stevens in cooperation with Leigh Connell, Theodore Mann, and José Quintero had tentative plans to launch Blitzstein's version of the play with actress Siobhán McKenna under Quintero's direction. (Blitzstein also imagined for this production Maureen Stapleton as Kattrin, Robert Morse as Holey-Cheese, E. G. Marshall or Ed Begley as the Chaplain, and Theodore Bikel, Eli Wallach, or Jack Warden as the Cook.) On that same day, Stefan Brecht wrote to the composer that the producers had not definitely selected his version, and that they were considering having either Auden or Richard Wilbur at least write the lyrics, although he assured Blitzstein, "Provided the lyrics are redone, I should be delighted to see them use your translation." While in Berlin in July 1959, Blitzstein went over his translation with Dessau and presumably discussed the script as well with Weigel, a famous Mother Courage, during their time together. Meanwhile, producers Lee Paton and Robert Welber announced their own plans for a Broadway mounting of the play as adapted by Eric Bentley, with Britten and Milhaud alternately mentioned as composers. Both rival production teams claimed the right to present the play's New York premiere, with Stefan Brecht backing the Blitzstein faction; but by the time the dust settled in early 1962, after a legal battle that established Bentley's rights, the two groups had dissolved. On March 28, 1963, the play finally opened on Broadway in a new version by Bentley produced by Cheryl Crawford and Jerome Robbins with Dessau's music used over Robbins's objections.[69]

This latter production won a Tony nomination for best play, but closed after fifty-two performances. Whether Blitzstein's adaptation would have been more successful, all things being equal, remains hard to say, but his script offers a compelling blend of winsome humor and deep poignance, with special freedoms taken with the lyrics, as the opening of Mother Courage's "Lullaby" might suggest: "Baby is sleepin'—/What noise is out there?/Neighbor's kid wailin'/But my kid don't scare./Neighbor's kid is raggèd/But you wear a gown/From the nightgown of an angel/I hemmed upside-down."[70]

Blitzstein's adaptation sat on the shelf for decades until his centennial in 2005, when, thanks to the exertions of Leonard Lehrman, director David Fuller used the script for a revival of the play by the Jean Cocteau Repertory (later, the Exchange) at the 140-seat Bouwerie Lane Theatre in New York's East Village. The production, which starred Lorinda Lisitza and ran for a little over a month, received mixed reviews, although the critics by and large commended Blitzstein's translation, its dated slang notwithstanding. "Some day the Blitzstein script may have an impact which will enhance the resonance of *Mother Courage and Her Children* . . . but it probably will need the theatrical muscle and imagination of a new age Orson Welles to reach a significant audience," wrote Brad Bradley, who thought the adaptation "possibly even better in creating an internationally meaningful vernacular than does his [Blitzstein's] earlier service to *The Threepenny Opera*." Following this premiere, actress Estelle Parsons and director Richard Block hoped to collaborate on a largely student production of the Blitzstein adaptation, which both thought "certainly the best of the available English versions of the play," but unforeseen circumstances, including conflicting commitments, prevented such plans from materializing.[71]

In the early 1960s, Blitzstein further became involved with the show *Brecht on Brecht*, a theatrical presentation of excerpts of the playwright's prose, poetry, and drama arranged by George Tabori, and presented by the Greater New York Chapter of the nonprofit American National Theatre and Academy (ANTA) at the Theater de Lys, initially for a few performances beginning on November 14, 1961, and then, as produced by Cheryl Crawford, for an extended run starting on January 3, 1962. Blitzstein's contribution essentially consisted of two of his *Threepenny Opera* songs, "Pirate Jenny" and "Solomon Song," sung once again by Lotte Lenya, but with the latter number featuring a newly translated stanza about the "wissensdurstigen Brecht," which Blitzstein rendered as "that hound for answers, Brecht."

For songwriter Bob Dylan (b. 1941), *Brecht on Brecht*, but especially "Pirate Jenny," proved a revelation, expanding the folk singer's "little shack in the universe . . . into some glorious cathedral, at least in songwriting terms." Apparently obtaining the off-Broadway cast album to *The Threepenny Opera*, Dylan closely analyzed "Pirate Jenny," with its "ship, a black freighter" (Blitzstein's memorable take on Brecht's "ship with eight sails"), and began to compose songs inspired by that number, including "When the Ship Comes In" (1963). Several annotators even contend that Dylan's contact with "Pirate Jenny" marked a decisive turning point in his artistic development, typically crediting Brecht in this regard, with only a rare observer like Sean Wilentz acknowledging Blitzstein's mediating role: "The words that laid Dylan flat on his back, and forever changed his thinking about songs and songwriting, came from an inventive, powerful new American translation of Brecht's German lyrics, written by Marc Blitzstein." The relevance of "Pirate Jenny" to the protest movements of the 1960s and a rising generation of popular musicians could be evidenced further by performances of the song by Nina Simone (1964) and Judy Collins (1966).[72]

Near the end of his life, Blitzstein also translated, possibly with *Brecht on Brecht* in mind, a Brecht lyric set to music by Eisler, "Ballad of Mary Sanders, the Jews' Girl" (1935), a stinging response to the Nuremberg Laws of September 1935, which, among other things, prohibited sexual relations between gentiles and Jews. In the poem's last stanza, the townspeople heckle Marie Sanders, "the Jews' girl," who's driven around town in her slip, her head shorn, with a sign around her neck because of her Jewish lover or husband. Blitzstein, who completed his final version on March 6, 1962, replaced Brecht's reference to the anti-Semitic propagandist Julius Streicher with that of Hitler: "The flesh goes gray in the pretty houses,/Tonight the Fuehrer speaks again./God almighty, if they had half an ear,/Can't they tell what is happening to them?" Brilliantly fitted to Eisler's powerful music, this adaptation stands as one of Blitzstein's crowning achievements as a translator.

From modest beginnings, Blitzstein's interest in adapting foreign songs, plays, and operas increasingly preoccupied him in his later years. He devoted himself to such projects not only in order to help make some admired works more accessible to an American public but for his own personal satisfaction and stimulation. Indeed, he undertook most of these adaptations without any clear prospects for publication or performance, even if in the case of *The Threepenny Opera*, such efforts proved among the most lucrative of his career.

This side occupation, which drew on his command of various languages, brought the composer into friendly contact with such congenial figures as Verdi, Offenbach, Bizet, Prokofiev, Dessau, Eisler, Weill, and Britten, but with no one more so than Brecht, whose importance to Blitzstein, although decisive since at least the mid-1930s, seems to have become that much more so after the war. This presumably involved Brecht's use of modernist techniques in the interest of a progressive social message related to—but independent of—dominant trends in both the Western democracies and the Soviet bloc, a position that made him all the more valued in the context of the Cold War. "Brecht's libretto offers no rostrum, no facile remedy for the chaos and disaster it excoriates," said Blitzstein of *Mahagonny*. Deeply shaken by Brecht's death in 1956, he became all the more determined "to get his work done here." No artist in any medium probably meant more to Blitzstein, who in turn served Brecht's legacy with extraordinary imagination, vigor, and skill.[73]

Reuben Reuben (1949–1955) and This Is the Garden (1956–1957)

After completing *Regina* in late 1949, Blitzstein began a new musical drama for which he composed the "Rose Song" (dedicated to Mina Curtiss) in February 1950. In April, he declared the piece "nearly half-finished!" and over the summer the *New York Times*, having reported the show's working title, "Reuben Reuben," in May, announced a Cheryl Crawford production for the coming season. But it would take another five years to complete and produce the work. Blitzstein struggled especially with the libretto, telling Mina Curtiss in 1952, "I think I abuse the talent by insisting on self-collaboration." Seeking at least some guidance from Crawford and director Robert Lewis, he also decided in early 1953 to have a "session" with Lillian Hellman, "who is hard, knowledgable [sic], and decent; she promises to let me have it with both fists. If I can get mad enough at her, something may come of it; aside from the off-chance that she may be actually helpful."[1]

As had long been his custom, Blitzstein traveled about while working on the piece, including stays with Mina Curtiss in Ashfield and his sister Jo in Brigantine. In the fall of 1951, he repaired to Bermuda, where he resided at the twelve-acre estate in Southampton that friend Anna Wiman had inherited from her father, producer Dwight Deere Wiman, and from where Blitzstein wrote a series of letters to Curtiss that reported on the "palatial" grounds, the town's "dull" bar scene, the "enormous amount of homosexuality among the married upper classes," and, begging forgiveness for sounding a "typically colonial-tourist" note, the "natives, both colored and Portuguese," whom he found "enchanting, both physically and in terms of nature." And in early 1952, he spent two months at Yaddo, his third residency there.[2]

The work finally started to fall into place in the course of 1953. In July, he told David Diamond, "I am . . . wildly happy with the opera. In a way it's a rejuvenation for me; I never wrote so easily, so well, or with such flair. The big problems of the text itself are nearly ironed out now." And in November, he wrote Bernstein, who he hoped might conduct the premiere, "I think it is a sublime 'lightweight'; so sublime it may not be lightweight at all: have I got into a Mozartean groove?" But difficulties continued to arise, and in August 1954 he wrote Curtiss, "Reuben has a way of deserting me at the very stage where I think it's all plain sailing. It can be fatigue, of course, but I think more than that: I've been too long at it. . . . they [Crawford and Lewis] want it *finished*, as I do desperately." Finally completing a satisfactory draft in the early fall of 1954, he signed a contract with Crawford on December 18 specifying a $4,000 advance against royalties and an additional $4,000 for the orchestrations exclusive of copying, terms that had been agreed on over a year earlier.[3]

Blitzstein continued to revise and orchestrate the work (for four winds, six brass, harp, piano, percussion, and strings) right up until the world premiere in Boston on October 10, 1955, assisted by his copyist Arnold Arnstein and eventually orchestrators Hershy Kay and Bill Stegmeyer as well, although he prepared most of the orchestral score himself. In early 1955, he also sought the advice of lyricist Johnny Burke (best-known for his songs with Jimmy Van Heusen) about the libretto, and over the course of the year, further consulted with such members of the company as choreographer Hanya Holm, musical director Samuel Krachmalnick, and actor Eddie Albert.[4]

Although work on the piece necessitated turning down such tempting offers as providing music for Crawford's 1951 production of Ibsen's *Peer Gynt*, Blitzstein had neither the means nor the inclination to devote himself exclusively to this one composition over so long a period, and he accordingly undertook other projects during its lengthy genesis, including adapting *The Threepenny Opera*. But the work, essentially six years in the making, occupied him longer than any other of his career, as evidenced by an extraordinary trail of hundreds of pages of notes, sketches, and music, many of them scrupulously dated.

In February 1950, Blitzstein described the piece as a "picture of New York: the gaiety, plight, awareness and unawareness of anger, bitterness, insouciance, ardor, urgency, even wisdom, mellowness. All trapped: fighting the trap, or supine within it." And in March, he summed up the story as involving a protagonist, Reuben, intent on committing suicide at dawn, goaded on by a bartender and saved by the heroine, Nina. In part he intended the work as a modern take on Goethe's *Faust*, with Reuben as Faust, the bartender—variously named Jimmy and Tad, but eventually Bart—as Mephistopheles, Nina as Gretchen, and the action transpiring on Walpurgis night (typically celebrated on the last day of April, although Blitzstein set the opera in September, presumably to coincide with the work's depiction of the feast of San Gennaro). By happenstance, Stravinsky embarked about this same time on his own Faustian opera with W. H. Auden and Chester Kallman, *The Rake's Progress* (1951), which Blitzstein apparently did not witness until its American premiere in early 1953 and which he thought, in any case, "a bore of an opera-buffa," with "three lovely airs" and some "beautiful scoring," but perverse in its "withdrawn-remote text" and "the even more sedate score," the bearded Baba "as nasty a piece of transvestiture as I ever want to encounter: since overt homosexuality is non-negotiable on an operatic stage, Rakewell takes the monstrosity to wed and to bed."[5]

In his notes for *Reuben Reuben*, Blitzstein alluded not only to Goethe, but to many other literary figures, including Homer, Aristotle, Shakespeare ("get Shakespearean" he told himself with regard to the "Rose Song"), Byron, Keats, Heine, Rimbaud, Shaw, Conrad, Proust, Joyce, F. Scott Fitzgerald, William Faulkner, Hart Crane, and Jean Genet as well as critics John W. Aldridge, Kenneth Burke, Benedetto Croce, and especially Paolo Milano. He further gleaned something from James Bridie's hit play *Daphne Laureola* (1949), a satirical look at postwar Britain that played on Broadway in the fall of 1950; and from James Jones's novel *From Here to Eternity* (1951), which Blitzstein described to Bernstein as "fearfully impressive, and heartbreakingly childish; and also wrongheaded to a degree. First steps in lumpenfascism; (a term which will depress you all over again)—but a *through* [sic] job, with that totality and utterness which gets me even when I howl in protest" (as opposed to William Goyen's 1950 novel *The House of Breath*, whose "poetry and sex" seemed to him "like one long puling wail, it's like fifteen *Partisan Review* stories in a row").[6]

Blitzstein's notes referenced the other arts as well, including John Huston's gritty film portrait of urban crime, *The Asphalt Jungle* (1950), and Jerome Robbins's ballet about predatory female insects, *The Cage* (1951), but especially the great silent film comedies of Charlie Chaplin, Buster Keaton, the Keystone Cops, and Harold Lloyd, whose antics helped inspire the first-act finale, with Reuben hanging from a chandelier above a jeering crowd. The relatively few musical allusions among Blitzstein's notes, meanwhile, mostly concerned Verdi, Offenbach, Weill, and Britten, precisely those composers whose operas engaged him during these years as either director or adapter, suggesting that he partly undertook these projects in light of his ongoing original work. *The Threepenny Opera* in particular embodied that "hard-boiled mood . . . with pity and terror and comedy coming through" for which he aimed, while Verdi's ability to sustain a scene by way of an underlying rhythm—"it stays a waltz, or a polka, right through the plot," he observed with regard to portions of *La Traviata*—provided a model for some of his own formal procedures. Along with Mozart, whose bicentennial he celebrated in June 1956 at the Stratford Festival by participating on the panel "What Mozart Means to Modern Music," Verdi also helped Blitzstein toward a new simplicity: "Listening to the Verdi *Requiem*," he wrote to himself in early 1951, "I see my way to the simplest of musical means. The sheer G-major to B-flat-major quiet cadence [presumably the end of the 'Dies irae'] makes my heart break." Blitzstein found further musical inspiration elsewhere, jotting down among his *Reuben* sketches themes from Bernstein's *Age of Anxiety* (1949) and Burton Lane's ballad "Too Late Now" (1951).[7]

Blitzstein's writings shed additional light on his artistic views during this period, including his 1950 article "Notes on the Musical Theatre" for *Theatre Arts*, and his April 22, 1956, Ford Hall Forum lecture "American Opera Today" delivered at the New England Conservatory's Jordan Hall, two essays that reveal a subtle shift of emphasis from that of the late 1940s: a maintained respect for such musicals as *Show Boat* and *Oklahoma!*—"opera can certainly learn from them, particularly in the matter of communicativeness," he argued—but with a sharper distinction drawn between the Broadway musical and the more integrated "lyric theatre" of Thomson, Gershwin, Weill, Menotti, and himself, the latter repertoire compared rather to the *opéras comiques* of France and the theater pieces of the Weimar Republic.[8]

In his article for *Theatre Arts*, he took special note of Menotti's *The Consul*, which had premiered in Philadelphia on March 1, 1950, and then on Broadway on March 15. Deeming the opera "less adventurous" than Menotti's *The Medium* (1946)and "naive in every department—musical, literary, political—except theatrical, where it is completely sure and knowing and shrewd," he thought its drama "more Grand Guignol than Kafka, more thriller than thrilling—on the edge of cheapness" and deplored its "political equivocation and safeness," which he described as "if anything, anarchic." And yet he argued that with its "landslide success"—the opera enjoyed 269 performances on Broadway and won some prestigious awards—"a new form has come into its own on our theatre scene. Call it the music-play, the lyric theatre, the musical theatre, what you will; it is perhaps the first true American musical form (just as jazz is probably the first true American musical idiom)." Whether in his own story of a suicide averted, rather than one committed, Blitzstein intended *Reuben* in part as a response to the Menotti work—he penned an early précis of *Reuben* on March 16, 1950, the day after *The Consul* premiered on Broadway—the two works shared some common concerns.[9]

While at work on *Reuben*, Blitzstein wrote too a review of Menotti's subsequent opera, *The Saint of Bleecker Street* (1954), in which he declared the piece "a triumph in technical-theatrical matters, but a sad failure in its choice of theme, or the capacity to make that theme negotiable," explaining with respect to its opposition of religion and skepticism, "Since religion is an eminently suitable subject for operatic treatment, while skepticism, being ideational, offers almost no chance for any emotional outpouring, we watch the Church-theme walk all over its opponent. Were the incest-motif [between Michele and his sister Annina] developed, were we made to grow within it and be purged by it, as in classic Greek tragedy, or Strauss' *Elektra*, or Stravinsky's *Oedipus Rex*—then indeed we might have something." By striking coincidence, the first acts of both *Saint* and *Reuben* included depictions of Little Italy's San Gennaro festival, scenes that threw the differences between these two works into sharp relief, although Blitzstein singled out Menotti's handling of just this section, among some others, as "full of lyricism and ingenuity, with sumptuous orchestral sounds, and interesting play of stage and pit." Still, singing "The Black Swan" from *The Medium* at a 1956 Ford Hall Forum lecture on American opera, he opined that that earlier opera remained the composer's "best work to date."[10]

During these same years, Blitzstein also published a short review of the one-act opera *Double Trouble* (1954) by Weill's contemporary Richard Mohaupt, a work he found "skillful to a degree" and "continuously engaging," although with the sort of "paucity of good tunes" that he thought, with the exception of Weill, characteristic of modern German opera. Some further musical commentary appeared in Blitzstein's correspondence from this time. In a 1955 letter to David Diamond, for instance, he described Lukas Foss's *Parable of Death* (1952) as "lousy," "Uttermurk," "grandiose, and utter nonsense."[11]

With respect to *Reuben*, Blitzstein early on distinguished three types of comedy: "comedy which is all innocence," "comedy which is burlesque-to-satire," and "comedy which comprehends Tragedy, which interpenetrates the tragic, is not different from it; which surrounds it." Whereas in the past he had written comedies largely of the second type, he intended this new work to exemplify the third type, periodically alluding to "the comic-tragic thing which I have been seeking," an approach he seems to have associated especially with Chaplin.[12]

At first, he imagined that aside from the hero and heroine, Reuben and Nina, the cast members would take on double and triple roles in order that they might be "seen by us both realistically and as they appear to Reuben," a young veteran given to hallucinations. He thought, for example, that the villainous Bart might reappear as various authority figures, including a priest, a major, a doctor, and Reuben's father, an idea that had it been realized might have heightened the connection between the opera and Berg's *Wozzeck*. In the end, he backed away from this conceit, although not entirely, with most of the minor cast members of its one and to date only production assuming multiple parts.[13]

Blitzstein's sketches flesh out what can be learned about the characters from the libretto. In his mid-twenties, Reuben, an air force radio-gunner who has recently served with the occupation forces in Germany, has just received a medical discharge from an army hospital at Maxwell Field, Alabama, and has arrived, for the first time in his life, in New York. He grew up motherless among a circus in the Midwest. His father, Pop, a trapeze artist known as "the human dart," was a "poetry-loving" pacifist "scornful of human-kindness or communication" who would lapse into silence and write notes to his son. Some months before the start of the action, Pop plunged to his death from the high wire before an "enthralled audience," leaving behind this note to his son: "I wish I could take you with me. I never wanted you to grow up in this crazy world." Along with some "harrowing" wartime experiences and general postwar tensions, Pop's suicide has left Reuben a "psychically crippled man full of guilt and fear" suffering from selective mutism, that is, the inability to speak in certain situations. He mutters the jingles "Reuben and Rachel" and "Shave and a Haircut"—making up his own lyrics that reveal his anxiety—or juggles balls to help calm himself. Vacillating between despair and exaltation, when he finds himself able to speak, he sometimes becomes grandly and bizarrely loquacious. Blitzstein fashioned some of Reuben's crazed talk after examples of schizophrenic speech cited in Louis Berg's 1933 book *The Human Personality*, while the opera's title, drawn from the first line of the 1871 song "Reuben and Rachel" (music, William Gooch, lyric, Harry Birch), "Reuben, Reuben, I've been thinking," further points to his unintegrated personality.[14]

Although the composer's former boyfriend Bill Hewitt no doubt served as a model for Reuben, Blitzstein likely had in mind, as in *No for an Answer*, the time's disaffected youth more generally, a generation represented not as before by Paul Bowles but by his successors, the so-called Beat writers, including Jack Kerouac, who like Hewitt was an emotionally disturbed veteran. At the same time, Blitzstein seems to have drawn on his own psychological problems ("the tragic-lost acute stage of R's sickness can be helped at first hand by your own," he wrote in his notes) as well as those of producer Irene Selznick, who apparently suffered from some form of mutism. Moreover, he had such varied figures as Androcles, Heine, Schubert, and Chaplin in mind when he wrote of Reuben's character as revealing "the pure-in-heart, the childlike—perky, ridiculous, every once in a while to himself too," further commenting that Reuben in the course of the play "becomes Chaplin. That is, from a lostness and a dilemma-ridden guy, he becomes the boy with real resistance to outside assault."[15]

Of modest circumstances like Reuben, Nina has just found employment as a telephone operator. (In earlier drafts, she's an actress as well, but Blitzstein later fudged on this detail, dropping the "too" from her question to Reuben, "You're in show business, too?") As explanation for the hostility she shows Cop Kerry in her opening scene, Blitzstein notes that she once had reported an assault to the police, who subsequently harassed her. "Natural," "healthy," and "carefree"— "She throws off filth, disease, evil"—she helps make Reuben "whole," while he reveals to her "the terror and hardship and dark side of life." Much as Hewitt presumably inspired some aspects of Reuben, so his girlfriend Luellen, surmises Eric Gordon, possibly provided inspiration for Nina.[16]

For the character of Bart, the malevolent bartender, Blitzstein took some cues from Billy McGlory, an infamous New York saloon keeper of the late nineteenth century about whom he read in Herbert Asbury's colorful history of *The Gangs of New York* (1926), a book that he also consulted while adapting *The Threepenny Opera*—a link that intimates other similarities between these two stage works. The owner of the bar-and-grill that constitutes the opera's principal mise-en-scène, the "runty but powerful" Bart, a precinct boss, runs various rackets. ("Never can tell about bartenders," commented Blitzstein in his notes.) About to be deposed by his top henchman Malatesta (an Italian gangster who never appears), Bart desperately awaits some sign that his luck will change. Blitzstein described him "on the realistic level" as a repressed homosexual whose interest in Reuben is "sadistic, and tease-playful," though "on another level" as "Mephisto, embodiment of evil." Meanwhile, Bart's girlfriend, the Countess, a nightclub singer, apparently evolved from early plans to have a "vamp, coquette" who could serve as Helen to Nina's Gretchen.[17]

The opera takes place on a warm September Sunday night, from 9:30 to dawn, at the present time (that is, the early 1950s) on Manhattan's Lower East Side. The scenario that follows mostly derives from a script, a piano-vocal score, and a roughly corresponding orchestral score assembled in the spring and summer of 1955, materials extensively modified in advance of and during the Boston run in October.[18]

Act I. Scene one. The Street, 9:30 P.M. After the overture ("Monday Morning Blues"), the curtain rises to reveal, in pantomime, Fez, a petty hustler, giving the young punk Blazer a pickpocket lesson (on Third Avenue near 12th Street, according to the composer's notes, which also reveal the derivation of their names: Fez, the fake Armenian, from his hat; Blazer, from his fluorescent jacket). After they exit, Reuben enters. A troubled veteran unable at times to talk and just discharged from the army for medical reasons, he reminisces about his early life in the circus and declares his intention to give away his belongings ("The Circus"). Spouting phony Armenian, Fez returns, suspiciously eyes Reuben, and leaves. Jane, lost, enters and asks Reuben's help finding the BMT subway; but unable to speak, he frightens her away. Fez, still jabbering, enters and exits. Reuben resolves to talk, imagining a harmonious conversation ("Thank You"). Fez reappears, and disarmed by Reuben's ingenuousness, drops his Armenian disguise and warns the young veteran, "The woods are full of thieves!" Mr. and Mrs. J. Doakes (according to notes, an Irish-American couple) enter squabbling, which unnerves Reuben. When Jane reappears, Mr. and Mrs. Doakes point her in the right direction, and the three, joined in the background by Reuben, hold a polite conversation ("Never Get Lost"). After Jane leaves, the Doakeses resume their quarrel until they finally notice Reuben and exit as well. Decrying the world and sensing danger ahead, Reuben decides he needs a drink.

Scene two. The Bar, 10:00 P.M. Four Barflies—Doc, Ignatz, Lonesome, and Mr. Chipper—confide their problems to Bart, the precinct boss who owns the saloon ("Tell It To Bart"). Worried that he's about to lose power to an Italian rival, Malatesta, the superstitious Bart anxiously awaits a lucky sign, flipping coins with his lover, the Countess, a sex-crazed nightclub entertainer ("It's In the Cards"). The Barflies resume their chit-chat, ignored by Bart ("Tell It To Bart"/"It's In the Cards"). Bart takes the entering Reuben as providential, as he tells the Countess, who departs. As the Barflies daydream, Reuben, by way of written notes, orders a drink and informs Bart about his Pop, a trapeze artist known as the "human dart," who, blaming "world tension," jumped to his death. As the Barflies talk about some recent suicides, Reuben gives Bart another note that reads "A high place," and Bart tells his bewildered assistant Harry to help Reuben find such a spot. As Harry and the Hopalong Kid, a boy passing by the bar dressed as Hopalong Cassidy, mime a shootout, the boy's shadow appears like a monster to Reuben. Panicked, Reuben finally utters the words "Bridge, that's where," and after delivering a speech at once hostile and euphoric, departs for the Manhattan Bridge ("Shave and a Haircut"). Bart orders Harry to tail Reuben and telephones Malatesta to lay odds that Reuben will kill himself by dawn, while the Barflies take all in stride ("Tell It To Bart," reprise).[19]

Scene three. The Bridge, 10:30 P.M. Having just landed a job as a telephone operator, Nina, a young Italian American, amuses herself by daintily spitting over the rail of the Manhattan Bridge ("Song of the Arrow"). Assuming that she means to jump, Reuben attempts to rescue her, but she takes his action for an assault. Cop Kerry comes to Nina's defense, but she, realizing that the mute Reuben meant to save her, poses as his girlfriend and chastises the officer. As Reuben and Nina depart, shadowed by Harry, Cop Kerry wonders why people pick on him ("Cop's Lament").

Scene four. The Bar, 11:00 P.M. Confirming his bet with Malatesta, Bart anticipates a change in his luck ("It's In the Cards," reprise). Nina and Reuben enter, and over beers, Nina muses on their budding relationship ("Such a Little While") and invites Reuben to accompany her to Mulberry Street in Little Italy for the San Gennaro festival. As Nina freshens up in the ladies' room, Bart encourages Reuben to talk about his father both at the festival and at a nightclub he owns, The Spot, and then leap from the bridge at dawn, promising him a night to end all nights ("Have Yourself a Night"). On her return, Nina senses Bart's evil intentions and the two argue as Reuben, rattled, slips out, followed by Harry and then Nina ("Have Yourself a Night," reprise).

Scene five. The Carnival, 11:30 P.M. Reuben and Nina seek each other among the crowd celebrating the feast of San Gennaro ("San Gennaro"). Attilio, a street vendor, expresses his romantic desires ("With a Woman To Be"). As Nina happily espies Reuben, a quartet of friends serenade her, the ardent Attilio eventually joining in ("The Hills of Amalfi"/"With a Woman To Be"). After taunting each other, two guttersnipes, Gisella and Blazer, tenderly dance as Reuben expresses his love for Nina ("Rose Song"). Reuben entertains the crowd with juggling, magic tricks, and other feats. Bart enters and prompts Reuben to make a speech about his father as planned, but the latter instead sings of love ("Miracle Song"). As Bart has Harry start a brawl, Reuben attempts to stop the fighting, but Nina pulls him away.

Scene six. The Column, 12:30 A.M. On a bench in a park-like triangular street intersection near the festival, Reuben, remorseful over the brawl, falls into a restless sleep in Nina's arms ("Sleep"). After he awakens, Reuben and Nina confess their love ("Love At the First Word"). The Countess appears, persuading Reuben and a reluctant Nina to join her at The Spot, the nightclub where she performs ("The Spot").

Scene seven. The Spot, 1:00 A.M. The action dissolves directly into a setting described by Blitzstein as "tawdry, garish, sleazy, a Greenwich-village imitation of a fashionable night-club uptown." The Countess performs a campy song about love ("Mystery of the Flesh") and the three Spot Girls—Dee Dee, Shoo Shoo, Pot Pot—lisp their way through a comic chorus-girl number on the same subject ("Yeth, Yeth"). Disturbed by an altercation between a rude white patron, Mr. Smythe, and a courteous black waiter, Smith, Reuben exchanges their positions, eventually getting

them into the same jacket, at which point, stuck, they confusedly waltz to the Countess's music ("Mystery of the Flesh," reprise). When the Countess joins Reuben,
Nina, and Bart at their table, she upsets all three by alerting Reuben and Nina to
Bart's bet. Reuben ascends to the nightclub's chandelier as a curious crowd gathers
below ("Thank You," reprise). Bart prods Reuben to jump, while Nina, fearful of
Bart's henchmen, tells him to remain above. Reuben, feeling abandoned, imagines
the taunting spectators below as figures at the circus, and when firemen, called by
the Countess, arrive and spread their net, he cries "Make way for the Human Dart"
and jumps, reenacting his father's death ("Circus Finale").[20]

Act II. Scene one. The Wards, 2:30 A.M. After an entr'acte ("Miracle Song" and
"San Gennaro"), the second act opens in a mental institution (Blitzstein had in
mind New York's public Bellevue Hospital), where Reuben and Nina have been
brought and placed in the men's and women's wards, respectively. As a brick-like
partition slowly descends center stage, dividing the two wards, the inmates sing
an eerie song of love ("Moment of Love"). A dance follows, one embodying "a reduction ad absurdum of non-communication in our outside world" ("Ballet").
Reuben assists a young male resident, Ury (described in sketches as a "Rimbaud-
[James] Jones-Genet figure," intimating a character of defiant nonconformity),
while Nina helps another inmate, a young African-American woman named Zoë.
Feeling that they have been rejected by each other, Reuben and Nina express
their loneliness ("There Goes My Love"). Xavier and Yolanda, two inmates caged
in solitary cubicles, have "a very personal love-moment," and Ury slashes his
wrists with a spike. After arriving attendants release Reuben and Nina, the male
attendant moves to strike Ury across the face, saying, "Why you no-good sonofa-
bitch" ("Moment of Love," reprise).

Scene two. The Bedroom, 3:00 A.M. Nina and Reuben have retreated to the
former's small studio apartment in Little Italy, still followed by Harry, who
arranged their release from the asylum and now waits outside. The lovers quarrel,
but Reuben, who feels reborn after his simulated death, asks Nina to help make
him whole ("Be With Me"). Reuben tells Nina that he needs to go to a party at
Bart's in order to see if he can face the man, but before they leave, she sings him an
old song learned from her mother ("Mother of the Bridegroom").

Scene three. The Bar, 4:30 A.M. After an interlude, the scene switches to Bart's,
where a large group—nearly the entire company—has assembled ("Tell It To
Bart," reprise). Lonesome holds a conversation with another Barfly ("Hard to
Say"). As Lonesome dozes, the Countess sings him a seductive lullaby
("Upstairsy"). On awakening, Lonesome sings a ditty with Cop Kerry ("Musky
and Whisky"/"I Can Mix All Kinds of Pleasures"). Reuben and Nina arrive, followed by Harry. Bart takes credit in getting Reuben "a nice dame to coozy him
tonight" ("Have Yourself a Night," reprise). Eager to hit Bart for insulting Nina,
Reuben restrains himself by discussing the pitfalls of communication with the
crowd, eventually leading all in a wordless chorus ("Reuben Talks"). Bart still

believes that Reuben will kill himself ("We Got a Pact"). However, Reuben, noting a horseshoe hung upside down on the wall, tells Bart that his luck has run out, at which point Bart violently hurls the horseshoe at a mirror, breaking it, and Reuben knocks him to the ground. After the crowd disperses, the Countess tells Nina and Reuben to leave her with Bart, explaining, "One, I'm a nymph. Two, I'm a lush. Three, I like the man. Go home." Harry quits Bart for good, and the Countess, alone with Bart, cares for his wound, as Bart swears he will never forgive her ("Upstairsy," reprise).

Scene four. The Bridge, Dawn. After a weekend on the town, a Southern gob, Henry Lippincott, returns to his ship in Brooklyn by way of the Manhattan Bridge ("Monday Morning Blues"). Meeting Reuben and Nina, he asks that they wave to him as he crosses over. Reuben and Nina resolve to "start again" whatever happens ("Such a Little While," reprise). As the sun rises, Reuben and Nina call out each other's names as they wave goodbye to the departing sailor.

The opera forms a parable about human contact, alternately thwarted and fulfilled. Virtually every detail of the libretto, right down to Nina's job as a telephone operator, serves some symbolic purpose in this regard. As in Blitzstein's previous allegories, and such classic ones as *Everyman* and *The Pilgrim's Progress* that he esteemed, the work's larger dramatic arc moves toward redemption, in this case, from Reuben's psychosis to his final cure in the penultimate scene as he stands up to Bart—a personal growth given life-affirming expression in the final scene as Reuben waves to the departing sailor while calling out his own name with Nina's. This coupling of names, echoed by Nina as the curtain falls, brings the drama full circle, as it recalls the popular song "Reuben and Rachel," a comical duet about isolation that Reuben anxiously sings at his first entrance (the lyrics altered to evoke a "world all made of glass").

In keeping with the allegorical spirit of the work, Blitzstein avoided allusions to contemporary events, although his notes reveal that the threat of nuclear warfare undergirded the drama, including Pop's decision to kill himself, according to one draft, on the morning of the first Bikini atom bomb test on July 1, 1946, an event "which proved," the composer wrote in 1951, "that the atom was to be used for war, not peace." Blitzstein more generally correlated the notion of suicide at dawn with atomic bomb tests at sunrise, making the final scene, in this context, all the more poignant. "Bart is Mephisto because he shows himself up as totally indifferent, egging on the isolation of people," he noted at one point. "It is a step from this to the atom-bomb, the actual decimation of 'the others.'" In yet another jotting, he identified the opera's theme as "Why stay alive in a life so dedicated to self-destruction." But notwithstanding some allusions to explosions—including Lonesome's remark "I wish they'd blow up the world, start another one," Reuben's cry "Everything'll explode," and even more subtly, Bart's use of the phrase "dawn's early light" from "The Star-Spangled Banner"—all of this remained subtexual.[21]

Other topical matters took metaphorical expression as well. Blitzstein considered the crowd's changing reaction to Reuben "from alarm to suspicion to hostility to 'prejudged guilt' and utter condemnation" in the first-act finale, for instance, as reflecting "all the steps" of the House Un-American Activities Committee, and drew a parallel as well between this same scene and the "nauseating spectacle" of the thousands of New Yorkers who gathered to watch a police shootout with a deranged gunman. Similarly, he intended the Smythe-Smith sequence as commentary on racial inequality, and the asylum scene, on contemporary alienation. "With all our new gadgets for communication,—we use them to *stop* communication," he ruminated. "We don't want to understand the other fellow." Some of these preoccupations might have been more obvious had he retained the character of Bobilly, an elderly public relations man who in early drafts brings Reuben to The Spot—a function taken over by the Countess—in the hopes of enlisting his support in promoting Cold War anxieties. But Blitzstein early on decided to avoid anything so explicitly political, one reason, perhaps, for the ultimate excision of Bobilly. "No need to go into the political aspects . . . ," he wrote in 1951. "R[euben] plans to die *because he can't talk*—that's clear enough. . . . keep the actual story free of cant and thesis."[22]

But if such restraint arguably mirrored the day's repressive political climate, to the point that Reuben's mutism could be read as symbolic of the muzzled popular front, the work's concern over the threat of nuclear annihilation and the debasement of public discourse placed the opera still in the tradition of the composer's socially conscious work, with Reuben's final oration even recalling Larry Foreman's speeches in *The Cradle*. Blitzstein's work had long combined the allegorical and realistic to some degree, and if the weight now shifted to the former, as it did in Arthur Miller's *The Crucible* (1953), which the composer apparently admired, this did not mean a retreat from social engagement, even if addressing such matters in the context of a romantic comedy represented something new.[23]

Blitzstein referred to the work as a "musical play" on the title page of his finished typescript but more casually as an "opera," a term appropriate enough given the piece's relative dearth of spoken dialogue and its musical seriousness and sophistication. At the same time, only a few roles require operatic singing in the conventional sense, most notably that of Nina, whose part requires considerable vocal agility.

The work similarly achieves some middle ground formally, with a considerable number of songs nestled within a large and complex musical structure. The Boston program listed no fewer than twenty-eight titled numbers (all mentioned in the above scenario, which further includes two titles from the composer's score, "The Circus" and "Circus Finale"), many arriving at endings firm enough for applause whether or not the music actually stopped. Chappell quickly published five of these numbers, republished decades later by Boosey & Hawkes along with an additional eight songs (leaving unpublished, ironically, the number perhaps most in a popular mold, "There Goes My Love," which Blitzstein strove to make "the kind of song one could *hear* Eddie Fisher singing").[24]

These sundry set pieces exploit a wide range of styles, but aside from, say, "Mystery of the Flesh" and "Yeth, Yeth" (which function like "Fraught" and "Dimples" in *No for an Answer*, that is, as nightclub entertainment), they generally eschew the sort of parody found in Blitzstein's earlier theater pieces. Rather, the varied allusions emerge in tandem with rather naturalistic character delineation: circus music with Reuben; folkloric strains with Nina; daemonic operatic tropes with Bart; Irish melody with Cop Kerry; Neapolitan song with Attilio; nightclub music with the Countess; and the blues with sailor Lippincott. At the same time, the score as a whole presents a highly individual profile, the harmonies characteristically flavorful, sometimes gorgeous, with spicy dissonances and unexpected turns, the music meticulously orchestrated, with a wealth of subtle sonorities. Much of the score leans, more or less explicitly, in the direction of jazz, with the influence of Bernstein occasionally suggested. The opera also features a new melodic ease—that "Mozartean groove"—that distinguishes it from much of Blitzstein's previous work. Tellingly, he recycled relatively little music for this piece, although he derived "Miracle Song" from "Home for a Hero" from the similarly tuneful *Goloopchik*.

The work's lyricism extends to much of the music connecting the actual numbers, so much so that sections of recitative—for instance, the altercation between Mr. and Mrs. Doakes or the dialogue between the Countess and Bart near the end of the first act, marked "slow boogie"—form sort of songs in their own right. In other instances, inspired in part by Verdi, the orchestra carries the melodic argument, sometimes varying one of the show's songs, at other times developing a new idea. Blitzstein masterfully manipulates these diverse melodies, not just motives, to create larger, often rounded or otherwise symmetrical structures.

For its composer, the work also makes unusually prominent use of ensemble singing, including a number of duets and quartets and a complex first-act finale reminiscent of the galloping conclusion of *Regina*'s second act. Whether Blitzstein earlier had been wary of ensembles because of their potential sacrifice of textural clarity and dramatic naturalism, he ingeniously circumvented such pitfalls, as he had in "Francie" from *No for an Answer* and the original "Night" from *Regina*, by initially presenting, for example, Bart's "Have Yourself a Night" and Nina's "Sleep" as solos, in the course of which Reuben eventually adds a mesmerized vocalise to the former, a dozing hum to the latter. In some other instances, he essentially combined two distinct numbers, each with its own text, only after presenting them separately, including "Tell It To Bart"/"It's In the Cards," "The Hills of Amalfi"/"With a Woman To Be," and "Musky and Whisky"/"I Can Mix All Kinds of Pleasures."

Blitzstein participated fully in the casting of the show, a major undertaking in itself, especially finding someone to play Reuben, with all the role's taxing dramatic, musical, and physical requirements. Early on, Blitzstein mentioned as possible Reubens Alfred Drake and José Ferrer, although by late 1953 he regarded

Donald O'Connor and David Wayne as the two front-runners. A list compiled by
Cheryl Crawford dated March 1954 included over one hundred potential candidates, from comedian Danny Kaye, crooners Eddie Fisher and Frank Sinatra, and
dancer Bob Fosse to such dramatic heavyweights as Marlon Brando and Montgomery Clift. Meanwhile, Crawford tried unsuccessfully to interest Michael Kidd
in staging the dances before turning to Hanya Holm.[25]

In her attempts to recruit one or another artist, Crawford enthused about the
piece, writing to Brando, "You will hear the best theatre work I have heard in my
twenty-seven years of theatre"; to Donald O'Connor's agent, "it is not only one of
the greatest and most original musicals of all time but definitely the greatest part for
a young actor-singer-dancer"; and to Michael Kidd, "It's just a masterpiece, that's
all." And in early 1955, contacting Rodgers and Hammerstein on behalf of Blitzstein and herself to see if they would listen to the composer play through the score
so as to "get your opinion as masters," she wrote, "I think it is a most astonishing
work, quite different from 'Regina' with lovely melodies, warmth and a rare imagination. In fact, far and away the most exciting work I have ever been connected with."[26]

By the summer of 1954, Eddie Albert had emerged the most likely contender
for the title role, and although Crawford continued to entertain other possibilities, including Mickey Rooney, she finally signed Albert that fall, even though the
actor's prior commitments, including a turn as Ali Hakim in the film version of
Oklahoma! (1955), necessitated further delays. A recent Oscar nominee for his
supporting work in *Roman Holiday* (1953), Eddie Albert (b. Edward Albert Heim-
berger, 1906–2005) had wide-ranging abilities suited to the part of Reuben, including a winsome personality and a pleasant singing voice (as perhaps best
remembered from the theme song for the television show in which he later starred,
Green Acres). Moreover, he had worked in a circus and had served in the military,
so he could draw on those experiences as well. Blitzstein's greatest reservations
concerned his age, as he had imagined a man in his twenties, not someone pushing
fifty. "He is wonderful, lovely, but a bit old," the composer wrote David Diamond
in September 1954, adding to Mina Curtiss the following month, "he seems just
not young, fresh, turbulent enough." But in March 1955, especially impressed
with the actor's readiness to master the physical demands of the part, Blitzstein
told Leonard Bernstein that Albert would be "immense."[27]

For the role of Nina, Blitzstein initially considered, among others, Brenda Lewis
and Mary Martin, but by April 1954, it had become, he wrote Diamond, "a toss-up
between Anna Maria Alberghetti and Patrice Munsel—both stunning, both really
moving, in two quite different ways." In May, the *Times* even reported that Munsel,
an opera star specializing in light coloratura roles, had been "going over the music"
with Blitzstein, and in fact, she made demo recordings of "Song of the Arrow,"
"Sleep," and "Mother of the Bridegroom" with the composer, who assumed the part
of Reuben in "Sleep"; but by June, she had decided that, although "intrigued" by
the score, eight performances a week would be too taxing on her voice.[28]

In the end, Crawford cast as Nina the then unknown Evelyn Lear (b. Evelyn Shulman, 1926–2012), who had accompanied her husband Tom Stewart on his audition for the show, and whom Crawford agreed to hear at Stewart's request "for good luck, happiness and peace in the family." In later years, both Stewart (here assigned three small parts, including one of the Amalfi quartet) and Lear would have major operatic careers, he as a Wagnerian bass-baritone, she as a starring soprano in the operas of Richard Strauss and Alban Berg. Given Lear's "natural heaviness," Blitzstein wondered whether the role's "perkiness" and "insouciance" lay within her reach, but he deeply appreciated her dramatic and vocal gifts, writing to Diamond, "so beautiful of voice, so human of face, so brilliant a theatre-person . . . that I am beside myself with pleasure and gratitude."[29]

Crawford further signed as Bart, George Gaynes (b. George Jongejans, 1917), an operatic baritone who had been in Bernstein's *Wonderful Town* (1953), and as the Countess, Kaye Ballard (b. Catherine Gloria Balotta, 1925), the uproarious actress who recently had won plaudits for her performance in Jerome Moross's *The Golden Apple* (1954) as another comic Helen figure. The cast also included, in the featured role of Attilio, future recording star Enzo Stuarti, and, as Blazer and Gisella, the young dancer-actors Timmy Everett and Sondra Lee.

Meanwhile, assisted by such singers as Richard Armbruster and Alice Ghostley, Blitzstein made demo recordings and held backers' auditions, leaving behind a tape of his own delightfully comic performances of "Musky and Whisky" and "Hard to Say." Cheryl Crawford raised about $200,000 for the production, which involved a cast of over thirty, additional singers and dancers, and a sizeable pit orchestra. As mentioned, Robert Lewis directed, Hanya Holm choreographed, Samuel Krachmalnick (whom Blitzstein described as "very able, a superb coach; and excited about the work") conducted, and copyist Arnold Arnstein and orchestrators Hershy Kay and Bill Stegmeyer assisted in the musical preparation. In addition, the husband-and-wife team of William and Jean Eckart, who earlier in the year had designed another show inspired by the Faust legend, Jerry Ross and Richard Adler's *Damn Yankees* (1955), created the lighting, costumes, and sets, which took inspiration from Edward Hopper and which Blitzstein thought "beautiful." (When the composer first met the Eckarts, he assailed their association with *Damn Yankees*, asserting that the show "demonized gays" by portraying the devilish Mr. Applegate as "an old queen.")[30]

Rehearsals began in New York on September 8, with an initial run-through on September 25. Crawford took a risk in bypassing New Haven in favor of an opening in Boston, where Blitzstein and the company arrived in early October in advance of a planned three-week run starting October 10, preceded by a couple of dress rehearsals before small audiences, at the Shubert Theatre, where the show closed prematurely on October 22.

Throughout this period, Blitzstein revised and edited the work, with a preserved tape of one of the Boston performances documenting the considerable extent to which he rewrote the piece. He continually tweaked the libretto, sometimes eliminating some off-color slang, Gisella's taunting "Git a hand-job" becoming, for instance, "I go around with an older crowd." More dramatically, he cut various portions of the score (including "Hard to Say") and dispensed with a considerable amount of sung recitative in favor of spoken lines (although often in such instances retaining the musical accompaniment). His notes suggest that he accomplished some of this in sessions with Robert Lewis and Samuel Krachmalnick in early September, before rehearsals began, but evidence points to a number of changes along these lines made after the Boston premiere, including the deletion of "Miracle Song" and "Yeth, Yeth."[31]

The motivations behind these revisions presumably involved a number of factors. With regard to the extensive reduction of sung lines, Blitzstein might have felt the cast unable to manage so much singing, or he might have thought the work stronger this way, or both. The need to shorten the playing time became an important consideration as well. Surely not coincidentally, Crawford had supervised a similar overhauling of *Porgy and Bess* in 1941, although the Gershwin opera proved more amenable in this regard, with recitative derived from a straight play, making the reversion back to speech natural enough, whereas Blitzstein conceived virtually his entire text in relation to music, so that the now-spoken portions often sounded like lyrics shorn of their melodies, as indeed they were.

On opening night, numerous attendees—estimates range from three hundred to about half the 1,500-or-so-seat house—walked out in the course of the performance, while others stayed and cheered. "It was a memorable night in the theater here," stated the *Boston American*, "because seldom have so many persons displayed such feeling against a show while so many others were loudly applauding." In her 1977 memoirs, Crawford, after admitting her mistake in advertising the work as a musical rather than an opera, recalled the premiere as follows: "Muttering bitter words under my breath, I stood at the head of one aisle, feet apart, arms akimbo, so that the lemmings would be forced to squeeze past me into the dark night. I was mad: mistaken announcement or no, so much blood and talent had gone into the show. Today, with the new sounds of music and new styles of writing, I doubt if it would seem at all obscure." Blitzstein wrote to Mina Curtiss, "Up until five minutes after *opening-night* curtain in Boston, there was not one person connected with the production who wasn't sure we were wonderful. And a moment later, we were ashes. We all knew it. The actors onstage went berserk, forgot lines, gave dizzily unreal performances that made my poor conductor in the pit try desperately to meet them at least in terms of musical bars."[32]

Although admiring of the production, the critics generally disliked the piece, especially Cyrus Durgin (*Boston Globe*), who wrote, "Speaking personally, not in 25 years around the Recording Angel business have I experienced so obscure, unfunny, musically dry, pretentious, solemnly nonsensical and boring a musical as this." Even the more sympathetic reviewers found the work baffling, including Elliot Norton (*Boston Post*), who reported "occasional moments of grandeur and exaltation," but found the work largely "incoherent," with some of it lapsing "into downright dullness." The most positive reviews suggested that the piece was "way over the heads of the first-night audience," with Alta Maloney (*Boston Traveler*) stating that the first-nighters by and large "paid respectful attention to honest, hard-working performances with extremely difficult material." Few of these mostly drama critics seemed cognizant of the score—Norton later admitted that as a "contemporary opera, an essentially serious drama set to music," the work "shouldn't have been launched in such an atmosphere"—although George Ryan (*Boston Pilot*), a rare exception, thought the music "uncommonly beautiful in all but the recitative portions." All the critics at least agreed that the work, even in this form, constituted an "opera" or "folk opera," with *Variety* writing, "This is not 'The Saint of Bleecker Street,' nor is it 'Pajama Game,' but it is apparently intended as a development of 'Pajama Game' toward 'Bleecker Street' in the classical musical form."[33]

During the work's brief run, several persons who had seen the production wrote Blitzstein wholehearted letters of support, from the night clerk at the Brunswick Hotel who found the work "very moving emotionally" to musicologist Victor Yellin and music critic Leonard Burkat, who both thought the opera, like George Ryan, "beautiful." "I think that what shakes people," added Burkat, "what makes them nervously laugh in the wrong places, is that it is a nasty story that is not about somebody else . . . but is about themselves." Attorney Seymour Bluhm, in a letter to the *Globe*'s Cyrus Durgin accusing him of hurting "the cause of creative theatre," also declared the work "excellent and unusual." The surviving archival tape lends credence to these more appreciative responses, with hearty applause after some of the numbers, in particular the "Rose Song," and whistling and cheering at the final curtain.[34]

In the days following the premiere, Crawford expressed her conviction that, notwithstanding the reviews, she had a hit on her hands, and Blitzstein feverishly continued revising the opera, mostly by rewriting lyrics and making cuts. "We are working on it night and day," stated Crawford, who brought in poet Norman Rosten and playwrights Robert Anderson (*Tea and Sympathy*, 1953) and N. Richard Nash (*The Rainmaker*, 1954) to help doctor the piece. On October 13, Anderson enumerated extensive suggestions in the form of notes as well as in a letter addressed to Crawford, Blitzstein, and Lewis in which he urged clarification of motives regarding the pact between Bart and Reuben and greater suspense by having Reuben court a more resistant Nina in the course of the drama, writing "I know this involves work way beyond what you can do in the time available—or perhaps than you want to do—but it gives a pattern towards which I think you should work." Blitzstein possibly made some slight changes in light of these criticisms, but in large part, he stood his ground, writing to himself on the evening of October 14, "But surely it is R[euben] with *his* conflict, between running towards death, and towards life (the B[art]-N[ina] equation) who should retreat and advance as regards Nina. It is *his* story, not hers, we want to root for. So if we can keep *him* in flux . . . *then* we have the will-they-won't-they thing that keeps the play moving."[35]

Crawford at first announced that the opera would play two weeks in Boston so that the company could incorporate major revisions before the scheduled opening in New York on November 8 at the ANTA Theatre. But by October 17, she had decided that, after a final performance that Saturday night, the show would close for good, although she voiced her determination to mount the piece at some later date: "I don't know how long it will take—a month, two months, three months, a year—but we're going to make it right . . . I realize now that when you have been with a production as long as I have with this one you can persuade yourself that your audience will see it through your eyes. Opening night here I learned that wasn't always so. The show didn't confuse me because I'd been with it so long and known it so well, but the customers were bewildered and annoyed." (Crawford subsequently arranged for her backers to receive a small percentage in her next two productions and managed to return about $30,000 to investors as well.)[36]

The production similarly taught designers William and Jean Eckart that their "enthusiasm for a show" did not necessarily provide "a barometer of the taste of the general public," as they too had "loved" the work—they would recycle some of its scenic ideas for Stephen Sondheim's 1964 musical *Anyone Can Whistle*—and in tryout had been "moved to tears of joy—leaving us totally unprepared for the audience reaction in Boston." Kaye Ballard, for her part, had such faith in the material that she even became a backer, but shrugged off Blitzstein's seeming unwillingness to overhaul the piece, telling the Eckarts, "The trouble with Marc is that he *likes* living on East 12th Street."[37]

On October 17, Blitzstein said his farewells to Lewis over the telephone, but after leaving for New York the next day, wrote him a letter, carbon-copied to Crawford, in which he reproached the director for giving up on the piece after opening night, in contrast to *Regina*, when throughout the tryout period and even after the New York opening, he "filled the players with your love of and belief in the work." Lewis's reply, also sent to Crawford, included the following:

> Your note was no surprise to me. All of us who have knocked ourselves out on the show; Hanya, Eddie, myself, etc. have been waiting for you to turn on us and blame us, because we have all, at one time or another, been witness to your ingratitude. The simple fact of the matter is that you were unable to do the job required to put the show over. . . . In this case [as opposed to *Regina*] what was required was either a new format with an additional writer writing dialogue scenes which you could and should not accept as it would change the piece into a regulation musical, or, a re-write in your own form by yourself which I think will take you months or years. The piddling things that you could only do now in the time given, always avoiding the central problem, were too embarrassing to present to the cast at all—much less with enthusiasm.

Lewis expressed his continued pride in the work, but agreed with the company "that giving you back your baby now, still alive and kicking, was the only way that you could ultimately have a success with it, and that is what we all wanted for you."[38]

A more conciliatory go-round followed, with Blitzstein assuming the main responsibility for the show's failure but expressing frustration—as he did in letters to friends as well—that he never received the right help "in time," and Lewis reminding him that "on opening night every name, great and otherwise, in American playwriting was offered you." Blitzstein also denied the charge of "ingratitude," saying, "I feel I covered you all with my love and appreciation," to which Lewis responded by stating that he didn't "want any gratitude. My payment was in the thrill and pleasure of working on such superb material. . . . You are still the best composer in this field, in my opinion." Lewis further noted the "irony" that Blitzstein's "play about non-communication was not communicated to the audience," but equally ironic seems to have been the breakdown of communication between director and composer.[39]

The critics and gossip columnists got wind of such backstage drama, their somewhat sensationalized accounts typically presenting Blitzstein in the more unflattering light as an author unwilling to make changes requested by Crawford, "one of the nicest and most important women in the theater." Walter Winchell reported that the composer had "nixed the free help" of Arthur Miller and Tennessee Williams, while Dorothy Kilgallen wrote that the "Sardi set" was "sharply divided into two camps. Friends of composer Marc Blitzstein hold producer Cheryl Crawford responsible for the flop; Miss Crawford's admirers say Blitzstein stubbornly refused to make the necessary changes in his material even when the audiences booed."[40]

Meanwhile, Blitzstein advised Mina Curtiss, overseas at the time, that she need not be concerned about returning for a New York opening. Briefly recounting the events of the last few weeks, he confessed that he had "made a great initial mistake" (he assured her that he would tell her more about that when he saw her) and described his state as "exhausted, and healthy," writing, "I have maintained a steady and healthy view of what seems (to me, of course) a staggering and brutal experience; and I don't have notions of killing myself off quickly by collapsing at this point." (He parenthetically described, as "a beating I shall cherish," a man who shook his fist at him during a performance saying, "Why shouldn't *you* suffer as we are suffering.") He further reflected,

> If I felt I was right all the time, and insisted on going back to my original score-script; or, if I felt it was all hopeless—I should be deeply worried about myself. I am neither. I now know that *this* story, I cannot tell alone; I need help, real collaborative help. I am prepared to find it. Cheryl says the moment I do, she will re-produce. She says she is a fighter. I think she is.[41]

Blitzstein duly sought the advice of playwright William Inge, then at the height of his prestige, having had a series of distinguished hits on Broadway, most recently *Bus Stop* (1955). After reading the script twice and hearing some of the score, Inge described the opera to Blitzstein, according to the latter's paraphrase of November 10, as "completely right on its own terms. . . . Its reality is a 'dream-like' reality, and should be presented as such with full knowledge and courage." Although Inge, like Anderson, mentioned the impossibility of a traditional "rewrite" given the "interplay" of text and music, Blitzstein asked him if he at least would work with him on a revision "with whatever billing or credit he might choose." Inge explained that he had other obligations, but would let Blitzstein know in a few days. Presumably, he declined the offer.[42]

In February 1956, Blitzstein told David Diamond that the production had "wrecked" his relationship with Lewis, but that he and Crawford had "come through very well. She still says she will put it all on again, as soon as the book is right." As late as October 1957, he looked ahead to retooling the work, telling David Diamond that he considered his musical *Juno* (1959) a "fine warmer-up" for such an endeavor. However, he never seems to have undertaken any serious revision of the opera, finding rather other uses for some of the music.[43]

At some point, Blitzstein clipped out a *Pogo* comic strip by Walt Kelly, which the composer titled, "My Life in Boston, 'Reuben Reuben.'" The strip shows Barnstable Bear, a pot stuck to his rear end, asking Albert Alligator and Mis Sis Boombah for help. Albert and Mis Sis proceed to apply plungers to him, leaving him not only with the pot but the two plungers attached to his body. Albert suggests that he get a job at the circus as a "legendary beast," and Mis Sis that he wag his tail to show his appreciation. "I ain't as grateful as you mebbe s'poses," responds Barnstable.[44]

But if Blitzstein kept his sense of humor about what he typically called "a disaster," and showed as good a face to friends as could be expected ("Marc is taking it marvelously," Bernstein wrote to Diamond), the experience must have been wrenching. He had worked tirelessly on the opera, off and on, for some six years, only to see his efforts crumble within days into dashed hopes and ruined friendships. His nephew Christopher recalled that the work's reception "was a terrific blow. . . . Creatively, it exhausted him, all but killed his morale." For a few months, his compositional activity slowed. But by June 1956, the familiar routine of his summer set-up in Brigantine had helped gird him for "settling into actual disciplined work," and by the spring of 1957 he had completed a major new work, *This Is the Garden*, for chorus and orchestra.[45]

Meanwhile, the opera became so forgotten that when in 1964, the year of the composer's death, Peter De Vries published a darkly satiric novel also entitled *Reuben, Reuben* (with the comma), which in turn gave rise to a play (*Spofford*, 1967) and a film (*Reuben, Reuben*, 1983), the similarity of title passed unremarked. Whether De Vries borrowed the title or anything else from the opera, the two works actually explored some similar themes, including suicide and the anxieties of modern life.

The general unavailability of the score inhibited much in the way of critical study. In advance of its premiere, British composer-critic Wilfrid Mellers, examining some excerpts Blitzstein had sent him, noted a new simplicity in the music, an "innocent lucidity" in the satirical numbers, and a "strange, almost hallucinatory" harmonic quality in "Moment of Love"—this last an astute observation given that Blitzstein originally intended the Bellevue scene as a "dope scene." In his own discussion of the opera, Eric Gordon observed, "The music to which Blitzstein set this most vexatious libretto turned out be the most seductive, ecstatic, lush, and lyrical score he ever wrote," and declared the work as a whole, his "best synthesis of 'art' and 'popular' music styles."[46]

The piece at least acquired a fabled reputation as one of the most intriguing failures in the history of the American musical theater. In his survey of such "flops," Ken Mandelbaum, for instance, described the opera as "impenetrable but fascinating" and "easily the most difficult work ever presented to an audience under the guise of a Broadway-style musical," with "a dissonant, fragmented score punctuated with occasional lyrical passages of extraordinary beauty." And Ethan Mordden regarded the work as "floppo surrealism," although he thought a writer of Blitzstein's "caliber" actually "incapable of creating floppos" and regarded the opera as admirable in its "desire to create something genuinely original, with its own sound, characters, and worldview," even if crippled by its "meandering story" and "lack of melodic inspiration."[47]

Moreover, several of the opera's numbers enjoyed the occasional airing. Leonard Bernstein sang some of "Musky and Whisky" at a 1985 memorial concert for Blitzstein (misremembering this "little pearl of wit" as coming from *Juno*, which also had drinking songs). Helene Williams, Ronald Edwards, William Sharp, and Dawn Upshaw all recorded songs from the opera, Upshaw combining "Never Get Lost" with "Take Me to the World" from Stephen Sondheim's musical *Evening Primrose* (1966).[48]

Part of a 1994 release, *I Wish It So*, that featured songs by Weill, Blitzstein, Bernstein, and Sondheim, this latter medley—like the album itself—drew on the widely held perception of Blitzstein (along with Weill and Bernstein) as a forerunner to lyricist-composer Stephen Sondheim (b. 1930). In the album's liner notes, producer Tommy Krasker wrote, for instance, "although his [Sondheim's] work has not veered toward American opera as envisioned by Weill, Blitzstein, and Bernstein, he is fulfilling their ideals through his theatrical daring, musical sophistication, and undeviating faith in the commercial stage." Other commentators similarly observed some such lineage, with Jamie James, for example, stating in a 1992 *New York Times* piece about *Regina*, "Leonard Bernstein and Stephen Sondheim are clearly indebted to Blitzstein." Sondheim, who remembered meeting Blitzstein only once, indeed acquired a wide familiarity with the composer's output, obtaining recordings of *The Cradle, No for an Answer,* and the *Airborne Symphony,* attending the Broadway productions of *Regina* and *Juno,* and sitting in on a backers' audition for *Reuben Reuben*; but notwithstanding his admiration for the opening chorus of *Juno* (surely a precursor to the opening of his own 1979 musical, *Sweeney Todd*), he found in Blitzstein's work "an academicism, a lack of natural grace and spontaneity, a clumsiness"—he recalled that he went to the *Reuben Reuben* audition only at the urging of Cheryl Crawford—and rejected the idea of any indebtedness to Blitzstein on either his part or even Bernstein's, a denial so extreme as to suggest some unnamed anxiety or resentment.[49]

For all the attractiveness of its score, the prospects for reviving *Reuben Reuben* remain problematic not only because of the lack of available materials, but because any production would have to decide whether to adapt the more fully operatic score or attempt to duplicate the Boston version. Although Blitzstein frowned on "going back to my original score-script," mounting the piece as originally conceived seemed to offer the more attractive option. Indeed, had *Reuben Reuben* been presented that way in the first place—perhaps by an opera company—its history might well have been very different. So rich and masterful a work deserved a second chance in any case.

In 1956, Blitzstein accepted a $500 commission from the Interracial Fellowship Chorus of Greater New York for a work for mixed chorus and small orchestra in celebration of the group's tenth anniversary. The chorus had been founded in 1947 by the Interracial Fellowship, an organization "devoted," according to one source, "to the fostering of interracial and interfaith understanding through a variety of social and cultural activities." In order to help achieve such goals, the chorus's young leader Harold Aks, a Juilliard graduate, and his associate David Labovitz, both Jewish Americans, actively recruited members from minority groups, dispensing with auditions, thought to be a barrier to minority participation, but rather offering classes in sight-reading prior to rehearsals. After the fellowship disbanded in 1952, the chorus continued primarily under the auspices of its sponsoring organization, the Interracial Music Council.[50]

On average composed of about one hundred women and fifty men, the chorus gave two concerts annually, usually at Town Hall, and often including sacred works by such masters as Buxtehude, Bach, and Haydn, but also new pieces, including Wallingford Riegger's cantata *In Certainty of Song* (1950). Singer Mordecai Bauman, concerned about Blitzstein's malaise following *Reuben Reuben*, reportedly helped facilitate this commission by promoting the idea with Aks, who overcame some qualms regarding the composer's suitability for a job of this sort.[51]

Starting as early as June, Blitzstein worked on the commission throughout the latter half of 1956 in Ashfield, Manhattan, Brigantine, and Mexico. He originally had planned to spend just the month of September south of the border, but finding the time there so restorative, he decided to extend his trip another month. Indeed, he wished he could remain in Mexico "indefinitely," as he told Mina Curtiss, adding to David Diamond, "I had forgotten what being away from [the] United States is like, in a new climate, with different people and a different language; and how wonderful a tonic it could be." He stayed mostly on his own in Cuernavaca, renting a house with a swimming pool and a "maid-cook-laundress," Casilda, whom he described as "a dream—short, fat, sparkling at the eyes, and infinitely worldly, and robustly efficient at her jobs." The Mexican people generally impressed him deeply, including the craftsman who designed a board for his piano with great care, "something we have forgotten all about at home." For diversion, he met with friends in the zocalo. "I am surrounded by that warm, patient, and sometimes violent character which is the Mexican," he wrote, further attributing to the country dwellers "an immense stolidity and impassive resistance to the encroachments of civilization, but full of warmth, charm and sweetness, too."[52]

After his return to New York and a two-week vacation in early February 1957 with Jo and Ed Davis and Leonard and Felicia Bernstein in Cuba (where he had gone, in part, to recuperate from a bout of pneumonia), he completed the work, *This Is the Garden: A Cantata of New York*, which he dedicated to his mother. The use of the term "cantata" perhaps suggesting otherwise, the piece included no solos, although it called for a double chorus in one number, "Hymie Is a Poop."[53]

Blitzstein, who wrote the text himself, conceived the six-movement work as a series of street ballads, as "real folk-lore of city streets," having partly in mind the corridos of Mexico. He seems to have given some thought as well to *The Cantos* of Ezra Pound, hence such working titles as "Cantos of the East Side" and "New York Cantos." All six movements involve diverse public New York settings to the point that Blitzstein considered such other titles as "Delancey to the Triborough," although as he explained in program notes, he did not intend the piece as a "travelogue," but rather as a study of "certain aspects of the life today of city people which have struck my imagination." Eventually he settled on the more metaphorical title, "This Is the Garden," borrowed from a 1923 poem by E. E. Cummings, "this is the garden:colours come and go" (which his friend David Diamond had set for chorus some twenty years earlier), in which people in a world "where other songs be sung" stand "enraptured, as among/the slow deep trees perpetual of sleep/some silver-fingered fountain steals the world." In a September 1956 letter to Diamond, after describing the work as "a suite about the New York 'outside,' each number having something to do with the human spirit breaking through the city, or failing to," he referenced yet another poem, Federico García Lorca's "Dawn" from *Poet in New York* (as translated by Stephen Spender and J. L. Gili), citing in particular the lines in which New Yorkers "know they are going to the mud of figures and laws,/to artless games, to fruitless sweat." Blitzstein's own lyrics for the work read as poems in their own right.[54]

The opening chorus, "The Lex Express," depicts a hectic morning subway ride at the end of which the initially high-spirited commuters swear and laugh "that helpless laugh" (the subway ride music adapted from "Steel Rolling Mill" from *Valley Town*). "I'm Ten and You'll See" imagines the fantasies of an impoverished ten-year-old. "Harlan Brown, Killed in the Street" describes the reactions of passersby to a man found dead in the street. "Hymie is a Poop" tells the story of a shrewd immigrant, Pepita, who without waking her clueless husband Jaime (the name later changed to its phonetic equivalent, Hymie), delivers her baby on the stoop of her brownstone in order to make a stir and obtain some needed cash. "In Twos" pictures lovers walking outdoors, a haven from home. And "San Gennaro" portrays the festival of San Gennaro in Little Italy (as in *Reuben Reuben*, from which the music derives, although reorchestrated, including the novelty of an opening harmonica solo). The chorus throughout functions dramatically in such sundry roles as commuters, gossips, and observers.

As an outline among his papers makes explicit, Blitzstein wanted this work to reflect a range of activities, ethnicities, and moods: (1) "The Lex Express," work/8:00 A.M./"straight American"/"bored, tired, irritated, early-morning-vigorous"; (2) "I'm Ten and You'll See," childhood/[no time or ethnicity specified]/"brutality, fantasy, spirit, get dirty"; (3) "Harlan Brown, Killed in the Street," death/4:00 P.M./African American/"awed, uneasy, pseudo-philosophical, superstitious, mysterious, sinister, it-wasn't me"; (4) "Hymie is a Poop," birth/4:00 A.M./Puerto Rican/"gay, spiteful, admiring"; (5) "In Twos," love/10:00 P.M./Irish and Jewish/"impersonally de-scribing, envious, superior, titillated, touched-even-moved"; and (6) "San Gennaro," play and religion/12:00 A.M./Italian Catholic/"boisterous-rowdy, out-for-fun, child-like-piety, solemn, happy, paeanic." (Blitzstein's notes also suggest that Harlan Brown was run down by a car.) Such a portrait of a day in the life of New York establishes the cantata as a sister work to *Reuben Reuben* over and above the borrowing of the "San Gennaro" chorus. Relatedly, the work shares with *Reuben Reuben* a bleakly comic view of the city (darker than that found in, say, *I've Got the Tune*, and one that accords with the common postwar perception of New York as a meaner place to live than previously), although in both works "San Gennaro" serves as a reminder of com-munal joy (with, in the cantata, the saint's ability to survive "fiery hell" neatly an-swering the "unbelievable hell" of the first movement's subway ride).[55]

Also as with *Reuben Reuben*, Blitzstein hinted at connections between such urban distress and the political climate, here by way of a dig in "In Twos" at the Democratic Representative Morgan Moulder, a longstanding member of the House Un-American Activities Committee who had investigated musicians in Los Angeles in the spring of 1956 as he would the following April in New York. Originally, Blitzstein had written, "How else are they [lovers] to fight the mildew? And how else are they to stand against cities, they say,/Except by staying close, ever closer?" but then, in a pun on mold and Moulder, changed the phrase "fight the mildew" to "fight the moulder" and eventually "fight off moulder." Commen-tators further have viewed "In Twos," with its avoidance of any gender identifica-tion and its suggestions of illicit love, as a coded gloss on homosexual relationships, with Eric Gordon, for instance, deeming the movement "a Whitman-like message to future generations that could not then be safely uttered," although as men-tioned above, the composer at least began with the premise of an Irish-Jewish romance, a conceit that suited the interfaith ideals of the Interracial Fellowship.[56]

That *West Side Story* (1957) similarly featured, in its earliest incarnation, a New York Catholic-Jewish romance intimated other correspondences between these two pieces, composed by Bernstein and Blitzstein not only at about the same time, but during a period in which they saw much of one another, including not only the aforementioned vacation in Cuba, but trips by Blitzstein to Martha's Vineyard in early June 1956, and to Boston later in November to help advise Bernstein and Lillian Hellman on *Candide*. Tellingly, both works also deal with urban violence, juvenile delinquency, and New York's Puerto Rican community. Justin Smith notes in particular a resemblance between "The Lex Express" and the opening to *West Side Story*, while similar correlations could be drawn between "Hymie is a Poop" and "Mambo," "In Twos" and "One Hand, One Heart," and "San Gennaro" and "I Feel Pretty." At the same time, the differences between the two works seem as striking as any similarities, with Blitzstein coming closer to Stravinsky and Copland, but also Weill, whose "Love Song" from *The Threepenny Opera* apparently served as a model for "In Twos." In any event, Bernstein allegedly did not care for *This Is the Garden*, whose premiere he attended, while Blitzstein described *West Side Story* to Diamond as "full of talent, remarkable in many ways, in the end a wrong 'un, and I'm not sure why. I don't find it a 'phony,' as [Harold] Clurman does; but it does go condescending at times ('Ah-the-poor-workers' mood of some of the stuff of the thirties), and uncomfortably affectionate. The music has drive but little poetry; the text [by Arthur Laurents] has craft but *no* poetry; ditto the lyrics [by Stephen Sondheim]. [Jerome] Robbins' job has much poetry (very needed in this work), which he seems afraid of, and covers up regularly, with bounce, violence, what-not."[57]

The cantata's indebtedness to Brecht-Weill, already noted with regard to "In Twos," could also be discerned not only in terms of the work's social content, but in its highly gestic suggestions of physical movement: sauntering and jostling in "The Lex Express"; skipping, marching, and flying in "I'm Ten"; staring and mourning in "Harlan Brown"; gossiping and promenading in "Hymie"; strolling in "In Twos"; and dancing, singing, and praying in "San Gennaro." The work's melodies similarly mimic such nonverbal sounds as cries, gasps, and hums; the two-note motive, for instance, that frames "The Lex Express," and that appears as well at the words "step down," seems to embody "that helpless laugh" mentioned in the text's last line.

Blitzstein described the "musical forms" of the work's separate movements as "quite simple: usually song-form, a-b-a, or a-b-c-b-a," but their diversity serves their individual poetic meanings. The first movement, for example, unfolds an unusual two-part design in which the first half depicts the ambling commuter and the second half his hellish subway ride, with a brief reminiscence of the opening music serving as a coda. The episodic second movement neatly reflects the impulsive daydreams of its ten-year-old protagonist. The outer sections of the third movement, in which each voice section enters singly, suggest the isolation of the spectators, the middle section, in which the chorus sings together, the "linking moment" of their shared grief and relief. The rondo form of the fourth movement enhances the humor of the narrative, with the refrain achieving full comic resonance only at the end, like a punch line. The through-composed fifth movement spins out a long line akin to the poem's meandering lovers. And the final movement's use of verse-chorus song form suits its evocation of a folk festival. "Music as close to pop as necessary," wrote Blitzstein in his notes, "spread and extend." The work's shifting tonalities similarly amplify the work's panoramic intentions, although the piece ultimately comes to rest on a tone center (C) whose major scale largely provides the pitch centers for the carefully connected individual movements, thereby helping to provide some overarching structure.[58]

The Interracial Fellowship Chorus and Interracial Orchestra under Harold Aks premiered *This Is the Garden* on May 5, 1957, at a concert at Carnegie Hall that also featured shorter pieces by Gabriel Fauré and, according to the program, the first complete American performance of Haydn's *Creation Mass*. A few days prior to the performance, the *Times* reported that a number of chorus members had objected to Blitzstein's piece, apparently on account of its difficulties, and that the group had held a debate on whether to perform the piece: "Partisan feeling ran high, but the Blitzstein work eventually won out."[59]

At the premiere, the "sizable house" gave the work, which concluded the program, "a rousing reception." The critics also liked the piece, thought "vivid" and "charming" by Jay Harrison (*Herald Tribune*), "jazzy" and "wistful" by Harriett Johnson (*New York Post*), and less approvingly, "jaunty, sentimental, mocking, pathetic and not very deep" by Howard Taubman (*New York Times*). In a letter to David Diamond some months later, Blitzstein commented, "The cantata was good; it didn't get quite the performance it rated, and still it was clear to me that (the pseudo-modest, actually arrogant statement) I hadn't made any serious mistakes. There were areas of disappointment: enunciation, which I had counted on, worked only fitfully. Choral Director Aks got nervous, whipped tempos at points to frenzy. And still it came off. Notices goodish."[60]

A published piano-vocal score appeared in 1957, prompting a laudatory review by *Musical America*'s Robert Sabin, who thought its "slangy, salty, wise-cracking" qualities "a relief, after the Victorian stuff that many of our choral composers are still turning out." In a 1967 note on Blitzstein, Copland treated the piece as one of the major achievements of the composer's later years, less "successful" than his other large choral work, the *Airborne Symphony*, but similarly "charged with a telling immediacy of musical effect, dissipated on occasion by banalities in the texts," and concluded that "despite weaknesses, both these cantatas deserve to be heard more often for the qualities they indubitably have."[61]

Despite such endorsement, performances of the work proved rare. JoAnn Rice conducted the piece, with piano accompaniment, in Brooklyn with the Stonewall Chorale, the nation's oldest gay and lesbian chorus, in June 1987; in

Irvington-on-Hudson with the Hudson Valley Singers in May 1990; and at New York's Merkin Hall with the Florilegium Chamber Choir (joined in this one piece by the Hudson Valley Singers) in June 1991. And Dan Perkins revived the piece, also with piano, with the Manchester Choral Society in Manchester, New Hampshire, in May 2010. Whereas Rice and her choirs readily warmed to the music, Perkins found that segments of his New Hampshire community chorus, like those in the Fellowship Chorus, resisted the work, in part because of difficulties that occasionally made it necessary for the pianist to double the voice parts; but in the end, the cantata, rendered with some stage movement that highlighted the piece's inherently dramatic qualities, won over singers and audience alike. As for why the work, described by Justin Smith as containing "inspired moments, a compelling structure, and an immensely appealing exuberance," found so few performances, Rice cited not only the relative unavailability of the music, but those "quintessentially New York" features that made it something of a "niche piece."[62]

More Music for Shakespeare (1950–1958)

In the course of the 1950s, Blitzstein provided the music for no fewer than four Shakespeare productions, beginning with his score for a 1950 Broadway staging of *King Lear* produced by Robert L. Joseph and Alexander Cohen and starring Louis Calhern under the direction of John Houseman, who insisted on Blitzstein's involvement. Presumably pleased to be collaborating once again with Houseman, whatever reservations he might have had about the director's work, Blitzstein drafted the music in Brigantine over the summer and signed a contract dated September 7 that specified a fee of $1,000 and a small percentage of the gross receipts.[1]

Often regarded during these years as a hoary melodrama for superannuated thespians, *King Lear* had had, as elsewhere, a fitful history in New York, notwithstanding the exceptional success of *The Jewish King Lear* (1892), a free adaptation, complete with happy ending, that became a staple of the Yiddish theater for a few decades. However, Houseman believed that the postwar period offered a more appreciative climate: "After the organized horrors of the Final Solution and the general acceptance of torture and civilian massacre as legitimate weapons of war climaxed by the dropping of the Bomb, mankind was ready to accept Shakespeare's grim view of the world in *King Lear*."[2]

On reading the play, which he had not done since college, Blitzstein wrote to Mina Curtiss about some aspects of the work that he found bothersome, including the discrepancy between the "small natures" of Lear and Gloucester and their "grandiose destinies," the king's fate described as "the grandest, most tempestuous heart-break in literature (and it *is*)." He further thought the disguises of Kent and Edgar a period contrivance that "has, for us, to be swallowed whole" and criticized the "quick pacing" of the play's final scene "as though Sh[akespeare] were bored by it, had a date, and scampered through it, cutting and hacking as he went." "The meat of the work," he concluded, "is Lear's grand storm; Gloucester's smaller agony; the meeting of Lear and Cordelia."[3]

Presenting Blitzstein with a list of thirty-four cues (many of these broken down into smaller ones), Houseman not only provided such signifiers as "Goneril theme" and "Lear hunting horn motif," but even more specific guidelines: "I need the schmalz so that I can shatter it with Edgar's appearance, which is a piss-cutter" (cue 10: end of II, ii); "if you could devise some grotesque, macabre, mad little accompaniment to the mock-trial, this would be simply great" (cue 20: III, vi); "The thing is that I would appreciate any aids I can get in coloring and clarifying the Goneril-Regan-Edmund sub-plot. A recognizable fanfare-theme to differentiate the two contending bitches might help. (Very brief, of course)" (cue 23: openings of IV, ii, and IV, v). Houseman allowed Blitzstein latitude in these matters—"I have such confidence in your theatrical sense that I will move and adjust lines almost anyway you want," he wrote to him from Malibu—but the composer, who scored the music for an offstage ensemble consisting of flute (doubling on piccolo), trumpet, French horn, Hammond organ (doubling on prepared piano, celesta, and solovox, an early synthesizer), percussion (including sandpaper and ratchet or washboard), and thunder drum, proved highly accommodating.[4]

A number of cues wound up consisting of short bits of music, often fanfares, used to accompany entrances and exits or to mark a transition from one scene or another. For the Fool's ditties, Blitzstein adopted, as in his operatic work, a variety of approaches, composing two fully accompanied songs, the jaunty "Fool's Song I" ("[Oh,] Fools Had Ne'er Less Wit in a Year") and the poignant "Fool's Song II" ("[Oh,] He That Has and a Little Tiny Wit," dedicated to his nephew Stephen); and four "jingles" merely punctuated by fool's bells and other percussion, the vocal part alternately involving rhythmic speech ("Have More Than Thou Showest"), unmetered speech ("That Lord That Counsell'd Thee," apparently cut), and sung melody ("Fathers That Wear Rags" and "That Sir Which Serves and Seeks for Gain"). Characteristically, Blitzstein imagined stage gesture in conjunction with these numbers; for "Have More Than Thou Showest," he directed the Fool to play the bells with his left hand and to synchronize the glissando xylophone punctuations with a slide of the back of his right thumb "across his rear."[5]

Blitzstein also wrote some notable music for the storm and battle scenes as well as for Lear's departure for Gloucester's castle and his reunion with Cordelia. For the departure scene, he used as underscoring the lovely "Fool's Song II," while for the reunion scene he reprised the music for Kent falling asleep in the stocks—the "schmalz" requested from Houseman—so that the score cross-referenced Kent's sleep with Lear's. Blitzstein employed other unifying gestures, such as adapting the grim overture for the "dead march" that concludes the play, and some of the "Fool's Song I" for the mock trial, made "grotesque" and "macabre" as requested by Houseman.

The extended storm sequence, embracing several scenes, posed the special problem of evoking, in Houseman's words, "the reality of the storm without interfering with the audibility of the characters. . . . With Marc Blitzstein's help I tried everything. I brought in the huge, dilapidated thunder-drum that had been so dear to Orson [Welles]'s heart; we played recordings of real thunder; we indicated the storm with turbulent music; we made unrealistic electronic thunderclaps with which Calhern had to compete for the attention of the audience. I think, finally, that we hurt rather than helped him with our efforts." For certain storm cues, Blitzstein wrote highly chromatic lines for the piccolo, trumpet, horn, and solovox in unison accompanied by trills alternately on the woodblock and snare drum (without snares), passages that surely sought to capture the tempest raging not only outdoors but in Lear's mind.[6]

Trimming the script to a playing time of two hours and forty-five minutes, Houseman hoped to present the five-act work in two acts; but this proved overly taxing for Calhern and the director accordingly divided the piece into three acts, which necessitated some last-minute alterations on Blitzstein's part. The show opened on December 25, 1950, at the National Theatre, with sets and lighting by Ralph Alswang, costumes by Dorothy Jeakins, and the offstage ensemble led by Max Marlin. In addition to Calhern, the cast featured Edith Atwater (Goneril), Jo Van Fleet (Regan), Nina Foch (Cordelia), and Norman Lloyd (Lear's Fool).

Houseman's belief that a postwar audience might be better prepared to receive the play found some vindication in Thomas Dash's comment in *Women's Wear Daily*, "With treachery, faithlessness, and murder afoot in the world, this macabre Shakespearean Grand Guignol strikes a pertinent note." But although the critics widely admired the production, including Blitzstein's music, which they deemed effective, even terrifying (though at times too overpowering, a defect presumably remedied after opening night), they remained rather cavalier about the play itself, some of the more sympathetic citing British essayist Charles Lamb's claim that the work ought better be read than staged. The show closed on February 3, 1951, after forty-eight performances.[7]

Blitzstein himself sounded upbeat about the production, telling Mina Curtiss,

> John [Houseman] has really done a beautiful job with the actors, who range from a realistic Lear (Calhern) to a highly stylized but electrically effective Edmund (Joe Wiseman, whose eccentric beauty I die for). Ralph Alswang's set is wonderfully ingenious, works miracles, and still shows horrid lapses of taste in detail. My music for the storm is considered a stroke of inspiration: a high keening sound, melodic but tortured, in three [sic] instruments in octaves at once, with a trilled wood-block underneath, and all surrounding and curiously supporting the raging Lear.[8]

When Houseman next directed the play in 1964, with the UCLA Theater Group, he again used the Blitzstein score, now conducted and recorded by film composer David Raksin; starring Morris Carnovsky, the production opened on June 6 for a three-week engagement at UCLA's Schoenberg Auditorium—the *Los Angeles Times* liked the score's "dark forbodings"—before moving on to the Pilgrimage Theater on July 10 for another few weeks. Yet another *Lear* directed by Houseman, this one a touring show with the Acting Company, also featured Blitzstein's score, here conducted by Stephen Colvin. Starring David Schramm, this production opened at New York's American Place Theatre on April 9, 1978, the notices similarly commending the music for evoking the "feeling of an age long past" (*Newsday*) and for combining "a sense of the timelessly ancient and modern worlds" (*New York Post*).[9]

When Orson Welles, who in 1953 had appeared on American television as Lear in a highly abridged version of the play with music by Virgil Thomson, returned to New York from Europe in 1955 under contract to producers Henry Margolis and Martin Gabel with the hope of establishing a repertory company on Broadway after the fashion of the Mercury Theatre, he decided to direct and star in his own *Lear* in alternation with another Jacobean classic, Ben Jonson's *Volpone* (1606), a comedy about the corrosive effects of greed; and he asked Blitzstein to compose the music for both plays. Although Blitzstein only recently had completed a *Lear* score, he agreed to write an entirely new one for Welles, his contract of November 14, 1955, specifying $1,000 for the music plus $50 per week for the run of the show and a small percentage of the box office receipts, as well as similar terms for *Volpone* should that production go forward.[10]

In meetings that fall, Blitzstein and Welles decided on a similar five-piece ensemble that could be used for both *Lear* and *Volpone*. Welles further expressed his wish, as Blitzstein recorded in minutes, to present *Volpone* as "a kind of 'musical,' with songs, numbers, dances, production-pieces," including magic tricks, one of the actor's specialties, the music sporting "gay, tart, heartless, brilliant, juicy stylish popular-venetio-serenadeo pieces," the Ben Jonson texts not limited to this particular play but culled from the poet's entire oeuvre. With respect to *Lear*, Welles proposed "a whole new conception, musically," one that would emphasize the play's more "lightly-emotional" moments, such as the scenes between Lear and his Fool, rather than the more heroic ones; and hence, the agreed on preference for an amplified harpsichord over the more orchestral Hammond organ, and Welles's decision to use, in addition to live music, "symbolic abstract" electronic sounds for the storm and battle scenes.[11]

Unable to secure a Broadway house for an extended engagement, Welles planned to present both shows at New York City Center over a six-week period, but financial pressures forced him to limit production to a two-and-a-half-week run starting January 12 (plus six preview performances) of just *Lear*, although the press announced a possible *Volpone* later in the season with comedian Jackie Gleason playing Mosca to Welles's Volpone. "Dearest Marc," the director assured Blitzstein in early December, "We are doing *Volpone* but not at City Center. Patience and fortitude." By this point, Blitzstein had started to canvas Jonson's collected works in consultation with Welles and presumably had completed those *Volpone* sketches found among his papers, including drafts, some only fragments, of an overture and five songs: one in the style of a "jazzed waltz" for Castrone and Volpone, "Come, My Celia" (from *Volpone*); one for Volpone and vocal quartet, "Song of the Glove" ("Thou More Than Most Sweet Glove" from the satire *Cynthia's Revels*); one for Celia, "Men, If You Love Us" (the first stanza of "In the Person of Womankind"); and two for Mosca, both entitled "Mosca's Song" ("Buz, Quoth the Blue Flie" from the masque *Oberon, The Faery Prince*; and a "slow tango" to the famed lyric "His Excuse for Loving"). Blitzstein selected several other Jonson lyrics from both *Volpone* and elsewhere, but ostensibly he never got so far as to set them.[12]

Although Welles's plans for a Broadway *Volpone* never materialized, in April 1956, after he had left New York for Hollywood and entered into an association with Desilu Productions, he still hoped to launch a musical version of the play, apparently as one of a series of hour-length television films announced that spring, and asked Blitzstein to mail him the Jonson lyrics the two had decided on. But nothing came of this either, and the composer eventually found other uses for some of the music.[13]

As for *King Lear*, Welles asked Otto Luening and Vladimir Ussachevsky to create the electronic portion of the score. Both on the Columbia music faculty, Luening (1900–1996) and his former student, the Manchurian-born Ussachevsky (1911–1990), had made a splash in the early 1950s as pioneers of *musique concrète*, that is, electronically manipulated instrumental and vocal sounds. Welles himself visited their studio, selecting and naming the sounds he wanted for as many as forty-four cues and declaring electronic music "the greatest thing that has happened for the theater since the invention of incandescent light," according to Luening, who marveled at the director's sharp ear and keen memory. Assisted by composer Chou Wen-chung and engineer Stanley Tonkel, Luening and Ussachevsky worked tirelessly on the score, which used some purely electronic sounds generated by oscillators but mostly recorded live sounds. Spending time with Luening and Ussachevsky at their studio in late November, Blitzstein deemed the two "the most enterprising and capable experimenters with sound-tape, electronic-sound, Ampex, etc." (this last, a reference to a brand of tape recorder), and he served as an intermediary between them and Welles, helping to supervise the timing and placement of the electronic cues.[14]

For his own music, Blitzstein faced the challenge of obtaining a harpsichord, an instrument then difficult to rent. Guided by harpsichordist Ralph Kirkpatrick, he arranged the purchase of a small John Challis that had been advertised in the *Times* and retained musicologist and technician Sibyl Marcuse to keep the instrument tuned. According to his manuscripts, he finished the score on December 28, 1955, but some evidence suggests that he continued working on the piece into 1956.

Arranging the music for flute (doubling on piccolo and clarinet), trumpet, French horn, amplified harpsichord, and percussion, Blitzstein provided Welles with a very different score than he had Houseman, in part because of Welles's distinctive concept of the work, but also because the electronic sounds relieved him of some responsibility. In addition, Welles had prepared a more condensed version of the play, one that ultimately ran about two hours and fifteen minutes without intermission but that included small interpolations from other plays. Once again, the composer framed the whole with an overture and final funeral march alike in style and mood, but in contrast to the high drama of the Houseman score, this framing music proved gently melancholy, its classicism reminiscent of Gabriel Fauré's incidental score to *Pelléas et Mélisande*.

Also as before, Blitzstein composed two full-fledged songs for Lear's Fool: "Fool's Song I" (which conflated, probably at Welles's request, Feste's "When That

I Was and a Little Tiny Boy" from *Twelfth Night* with "He That Has and a Little Tiny Wit" from *Lear*) and "Fool's Song II" ("Fools Had Ne'er Less Grace in a Year"), both numbers reminiscent of "Fool's Song I" from the 1950 *Lear*, but more direct and brusque in mood. He also provided a "Drinking Song" for the Fool and the "riotous" knights, the text stitched together from *Henry IV, Part 2* (V, iii), with a short instrumental reprise of the song used subsequently for Kent in the stocks.

Blitzstein further devised a lengthy harpsichord solo to accompany much of the scene in which Edmund hoodwinks his father Gloucester and brother Edgar, thereby helping to amplify that section's comic undertone. The score also features a tenderly waltz-like passage for Lear's departure for Gloucester's castle, a dramatic turning point that had elicited a similarly heartfelt response in the composer's previous *Lear* score; and a brooding passage—the score's most harmonically complex moment—for Cordelia's short scene on the Dover road.

King Lear opened on January 12, with Welles joined by a cast that included Geraldine Fitzgerald (Goneril), Viveca Lindfors (Cordelia), Sylvia Short (Regan), and Alvin Epstein (Lear's Fool). Theodore Cooper designed the sets, Robert Fletcher, who also played Edgar, the costumes. Blitzstein, leading the five-piece ensemble from the harpsichord, received prominent billing for the "musical score," with Luening and Ussachevsky mentioned only near the end of the playbill for the "tape recorder sound score."

To judge from the notices, the times remained rather inhospitable with regard to the work, described as "baffling" (in that Lear seemed so unlikeable a hero) by both the *Daily News* and the *Journal-American*, not to mention "creaky and dubious" by *Variety*. In any event, the production received poor reviews, considerably more so than had Houseman's, with many criticizing Welles's acting and direction as bombastic. A few critics briefly noted the originality of Blitzstein's contribution, but none mentioned Luening and Ussachevsky aside from the *Musical Quarterly*'s Henry Cowell, who conversely had nothing to say about the Blitzstein score.[15]

During the preview week, Welles fractured his left ankle, and on opening night, hobbling about with a cane, injured his other leg. The following evening, he appeared by himself in a wheelchair and entertained the great majority who elected to stay with commentary about the play and selected monologues. Until the show closed after twenty-one performances on January 29, he performed his part in a wheelchair, pushed around stage by the Fool, Alvin Epstein. In later years, critic Mel Gussow, who like Otto Luening remembered Welles's Lear at City Center as the most memorable of his life, wrote that the wheelchair "encompassed a universe: it became a metaphor for Lear's enforced retirement and isolation." But the accident hurt sales, and even under the best of circumstances, the production, reportedly the most expensive play in City Center's history to that date, could not recoup its investment after so short a run, a situation compounded by the cancellation of a planned ten-week tour.[16]

Soon after, on March 4, 1956, the *New York Times* announced that the outstanding Greek-born conductor Dimitri Mitropoulos, director of the New York Philharmonic since 1951, had commissioned Blitzstein to write a one-movement orchestral piece based on the composer's two *Lear* scores (1950, 1956). The circumstances surrounding this commission remain unknown, but presumably Leonard Bernstein, soon to succeed Mitropoulos and a close personal friend of both men, played some role. Blitzstein seriously started in on the piece later in 1956, but partly because of various health problems, including a kidney-stone attack in early 1958, he did not complete the work, *Lear: A Study*, until shortly before Mitropoulos gave the first and to date only performances of the piece at Carnegie Hall on February 27 and 28 of that year. Scored for full orchestra supplemented by two cornets and a large percussion battery, the work bore a dedication to the composer's sister Jo.[17]

For the Philharmonic's program book, Blitzstein provided some remarks about the play and its main character:

> Shakespeare's "King Lear" has been with me for a long time. For me it is his most compelling tragedy: of all his works it seems the one which announces the modern epoch. The hero Lear *attains* tragic dimensions as the play proceeds. He is quite unlike the heroes of Greek tragedy, who are fully-realized characters in conflict with unyielding fates. Lear is a king: but a boastful barbaric king, a playboy, a carouser and hunter with his knights. He receives the true and false loyalties of his three daughters with little or no sensitiveness or differentiation. When friction, ingratitude, insubordination develop, he meets them with lordly petulance, later with irresponsible fury and explosiveness. It is only through the ravages of trial-by-storm, of pain to the point of madness, that the bullying child at last comes into his own as full protagonist, strong and beautiful in self-knowledge. And by a stroke of irony which is pure Shakespeare, it happens too late, at the moment of death itself.

Blitzstein further informed the Philharmonic's press department that the work's three parts represent "a) the stripe of man and king; b) the nature-storm and the inner storm; and c) growth, serenity and death."[18]

The work's first part, Maestoso, meant to reflect "the stripe of man and king," actually comprises, remarkably enough, a fairly literal transcription of the opening passacaglia from Blitzstein's 1929 opera, *Parabola and Circula*. The more chromatic second part, Allegro leggiero, contains the "keening" storm music from the Houseman production, but also music of undetermined origin, perhaps newly devised for this piece, thereby possibly explaining why this section caused the composer particular "grief and effort." Arriving after a brief reminiscence of the passacaglia, the delicately scored third part, Adagietto, ingeniously alternates two cues from the Welles production: the concluding funeral march and the poignant music for Lear's departure for Gloucester's castle, finally fused in a bittersweet ending that well captures that sense of "growth, serenity and death" mentioned by the composer. The extensive use of music from *Parabola and Circula* naturally raises questions about that opera's relation to the Lear story, but in any case, the adapted passage neatly matches the general tenor of Blitzstein's *Lear* scores, resemblances accentuated by a slight rewrite of the music for Lear's departure.[19]

After the performances at Carnegie Hall on Thursday night and Friday afternoon, Blitzstein wrote Diamond, "All the composers love it: [Alexei] Haieff, [Carlos] Chávez, Lenny [Bernstein], Bill Schuman, etc. The *Trib* (Jay Harrison) gave it a rave, the *Times* (Harold Schoenberg [sic]) a scurrilous notice. It sounds; very big, clear, short, with a spread serene finish which was the only thing Mitropoulos had trouble with. In general, he played it beautifully, particularly on the Friday afternoon, when it had a real audience success." Schonberg, like Harriett Johnson in the *New York Post*, seemed less "scurrilous" than lukewarm, finding the music "grim and dissonant enough" and "well scored," but otherwise "tenuous" and "neutral." However, Jay Harrison, although he guessed that Mitropoulos's performance "did not quite come off," truly did rave: "Blitzstein has . . . produced a first-rate piece of music, a work of vigorous imagination, bold color and strong contrasts. It rages and broods, fumes then goes contemplative, declaims then whispers, roars then retreats to silence. And it is masterful in its construction, compelling, therefore, in a purely formal sense from beginning to end."[20]

As Schonberg predicted, the piece made little dent, although Ned Rorem (b. 1923) by his own admission "filched" a prominent grace-note motive from the work for his tone poem *Eagles* (1958), as he later would borrow a gesture from *Regina* for his opera *Miss Julie* (1965). Rorem, as mentioned earlier, had met Blitzstein at Tanglewood in the summer of 1946, and that fall, the twenty-three-year-old Juilliard student interviewed him for a sociology class, the start of a lifelong friendship. Rorem, who discerned a resemblance between Blitzstein and the mustachioed character actor Keenan Wynn, impressed the older man with, among other things, his dashing good looks, although their relationship never became sexual (Rorem claiming that Blitzstein's preferences in that regard ran more toward heterosexual men).[21]

Blitzstein became a supportive although not uncritical mentor to Rorem, steering him away from "libretto land" by rewriting the young man's text for *The Robbers* (1956) and giving him flack over some "arty-arty *Harper's Bazaar* photos" that he and friend William Flanagan (1923–1969) had taken. He also wrote a short essay, "On Two Young Composers," that served as marketing copy for a February 24, 1959, concert of songs by Rorem and Flanagan at Carnegie Recital Hall and that praised Flanagan's "sensitive, personal, and remarkably sure" melodic "curve" as well as Rorem's "gift of daring. . . . It is a long time since anyone brought off the grand style, outsized sweeping line, thunder and all, that marks his stunning

'The Lordly Hudson.'" Rorem had limited sympathies for Blitzstein's political beliefs and mixed feelings about the music as well, stating a highly selective preference for "Emily," "Birdie's Aria," and especially the song cycle *From Marion's Book*. "We barked up very different trees," recalled Rorem, who noted a similarity of language described as "diatonic, lyric, simple," but who also expressed disappointment over Blitzstein's coolness toward Ravel, Cocteau, and Poulenc, and whose sweeping *Eagles* indeed seemed some distance from the sober theatricality of *Lear: A Study*. Flanagan, at least in 1958, seemed more wholeheartedly enthusiastic about Blitzstein, calling *Regina* "an opera of blood-curdling power that, for all its faults, is as rich in purely musical value as any composed in the decade since it was first performed on Broadway."[22]

Lear: A Study remained the only major instrumental piece of Blitzstein's later years, and even this effort derived from his theater work. Otherwise, regarding instrumental music, he wrote only some occasional piano pieces: the solemn *Innocent Psalm* (1953) "for the Bernstein baby," that is, his goddaughter Jamie Bernstein (b. 1952), the oldest child of Leonard and Felicia; a stately wedding piece, *For Kit's Wedding*, dated May 15, 1953, in celebration of his nephew Christopher's marriage to Sonia Fogg on June 6 of that year; the festive *Wedding Piece for Stephen and Joyce*, in honor of his other nephew's marriage to Joyce Kidder on July 30, 1955; and his last completed piece, the ruminative *Lied* ("On his birthday, a portrait of Ben Cooper contemplating his two women") on the occasion of his host Benjamin Cooper's birthday on June 28, 1963, the "two women" a reference to Cooper's wife, soprano Brenda Lewis, and their baby daughter Edith.

Blitzstein performed the wedding pieces himself: *For Kit's Wedding* at an upright piano prior to the ceremony at the Fogg home in Philadelphia; *Wedding Piece* as Joyce Kidder descended the staircase of her parents' home, also in Philadelphia. Likewise, he performed *Lied* for the Coopers at their home in Weston, Connecticut, and presumably played *Innocent Psalm* for the Bernsteins. All four vignettes seem characteristically dramatic, and the composer tellingly recycled the two wedding pieces for his 1958 incidental score to *A Midsummer Night's Dream*. At the same time, the strictly three-voice *Innocent Psalm* and four-voice *Lied* contain a certain severity as well: the neoclassical dramatist in a nutshell.[23]

Blitzstein's association with Shakespeare during these years—surpassed only by his preoccupation with Brecht—continued with his 1958 residence at the American Shakespeare Festival in Stratford, Connecticut, where he provided music for *A Midsummer Night's Dream* and *The Winter's Tale*, and supervised Virgil Thomson's music for *Hamlet*, a score originally written for a 1936 Broadway staging of the play.

The Stratford Festival had opened its doors only three years earlier, in July 1955. John Houseman, who served as artistic director from 1956 through 1959, engaged Thomson for his first two seasons there, followed by Blitzstein in 1958. Given the presence at Stratford of such figures as Houseman, Thomson,

Blitzstein, lighting designer Jean Rosenthal, and actors Will Geer and Hiram Sherman, the festival could be seen as a descendant of the Federal and Mercury Theatres, which had given birth to *The Cradle* some twenty years earlier.[24]

Blitzstein accepted the terms of $600 for each of the two scores, along with an additional $25 per performance. As he worked on *A Midsummer Night's Dream* throughout April and May, he broadened his knowledge of Renaissance music, including, apparently, familiarizing himself with a recent recording of Shakespeare songs by countertenor Alfred Deller and the Deller Consort. Completing a draft of the score for flute (doubling on piccolo), oboe (doubling on English horn), trumpet, horn, violin, cello, lute (doubling on bass), harpsichord (doubling on celesta), percussion (two players), countertenor, and soprano on May 29, he revised the music fairly significantly during the weeks leading up to the show's premiere on June 20.

The production's young director Jack Landau—who in 1967 met a violent death similar to Blitzstein's—used a slightly abridged version of the play divided into three acts or "parts," and presented the work in the style of a masque on the occasion of a Tudor nobleman's wedding, with the overture featuring the "rude mechanicals" readying the entertainment. David Hays designed the scenery, Tharon Musser the lighting, Thea Neu the costumes, and George Balanchine the choreography. The cast featured Jack Bittner (Theseus), Nancy Wickwire (Hippolyta), Richard Waring (Oberon), June Havoc (Titania), Richard Easton (Puck), and an all-star group of "mechanicals" that included Sherman (Bottom), Geer (Snout), and Morris Carnovsky (Quince). From the keyboard, Herman Chessid led the ten-piece ensemble and the two featured singers: countertenor Russell Oberlin (A Master of Revels, a character added to the original script) and soprano June Ericson (A Fairy or, as alternately identified, the First Fairy).[25]

Blitzstein wrote a particularly ample score for this production, encouraged not only by the relatively rich instrumental resources at hand, but by the play's congeniality to musical treatment. He even drew on period lyrics for supplemental vocal numbers, in the end setting six texts: two from the play—the fairy chorus "You Spotted Snakes with Double Tongue" ("Lullaby") for the First Fairy (and reprised for Titania's sleep with Bottom), and Bottom's ditty "The Ousel Cock So Black of Hue" (set unaccompanied in the context of a larger set-piece)—and four others—"Whilst Youthful Sports are Lasting" (the second and third stanzas of Elizabethan composer Thomas Weelkes's "To Shorten Winter's Sadness") for the Master of Revels (just before Egeus's entrance, I, i); a slightly varied version of this song, "Farewell My Joy" (using another madrigal text by Weelkes) for the Master of Revels (part of a "transformation" interlude linking Acts I and II, although in this version within Act I; and reprised for the exit of the mortals at the play's end); "On the Plains, Fairy Trains" (a Barnabe Barnes text set to music by Weelkes) for the First Fairy (for the same transformation scene); and "Sweet is the Rose" (a sonnet by Edmund Spenser) for the Master of Revels (at the top of III, ii, serving here to open this version's second act).

Most of the work's thirty-six cues (several ostensibly cut before opening night) color the royal court of Theseus and Hippolyta and the fairy kingdom of Oberon and Titania as opposed to the tradesmen and the young lovers, whom Blitzstein left largely unmusicalized, with such exceptions as a series of short comic cues for the Pyramus and Thisbe play-within-a-play. Theseus and Hippolyta have their own themes (his, a fanfare; hers, a "courtly march" adapted from the wedding music Blitzstein wrote for his nephew Christopher), while Puck has two (a soft, staccato leaping theme, and music derived from "Abel Offers the Lamb" from the composer's ballet *Cain*). Other recurring leitmotives include those for "love" and "love-juice."

The more extended instrumental cues include the overture, which incorporates Bottom's ditty; a sultry "Tango" that depicts the infatuated Titania; a joyous "Wedding March" (adapted from Blitzstein's *Wedding Piece* for nephew Stephen) that, like the popular "Wedding March" from Mendelssohn's *Midsummer* score, sets the tone for the final act (which in this version occurs within the third act); a robust "Bergomask" for the players, as specified by Shakespeare, followed by a more stately "Pavane" for the larger company; and the delicate "Fairy Blessing" that accompanies Oberon's concluding recitation, capped by a return of Puck's music for the epilogue. Sadly, Balanchine's choreography in this rare collaboration with Blitzstein does not seem to have survived.

For this score, Blitzstein imaginatively exploited musical space in order to enhance stage movement and scenic contrast. Immediately following the overture, for example, he wrote an offstage fanfare, played by half the ensemble, for Theseus, followed by an onstage march, played by the other instruments, for Hippolyta, and then combined the two musics as the lovers meet, thereby establishing their individuality and foreshadowing their union. For the arrival of the fairies, he similarly constructed an elaborate transformation scene in which, against the final strains of "Farewell My Joy," the First Fairy's song "On the Plains" steals in, overlapping the Master of Revels's disappearing "fa-la-la's"; as oboe switches to English horn, bowed strings to plucked, snare and bass drum to vibraphone, and harpsichord to celesta, with triads dissolving into clusters, a new sound vista seamlessly emerges. (Benjamin Britten coincidentally made use of similar contrasts in his 1960 operatic adaptation of the play.) For the awakenings of Titania and Bottom, Blitzstein conversely composed passages that embellished the transition from fairy to mortal realms.

At the same time, he drew correspondences between these two domains; the music that accompanies the initial entrance of Oberon and Titania, for instance, daintily parodies that for Theseus and Hippolyta, while the "Fairy Blessing" similarly mimics the "Bergomask." In such ways, Blitzstein helped dramatize the notion that the mortal and fairy worlds mirror each other. As to musical style, the term "Elizabethan-romantisch," used by the composer in reference to the "Tango," aptly describes the score as a whole, with its echoes of Morley, Brahms, and

Debussy. On the other hand, the soft, somber, dissonant fog music, like an eerie hymn, seems pure Blitzstein.

The critics lauded virtually every facet of the production, including the "gay, amusing" score, John Chapman (*Daily News*) deeming the music "far more impressive and enjoyable than the run-of-the-mill stuff one usually associates with Shakespeare productions." Harriett Johnson even published an article in the *New York Post* devoted exclusively to the score in which she wrote that the music provided "enchantment to enchantment as the play proceeds" and without which "the play's impact would suffer, while instead it gives the effect of adding momentum to a swiftly paced production that is as aerial as Puck himself."[26]

Blitzstein wrote a more subdued but no less enchanting score for *The Winter's Tale*, composing his thirty-six cues mostly in a "gruelling" ten-day period straddling June and July. Houseman and Landau co-directed, each taking charge of different sections of the play. (In a letter to his copyist Arnold Arnstein, Blitzstein, warning of possible last-minute revisions, complained of "the vagaries of directors, of which we have two on this one.") Dorothy Jeakins created the costumes, Jean Rosenthal the lighting, and once again, David Hays the scenery, and George Balanchine the dances. At the suggestion of Lincoln Kirstein, the production employed tarot card imagery, an idea that, as Houseman recalled, helped reconcile the play's unusual "blend of ritual and reality." John Colicos (Leontes), Nancy Wickwire (Hermione), and Nancy Marchand (Paulina) headed a strong cast, and Chessid once again led the same ten-piece ensemble from the harpsichord.[27]

One of Shakespeare's final plays, *The Winter's Tale* (ca. 1610) falls into two large parts. Acts I through III unfold a tragedy, mostly set in Sicily, in which the deranged jealousy of Leontes, King of Sicily, leads to the attempted murder of his presumed rival Polixenes, King of Bohemia; the banishment of his infant daughter Perdita; and the deaths of his wife Hermione and their son, along with a loyal member of court. Acts IV and V, transpiring sixteen years later, form in contrast a pastoral comedy mostly set in Bohemia, one that involves the romance of Perdita (raised a shepherdess) and Polixenes's son Florizel, the reconciliation of the young lovers with their kingly fathers, and finally a statue of Hermione that comes to life. The first large section moves from Sicily to Bohemia, the second, from Bohemia back to Sicily. Stratford presented the play, somewhat pruned, in three acts, with the first act comprising Acts I and II; the second, Acts III and IV; and the third, Act V.

Much as Blitzstein created separate but related sounds for the mortal and fairy realms in his *Midsummer* score, so he structured his music for *The Winter's Tale* around opposing images of Sicily as "cruel, sophisticated, the winter and early spring—styled—gay sometimes" and Bohemia as "sunny, vernal, abundant, open rustic—summer and 'ripe autumn.'" The overture, a martial prelude that seeps over as underscoring for the opening dialogue, immediately sets the tone for Sicily, or more specifically, as the composer wrote in his notes, "Everything is

hunky-dory in Sicilia." Hermione has her own signature theme, a stately sarabande that contrasts with Leontes's agonized music. Blitzstein develops some of
these materials throughout the work in order to help strengthen the play's tenuous unity as well as to enrich the drama: a "junior version" of the overture
accompanies the arrival of Perdita and Florizel at the court of Leontes; a delicate
reworking of Hermione's theme signifies the infant Perdita in the storm scene;
and a "purged" rendering of Leontes's "night-agony" depicts his restored sanity.[28]

Blitzstein establishes the contrasting world of "sunny" Bohemia in the play's
second half by way of brightly scored instrumental cues along with sprightly
songs, dances, and short comic snatches, such as those for the exchange of clothes
between Florizel and the thief Autolycus. Near the end, the score even contains a
cue entitled "Farting Fanfare" for the rustic father and son, Shepherd and Clown,
in their new attire as gentlemen, with downward horn glissandos placed in
humorous, chromatic contexts.

Blitzstein also set all five of Autolycus's songs, which appear in fairly quick suc-
cession in the play's second half: "When Daffodils Begin to Peer" ("Shepherd's
Song," first three stanzas only); "Jog On, Jog On"; "Lawn As White As Driven
Snow" ("Vendor's Song"); the "merry ballad" (Shakespeare's phrase) in three
parts, "Get You Hence, For I Must Go," with shepherdesses Mopsa and Dorcas
("Trio"); and "Will You Buy Any Tape" (a revamping of the "Vendor's Song"). The
"Vendor's Song" and the "Trio," the two big numbers, feature full orchestral accompaniment, with the former responsive to the Servant's amazed description of
Autolycus: "He sings several tunes faster than you'll tell money; he utters them as
he had eaten ballad and all men's ears grew to his tunes." (For the "Vendor's Song,"
Blitzstein also took some liberties with the text, including adding his own "didle-
didle's.") The other three songs, although essentially unaccompanied, sometimes
have instrumental frames, as in the case of "Shepherd's Song," which opens and
ends with a plaintive oboe solo in a contrasting modality to the song proper. As
with the *Midsummer* score, these settings show the influence of Elizabethan music
and perhaps British folk music as well.

As Autolycus, Earle Hyman, an African-American actor who had portrayed
Othello at Stratford the previous season and who later became a familiar television presence as Bill Cosby's father on *The Cosby Show*, struggled with his songs,
despite extensive coaching with the composer, who during a run-through admonished him for merely marking rather than singing his music. Fortunately, in the
"Trio," he had the support of two solid singers, June Ericson (Mopsa) and Barbara Barrie (Dorcas), who remembered Blitzstein as a warm and encouraging
mentor.[29]

Blitzstein also added some romantic luster to this production by way of two
Ben Jonson settings salvaged from the aborted *Volpone*: "Song of the Glove," a
solo for countertenor with lute accompaniment that prepares the entrance of Florizel and Perdita; and "Men, If You Love Us" (which had existed at least in some

preliminary guise), a solo for unaccompanied soprano (or alternately a duet for two unaccompanied sopranos) that serves as a transition to the final scene.

Some of the score's more noteworthy cues also include the dolorous introduction that precedes the trial scene; the storm music, which employs a muted, flutter-tongued trumpet in a high register to suggest "a savage kind of ram's horn (shofer)"; a ticking episode for Time's soliloquy; the play's "dance of Shepherds and Shepherdesses" (but not its "dance of twelve Satyrs," part of a sheep-shearing festival scene cut), for which Blitzstein wrote a rustic "Passepied" incorporating rhythms suggested by Balanchine; and Hermione's magical transfiguration, in which the composer strove for "beauty, grace, a religious mass-like feeling, continuing to the end of the play, swelling to a great Hosanna-like finish." At least in intention, this finale recalls the ending of his 1932 opera *The Condemned*, another work involving imprisonment, death, and redemption, a connection that helps explain—as does, perhaps, the composer's own contemporaneous travails with the House Un-American Activities Committee—the inspired quality of this particular incidental score.

Opening on July 20, *The Winter's Tale* proved another festival favorite, and although Blitzstein's score received less notice as compared to *A Midsummer Night's Dream*, *Variety* deemed the music "helpful throughout." Stratford revived *A Midsummer* in the spring of 1959, primarily for student audiences, and then launched a successful coast-to-coast tour of both plays in the fall of 1960, with Bert Lahr in the roles of Bottom and Autolycus.[30]

In 1958, Blitzstein assembled six numbers from these two productions as *Six Elizabethan Songs* for tenor or soprano and piano, dedicated to Leonard Bernstein, and published the following year by Chappell in the following order: "Sweet is the Rose," "Shepherd's Song," "Song of the Glove," "Court Song" (that is, "Farewell My Joy"), "Lullaby," and "Vendor's Song." (Blitzstein attributed the words of "Sweet is the Rose" to "Amoretti," the Spenser collection from which the poem comes, and those of the "Court Song" to anonymous.) The circumstances of its premiere remain unknown, although Katherine Ciesinski performed five of the six songs with pianist Brian Zeger on December 1, 1991, at Curtis Hall in Philadelphia, while Brian Porter performed the whole set with Donald St. Pierre on March 2, 2005, at the Curtis Institute, and Karen Vuong with Leo Marcus four days later in Los Angeles.[31]

In 2003, Boosey & Hawkes republished these six numbers along with "Fool's Song" (that is, "Fool's Song II") from the 1950 *King Lear*, "Whilst Youthful Sports" from *A Midsummer Night's Dream*, and "Autolycus-Dorcas-Mopsa Trio" (that is, the trio "Get You Hence, For I Must Go") from *The Winter's Tale*—a largely unknown treasure trove of delectable songs that imaginatively bestow their exquisite texts with music that mediates between past and present.[32]

Blitzstein's abilities as a composer of incidental stage music—an achievement rivaled by few other Americans—helped endear him to New York's theater community all the more. However, none of this work achieved the status of, say, Copland's *Quiet City*, derived from music for a play by Irwin Shaw. The strengths of Blitzstein's incidental scores tended rather to concern their integral relation to the productions at hand, so that their effectiveness depended in large part on stage use, as Houseman demonstrated in his repeated employment of the 1950 *King Lear* score, and, less fully, Richard Linklater in his recreation of the Mercury Theatre's *Julius Caesar* in the film *Me and Orson Welles* (2009). At the same time, the songs for the Shakespeare plays, even independent of any theatrical context, continue to delight, while *Lear: A Study* might one day prove a cherished work as well.

22

Juno (1957–1959)

On April 16, 1958, Blitzstein received a subpoena to appear before an executive session—often the prelude to a public hearing—of the House Un-American Activities Committee (HUAC) at the Foley Square federal courthouse in New York. He arrived at court on May 8 accompanied by his counsel Telford Taylor, a notable critic of McCarthyism who had been one of the chief prosecutors at the Nuremberg military trials.[1]

Congress established HUAC in 1938 as a means of investigating "subversive and un-American propaganda," initially meaning primarily fascist and racist activities; but under its first chairman, Martin Dies, the committee quickly made communism its principal target, holding hearings on alleged communist infiltration into the Federal Theatre Project that led to that program's demise in 1939. Made a standing committee in 1945, HUAC continued its sweeping and often ruinous investigations of artists, among others, after the war, an agenda complemented by probes led by Wisconsin Senator Joseph McCarthy and fueled by such vigilante publications as *Red Channels* (1950).[2]

Staffed with politicians and attorneys, HUAC focused on the political associations of artists as opposed to their work. "We do not feel that the performance of a concerto by a Communist is in itself subversive," allowed Representative Morgan Moulder (the same Moulder sideswiped in Blitzstein's *This Is the Garden*). "But we do feel that the presence of the activities of Communists, of persons loyal to the international conspiratorial apparatus in the Soviet Union, do [sic] constitute a subversive threat regardless of the profession in which these persons are engaged." But even this understated the scope of the committee, who investigated citizens with highly tenuous or remote connections to communism and the Soviet Union, although by the time of Blitzstein's subpoena, the Supreme Court had begun to curtail the committee's more flagrant abuses of First Amendment rights.[3]

HUAC long had kept a file on Blitzstein, including reports by two informants, Louis Budenz and Howard Rushmore, who stated that according to V. J. Jerome, the cultural czar of the American Communist Party (CPUSA), the composer was a party member. In late November 1956, a committee staff member—apparently attorney Dolores Scotti, a leading HUAC researcher—confronted the composer with his record in order to learn what "information he might possess relative to Communism, especially in the entertainment field," but Blitzstein, after denying that he could have been so "identified," said, according to government records, "If I am officially called I will do my duty, but I do not wish to speak to any member of the Committee otherwise. I do not feel I must explain any errors and mistakes I may have made in the past which are my private concern and I certainly do not wish to discuss what other people have done." In another memo to Staff Director Richard Arens, this one dated April 1958, Scotti spoke of the difficulty in serving Blitzstein a subpoena— "[he] is frequently out of the country or is evasive and slippery"—and recommended that "considering his very lengthy record," he submit to a long executive session.[4]

Subpoenaed witnesses had a range of options with regard to testimony, including remaining silent under protection of the Fifth Amendment. But whatever tactic adopted, witnesses, at least those called publicly, typically suffered negative repercussions, some quite severe, although the New York theater world offered something of a safe haven, as discussed earlier.[5]

In his private session, Blitzstein faced a three-man subcommittee comprising Representatives Morgan Moulder, Bernard Kearney, and Gordon Scherer, along with Staff Director Arens and Investigator Scotti, with Kearney acting as chairman for Moulder, who arrived in the middle of the composer's testimony. Asked about his political activities—Arens, who led the questioning, referred to his "communist front record" as "one of the most extensive" he had ever seen—and about such associates as Lillian Hellman, Brenda Lewis, Will Geer, and Stratford stage manager Bernard Gersten (scheduled to testify directly after him), Blitzstein admitted to being a Communist Party member from 1938 to 1949, but refused to discuss anyone else's politics or to name any names. At the first such request, to name the person who solicited him to join the party, Blitzstein asked to read a prepared statement, which Kearney permitted. This short statement acknowledged a citizen's "obligation" to provide "information which may be of aid to an authorized legislative inquiry," but continued as follows:

> I do not believe that the House of Representatives has authorized your Committee, or that it could constitutionally authorize it, to question individuals with respect to their political associations, beliefs and/or activities. The powers of Congressional committees in legislative investigations are limited by the Constitution, as set forth in the Bill of Rights and especially in the First Amendment....
>
> Even with such serious legal questions being raised, I do not wish or mean to restrict my testimony simply in order to challenge your Committee's authority. It is because I would not feel legally or morally justified in answering questions put to me which lie beyond Constitutional limitations, or which are not pertinent to any authorized subject of inquiry, in cases where persons other than myself might be unnecessarily involved or damaged; persons whose activities, as far as I have observed them, were innocent of anything unlawful or dangerous to our Nation or its security.

Blitzstein subsequently held firm, repeatedly declining to disclose any information about others, even the number of persons in the entertainment field he could identify as communist, a question he regarded as "leading."[6]

Blitzstein's admission of possible "errors and mistakes," as reported by a HUAC staff member in November 1956, suggests that he had reassessed his political past, understandable enough in light of Khrushchev's denunciation of Stalin and the Soviet invasion of Hungary, which reportedly disturbed him deeply. Now, his 1958 testimony pointed explicitly to dissatisfaction with the Communist Party:

MOULDER: "Is your political philosophy the same now as it was then [the 1930s]?"

BLITZSTEIN: "It is very hard to say, sir. I don't believe—I have come to the conclusion that I am not a very political thinker."

MOULDER: "What do you understand the objectives and purposes of the Communist Party to be as of today?"

BLITZSTEIN: "Frankly, I do not know. I find today that I disagree with many of the Communist Party policies and in particular the attempt to interfere with my individual freedom of thought."

————

KEARNEY: "You also stated, I believe, a few minutes ago in words or substance that you joined during the Depression and always believed in the rights of minorities. I presume that you felt that the Communist Party was a believer in the rights of minorities. Do you still hold that opinion today?"

BLITZSTEIN: "I am very confused on the subject, sufficiently confused."

————

ARENS: "What caused you to disassociate yourself or become disassociated from the Communist Party?"

BLITZSTEIN: "Largely the fact that my thinking changed from, or, rather, moved much more closely to my own craft and art. . . . It was also a sense of disaffection for the way in which the Communist Party seemed to be tailing the line always proposed by the Soviet Union. Many aspects of that line and many aspects of the policy such as the one you, Mr. Chairman, brought up, I resented and objected to" [an allusion to Kearney's mention of the Soviet "campaign against the Jews in the satellite countries in Eastern Europe today"].

————

ARENS: "Are you now against the Communist Party, against the activity of the Communist Party?"

BLITZSTEIN: "Yes, sir, I think I am."

At the same time, Blitzstein defended the CPUSA as a "political party" as opposed to "an international conspiracy." Nor did his testimony, even under duress, represent a blanket disavowal of all CPUSA policies, let alone socialism or Marxist theory.[7]

The committee subsequently subpoenaed Blitzstein to appear at an open hearing at Foley Square on June 18. Telford Taylor argued for a postponement, given the date's proximity to the June 20 opening of *A Midsummer Night's Dream* at Stratford, where the composer had been working, and stated Blitzstein's willingness to go to Washington at a later date at his own expense; but Committee Chairman Francis Walter insisted on his presence as ordered. However, on the day of the hearing, after questioning a number of other witnesses, including Gersten, the committee decided for whatever reason to end the proceedings before getting to Blitzstein. Nor did they ever ask him to return. (Gersten's appearance, incidentally, led to some local picketing at Stratford, and even to the resignation of some of the festival's most important trustees, but John Houseman and Lincoln Kirstein stood by him, in part because the company's communists and fellow travelers—of which Houseman counted himself as "the most notorious"—would not have tolerated a dismissal.)[8]

On July 20, Blitzstein gave a brief summary of this entire episode to David Diamond:

> I was due to appear before that committe [sic] last month; had my "private" session with them, and hired a wonderful lawyer, Telford Taylor. I did *not* take the Fifth Amendment; I challenged their authority to question me at all on the subject; then *voluntarily*, for the record, answered questions of membership, etc., saying I had nothing to hide, and was innocent of any legal or moral criminality. This disturbed them no end: they wanted me to be a "menace" or to "return to the fold" as a "confessor" and informer. So, at the last minute (literally, just before I was about to step to the bench), they struck my name off the list; there was not even a hint publicly that I had been there. In a way, I felt cheated; but I am told I am very lucky.[9]

Meanwhile, the FBI maintained its own file on Blitzstein and in early 1959 attempted to interview him, an action "warranted in view of the fact that the subject could, if he would, provide considerable information of interest to this Bureau." However, according to an FBI memo, when special agents—who described the composer as "cold in his manner" and "soft spoken," with "theatrical mannerisms"—approached him on March 25, he told them he had nothing to add to his HUAC testimony and that "he resented the attempts of the FBI to interview him as he considered it an invasion of his privacy." This same report recommended that no further efforts be made to interview him, and that, given the lack of any documented "subversive activity" over the last five years and his "sufficiently cooperative" testimony before HUAC, he remain off the security index. Nonetheless, the bureau continued to monitor his activities, including his trips abroad. And in August 1960, following the controversial announcement of a Blitzstein opera about Sacco and Vanzetti for the Metropolitan Opera, the FBI once again placed him on a security list by way of a reserve index card, which they canceled only upon notification of his death in 1964.[10]

In May 1957, prior to his testimony before HUAC, Blitzstein signed a contract with writer Joseph Stein to provide the score for a musical adaptation of *Juno and the Paycock* by the Irish playwright Sean O'Casey. Blitzstein and Stein intermittently worked on this project over the next twenty months, with Blitzstein writing the lyrics and music and Stein the book, and the show opening as *Juno* in early 1959.

Born in New York to Polish-Jewish immigrants, Stein (1912–2010) earned a master's degree in social work but started writing comedy sketches for radio in the early 1940s and eventually left his job as a psychiatric case worker in order to devote himself full-time to writing, including co-authoring with Norman Barasch the script for a 1946 radio program hosted by Hildegarde that featured Blitzstein in a guest appearance, and joining the staff of a leading television variety program, *Your Show of Shows*, in the early 1950s. Meanwhile, in the late 1940s, he began providing material for Broadway revues in collaboration with fellow radio writer Will Glickman, with whom he went on to co-author his first Broadway book musicals, both hits: *Plain and Fancy* (1955) and *Mr. Wonderful* (1956).[11]

About the time *Mr. Wonderful* opened in March 1956, Stein gave serious thought to adapting *Juno and the Paycock* for the musical stage. He had been "overwhelmed by the power of the play" and thought its language and story, which he described as "bursting with humor and wit and drama and emotion," amenable to musical treatment. "The earthiness of the characters appealed to me, as they do in pretty much all my work," reflected Stein, whose later musicals included *Fiddler on the Roof* (1964), *Zorba* (1968), and *Rags* (1986).[12]

Surely not by accident, Stein conceived or at least pursued this idea proximate to the March 1956 Broadway opening of *My Fair Lady*, an extraordinarily successful musical adaptation of G. B. Shaw's *Pygmalion* (1913). Tellingly, when Stein met with O'Casey in Torquay, England, in July 1956 in order to secure rights to the material, he described the score of *My Fair Lady*—he brought with him the cast album to play, only to find that the playwright did not own a record player—in order to give a sense of what could be done along these lines.[13]

Stein recalled how O'Casey, who had had little experience with musical shows, grew increasingly more enthusiastic about the planned work until the "whole idea of the musical.... seemed to take distinct and concrete shape in his mind. I had the feeling that he saw it ... come to life on the stage." The discussion of *My Fair Lady* also touched a vulnerable spot: the playwright's lack of financial success as compared to Shaw. O'Casey himself later admitted that although he had doubts about a musical version of *Juno*, "the chance of dollars was too much for me." Moreover, he found Stein and his wife Sadie "a very charming and likeable couple." Selling the exclusive rights to musicalizing the play to Stein and co-writer Glickman for

$1,500, he told a friend in May 1956, "I know that it [the show] won't be a 'Don Giovanni' or a 'Boris,' but there's room for things interesting as well as things magnificent: a seed pearl has its loveliness as well as a Kohinoor diamond; but I hope it may have the gentle sparkle even of a seed pearl."[14]

Sean O'Casey (b. John Casey, 1880–1964) grew up in Dublin in a lower-middle-class Protestant family and worked as a laborer before establishing his reputation as a writer in the 1920s with three plays set in Dublin against the backdrop of recent Irish history: *Shadow of a Gunman* (1923), *Juno and the Paycock* (1924), and *The Plough and the Stars* (1926). However, the rancor ignited by especially *The Plough and the Stars* prompted him to relocate to England, where he remained the rest of his life, settling in Torquay with his family in 1937. In his later years, he continued to stir controversy, both for his plays and, as a staunch supporter of the Kremlin, his politics.[15]

Juno and the Paycock takes place over a two-month period in the fall of 1922 during the Irish civil war (1922–23), which pitted "free staters," who supported the Anglo-Irish treaty of 1921 establishing Ireland as a self-governing dominion within the British empire, but which granted the Northern counties the option of remaining part of Great Britain, against the "diehards," who wanted a unified island republic. Each of the play's three acts unfolds in the small Dublin tenement apartment occupied by Jack and Juno Boyle and their young adult children, Mary and Johnny. An idle laborer who fancies himself a captain with a seafaring past, the cocky "Captain" Boyle—the story's "paycock"—spends much of his time drinking with his tenement mate, the obsequious "Joxer" Daly. His down-to-earth wife, a working woman, keeps the family afloat, for Mary, a girl with upward ambitions, has gone on strike, while the crippled Johnny, a former freedom fighter who took a bullet to the hip during the 1916 Easter Rising and who lost an arm fighting on the rebel side in the civil war, remains out of work as well. Boyle christened his wife Juno because of sundry connections with the month of June, but the character's name and the play's title also serve as a reminder of the Aesop fable about the Roman goddess Juno and the discontented peacock, the O'Casey play ending with the similarly vain and disgruntled Boyle complaining, "th' whole worl's in a terrible state o'chassis" (that is, chaos).[16]

The work's other characters include Mary's former boyfriend Jerry Divine, a union official; her new, relatively worldly beau Charles Bentham, who in the course of the action gives up his position as a schoolteacher to pursue a career in law; and a few residents who live in the same tenement as the Boyles and Joxer Daly, including the chatty and well-intentioned Maisie Madigan; the prorepublican tailor "Needle" Nugent; and Mrs. Tancred, who has recently lost her son Robbie in the civil war. Robbie, a diehard, had been Johnny's commanding officer at one point, and the play turns on the eventual revelation that, apparently out of some sort of resentment, Johnny informed on Robbie, an act of betrayal that has left him racked with fear and guilt.

However, the main action concerns news, brought by Bentham near the end of the first act, that Boyle has been left a considerable amount of money by a deceased cousin. In Act II, a few days later, the Boyles celebrate in their newly furnished flat with Bentham (now engaged to Mary), Mrs. Madigan, and Joxer Daly, a party interrupted by Robbie Tancred's funeral procession. The final act takes place two months later. Boyle has kept from his family the fact that they are not to receive the inheritance because of an oversight by Bentham in drafting the will. Meanwhile, Bentham has left for England, leaving Mary heartbroken. As Juno takes Mary to see a doctor, Nugent and Mrs. Madigan come to collect on their debts. Juno returns to inform Boyle that Mary is pregnant and that Bentham is the child's father. When she suggests that they use their forthcoming inheritance to move, Boyle tells her about the botched will and insists that Mary is not to return home. When Juno threatens to leave in that case as well, Boyle indifferently departs for a pub with Joxer.

After Mary returns, Juno leaves in pursuit of Boyle, and Jerry arrives, offering Mary unconditional love based on his socialist beliefs; but when he learns about Mary's predicament, he sadly departs. After Johnny, too, castigates Mary, she rushes out, leaving him alone. Two militia men arrive and drag Johnny away to face questions about Robbie Tancred's death. In the brief final scene, an hour later, Juno learns that Johnny has been killed, and tells Mary that the two of them will move to her sister's and raise the baby together. "My poor little child that'll have no father!" exclaims Mary. "It'll have what's far better—it'll have two mothers," responds Juno, who now realizes that she should have had more compassion for Mrs. Trancred: "Ah, why didn't I remember that then he [Robbie] wasn't a Diehard or a Stater, but only a poor dead son!" After echoing Mrs. Tancred's words—"Sacred Heart o' Jesus, take away our hearts o' stone, and give us hearts o' flesh! Take away this murdherin' hate, an' give us Thine own eternal love!"—Juno leaves with Mary. Boyle and Joxer return to the empty apartment stone drunk and both collapse.[17]

O'Casey called Juno and the Paycock a "tragedy," but commentators often refer to the play as a "tragicomedy," for the dialogue crackles with enormous wit and the characterizations recall the comic tradition of Shakespeare and Dickens, somewhat filtered through music hall and other popular entertainments. At the same time, a sense of pathos, even desperation, hovers about the piece, as the characters attempt to escape from their hapless lives through one means or another: Boyle, drink and tall tales; Johnny, nationalism; Mary, romance; Jerry, socialism; Bentham, theosophy. Even Juno, the play's least deluded character, has a myopic devotion to her family that limits her sympathy for the outside world. O'Casey suggests that at least in part the circumstances of poverty and political strife have thus blinded his characters, although Juno matures to a deeper understanding that gives some hope to her benighted world.

When Stein decided to adapt the play, he thought of Blitzstein, a "consummate writer" of the "Brecht school" (he especially admired The Cradle), as someone who could provide the kind of music he thought the show needed. Approaching the composer in April 1957, Stein found him not only receptive but "fascinated" by the idea. "When Marc and I met," he recalled, "we immediately felt a kinship. We had a feeling that we saw the work the same way and that the music would give the play an extra dimension. The collaboration was immediately successful."[18]

In October 1957, Blitzstein explained to David Diamond that he "jumped at the chance" to work on this project, "1) because I love the play, and think it may work as a musical; 2) because someone else would do the 'book,' and I have longed these many years for an attempt at what is loosely called 'collaboration'; and 3) it seemed like a fine warmer-up for my re-working of 'Reuben Reuben,' which I shall tackle as my next theatre-piece." Moreover, he liked Stein, whom he thought "a dear," describing the writer and his wife Sadie as "simple good people with nothing (as yet) of commercialism rubbed off on them." And as suggested above, he admired O'Casey as well, telling David Diamond after Brecht's death in 1956, "we don't have his [Brecht's] like any more, with the exception of O'Casey, in terms of stature." The composer's HUAC hearing in May 1958 similarly evidenced his high regard for the Irish playwright, for when Richard Arens, no doubt aware of the *Juno* project and O'Casey's communist sympathies, asked in session, "Do you know or have you ever known a person by the name of Sean O'Casey?" Blitzstein answered, "I have never known Mr. O'Casey personally. I have known him obviously as all students of drama have known him as one of the chief writers of drama of the twentieth century."[19]

Furthermore, *Juno and the Paycock* had many features that would have attracted Blitzstein, including its working-class characters, its ironic dismantling of romantic illusions, and its blend of comic and tragic elements, not to mention a central female protagonist, like the Moll in *The Cradle*, Clara in *No for an Answer*, and Alexandra in *Regina*, who grows in social consciousness by the play's end. Nor had the subject of the guilt-ridden informer—which had figured so prominently in *No for an Answer*—become any less relevant during these years. And as suggested by his arrangement of an Irish popular tune, "Dublin Street Song" (1941), and his Irish tenor aria, "Cop's Lament," from *Reuben Reuben* (1955), Blitzstein seemed predisposed to the challenge of writing music and lyrics appropriate to the play's Irish setting and characters.

A few days before Blitzstein signed the May 1957 contract, which specified 5 percent of box-office receipts to Stein's 3 percent and O'Casey's 1.5, the *Times* reported that because of "a division of opinion, emphatically not a rift," Glickman had "bowed out" from the project. Indeed, Stein and Glickman continued to collaborate on the Jerry Bock–Sheldon Harnick musical *The Body Beautiful*, which opened in early 1958. Glickman, who sold his share of the rights to the composer, purportedly thought Stein and Blitzstein too serious in their approach to the material.[20]

Blitzstein worked hard on the musical from the late spring to the early autumn of 1957, especially in June and July, and by early August he and Stein had readied a nearly complete show. "I worked for seven weeks," Blitzstein wrote to Diamond, "and actually began it and finished it within that time—the only job I've done at that kind of white-heat since 'The Cradle Will Rock,' twenty years ago. And I like it." Stein later confirmed, "We both worked at white heat. We were both completely in love with the project, and within two months the basic scope [score?] and book was finished." Blitzstein anticipated a possible production for the spring of 1958 and then perhaps a film version with James Cagney, for whom he auditioned the score during the summer of 1957.[21]

Stein kept O'Casey abreast of their progress, writing to him on July 24,

> Marc has completed a good part of the score, and I feel you will be delighted with what he has done. The songs are tuneful and charming, and most important, exactly in character with the people, the locale and the story.... As for the book, I have tried to remain faithful to the characters and line of the story in the play. The plot is identical and builds, exactly as it does in the play, to the same climax. . . . All in all, we feel very good about the work, and I hope you will feel that we have treated the play with honesty, and have done it a fair measure of justice.

Stein's alterations indeed proved mostly minor, but sometimes telling nonetheless, as in having the two women's final destination not another apartment in town, but more bucolically, a farm a few hours away. Juno also appears less flawed, with no depiction of her callous lapses regarding Mrs. Tancred ("In wan way, she deserves all she got"). A more obvious change, this one devised by both book writer and composer, involved the introduction of four gossips, or "biddies," "crones," or "norns" as Blitzstein variously referred to them, who serve as a commenting chorus, and who include, along with Mrs. Madigan, three newly invented characters, Mrs. Brady, Mrs. Coyne, and Miss Quinn—a conceit that recalled not only the four Barflies in *Reuben Reuben*, but the gossips of another tenement drama, Kurt Weill's *Street Scene*. In short, Stein and Blitzstein added some sentiment and humor that brought the play closer to American musical theater traditions, as O'Casey realized would need be the case: "I think the musical should be brighter in spirit and look than the play, for it is another form and, actually, a different work," he wrote to Stein on May 10, 1958, adding on May 21, "but mind you dont [sic] go too far and make it too gaudy."[22]

Stein also reshaped the three-act original into two acts, each broken down into smaller scenes. In this way, he could place some of the action, as Blitzstein urged, outdoors, the final mise-en-scène—not unlike Edward Hopper's famous *Nighthawks* (1942)—a depiction of both a street and Foley's bar, so that the departing Juno and Mary, and the inebriated Boyle and Joxer, could be seen simultaneously. Such an approach, somewhat cinematic in quality, proved particularly fluid for the party scene at the top of the second act as the action moves from the Boyle home to their backyard. Stein also added a few scenes in order to frame and amplify the drama, including one for Mary and Bentham on Ireland's Eye (an island overlooking Dublin Bay) that enlarges their story.

In large part following Stein's suggestions for song spots, Blitzstein completed fifteen numbers in conjunction with the August 1957 libretto: "Daarlin' Man," a number for Boyle, Joxer, and the ensemble, set in Foley's bar, that plays on Joxer's fawning behavior toward Boyle; "I Wish It So," a solo for Mary that reveals her unrest (regarding this number, Blitzstein wrote in his notes, "Remember, a spitfire!"); "Song of the Ma," a number about motherhood for Juno; "Quarrel Song" for the bickering Juno and Boyle; "What Is the Stars?" in which Boyle reminisces with Joxer about his supposed life as a sailor (with interjections, later dropped in production, by a coal-block vendor); "One Kind Word" for Jerry but with some spoken lines by Mary (whose chiding remark, "You've always been glib and light of speech, and sometimes I think you're fooled by your own smoothness," a line cut from the final script, offers a key to the song); "From This Out" for Boyle, Juno, Mary, Joxer, and a small ensemble, in which Boyle envisions himself remade by his new wealth; "Ireland's Eye," a solo for the Young Salt, and "You're the Girl" for Bentham and Mary, both introduced in the interpolated scene on Ireland's Eye, the former an air of sexual yearning that forewarns Bentham's infidelity and the latter a song of seduction; "Troubles" (later retitled "You Poor Thing") in which the four gossips complain about their problems; "Music in the House" for Boyle and the ensemble, a number near the top of Act II that features Boyle's newly purchased gramophone as a symbol of middle-class prosperity and that features two simulated period recordings that function as parodies: a sentimental mother song, "It's Not Irish (to Deny Your Poor Old Mother)," sung by an Irish tenor, and the instrumental "Liffey Waltz," to which the ensemble eventually joins in (the tunes of "Music in the House" and "The Liffey Waltz" at one point appearing in counterpoint); "Bird Upon the Tree," a duet corresponding to the one sung by Juno and Mary in the original play; "Hymn" for the Young Die-Hard and the ensemble during Robbie Tancred's funeral; "Farewell Me Butty," an expansion of the spat between Boyle and Joxer that occurs just prior to Juno's return from the doctor; and "Lament" (later retitled "Where?"), sung by Juno after Johnny's death. By this point, Blitzstein also had sketched out the first-act ensemble finale "On a Day Like This," a number delineating the dreams of the Boyles and the other tenement residents.[23]

Blitzstein further wrote reprises for several of these songs, including "You Poor Thing," "One Kind Word," "I Wish It So," "Song of the Ma" (as part of "Where?"), "Bird Upon the Tree," and "Daarlin' Man," the latter five used in quick succession along with "Where?" for the show's denouement. Although Blitzstein altered some of the words of these reprised songs in response to their new dramatic contexts, he also kept some of the lyrics, allowing them to resound with new meanings, most poignantly "Bird Upon the Tree," hummed and sung by Juno and Mary as they prepare to leave, its theme of freedom here underscoring their newfound liberty, the song's nature imagery now conjuring the countryside to which they are headed. Blitzstein reminded himself while composing this duet, "In writing this, think of the end of the play as well! Despite its sweetness and simplicity, it must also have the kind of possibility of sweep that can swell after they sing it together as they pack to go." True enough, he followed the reprise of "Bird Upon the Tree" with a soaring instrumental development of its main theme as a transition to the short final scene, which contains a brief reprise, now more pathetic than comic, of "Daarlin' Man" for Boyle and Joxer. Underlining the bifurcated structure of this finale, with its simultaneous depictions of birth and decay, freedom and servitude, Blitzstein articulated this reprise of "Daarlin' Man" with reminders of the "Bird Upon the Tree" motive and, triumphantly at the end, the main theme from "Song of the Ma," suggesting some victory for Juno despite the tragic fates of her two children.[24]

Blitzstein, in his lyrics, like Stein in his dialogue, aimed to complement the colorful language of the largely retained O'Casey text without too great a sacrifice to his own creative impulses. To accomplish this, he compiled lines from the play, as he had for his adaptation of *The Little Foxes*, which he then reshaped accordingly. In "Song of the Ma" and "What Is the Stars?" he further used portions of two lyrics that O'Casey had sent to Stein in October 1956 "as (I think) the best I could do." At the same time, the composer largely dispensed with those various lyrics found in the play itself, with the principal exception of the funeral procession song, which Blitzstein set virtually verbatim as "Hymn," although he substituted "God" and "Heaven" for Jesus's name.[25]

Meanwhile, he put to use his growing familiarity with Irish music. He adapted, for instance, the traditional air "Molly, My Dear" ("At the Mid' Hour of Night") for the verse of "I Wish It So," preserving the basic shape of the tune, and at the phrase beginning "I'm sleepin' at night," quoting the melody fairly literally but just altered enough and so harmonized as to maintain a strongly personal flavor. (Blitzstein originally conceived the entire song as in a meter of 6/8, but he had the happy inspiration to recast the chorus, one of his best-loved melodies, into 2/2, thereby throwing the chorus into that much greater relief.) He similarly used the traditional melody "The Hills of Donegal" for the "them was days" portion of "What Is the Stars?" Otherwise, at least in these earlier stages, he largely refrained from using folk material, although in the case of "Bird Upon the Tree," he seems to have had in mind, as suggested by his notes, the tune "Bunclody," whose melodic turns and general structure he ingeniously adopted, as he did the song's bird imagery.

To whatever extent the other numbers drew on authentic sources, the score as a whole cut a distinctively Irish profile both in word and tone, with the main exception of "You're the Girl," a Cole Porter-like number befitting Charlie Bentham, a "micky dazzler" who represents for Mary the glamorous life for which she yearns. Intended as the show's "*real* schlager-tune" [hit song], this extravagantly

romantic number registers a subtly parodistic undertone as opposed to the clearly
burlesque quality of the composer's earlier Porter takeoff, "Fraught," from *No for
an Answer*. However, like several other numbers from the original score, "You're
the Girl" never made it to Broadway, Blitzstein later writing on the musical manuscript, "This one never used, I'm happy to say."[26]

Otherwise, Irish influences can be discerned in nearly all of the numbers, from
evocations of drinking songs and sea shanties to more modern dance and vaudeville styles, with "Music in the House," somewhat like the party scene in *Regina*,
operating as a send-up of bourgeois taste, although here decidedly Irish. "The
whole meaning of this number . . . ," wrote Blitzstein, who also considered using
bits of Beethoven's Fifth Symphony and American ragtime, "is the wonder and
marvel of the 'new idea' of having music, whichever music you want, whenever
you want it, beautifully sung and played; the old-fashioned, quaint if you like,
innocence of poor people in Dublin in 1922; before radio, with gramophones the
exclusive privilege of the rich."[27]

Although the score came, for Blitzstein, unusually close to the work of, say,
Richard Rodgers or Frederick Loewe, its almost relentlessly ironic if sympathetic
view of an urban underclass plainly stood out from mainstream Broadway musicals. Relatedly, its harmonic language, although on balance conventional enough,
featured a subtlety rare even by the standards of Weill or Bernstein—the chords
freshly spaced, the harmonic movement often unexpected, the whole saturated
with considerable dissonance, usually mild, but sometimes wrenching, as in
"Where?" or barbed, as in "Farewell Me Butty"—all helping to shade the drama
and the words. Moreover, although Blitzstein made greater use of four-measure
phrases in this score than was his wont, and to some degree accommodated popular song forms as well, he made trenchant use of formal irregularity, providing "I
Wish It So," for instance, with a coda that settles on the last line of the song's verse,
and using five-measure phrases as the norm in "Daarlin' Man," with the odd fifth
measure comically used to accompany some interjection or other by Boyle or
Joxer. Several numbers leave conventional song forms so far behind, or grow so
complex and agitated, as in "From This Out" and "Ireland's Eye," as to become at
times practically unhinged.

Some novel gestures further brought the score's adventurousness to the fore,
such as the juxtaposition of speech and song in "One Kind Word" (reminiscent of
"Francie" from *No for an Answer*) or the mechanistic passage in "Music in the
House" that accompanies Boyle as he winds up the gramophone, music that
makes the blaring arrival of "It's Not Irish"—aptly described in an early review
as "the mother song to end all mother songs"—all the funnier, much as the return
of "The Liffey Waltz" appears that much more disturbing on the heels of the
"Hymn." "Music in the House" contains yet another surprise, the repetition of
two short phrases, the first bumpy in its irregularity, to mimic a skip in the simulated gramophone recording of "The Liffey Waltz." In short, although not one of

Blitzstein's more daring or ambitious efforts, the music, for all its accessibility, proved typically inventive, challenging, and masterful, the lyrics correspondingly innovative, bold, and adroit.[28]

Presumably in the summer or fall of 1957, Blitzstein made demo recordings of the score as described above, brilliantly rendering the varied principal roles with humor and skill, his piano playing equally deft. For his warmly comic portrayals of Boyle and Joxer, he employed that high-pitched raspy voice that he had used for the Barflies in his demo recordings for *Reuben Reuben*, but here with a brogue that made him sound that much more like Barry Fitzgerald, the actor who had originated the part of Boyle. In all the numbers, he characteristically took considerable freedom with tempo and rhythm for dramatic effect.[29]

In the spring of 1958, Stein sent copies of these recordings to O'Casey, who listened to them with his family. The Irish playwright and his wife Eileen responded favorably, especially the latter, who thought a number of the songs "very catching and charming." O'Casey himself reserved judgment, but he told Stein that after hearing Poulenc's *Chansons françaises* on the radio, he told his wife, "Well, the music of *Juno* is as good as that," to which she commented, "Better; a lot better." After the show opened to poor reviews in March 1959, O'Casey admitted to New York drama critic Richard Watts Jr. that although his family had liked the music, he "could see nothing of mirth or melancholy in any of it; and the dialogue I read didn't please me at all." But in his correspondence with Stein, he only went so far as to note a few infelicities in the text, prompting revisions in turn.[30]

Meanwhile, in the fall of 1957, the Playwrights' Producing Company acquired the property. A consortium of mostly playwrights established in 1938 with the aim of producing their own work, the company's members currently included, among the original founders, Maxwell Anderson and Elmer Rice but also playwright Robert Anderson and producer Roger L. Stevens, who by this point had assumed leadership of the group, and for whom Blitzstein auditioned the score. The company, which dissolved in 1960, increasingly had begun to launch the work of artists outside the group and to engage co-producers as well, in this case, entering into agreements with Oliver Smith and eventually Oliver Rea, with Lyn Austin named associate producer. In the past, the company had produced several shows by Kurt Weill, a one-time partner in the firm, but otherwise it had had little to do with musical theater.[31]

The producers assembled a first-rate team, including the rising British director Tony Richardson, best known at the time for his work on John Osborne's play *Look Back in Anger* (1956), which had arrived on Broadway in the fall of 1957. (O'Casey's own choice, Robert Lewis, the director of the Scottish-themed *Brigadoon*, remained unlikely given the latter's rift with Blitzstein over *Reuben Reuben*.) They also signed choreographer Agnes de Mille (1905–1993), whose credits included *Rodeo* (1942), *Oklahoma!* (1943), and, perhaps more to the point, *Brigadoon* (1947), revived on Broadway in the spring of 1957. (Blitzstein's frayed relationship with Jerome Robbins, damaged by the latter's HUAC testimony, surely precluded his involvement as well, not that Robbins necessarily would have welcomed working on a show about a guilt-ridden informer.) Co-producer Oliver Smith designed the sets, Irene Sharaff the costumes, and Peggy Clark the lighting. Presumably consulted in all these decisions, Blitzstein selected as music director Robert (Bobby) Emmett Dolan, a prominent Hollywood composer and music director eager at this point to return to Broadway, where he initially had made his mark.[32]

By May 1958, two marquee names, Shirley Booth (1898–1992) and Melvyn Douglas (stage name of Melvyn Hesselberg, 1901–1981), had been enlisted for the parts of Juno and Boyle. Neither Booth nor Douglas was particularly associated with musical theater, although the former, who had starred in two Arthur Schwartz musicals earlier in the decade, could at least carry a tune, as Blitzstein knew from having worked with her on the premiere of his 1937 radio opera, *I've Got the Tune*, and the 1947 City Center revival of *The Cradle Will Rock*. By contrast, Douglas, who had staged the American premiere of O'Casey's *Within the Gates* in 1934, had virtually no singing voice even as compared to Rex Harrison, whose success in *My Fair Lady* might have encouraged the producers in this direction.

Over the summer, Tony Richardson arrived in New York for some auditions as well as meetings with Stein, Blitzstein, de Mille, and Oliver Smith (who proposed that the show open with a "dramatization" of Robbie Tancred's murder, an idea eventually adopted). However, after returning home, Richardson ran into some scheduling conflicts, and in October he resigned from the show. "I believe in your wonderful, original and daring work more than I can say," he wrote to Blitzstein, "and it really is the greatest disappointment in the theatre that I have ever had that I can't do it. I was so thrilled and delighted when you asked me to and so much loved working with you when I was last in New York." Within days, the producers announced as his replacement Vincent J. Donehue, who recently had won a Tony Award for his direction of *Sunrise at Campobello* (1958). Although distressed that Richardson backed out of the show, Blitzstein later came to terms with the matter, writing in early 1961 to his mother-in-law Lina Abarbanell, who had served as the musical's casting director, "I have more-or-less forgiven him [Richardson] his 'naughtiness' regarding *Juno*—my god, if I have forgiven Orson [Welles] all his misbehaviors, who is Tony to imagine himself in *that* class?"[33]

Casting continued throughout 1958. Touted by O'Casey, the Dublin-born Jack MacGowran, a veteran of the Abbey Theatre, assumed the role of Joxer Daly. The producers further signed singers Monte Amundsen (Mary) and Loren Driscoll (Jerry) and dancers Tommy Rall (Johnny) and Gemze de Lappe (Molly). Other cast members included Earl Hammond (Charlie), Nancy Andrews (Mrs. Brady), Beulah Garrick (Miss Quinn), Jean Stapleton (Mrs. Madigan), Sada Thompson (Mrs. Coyne), Liam Lenihan ("Needle" Nugent), Robert Hoyem (I.R.A. Singer [Young

Die-Hard]), and Arthur Rubin (Foley), who also provided the voice for the recording of "It's Not Irish." All told, the cast contained twenty-four principals along with another ten singers and seventeen dancers, including Glen Tetley in a featured spot.

Working with de Mille, whose choreography borrowed from Irish step dancing, Blitzstein prepared the music for the dance sequences in the songs "Daarlin' Man," "On a Day Like This," and "Music in the House" as well as two ballets: the first-act "Ireland's Eye" (originally "Lovers' Walk"), a flirtatious dance that sets the stage for Mary and Bentham's romantic scene; and the second-act "Johnny's Dance" (also just "Johnny"), in which an anguished Johnny dances feverishly with his girl-friend Molly on the day of Robbie Tancred's funeral. (Stein and Blitzstein early on imagined a dancing rather than a singing actor for Johnny, who has relatively few lines in the O'Casey play.) No doubt with de Mille's encouragement, Blitzstein made extensive use of traditional melodies for most of these dances: "Daarlin' Man," various reels, including "Lady Nelson's Reel"; "On a Day Like This," a series of jigs, the first one (for two men), an original effort, the others consisting of "Ride a Mile" (a slip jig in traditional 9/8 time for Glen Tetley), "Follow Me Up to Carlow" (a shillelagh dance for four men), and "Rocky Road to Dublin" (for Juno, Boyle, and the ensemble); "Ireland's Eye," the air "The Song of Sorrow" ("Weep On, Weep On"), arranged with drones in imitation of bagpipes; and "Johnny's Dance," after an extraordinary four-voice canon based on the main theme of "The Liffey Waltz," the tunes "Avenging and Bright" and "Marquis of Huntley," with "Callino casturame" serving as a refrain, and the "Reel of Tulloch," juxtaposed with the "Hymn," as the coda. Blitzstein consulted a variety of written sources for these tunes, but he apparently had such Irish acquaintances as writer Denis Johnston and actress Geraldine Fitzgerald sing melodies to him as well. In a few instances, he knowingly employed non-Irish tunes, as in the case of the English "Lady Nelson's Reel" and the Scottish "Marquis of Huntley" and "Reel of Tulloch," so long as he felt no incongruity ("too Scottish," he wrote over a rejected tune).

Blitzstein also prepared other instrumental sections, including the overture, an entr'acte, and a second-act prelude, as well as interludes and curtain calls. For the overture, he transformed "Where?" into a majestic opening, somewhat like a martial jig, that portends the ultimate tragedy. One particularly moving inter-lude, the scene-change music that follows the tempestuous "Johnny's Dance," puts forth the melancholy Irish tune "The Valley Lay Smiling Before Me" with great simplicity and tenderness.

In preparing the full score for six winds, five brass, piano/celesta, accordion, gui-tar/mandolin/banjo, percussion, and strings, Blitzstein enjoyed the assistance of two of Broadway's finest orchestrators, Robert Russell Bennett and Hershy Kay, both of whom scored nearly the entire musical, with the composer essentially orches-trating only "Bird Upon the Tree." However, Bennett and Kay carefully followed Blitzstein's suggestions for specific colors and moods and scrupulously adhered to his short score, using percussion circumspectly. As a result, the work featured an unusually elegant sound for a Broadway musical, as epitomized by Kay's subdued scoring of "Where?" not to mention Blitzstein's own music-box orchestration for "Bird Upon the Tree."[34]

Although "Juno" long had served as the show's working title, by the fall of 1958, Stein and Blitzstein temporarily had settled rather on "Daarlin' Man," the name derived from the song lyric that framed the musical. O'Casey, who liked neither title, suggested rather "Juno and Jack," writing to Stein in December 1958, "it is short, crisp, and musical. It is alliterative, and suggests a connection with the Nursery song, 'Jack and Jill' (as 'My Fair Lady' does with another); Jack falling, and Juno tumbling after him, as happens in the play. It also gives a fair showing to the 2 chief characters." But by this time, Stein and Blitzstein had reverted to "Juno" as the work's title.[35]

Rehearsals began in mid-December, with the show opening at Washington's National Theatre on January 17, 1959. The musical, at this point, approximated that drafted by Stein and Blitzstein during the summer of 1957, although the production had dropped "Quarrel Song," "Ireland's Eye" (the song, not the ballet), and "You're the Girl," and added two others: "His Own Peculiar Charm," a whimsical solo for Juno loosely derived from "Hard to Say" from *Reuben Reuben*, and sung to Bentham at their first meeting as a means of establishing Juno's affection for Boyle; and a replacement for "You're the Girl," namely, "My True Heart," in which Bentham repeats Mary's ardent melody against a light, swinging accompaniment, "as if," wrote the composer in his notes, "he had used the words a dozen times before." Blitzstein seems to have made at least some of these revisions in response to popular taste, with Bentham's strain in "My True Heart" even suggesting some absorption of rock and roll. (If Blitzstein could hear Eddie Fisher singing "There Goes My Love" from *Reuben Reuben*, he might well have imagined the likes of Elvis Presley performing this music.) Tellingly, a caricature of the composer filed among his papers has him saying, in a speech bubble, "I'm sorry Oliver [Smith?], but I refuse to turn 'Music in the House' into a rock & roll number. I think its [sic] very commercial the way it is."[36]

The reviews of the Washington world premiere lauded the production, especially "Johnny's Dance," thrillingly performed by Tommy Rall, whose rigid left arm revealed a hand stump, a startlingly sober gesture for a Broadway musical. Oliver Smith's large, mobile set, which twice won applause on opening night, also elicited praise. But the critics agreed that the work seemed curiously disjointed, with numbers that embellished rather than advanced the story, "a play which takes time out for a song or dance here or there" in the words of *Variety*. Lillian Hellman and Leonard Bernstein, who attended the premiere, voiced similar concerns to Blitzstein, although Hellman assured him that the work "is going to be fine, almost is now." The producers quickly announced that the show would play an extra week in Boston and open in New York on March 5 rather than February 26 as planned.[37]

As the company plunged into extensive revisions, composer Frank Loesser traveled to Washington at Blitzstein's request and offered what help he could, although he and his soon-to-be wife Jo Sullivan, who had worked with Blitzstein on *Let's Make an Opera* and *The Threepenny Opera*, generally thought the show in good shape. By the time the musical opened in Boston at the Shubert Theatre on February 4, various scenes had been repositioned and shortened, including the removal of the ballet "Ireland's Eye" and the songs "From This Out" and "Farewell Me Butty" (although Blitzstein worked some of "From This Out" into "On a Day Like This"), while a second-act number, "For Love," had been added for Mary, who reprised the song at that spot where previously she had reprised "I Wish It So." To judge from the reviews, such changes hardly made a difference, the Boston critics maintaining that, for all its assets, the work failed to enhance or even suit the original O'Casey play. Elinor Hughes, who described the show as "less a musical or even a musical play than it is O'Casey's play with interpolated songs and dances," reflected in a follow-up piece, "It is quite possible that 'Juno and the Paycock' could have been made into an opera, and in that medium its essentially serious subject matter and strong dramatic characters could have been translated into powerful musical terms that would have paralleled its effectiveness as a drama."[38]

Soon after the Boston opening, the producers dismissed Donehue, who asserted that he had reached a stalemate with Stein and Blitzstein over needed changes in the material and who finished the year as the director of *The Sound of Music*. Flying in from the West Coast to attend a performance on February 7, director-actor José Ferrer agreed to take over the production. Just prior to the New York premiere, Blitzstein wrote Mina Curtiss that Ferrer "has been excellent in the emergency; and we have zoomed to something close to my original conception. But how close, and how improved we are I can't tell."[39]

By this juncture, the atmosphere had become increasingly acrimonious. In his memoirs, Douglas recalled how MacGowran, a heavy drinker, exploded at one rehearsal, "No one here knows a fuckin' thing about O'Casey or this fuckin' play." Booth, agreeing with those critics who thought her miscast, grew aloof to the point of apathy, exasperating her colleagues. Ferrer thought Blitzstein "difficult and petulant," while the composer regarded Booth "an inert slug" and de Mille a "bitch" and a "horror." That during tryouts, de Mille (who remembered Blitzstein as "small and furtive, with a rodent quality") brought in Trude Rittman (1908–2005), the eminent German-born Broadway arranger, and then presented Blitzstein with a new Rittman ballet, "Dublin Night," to replace the cut "Ireland's Eye," Blitzstein found particularly galling. "I met the challenge, but withered inside," remarked the composer, who, retaining the basic outline of Rittman's draft, enlivened the rhythms, refined the harmonies, varied the textures, and apparently also appended a new dynamic coda—what Rittman later called "adding here and there his personal touches." Wrote Blitzstein to Curtiss, "The last weeks of try-out were continuous and ever-mounting torment. I must have written two full scores, the final result being an amalgam of both, achieved by me fighting tooth-and-nail with all the assorted 'temperaments' involved."[40]

By the time the show arrived in New York in March, it featured three new songs: "We're Alive," a number added to the opening pantomime showing the death of Robbie Trancred that contained a choral expression of Irish fortitude and mourning; "We Can Be Proud," a lusty patriotic song sung by a male quartet in Foley's bar; and "Old Sayin's," a comical duet for Boyle and Juno that replaced the cut "Quarrel Song." (Blitzstein also had written yet another solo for Juno, alternately called "Mem'ry Green" and "The Girl I Used to Be," ostensibly to replace "His Own Peculiar Charm," now dropped from the show, but that number failed to stick.) For the effective "We're Alive" opening, whose refrain, "as the old woman said," provided a mythical resonance to Juno's story, Blitzstein adapted two traditional tunes, "The Shan Van Vocht" and "The Foggy Dew," for the chorus and another folk melody, "I'm the Boy for Bewitching Them," for the instrumental interlude and the coda. The first-act ballet, "Dublin Night," rightly credited to both Rittman and Blitzstein, similarly used the traditional tunes "Yellow Horse," "Sixpence," and, climactically prepared by rhymed shouts of "up the rebels," the ancient "Callino casturame," a theme associated in the musical with Irish resistance.[41]

The chanting of "up the rebels" in "We're Alive" and "Dublin Night," not to mention the presence of British soldiers and the ad libitum cries of "the British" in "We're Alive," underscored the fact that Stein and Blitzstein by this point had reconceived the play as taking place during the Irish war of independence as opposed to the Irish civil war, with the year of the action duly pushed back from 1922 to 1921, although the souvenir program book still made reference to the civil war. The musical always had been somewhat hazy about Irish history, changing, for instance, O'Casey's phrase, "Diehard or a Stater" to "Die-hard or a rebel," although the diehards were the rebels; retaining that particular phrase in connection with the Anglo-Irish war made even less sense. More generally, reconfiguring the play's background meant some undermining not only of its plot, but its moral essence (although the original context easily could be restored simply by eliminating a few phrases).[42]

The show opened at Broadway's capacious Winter Garden Theatre on March 10, 1959. The revisions undertaken in Boston under Ferrer's direction apparently helped considerably, for the New York reviews overall proved better than those in Washington and Boston (except for Booth's performance, which came in for tougher criticism). "Although it's considerably short of a triumph," reported *Variety*, "'Juno' is much better than had been indicated by the advance reports from out-of-town." Blitzstein himself wrote to Curtiss a few days after the show opened, "It is a good work—certainly far from the one I conceived; but good enough." But although the notices complimented many aspects of the "impressive" and "irreproachable" production, including Blitzstein's score, thought "frequently memorable" by Thomas Dash, the reviews remained, in the end, unfavorable—"respectful but disparaging," in Blitzstein's words.[43]

As in Washington and Boston, the New York critics had two principal objections: that the show fell short of the O'Casey play (remarked Kenneth Tynan, "It is always an impertinence for talent to halt the flow of genius"); and that its separate elements failed to cohere into a unified whole. Both observations recalled the early reception of *Regina*—perhaps that much more unsympathetic here because only drama critics reviewed this particular piece. But for all the praise lavished on O'Casey, the reviews failed to note, aside from *Variety*, that the Irish playwright never had been particularly successful with Broadway audiences. Nor did they mention that O'Casey himself eschewed the conventions of the well-made play, so much so that the musical's shifting tone and episodic structure could be seen as a daring response to the playwright's radical vision.

The tepid reviews spelled doom. Robert Russell Bennett, who thought Blitzstein a composer "of great distinction," and *Juno* "a better than average show," recalled, "At the premiere there were more than the usual bravos and salvos of applause, it seemed to me, but the next morning the reviews were murderous and the show died at birth. Marc Blitzstein called me on the telephone . . . and he thanked me with great sincerity for my help—which was a very rare experience for me, but Marc was a rare musician." A few days after the opening, Blitzstein, exhausted, left for Acapulco—"fled, the word is, I think," he wrote Curtiss—with his friend Morris Golde. The show, which closed deep in the red on March 21 after sixteen performances, received not a single Tony nomination.[44]

The work's ill fortune "neither surprised nor shocked" O'Casey, who maintained that, doubtful about the enterprise from the start, he had suggested that Stein adapt rather *Red Roses for Me* or *Purple Dust*, two of his plays thought "more suitable and more flexible for a gay alteration." He only regretted the disappointment the show's failure afforded Stein, Blitzstein, and the others "who worked so damnably hard to make the venture go."[45]

On March 28, music director Robert Dolan wrote Blitzstein that on his return to Los Angeles, he played the music for fellow film composer Hugo Friedhofer (long appreciative that Blitzstein years earlier had persuaded William Wyler of the merits of his score to *The Best Years of Our Lives*), who liked the music so much that he had Dolan perform some of the score for several film music colleagues. Dolan, grateful himself that Blitzstein "took a chance" on him, further urged the composer "to keep your voice ringing in the theater . . . no matter how discouraging Juno turned out to be," stating that the production's problems lay outside the work:

> One major fault . . . was Oliver Smith's scenic conception. . . . They [the sets] were lumbering, oppressive and overblown. The next fault to greet the audience's eyes was some really major miscasting. Poor Melvyn can

never be Jack Boyle and Shirley, I am beginning to think, can never be *anything* two performances in a row. She was the biggest shock of all to me. Running her a close second was Agnes whose neglect of the principals' numbers was unpardonable.... Because sleeping dogs are supposed to be left undisturbed I will waive comment on the press department of the Playwrights Co.... Finally, the critics displayed a new-found reverence for O'Casey ... that carried as much sincerity as [Richard] Nixon's TV apologia in 1952 with his wife by his side.

I hope you will never be benign about Juno's fate. I could never forgive that. This score was written with deep conviction. If you dismiss your convictions you have nothing left.

And on March 19, Oliver Rea wrote a consolatory letter of sorts to Abarbanell, saying, "It is a little early for me to attempt to express in words my pride in having had the opportunity to work with you and Marc on *Juno*."[46]

Chappell published, in somewhat simplified arrangements, four songs from the score, including "I Wish It So," which they also anthologized and which became the show's best-known number, with recordings over the years by Rosemary Clooney (1963), Judy Kaye (1986), Karen Holvik (1991), Dawn Upshaw (1994), and Helene Williams (2001). Later, Boosey & Hawkes released more authentic versions of these four songs, along with other numbers, including some that had never made it to Broadway.

In 1959, Columbia released an original cast album well-received by the critics, although, given the amount of material cut and the limited singing ability of its two leads, one that failed to do the score full justice. (Nor did the album's lighthearted cover art, taken from the show's publicity, accurately convey the work's tone.) Cheering producer Goddard Lieberson's decision to record this Broadway flop, *HiFi Review* deemed the music rich in "dramatic appeal and lyrical beauty" and the stereo engineering superb. In another review, Virgil Thomson found the score "more earth-bound than earthy" and "a bit word heavy for taking flight," but thought the orchestral sound to possess "a variety and an evocative power far superior to the deafening ways of the routine Broadway 'musical'" and the work, like all of Blitzstein's, to have "character and savour."[47]

Blitzstein brought the cast album with him to Europe in the summer of 1959, meeting in England with Oscar Lewenstein, who had co-produced the British premiere of his adaptation of *The Threepenny Opera*, about a London mounting, and in Ireland with the Anglo-Irish director Tyrone Guthrie about a production there. After playing the recording for Guthrie, Blitzstein wrote in his journal, "He is impressed by the melodic gift, loves the treatment of the women, carps at Boyle and Joxer (says I haven't plumbed *their* depths; too American and music-hall in treatment)—I think he likes it—I'll find out (tomorrow?) whether he will do it." But no European production ever materialized.[48]

While in England, Blitzstein also telephoned Sean O'Casey, hoping to pay him a visit, but the playwright, with his wife Eileen away, asked not to be disturbed. "He was crotchety, petulant, and blames Jo[seph] Stein and me for the 'Juno' failure," wrote Blitzstein in his diary. Over the phone, O'Casey repeated his complaint about the play as inimical to musical treatment, professing to "hate the thing [the play] myself," but adding, "still, go and do it in London if you can; heaven knows I need the success as much as you do."[49]

In 1964, following his great success with *Fiddler*, Stein hoped to interest that show's producer, Harold (Hal) Prince, in a revival of *Juno*, but nothing came of that either. However, in the 1970s, director-lyricist Richard Maltby Jr. and actress Geraldine Fitzgerald collaborated on and launched a loose adaptation of the piece, *Daarlin' Juno*, that included new lyrics by Maltby (whose later credits included co-writing the lyrics to *Miss Saigon*). The show played for about a week at the Williamstown Theatre Festival in August 1974, with Fitzgerald (Juno) and Milo O'Shea (Boyle) under the direction of Arvin Brown and the musical supervision of Arthur B. Rubinstein and Herbert Kaplan, who modeled the small instrumental ensemble after an Irish village band; further revised, the show ran for about a month at the Long Wharf Theatre in New Haven in May and June 1976, again with Fitzgerald and O'Shea under Brown's direction but with Thomas Fay as musical director. *Daarlin' Juno* so altered *Juno* as to constitute an essentially different work, but the original musical remained so obscure that *Times* reviewer Mel Gussow could unquestioningly report that the adapters had "attempted an act of theatrical restoration" and comment about Blitzstein's "deficiencies" as if he had witnessed the real thing. Ken Mandelbaum more knowingly commented, "*Juno*, while not an opera, has a definite operatic grandeur, and scaling the score down and eliminating some of it altogether did the show no service. The lyrics, and even sections of the music, were needlessly rewritten."[50]

In October 1992, a small off-Broadway theater on East 15th Street, the Vineyard, launched a more faithful but still freely altered version of the work, with a slightly revised book by Stein, new lyrics by Ellen Fitzhugh, and some reinstated songs adapted by musical supervisor Grant Sturiale. Vineyard artistic director Douglas Aibel explained that he had fallen in love with the work after hearing the cast album at age twelve and had long wanted "to mount the show on a scale that didn't reduce the score, that allowed for the size and scope and passion of the music." Directed by Lonny Price and starring Anita Gillette (Juno) and Dick Latessa (Boyle), the production, which featured a single piano accompaniment performed for part of the run by Jason Robert Brown, the future composer of *Parade* (1998), had an intimacy that precluded inclusion of the ballets or full treatment of the production numbers. In their reviews for the *Times*, drama critic Mel Gussow reiterated his complaint about the redundancy of Blitzstein's contribution, whereas music critic Stephen Holden more positively deemed the piece a "well-made musical" with a score of "freshness and vitality" that seemed the "opposite in tone from the sophisticated Broadway music of Richard Rodgers or Leonard Bernstein." Leonard Lehrman, in *Opera Monthly*, similarly welcomed the Vineyard's "admirable attempt to rescue Blitzstein's gorgeous score."[51]

With productions few and far between, the highly prized original cast album, reissued on CD in 2002 by Fynsworth Alley, largely provided the basis for later evaluations of the musical by such mavens as Ken Mandelbaum, Ethan Mordden, and Marc Miller, all of whom agreed that the show remained, in Miller's words, "one of Broadway's most tantalizing failures." Mandelbaum, who thought the music "rich and magnificent" and the prologue "one of the musical theatre's most stirring openings," observed that "Blitzstein's most accessible score was still more complex than Broadway audiences were used to at the time and was not easy to fully appreciate on a first hearing." Mordden noted that the work's "truly memorable score" derived "logically out of the story, yet there are imaginative stunts as well." And Miller found the music "overpowering" and the cast album "a thing of surpassing beauty. . . . though it takes several listenings for this score to fully yield its riches."[52]

Meanwhile, Agnes de Mille, who had filmed much of her *Juno* choreography with the dancers in rehearsal clothes in 1959, returned to these preserved dances, which included the slip jig and the three ballets ("Ireland's Eye," "Dublin Night," and "Johnny's Dance"), near the end of her career in the mid-1980s and shaped them into a half-hour ballet, *The Informer*. Also set at the time of the Anglo-Irish war, the ballet, freely based on Liam O'Flaherty's novel and John Ford's film of the same name, concerned a love triangle involving two men and a woman, with one of the men, a wounded one-armed veteran like Johnny, informing on the other. Composer John Morris and pianist Martha Johnson, a longtime de Mille associate who had been the rehearsal pianist for the original show, constructed a score based almost exclusively on the slip jig and the three ballets, except for one dance movement by Johnson, "Keening," and even that incorporated Blitzstein's setting of "The Valley Lay Smiling." Programs and publicity described the music as "old Celtic tunes" arranged by Blitzstein, Johnson, Morris, and Rittman, and orchestrated by William D. Brohn, but Blitzstein plainly deserved credit as the score's principal author.[53]

The American Ballet Theatre premiered *The Informer* on March 15, 1988, in Los Angeles and gave the first New York performance on May 10, the *New York Times* declaring the piece "a highly deserved personal triumph" for de Mille. Revived by Ballet Theatre the following two seasons, the work, whose anguished solo for the one-armed veteran proved a high point as it had on Broadway, afterwards slipped into obscurity, although Lynn Garafola, who placed it in the tradition of Fokine, thought the ballet admirably "old-fashioned" in its craft and high-mindedness and deserving of a place in the repertory.[54]

On March 27, 2008, *Encores!* under the artistic directorship of Jack Viertel, presented a revival of *Juno*, with the original orchestrations, in the form of a staged concert production at New York City Center, the site of so many historic Blitz-stein events over the years. The cast featured Victoria Clark (Juno), Conrad John Schuck (Boyle), Celia Keenan-Bolger (Mary), Dermot Crowley (Joxer), Michael Arden (Jerry), Clarke Thorell (Bentham), and Tyler Hanes (Johnny). David Ives tweaked the script, Joshua Clayton helped prepare the score, Garry Hynes directed, Warren Carlyle staged the dances, and Eric Stern led the onstage thirty-piece orchestra.

The production proved faithful to the original Broadway show. Viertel, who thought the work a "close formal relative" to Carousel and Lost in the Stars, believed that "Stein and Blitzstein got it pretty close to right the first time" and that the book needed only "minor adjustments." The end result included a shortened script, the restoration of the reprise of "I Wish It So," and the reinstatement of "Farewell Me Butty," Viertel explaining that Encores! could not support so long a scene without a musical number. In addition, choreographer Carlyle dispensed with the first-act ballet but rather, in collaboration with Stern, combined portions of "Dublin Night" with "Johnny's Dance" to create one long second-act ballet.[55]

Put together in a mere two weeks, this revival won cheers from the audience—as in the original production, "Johnny's Dance" brought down the house—and something close to a rave by Everett Evans (Houston Chronicle), who thought the book "sturdily constructed, especially powerful in the closing stretch's inexorable march to tragedy." And although Ben Brantley (New York Times) and David Fin-kle (TheaterMania.com) echoed earlier criticisms about the work's lack of cohesion, both acclaimed the score, described by Brantley as translating "Irish folk vernacular into a style that is part Broadway perkiness, part twentieth-century anxiety. . . . Even the most buoyant love songs and ensemble numbers are inflected with an underlying grimness, as if hope could never be expected to fly free in the rotting tenements of Dublin."[56]

Such observations, including Ethan Mordden's depiction of the musical as "the grimmest of the decade's musical plays," perhaps overstated the work's somber qualities, given the high spirits of "Daarlin' Man" and "What Is the Stars?" and the exuberant joy, even if illusionary, of "On a Day Like This" and "The Liffey Waltz." At the same time, a more ample rendering of the finale than heard either on the cast album or in the Encores! production, with the expanded "Bird Upon the Tree" swelling heroically, would help redress what Virgil Thomson called the work's "earth-bound" qualities and afford something more redolent of the sweep that lifts Regina at its end. Retaining such other sections as the "Valley Lay Smiling" interlude and restoring the ballet "Ireland's Eye" presumably would enhance the work's pacing and emotional range as well. In any case, Encores! showed the work to be a lovely and poignant musical well deserving of stage presentation.[57]

23

Final Years, I (1959–1961)

After he returned home from the war, Blitzstein did not venture overseas for over ten years, presumably because of anticommunist passport restrictions. But on March 9, 1959, the day before *Juno* opened on Broadway, he wrote Mina Curtiss that his attorney Telford Taylor thought he could "chance a passport now," and securing one that spring, he visited Rome, Florence, Paris, Frankfurt, Berlin, London, and Dublin over the summer.[1]

Before departing, Blitzstein was inducted into the National Institute of Arts and Letters at its May 20 ceremonial in New York. He had been nominated for membership by Virgil Thomson, with seconds from Copland and Douglas Moore, and in early 1959, he was elected to the institute, which sought to foster the arts through the dispensation of awards and grants among other activities. "They make me a member of the Institute today," wrote Blitzstein to David Diamond. "My word. Me, an Academician!" The only musician admitted that year, Blitzstein joined his old friend painter Julian Levi among the new inductees.[2]

Copland had shown his continued support for Blitzstein the previous summer as well by selecting him as one of eight composers showcased at the Berkshire Music Center, further privileging him, as with only Ives, Sessions, and himself, with a concert devoted entirely to his music. Presented under the auspices of the Fromm Music Foundation, this all-Blitzstein concert, given on July 25, 1958, and prefaced by introductory remarks by the composer, featured a performance of *Triple-Sec* along with various songs and chamber pieces. The Argentine-born Mario Davidovsky, later known for his electroacoustic compositions but then a Tanglewood student, recalled that he left in the midst of this event furious that he had to listen to "that kind of light music," leading Copland to "patiently" tell him "about what Broadway was and the importance of show music. He [Copland] took the time and trouble to give me examples of local Argentinian tango and Brazilian samba composers to trace a parallel with what Blitzstein was doing." For all this, Blitzstein's relationship with Copland long had settled into one of warm but distant collegiality; his closest musician friends remained Leonard Bernstein, whom he saw fairly often, and David Diamond, to whom he wrote with some regularity.[3]

As a member of the National Institute, Blitzstein quickly asserted his leadership qualities, serving on the Grants Committee for Music (1959–61, chairman, 1960),

the Revolving Fund Committee for Music (1960–61), and the Departmental Committee (1962–64). He himself nominated for grants Ramiro Cortés, Ned Rorem,
Mordechai Sheinkman, and Lester Trimble in 1960; Ernst Bacon, Mel Powell, Ned
Rorem, and William Sydeman in 1961; and William Flanagan, Frederic Myrow,
and Ned Rorem in 1962, recommendations that revealed some familiarity with a
variety of younger composers, while intimating a special regard for Rorem.

Leaving for Europe in June 1959, Blitzstein spent the first leg of his travels in
the company of a longtime friend with whom he had grown increasingly close,
Irene Diamond (1910–2003), a talent agent whose achievements included getting
producer Hal Wallis to make the film *Casablanca*, and who, thanks to her husband
Aaron's real estate fortune, more recently had become involved with philanthropic activities, many devoted to the arts, but also in later years to include gun
control and AIDS research. She and Blitzstein rented a Fiat and traveled from
Rome to Florence to Milan and from there flew to Paris, where they rendezvoused
with Irene's husband. The composer continued on to Frankfurt, Berlin, London,
and Dublin on his own, before returning home in late July.[4]

In part, Blitzstein visited these various cities, as mentioned earlier, in order to
help promote European interest in *Regina* and *Juno* as well as to advance his
ongoing Brecht-related projects, which prompted meetings with Helene Weigel,
Elisabeth Hauptmann, and Paul Dessau in Berlin and John Willett in London. But
the trip had its purely social side as well, including time spent with composer
Alexei Haieff and humorist S. J. Perelman in Rome; David Diamond and his pupil
Francis Thorne in Florence; Virgil Thomson and arts writer Rosamond Bernier in
Paris; actors Pinkas Braun and Gisela Fischer in Frankfurt; composers Hanns
Eisler and Boris Blacher and music critic Paul Moor in Berlin, writers Lester Cole
and Donald Ogden Stewart and director Sam Wanamaker in London; and in Ireland, Canadian author Robertson Davies, whom he met at director Tyrone Guthrie's home in County Monaghan, and actor-playwright Micheál Mac Liammóir.
Keeping a journal throughout, he described Rome as "a dream-city," Paris as "the
great incredible queen and sweetheart and hussy she always was," and London as
"so devastatingly *square*, so doggedly old-fashioned in its effort to *stick* the world."[5]

Blitzstein also left behind impressions of various cultural outings, including in
Paris, Offenbach's *La vie parisienne* at the Palais Royal ("poor, coy and cute"), the
film *Black Orpheus* ("adorable"), and Anouilh's *L'Hurluberlu* ("poorish"); in
Frankfurt, a rehearsal of *Elektra* (the production "poor," although Inge Borkh
"immense"); in Berlin, Brecht's *Arturo Ui* ("middling good Brecht play marvelously produced") and *The Mother* ("a *lehrstück* lesson of enormous power"); and in
London, Shelagh Delaney's *A Taste of Honey* (he "liked the second act"), Hugh
and Margaret Williams's *The Grass is Greener* ("a good comedy of manners, saying
nothing very skillfully"), Brendan Behan's *The Hostage* ("there is something right
about it—a stab of vitality"), Marguerite Monnot's *Irma la Douce* (the 1958
British adaptation), and Arnold Wesker's *Roots* ("the best play I have seen here,

until its final message-y dénouement"). Compared to previous European stays, he tellingly devoted that much more attention to opera and theater than to the musical scene per se, much as his social world by this time had become increasingly dominated by theater and film people rather than musicians.[6]

After he arrived home, Blitzstein told Ned Rorem, "it was a glorious trip, from all points of view—including amours and the business-aspect." Concerning the latter, the composer seems to have been overly optimistic given that no European production of *Regina* or *Juno* materialized; nor did any of the Brecht-related projects pan out. But the trip had at least one important professional ramification. While in Rome, he saw the left-wing music critic Fedele D'Amico, whom he apparently had known in Italy in the early 1930s, and who, recalling the composer's choral opera inspired by the Sacco and Vanzetti affair, *The Condemned* (1932), presented him with a small 1927 German monograph about the case by the anarchist journalist Augustin Souchy, which D'Amico inscribed in French, "in remembrance of our first meeting." This encounter helped trigger Blitzstein's decision to write an opera about Sacco and Vanzetti, a project that occupied him for the rest of his life.[7]

Notwithstanding the continued success of *The Threepenny Opera*, Blitzstein still faced the necessity of earning money, especially now that he was helping to support both his mother and mother-in-law, and upon returning home, he turned his attention to, among other things, possible writing assignments, including an article on musical theater for the *Saturday Evening Post*'s prestigious "Adventures of the Mind" series that, if accepted, would have brought him $2,500 and a piece about Brecht-Weill for *Horizon* magazine for a promised $500. However, he completed neither essay, presumably in part because a Ford Foundation grant awarded in early 1960 satisfied his financial needs for the moment. The *Horizon* article seems not to have gone much past the research stage, although the author's notes contain some critical observations, including mention of Satie and Milhaud as precursors to Brecht-Weill. By contrast, he accomplished a fair amount of work on the *Evening Post* essay, a sweeping view of musical theater that would have considered opera as a vehicle for social commentary, including references to works by Mozart, Bizet, Musorgsky, Leoncavallo, Charpentier, Mascagni, Berg, and Weill. This article also seemed poised to address the difficulties in establishing a serious musical theater tradition on Broadway because of "money-panic (great outlay of expense; wish to *mollify* the critics and the public, placate them . . . so as to recoup)" and "that out-of-town nightmare, the 're-write,' whereby many of the original concepts get lost, and *all* of the form goes to pot."[8]

In May 1960, Blitzstein did publish, however, a short review of a recording of works by Lili Boulanger (1893–1918) conducted by Igor Markevitch, an album supervised by Lili's older sister Nadia. He seems to have undertaken this article, for all its brevity his last important critical piece, out of sheer admiration for Lili's music, although lingering affection for Nadia, his former teacher, probably played a part as well. In any case, he made the rather novel case for Lili not merely as a precocious talent who died tragically young, but as an "extraordinary," "original," and "uncompromising" composer whose *Pie Jesu* influenced Poulenc's *Dialogues of the Carmelites* and whose *Psalm 24* anticipated Honegger's *King David*. He further compared *Pie Jesu* to the *Kindertotenlieder* of Gustav Mahler, whom he likewise regarded as a prophetic figure, writing that "both works have an ineffable inno- cence and an unerring personal singing line." "Let us hear more of her [Lili]," con- cluded Blitzstein. "Let us know what we have missed, and what we have been offered." Nadia lost no time telling Blitzstein how much she appreciated the review: "Feel how profoundly I am touched—your article is so understanding, so human,— it is for me an invaluable tribute." Blitzstein's enthusiasm for Lili possibly helped resolve Bernstein's decision to invite Nadia to conduct the New York Philharmonic in February 1962 in a concert featuring her sister's work.[9]

By this time, Blitzstein largely had set aside writing assignments and lecture engagements in order to concentrate on his Sacco and Vanzetti opera. However, in the spring of 1962, he took some time away from Yaddo, where he had been in residence, in order to give the first of Brandeis University's second annual series of Adolph Ullman Memorial Lectures in the Creative Arts, delivering his address on April 2 and taping it the following day for WGBH-TV. Discussing his career in musical theater at some length, he stated, with respect to his sense of "engagement or commitment" that dated back to *The Condemned* (1932), "In the days of the thirties it was strict, even sectarian. It is now rather looser, more flexible and broader, but many things remain. I believed then, as I do now, in the right of all men to have no need to ask favors in order to exist with dignity." Such concerns, he argued, placed him within an operatic tradition that controversially addressed "social and political problems," citing a list of works comparable to those men- tioned in his notes for the *Saturday Evening Post* article but that now additionally included *Fidelio, Die Meistersinger, Nabucco, Simon Boccanegra,* and *Andrea Ché- nier.* Regarding his musical technique, he admitted that, in an age of twelve-tone and chance composition, he wrote "conservative" music, but he confessed his delight and gratitude "that others wish to move the whole range of possibilities in music forward. And I have an intense interest, not only as a listener, in the most recent schools, because if I am anything I am an amalgamator, a kind of musical amalgamator, and I will get around to all the new schools." Finally, he urged his listeners to take a philosophical approach to life: "If there's a single good thing that has happened because of the bomb . . . it is that no one, repeat no one, can evade the crucial questions, 'Who am I? How am I to live? By what and with what values?' I have no easy answers for myself and so I can have no easy answers for you. The one thing we can ask is that our lives have some meaning." "The Brandeis lecture was a wow," Blitzstein informed his sister, further mentioning that he thought the university possibly interested in offering him a position, although nothing of that sort seems to have transpired.[10]

Later in 1962, Blitzstein published his last article, a short piece "On the Threepenny Opera" for *Musical Show*, the house organ of the Tams-Witmark Music Library, which had taken over licensing responsibilities for the composer's adaptation of the work. "It is fine to know that what began as a labor of love has blossomed into a national-wide accolade," wrote Blitzstein; "and that the 'Threepenny Opera' will no longer be just a name on everybody's tongue, but a part of everybody's theatre experience."[11]

Finally, in a 1963 interview with John Gruen, published after the composer's death, Blitzstein once again took up the subject of opera as a vehicle for social comment, here made that much more explicitly personal. "I found myself wishing more and more to say things to more and more people," he told Gruen. "I found I could do this by writing operas. I could express my ideas far better in this idiom than, let us say, in the writing for string quartet. I find I am a protester. I am, for my sins, a kind of nonconformist, but—and this may surprise you—I discovered that I was absolutely in [the] tradition of all opera; not just the apex of opera—that is the nineteenth-century opera—but starting way back with dear old Monteverdi. Most every opera has a sociopolitical theme." To illustrate his point, Blitzstein cited a few additional titles to those previously mentioned in such discussions, including *The Magic Flute, The Barber of Seville, La Traviata, Aida, Madama Butterfly, Porgy and Bess,* and *The Consul,* as well as *The Ring of the Nibelungen,* which he described as "a semi-Fascistic picture of gods and goddesses as *Übermenschen*—that is, the type of Nordic supremacy which Hitler switched to Arian supremacy" (he also referred to *Die Meistersinger* as "a picture of medieval unions"). When Gruen suggested that the great operas survived "because of their music, more than their message," Blitzstein responded, "I would be very unhappy to think that it was true that my message is more important than my music. I would hope that ultimately somebody would feel that the music did not only *not* stand in its way, but that the music was as much of the projection of the message."[12]

As for his creative work, in the fall of 1959, Blitzstein accepted a $600 commission for a set of songs for soprano Alice Esty; and in early 1960, he agreed to provide, for the same amount, the incidental music for Lillian Hellman's play *Toys in the Attic.* Aside from the short piano piece *Lied* (1963), these would be his last completed compositions.

That same fall, Blitzstein also began preliminary work on an animated film musical adaptation of E. B. White's children's book *Charlotte's Web* (1952), already recognized as a classic although of recent vintage. A tale about a sweetly innocent pig, Wilbur, rescued from death first by Fern, an eight-year-old farm girl, and then by Charlotte, a crafty spider, the story had features, including its concern with social responsibility, that naturally would have appealed to the composer, who might have regarded it, like *Reuben Reuben,* as a "comedy which understands Tragedy." In any event, Blitzstein and his agents at William Morris hoped to interest Martin Jurow or some other producer in financing the enterprise, with the film to be made by Japanese animators and processed and distributed back home.[13]

Blitzstein decided to collaborate on at least the script with the daughter of Richard Rodgers, composer-writer Mary Rodgers (b. 1931), who by this point had written the narration and lyrics to the children's revue *Three to Make Music* (1958, televised 1959, with music by her sister, Linda Rodgers Melnick), and the music for the fractured fairy tale, *Once Upon a Mattress* (1959), two efforts that revealed her abilities— long before her series of successful juvenile books, including the popular *Freaky Friday* (1972)—in working with children's literature. Mary Rodgers originally met Blitzstein through Leonard Bernstein (whom she knew through her childhood friend Stephen Sondheim), and although she "didn't really like" Blitzstein's music, she enjoyed his company—she found him "brusque" but "charming"—and agreed to meet with him regularly to discuss the film. Blitzstein went so far as to draft a scenario, along with a few ideas for lyrics and a list of twelve possible song spots, including a concluding "sad duet" for Wilbur and Charlotte; but when he and Rodgers met with E. B. White at the Algonquin Hotel to discuss rights, they found him unwilling to relinquish what he regarded as his favorite property. Had the project gone forward, Blitzstein presumably would have written the music and lyrics himself; a surviving fragment of the song "Glee for Jamie," written for his goddaughter Jamie Bernstein, perhaps hints at what some of the score might have sounded like.[14]

Set in New Orleans at an unspecified time, Lillian Hellman's *Toys in the Attic* centers on the interrelationships among five characters: the ne'er-do-well Julian Berniers; his two devoted, unmarried sisters Anna and Carrie; his young, insecure wife Lily; and Lily's patrician mother Albertine Prine. In an interview given shortly before the work's premiere, Hellman, denying that she ever had been "very concerned, in a literary sense, with the world," described her intention in this new play to explore the destructiveness of certain kinds of love and to argue for the need "to live by your own standards, even if you're going to be lonely and unpopular." Produced by Kermit Bloomgarden and directed by Arthur Penn, the play opened at the Hudson Theatre on February 25, 1960, with scenic designs and lighting by Howard Bay, costumes by Ruth Morley, and a cast that starred Jason Robards Jr. (Julian), Maureen Stapleton (Carrie), Anne Revere (Anna), Irene Worth (Albertine), and Rochelle Oliver (Lily).[15]

Blitzstein's score included the four cues specified by the text: "French Lesson," a recurring tune that represents one of the *French Lessons in Songs* that Carrie purchases in advance of her planned trip to Europe with Anna; a fuller version of this melody possibly intended to serve as the waltz Carrie plays at the spinet at her brother's request; "Big Day" ("Julian's Song"/"Bernier Day"), a setting for voice, banjo, and piano of Julian's jubilant lyric, written by Hellman, at the top of Act III (the banjo surely tailored to Robards, who accompanied himself in the number); and a bit of "Eusebius" from Schumann's *Carnaval* for piano, played by Anna, who refers to the music as Carrie's "favorite."[16]

For "French Lesson," or so his sketches would suggest, Blitzstein recalled such popular tunes as Kern's "The Last Time I Saw Paris," Rodgers's "Dites-Moi," Porter's "I Love Paris," and Louis Guglielmi's "La vie en rose," but ultimately wrote something closer to a French folk tune, one humorously singsong in response to the number's pedagogical intentions. Similarly, he structured "Big Day" around a charming Louisiana folk tune as arranged by Mina Monroe and Kurt Schindler, "Tan patate-là tchuite" ("When your potato's done"), retaining the piece's design but accommodating the melody to fit Hellman's lyric. For Carrie's favorite piece, Blitzstein considered Mendelssohn, Gottschalk, and Grieg before settling on Schumann's dreamy "Eusebius," apparently just the first two bars played by the right hand alone. Albeit limited in scope, the score helped flesh out the characters of the rambunctious Julian, with his remembrance of the simple life on the bayou, and his genteel sisters, with their dream of a visit to Paris.[17]

Toys in the Attic garnered several raves, but mostly mixed reviews that, while respectful of its craftsmanship, took issue with some of its contrivances. "It starts out as an inquiry into the moral consequences of wealth," wrote Kenneth Tynan in the *New Yorker*, "and ends up as a treatise on abnormal psychology." The critics overlooked Blitzstein's contribution, some use of which might have enlivened George Duning's rather synthetic score for the play's 1963 film adaptation.[18]

Since the late summer of 1959, Blitzstein had been concentrating primarily on an opera he never lived to complete (one whose working title, *Sacco and Vanzetti*, can serve here as well). Knowing that he was in for the long haul, he no doubt pursued some of the literary and musical projects mentioned above in part to help sustain him for the duration, although as mentioned, in early 1960 he received support for the opera in the form of a grant from the Ford Foundation.

Having recently helped to finance festivals of American opera with the New York City Opera, the Ford Foundation announced in October 1959 that they had established a $950,000 fund to be dispensed to four opera companies—the New York City Opera, the Metropolitan Opera, the Lyric Opera of Chicago, and the San Francisco Opera—for productions of new or recent American operas, including fees to composers and librettists as needed. As early as December 1959, Ross Parmenter in the *Times* mentioned Blitzstein's work-in-progress—"a real opera, not for Broadway, with a contemporary American theme ... very serious"—as a likely candidate for this initiative.[19]

As Blitzstein prepared the music for *Toys in the Attic* in early 1960, he met with General Manager Rudolf Bing and Assistant Manager John Gutman of the Metropolitan Opera as well as with Director Julius Rudel of the New York City Opera about Ford Foundation funding for his Sacco and Vanzetti opera, which he proposed to finish in two years (meaning a possible production, as far as the Met was concerned, in 1963 at the earliest). Both companies offered to recommend him for a Ford Foundation grant, and although Bing refused to commit himself to a production until he had had the opportunity to examine about an act's worth of the score, he promised an additional $1,000 against future royalties. Blitzstein also spoke with the foundation's director, W. McNeil Lowry, who explained that on average a total of $6,000 had been earmarked for the author or authors of each commissioned work, that Blitzstein would get the same amount of money whether he went with the Met or the City Opera, and that copying costs would have to be assumed by the opera company or a publisher. Blitzstein subsequently asked the foundation for $15,000, explaining that the opera would take him two years to write and that he would need $7,500 per year to meet his expenses.

The $1,000 sweetener aside, Blitzstein surely regarded the prospect of writing an opera for the Met, the nation's preeminent opera house, as too tempting an opportunity to turn down. In any event, on February 9, he informed Bing that he had chosen the Met, and two days later, after the City Opera's revival of *The Cradle* opened, he told Rudel as well. "He [Rudel] takes it with considerable grace, saying 'Very well. Good luck. Try your wings,'" wrote Blitzstein in his journal, although some months later he told Diamond, "I picked the Met, with the usual hard feelings on the other side." Meanwhile, the foundation came through with a two-year, $15,000 grant to be paid in quarterly installments, of which William Morris, Blitzstein's agent, agreed not to take their usual 10 percent.[20]

On February 26, word of a new Blitzstein opera on the subject of Sacco and Vanzetti broke in many newspapers, even making the front page of the *New York Herald Tribune*. The story was also picked up by *Time* and *Newsweek*, which in an article entitled, "Opera—Strange Venture," stated, "In a day of deadening conformity, it was remarkable news that a respected foundation was subsidizing an operatic treatment of one of the most controversial episodes of modern U.S. history: The Sacco-Vanzetti case." The *Herald Tribune* had attempted to downplay the seeming strangeness of the Ford Foundation's involvement by reporting that Henry Ford had been sympathetic to Sacco and Vanzetti, although this perhaps only furthered the false impression left by the article that the foundation itself had selected the opera's subject material. At any rate, the *Tribune* subsequently published a clarifying letter from the composer, who explained, "Contrary to many people's assumption, the Ford Foundation does not under any circumstances suggest, approve or disapprove the theme or subject-matter of the new works to be commissioned as part of its opera plan. That aspect concerns the opera companies and the opera composers and librettists involved, and only them."[21]

The announcement brought Blitzstein letters of congratulations from various well-wishers. Constance Askew, the noted arts patron, thought Sacco and Vanzetti "the perfect subject" for him, while Mary Weaver, widow of composer Powell Weaver, similarly wrote, "Here, surely, is a theme on which you will have the strongest convictions, and yours has, at least as far as your work has gone, been a lifetime of any intolerance with injustice." Experts on the case offered their assistance, including Gardner Jackson, an investigative reporter who had served on the Sacco-Vanzetti Defense Committee and who wrote Blitzstein on March 16 that the announcement of the opera "causes deep rejoicing in my wife and me, as, we're sure, it must in many others." Both George Braziller and *Esquire*, which had included the complete Gian Carlo Menotti text to Barber's *Vanessa* in their December 1957 issue, expressed interest in publishing the libretto.[22]

At the same time, negative responses began to surface. The reactionary *National Review* led the charge by posting a March 12 editorial presumably written by the journal's editor, William F. Buckley Jr., that misleadingly stated that the Ford Foundation had commissioned Blitzstein "to write the myth of the martyrdom of Sacco and Vanzetti into our musical culture," which the editorial deemed "a typical venture in ritualistic Liberalism." George Sokolsky soon after published similar diatribes in the *New York Journal-American* and the *Daily Kennebec Journal*, as did Edward B. Simmons in the *New Bedford Standard*. But whereas the *National Review* merely referred to Blitzstein as "a noisy, belligerent fellow traveler," Sokolsky, in his March 30 piece for the *Journal-American*, reported for the first time publicly that Blitzstein had been a member of the Communist Party, even giving his years of membership, which leaves little doubt that he obtained this classified information through the FBI, with whom Sokolsky had close relations, or some other government agency.[23]

The revelation of Blitzstein's party membership added fuel to the fire. A July posting in *U.S. News and World Report* decrying Sacco and Vanzetti as the "heroes of an American folk opera, now planned," contained, in bold print, the subheader, "Composer: an ex-Red." And in September, after the board of the 600,000-member National Federation of Music Clubs formally opposed the proposed Metropolitan production citing the composer's past Communist Party membership, the *Boston Herald* called for a "counter-opera" that would proclaim "the triumph of the courts of Massachusetts against the onslaught of Communists, fellow-travelers, petty logicians and misguided jurists." Meanwhile, private citizens made phone calls and wrote letters criticizing the commission to Congress, the Ford Foundation, and the Metropolitan Opera. Meeting with Blitzstein in March 1960, Bing did not seem "fazed" by such reaction, even stating that the inevitable picket by the American Legion could "only help business," although he seemed concerned that the opera not be "inflammatory" or "rabble-rousing," to which the composer refused to make any promises. In any case, the Metropolitan officially asserted that what mattered most was "whether or not the work will be good," the president of the Opera Association, Anthony Bliss, stating in one instance, "We do not feel that we should prejudge Mr. Blitzstein's work, especially since he has assured us that his political leanings are no longer of a leftist nature," and on another occasion, "Mr. Blitzstein avows that he no longer maintains his past political affiliations." Although not happy about the situation, the Ford Foundation simply defended the right of its grantee institutions to make their own artistic decisions.[24]

In May 1960, in the midst of this controversy, Blitzstein retired to Martha's Vineyard, finding a place to rent in the Katama area of Edgartown. He chose the locale not only in order to be able to work on the opera undisturbed in the sort of coastal area he favored, but also to be near the vicinity where the events of the Sacco and Vanzetti case transpired and to be able to make research trips to the mainland as needed. Over the summer months, he in addition completed the song set *From Marion's Book* that he had promised soprano Alice Esty.

In the course of the 1950s, Esty had appeared regularly in concerts of mostly American and French songs, presenting premieres of commissioned works by Georges Auric and Francis Poulenc among others. In May 1959, her pianist David Stimer, described by Ned Rorem as a "more than competent Svengali," wrote Blitzstein to inquire whether he would be interested in writing Esty a set of songs for a concert that would also feature new works by Rorem and Virgil Thomson. The critics generally admired Esty's spirit of adventure more than her vocal abilities, but Blitzstein seemed respectful of her talents—he referred to her as "a good and rich soprano" in a letter to David Diamond, for whom he hoped to secure a commission as well—and, encouraged too by the involvement of Thomson and Rorem, decided to accept the terms of the $600 commission, namely, a song set of about ten to fifteen minutes in length to contemporary verse, with Esty given exclusive performance and recording rights for two years.[25]

Esty also required that the selected texts meet her approval. In his May 1959 letter informing Blitzstein that Thomson and Rorem would be setting Kenneth Koch and Theodore Roethke, respectively, Stimer recommended as possible poets John Betjeman, Elizabeth Bishop, Dylan Thomas, and Richard Wilbur. The last-named, who had written most of the lyrics to Bernstein's *Candide*, duly submitted to the composer at his invitation two poems in June; but Blitzstein found them, as he told the poet, inhospitable to musical treatment. In the end, he instead returned to E. E. Cummings, five of whose poems he had set in 1929 for his previous song set, *is 5*; and whose poem "this is the garden" had provided the epigraph for his 1957 choral work of the same name.[26]

For this new work, Blitzstein recycled one of the numbers from *is 5*, namely, the haunting "when life is quite through with" (at this point, only "Jimmie's got a goil" from *is 5* had been published), but otherwise selected six of the poet's later poems: "silent unday by silently not night" from *no thanks* (1935); and "what if a much of a which of a wind," "yes is a pleasant country:" "open your heart:" "until and i heard," and "o by the by" from *1 x 1* (1944). (Blitzstein also embarked on a setting, left unfinished, of "maggie and milly and molly and may" from the 1958 collection *95 Poems*.) Ordering them as follows—"o by the by," "when life is quite through with," "what if a much of a which of a wind," "silent unday by silently not night," "until and i heard," "yes is a pleasant country:" and "open your heart:"—he titled the finished piece "From Marion's Book" in reference to the dedication to Cummings's wife Marion Morehouse—"marion's book"—that prefaced *1 x 1*.

On August 19, 1960, presumably in response to some questions about the work, Blitzstein sent Esty and Stimer "a breakdown of my understanding of the cummings songs I have set. Not my feeling about them; I hope I have put that in the music." With respect to "o by the by," he wrote that the image of a kite "must be kept throughout, of a comical volatility. Poignance at the diving and the climbing. . . . And then a final frustration (comic again) as the string is let go." About "when life is quite through with," he stated, "Elegiac, muted; at the grave of the beloved." He described "what if a much of a which of a wind" as "a kind of young, roistering paean to the indomitableness of man." "Silent unday by silently not night," deemed "The most ambitious of the lot," elicited these thoughts: "Death, purgatory, trans-figuration; or, death-not-death, raging breaking-apart, the rising of the phoenix." For "until and i heard," he advised, "Light as a feather, yet soaring, with a lyrical rising to the triumphant 'grave gay brave bright cry of alive.'" "Yes is a pleasant country:" he thought "Tiny, slight, but not trivial or facetious." And for "open your heart:" his favorite of the songs, he suggested "big climaxes and sudden hushes; and then the last phrases, quieter and quieter, to the endless word 'ocean.'"[27]

Blitzstein's selection of poetry so steeped in evocations of the natural world—sometimes depicted musically, as in the whirls of "what if a much" and the chirps in "until and i heard"—intimated his own deep appreciation for nature. "I have found myself shocked more than once by the easy way in which people had consigned him [Blitzstein] to the file marked Urban, Radical, Bohemian, Angry, whatever..." wrote Leonard Bernstein in a memorial tribute to the composer. "My most vivid images of Marc are all connected with nature: by the sea, in the woods, on a boat, in the sun, in the snow. . . . It was a child of nature who had written those notes that seduced my soul, those thousands of special, mysterious notes that can never be forgotten." While in Edgartown, Blitzstein admitted in particular his fondness for "the desert, the sea, dunes, a spread" over "spectacular landscapes," writing, "I love endless vistas; and spectacular landscapes are likely to be too focussed for me: a peak, or canyon, or gorge, or range. Singleness, rather than variety of multiplicity, is to my taste." Such inclinations took special expression in the final song of this new Cummings cycle, "open your heart:" with its rich and slow-moving harmonies, reflective of the poem's "summitless" imagery, that come to rest on an ambiguous major-minor polychord at once serene and melancholy.[28]

From Marion's Book encompasses not only a wide emotional range, as suggested by the composer's remarks above, but a fairly broad stylistic one as well, although largely characterized by clipped phrases and prickly harmonies, with the long lines and luxuriant chords of "open your heart:" forming the principal exception, all in response to the poetry. Blitzstein had employed this sort of colorfully dissonant language especially in his music from the late 1920s and early 1930s, thus enabling him to find room in this new work not only for "when life is quite through with" from his previous Cummings set, but some of the austere interlude for the exhausted pris-oner from *The Condemned* (1932) as the basis for the accompaniment for "silent unday by silently not night." He relatedly gave thought to the use of a twelve-tone row for this work, a technique that had not really engaged him since the early 1930s.

In its musical style then, no less than in its choice of poet, *From Marion's Book*, like the contemporaneous *Sacco and Vanzetti*, suggested a return of sorts to the world of Blitzstein's first maturity. At the same time, this new Cummings set revealed a ripened mastery, full of warmth and wit, that not incidentally paralleled Cummings's own development, as the cycle drew on the poet's later work.

Having already introduced the Thomson and Rorem sets in April 1960, Alice Esty, accompanied by David Stimer, premiered *From Marion's Book* at Carnegie Recital Hall on March 13, 1961, on a program that also included songs by Poulenc and commissioned pieces by Paul Bowles and Germaine Tailleferre, a performance that Blitzstein, back in Rome, could not attend. The piece, which Eric Salzman (*New York Times*) thought to contain "a kind of bit-of-everything bounce and bite that was sometimes effective," provided, wrote Martin Bernheimer (*Herald Tribune*), "the most humor of the evening."[29]

David Diamond quickly recognized the work's distinction, his observations assuming special significance in light of his close personal and professional association with Cummings: "They are excellent in that [Cummings] remains himself yet Marc's personality musically transforms the words into pure Blitzstein, a happier blend of poet and composer I don't know. Aaron [Copland] *almost* achieved it in his Dickinson songs. But Aaron's is the better music." And Ned Rorem similarly remembered *From Marion's Book* as "for my metabolism, his [Blitzstein's] very best work. . . . Marc's concert songs do not, by definition, pander to the big audience. Not that such pandering is in itself wrong; it's wrong only when an intellectual aims at the hoi polloi. . . . Marc tempered his language according to whom he was addressing." However, the cycle never established itself, although singers occasionally revived one or another of the numbers, William Sharp, for instance, including "o by the by," "until and i heard," and "open your heart:" (along with "Jimmie's got a goil") on a recording of Blitzstein's songs.[30]

After about four months on Martha's Vineyard, where he occasionally saw Lillian Hellman and Leonard Bernstein, Blitzstein left in the fall of 1961 for a nine-month sabbatical in Rome, presumably in order to absorb some Italian atmosphere for the opera, but also because he loved the city. Subletting his apartment to Mordecai and Irma Bauman, he flew to Paris in November, rented a Peugeot, and drove to Rome, stopping on the way in Florence to pick up David Diamond, who accompanied him to the capital. About a week after his arrival, he found a small attic apartment located at 52 Colonna Antonina, whose balcony afforded "a view of antiquity that makes me breathless," as he told his mother. The apartment also afforded good proximity to fine restaurants—what with his enthusiasm for Roman pasta, he temporarily gained some weight during this stay—and spots of local interest, including gay cruising areas. "When I get to dreaming," he wrote Copland in December, "I wander over to the Foro Romano [Roman Forum]; when I get horny, it's the via Veneto."[31]

Blitzstein led a relatively busy social life while in Rome. He saw with special frequency correspondent Curtis Bill Pepper and his wife, sculptor Beverly Pepper, an American expatriate couple at whose residence he met interesting guests, including on one occasion Alice B. Toklas. He also spent time with old friends like Martha Gellhorn, Lillian Hellman, Leonard Lyons, and Orson Welles, and a number of composer colleagues, including Jacob Avshalomov, Arthur Berger, Gail Kubik, Alexei Haieff, Robert Moevs, Robert Palmer, Francis Thorne, and of course David Diamond—some in residence abroad, others simply passing through. Robert Palmer, who knew Blitzstein only slightly from Tanglewood, visited the composer at his apartment, and the two played through part of the Sacco and Vanzetti opera together at the piano. "My major impression of him was that he was such a kind, gentle man," Palmer later recalled. "We immediately had an affinity. . . . it was one of the greatest experiences of my life to meet such a person and share music with him."[32]

Blitzstein also mingled with the locals, whom he described as "so theatrical here, making an operatic production of the smallest thing" and as "cynical, sad, happy and stubborn. I love them." His closer Italian friends included actor Mario Tarchetti and his wife Lucille, and music critic Fedele D'Amico, one of the few local musicians he did not find "dull," and his wife Suso Cecchi D'Amico, the prominent screenwriter who worked especially closely with Luchino Visconti. In addition, he met such luminaries as writer Alberto Moravia, whom he liked, actress Anna Magnani, whom he did not, film directors Federico Fellini and Franco Rossi, and painter Carlo Levi. And although in February he told Diamond that he imagined himself "too crotchety and old" for love, about this same time he also embarked on an affair with a younger, attractive Italian, Adolfo Velletri, writing Diamond in early March,

> I have a quiet love-life: not exciting, not right, but full of that uniquely Italian mothering-by-lover that is so touching. Do I want mothering, six slightly wilted carnations on my birthday, almost daily post-cards, the darning of a cigarette-hole in my impermeabile? Do I? Clearly I do, in some part of me; or I'd give it up; and I don't. I used to hear that Italy was the place where a woman was made to feel a woman. Apparently they work it on both sides of the fence, and over it and beneath it too. God love them.[33]

While in Italy, Blitzstein saw several movies, including Fellini's *La dolce vita* and Visconti's *Rocco and His Brothers* (the latter with a screenplay by his friend Suso D'Amico), and some plays as well, including a hit drama about Sacco and Vanzetti by Mino Roli and Luciano Vincenzoni ("good boys" who became friends) and Giovanni Testori's controversial play about homosexuality, *L'Arialda* (Blitzstein "stood it for one act"). Although he chose Rome, as he told Mina Curtiss, because he knew that the musical season would be "abundant and poor, so I can forget it," he occasionally went to concerts as well. In late November, he attended with Fedele D'Amico the dress rehearsal of an all-Stravinsky concert including the recent *Movements* for piano and orchestra (1959) and other works that he had never heard, telling Leonard Bernstein, "[Robert] Craft conducted abominably, Stravinsky himself very well, but showing his alarming sudden decrepitude." And in April, he spent two weeks at the International Festival of Contemporary Music of the Venice Biennale, driving there and back in his Peugeot with producer Ethel Reiner (who had co-produced *Candide* on Broadway) and where he attended, among other events, Britten's chancel opera *Noye's Fludde*, the world premiere of Luigi Nono's twelve-tone opera *Intolerance 1960*, and a concert of electronic music; one day he also slipped away to Yugoslavia for lunch, but in the main, he spent his time exploring the city's byways and marveling at its glorious architecture and art. "I fell madly in love with Venice, a city I had snooted for years," he wrote Diamond. "But Rome remains my idea of real wonder and glory."[34]

As for the festival, he thought it a "bust" except for Nono's antifascist opera, which the Italian composer, wrote Blitzstein to his sister, "had written originally as a paean to [Fidel] Castro and fulminating against the USA, but which his publishers salved down so it became simply a 'liberal-type' plea. A full-scale riot took place, with screams, fights in the aisles, stench-bombs (right by my row), and fascist leaflets, all organized by the reactionaries. You couldn't tell sometimes which whistle was in the score, which from the house." He found Nono's "serious, intense, long-breathed and almost continuously adagio" music "impressive," as he further informed Diamond, but the libretto "tedious, impersonal," and the production "sheer sabotage."[35]

Blitzstein occasionally shared his own political thoughts during this period with friends and family. In letters to his sister and Mina Curtiss, for instance, he commented sardonically about John F. Kennedy's January 20, 1961, inaugural ceremony, which he had heard over the radio; quoting Kennedy's statement, "If a free society cannot help the many who are poor, it cannot save the few who are rich," he told Jo, "So THAT is to be the keystone: save the poor *for* the rich. Well, what else did we expect?" And yet he wrote more optimistically to his mother, "Who knows? He [Kennedy] may turn out all right." He reported on right-wing student demonstrations against South Tyrolean autonomy ("so students can be *lumpen* too") and left-wing student protests against the murder of Congolese leader Patrice Lumumba ("The same yelling transformed at intervals to rhythmic chanting, and the same cracking of heads by the polizia, only this time there were more polizia and more cracked heads, of course"). And he showed concern as well over the response of the United Nations to the Lumumba affair (although he couldn't give Khrushchev "much either for trying to break up the UN, clearly his tactic of the moment"); America's lagging space program (the first manned flight by Soviet astronaut Yuri Gagarin on April 12 thrilled him); and the country's Cuban misadventures.[36]

In early May, Blitzstein spent a few days in Positano on the Amalfi coast as a guest of Edna Lewis, an artist whose workshop had helped turn the town into a popular arts colony. He and Lewis had a mutual friend in Morris (Moish) Golde (1920–2001), the New York businessman and arts lover with whom Blitzstein had become particularly close over the previous decade. Golde, who occasionally made his 123 West 11th Street apartment available to Blitzstein when the composer's own studio was otherwise occupied, moved centrally among some of New York's most sophisticated gay artists, including poets John Ashbery and James Schuyler and composers Virgil Thomson and Ned Rorem. (Rorem, who embarked on an affair with Golde in 1943, found him, for all his "butch swagger," the "most cultivated man I knew," and referred to him—at least after Blitzstein's death—as "my most leftist friend.")[37]

Another friend, the feminist writer Janet McDevitt, joined Blitzstein on the drive down to Positano, the two touring en route Amalfi and Ravello, towns that the composer had visited in 1930. On the trip back by himself—McDevitt remained in Positano—his car broke down, leaving him stranded in Naples for a few days. After returning to Rome, he attempted to end his romantic relationship with Adolfo Velletri, writing in his journal on May 19, "I break the news, am curiously saddened," and informing Golde the following day,

> I myself have just had the saddening experience of sending packing someone really in love with me. It was hopeless, and I did the right thing; but I feel a heavy void, and the nasty sense of having been cruel; I suppose I wasn't, but it feels that way. I have the insane impulse to phone and say "Come up" and start the whole mess over again, simply because I can't stand the memory of the look in a pair of eyes. I won't, though.

But in response to Velletri's pleas, Blitzstein continued to meet with him, even as he apparently saw other men.[38]

In late June 1961, Golde arrived in Rome with his friend Gene Myers, and the two accompanied Blitzstein for another holiday in Positano before the composer headed home in early July, the opera still not finished.

Final Years, II (1961–1964)

Blitzstein returned to New York in July 1961 with his Peugeot, which he kept garaged at the Drake House, an apartment building in New Rochelle owned by his friend Aaron Diamond. At first he chose not to respond to the sentimental letters and postcards sent to him by Adolfo Velletri, but in November, he wrote Velletri a letter in English, which he then translated into his "atrocious Italian," saying, "It is so much better for both of us, believe me, that this communication be ended, once and for all. I wish you well with all my heart. I shall answer no more letters. One day you will forgive me, even understand." This seems to have been the end of it.[1]

Declining an offer to return to Italy as a resident at the American Academy for the fall, Blitzstein continued work on the opera in late summer in Brigantine and then in the fall in New York, where he attended Ossie Davis's play *Purlie Victorious*, the debut of Douglas Moore's *The Wings of the Dove* at City Center, a dress rehearsal of Puccini's *The Girl of the Golden West* at the Met with Leontyne Price and Richard Tucker, and the premiere of David Diamond's Eighth Symphony presented by Bernstein and the New York Philharmonic. With the end of his two-year grant period fast approaching, Blitzstein met with Rudolf Bing on October 9 and requested an extension, saying that although he had a "pile of stuff," he needed about six more months before he could audition the work and a full year in order to complete it. Bing seemed "dubious" and indeed Blitzstein received notice from the Ford Foundation in November that an extension had been denied. The composer immediately wrote back explaining that he had "miscalculated the difficulty of the task and the amount of time required to do the libretto, composition and orchestration of the opera," adding, "I have worked, I am working, with all possible speed and energy, solely on the opera. I now see that I shall need certainly another year. And so I shall have to seek financial help elsewhere during the final period of work. Never fear; the opera will get finished."[2]

A few days later, he received a letter from Elizabeth Ames, executive director of Yaddo, stating that she had heard from writer and board member Malcolm Cowley that Blitzstein had some interest in working that winter in Saratoga and that she would be "delighted" to recommend him for a residency. Blitzstein accepted the offer, and in late November arrived for his fourth and final residency at Yaddo, having worked there in 1931, 1939, and 1952 as well. Staying in West House in the large "pink room" studio (so called because of its pink decor) as he had the previous time, he remained at Yaddo for five months, discouraging friends and family from visiting him so that he could devote himself uninterruptedly to his work. At the same time, he welcomed the arrival at Yaddo of writer John Cheever, an "old friend" with whom he could "make good conversation," and enjoyed the company of other residents as well, to judge from this recollection by French literature scholar Wallace Fowlie:

> His was a mind trained on the arts, not only music but painting and literature, and a mind cultivated on worldliness that had never been tricked by mere worldliness. I listened avidly to the speech of Marc Blitzstein, to whatever he might say to the small group that gathered for drinks before dinner in West House, and to the stories he might tell during dinner in the winter dining room, and to the continuous talk after dinner in the small library beside the dining room. He spoke as if he had been silent for too long during the workday hours. He spoke with wit and perceptiveness as if he had rehearsed his thoughts and stories. Wit he had, but no trace of malice. His words that entertained and delighted all of us were slightly contradicted by the expression of sadness that often passed over his face.[3]

Soon into his stay at Yaddo, Blitzstein attempted to cut down on coffee and cigarettes after feeling some heart pain and an irregular heartbeat. That he first noticed such symptoms on December 17, 1961, the day, as he observed, that *The Threepenny Opera* closed, could not have been merely accidental, as this meant a loss of income and additional stress at a time of considerable uncertainty regarding future prospects.

He at least obtained some financial relief in the form of a tax deduction for an initial donation of his papers to the Wisconsin Center for Theater Research. Cofounded by the University of Wisconsin at Madison, which provided its operating budget, and the Wisconsin State Historical Society, which processed and housed its holdings, the center, under the directorship of Robert Hethmon, speedily located some desirable collections and by March 1961, when they first approached Blitzstein, still in Rome, they already had reached an agreement with the Playwrights' Producing Company, and had received promises of intent from playwrights Paddy Chayefsky, Paul Green, and Lillian Hellman as well (although only Chayefsky in the end deposited his papers there). In time, the archive—which eventually became the Wisconsin Center for Film and Theater Research— obtained the papers of S. N. Behrman, Moss Hart, George S. Kaufman, Herman Shumlin, Dwight Deere Wiman, and other prominent Broadway playwrights, producers, directors, actors, and designers, as well as significant film, radio, and television collections, including material related to the Hollywood Ten and the corporate records of United Artists. On the other hand, although they hoped to acquire the papers of Harold Arlen and Kurt Weill, and did procure some material from Stephen Sondheim, they never gained a music collection of comparable importance to that of the Marc Blitzstein Papers.[4]

The center assumed responsibility for the packaging, mailing, and future care of items, but as a rule did not pay cash settlements or cover appraisal fees for the purposes of tax deduction. However, when Hethmon, as he later reported, met with the composer in the latter's apartment in October 1961, Blitzstein, putting the "matter frankly on a take-it-or-leave-it basis," stipulated that the center bear the expense of an appraisal, saying that another institution had expressed interest in purchasing his papers; he further requested that the appraisal move forward promptly so that he could take a deduction for the current tax year. Judging from Blitzstein's "living quarters that he is not affluent," and given too the importance of the collection, Hethmon successfully argued that the university make an exception, as they had agreed to do in the case of Lillian Hellman, and have the collection appraised.[5]

By the end of the year, Blitzstein, after consulting with his attorney Abraham Friedman and his accountant David Algase, had donated material related to *Cain* and *The Guests* valued at $5,100 to the center. The appraiser, Lew David Feldman of the House of El Dieff, continued assessing Blitzstein's papers into the next year, and in April 1962, put the estimated worth of the materials thus far examined, including many things stored in Philadelphia at 6436 Overbrook Avenue (where nephew Christopher now lived), but excluding, among other items, the composer's correspondence, at $83,160. As early as February, Blitzstein knew that the value of his papers would exceed $75,000, which, he told Mina Curtiss, "sent Lillian [Hellman] stark crazy (she having been calculated, [by] another appraiser, at $40,000, but then she got half in cash)." Blitzstein continued to donate material in the years that followed, as would Jo and Ed Davis after his death; others made gifts as well, including Norman Cazden, who donated the manuscripts to the *Scherzo* for piano and the Concerto for piano and orchestra to the center in 1964. By 1989, the collection, which also included Eva Goldbeck's papers, contained 113 boxes of material (copied onto 71 reels of microfilm), 23 tape recordings, and 114 disc recordings.[6]

Robert Dietz became the first scholar to make extensive use of this collection, beginning his research, with Blitzstein's permission, during the composer's lifetime and completing a doctoral thesis on the Depression era operas in 1970. Paul Talley likewise examined the archive for his 1966 dissertation on the opera librettos. All subsequent serious Blitzstein research similarly has drawn on this remarkable collection, now widely available in microfilm format via interlibrary loan.[7]

In early 1962, while at Yaddo, Blitzstein received two offers that helped support his ongoing work on *Sacco and Vanzetti*, namely, invitations to spend a residency in Israel over the summer and then one at Bennington College for the following academic year.

Blitzstein began his Israeli sabbatical by participating in an "Israeli-American Dialogue" sponsored by the American Jewish Congress (AJC), an advocacy group long active in Jewish and Zionist causes. Meyer Weisgal, the Polish-American-Israeli writer who had produced Kurt Weill's *The Eternal Road* in 1937 and who at the time chaired the executive council of the Chaim Weizmann Institute of Science, seems to have had a hand in selecting the composer for the symposium's arts panel; he had known Blitzstein for a number of years, as had his nephew, composer Hugo Weisgall, and his son, actor Michael Wager, who recently had appeared as Sasha in the 1960 City Opera production of *The Cradle*. Meyer and the Weizmann Institute in any case arranged for Blitzstein to remain in Israel for another six weeks following the conference.

Held in Jerusalem on June 12–14, the "Israeli-American Dialogue" featured addresses by Prime Minister David Ben-Gurion and other Israeli dignitaries, with the Americans, aside from Blitzstein's panel, represented mostly by members of the AJC. The organizers hoped that this conference might improve understanding between the United States and Israel, strained in recent months over Israel's development of a nuclear arms program and its reprisal raids against Syria (which brought a reprimand by the United Nations in March 1962), although such aspirations faced a stiff challenge from Ben-Gurion, whose acclamation of Jewish life in Israel as opposed to that in the Diaspora distressed American Jews both at the conference and back home.[8]

Taking place on the afternoon of June 13, Blitzstein's session, which focused on "Jewish commitment in the creative arts," featured three other Jewish-American artists—choreographer Anna Sokolow (whom Blitzstein described as "sweet"), artist Jack Levine, and producer Harold Prince—along with six Israeli artists, including the Czech-born keyboardist-composer Frank Pelleg and the American-born writer Meyer Levin (whom Blitzstein thought an "absurd and unattractive ego-maniac"). Aside from Sokolow, the invited Americans had little connection with either Israel or Judaism per se, but all four had known leftist sympathies, perhaps one reason that they were invited to attend.[9]

Blitzstein and his co-panelists delivered short statements followed by an open discussion (transcriptions of which later appeared in the AJC's in-house organ *Congress Bi-Weekly*), with the composer's characteristic graciousness on display, as in the manner he admitted his chagrin in visiting a country without knowing its language and the way he put questions to the Israeli participants in the open forum. "I have come here because I want to find out about Israel," he stated; "particularly because I want to find out about Israeli art, and the people who make it, which is even more important, and, incidentally, to expose myself to you."[10]

In his short address, Blitzstein emphasized the progressive dimensions of his Jewish identity, quoting Theodor Herzl on the "personal pang" Jews worldwide felt at the Dreyfus affair, but adding that he also felt a "great personal pang at the thought of the gas ovens" and "the plight of Sacco and Vanzetti." He even suggested the advantages of being Jewish in writing about the latter incident, an idea stated more explicitly in his Israeli journal: "Have to be jewish to feel for Sacco-Vanzetti (or, it doesn't hurt)." "It is possible that anti-Semitism is the biggest reason for my feeling a Jew," he further told his audience, "and, were it to be wiped out from the earth, I might cease being a Jew, or cease feeling as a Jew." When he hears people comment that his music "sounds very Jewish," he "startles" himself "constantly" by realizing that they're "quite right" even if there's "not a hint of an Oriental mode." Although an "anti-mystic," he finds this phenomenon "possibly, mystical," stating, "I believe in the entire continuity of Jewish life, Jewish survival, in the making of a Jewish nation, such as we now have—and I say that spontaneously, naturally. I remember walking through Jerusalem yesterday for the first time in my life, and someone was pointing out how close the Jordan border was, and I pointed to one spot and said, 'Is that *us*?' Clearly, I feel Jewish!"[11]

Blitzstein's association of Jewishness with otherness as found in his conference talk surfaced elsewhere during his time in Israel. "What with the jewish-bit and the homosexual-bit on Broadway, I might even think myself belonging to a *majority*, god forbid," he wrote in his journals. In a similar vein, he told the leftist Israeli newspaper *D'var Hashavuah* that as a socialist, a serious composer, and a Jew he belonged to three distinct minorities. And in what appears to be the draft of an August 17 letter to his friend Julia Algase, he framed this issue not only in terms of his own identity, but that of the whole Jewish people: "Religiousness, the *need* to keep the faith, was (and apparently still is) for the *Diaspora*, the still up-and un-rooted. But *in Israel*, they throw it off. No need *to be a Jew*. No need to answer *Anti-Semitism* with *Semitism*."[12]

In his travel diary, Blitzstein penned other thoughts apparently in preparation for either his panel presentation or subsequent interviews given in Israel. In one instance, he wrote, "I am what can be called a 'musical materialist' (in Albert Schweitzer's term)—my use of music is as a reflector, depicter, a 'graphic' representation of all the human experience. Only in one point in musical history does this become 'program' music (odious word). But 'absolute' music also shows this, the most basic function of music. There is, frankly, no absolute music!" In another entry he stated, "Art is *not* communication (a 2-way street), but propaganda—i.e., persuasion—although to make you feel as I do—done so well, so irrefutably that it is in its way unanswerable," further compiling a list of "'propaganda' artists," all painters, including "not only" Hogarth, Daumier, Grosz, the Mexican muralists, and others one might expect, "but also, Rembrandt, Velasquez, Goya, El Greco— and, if you please: *All* the religious Renaissance painters."[13]

Blitzstein informed family members that although many considered the Jerusalem conference "a big success," he found it "depressing and a bust, except for some startling 'talking-back' to Ben-Gurion who thinks all American jews ought to be bi-lingual, and then just Hebrew-speaking as they make an 'aliya' (mass-migration) here," an attitude with which he seemed to have had some sympathy, comparing the challenges posed by poorly educated immigrants in Israel with those in the United States. He himself attempted to learn some Hebrew and expressed his intention of returning to the country, telling one reporter at the end of his visit, "I certainly didn't come looking for a home—but in a way I've found one."[14]

After the conference, Blitzstein spent the remainder of the summer in Israel courtesy of the Weizmann Institute. As he looked for a place to stay, he spent a week in Rehovot, the institute's home, before he "flew the coup," as Meyer Weisgal put it, and settled into a small cliffside home overlooking the Mediterranean on the grounds of a prominent Israeli geologist, Leo Picard, in Beit Yannai near Kfar Vitkin, two settlements located midway between Tel Aviv and Haifa. The cottage itself he thought "the most satisfying house I've ever had, better than Rome or Edgartown or Capri; I have to go back to Mallorca for comparisons. Not grand or *luxe*; but exactly suited to my needs, and gorgeous as to garden, view and seascape." Assisted by a Jewish Yemenite maid, he maintained a rather isolated routine of working on his opera and swimming, with regular jaunts in his rented 1962 Morris-Oxford sedan to nearby Netanya for meals, and occasional excursions into Tel Aviv and elsewhere for various activities, including performances of Brecht's *Galileo* at the Cameri Theatre and Puccini's *Turandot* with the Israeli Opera, a reception in Jaffa with Golda Meir and the French ambassador on Bastille Day, and, at Anna Sokolow's invitation, a wedding party with Sara Levi-Tanai's Inbal Dance Theater (a dance ensemble based on Yemenite traditions) during which he "joined forces with the singing and swaying circle around the bride." He also attended an Inbal rehearsal, telling his sister afterwards, "I ... practically cried at the beauty of the girls and the men, the swift simplicity of their story-telling-in-dance, and the severe linear heartbreaking music. I tried to tell Sara, their leader, what I felt. She just patted my hand, and said: write for us. Who knows? maybe." Perhaps with such thoughts in mind, he began notating snatches of local melody and birdsong, going so far as to set one tune with personal, pungent harmonies. "I feel capable of anything now," he wrote Jo. "I am having sex and fun as well as the closest thing I'll ever have to serenity and joy."[15]

In the second week of August, Blitzstein took an extended break and traveled north to Haifa, where he met with distant relatives; to Nazareth, where he heard some memorable choral music as part of a Moslem wedding processional; and on to Tiberias, where he took a swim in the Sea of Galilee before proceeding to Safed, which he compared to Provincetown. During this same week, he also met with Israeli composers at a meeting at the Milo Club in Tel Aviv.

Whatever his feelings about individual places—he found Jerusalem "beyond words wonderful and awesome," Tel Aviv "dreadful, but jumping with culture," and Haifa "dream-beautiful, on the hill like San Francisco, but parochial German-jewish"—he thought the country as a whole "a stupendous effort, and I still don't know on what it basically rests: a United Nations partition decision, which kicked millions of Arabs out to their not un-natural resentment. But such scholarship, and such building, and such making green what was sandy rock, miles and miles of it." Enthralled by the hilly landscape en route to Safed, he wrote in his journal, "This is all brought here and struggled for and *done*, against drought, against malaria, against soil, against enemies. Jesus, I'm a goner."[16]

As in his stays elsewhere, Blitzstein also enthused about the local populace, telling Jo, "The natives are marvelous, and spoken Hebrew has a wonderful softness," and writing to Morris Golde,

> I find the people so various, so multiple in their qualities and defects that I am likely to live on the memory for a long time. Maybe not memory; maybe actual coming again. This place is one I haven't exhausted by any means. Perhaps I'm lucky; perhaps I've arrived at a time when things are happening which will never happen again. For one thing, the many-laguage[sic]-many-customs aspect; it must all soon simmer down to a unified nationalism, the *sabras* [natives] already show the signs.[17]

However, in this instance, he sometimes couched such observations in contrast to presumably Jewish-American tourists, deemed "of course the worst," and American Jews in general. "Nobody here really looks like a jew, except a couple of Arabs," he wrote Curtiss. "The type ('sabra,' if they were born here) is a beautiful specimen, tall rangy, rugged and 'intellectual'; the girls have tiny waists and good style. Noone [sic] is fat." And he told Jo, "everyone is sweet, cordial, and all have hair-raising stories," which, he added, "keeps Israel from being Miami or the Catskills: it is their own land, they have gone through unspeakable pain and struggle to get here, and they have put all of the greatest of human and moral effort to make the land work. And I gather they are at last self-sustaining; and not a mere satellite of rich American Jewry." All this, as with other statements made over the years, more than suggests a critical stance toward bourgeois American Jewry (as with bourgeois Americans as a whole), notwithstanding the fact that anti-Semitism deeply offended him and that so many of his closest friends were Jewish Americans, several of whom possessed considerable means.[18]

In February 1962, William Fels, the president of Bennington College, wrote Blitzstein, asking if he'd like to be considered for the school's John Golden Foundation playwright-in-residence fellowship for the following year, having heard from Wallace Fowlie that he might be so inclined. The fellowship included a $5,000 stipend with an apartment and meals provided by the college during the two resident terms, from mid-September through mid-December and from mid-March through mid-June (although for tax purposes, the grantee had to declare the room and board as income, as the composer later learned). Intrigued, Blitzstein visited the campus in March. After waffling on both sides, in mid-May, he received an official offer from Dean Harry Pearson, who also notified him that, because a member of the drama department would be on leave, he would be expected to give five tutorials in playwriting each semester, to which Blitzstein agreed. Following his return from Israel and some time in Brigantine and New York, he alighted on the Bennington campus in September 1962 to begin his residency, occupying an apartment in Swan House, one of the student dormitories.[19]

Bennington College opened its doors in 1932 in the town of Bennington, Vermont, as a small women's college, although it admitted men to its theater program as early as 1935 and would become fully coeducational by 1969. With its small student body and a progressive curriculum that emphasized individual study, often in the arts, including a notable dance program, the college resembled the Dartington School in England with which Blitzstein had had a brief association in the 1930s. Such institutions seemed kindly disposed to Blitzstein; indeed, not many American colleges during this period would have asked a former Communist Party member of long standing to join the faculty. But in any event, as with Dartington, he found himself increasingly disenchanted with the college during his short time there.

Blitzstein apparently interviewed a number of students before deciding on the three women and two men for his playwriting tutorial for the fall. The students, who worked on straight plays or musical theater scripts, met with him privately one hour each week, usually in the late afternoon. By semester's end, Blitzstein found that all of them had done good if not exceptional work, except for one of the men, whom he dropped from the spring roster, adding a female student in his stead.[20]

In addition, he held two-hour "jam sessions," typically on Wednesday nights, in which the students read their work for each other, including assigned exercises, with Blitzstein setting up a certain scene or problem, including one requiring a short dialogue in which someone "starts *ignorant*, or with a *mistaken notion* about another person" and "ends up with a new *realization* and a new problem." The class also considered selected texts, including Brecht's *Mother Courage* and Blitzstein's own *Regina* libretto. "We examined the theatre of the absurd, the theatre of myth, the theatre of action, of propaganda, of naturalism, realism, surrealism; theatre with and without music (since I am a theatre composer, we lingered there), with and without scenery, theatre-in-the-round and on-the-square (street-corner theatre)," wrote Blitzstein in a report submitted to the college after he completed his tenure. "The tutorials also read from their works-in-progress; there I must say the sparks really flew." He continued, "Since I have a clear *parti-pris* for one kind of approach, and since I have no aspiration to a career as a teacher, I let them have it. . . . I think maybe this is the real value of a one-man-for-one-year set-to with remarkable students." Meanwhile, his evaluations of his tutorials, even when observing limitations of one kind or another, showed real appreciation for their efforts, including satisfaction with one student who "is quite seriously concerned with, and moves easily in, the style and machinations of a kind of playwriting which has been badly named 'Theatre of the Absurd,'" even though his "own predilections" made him "less than content."[21]

When asked about his year in academia, Blitzstein typically quipped that he was "both too vain and too impatient" to consider himself a "real teacher," but he nonetheless admitted, as in his end-of-the-year report, that he "succeeded at Bennington beyond my expectations, if verbal and written testimonials from the five students are to be believed." Moreover, he told the *Washington Post* "that in the act of revealing something to them [his students], I am also revealing it to myself." He seems to have made a particularly deep impression on the young woman interested in absurdist drama, Reed Wolcott, who left him the mash note, "I love you sheepishly," in May, and who wrote, in a long letter the following October, "I've never loved or admired anyone as I do you. . . . Because you are the finest teacher who has ever taught me and the greatest man I've ever known. . . . Because your courage and integrity which was in everything you did and said taught me that there are good people left and things to live and fight for." After Blitzstein's death, Laurence Hyman, the son of Bennington literature professor Stanley Edgar Hyman and writer Shirley Jackson, and the one male student who worked with him both semesters, eulogized him as follows:

> As a tutor he was truly enlightening, and would quietly listen to groping student scripts and libretti, never trying to change or improve upon faulty parts, but kindly hinting, suggesting. His imagination was seemingly endless and he had a way of reviving life and vitality in plays that had long ceased to excite their writers. He took every student work seriously and furiously insisted that there was no such thing as "bad art," but some art was better, more consistent and reasonable than other art.[22]

Blitzstein spent most of his time at Bennington on his own dramatic work, including, by November, a new project: two one-act operas, *Idiots First* and *The Magic Barrel*, based on stories by his colleague in the English department, Bernard Malamud. He simultaneously developed a warm friendship with the author and his wife Ann, occasionally having dinner with them and their children at their home, including the writer's preteen daughter Janna, who later remembered Blitzstein as "a slim, small, balding man with a mustache, irascible and averse to being pushed." She recalled in particular a dinner at their home with critic Alfred Kazin and his family at which Blitzstein, after finally agreeing to perform something from *The Threepenny Opera*, took Janna and the Kazin's daughter into the room that held the piano, shut the door, and "intently, fiercely, pounded out and sang 'Pirate Jenny' only to us. . . . I felt rapturous hearing it so intimately, and pleased by the power reversal Blitzstein had accomplished. I remember looking around at one point and seeing the Kazins and my mother and father piled together, peering over one another into the room, listening through the narrow space they had boldly cracked between door and jamb."[23]

Blitzstein spent the long semester break mostly in New York, where he took care of dental work and other health needs. He also had to attend to his seriously ill mother-in-law, Lina Abarbanell, and then arrange her funeral and settle her estate following her death on January 6, which left him, as he wrote David Diamond, "bereft in a way I wouldn't have thought possible." After Blitzstein's own death a year later, playwright Alden Nash wrote to Lillian Hellman, "I rather sense that with her [Abarbanell's] passing Marc felt left very much alone in the world," a sentiment that however exaggerated nonetheless intimated Lina's importance to him not only as a second mother but as his last real link to Eva.[24]

During this winter holiday, Blitzstein attended various social and cultural events, including attending a January 25 recital at Carnegie Hall sponsored by the International Society for Contemporary Music (ISCM) of recent chamber works by American composers Allan Blank, Peter Westergaard, Mark Brunswick, Seymour Shifrin, and Harvey Sollberger, along with Alban Berg's *Lyric Suite*. Blitzstein scribbled some remarks on his program, writing next to Brunswick's piece, "Lady-Sessions, tantrums and all" (a reference to Brunswick's friend Roger Sessions), and next to Sollberger's name, "The concert-form is dead—otherwise we might see and hear this without busting our sides." With respect to the Berg quartet, he wrote, apparently with some of the slow fourth movement in mind, "find it and set it: 'I can do this trauma so much better than you/I can etc.,'" and remarked more generally, "a giant among non-entities: what I have against him [Berg] is the telling us *how*-it-is—'delirando,' 'estatico' etc.,—more than the *word*, the attitude; compulsory hypnotism-music." In yet another corner of the program, Blitzstein wrote, "a concert of the ever-old music newly-composed (get them off their ass)," and below, the names Bernstein, Copland, Haieff, Rorem, and his own, suggesting some opposition between this latter group of composers and the modernist establishment as represented by the ISCM.[25]

Over the break, he further took in Tony Richardson's 1962 film *The Loneliness of the Long Distance Runner*, a preview of Lillian Hellman's 1963 satire *My Mother, My Father and Me*, and a number of concerts with Bernstein and the Philharmonic at the new Philharmonic (later, Avery Fisher) Hall at Lincoln Center, including performances on separate occasions of Mahler's Fifth Symphony, Roberto Gerhard's First Symphony, Janáček's *Glagolitic Mass*, Bernstein's *Symphonic Dances from "West Side Story,"* and Copland's *Connotations*. He also accompanied the Bernsteins on tour with the Philharmonic to Miami, where one evening he apparently caught comedian Milton Berle's act at the Fontainebleau Hotel.

Blitzstein resumed his more provincial life in Bennington in mid-March, although in April he returned to New York to attend a Passover seder at the home of his friends Benjamin and Julia Algase, both progressive attorneys (Benjamin was the brother of his accountant David Algase); and in May, he traveled to Washington to see Alan Schneider's production of *The Threepenny Opera*. At Bennington, meanwhile, he socialized not so much with the music faculty (which included his longtime associate Henry Brant) as with Malamud, Stanley Hyman and Shirley Jackson, drama professor William Sherman, and language professor Georges Guy. He also butted heads with other faculty in defense of a student initiative to divert money from some school dinners to the Bennington Civil Rights Committee. The previous fall, he had written Diamond about his appointment, "Enjoying it too, although I'll never really belong to the 'groves of academe,'" and that spring semester he similarly wrote Jean Dalrymple that he had been happy at Bennington. But he also mentioned tensions between the music and drama departments in a letter to Wilfrid Mellers, and in September 1963, after departing from the school, he wrote to Diamond, "After Lina [Abarbanell]'s death, which cut me sharply and left a considerable void, I plugged back to Bennington, not liking teaching, finding faculty life heavy and loathsome. The ray of light was Bernard Malamud."[26]

Meanwhile, Blitzstein happily learned in February that he had received an unsolicited $4,000 grant from the Chapelbrook Foundation to be paid in installments over a one-year period. Established in 1953 by his friend Mina Curtiss (and dissolved in 1973), the foundation gave grants to established artists, often poets, typically through an application process; but in this case, the trustees unanimously voted to present Blitzstein with an honorary gift "in recognition of his distinguished contributions to the field of music as a composer and in the hope of facilitating the continuance of his creative work." Curtiss, aware of Blitzstein's difficult circumstances, presumably initiated this bequest. Having tactfully refrained from applying for a grant in the past, Blitzstein accepted the offer ("understatement of the year," he noted to himself) and requested that the grant be paid in two $2,000 installments, one in July, the other in January. (In the end, the foundation transmitted the second payment, which failed to reach him before his death, to his estate.)[27]

After leaving Bennington in mid-June, Blitzstein spent some six weeks at the home of his friends soprano Brenda Lewis and her husband Benjamin Cooper in Weston, Connecticut, where he wrote his last completed piece, *Lied*, on the occasion of Cooper's birthday. He then spent about two months in Brigantine before returning to New York in late September. As of mid-September, he still did not know where he would spend the winter, but he told Diamond it would be "almost anywhere but New York, where I can't work." Ultimately, he decided to spend five months, November through March, on the island of Martinique, an overseas region of France in the eastern Caribbean. In a letter to Morris Golde, he suggested that he chose Martinique because he thought the place an affordable "tourist-backwater," but in any case, such an adventure epitomized his credo, expressed to his Bennington students and others during these years, that for artists, "The world should be our oyster."[28]

In the course of October, prior to his departure, Blitzstein attended Jerome Moross's musical theater piece *Gentlemen, Be Seated!* at City Center, an all-Stravinsky recital by Bernstein and the Philharmonic, and a new play by Edward

Albee, *The Ballad of the Sad Cafe*, followed by a postperformance party hosted by Albee and his lover, playwright Terrence McNally. Before leaving for the Caribbean, he left for reasons unknown much of his *Sacco and Vanzetti* materials in the trunk of his car garaged in New Rochelle.

After arriving in Martinique on October 23, Blitzstein rented a Peugeot and stayed for a short while at the Auberge de l'Anse Mitan in Trois-Îlets near Fort-de-France before finding a three-bedroom home to rent in Frégate near François on the Atlantic coast, with a view of the ocean and easy access to stunning beaches. With a local maid in attendance as well, the arrangement resembled that in Israel and to a lesser extent Rome, but without their "cushy splendors"; on the contrary, he had to contend with power outages, voracious mosquitoes, poor roads, and other annoyances, including the "shenanigans" of the natives. Although he had planned to stay until early April—he had a return ticket dated April 4—he even thought about quitting the island altogether. But he found the people "beautiful (East Indian, Carib, Negro and French make stunning varieties), of deep and gallant courtesies," and the rustic conditions "exactly what I've been looking for: in three years (five or six at most) it [Martinique] will be Frigidaired, concreted, pulled and pushed and driven into the spoiled American tourist fingers."[29]

Whatever his initial reservations about Kennedy, news of the president's November 22 assassination deeply distressed him, and feeling an "atavistic wish to be home 'with my people,'" he attended a commemorative mass for the slain leader in Fort-de-France. "As to what kind of president Johnson will make, and whether he will be re-elected, I don't dare think," he wrote to his mother. Bernard Malamud later related that the Kennedy assassination left Blitzstein in "a terrible state," making it difficult for him to work: "he didn't know what to do with himself, and had an absolutely horrid feeling of what America had come to." Arriving on the island in late November, Morris Golde similarly remembered Blitzstein as "despondent," but that seems to have been the result also of various "personal troubles and problems" that he had "more-or-less solved" by the time Golde left. In any case, his mood subsequently brightened. He made friends among the locals, becoming "intellectually enamored" of a Swiss priest, Père Mayer, "who smokes, drinks, wears shorts on leave, and curses superbly; he is also a music-fanatic and can talk Schönberg and [Pierre] Boulez with me." On December 12, he wrote to his mother, regarding his stay, "What a sight; what calm; what fun; and what good work as a dividend."[30]

On December 19, Blitzstein penned what appears to have been his last letter to Bernstein, an unusual missive consisting of nothing but a dream that he had had that morning: As he mills about a "great convention or something" in the "new" Philadelphia, Lillian Hellman fetches him in a chauffeured limousine and takes him to his suite in a posh hotel, where she and her ex-husband Arthur Kober go "into a long, presumably comic (distasteful to me, I recall) session of making-fun-of-luxury-while-enjoying it." A "mousy" girl in red, who appears to be Hellman's "duenna," and a "huge beautiful thirty-year-old negress" enter, and against the tearful protests of the latter, Hellman begins to "draw out" the black woman's right breast, saying, "But it's *wonderful*, Jerry; I *like* it!" and comments on the resemblance between the woman's nipple and "a man's 'thing.'" "And as I looked," Blitzstein continues, "I saw that indeed it was like a tiny circumcized prick; dark of course, but with a blond-flesh tip" (adding in an asterisked footnote, "This part is the most obviously autobiographical; but then I guess all of it is"). As the others depart, Blitzstein says something reassuring to the girl in red, "such as she must be used to this kind of thing, and would recover as always. I closed the door behind them; and woke up." Hellman biographer Deborah Martinson suspects some connection between the black woman and Hellman's childhood nanny Sophronia (the inspiration for Addie in *The Little Foxes*), the girl in red and Hellman's secretary Rita Wade, and Jerry and her first lover, known only as "Jerry V."[31]

At the same time, as Blitzstein himself realized, this recorded dream, a rarity among the composer's papers, essentially represents an autobiographical statement, as immediately evidenced by the setting in Philadelphia, his home town. Beth Martin, a depth psychotherapist, notes the presence of three females—the girl in red, the large black woman, and Hellman (at fifty-eight, the same age as Blitzstein)–that fit the Jungian archetype of maiden-mother-crone; and she sees the dream as a metaphor for the creative cycle, with the mother figure fulfilling the untapped potential of the maiden and renewing the waning powers of the crone—an apt interpretation given Blitzstein's current worries about *Sacco and Vanzetti*. Composer Edward Applebaum, another student of Jungian psychology, further finds encoded in the dream some ambivalence and guilt over class and sex. Meanwhile, the background of the "great convention" in Philadelphia, with its "new boulevards and old Georgian architecture," echoes the Philadelphia Convention of 1787 that gave rise to the United States Constitution, thereby suggesting some convergence of personal and public concerns, intriguingly amplified by having the symbol of revitalization a black woman.[32]

Residing in spacious living quarters for a change, Blitzstein hosted small dinner parties in Martinique, and after Jo and Ed Davis visited for a day in late December while cruising the Caribbean, invited them to return for a longer stay. He offered to host Irene and Aaron Diamond in March as well. (Irene wrote to him on December 5, "I miss you *terribly*," and again on December 31, "There is a real longing for you always.") He also sent Rudolf Bing and John Gutman of the Metropolitan Opera a copy of Sacco's second-act aria, "With a Woman To Be," to give them finally "a taste of what my opera on Sacco and Vanzetti might be like." He suggested, further, that they get for audition purposes a "dramatic tenor," writing at first "who knows the Italian school, but doesn't overdo it," later changed to "(Sacco is a tortured man and shows it)." In a response dated January 4, Gutman informed him that he had asked tenor Nicholas Di Virgilio to learn and perform the number.[33]

On January 12, Blitzstein wrote a letter to his mother that he asked her to save, explaining, "It's the only time I have analyzed what I've seen here." After discussing the power wielded by the interbred white upper class and the socioeconomic causes undermining the institution of marriage among the black lower class, he commented, "An explosion of some sort is due, I'd say. For one thing the Communist Party is very powerful here politically, although the unions are economically weak," adding, with regard to the island's compulsory education, "So we have Marguerite [his maid], high-school educated, beautifully trained *as a servant*, with no real future ahead of her." And in another letter to his mother a few days later, after waxing poetic about the island's sunsets and sunrises ("when the light takes on a startling supernal glare, total white without modulation, like lighting suspended in space. . . . I call it the Second Coming light; it's really staggering and Biblical"), he further discussed life among the island's poor, including the prohibitive cost of meat: "So only the rich get to eat meat." Blitzstein remained alert to social and economic injustice to the end.[34]

On January 21, after dinner with some friends in François, Blitzstein went out drinking in some dockside bars in Fort-de-France and fell in with three young seamen, two Portuguese-born merchant sailors from Venezuela currently working in the local fishing industry and a native apprentice fisherman still in his teens. After Blitzstein reportedly slipped into a deserted alley with one of the three for some sexual encounter, the seamen attacked him, taking his wallet and watch and leaving him badly beaten. Half-undressed, Blitzstein managed to get to a public square, the Place de Stalingrad, where he was discovered calling for help in the early morning hours and taken to Fort-de-France's Clarac Hospital.[35]

When United States Vice-Consul William Milam arrived at the hospital that morning, he found Blitzstein in a gurney waiting to be examined and, although aware of the composer's good French, arranged for him to see a doctor who spoke fluent English. This doctor subsequently assured Milam that Blitzstein, although badly bruised and in pain, would live. The composer recovered well enough to identify the three "bastards" to the authorities but asked that his family be told only that he had been in an automobile accident.[36]

That evening, Milam telegrammed Jo Davis in Philadelphia, "Marc Blitstein [sic] hospitalized. Auto accident. Your presence needed if possible. Telephone American consulate." But as the Davises were out to dinner when the message arrived, the telegram initially was read to the composer's eighty-one-year-old mother, who had moved in with her daughter. Meanwhile, Blitzstein's condition deteriorated, his face yellowing; long plagued by jaundice, the likely result of excessive alcohol use, he died of a ruptured liver, probably some time between 8:45, when Milam mailed his telegram, and 9:52, when he sent a second one, which read in part, "Regret notify death your brother Marc Blitztein [sic]," and which requested funds for the disposition of his remains. Davis, who had since returned home, received this second telegram, but kept the news from her mother for the time being.[37]

And so Marc Blitzstein died on January 22, 1964, at age fifty-eight, just shy of his fifty-ninth birthday, the apparent victim of a gay bashing. With his penchant for sexual cruising, he long had placed himself in jeopardy, and indeed had been mis-used over the years by pickups, typically in the matter of petty theft, although Bill Hewitt recalled saving him from bodily harm at the hands of an Irish guardsman during the war. But he ran an increased risk in Martinique, which widely promoted "hypermasculinity," according to a 1996 study that claimed a distinction between Hispanic machismo permissive of "sexual conquests of other men" and Martiniquais hypermasculinity in which "any admission or accusation of sexual relations between men threatens male status and reputation." Some friends and family imagined too that Blitzstein might have survived had he been treated in an American hospital, but his case well might have proved fatal even under the day's best medical care.[38]

Ned Rorem, among others, noted the seeming irony that Blitzstein died at the hands of "the very type he had spent a lifetime defending," comparing his fate with that of communist film director Pier Paolo Pasolini, murdered by a hustler. But in fact, Blitzstein's dramatic pieces over and again presented such hooligans with repugnance, his compassion for Mike Stretto in *No for an Answer* notwith-standing. His work, which so often explored the theme of goodness challenged or destroyed by evil, could even be seen as a protest against the brutality that eventu-ally engulfed him.[39]

On January 23, the press reported that the composer had been killed in a car accident and at that evening's New York Philharmonic concert, Leonard Bernstein dedicated his performance of Beethoven's "Eroica" Symphony to Blitzstein's memory; reported Eric Salzman in the *Herald Tribune*, "The work was performed as if the conductor were rewriting Beethoven as he went along in order to express his personal grief. It was an incredible, agonized, unbearable reading which, with its bursts of nervous energy, and wild relentless drive, left detail, clarity, accuracy and indeed everything but anguished, frenetic intensity far, far behind."[40]

The front-page obituary that appeared the next day in the *New York Times* summarized the composer's many accomplishments and quoted Leonard Bernstein as saying, "Mr. Blitzstein was so close a personal friend that I cannot even begin to measure our loss of him as a composer. I can think only that I have lost a part of me; but I know also that music has lost an invaluable servant. His special position in musical theater is irreplaceable." In another section of the paper, Ross Parmenter offered an appreciation of Blitzstein's theatrical work, calling *Regina* "one of the best operas written by an American."[41]

The following day, January 25, the world learned that Blitzstein actually had been beaten to death during a robbery and that his three assailants—who, according to the Martinique police, had become embroiled in "a dispute" with Blitzstein—had been arrested. Meanwhile, Jo Davis made arrangements for the body to be shipped back home, and after cremation on January 27, for the ashes to be buried in a family resting place at Philadelphia's Chelten Hills Cemetery in a private ceremony without any religious service, in accordance with the composer's wishes. Blitzstein originally intended to divide his estate between his mother and Lina Abarbanell, but with the latter deceased, all his assets went to Anna. His will further named Jo and Ed Davis as trustees, with Copland and Bernstein as literary executors.[42]

Jo Davis received numerous condolence cards, a testimony not only to her brother's wide circle of friends, but her own. Burton Lane, the composer of *Finian's Rainbow*, wrote, "Marc was a personal friend of mine and I deeply mourn his loss"; journalist I. F. Stone, "He radiated a benevolence and joy we [Stone and his wife] shall never forget"; Bernard Malamud, "How charming, delightful, how human and dedicated a person he was. And how tragic the loss"; and David Diamond, "I have lost one of the *most* loyal, devoted friends, and a companion equal to no other!" Helen Rosen, wife of famed ear surgeon Samuel Rosen and a longtime progressive activist, recalled, "Through the tough 30's, the confused 40's and the sad 50's, Marc was always a bulwark of straight thinking and of strength and integrity found in very few of our generation." New friends from Martinique, Lollie and George Peckham, wrote, "He loved people—no matter what race, color, creed, nationality, or kind of clothes they wore. Perhaps this inquisitiveness into what makes people tick might have been the cause of his demise." And the composer's sixty-one-year-old New York maid Elizabeth Pond stated, "It is very hard for me to get use to whats [sic] before me after 11 years of service to such a nice and very considerate person as Mr. Blitzstein, not just a boss but a friend to my grandson and I whom he often talked to." Those who knew the composer best typically remarked on his gentleness, vitality, and wit.[43]

Lillian Hellman took the lead with regard to public commemoration. On January 31, she appeared as the featured speaker at a memorial service held at the Helen Hayes Theater and attended by about 120 people (Leonard Bernstein, in Boston for, appropriately enough, a performance of his *Kaddish Symphony*, could not attend), the *New York Times* reporting that she "told of her long, sometimes stormy relationship with the composer. She spoke of his outspokenness, honesty and bravery and regretted that wider recognition had not come to him." (Among her notes, presumably for this eulogy, Hellman wrote, "Had a chip on his shoulder and often fought. But always in the fight there was an attempt to tell the truth and if you had any respect for the truth, you came out better for it.") On February 2, she also published at her own expense a brief reminiscence, "Marc Blitzstein Remembered," in the *Times*. And she spearheaded a benefit memorial concert to raise funds for a Marc Blitzstein Musical Theater Award to be given by the National Institute of Arts and Letters (whose council quickly approved the idea) to a composer, lyricist, or librettist in order "to encourage the creation of works of merit for the musical theater."[44]

Supervised by David Oppenheim, a close associate of Bernstein's and a notable record and television producer, this memorial concert took place at Philharmonic

Hall on April 19. The program featured excerpts from *Regina*, with Hellman narrating and Julius Rudel conducting; an aria from each of his operas-in-progress ("How I Met My New Grandfather" from *Idiots First* sung by José Ferrer; "Then" from *The Magic Barrel* sung by Anita Ellis; and "With a Woman To Be" from *Sacco and Vanzetti* sung by Luigi Alva), all three orchestrated by Hershy Kay and conducted by Bernstein; and after intermission, a playback of Blitzstein's 1956 discussion of *The Cradle Will Rock* as recorded by Spoken Arts, and excerpts from that opera with Leonard Bernstein on the piano—brilliant performances by an impressive array of musical theater and operatic luminaries. "If any of your favorite theatrical people were missing from the stage," stated Alan Rich in the *Herald Tribune*, "they were probably in the audience."[45]

The concert elicited a tepid appreciation by Harold Schonberg (*New York Times*) and more wholehearted tributes from Irving Kolodin (*Saturday Review*) and Leighton Kerner (*Village Voice*). "He was fertile in the invention of words and phrases, lines and rhymes that suited his characters as closely as the music in which he depicted them," opined Kolodin, who also praised the composer's "pungent and discriminating" criticism, while Kerner stated that even after the "marathon program" ended at midnight, "this Blitzstein-fan-disguised-as-a-reviewer would willingly have stayed for a run-through of 'No for an Answer' and 'Reuben, Reuben.'"[46]

Although many of Blitzstein's family, including his mother, attended the concert, Jo Davis chose rather to travel to the Soviet Union as national literature chairman of the American section of the Women's International League for Peace and Freedom for the second Soviet-American Women's Conference. "She did not like ceremony of any sort," recalled her son Christopher, "felt its falseness, was very private, hated showing off and parading emotion, didn't like to deal with sympathy, etc., and on the whole, I think, was glad to be out of the country for the memorial." In contrast to Hellman's assertions, Davis also had doubts, shared by David Diamond, about whether her brother would have liked such an event. "I had many great talks in the 29 years I knew Marc about Death and the Artist after death. I KNOW he would not have approved," wrote Diamond to Davis. "But that evening was more than a Memorial event. It made people—I am sure—remember again what this man's Awareness and Agape sense was. And will always be." In any case, Davis and her family deeply mourned the loss of so beloved a son, brother, and uncle. "I live with him daily," she wrote Bernstein in March 1965, "and sometimes I can even get passed [sic] the last horror and continue a 'life' that for me cannot die."[47]

The program book for the Lincoln Center memorial concert featured reminiscences from friends who emphasized different aspects of the composer's accomplishment and character: Copland, his humanity and contribution to American musical theater; Mina Curtiss, his work ethic, knack with animals, generosity, and liveliness; Minna Lederman, his volatility, curiosity, and loyalty; Lillian Hellman, his humor; Bernstein, his closeness to nature; Claire Reis, his excellence as a public speaker. Some of Copland's remarks appeared contemporaneously in the journal *Perspectives of New Music*, Lederman's, in *Show: The Magazine of the Arts*, while Bernstein later included his tribute in his book *Findings* (1982).[48]

At the memorial concert, Bernstein announced, to moans in the audience, that although the estate had recovered the composer's drafts for the Malamud operas, including a nearly complete *Idiots First*, they had not been able to locate any of the *Sacco and Vanzetti* score aside from the aria on that evening's program. No one apparently knew that Blitzstein had stored drafts and sketches for the opera in the trunk of his Peugeot, which Aaron Diamond had removed after the composer's death to a used-car lot in Queens for sale. But reading about the lost work in reviews of the concert, the manager of the car lot checked some cartons he had found in the vehicle's trunk and discovered them to contain the missing manuscripts, which he returned to the estate, and which included, reported Bernstein, two "substantially finished" acts of *Sacco and Vanzetti*. The *Times* further quoted Irene Diamond as saying, "He [Blitzstein] was very meticulous. It was not like him to leave the manuscript stored in the car."[49]

On June 6, 1964, a number of Bennington students presented "An Homage to Marc Blitzstein" at the Carriage Barn, produced and directed by the composer's former student Reed Wolcott, who had assisted Oppenheim on the Lincoln Center memorial. So elaborate a tribute, including scenes from various operas and an exhibition of materials on loan from the Wisconsin Center for Theater Research, testified to the impact that Blitzstein had made during his one short year at the school, witnessed as well years later by Bernard Malamud's daughter Janna, only twelve at the time:

> Blitzstein's death became an emotional gateway for me into the whole world of politically aware art and social justice commentary. Coming close on the heels of the John F. Kennedy assassination and the first civil rights killings, its brutality eddied into the larger collective mood of civil drama and solemnity, of innocence lost, which would soon become the Vietnam protests. I think it also may have marked the beginning of a different kind of conversation between my father and me. I became more cognizant of his world, more interested in eliciting his opinions about news stories, books, and events.[50]

In its 1965 proceedings, the National Institute included a memorial by Malamud along with another reminiscence by Leonard Bernstein, who expressed that same sense of loss that he voiced to Nadia Boulanger in a letter written the previous November: "I cannot stop thinking about Marc Blitzstein, whose death was to me like the loss of my right arm, or my eyesight. I cannot yet understand that he is not here. And it is not only grief—it is quiet and regret and bewilderment." Based on a speech given some months earlier, Bernstein's National Institute piece (republished, like the memorial concert remembrance, in *Findings*) referred to Blitzstein as a "survivor" who produced a "long chain of beautiful work-failures," as mentioned earlier, and had this to say as well: "Gallantry, vitality. Wry, Talmudic humor. A fresh, slanted view of everything. A secret affair with word-notes. Loyalties of improbable intensity, in unlikely places. Endless affection, grace. Endless capacity to suffer through quarrel, to find truth, or if not, to invent it. All these have been yours."[51]

The memorial concert at Philharmonic Hall netted a profit of over $14,000, with film and theater personages and prosperous attorneys many of the major contributors, including Hellman's friend, Philadelphia lawyer Arthur W. A. Cowan, who alone raised $1,500. Organized by Hellman, the first Marc Blitzstein Award committee—consisting of herself, Copland, Bernstein, and Lukas Foss—gave the initial $2,500 prize to composer William Bolcom. Because of the relatively small endowment and difficulties in determining suitable awardees, the institute (which later merged with the academy) gave the award not annually, as originally planned, but rather periodically, and eventually raised the amount to $5,000 as well. In the decades following Bolcom, the award went to three other composers (Jack Beeson, 1968; Richard Peaslee, 1988; and John Kander, 2012); three librettists (John Olon-Scrymgeour, 1976; Charles Kondek, 1997; and Arnold Weinstein, 2002); one lyricist (Sheldon Harnick, 1993); and one writer-composer (Rinde Eckert, 2005).

In late May 1965, a French court convicted Blitzstein's three assailants of involuntary homicide and theft. By this time, the police had found some of the stolen money in the cabin of the sailors' fishing vessel. The court sentenced Armando Fernandes, twenty-seven, to three years; Alfredo Rodriguez, thirty-five, to fourteen months; and Daniel Yves Charles Nicolas, eighteen, to a fourteen-month suspended sentence and three years of probation. Vice-Consul Milam, already assigned elsewhere, imagined that the police chief and prosecutor would have pursued tougher retribution had they not disapproved of Blitzstein's "moeurs" ("morals"). Moreover, none of Blitzstein's family chose to attend the trial, which might have made a difference in this regard as well. "There was none of that savage response that has to do with vengeance," recalled Christopher Davis. "There was also an element of denial and evasion; we were so upset we wanted nothing to do with it."[52]

The Unfinished Operas

In 1963, Blitzstein stated that he chose the Sacco and Vanzetti affair as the subject of his opera-in-progress "because it is one of the noblest and entirely felt subjects in the consciousness of the world. It is a subject known not only to the intellectual world but even more so to the workers and peasants the world over. . . . I think the Sacco-Vanzetti story can never be told too often in terms of reminding us of a justice which miscarried." Privately, he also placed the affair in the context of the American experience: "This is a 'land of freedom'—we exist as an *idea*, as well as a country; that idea is the principle of *freedom* for the *individual*—the very thing exemplified by the characters and lives of S[acco] and V[anzetti]. And the tragedy of the story is how far we went astray as a nation and a govt; we *killed* the images of our ideal. This of course gets beyond [the] USA, and falls into the trap of 'man's inhumanity to man'—what happens is that the *condoners* reap the whirlwind."[1]

That Sacco and Vanzetti held universal as well as national meanings for Blitzstein could be deduced from other jottings found among his papers, such as an undated note that summarized the opera in terms of "1) [the] individ[ual] vs. society (*anywhere*); 2) the *nature* of man himself; 3) the fight of *man* to rise above animal, in *this* respect, and in others." In early 1960, he further described the work's theme as follows: "Two small good people, frightened, making mistakes—*grow* like thunder in their martyrdom; the persecutors dwindle at the same time. And it proceeds to death itself." At the same time, he did not view the story as furnishing a compelling argument against the death penalty per se, observing that a better case in this regard could have been made if the defendants had had less financial support (whereas with the money behind them "they might almost have been millionaires") or if they more likely had been guilty, as in the case of Caryl Chessman, a convicted thief and rapist whose execution in 1960 became a cause célèbre among death penalty abolitionists.[2]

Blitzstein's decision to undertake a Sacco and Vanzetti opera in the fall of 1959—he started to notate ideas on Labor Day, September 7—signaled not merely a return to longstanding preoccupations, as manifested above all by his 1932 choral opera *The Condemned*, but also a sensitivity to current concerns that went far beyond the stimulus provided by Fedele D'Amico's gift of a monograph on the subject in the summer of 1959. Interest in the case was in the air. In May 1958,

CBS Television broadcast a two-part show about the affair, and later that year, Representative Alexander Cella filed a resolution with the Massachusetts state legislature urging that Sacco and Vanzetti be pardoned posthumously, leading to an open hearing on April 2, 1959, a transcript of which Tom O'Connor—secretary of the Committee for the Vindication of Sacco and Vanzetti—some time later sent to the composer inscribed "to Marc Blitzstein, with whose opera the Sacco-Vanzetti case will take its place among the classic legends of humanity." (The state legislature rejected the resolution as beyond their purview, but the hearing set the stage for an exoneration of the two men by Governor Michael Dukakis in 1977.)[3]

This revitalized interest intensified in the early 1960s as evidenced by a series of dramatizations, all sympathetic to the two anarchists, including a two-part NBC Television docudrama directed by Sidney Lumet and written by Reginald Rose, *The Sacco-Vanzetti Story* (1960); an off-Broadway musical by Armand Aulicino and Frank Fields, *The Shoemaker and the Peddler* (1960); an Italian play by Mino Roli and Luciano Vincenzoni, *Sacco and Vanzetti* (1960), quickly translated and presented worldwide; an American play by Robert Noah, *The Advocate* (1962); and a French play by Armand Gatti, *Public Song Before Two Electric Chairs* (1964). Concurrently, several new studies about the case emerged, some challenging the prevailing presumption of the two men's—or at least Sacco's—innocence, including Robert Montgomery's *Sacco-Vanzetti: The Murder and the Myth* (1960), James Grossman's "The Sacco-Vanzetti Case Reconsidered" (1962), and Francis Russell's *Tragedy in Dedham* (1962), publications that led to heated exchanges among scholars and pundits.[4]

In attempting to account for the renewed attention to the case in the 1960s, Lisa McGirr points to contemporaneous movements for greater social justice around the world and a corresponding search for "moments of such solidarity in the past for inspiration." The late 1920s and early 1960s tellingly had some relevant parallels, including widespread postwar disillusionment with the United States. A number of commentators in both eras even equated sympathy with Sacco and Vanzetti with anti-Americanism, although the plays mentioned above, like Blitzstein's opera, tended to view the incident not simply as a struggle between radical immigrants and the Commonwealth of Massachusetts, but also as a moral argument unfolding within the establishment itself, with sundry law officers, attorneys, and citizens embodying various virtues and failings. In a handwritten critique of an article by Robert J. Clements that argued that the Roli and Vincenzoni play had an anti-American agenda, Blitzstein (who, as mentioned, came to know the playwrights in Rome) wrote, "Vincenzoni was appalled and alarmed at the effect of 'Anti-Americanism' of the play. He hated the invitation from the Soviet embassy. (He had earlier 'baited' me by saying 'Why is only the Soviet Union silent during the revival of interest in the case?')"[5]

Indeed, although communists long had made common cause with a broad leftist coalition in defending Sacco and Vanzetti, the two men themselves identified more with the anarcho-communism of Peter Kropotkin and Luigi Galleani than with Marx and Lenin. Some of the staunchest defenders of Sacco and Vanzetti—from anarchists like Aldino Felicani, who founded the Sacco-Vanzetti Defense Committee in 1921, to conservatives like Michael Musmanno, a Pennsylvania Supreme Court justice who as a young attorney had volunteered on behalf of the two men—could be, as Blitzstein well knew, vehemently anticommunist and probably would not have welcomed the comparisons made by the composer and others during these years between, on the one hand, the two anarchists and, on the other, Julius and Ethel Rosenberg, executed in 1953 for allegedly conspiring to commit espionage. "This blind-spot/Achilles-heel is part of the nature of many left-wing dissidents in the orthodox left," wrote Blitzstein. "The real enemy is imperialistic capitalism; but the larger-hulking foe, the immediate antagonist, is the 'Stalinist,' on whom they shower the strongest vituperation. It works the other way too: cf. [the] CP's [Communist Party members] vs. Social Democrats; in Germany (pre-Hitler and later), in Spain, etc." Blitzstein in contrast seems to have considered the lessons of Sacco and Vanzetti as applicable to a variety of dissenting worldviews.[6]

On a more practical level, with its two Italian protagonists, the story offered Blitzstein possibilities for more Italianate singing than typical of his work. "Since it [the opera] dealt with two immigrant Italian Americans," stated Leonard Bernstein, "Blitzstein could allow his music to soar in an Italian way that lends itself to operatic treatment." Blitzstein surely reasoned that along with the broad appeal of the drama, this more traditionally operatic approach ("My Sacco-Vanzetti opera," he remarked, "will be a 'grand-opera,' not in the Meyerbeer sense of thunder and guns—and yet, on second thought, I may have very much of a twentieth-century equivalent to it") could help find the work the international audience that had eluded *Regina*. "Watch out for local *references* (American)! . . ." he cautioned himself. "This is a work remember, to be translated, done elsewhere, in many other languages."[7]

While working on the opera, Blitzstein extensively researched the case, painstakingly quoting and annotating historical documents. By April 1960, he could even serve as a consultant to NBC's *Sacco-Vanzetti Story*, to judge from his editing of an early draft of the Rose teleplay and his presence at the network's Avenue M studio in Brooklyn for the May 15 filming. He paid special attention to the two men's published letters, arranging lines from them much as he had done with the original source material for *Regina* and *Juno*. In addition, he conversed with such longtime Sacco-Vanzetti activists as Aldino Felicani and Gardner Jackson, as well as with Sacco and Vanzetti's lawyer, Herbert Ehrmann, who authored a landmark 1933 study about the case, and Harvard English professor Harry Levin, who told him that he had heard the principal member of the advisory committee that had defended the court's guilty verdict, Harvard President A. Lawrence Lowell, say, "You know all Italians are liars." On his copy of a 1958 article on

"Sacco's Struggle for Sanity" by psychiatrist Ralph Colp Jr., Blitzstein scrawled, "*Everything* is grist."[8]

Blitzstein's notes also referenced previous works that had dealt with the affair, including Upton Sinclair's *Boston*, Maxwell Anderson's *Winterset*, and the scripts by Rose and Roli-Vincenzoni, along with the Sacco and Vanzetti drawings by Ben Shahn, an artist with whom he strongly identified and who he hoped might do the set designs for the opera. He further cited Arthur Miller's *View from the Bridge* as a model for Italian-American dialect; Lillian Hellman's *Watch on the Rhine* for his portrait of Elizabeth Glendower Evans, a humane Boston Brahmin in the mold of Hellman's Fanny Farrelly; and Robert Lowell's poem "Children of Light" for the "mood and notion" of the chorus representing the Commonwealth. Yet other works attracted attention because of their inventive use of montage, such as William S. Burroughs's novel *Naked Lunch*, Ingmar Bergman's films *Wild Strawberries* and *The Magician*, and Tony Richardson's film *The Loneliness of the Long Distance Runner*, whose complex scenario he outlined in detail while sitting through the movie a second time. He additionally alluded to a number of other literary works ranging from the Bible, Sophocles, Juvenal, Dante, and Shakespeare to Dostoyevsky, Jean Genet, Albert Camus, James Baldwin, and Allen Ginsberg, mentioning too such operas as *Carmen*, *Otello*, *Wozzeck*, *Moses und Aron*, and *The Consul*. However, he apparently had in mind, above all, Georg Büchner's *Danton's Death* and *Woyzeck*, and the work of Bertolt Brecht, including *The Measures Taken*, *Saint Joan of the Stockyards*, *Life of Galileo*, *Mother Courage and Her Children*, and *The Resistible Rise of Arturo Ui*—plays variously admired for their tone, structure, and content, including their use of historical figures and events.[9]

"I have determined to get well along on the libretto before writing a note of music," he wrote Mina Curtiss from Edgartown in May 1960, after months of research. "It's good discipline for me, who have always run to the piano for too-easy, too-quickly rewarding results before stopping to think and plan." But shaping so much material into a workable libretto proved arduous. "The opera is hard, hard," he told Ned Rorem in June. "I do nearly twelve hours a day." He occasionally consulted with such friends as Lillian Hellman, Joseph Stein, and George Tabori, but he worked largely on his own, reluctant to show his material to anyone.[10]

During the early part of his Rome sabbatical, his work went well, and by the end of 1960, he seems to have completed much of the first of three intended acts and made some headway on the second as well. But he became increasingly bogged down in the course of 1961, often alluding to problems with the text. "I have torn up more on this one than I ever wrote on another," he wrote Mordecai and Irma Bauman in January. In February, he told Lina Abarbanell of being in "somthing [sic] of a funk," and in May, he wrote David Diamond about emerging from "the creative dumps." While at Yaddo in late 1961 and early 1962, he spoke of a "break-through" and a "turning-point," but his momentum soon stalled once again. In the fall of 1962, after close to three years of herculean effort, he turned his attention to a new project, composing two one-act operas after Bernard Malamud, although he continued to work on *Sacco and Vanzetti* as well.[11]

Such hardship took its toll. "The ups and downs of my moods won't bear investigation, much less description," he wrote Leonard Bernstein in December 1961. Frequently touchy about his work, he now appeared at times utterly overwrought. On one occasion, in 1961, he raged at Minna Lederman after she asked him, during the intermission of a concert, if he had finished the opera, at which he shouted at her, "Finished—what a word! Of course it is! Of course it isn't!" Recalled Lederman, "He continued in this disjointed manner for some time, his eyes flaming. 'What can you mean? What a question!' I drew away, afraid he would fall in hysterics, and turned toward the hall. He swallowed tears of rage and followed me." Ann Thorne, wife of composer Francis Thorne, related an almost identical story about Blitzstein exploding at the dinner table when asked about his progress in Italy, but here the Thornes' young daughter reduced all to laughter by saying, "I think that's a very obvious question to ask a composer."[12]

Some commentators have conjectured that Blitzstein might have had trouble completing the opera because of doubts about the men's innocence raised by Francis Russell and others, but the evidence supports no such contention. On the contrary, in response to James Grossman's article, Blitzstein asked how the author, after acknowledging the unfairness of the trial, could "derive any facts in making conclusions from an unfair trial?" And with regard to Upton Sinclair's revelation about defense attorney Fred Moore's admission of the men's probable guilt, a linchpin in the revisionist argument, he wrote that Sinclair "should have known" an August 1924 letter from Sacco to Moore "full of vituperation and hostility." "My conception assumes their [Sacco and Vanzetti's] innocence (an assumption justified by the over-all evidence and research, in which latter division you have played so large a part)," he assured Michael Musmanno in June 1963 after receiving from the judge his review of the Russell book in the *Kansas Law Review*. "It proceeds to what I feel is a true operatic theme: the rise to nobility and yes, glory, both intellectual and spiritual, of two simple men, in collision with specific chicaneries within the Establishment (here the Commonwealth), driven chaotic and ultimately murderous amid a universal cry for justice." Blitzstein's papers point rather to his being overwhelmed by the amount of material on the subject and the desire to encapsulate the details of a complicated social and legal incident and to pare the work "down to a single focus," including addressing "polemical points" that most other dramatizations had sidestepped. That he chose to employ a rather complex musical language for the opera presumably made the work only that much more taxing. Commented his sister Jo, "Marc couldn't bring the characters to life without making it very heavy. He just couldn't find a balance between script and music."[13]

In any case, Blitzstein had every intention of returning to the project after finishing his Malamud operas, and as late as December 1963, while in Martinique, he continued to draft ideas for the work. Had he lived, he likely would have completed the opera; he had enormous perseverance—it had taken him about four years to write *Regina*, based on a famously well-constructed play, and six years to write *Reuben Reuben*, which had required relatively little research—and he usually saw his pieces, however intractable, to completion, especially ones as ambitious as this. Whether the Met would have launched the work remains another matter.[14]

From the start, Blitzstein chose to focus on the figures of Ferdinando Nicola (Nick) Sacco (1891–1927) and Bartolomeo (Barto) Vanzetti (1888–1927)—a natural enough decision, although Hellman advised that he avoid them altogether, arguing that the composer's gifts lay more in the direction of satire than tragedy, Blitzstein countering by citing the uninspiring example of Maxwell Anderson's *Winterset*, which only alluded to the case. He also decided fairly quickly on a large cast of supporting characters, including Sacco's wife Rosa and their small boy Dante (a silent part); the men's anarchist colleagues Mike Boda and Ricardo Orciani (the latter silent); the owners of the Elm Square garage, Ruth and Simon Johnson, whose tip to the police led to the two men's arrest; the arresting officers Thomas Connolly and Earl Vaughn (the latter silent); Police Chief Michael Stewart; witnesses for the prosecution Mary Splaine and Michael Levangie; District Attorney Frederick Katzmann; defense attorney John McAnarney; Sacco-Vanzetti supporters Elizabeth Glendower Evans, Aldino Felicani, Mary Donovan, and Tom O'Connor; Judge Webster Thayer; jury foreman Walter Ripley; the convicted murderer who confessed to Sacco and Vanzetti's alleged crimes while in jail, Celestino Medeiros; journalist Philip Stong; the governor of Massachusetts, Alvan Fuller; and the governor's advisory committee—A. Lawrence Lowell, Samuel Stratton, and Robert Grant—who sided with the court. In view of the far greater number of actual participants in the affair, Blitzstein decided to have some of these characters assume representative functions and accordingly adjusted the record in order to have, say, Levangie proclaim something stated by another witness.[15]

Perhaps the most unusual decision in this regard was in having McAnarney personify the defense as opposed to either of his two younger brothers, who took more active roles in the case, not to mention radical attorney Fred Moore, who headed the team until William Thompson became chief counsel in 1923. But McAnarney's high position in Boston society, like that of Elizabeth Glendower Evans, served specific dramatic purposes. Stated Blitzstein in his notes, "John W. [McAnarney] is . . . the *male* side of the true traditional American conservative; integrity is his personal hall-mark, and the quality he demands in others. . . . E. G. Evans is of course the other, *female*, side of the coin; and in the opera, she can be the more colorful." Blitzstein further described Evans, Sacco's "Auntie Bee" who helped teach the prisoners English, as an "old-style conservative, wealthy, educated and enlightened, who believes fiercely in the heritage and traditions of the United States, which include the possibility, even the desirability of dissident opinions," the character thereby evoking, as Eric Gordon observes, a strong kinship with Clara Chase, the female protagonist of *No for an Answer*.[16]

Adapting an unusual conceit central to *The Condemned*, Blitzstein planned to depict some of the more official characters, including the prosecutors, the judge, and the Lowell Committee, by way of two-voice men's choruses (comprising alternately twenty tenors, twenty basses, and twenty mixed male voices) who, when needed, would step out of a full hundred-voice mixed chorus that symbolizes the Commonwealth as a whole, a concept aimed at dramatizing the state's institutional force. (Aware that Police Chief Stewart had "balked" at his portrayal on the NBC dramatization, Blitzstein eventually decided to omit that character; at one point, the composer apparently considered simply substituting fictional names for most of the supporting cast and even locales, but in the end he decided against this idea.)[17]

Inspired by Schoenberg's *Moses und Aron*, Blitzstein further thought to juxtapose speaking and singing choruses. As another novelty, he imagined, in early 1963, two unspecified points in the drama at which a taped chorus would be superimposed over the live chorus, thinking that excerpts from "La notte" and "Il cielo in una stanza," two current Italian song hits performed by Mina (Anna Maria Quaini), might be sung in a high tessitura, recorded at a slow speed, and then transmitted at a high speed "so that the sound, especially of the soprani, will be higher than voices have ever been heard." He expected that he might confer with such colleagues as Vladimir Ussachevsky or Henry Brant about this.[18]

Working hard to differentiate Sacco and Vanzetti, Blitzstein conceived of the former as athletic, idealistic, and temperamental, the latter as intellectual, active, and even-keeled. He apparently underestimated Sacco's association with the Galleanist movement; he generally seems to have minimized both men's militancy, asserting that they opposed "force or violence of *any* sort" and that they "were unequipped by nature, by their psychological being, to hurt or to kill." At the same time, he refused to regard them as saints, an objection he raised with respect to the NBC drama, and increasingly came to recognize their willingness to "condone violence," underlining in his volume of letters by Sacco and Vanzetti, this statement by the latter: "The slave has the right and duty to arise against his master. My supreme aim, that of the Anarchist is, 'the complete elimination of violence from the rapports (relations).'"[19]

At one time or another, Blitzstein drafted various solos for his two protagonists: "Pesce, Anguille" and "The Whole Shoe" ("Song of the Craftsman"), numbers about their lives as fish peddler and heel trimmer, respectively; "Yesterday I Had to See Dentista," a humorous song for Vanzetti in strict terza rima, the interlocking rhyme scheme of the *Divine Comedy* that Shelley also had used, as Blitzstein noted, in his "magnificent" poem "Ode to the West Wind" (this terza rima idea suggested by a letter from Vanzetti to Elizabeth Glendower Evans in which he writes, "If I were poet and know the metre, I would write a song of it in third rhyme"); "With a

Woman To Be," a scene illustrating Sacco's deteriorating mental state; "The Books," a number for Vanzetti expressing his distress over some of his books damaged and misplaced by the authorities; "I Never Know, Never Heard" and "This Is What I Say," the respective remarks of Sacco and Vanzetti to the court following their sentencing; and "If It Had Not Been for These Thing," Vanzetti's stirring words as reported by Philip Stong, concluding, "That last moment belongs to us/That agony is our triumph." In addition, the composer sketched a second-act love duet for Nick and Rosa, "My Companionship."[20]

Blitzstein early on decided on a three-act format, with the first act covering the days surrounding the two men's arrest on May 5, 1920; the second act, their trial and long incarceration; and the third act, the events preceding their execution on August 23, 1927. The composer accordingly considered such titles as "The Seven Years of Sacco and Vanzetti." But he resisted a strictly chronological narrative, experimenting, as he had in the past, with flashback techniques, hence, his attention to such films as *Wild Strawberries* and *The Loneliness of the Long Distance Runner*. "Fuck continuity!" he told himself in September 1960. "It has been the bane of this whole thinking-period." At one point, he considered beginning the opera with a speakeasy scene on the night of the execution, not only to establish some period context, like the prologue to *Regina*, but so that the entire opera would unfold as a flashback. For this evocation of the roaring twenties, Blitzstein planned to feature two characters, Compère and Commère (shades of *Four Saints in Three Acts*), inspired by F. Scott and Zelda Fitzgerald, and a bop chorus, with in one version Commère jumping into a fountain. The scene then would have proceeded to a second part, an austere double chorus, "This Is the End of the Opera," that would have announced the opera's theme, as at the start of *Pagliacci*. However, he eventually decided against this idea and revamped the double chorus as a more general expression of institutional power, "Chair, Scale, Scepter," that he alternately seems to have considered for scenes one and four.[21]

In the end, the largely mapped out first-act libretto, coincidentally structured, as Blitzstein himself observed, like the opening act of Roli and Vincenzoni's play, formed a rather straightforward narrative. After the opening chorus (scene i), Nick and Rosa rehearse at home the climactic letter scene from Ibsen's *A Doll House* in Italian (the Saccos reportedly performed such plays for various worker causes, although Blitzstein chose this particular one as a foil to Nick and Rosa's happy marriage); Vanzetti arrives with news of the arrest and suicide of fellow anarchist Andrea Salsedo and suggests that he and Sacco collect incriminating radical literature (scene ii). At the Johnson garage at Elm Square, where friends Boda, Orciani, Sacco, and Vanzetti come to retrieve Boda's car, garage owner Simon Johnson and his shrewish wife Ruth—both portrayed as racist and greedy—tip off the police, and Officers Connolly and Vaughn arrest Sacco and Vanzetti (scene iii). After a choral number that includes some commentary by the Katzmann chorus (scene iv), the action moves to the Brockton police station, where Sacco and Vanzetti—separated on stage to simulate two distinct scenes happening at once—are questioned by District Attorney Katzmann (unaware of why they have been arrested and fearful of deportation, the two fatefully lie) and are identified by witnesses Splaine and Levangie (scene v). In a Brockton prison, Sacco and Vanzetti finally learn from McAnarney the reason for their arrest, leaving them "stupefied" and "frightened" as the act closes (scene vi). However, as late as 1963, Blitzstein considered other, less chronological ways to organize this first act.[22]

Moreover, various outlines and sketches suggest that the second and third acts, much less of which survives, might well have made greater use of flashback techniques. In any case, the second act likely would have included some depiction of the trial, with Sacco and Vanzetti, as in real life, placed in separate cages in court, a setting reminiscent of the asylum scene in *Reuben Reuben*; scenes in their separate cells (at times simultaneously visible), including some portrayal of Sacco's friendship with Elizabeth Glendower Evans; and a finale in which Sacco, moved to a psychiatric hospital after going on a hunger strike in 1923, recalls his courtship of Rosa ("With a Woman To Be") and then goes mad imagining the female inmates (represented by an offstage women's chorus) to be Rosa calling for their son. The third act presumably would have covered Medeiros's 1925 confession and a number of events that transpired in 1927, including the two men's sentencing, Vanzetti's oft-quoted interview with reporter Philip Stong, the report of the Lowell Committee, the final public protests, and the executions of Medeiros, Sacco, and Vanzetti.

Three portions of the piano-vocal reduction—the Elm Square garage scene, the chorus "Chair, Scale, Scepter," and the aria "With a Woman To Be"—exist in their entirety, but otherwise, only varying parts of the score survive, from much of the first-act scene at Sacco's home and Vanzetti's third-act aria, "If It Had Not Been for These Thing," to a large amount of the love duet and Sacco's mad scene, to only a bit of Vanzetti's "Pesce, Anguille," and virtually nothing but the text of "This Is What I Say." Leonard Lehrman, who completed the opera, estimates that at the time of his death, Blitzstein had finished only about 20 to 30 percent of the music and even that includes for the most part sketches. That Blitzstein completed more than what is preserved on paper, however, remains a distinct possibility; in fact, in notes following an October 9, 1961, session with Rudolf Bing, he claimed to have completed enough material to meet the Met's audition expectation of 40 percent music, 75 percent text. Even so, this would have been exclusive of the orchestration, which Blitzstein typically undertook only after completing a reduced score and which would have entailed considerably more work, especially as he seemed eager to take advantage of the Met's large orchestral resources.[23]

The extant music varies from the austere Stravinskian grandeur of the opening chorus and the parodistic melodrama of the Ibsen play-within-a-play to the haunting romanticism of Nick and Rosa's love duet and the solemn dignity of

Vanzetti's "If It Had Not Been for These Thing." At times, Blitzstein strove for comic relief, including some cutting irony in the Elm Square garage scene and the cheerful humor of "Yesterday I Had to See Dentista," with its incorporation, as in *Reuben Reuben*, of the jingle "Shave and a Haircut." But the surviving score over-all contains the sort of grim, dissonant language not really heard in Blitzstein's work for close to thirty years, with such severity not boding well for easy accep-tance, although the work's dramatic intensity might have carried the day. Indeed, "With a Woman To Be," as orchestrated by Hershy Kay and performed at the composer's memorial concert by tenor Luigi Alva under Leonard Bernstein, drew sustained applause from the audience and mostly positive remarks in the press.

Again, the work's dissonant language evoked not just the music of the composer's early maturity, but an engagement with contemporary trends, in particular, the vogue for twelve-tone music, as reflected by Blitzstein's interest in Boulez and admi-ration for Nono's *Intolerance 1960* and Copland's *Connotations*. He even sketched several twelve-tone rows and their standard permutations in conjunction with the opera, with his very first musical draft, dated December 8, 1959, referencing the twelve-tone method. But the surviving music shows little evidence of any strict twelve-tone writing. In 1962, he even admitted that he would rather listen to than compose serial music, saying, "for my kind of theater, serialism does not yet seem flexible enough." And in 1963, he added, "although I studied with Schönberg, I cer-tainly don't belong with the serial composers—cooked or raw. Not that I don't admire them enormously. In a curious way, I go to school to them—with my ear, that is, not my brain. I am a tonal composer and am more interested, for my own music, in the freshness of disclosure than I am in the novelty of ingredients."[24]

At the same time, the only extended completed scene, the one at the Elm Square garage, reveals a highly personal absorption of serial principles. Blitzstein con-structed this entire scene around a series of 137 pitches, as put forth, with only minor deviation, in the orchestral melody that accompanies Boda's opening lines (measures four to thirty, beginning on C and ending on $G^\flat$). Versions of this long row reappear throughout the scene, which consequently resembles a set of varia-tions. Perhaps most strikingly, at the concluding section beginning with Officer Connolly's "You're both under arrest," the row unfolds in augmentation in the ac-companiment, essentially bringing the scene to its end. Whether or not Blitzstein devised this series prior to actual composition, the general approach recalls his serial forays from the early 1930s, in particular, the chamber piece *Discourse*, another work left unfinished.

After Blitzstein's death, Leonard Bernstein, encouraged by such friends as Wil-liam Schuman to complete *Sacco and Vanzetti*, spent "a good deal of time" with the surviving manuscript, but found the piece "only half-composed, and full of unresolved choices. Who can guess at how you [Blitzstein] would have resolved them?" He also told John Gruen that working on the opera would "plunge him into great depression." In 1986, Jacob Druckman, at Bernstein's behest, approached Daron Hagen (b. 1961) about completing the opera after Bernstein had heard Hagen, then a composition fellow at Tanglewood, improvise at the piano in Blitzstein's style; but after looking through the sketches at Bernstein's studio later that year, Hagen also found the materials too fragmentary. However, composer Leonard Lehrman had long felt otherwise and in 1999 signed a contract with the Blitzstein estate that gave him authorization to reconstruct the opera, including permission to use other pieces in the Blitzstein catalog as needed, with compensation based on the sharing of royalties.[25]

Born in 1949, composer-pianist Lehrman grew up in suburban New York, studying privately with Elie Siegmeister before further work with Robert Palmer at Cornell and Nadia Boulanger in Paris. He developed an early affinity with Blitzstein during his undergraduate years at Harvard, where he supervised performances of *The Cradle*, *The Harpies*, and *I've Got the Tune*, and in later years, he completed Blitzstein's unfinished Malamud opera *Idiots First*, produced recordings of Blitzstein's music, edited the three-volume *Blitzstein Songbook*, and authored a bio-bibliography of the composer.

Lehrman finished his *Sacco and Vanzetti* piano-vocal score, dedicated to Robert Palmer, in early 2001 and the orchestration in 2003, with Sacco's niece Fernanda Sacco arranging for a literal translation of the libretto into Italian. About this same time, Lehrman, who had edited "With a Woman To Be" for the first volume of the *Blitzstein Songbook*, included his completions of four other solos from the opera in the second volume, and an essentially new song, based on "Hymn" from *Juno*, in volume three. For both the completed opera and the published excerpts, Lehrman distinguished, with varying degrees of specificity, his own work from Blitzstein's.[26]

Lehrman scored *Sacco and Vanzetti* for a large cast, but made provisions, as at its premiere, for smaller casts of ten singers and several actors via doubling of minor parts. With only a few finished set pieces at his disposal, he nonetheless created a three-act, seventeen-scene opera about three hours in length, filling out the libretto by writing some of the text himself and by culling other writings, including an excerpt from Governor Dukakis's proclamation on the trial issued in 1977, some thirteen years after Blitzstein's death. Lehrman also made extensive use of surviving drafts and further recycled, often with rewritten lyrics, passages from other Blitzstein works, especially *Reuben Reuben*, but also *The Condemned*, "Into the Streets," "Let's Be Blue," *Juno*, *From Marion's Book*, and *Lied*. In addition, he made passing allusions to pieces by Earl Robinson and Leonard Bernstein as well as his own cantata about the Rosenbergs, *We Are Innocent*. However, even with all this borrowing, which made the work something of a pastiche, he still needed to compose much of the score from scratch.

Lehrman's long familiarity with Blitzstein helped him flesh out fragments in a relatively seamless manner and create new set pieces in a roughly characteristic style. In a review of the work's premiere, Joseph Pehrson expressed surprise that the opera had "virtually no identifiable music of Leonard Lehrman in it. . . . It was as if, miraculously, Marc Blitzstein arose from the dead just to complete this important work." And in a study of Lehrman's creation of an aria for Vanzetti from a surviving remnant (published as "Vanzetti's Last Statement" and recorded by Marcus DeLoach in 2004), Melissa de Graaf deemed the result "as effective a completion of an unfinished piece as one could hope for." At the same time, Lehrman's music could not be expected to feature Blitzstein's kind of originality or formal cogency, and in another review of the premiere, Barry Cohen wrote that despite "the superficial similarity of styles" between the two authors, "music by a great composer can be heard between the notes. Ultimately, the heart was abandoned in this effort."[27]

Some of the borrowed passages arguably worked better than others. Whereas Blitzstein himself used a snippet of an Italianate melody from *Reuben Reuben* for Sacco's "With a Woman To Be," developed further in a manner suited to the opera's more serious intentions, some of Lehrman's quotations seemed less apt, such as the use of Bart's seductively devilish "Have Yourself a Night" from *Reuben Reuben* for thoughtful utterances by McAnarney, or the workers' song "Into the Streets May First" for a chauvinistic Memorial Day chorus. Relyricizing so much vocal music generally compromised Blitzstein's poetic welding of word and tone, as in the way the music for the Cummings song, "when life is quite through with/and leaves say alas," here accompanied the lyric "I brought you a plant./Also some books," sung by Elizabeth Glendower Evans to Sacco, although such discrepancies naturally would be more evident to listeners familiar with the original source materials.

Thanks in part to the involvement of soprano Brenda Lewis, who deemed Lehrman's completion "powerful," *Sacco and Vanzetti* received three modestly staged performances on August 17–19, 2001, at the White Barn Theatre, a small venue on the Norfolk, Connecticut, estate of Lucille Lortel, the recently deceased producer who had had a long association with Blitzstein. Vincent Curcio produced the work, Donald Saddler directed, Leo Meyer designed the lighting, and Lehrman led from the piano (assisted by Michael Pilafian) and assumed the role of jury foreman Walter Ripley as well. The cast, performing on book, featured Gregory Mercer as Sacco and James Sergi as Vanzetti. The mainstream press largely overlooked the event, but *New Music Connoisseur* published the aforementioned notices by Barry Cohen and Joseph Pehrson. Several internet reviewers and bloggers weighed in as well, including composer Daniel Felsenfeld, who, in a review for *Andante.com*, praised the work, in particular, the arias, which he thought "everything opera arias ought to be: they take you inside the thoughts of the character, offering an emotionally voyeuristic thrill."[28]

In November, *Opera News* published an article about the completion, "Dead Man Writing" (the title an allusion to Jake Heggie's opera about capital punishment, *Dead Man Walking*), by Joel Honig, who had not attended a performance of the work, but had observed Lehrman, Brenda Lewis, and composers Robert Palmer and Anton Coppola (whose own *Sacco and Vanzetti* recently had premiered with Opera Tampa) in a preperformance symposium on August 18 in Westport moderated by writer Joan Peyser. Declaring the work a "scam," Honig claimed that Blitzstein had been victimized: "the gold of his legacy has been melted down into cufflinks for someone else to display." *Opera News* subsequently published several letters of protest—Lehrman posted still others on his website—by writers who found it unconscionable that anyone would so denigrate a piece sight unseen and who objected to Honig's characterization of the symposium as well. Stephen Davis, representing the Blitzstein estate, whose motives seemed questioned, further expressed the belief "that there was sufficient material available to enable a composer with a thorough understanding of Blitzstein's music and spirit to rescue what otherwise might have been forever lost to the operagoing public," while Lehrman placed his effort within a "noble tradition" exemplified by operas by Borodin and Musorgsky completed by others.[29]

At the same time, *Opera News* also published a letter in defense of Honig from composer-conductor John Jansson, who argued that the tradition invoked by Lehrman—and here he mentioned *Turandot* and *Lulu*—involved works "substantially complete," whereas this work was "nowhere near completion." For Jansson, the appearance of Dukakis's words near the end of the work constituted "the final nail in the coffin," stating, "clearly there cannot be even the faintest shred of evidence to support its inclusion, unless, of course, Blitzstein was clairvoyant." Acknowledging Lehrman's "expertise" regarding Blitzstein, Jansson nevertheless deemed the enterprise "misguided." Honig himself offered a riposte, saying, "Aping a creator's mannerisms and cloning his material produces, at best, a plausible counterfeit."[30]

The controversy surrounding the opera clearly concerned issues of authorship and appropriation far more than the piece in and of itself. Had the opera come forward as a work of Lehrman's based on material by Blitzstein as opposed to a completion per se, some of this contentiousness might have been circumvented or at least minimized. So ambitious and complex an undertaking in any case needed to be considered on its own terms, ideally informed by more performances of the work as well as by familiarity with both Lehrman's and Blitzstein's larger output.

Whatever the fate of Lehrman's completion, the one number from the work that Blitzstein felt prepared to unveil, "With a Woman To Be," at least deserves to be remembered as one of his last important songs for the musical theater. "It has dignity, it has drama and pulse and rings like struck steel," wrote Jay Harrison in *Musical America* at the time of its premiere in 1964. Embracing the humanity of Nicola Sacco, this one aria might yet help win Blitzstein more of that international audience that he hoped to reach with the opera itself.[31]

After arriving at Bennington as playwright-in-residence in the fall of 1962, Blitzstein, as mentioned, befriended his colleague in the English department, Bernard Malamud, and decided to take a "breather" from *Sacco and Vanzetti* and adapt two of Malamud's stories, "Idiots First" and "The Magic Barrel," as one-act operas, jointly to be called *Tales of Malamud*. The two men signed a contract dated January 1, 1963, granting Blitzstein exclusive rights to the material and promising Malamud one-third of all proceeds, aside from those individual numbers that might be performed or published separately.[32]

Nine years younger than Blitzstein, Malamud (1914–1986), who had joined the Bennington faculty in 1961, was born in Brooklyn the son of Jewish-Russian immigrants. An obscure English teacher for many years, he came to national attention with his first novel *The Natural* (1952), but achieved even greater recognition with his next novel, *The Assistant* (1957), and two collections of short stories, *The Magic Barrel* (1958) and *Idiots First* (1963). Blitzstein presumably recognized an affinity between these later tales, mostly about poor, trapped Jewish immigrants, and his ongoing work on Sacco and Vanzetti. Indeed, about this same time, Malamud himself considered writing a novel based on Sacco and Vanzetti or some other case of social injustice, an aspiration that evolved into his prison novel *The Fixer* (1966), suggesting Blitzstein's possible influence on his evolving career.[33]

The Jewish milieu of Malamud's stories no doubt intrigued Blitzstein as well, his recent trip to Israel helping to predispose him in this direction. And although he never specified the sort of theatrical venue he had in mind for these operas, he might have sensed too the growing amenability to depictions of Jewish life on the Broadway musical stage, as indicated by the forthcoming musical based on the stories of Sholem Aleichem that opened in 1964 as *Fiddler on the Roof* with a book by Blitzstein's friend Joseph Stein. At the same time, the work's title intimates that the composer viewed his *Tales of Malamud* in the tradition of Jacques Offenbach's *Tales of Hoffmann*, an operatic adaptation of three fantastical stories by E.T.A. Hoffmann.

Tellingly, Blitzstein early on imagined adapting not two but three Malamud stories: either "An Apology," "The Death of Me," "The Loan," "The Mourners," or the unpublished "A Fool Grows Without Rain" (which the author made available to him) for the first act, followed by "Idiots First" and "The Magic Barrel" for the next two acts. At one point, he also considered adapting "Angel Levine," whose scene in a bar in Harlem naturally would have appealed to him. In his notes, he recognized the possibility of turning "An Apology" into a "parable of passive resistance. Not unlike the 'lunch-counter sit-downers' in the American South, or the British Trafalgar-Square anti-nuclear demonstrations." "The Mourners" and some other stories might have attracted him for similar reasons. However, in the end, he decided that "Idiots First" and "The Magic Barrel" could provide "a full evening." With the former about an ill man haunted by his impending doom and the latter about a rabbinical student who falls in love with a prostitute, these two stories had points in common with the Hoffmann tales musicalized by Offenbach, as Blitzstein surely appreciated.[34]

Beginning his adaptation of "Idiots First" (1961) in the fall of 1962, Blitzstein completed the libretto and much of the music in the course of a year, telling Bernstein in September 1963 that he had finished the work, although he continued to sketch scenes and did not leave behind a complete score. He conceived the opera as about an hour in length, with thirteen short scenes and a cast of eight singing and two speaking roles, with five silent actors as extras. Closely following Malamud's picaresque narrative, which showed resemblances to the composer's own *Reuben Reuben*, Blitzstein created separate scenes for even the merest mention of events, although he tweaked some of the dialogue and made other changes as well.[35]

Scene one. Mendel's Room. Awakening from a dream, Mendel (baritone), a widower haunted by an angel of death, Ginzberg (baritone), and fated to die at midnight this very evening (significantly, Friday night, the beginning of the Jewish Sabbath), prepares to send his thirty-five-year-old retarded son Itzak (tenor, Isaac in the original) by train to live with Mendel's eighty-year-old uncle Leo in California. Scene two. Pawnshop. Mendel receives only eight dollars for his watch from an uncaring pawnbroker (baritone), leaving him thirty-five dollars short for Itzak's railroad ticket. Scene three. Fishbein's Palace. Mendel asks the wealthy Fishbein (tenor) for money at the latter's palatial home, but the philanthropist, after offering Mendel and Itzak a meal and explaining that he gives money only to organized charities, has his butler Levinson (bass) show them the door. Scene four. Park Bench. Resting in a park, Mendel tells Itzak a story, but after Ginzberg passes by with Sabbath greetings, Mendel hurries away, his anguished outbursts drawing the attention of a policeman (actor). Scene five. Doorway. Mendel seeks out an old friend, but learns that the man died years ago. Scene six. Cafeteria. Mendel orders some food for his son in a cafeteria, but again flees at the sight of Ginzberg. Scene seven. Side Street. Mendel imagines Itzak happy in California. Scene eight. Pawnshop. Hoping to interest the pawnbroker in his furniture, Mendel returns to the pawnshop, which he finds closed.

Scene nine. Synagogue. Mendel wakes up a poor and sickly rabbi, Yascha (tenor), who has no money, but who offers him his new fur-lined coat, which Mendel successfully wrests from the clutches of the rabbi's outraged wife Ruchel (soprano). Scene ten. Pawnshop. Mendel espies the pawnbroker within, and insisting that the latter open his shop, pawns the rabbi's coat (this mimed episode added by the composer). Scene eleven. Train Gate. Mendel purchases a train ticket for his son, but Ginzberg, as a ticket collector, prevents Itzak from boarding, telling Mendel that it's past twelve; as Mendel lunges at him, exclaiming, "You bastard, don't you understand what it means to be human?" Ginzberg, seeing his own darkness reflected in Mendel's eyes, relents and allows Itzak passage. Scene twelve. Coach Seat. Mendel says farewell to his son. Scene thirteen. Train Gate. Seeking Ginzberg, Mendel collapses.[36]

For the scene in the park, Blitzstein added some comic relief by way of a story told by Mendel to Itzak, "How I Met My New Grandfather," about his terror at age nine on meeting his grandmother's new husband. Mendel relates this anecdote to comfort his son—and perhaps himself, given the resemblance between the grandfather and Ginzberg—an intention made clearer in a draft in which Blitzstein has Mendel say at the end, "So *you* see, nothing to be scared," a line later cut. The composer similarly fleshed out the cafeteria scene, which contains no dialogue in the original story, by having Mendel say, "Itzak, hurry up, make it quick," then "Don't eat so fast," then "Is good? So finish," a mode of Jewish humor consistent with Malamud's own.[37]

Blitzstein also extended the ending. Whereas Malamud concludes his story by writing, "When the train was gone, Mendel ascended the stairs to see what had become of Ginzberg," Blitzstein, mindful of the need for an effective curtain, has a staggering and laughing Mendel come downstage and say, at least in one draft, "Now I got to look for you? I beat you, Ginzberg. Where are you? Ginzberg," before sinking to the ground. The composer wanted to suggest, more than Malamud, some triumph even at the moment of death, the sort of characteristically affirmative ending he intended as well for *Sacco and Vanzetti*. But he remained unsure about the phrase "I beat you," with Mendel saying in other sketches, "Where are you, Ginzburg? Now I got to look for you? Ginzburg. Where are you, Ginzburg?" (with Blitzstein using here Malamud's 1963 revised spelling of Ginzberg).[38]

In conjunction with his scenario, Blitzstein sketched a set design dividing the stage into separate sections, with the idea that Mendel and Itzak would travel from one area of the stage to the other. That the composer conceived of the work in highly visual terms seems intimated as well by early references in his notes to Marc Chagall and Georges Rouault, whose designs for *The Prodigal Son* he had seen at the Ballets Russes in Paris in the spring of 1929. As for Blitzstein's own mise-en-scène, Paul Talley notes its connection to the mansion stagings used for such medieval dramas as *Everyman*, a fitting adaptation given the story's resemblance to such morality plays.[39]

A fair copy reduced score exists for most or all of scenes one through seven and scene nine, as do sketches for at least some material for four of the other five scenes. Attentive to the fact that Mendel and Itzak take a subway to Fishbein's home, Blitzstein also wrote two short interludes suggesting their ride there and back. The surviving scenes unfold subtle symmetrical forms that become more through-composed as the drama accelerates, a dynamic process left incomplete.

On stage the entire time, Mendel does most of the singing, including three solos that approximate formal set pieces: "Who Will Close the Door?" sung to Fishbein, and "How I Met My New Grandfather" and "Under the Sky in California," both sung to Itzak. As for Itzak, in addition to setting his occasional utterances, Blitzstein transforms those howls and mewls mentioned by Malamud into vocalized tunes and melodic bits, and as such, the character gets a solo of his own as he eats his eggs, a wordless song of joy that ultimately turns to fear as he and his father once more flee Ginzberg. Characters occasionally sing at the same time, as in the argument between Yascha and Ruchel, but this proves the exception, with the texture of the opera remaining overall very intimate.

The music features a deeply Yiddish quality, sometimes with folkloric overtones, as in the pawnbroker's music and "How I Met My New Grandfather," but even here with a dark coloring the composer's own. In his analysis of the opera, Leonard Lehrman attributes its Jewish flavor in part to a modal language that emphasizes such intervals as the augmented second and the tritone, although within this basic framework, the work contains a wide range of moods, from the dissonant eeriness of Mendel's dream, music somewhat reminiscent of Copland's *Vitebsk*, and the waltz-like pomposity of Fishbein to the whole-tone otherworldiness of Yascha and the metrical frenzy of his wife, with its echoes of Stravinsky and Bartók. (Alongside some sketches that resemble this latter music, Blitzstein wrote, in reference to Bartók's 1911 piano piece, "How is your 'Allegro Barbaro'?")[40]

Blitzstein recycled some existing materials for the score, including "Abel Offers the Lamb" from *Cain* for some of Itzak's music, and almost note-for-note, although with new lyrics, "Song of the D.P." from *Goloopchik* as Mendel's plea to Fishbein, "Who Will Close the Door?" Bernstein told Lehrman that he remembered Blitzstein singing this latter song "rigidly, *grimly* in tempo, not sentimental but stiff, and with a certain *noble* quality," adding, "Mendel becomes a big character in this song." Blitzstein also seems to have made some use of the 1961 Japanese hit tune "Ue o muite arukō" (music by Hachidai Nakamura, and popularized in the United States in 1963 as "Sukiyaki"), whose melody he transcribed among his sketches and whose principal rhythm he possibly appropriated for some accompanimental music in scene four.

He further made more conspicuous use of twelve-tone melody in *Idiots First* than in *Sacco and Vanzetti*, with Mendel's dream featuring a gauzy, mercurial twelve-tone figure comprising six pairs of tritones—the interval, as Lehrman points out, called the "devil in music" by medieval theorists. Annotating the initial appearance of this gesture in his manuscript, Blitzstein wrote, "The spells of weakness in Mendel get done by the row," with Lehrman identifying the motive—as well as a theme involving a second row later in the score—more specifically with Ginzberg. In addition to the use of chimes to mark the approach of the witching hour, Blitzstein also planned an array of sound effects, some indicated precisely in the score, including the ticking of a tin clock and the ring of a buzzer, others merely alluded to, including some "radio-jazz music" heard within an apartment in the doorway scene and Ginzberg's slurping his food in the cafeteria scene. Like other aspects of the piece, such use of sound intimated the continued influence of cinema on Blitzstein's theatrical output.[41]

Blitzstein started work on his other Malamud opera, *The Magic Barrel*, more or less in tandem with *Idiots First* and completed a rough draft of the libretto in August 1963. Again, he stayed scrupulously close to the original story, at least in his extant libretto, for he planned later to interject song lyrics and otherwise alter the text. Even in this preliminary version, he needed to write his own lines for the sixth and final scene, the meeting between Leo and Stella, as Malamud wrote no dialogue for this particular episode. Moreover, he decided to have the entire opera take place in Leo's room, with some of the action depicted as fantasies or flash-backs on another part of the stage.

Scene one. The Room and the Three Weddings. A February night. Leo Finkle (tenor), a lonely twenty-seven-year-old rabbinical student, hires a marriage bro-ker, Pinye Salzman (baritone), to find him a wife among the many women whose cards the matchmaker keeps at home in a barrel; Pinye describes three possible wives, none of whom appeal to Leo: the first is a widow, the second, too old at thirty-two, the third, crippled. Scene two. The Room. Next day. Pinye returns to assure Leo that the match formerly described as thirty-two years old, Lily H., is only twenty-nine and encourages him to meet her. Scene three. The Room and Riverside Drive. A week later. Describing his date with Lily (mezzo-soprano) to Pinye, Leo expresses dismay that the matchmaker not only lied about Lily's age but misrepresented him as a religious man, forcing him to tell Lily, "I came to God not because I loved Him, but because I did not." Learning that Leo has decided in favor of a love as opposed to an arranged marriage, Pinye leaves behind a packet of photographs of other women.

Scene four. The Room and the Photographs. A month later. Finally looking through the packet of photographs, Leo finds a snapshot of a woman apparently left there inadvertently and falls madly in love with her. After the woman, Stella (soprano), appears to him in a fantasy, he rushes out in search of Pinye. Scene five. The Room and Salzman's Tenement. Two hours later. Leo leaves word for Pinye with his wife Yetta (soprano), and Pinye arrives at Leo's, informing him that the woman he's in love with is "wild, without shame" and none other than his daughter Stella ("she should burn in hell"), but he agrees nonetheless to arrange a meeting (leading Leo to suspect that this had been Pinye's intention all along). Scene six. The Room. A spring night. Leo and Stella meet and sing a song of love together as Pinye chants the "Mourner's Kaddish" (the traditional Jewish prayer for the dead) and the chorus reprises the opening wedding music.

A romantic story that concludes with springtime rebirth, *The Magic Barrel* plainly would have made an effective companion to *Idiots First*, a grim tale ending in death. Both stories further contain complementary thematic elements that Blitzstein had long found congenial, with *Idiots First*, like *Sacco and Vanzetti*, exploring the capacity for human dignity, *The Magic Barrel*, like *Reuben Reuben*, the redemptive power of love. Such contrasts and similarities between the two tales—with *The Magic Barrel* also offering greater opportunity for spectacle—presumably would have been highlighted by the composer's idea of having the singers playing Mendel and Itzak also assume the roles of Pinye and Leo.

Regarding the score, only the opening portion of the first scene and a song for Stella, "Then," survive. The fragment from scene one reveals Blitzstein's innate dramatic flair, with Leo imagining various wedding ceremonies, portrayed by the chorus and dancers in an enclosed portion of the stage. For this scene, the composer not only drew on his study of traditional Hebrew melodies as found in Harry Coopersmith's *Songs of My People* and Gershon Ephros's *Cantorial Anthology*, but surely also on his recent attendance at an Israeli wedding with members of the Yemenite Inbal dance company.

Blitzstein wrote "Then" in Martinique in late 1963 and early 1964—his final song. "I finally got the real tune I had in mind for Stella for 'The Magic Barrel,'" he wrote to his mother on December 23; "and I like it." In this number, Stella wonders whether people who talk about love are "either wrong,/Or they don't mean me," each of its two stanzas concluding, "How long, how old/Must I get to be/Till for me/It's then?" Blitzstein considered introducing the song in scene four, presumably as part of Leo's fantasy, but he decided to use it in the final scene instead. At the 1964 memorial concert, Leonard Bernstein described the number, with some exaggeration, as "the closest Marc Blitzstein ever came to writing a straightforward popular song," adding, "Even so, it's not all that straightforward as you will hear in his treatment of the harmonies." The song recalls both the weariness of "Nickel Under the Foot" and the yearning of "I Wish It So," but the modal harmonies provide a distinctively troubled mood, with the final unresolved sonority (C-E♭-D-F♯-A) poetically reflective of the song's concluding question. On a more hopeful note, some of the love lyrics for the finale survive as well, including the Chagallesque stanza, "Your voice is all the violins/Your light is all the candles/Revolving in the sky./And now that I have seen you/And would not live without you/I have to ask forgiveness./I should have known."[42]

Two numbers from *Tales of Malamud*—"How I Met My New Grandfather" and "Then"—were premiered at the April 19, 1964, Blitzstein memorial concert by, respectively, José Ferrer ("with a Yiddish accent," wrote Harold Schonberg in the *Times*, "that would have made a row of blintzes stand up and salute") and Anita Ellis, the music orchestrated by Hershy Kay and conducted by Leonard Bernstein. Both songs also appeared in the first volume of the *Blitzstein Songbook* in somewhat modified form.[43]

At this memorial concert, Bernstein delighted the audience by announcing his intention of completing and orchestrating *Idiots First*. But he failed to follow through, explaining in the commemorative letter mentioned above, "A short scene to be written here and there, ten bars of accompaniment missing here, twelve bars there. It could be done, they tell me. Done? With what notes? Only yours, your own private and mysterious notes. Neither I, nor anyone I know, has access to your luminous caves where those word-notes are forged."[44]

At composer George Rochberg's suggestion, the Blitzstein estate approached William Bolcom about a completion, but nothing came of that either. But the young Leonard Lehrman, eager to take on the work, received permission from the estate to do so in 1970, and completed in late 1973 a short score for two pianos and chimes that won the support of the Davis family and various friends, including Elie Sieg-meister, David Diamond, and Leonard Bernstein. Lehrman subsequently com-pleted an orchestral version in January 1991, shortly before the death of his former teacher, Elie Siegmeister, to whom he dedicated the score. And in lieu of *The Magic Barrel*, he wrote his own companion opera, *Karla*, based on the Malamud story "Notes from a Lady at a Dinner Party" (1974, orchestration 1976), and eventually readied a trilogy by composing another Malamud one-acter, *Suppose a Wedding* (1996).[45]

With regard to *Idiots First*, Lehrman remained relatively faithful to the surviving material, although not slavishly so; indeed, he even made some minor revisions to the completed fair copy portions. In the end, scenes one through seven and scene nine constituted essentially the work of Blitzstein, as did scene thirteen, although for this final scene Lehrman had to rely on a pencil sketch rather than a more fin-ished version in ink; the other scenes represented largely the work of Lehrman based on an informed study of sketches and the opera as a whole. Given its length and centrality, scene eleven, with its climactic confrontation between Mendel and Ginzberg, presented the most daunting challenge to Lehrman, whose decision to relyricize such previous sections as "How I Met My New Grandfather," "Under the Sky in California," and Fishbein's waltz at least maintained the work's tone and style.

Idiots First debuted, in its two-piano version, at Cornell on August 3, 1974, with Paul Gibbons (Mendel) and Bill Castleman (Itzak) under Lehrman's musical direction. The Marc Blitzstein Opera Company, founded by Lehrman in 1971, gave the work's official premiere at the Monroe County Library in Bloomington, Indiana, on March 14, 1976, with Rick Davis (Mendel) and Lynn Whaley (Itzak) under Richard Duncan. Subsequently, the Bel Canto Opera Company presented the New York premiere on January 14, 1978, with Morris White (Mendel) and Charles Osborne (Itzak) under Lehrman, and the Center for Contemporary Opera (CCO) presented the first performance of the work's orchestral version at New York University on March 19, 1992, with James Sergi (Mendel) and Mark Tobias (Itzak) under Richard Marshall. At all these outings, the work preceded *Karla* on a double bill.[46]

Idiots First met with consistently favorable notices. Leighton Kerner (*Village Voice*) declared the Bel Canto performance, which Peter Davis (*New York Times*) had found "extremely moving," the "most important event" of the 1977–78 New York opera season exclusive of the Met and the City Opera, while Bernard Hol-land (*Times*) similarly commended the semistaged CCO production: "Blitzstein's talent for coherent and compelling vocal writing sweeps the opera along." William Zakariasen (*Daily News*) and Arlo McKinnon Jr. (*Opera News*), reviewing the Bel Canto and CCO performances, respectively, even deemed the opera "Blitzstein at his best," an assessment reached years earlier by Ned Rorem, for whom Blitzstein played the score before leaving for Martinique. The critics generally did not know the work well enough to comment on Lehrman's contribution per se, but they discerned no incongruity among its parts, Zakariasen writing, "The music is typical Blitzstein—full of catchy tunes colored with acid wit, and it's a tribute to Lehrman that one can't tell where he takes over."[47]

Lehrman's efforts notwithstanding, Blitzstein's three unfinished operas remain irretrievable in some fundamental ways. With *Sacco and Vanzetti* and *The Magic Barrel*, simply not enough material survives to give much sense of their ulti- mate shape and content. The working libretto and nearly nine contiguous scenes of *Idiots First* provide a more coherent torso, but even here, the music for the final scenes survives merely as rough drafts, if at all, not to mention the absence of an intended companion piece that would have framed the work thematically and musically. Nor did Blitzstein leave behind, other than a few indications in his vocal score, anything in the way of orchestration, although sonority seemed destined to play an important role in all these works.

This loss represents a serious one. From the time that excerpts from these last operas came before the public in 1964, commentators have surmised that this music signaled a new phase for the composer that reflected a deepening artistic vi- sion: a "subtler, more profound music," in the words of Irving Kolodin. Many ob- servers viewed this development in terms of the music's greater chromaticism, but the matter went deeper than this, encompassing innovative forms, novel sounds, and unusual stagecraft as well as some development in terms of dramatic content, an emphasis not so much on social activism and group solidarity as on the possibil- ities for human growth and meaning even in the face of suffering and death.[48]

From the perspective of Blitzstein's entire career, the unfinished operas—and *From Marion's Book* might be added here as well—represent a synthesis of the daring of his youth with the mastery and communicativeness developed over a lifetime of working in theater, film, and radio. Other artists of his generation followed a similar trajectory, often with limited success in their later years, and the question remains how fortunate Blitzstein would have been in this respect had he lived longer. He seems to have had in his favor, among other things, an unusual ability to absorb a wide range of new ideas, including the latest musical, literary, and cinematic trends both at home and abroad. Granted, his career had faltered in the course of the 1950s, but he had been stymied by an increasingly inhospitable environment, whereas now he was writing for an operatic world potentially more sympathetic to his ideals. The fragments that survive, although perhaps less immediately ingratiating than *The Cradle* or *Regina*, suggest that these late works at least would have helped maintain his position as a leader in the development of a native musical theater.

Conclusion

In late 1966, singers Norman Friesen and Mira Gilbert presented a revue of Blitzstein's music at the Provincetown Playhouse titled *Blitzstein!* Reporting on the show, which closed after seven performances, the *New York Times* described the composer's work as "socially irrelevant and theatrically dead—propaganda gone flat, like a tired old newsreel," the sort of dismissal that by this time had become rather commonplace. In contrast to Gilbert Chase's *America's Music* (1955), Wilfrid Mellers's *Music in a New Found Land* (1964), and H. Wiley Hitchcock's *Music in the United States* (1969), all of which had shown deep appreciation for Blitzstein, even historical surveys of American music, including Charles Hamm's *Music in the New World* (1983), tended to give the composer only fleeting attention. This decline of interest brought distinct disappointment to Copland, who in 1967 wrote, "It is saddening to think that he [Blitzstein] is no longer working at his appointed task. And it is disheartening to realize how little the present generation knows who he was or what he accomplished."[1]

In 1976, Muriel Balash produced and directed two half-hour television episodes on Blitzstein, "Marc Blitzstein: Composer with a Message" and "The Cradle That Rocked Broadway," that perhaps did little to stem such disinterest but that nevertheless contained poignant observations by friends and colleagues, including Copland, who explained, "He [Blitzstein] could have written sonatas and symphonies like the rest of us. But that wasn't interesting to him. He wanted to say something with his music, something outside the mere field of music, and that passion . . . to take a social attitude towards music and what it might do in the whole field of society: that was very special to him." And at the end of the documentary's second segment, Leonard Bernstein said, "One of the things that bothers me about Marc Blitzstein since his death is the rapidity with which his name's been forgotten; it's just heartbreaking, because the effect that he has had on American musical theatre is incalculable."[2]

A successful revival of *The Cradle Will Rock* by the Acting Company under the direction of John Houseman that premiered in 1983 helped signal some revitalized interest, as did an all-Blitzstein concert hosted by Houseman on April 28, 1985, at Juilliard's Alice Tully Hall in honor of the composer's eightieth birthday. Presented under the auspices of the Composers' Showcase (Charles Schwartz, artistic director), this latter event featured an array of songs, with Leonard Bernstein, to the delight of the audience, singing "Zipperfly" and a bit of "Musky and Whisky" at the piano, although most of the performers represented a younger generation, including singers Patti LuPone and Christopher Groenendaal and pianists Steven Blier and Michael Barrett, who went on to premiere and record the Piano Concerto (1931) under Lukas Foss the following year. A few years later, in the fall of 1988, the Soho Repertory Theatre, under the artistic directorship of Marlene Swartz, presented *The Blitzstein Project*, which had a short run at St. Bart's Playhouse in New York, and which featured two one-act rarities, *The Harpies* (1931) and *I've Got the Tune* (1937), along with some of the composer's songs. And on the day the show closed, Dennis Russell Davies and the American Composers Orchestra debuted Blitzstein's *Orchestra Variations* (1934) at Carnegie Hall. "Renewed interest in the composer appears to be developing," noted the *New York Times*.[3]

The next year, St. Martin's Press released the first full-length biography of the composer, Eric Gordon's *Mark the Music: The Life and Work of Marc Blitzstein*. A Yale graduate who had pursued master's and doctoral work in Latin American studies at Tulane, Gordon (b. 1945) came into contact with Blitzstein's work in 1977 while preparing a segment about Sacco and Vanzetti for a radio show he hosted in Hartford. Appalled by the neglect of so significant a progressive and gay artist, he embarked on his biography in 1979 and completed it ten years later, his study of Blitzstein's papers supplemented by well over a hundred interviews.[4]

The reviews of Gordon's biography offered something of a barometer regarding Blitzstein's still uncertain position: Don Shewey (*New York Times*), discussing the composer's "unsatisfying life," asserted that the legendary premiere of *The Cradle Will Rock* "now overpowers the show's cartoon-simple sentiments," whereas Brian Drake (*Opera Monthly*) described the same work as "beautifully structured, thrilling to watch, with a score that reveals new riches on every reading." As to Gordon's book itself, commentators extolled the author's extensive research, even if a few missed more substantial discussions of the music.[5]

These reviews took particular notice of Gordon's treatment of Blitzstein's sexuality and ethnicity and generally found the book commendable in this regard, although Lawrence Mass argued that the author had not "come to grips with the nearly total absence of tangible homosexual consciousness and parallel obscurity of Jewish consciousness" in Blitzstein's work, an "absence" that purportedly made his operas less durable than Britten's. By contrast, Robert Kendrick noted more simply and incontrovertibly, "The major elements of his [Blitzstein's] life—his commitment to radical politics, his homosexuality, and his immigrant Jewish background—permeate most of his music" (although it might be added that Blitzstein seems to have regarded his Jewish background and his homosexuality not as matters of pride so much as conferring a doubly oppressed minority status that helped sharpen his perception of social injustice and dysfunction in general, with his work exploring the corrosive effects of such discrimination on humanity as a whole). [6]

The rehabilitation of Blitzstein, although regularly challenged, continued apace in the decades following Gordon's book. Productions of both *The Cradle*—whose premiere inspired Jason Sherman's 1998 play *It's All True* and Tim Robbins's 1999 film *Cradle Will Rock*—and *Regina* occurred with increasing frequency, while the composer's adaptation of *The Threepenny Opera* held its own among many rivals. Revivals of such lesser-known pieces as *No for an Answer* and *Juno* found their way onto the stage as did the composer's translation of *Mother Courage* and Leonard Lehrman's completion of *Sacco and Vanzetti*. Publisher Boosey & Hawkes released three Blitzstein songbooks edited by Lehrman, whose bio-bibliography of the composer appeared in 2005, the year also of several centennial celebrations around the country. Performances and recordings of the songs and the early piano and chamber pieces, although sporadic, met with critical acclaim. And such chroniclers of American music as John Warthen Struble (1995), Elise Kirk (2001), and Joseph Horowitz (2005) treated the composer with renewed respect.[7]

Blitzstein's work found friends abroad as well as at home. Introduced to the music by Wilfrid Mellers while studying in England in the late 1950s, the distinguished Australian composer Peter Sculthorpe (b. 1929) acquired a lifelong attachment to Blitzstein, whom he came to regard as "one of America's great composers." While at Yaddo in 1966–67, he grew particularly fond of the City Opera recording of *Regina*, sections of which he listened to virtually every day. "My favourite parts of *Regina* are the achingly beautiful exchanges between Birdie and Addie, and, above all, Horace's 'Consider the Rain,'" he remarked in 2011. "I know of no other music that speaks so eloquently about America and what it could become. Sadly, there are now too many Hubbards. Like Blitzstein's libretto for *The Cradle Will Rock*, his libretto for *Regina* makes a powerful statement about the human condition."[8]

Blitzstein attracted other aficionados from around the world. Intrigued by the Acting Company's performance of *The Cradle* in London in 1985, British composer-conductor John Jansson (b. 1958) led the European premiere of *I've Got the Tune* at the George Wood Theatre in 1989 and a production of *The Cradle* at the Battersea Arts Centre in 1997, the year in which he also started a website devoted to the composer; deeming Blitzstein "a very good composer whose best work deserves to be heard more (or even, at all)," he also began editing the solo piano music with an eye to possible publication. Dori Parnes (b. 1963), a notable Israeli composer, translator, and activist, similarly discovered Blitzstein through the Acting Company's recording of *The Cradle*, a recording that "from the very first notes" left him "captured for life"; translating over thirty Blitzstein songs into Hebrew, Parnes believed that a number like "The Cradle Will Rock" had much to say to contemporary Israelis, although he became particularly fascinated by *Reuben Reuben*, which he dreamed of staging. Paul A. J. Oomens (b. 1966), a civil servant in the Dutch government and the founder and director of the KamerOperaProject, an organization dedicated to

twentieth-century chamber operas, had hopes rather of mounting a small-scale production of *No for an Answer*, finding its "superb feeling for the American language"
comparable to Musorgsky, and its themes of "economic crisis, narrow-mindedness,
the multicultural society, flexible, cheap labor and anxiety about immigration" as
relevant as ever.[9]

The lack of available and workable editions, a common source of frustration for
Jansson, Parnes, and Oomens as for doubtless others, surely hindered the composer from attaining a greater presence both nationally and internationally. But if
Blitzstein remained marginalized, that had long been his fate. His achievement
endured nonetheless.

In some ways, Blitzstein typified his generation of serious American composers.
Trained as a pianist in the classical tradition, by his teens he had started to write
his own compositions, his early work suggesting an absorption of Debussy and
popular American music. That he went on to study with such varied figures as
Alexander Siloti, Rosario Scalero, Nadia Boulanger, and Arnold Schoenberg perhaps made him in a way all the more representative. In any event, like many colleagues, he retained a modernist sensibility forged in the 1920s, even while
moving toward greater accessibility in his middle years and adapting some new
adventurous trends in his later ones.

And yet in the end, Blitzstein proved a highly unusual figure. First, his literary
and theatrical preoccupations had virtually no counterpart among serious American composers, activities that included not only producing an outstanding body
of criticism, like Virgil Thomson, and creating most of the librettos for his operas,
like Gian Carlo Menotti and Carlisle Floyd, but writing poems, sketches, and
scripts, performing in theaters and cabarets as well as on radio, directing stage
works, and translating and adapting dramatic and vocal texts in various languages. His catalog reflected such interests, as he composed mostly for the stage,
screen, and radio, including, among those scores that survive in their entirety, ten
musical dramas (including a radio opera), three ballets, ten incidental scores, and
seven film scores (including a film-opera). Of his few major concert works
composed after 1934, two, the *Airborne Symphony* and *This Is the Garden,* were
essentially dramatic cantatas, while a third, *Lear: A Study,* literally derived from
his stage work. Theatrical elements, including a sense of conflict and revolt, generally permeated his work—Virgil Thomson, who over time developed a greater
appreciation for the music to *Regina,* initially judged the opera "not very musical,
though it is unquestionably very, very, very, very theater"—making Blitzstein in
some ways less a musician's musician than an actor's musician.[10]

Another singular aspect of his life concerned his wholehearted engagement with
prolabor, antifascist, and other progressive causes as expressed not only in his music
but in his criticism, his propaganda work, and his association with various leftist organizations, including for a period the American Communist Party. True, in the early

1950s, presumably in response to red baiting, he retreated from social activism; and in the course of the decade, he revealed as well a more detached attitude with respect to the Soviet Union, which he had tended to idealize in the 1930s and 1940s. But even so, he remained dedicated to his social ideals, challenging the authority of the House Un-American Activities Committee and standing by his populist convictions. And he continued to write works that expressed such cherished beliefs as the dignity of the common man and the rights of workers, immigrants, women, and minorities, selecting Sacco and Vanzetti as the subject of his final major stage piece.

Blitzstein's inclination toward the theater and social protest perhaps warranted comparison sooner with Kurt Weill and Hanns Eisler, especially in their collaborations with Bertolt Brecht, than with any native-born American composer, although similar combinations of qualities could be found in the work of Leonard Bernstein, who, although generally more accessible, followed somewhat in his footsteps. To view Blitzstein as a kind of American Weill or Eisler, or as a predecessor to Bernstein, accordingly had some merit, although this ran the risk of minimizing his significance and individuality.

Blitzstein inherited both his attraction to the stage and his dedication to social justice especially from his father, an outspoken socialist who had some experience in vaudeville, although his mother's family could also claim thespians, including the celebrated Yiddish actors Boris and Bessie Thomashefsky. Blitzstein's only sibling, his sister Jo, tellingly developed parallel interests, including some involvement with theater and radio in her early years and a leadership position with the Women's International League for Peace and Freedom in her later ones.

This family heritage and his own astonishing precociousness notwithstanding, Blitzstein's mature aesthetic emerged over time, in part because his sort of achievement had little precedent, at least in American classical music, for he gleaned important lessons from Whitman and other poets and writers. His aesthetic crystallized with the masterful *Cradle Will Rock* (1936–37), which synthesized various approaches that had characterized his previous work and that he identified around 1930 as the "communistic" (work that addresses the average man), the "fantastic" (work that grapples with destiny), the "burlesque" (work that appropriates popular art), and the "classic" (work that encompasses mythic experience); and which revealed, moreover, the extraordinary incorporation of not only vaudeville, silent film comedies, Broadway musicals, and blues and jazz, but the music of Satie, Stravinsky, Eisler, Weill, and Copland, the poetry and fiction of the likes of Cummings and Hemingway, and the work of socially engaged playwrights, in particular, the work's dedicatee, Brecht, whose distancing effects and gestic techniques he adapted to more homegrown conditions and traditions. Blitzstein furthered and varied this achievement with, among other works, the naturalistic tragedy *No for an Answer* (1937–40), the ironic melodrama *Regina* (1946–49), the romantic comedy *Reuben Reuben* (1949–55), and the tragicomedy *Juno* (1957–59).

Although Copland singled out as especially noteworthy Blitzstein's ability to give convincing voice to "all those American regular fellows that seem so much at home everywhere except on the operatic stage," the composer's work typically raised questions of social awareness and responsibility among people of diverse backgrounds, with several of his dramas specifically involving educated characters faced with moral dilemmas. Even such prounion operas as *The Cradle* and *No for an Answer* focused primarily on the perceived need for the middle class to align itself with the working class, making the designation of such works as "proletarian operas" or "workers' musicals" somewhat misleading. Blitzstein had an unstinting concern for all humanity and an uncanny gift for vividly delineating a wide range of characters, not only as a musical dramatist, but even as a singing actor, as evidenced by his demo recordings for *Juno* with himself assuming a variety of roles.[11]

Two technical accomplishments stand out. First, using popular elements in a distinctive way, he created a truly vernacular musical theater, one sensitively attuned to the rhythm and intonation of varieties of American speech, including ethnic dialects. To this end, he avoided complexities that might detract from a work's dramatic power and authenticity, so that for all the melodic charm and harmonic sophistication of his music, and the adept handling of assorted poetic devices, attention remained focused on the vivid projection of text and character. Stated Leonard Bernstein in 1976, "Marc [Blitzstein] was and still is, as far as I'm concerned, the greatest master of the setting of the American language to music."[12]

A second major achievement involved the creation of new forms of musical theater. Although he occasionally worked along the lines of one or the other of the two dominant musico-dramatic traditions—number opera, with its alternation of song and recitative, and through-composed opera, with its continuous argument in the accompaniment—more characteristically, he molded speech, half-speech, sung recitative, song, and chorus, all variously coordinated with musical accompaniment, into block-like sections that took shape from the dramatic action, so that his work seemed at times best described as "plays in music" or "musical plays," terms he himself sometimes used as did some commentators. The combination of heterogeneous elements into discrete blocks—forms whose collage-like aspects made contact with cinematic montage—allowed him to mix dramatic modes in unusual ways, to experiment with flashback and other novel stage techniques, and to blur traditional genre demarcations. Such formal mastery and originality also surfaced in subtler and more small-scale ways, as in the architecture of his finely and ingeniously wrought songs.

Blitzstein himself distinguished his formal procedures not only from Weill and Eisler, but from his American colleagues, tending to place his work rather in the tradition of the *opéra comique*, which he defined as "a musical stage work which does not attempt the grand or noble level, and which is free to use speech or song as the occasion requires." He also evoked the example of Jacopo Peri and the creators of opera, stating, "the basic impulse is the same, the wish to write a play in terms of music, with a heightened and charged effect that music can give to the spoken word or the silent action." Comparisons further could be drawn, as seen above, with Musorgsky, about whom Blitzstein had shown special sympathy during his student days in Philadelphia, revealing such instincts to be deeply ingrained.[13]

Discerning critics recognized Blitzstein's achievement, and not just within the context of American music. Wilfrid Mellers, after enumerating several different methods of text setting in *The Cradle*, observed, "None of these techniques was in itself new; no one before Blitzstein, however, had used them so consistently, so coherently, and to such imaginative purpose." Others similarly acknowledged the composer's uniqueness, including Bernstein, who considered him a model for his own work. But Blitzstein's output, drawing on so large a compass of skills and ideas, and so fervent a commitment to social change, proved too personal and uncompromising for easy emulation or even appreciation. Indeed, his professional life, hampered by a milieu often indifferent if not hostile to his work, largely constituted one long uphill battle, notwithstanding some intermittent success. And how much greater the struggle had he not had the sympathetic support of such family members as his sister Jo and his wife Eva Goldbeck; such friends as Aaron Copland, Minna Lederman, and Mina Curtiss; such collaborators as Orson Welles, John Houseman, Leonard Bernstein, Lillian Hellman, Lotte Lenya, and Cheryl Crawford; such patrons as Alene Erlanger, Motty and Bess Eitingon, and Serge Koussevitzky; and the many musicians and actors devoted to his art and his ideals.[14]

A figure of considerable historical importance, Blitzstein remains at the same time a living presence, the creator of moving and entertaining works full of acid wit and aching desire, bitter anger and tender affection, dark despair and stirring optimism, works that expose life's hardship and cruelty but that celebrate its joy and valor as well. With searing honesty and ennobling hope, his words and music, much like his life itself, continue to illuminate both man's fallible nature and his glorious potential.

ABBREVIATIONS

AC	Aaron Copland
ACC	Aaron Copland Collection, Music Division, Library of Congress
ASC	Alexander Smallens Collection, Music Division, New York Public Library
BAL	Muriel Balash, *Composer with a Message* ("Part I: The Cradle Will Rock," 1964; "Part II: Marc Blitzstein: Composer with a Message," 1976; "Part III: The Cradle That Rocked Broadway," 1976), Creative Arts Television, Kent, CT, 1976
BLI	Marc Blitzstein, "Marc Blitzstein on Music," Adolph Ullman Memorial Lecture, Brandeis University, presented April 2, 1962; taped as a telecast, WGBH-TV, April 3, 1962; transcribed by author
BRA	Henry Brant, "American Composers, XXV: Marc Blitzstein," *Modern Music* 23/3 (Summer 1946): 170–175
CD	Christopher Davis
CDC	Christopher Davis Collection, Mugar Memorial Library, Boston University
CG	Cecil Goldbeck
CIMA	Curtis Institute of Music Archives
COP	Aaron Copland, *Our New Music: Leading Composers in Europe and America*, McGraw-Hill, New York, 1941; revised as *The New Music: 1900–1960*, Norton, New York, 1968
DD	David Diamond
DDC	David Diamond Collection, Music Division, Library of Congress
EG	Eva Goldbeck
GMF	John Simon Guggenheim Memorial Foundation
GOR	Eric A. Gordon, *Mark the Music: The Life and Work of Marc Blitzstein*, St. Martin's Press, New York, 1989
HAL	Edith Hale, "Author and Composer Blitzstein," *Daily Worker*, December 7, 1938
JD	Josephine Davis
KWF	Kurt Weill Foundation for Music
LB	Leonard Bernstein
LBC	Leonard Bernstein Collection, Music Division, Library of Congress

LC	Library of Congress
LED	Minna Lederman, "Memories of Marc Blitzstein, Music's Angry Man," *Show: The Magazine of the Arts* 4/6 (June 1964): 18, 21–23
LEH	Leonard J. Lehrman, *Marc Blitzstein: A Bio-Bibliography*, Praeger, Westport, CT, 2005
LH	Lillian Hellman
LHC	Lillian Hellman Collection, Harry Ransom Center, University of Texas-Austin
LL	Leonard J. Lehrman
MB	Marc Blitzstein
MBH	Marc Blitzstein, 5th Investigative/Files and Reference subseries, House Un-American Activities Committee, National Archives
MBP	Marc Blitzstein Papers, Wisconsin State Historical Society
MBS1	*The Marc Blitzstein Songbook*, Vol. 1, edited by Leonard Lehrman, Boosey & Hawkes, New York, 1999
MBS2	*The Marc Blitzstein Songbook*, Vol. 2, edited by Leonard Lehrman, Boosey & Hawkes, New York, 2001
MBS3	*The Marc Blitzstein Songbook*, Vol. 3, edited by Leonard Lehrman, Boosey & Hawkes, New York, 2003
MC	Mina Curtiss
MCC	Mina Curtiss–Marc Blitzstein Correspondence, Music Division, Library of Congress
MEL	Wilfrid Mellers, *Music in a New Found Land: Themes and Developments in the History of American Music*, Barrie and Rockliff, London, 1964
MM	*Modern Music*
NYHT	*New York Herald Tribune*
NYPL	New York Public Library
NYT	*New York Times*
ROR	Ned Rorem, *A Ned Rorem Reader*, Yale University Press, New Haven, CT, 2001
SD	Stephen Davis
TAL	Paul Myers Talley, *Social Criticism in the Original Theatre Librettos of Marc Blitzstein*, Ph.D. dissertation, University of Wisconsin, 1966
WHS	Wisconsin State Historical Society

NOTES

Chapter 1

1. GOR and LEH are the principal sources for information about the Blitzstein family (the latter drawing substantially on the work of family genealogists, Freya Blitstein Maslov and Marc Galanter); see also Freya Maslov, updated family tree, 2002. GOR, 4, writes that Marcus and Hannah moved first to Bessarabia, but given Mary's presumed birth in Podwoloczyska (according to birth records), his source might have confused Bessarabia with the nearby area of eastern Galicia. Similarly, he writes that the Blitzsteins lived four years in Liverpool, but if Mary was born in Galicia in 1887 and the family left for Philadelphia in 1889, this seems questionable. Given Alberta's death in Southampton in 1889, the family might have spent a year or so in that city and simply left for America from Liverpool. On the other hand, Freya Maslov heard from older relatives that the Blitzsteins moved to England at one point and then back again to Europe; and grandchildren recall Sam and Mary both saying that they were born in Liverpool: CD to author, January 24, 2011; SD to author, January 24, 2011; Carol Zaleski to author, September 4, 2007.
2. *Philadelphia: A 300-Year History*, edited by Russell F. Weigley (New York: Norton, 1982), 535 ("settled"); *Jewish Life in Philadelphia 1830–1940*, edited by Murray Friedman (Philadelphia: ISHI, 1983).
3. Harry D. Boonin, *The Jewish Quarter of Philadelphia, 1881–1930* (Philadelphia: Jewish Walking Tours of Philadelphia, 1999).
4. Boonin; Robert Leiter, "Opening the Door to the New World," *Jewish Exponent* (July 13, 1984): 85–87, 119; "Blitzstein Bank Promises Checks," *Philadelphia Evening Bulletin* (December 24, 1930), states that the bank was established in 1889.
5. Boonin, 31 (for photograph of the 1919 building designed by J. Horace Frank), 32 ("regular banking").
6. GOR and Boonin, 32, reprint these photographs; Harry Boonin, interview with author, September 1, 2007 (for Babushka's funeral).
7. GOR, 5; Boonin, *Jewish Quarter*, 65; Zaleski.
8. Zaleski; Helga Dudman, "Sacco and Vanzetti at Beit Yannai," *Jerusalem Post* (August 26, 1962).
9. Helen Hough, unpublished letter to the Blitzstein family, MBP; GOR, 18, places Gorky's visit in the context of the Moscow Art Theater's limited engagement in New York in early 1923, but the playwright, who visited Philadelphia in 1906, was in Germany at the time; SD, interview with author, August 29, 2007; MB, notes, MBP ("sound of"); Madeleine Goss, "Marc Blitzstein," *Modern Music-Makers: Contemporary American Composers* (New York: E. P. Dutton, 1952), 360.
10. Hough; MB to Julian Levi, January 9, 1934, Julian Levi Papers, Archives of American Art, Smithsonian Institution; HAL.

11. MB, marginalia, ISCM program (January 25, 1963), MBP; CD, interview with author, August 27, 2007, to author, May 23, 2011; SD, interview with author, May 28, 2011.
12. Goss, 361 (for Santa Monica High School); CD, *The Case Against Death*, unpublished memoir, 59, courtesy of the author.
13. EG, Journals, June 8, 1929, MBP.
14. Berenice Skidelsky, Journals, January 21, 1921, April 2, 1927, January 4, 1944, Berenice Skidelsky Collection, NYPL; MB to Skidelsky, November 9, 1921, MBP.
15. MB to JD, October 29, 1929; MB to EG, January 13, 1931 (see also MB to EG, November 18, 1930), MBP; Robert Leiter, "Mr. Vivid," *Pennsylvania Gazette* 82/5 (March 1984): 21–25 ("more like").
16. MB to JD, September 22, 1942, MBP; Leiter, "Mr. Vivid" ("could be"); CD, May 23, 2011, questioned Eric Gordon's assertion, "Anyone could see that despite the fact of having her own family . . . Marc was always the most important person to Jo" (GOR, 49), stating, "Jo had the strength and capacity to handle both, and neither her brother nor her family was excluded from her full love and support."
17. CD to author, August 30, 2010; HAL.
18. Skidelsky, Journals, January 21, 1921, Berenice Skidelsky Collection, NYPL; Berenice Skidelsky to JD, January 23, 1964, MBP; Elinor Hughes, "'Regina' Cherished Project of Composer Marc Blitzstein," *Boston Herald* (October 19, 1949); HAL; Goss, 361. According to standard accounts, Blitzstein began to take piano lessons—and give recitals—at age five; but his September 18, 1924, Application for Admission to the Curtis Institute, CIMA, claimed only eight years of study of piano, which would suggest that he started lessons at age eleven or twelve; still another source, Robert Leiter, "In 'Cradle,' a Phila. native son triumphs," courtesy of the author, states that MB started playing piano at age three and performed with members of the Philadelphia Orchestra at Witherspoon Hall at age five.
19. Robert A. Gerson, *Music in Philadelphia* (Westport, CT: Greenwood Press, 1940), 302; George Antheil, *Bad Boy of Music* (New York: Da Capo, 1981), 1, 16, 128; Constantin von Sternberg, *Ethics and Aesthetics of Piano-Playing* (New York: G. Schirmer, 1917), 19 ("Art"); Sternberg, *Tempo Rubato and Other Essays* (New York: G. Schirmer, 1920); Sternberg, "Against Modern'ism," *Musical Quarterly* 7/1 (January 1921): 1–7; Sternberg, "Music and Its Auditors," *Musical Quarterly* 9/3 (July 1923): 343–349.
20. Meryle Secrest, "For Threepence: He Doesn't Mind Being in Shadow," *Washington Post* (May 14, 1963) (age nine).
21. Gerson, 302.
22. Goepp, cited by *The Philcon* 1/1 (March 1928), courtesy of Sara J. MacDonald, University of the Arts, Philadelphia; "D. Hendrik Ezerman," *NYT* (January 7, 1928).
23. MB performed the Chopin B$^\flat$-minor Scherzo on June 3, 1919; the Chopin C$^\sharp$-minor Polonaise on February 7, 1919; the Brahms B-minor Rhapsody on February 6, 1920; the first movement of Saint-Saëns's Concerto in G minor on April 25, 1921; and two Chopin preludes and his Etude in G$^\flat$ major on June 1, 1921.
24. Unidentified clippings, *Philadelphia Morning Ledger*, *Philadelphia Evening Ledger*, and other papers, February 6, 1922; MB, "The Pearly Touch," MBP.
25. Skidelsky, Journals, February 19, 1922, Berenice Skidelsky Collection, NYPL.
26. Secrest ("For one"); Arthur Bronson, "Blitzstein To Rock The Cradle Again," *Philadelphia Record* (February 16, 1941) ("I'd have"); Application for Admission; J. Leon Lichtin, interview with author, August 13, 2007.
27. For nine preludes and *Pandora*, see work lists, MBP, and "American Youth to Have Its Fling in League Concert," *Musical America* 45/17 (February 12, 1927): 27 (*Pandora* here called *Pandora's Box*).
28. Howard Pollack, *Aaron Copland: The Life and Work of an Uncommon Man* (New York: Henry Holt, 1999), 32–33; for still other early fragments, see LEH, 32.
29. Blitzstein, "Musicredo," MBP.

30. MB to Berenice Skidelsky, November 9, 1921; MB, marginalia, "Poet-Student" (in this version, Blitzstein wrote "sits," not "settles"); MB, "Hint"; MB, marginalia, poems (for Aldington), MBP.

31. GOR, 18; Edward Potts Cheyney, *History of the University of Pennsylvania 1740–1940* (Philadelphia: University of Pennsylvania Press, 1940), 266.

32. MB to William E. Walter, August 18, 1925, CIMA (each lesson with Siloti, including train fare, cost $27); Charles F. Barber, *Lost in the Stars: The Forgotten Musical Life of Alexander Siloti* (Lanham, MD: Scarecrow Press, 2002).

33. Barber; GOR, 17; Siloti, letter of recommendation, December 29, 1927, MBP.

34. Hughes; MB, "The Book—Beginning. Me," ca. 1947 (for MB's planned autobiography, *Case Meets History*, see GOR, 301–302); MB to JD, July 21, 1929, MBP; GOR, 7.

35. DD to MB, December 14, 1943, DDC; MB to JD, November 6, 1943, MBP.

36. LED, 23; Aaron Copland, "In Memory of Marc Blitzstein (1905–1964)," *Perspectives of New Music* 2/2 (Spring–Summer 1964): 6; Irma Bauman to author, June 14, 2007.

37. Siloti; for other uses of "gifted," see LED (18), Copland (6), Bauman, and Nadia Boulanger's confidential report on MB, acknowledged October 10, 1932, GMF; Lehman Engel, *This Bright Day: An Autobiography* (New York: Macmillan, 1974), 81.

38. "Symposium on the Marc Blitzstein/Leonard Lehrman *Sacco and Vanzetti*" (August 18, 2001): http://ljlehrman.artists-in-residence.com/articles/operajournal8.html; MC, "Marc Blitzstein Remembered," program, Marc Blitzstein Memorial Concert (April 19, 1964), LBC ("involved"); Carmen Capalbo, interview with author, February 16, 2010; Jack Viertel, "Reviving Juno," *Playbill: Juno* (March 27–30, 2008): 10; Carol Zaleski to author, September 4, 2007.

39. CD and SD, interviews; CD, *A Kind of Darkness* (London: Rupert Hart-Davis, 1962); CD, *The Sun in Mid-Career* (New York: Harper & Row, 1973).

40. MB to JD, January 13, 1931, MBP; MB to CD, January 27, 1961, CDC.

41. MB to JD, August 29, 1929, October 29, 1929, November 25, 1929, December 24, 1929 ("during which"), MBP; Henry A. Murray, interview with Forrest Robinson, July 24, 1970, transcript, Henry Murray Collection, Harvard University.

42. MB to JD, November 25, 1929, MBP ("no intention"); SD, interview; Irma Bauman, interview with author, June 21, 2007.

43. GOR, 19; Eric Gordon to author, January 3, 2009 (which names Hewitt as the source for Blitzstein's negative reaction to being penetrated sexually).

44. George Chauncey, *Gay New York: Gender, Urban Culture, and the Making of the Gay Male World, 1890 to 1940* (New York: BasicBooks, 1994); MB to DD, February 11, 1961, DDC; CD, *The Case*, 225; GOR, 63, 255, 321.

45. MB to MC, February 17, 1953, MCC.

46. MB to DD, February 17, 1942, DDC; MB to MC, June 18, 1943, MCC; MB to LB, May 19, 1950, LBC.

47. GOR, 461; Joan Peyser, interview with author, December 28, 2009; MB, FBI file, April 22, 1949, June 14, 1955; the 1949 report states that MB "had been treated for a psychoneurotic condition at one time by Dr. Bernard S. Robbins (who was also acquainted with the subject socially)," with the connection between the treatment by Robbins and that by the Veterans Administration left unclear.

48. MB to JD, November 21, 1929, MBP.

49. MB [to Berenice Skidelsky], September 18, 1928, MBP.

Chapter 2

1. Diana Burgwyn, *Seventy-Five Years of The Curtis Institute of Music* (Philadelphia: Curtis Institute of Music, 1999).

2. MB, Application for Admission, received March 10, 1926, CIMA (a Curtis administrator adjusted this information to read "race: white" and "nationality: American [Jewish]"); MB to William E. Walter, August 18, 1925; Walter to MB, September 10, 1925, CIMA.

3. John Gruen, *Menotti: A Biography* (New York: Macmillan, 1978), 19, 22, 27–28 ("always"); Barbara B. Heyman, *Samuel Barber: The Composer and His Music* (New York: Oxford University Press, 1992), 35 ("He never"), 310 ("corrected"); MB, "Talk-Music-Dance; New York, 1933," *MM* 11/1 (November–December 1933): 35; see also Virgil Thomson, *Virgil Thomson* (New York: Da Capo, 1966), 68–69.

4. MB, marginalia, MBP.

5. MB, lecture notes, MBP; Curtis Institute School Records, CIMA; James A. Pegolotti, *Deems Taylor: A Biography* (Boston: Northeastern University Press, 2003), 144; MB to Miss James, October 7, 1925 (in which he mentions his intention of taking a course with Hermann Weigland, who taught German); yet another course on his transcript, "Orchestra. Senior," could signify various things.

6. MB, student essays, MBP.

7. MB, student essays, MBP.

8. Unidentified reviews of the Philadelphia Orchestra concert (July 13, 1926), MBP.

9. Pegolotti, 144. There was also this intriguing family connection between Blitzstein and Barber: Blitzstein's mother-in-law, Lina Abarbanell, made her Metropolitan Opera debut as Hansel playing against Barber's aunt, Louise Homer, as the Witch.

10. MB, "The Modern Movement in Music," 1928–29, MBP.

11. Burgwyn, 18; Léonie Rosenstiel, *Nadia Boulanger: A Life in Music* (New York: W. W. Norton, 1982), 222; Jérôme Spycket, *Nadia Boulanger* (Stuyvesant, NY: Pendragon Press, 1987), 68 (Spycket further states regarding Blitzstein and Boulanger that "their relationship proved to be pretty difficult," which does not seem at all to have been the case; the author might have confused Blitzstein with David Diamond); MB to Berenice Skidelsky, October 24, 1926, MBP.

12. LEH, 34; MB, tablet, MBP (this tablet also contains what seems to be caricatures of Boulanger and Schoenberg).

13. MB to Nadia Boulanger [late 1928], Nadia Boulanger Collection, Bibliothèque nationale de France, courtesy of the Fondation Internationale Nadia et Lili Boulanger; Nadia Boulanger, letter of recommendation, January 2, 1928, MBP.

14. MB to Berenice Skidelsky, October 24, 1926.

15. MB to Dorothy Smith, January 18, 1927, Dorothy Smith Dushkin Collection, Smith College (Smith later married music teacher David Dushkin, not to be confused with violinist Samuel Dushkin).

16. MB to William E. Walter, January 6, 1927, MBP ("imbibing," "Though I think"); Peter Gradenwitz, *Arnold Schönberg und seine Meisterschüler: Berlin 1925–1933* (Vienna: Paul Zsolnay, 1998), 27, 102; Joseph Auner, *A Schoenberg Reader: Documents of a Life* (New Haven, CT: Yale University Press, 2003), 192–193.

17. MB to Dorothy Smith, February 10, 1927, Dorothy Smith Dushkin Collection, Smith College.

18. MB to Nadia Boulanger, October 18, 1927, Nadia Boulanger Collection, Bibliothèque nationale de France, courtesy of the Fondation Internationale Nadia et Lili Boulanger.

19. For a more positive assessment of Schoenberg from an earlier American student, see Adolph Weiss, "The Lyceum of Schönberg," *MM* 9/3 (March–April 1932): 99–107; MB to William E. Walter, March 19, 1927, CIMA; Marion Bauer, "Whither Are We Wandering With Our New Music?" *Musical Leader* 52/16 (April 21, 1927): 10.

20. MB, "The Modern Movement" ("we always"); Sointu Scharenberg, *Überwinden der Prinzipien: Betrachtungen zu Arnold Schönbergs unkonventioneller Lehrtätigkeit zwischen 1898 und 1951* (Saarbrücken: Pfau, 2002), 195–200; MB to Nadia Boulanger, October 18, 1927.

21. MB to Nadia Boulanger, October 18, 1927.

22. MB, "Four American Composers," *This Quarter* 2/1 (July–August–September 1929), 163 ("It is only"); MB to William E. Walter, March 19, 1927; BLI; GOR, 28; MB, "The Modern Movement"; R. P., "Arnold Schönberg, on First Visit, Receives the American Press," *Musical Courier* 107/20 (November 11, 1933): 7.

23. MB to Nadia Boulanger, October 18, 1927; Roberto Gerhard to MB, February 11, 1963; MB, marginalia, MBP ("haunted"); see also Roberto Gerhard, "Schoenberg Reminiscences," *Perspectives of New Music* 13/2 (Spring–Summer 1975): 57–65.

24. MB, "The Modern Movement."

25. MB, "The Modern Movement."

26. MB, "The Case for Modern Music," *New Masses* 20/3 (July 14, 1936): 27 ("Schoenbergian"); "Masterworks," unpublished lectures, MBP ("bonafide"); "Talk-Music-Dance; New York, 1933," *MM* 11/1 (November–December 1933): 34 ("an extremely"); "Spring Season in the East," *MM* 8/4 (May–June 1931): 34 ("among").

27. BLI; BRA, 170; Gradenwitz, 111 ("die konzise Form der musikalischen Darstellung und das Prinzip der 'sich entwickelnden Variation'").

28. MB, "The Modern Movement" (Blitzstein mistakenly recalled that Wolpe, as opposed to Stuckenschmidt, incorporated the sounds of a slammed piano lid); MB, "Dancers of the Season," *MM* 8/3 (March–April 1931): 39, 41; George Antheil, *Bad Boy of Music* (New York: Da Capo Press, 1981), 29.

29. Although the 1930 census gives Madi's first name as "Madeline," at some point she seems to have dropped the second "e" (other variants of both her first name and her nickname, "Madi," can be found, including "Madeleine" and "Maddie"); HAL ("grandfather"); Helen Hough, unpublished letter to the Blitzstein family, MBP; Susan Braudy, *Family Circle: The Boudins and the Aristocracy of the Left* (New York: Knopf, 2003), 22, 76; see also Gerald Weales, *Clifford Odets: Playwright* (New York: Pegasus, 1971), 22; Margaret Brenman-Gibson, *Clifford Odets: American Playwright* (New York: Atheneum, 1981), 122–124; Myra MacPherson, *"All Governments Lie": The Life and Times of Rebel Journalist I. F. Stone* (New York: Scribner, 2006), 95–96; D. D. Guttenplan, *American Radical: The Life and Times of I. F. Stone* (New York: Farrar, Straus and Giroux, 2009), 44–46.

30. Aaron Copland and Vivian Perlis, *Copland: 1900 through 1942* (Boston: Faber and Faber, 1984), 330; Weales, 22; CD to author, April 13, 2009; MB, "Theatre Music," *MM* 17/3 (March–April 1940): 181–184; Guttenplan, 114; Brenman-Gibson, 638, writes that it is "certain" that Odets did not meet Blitzstein until 1932, when the latter was twenty-three, but in fact, Blitzstein was twenty-three in 1928.

31. MB to William E. Walter, March 19, 1927; Walter to MB, March 24, 1927, CIMA.

32. AC to the Edward MacDowell Association, April 1, 1928, Edward and Marian MacDowell Collection, Music Division, LC.

33. MB [to Berenice Skidelsky], November 16, 1927, MBP; AC, notes for "Youngest Americans," ACC, courtesy of Matthew Mugmon; MB to Louis Simon, March 20, 1928 (GOR, 32); MB to Nadia Boulanger [late 1928], MBP; Edwin H. Schloss, "Blitzstein Appears in Critical Recital," *Philadelphia Record* (April 22, 1933).

34. MB, "The Modern Movement"; MB, "Four American Composers"; MB to MC, June 3, 1939, MCC; MB to DD [1943], DDC; MB to AC, March 12, 1963, ACC.

35. GOR, 40, provides a 1928 date for "The Modern Movement," but various references suggest that the bulk of the lectures were written and delivered in early 1929; COP.

36. MB to Nadia Boulanger [late 1928].

37. MB, "On 'Mahagonny,'" *Saturday Review* 41/22 (May 31, 1958): 40.

38. MB, program notes, Riva Hoffman and Her Dancers, MBP; MB, "My Lady Jazz" (January 5, 1926): 17, 29 (MB, marginalia, MBP); MB, "Hin und Zurück in Philadelphia," *MM* 5/4 (May–June 1928): 34–36.

39. MB, "Four American Composers."

Chapter 3

1. In this undated catalog, Blitzstein gave the original movement titles of *Percussion Music*—"Flam," "Drag," "Paradiddle"—and for *Theater for the Cabaret*, he indicated eighteen as opposed to nineteen voices.

2. MB to Henry Allen Moe, August 17, 1929, GMF; presuming that *Three Songs to Words of A. E. Housman* (according to a work list, 1924, although perhaps 1924–1925), includes "From Far, From Eve and Morning" and "Into My Heart an Air" (whose fair copy bears a date of 1925), that would leave one Housman setting unidentified.

3. MBS1; MBS2; MBS3; Melissa J. de Graaf, review of the *Marc Blitzstein Songbook*, Vols. 1 and 2, *Notes* 60/1 (September 2003): 296–301; Barry Drogin, "Worth a Half-Century Wait," *New Music Connoisseur* 10/1 (Spring 2002): 26.

4. MB, 1929 Guggenheim Fellowship Application Form, GMF.

5. "Naegele Heard Here Again," *NYT* (January 8, 1927).

6. MB to Nadia Boulanger, October 18, 1927, Nadia Boulanger Collection, Bibliothèque nationale de France, courtesy of the Fondation Internationale Nadia et Lili Boulanger; Margaret Brenman-Gibson, *Clifford Odets: American Playwright* (New York: Atheneum, 1981), 124; George Antheil, *Bad Boy of Music* (New York: Da Capo Press, 1981), 156, 161.

7. GOR, 29; MB to Julian Levi, July 6, 1928, Julian Levi papers, Archives of American Art, Smithsonian Institution.

8. An incomplete translation of "After the Dazzle of Day" into French exists as well, penciled underneath the English in MB's manuscript.

9. MB [to Berenice Skidelsky], May 29, 1928, MBP.

10. Walt Whitman, *Leaves of Grass: A Textual Variorum of the Printed Poems*, 3 vols., edited by Sculley Bradley, Harold W. Blodgett, Arthur Golden, and William White (New York: New York University Press, 1980).

11. David Metzer, "Reclaiming Walt: Marc Blitzstein's Whitman Settings," *Journal of the American Musicological Society* 48/2 (Summer 1995): 241.

12. Metzer, 246–247.

13. "Negro Choristers Singing for Copland," *New York World* (December 30, 1928); *The Correspondence of Roger Sessions*, edited by Andrea Olmstead (Boston, MA: Northeastern University Press, 1992), 139.

14. Charles Sinnickson Jr., "Blitzstein Gives Lecture-Recital," *Philadelphia Record* (October 23, 1946); reviews of "Gods" and *Two Coon Shouts*, MBP; unidentified review of "Gods" ("the music"); Arthur D. Pierce, "Donner und Blitzstein," *Camden Evening Courier* (March 14, 1928) ("There is").

15. Reviews of *Four Songs* by Samuel Chotzinoff, *New York World*; Olin Downes, *NYT*; Oscar Thompson, *Post* (all December 31, 1928); Marion Bauer, *Musical Leader* (January 3, 1929); Robert A. Simon, *New Yorker* (January 12, 1929).

16. "League Concert Coming," *Musical America* 47/16 (February 4, 1928): 25.

17. Robert A. Simon, "Musical Events," *New Yorker* (February 25, 1928): 63; "League Concert Coming."

18. LED, 18 (concerning the slamming piano lid, Lederman confused MB's Piano Sonata with his *Percussion Music*); MB, program notes, Composers' Forum-Laboratory concert (April 15, 1936), MBP.

19. LEH, 170–171; Pierce ("Sonata in One Round"); Charles Glenn, "Meet Marc Blitzstein, People's Composer," *People's World* (June 27, 1941).

20. John Rockwell, "Music: The League at 25," *NYT* (February 17, 1980); Albrecht Duemling, "Marc Blitzstein zum 80. Geburtstag," *Neue Zeitschrift für Musik* (March 1985): 46 ("erstaunlich frisch"); Greg Stepanich, *Palm Beach ArtsPaper* (May 10, 2009); William G. King, "Music and Musicians: About Marc Blitzstein," *Sun* (October 19, 1940).

21. Louis M. Simon, "Stella Simon and Her Film, 'Hands,'" unpublished manuscript, 1989, Museum of Modern Art Film Study Center.

22. Jan-Christopher Horak, "The First American Film Avant-garde, 1919–1945," *Experimental Cinema, The Film Reader*, edited by Wheeler Winston Dixon and Gwendolyn Audrey Foster (New York: Routledge, 2002), 35–36; David Curtis, *Experimental Cinema* (New York: Delta, 1971), 35.

23. Hans Feld, "Ein Film von Händen," [Berlin] *Film-Kurier* (September 1, 1927) (for Kraus); GOR, 30 ("horribly"); Lori Pauli, "Stella F. Simon 1878–1973," *History of Photography* 24/1 (2000): 75–83.

24. Ischi, "Hände spielen Dramenhelden und Liebhaber," *Berliner illustrierte Nachtausgabe* (January 29, 1929); Josef Jentter, "Krawall in der Nachtvorstellung," [Frankfurt] *General-Anzeiger* ("Hände weg"); reviews, *Hände* clipping file, Museum of Modern Art Film Study Center.

25. "Sturm im Gloria-Palast," [Berlin] *Montag-Morgen* (February 18, 1929) (for Antheil); Artur Michel, "Skandal um Tamiris," [Berlin] *Vossische Zeitung* (February 19, 1929) ("Blues-Musik"); reviews, *Hände* clipping file.

26. GOR, 28, 34; James Ross Moore, "Ronald Jeans," *Oxford Dictionary of National Biography* (New York: Oxford University Press, 2004); "Wild Party in Night Club Harmonized in 'Hot' Opera," *Philadelphia Record* (April 30, 1929).

27. MB, "Hin und Zurück in Philadelphia," *MM* 5/4 (May–June 1928): 34–36; "Wild Party."

28. H. T. Craven, "Marc Blitzstein Operatic Satire Rocks Ballroom," *Philadelphia Record* (May 7, 1929).

29. Craven; Arnold Dresden to Raymond Walter, May 14, 1929; Alfred J. Swan to Frank Aydelotte, May 15, 1929; confidential reports on MB from Marian MacDowell, Pierre Monteux, Lazare Saminsky, and Alexander Smallens, GMF; Nadia Boulanger, letter of recommendation, January 2, 1928, MBP.

30. Lee Davis, *Scandals and Follies: The Rise and Fall of the Great Broadway Revue* (New York: Limelight Editions, 2000), 276; reviews of *Triple-Sec* by J. Brooks Atkinson, *NYT*; Robert Littell, *New York World*; Wilella Waldorf, *Post* (all June 5, 1930), MBP; Meryle Secrest, "For Threepence: He Doesn't Mind Being in Shadow," *Washington Post* (May 14, 1963); Howard Pollack, *George Gershwin: His Life and Work* (Berkeley: University of California Press, 2006), 145; CG to EG, June 19, 1930, MBP.

31. GOR, 59–60; MB to JD, June 23, 1930, MBP.

32. Willy Strecker to MB, November 4, 1954, MBP; for German retrenchment, see Michael H. Kater, "The Revenge of the Fathers: The Demise of Modern Music at the End of the Weimar Republic," *German Studies Review* 15/2 (May 1992): 295–315.

33. Arthur Berger, "Concert and Recital," *NYHT* (June 8, 1950).

34. Glenn; BLI.

35. "Contemporary Music," unidentified journal, March 14, 1928, MBP ("glorified bass drum").

36. David T. Little, *The Critical Composer: Political Music During and After "The Revolution"* (Ph.D. dissertation, Princeton, 2011), 30–33; Howard Pollack, *Aaron Copland: The Life and Work of an Uncommon Man* (New York: Henry Holt, 1999), 275.

37. LEH, 175; Sarah Cahill, interview with author, January 17, 2008; Allan Ulrich, "Marc Blitzstein Centenary Celebration, San Francisco," *Financial Times* (March 1, 2005); Jerry Dubins, review of *First Life: Marc Blitzstein*, *Fanfare* 33/3 (January–February 2010): 114–116; Blitzstein Centennial Concert, March 6, 2005, videotape, courtesy of Eric Gordon.

Chapter 4

1. "Blitzstein Upholds Music Modernism," *Philadelphia Record* (January 4, 1933).

2. Harry D. Boonin, *The Jewish Quarter of Philadelphia, 1881–1930* (Philadelphia: Jewish Walking Tours of Philadelphia, 1999), 33, 155 n85; see also articles on the Blitzstein bank in the *Philadelphia Evening Bulletin* (December 24, 1930, December 27, 1930, March 25, 1931).

3. MB to EG, January 13, 1931 ("an old man," "both cheerful"), March 27, 1931 ("vulturous"), MBP; "Samuel M. Blitzstein," *Philadelphia Evening Bulletin* (April 28, 1945).

4. MB, "Modern Music: Latest Developments" (1931), MBP; GOR, 63–64.

5. GOR, 37.

6. Eric Gordon, "The Met's First Hansel," *Opera News* 48/7 (December 24, 1983): 30–31; Edward Goldbeck, "A German Jew," *Chicago Daily Tribune* (December 26, 1915).

7. Henry A. Murray, interview with Forrest Robinson, July 24, 1970, transcript, Henry Murray Collection, Harvard University; *"In Old Friendship": The Correspondence of Lewis Mumford and Henry A. Murray, 1928–1981*, edited by Frank G. Novak Jr. (Syracuse, NY: Syracuse University Press, 2007), 112 ("lacked").

8. CG to EG, August 28, 1929, April 16, 1930, February 22, 1931, MBP.

9. GOR, 36; HAL; Charles Pearce to EG, May 8, 1935, MBP.

10. EG, *The Broken Circle*, MBP (an excerpt from the novel appeared as "Arc" in *The Second American Caravan: A Yearbook of American Literature*, edited by Alfred Kreymborg, Lewis Mumford, and Paul Rosenfeld [New York: Macaulay, 1928], 726–738).

11. Glenway Wescott, letter of recommendation, October 10, 1929, MBP.

12. EG to her parents, June 19, 1929; AC to EG, December 11, 1929, March 10, 1931; EG to AC, March 6, 1931, MBP.

13. MB, critique of *The Broken Circle*, MBP.

14. GOR, 37; EG, Journals, July 18, 1929, MBP ("You will").

15. EG, Journals, September 5, 1929, September 7, 1929; CG to EG, August 26, 1929 (see also August 4, 1929), MBP.

16. MB to EG, September 13, 1929, September 18, 1929, MBP.

17. "Chronology of Activities, Compositions, and Writings of Marc Blitzstein from 1905 to 1942," MBP; 1940 Guggenheim Fellowship Application Form, GMF; MB, "'Threepenny Opera' Is Back," *NYHT* (March 7, 1954); MB, "On 'Mahagonny,'" *Saturday Review* 41/22 (May 31, 1958): 40, 47 ("in execrable"); MB, "Prize 'Dreigroschen,'" *Saturday Review* 41/43 (October 25, 1958): 64–65 ("adored"); MB to Berenice Skidelsky, October 8, 1928, MBP; Eike Fess to author, October 30, 2007; Blitzstein's casual mention of *The Threepenny Opera* in his 1928–29 "Modern Movement" lectures hardly solves this conundrum.

18. MB [to JD], October 7, 1929, MBP; EG to Marian MacDowell, November 9, 1929, Edward and Marian MacDowell Collection, Music Division, LC; EG, Journals, December 1, 1929; MB to Berenice Skidelsky, October 31, 1931, MBP.

19. MB to JD, November 11, 1929; EG, Journals, December 4, 1929; MB to EG, March 11, 1931; EG to MB, April 1, 1931, MBP; CD, *The Case Against Death*, an unpublished memoir, 233, courtesy of the author.

20. MB to JD, December 4, 1929, MBP.

21. EG, Journals, February 8, 1930, MBP.

22. CG to EG, February 25, 1930; EG, Journals, May 6, 1930; EG to CG, November 30, 1930, MBP; Willy, *The Third Sex* (Urbana: University of Illinois Press, 2007), 25 ("sodomic"); MB to Alexander Smallens, October 24, 1930, ASC ("ruthlessly").

23. EG, Journals, May 12, 1930, MBP; EG to AC, postmarked May 16, 1930, ACC; *The Correspondence of Roger Sessions*, edited by Andrea Olmstead (Boston: Northeastern University Press, 1992), 139.

24. EG to CG, November 30, 1930; EG, Journals, various June and July entries, MBP.

25. MB to EG, August 11, 1930; MB to AC, August 19, 1930, MBP.

26. EG, Journals, September 19, 1930, October 12, 1930; MB to EG, October 7, 1930; EG to CG, November 30, 1930, MBP.

27. EG, Journals, December 7, 1930, March 2, 1931, MBP.

28. MB to EG, February 16, 1931, March 27, 1931, May 26, 1931, June 8, 1931, MBP.

29. MB to EG, January 13, 1931 ("beautiful"), March 27, 1931 ("I was prepared"); EG, Journals, March 29, 1931, MBP ("ausserordentlich"); MB to Alexander Smallens, June 5, 1931, ASC ("release").

30. MB to EG, February 16, 1931; CG to EG, June 14, 1931, MBP.

31. EG, Journals, July 28, 1931, MBP.

32. EG to CG, September 30, 1931 ("permanent"); MB to EG, September 16, 1931, September 18, 1931, October 2, 1931; EG, Journals, October 16, 1931 ("I think," "His letters"), MBP.
33. MB to EG, January 13, 1931, September 23, 1931; JD to EG, September 24, 1931, MBP.
34. EG, Journals, November 15, 1931, December 30, 1931, MBP.
35. HAL.
36. MB, 1929 Guggenheim Fellowship Application Form, GMF; MB, notes; MB to JD, December 4, 1929, August 8–14, 1931; MB to EG, September 18, 1931; "November 7: 1917–1931," program in Russian, MBP (see also GOR, 72); for suggestions of Eva's influence, see, for instance, LED, 21: "It was clear that Eva shared, perhaps helped to mold, Marc's emerging political convictions."
37. Malcolm Cowley, "Echoes of a Crime," *New Republic* 84/1082 (August 28, 1935): 79; Murray Kempton, *Part of Our Time: Some Ruins and Monuments of the Thirties* (New York: Simon & Schuster, 1955); Moshik Temkin, *The Sacco-Vanzetti Affair: America on Trial* (New Haven, CT: Yale University Press, 2009).
38. EG, Journals, March 15, 1932, July 12, 1932, September 22, 1932, MBP.
39. MB, "A Musician's War Diary, Part III," *New Masses* 50/9 (August 27, 1946): 12; Irving Howe, with the assistance of Kenneth Libo, *World of Our Fathers* (New York: Harcourt Brace Jovanovich, 1976); Vivian Gornick, *The Romance of American Communism* (New York: Basic Books, 1977); Arthur Liebman, *Jews and the Left* (New York: John Wiley & Sons, 1979); Maurice Isserman, *Which Side Were You On? The American Communist Party during the Second World War* (Middletown, CT: Wesleyan University Press, 1982); Murray Wolfson, *Marx: Economist, Philosopher, Jew: Steps in the Development of a Doctrine* (New York: St. Martin's Press, 1982); *Essential Papers on Jews and the Left*, edited by Ezra Mendelsohn (New York: NYU Press, 1997); *Dark Times, Dire Decisions: Jews and Communism*, edited by Jonathan Frankel (New York: Oxford University Press, 2004); Alan M. Wald, *Trinity of Passion: The Literary Left and the Antifascist Crusade* (Chapel Hill: University of North Carolina Press, 2007), 180–186; Archie Brown, *The Rise and Fall of Communism* (New York: HarperCollins, 2009), 129–132; Karl Marx, "On the Jewish Question," *The Marx-Engels Reader*, edited by Robert C. Tucker (New York: W. W. Norton, 1972), 24–51.
40. Gert Hekma, Harry Oosterhuis, and James Steakley, "Leftist Sexual Politics and Homosexuality: A Historical Overview"; Laura Engelstein, "Soviet Policy Toward Male Homosexuality. Its Origins and Historical Roots"; and Harry Oosterhuis, "The 'Jews' of the Antifascist Left: Homosexuality and Socialist Resistance to Nazism," *Journal of Homosexuality* 29/2–3 (1995): 1–40, 155–179, 227–257; Stuart Timmons, *The Trouble with Harry Hay: Founder of the Modern Gay Movement* (Boston: Alyson, 1990).
41. Hekma; Oosterhuis; Randall Halle, "Between Marxism and Psychoanalysis: Antifascism and Antihomosexuality in the Frankfurt School," *Journal of Homosexuality* 29/4 (1995): 295–317; Timmons, especially 160, 186, 294–295.
42. MB to JD, August 8–14, 1931, MBP; see also MB to Alexander Smallens, August 14, 1931, ASC.
43. MB to JD, December 24, 1929, MBP.

Chapter 5

1. MB to Henry Allen Moe, August 17, 1929, GMF.
2. MB to JD, November 25, 1929, MBP; according to sketches, Blitzstein intended "Jimmie's got a goil" as the second number, but apparently changed his mind subsequently.
3. Carol J. Oja, "Cos Cob Press and the American Composer," *Notes* 45/2 (December 1988): 242–243; MBS3.
4. MB [to EG], August 29, 1929, MBP; Christopher Sawyer-Lauçanno, *E. E. Cummings: a biography* (Naperville, IL: Sourcebooks, 2004), 429; DD, Journals, May 31, 1945, DDC.
5. "Olin Downes Addresses League," MBP ("moments"); David Ewen, "New Blood in American Music," *Musical Courier* 107/12 (September 16, 1933): 6 ("formless").

6. MB to Berenice Skidelsky, October 31, 1929, MBP; EG to AC, November 8, 1929, ACC (for completion of the opera on November 7); MB to JD, November 11, 1929, MBP.

7. MB, sketches, MBP; BLI.

8. Blitzstein, *Parabola and Circula*, two measures before rehearsal 32 ("All we") and six before rehearsal 73 ("All of"), in both the fair copy orchestral and piano-vocal score, MBP; MB to JD, August 21, 1933, MBP.

9. MB, notes, MPB.

10. BRA, 170.

11. MB to Berenice Skidelsky, March 9, 1930, MBP; MB to Alexander Smallens, September 16, 1930, ASC.

12. MB to EG, January 13, 1931, MBP.

13. GOR, 443; William G. King, "Music and Musicians: About Marc Blitzstein," *Sun* (October 19, 1940); MB, "Marc Blitzstein's 'The Guests' To Premiere This Thursday," *New York Star* (January 17, 1949); BLI.

14. EG, Journals, May 12, 1930, MBP.

15. MB to EG, January 13, 1931, February 16, 1931, MBP; MB to Alexander Smallens, September 5, 1930, ASC; EG, Journals, October 1, 1930; EG to CG, November 30, 1930, MBP.

16. MB to EG, February 16, 1931, MBP.

17. EG, Journals, April 29, 1931, MBP.

18. GOR, 62; "Contemporary Music," *Philadelphia Evening Bulletin* (February 26, 1931); James M. Keller, "Americans in Paris," *Chamber Music* 26/5 (September–October 2009): 78–82; Jerry Dubins, review of *First Life: Marc Blitzstein, Fanfare* 33/3 (January–February 2010): 114–116.

19. EG to CG, November 30, 1930; MB to JD, May 22, 1930, MBP.

20. MB, "Premieres and Experiments–1932," *MM* 9/3 (March–April 1932): 121.

21. MB, "Cain," MBP (a slightly varied scenario appears not among the *Cain* materials, but among the composer's written work).

22. MB, "Cain"; MB to EG, May 22, 1930, MBP.

23. EG to CG, November 30, 1930; MB to JD, June 23, 1930; MB to EG, November 19, 1930, January 13, 1931; EG, Journals, September 19, 1930, MBP; Aaron Copland, "Neglected Works: A Symposium," *MM* 23/1 (Winter 1946): 8; Douglas Moore, confidential report on MB, received September 28, 1932, GMF.

24. MB to EG, November 3, 1931; Oscar Wagner to MB, November 16, 1931; MB to JD, December 9, 1931; EG, Journals, January 8, 1932, January 12, 1932, MBP.

25. John Martin, "Zemach's Dancers Delight Big House," *NYT* (January 26, 1931); MB, "Dancers of the Season," *MM* 8/3 (March–April 1931): 41.

26. MB to EG, February 5, 1931, MBP; GOR, 66; "Marc Blitzstein's 'The Guests.'"

27. "Abel Offers the Lamb," *This Quarter* 3/3 (January–February–March 1931): 440–441; Harold Morris, *Contemporary American Music* (Houston: Rice Institute, 1934), 128, 135–136; Robert A. Simon, "Musical Events," *New Yorker* (December 14, 1935): 111; Louis Biancolli, "Young Composer Plays Own Work," *World-Telegram* (April 16, 1936); Steve Smith, "After Almost 80 Years, A Score Gets a Hearing," *NYT* (June 9, 2008).

28. Aaron Copland and Vivian Perlis, *Copland: 1900 Through 1942* (Boston: Faber and Faber, 1984); Carol J. Oja, "The Copland-Sessions Concerts and Their Reception in the Contemporary Press," *Musical Quarterly* 65/2 (April 1979): 212–229.

29. Ralph Steiner, *A Point of View* (Middletown, CT: Wesleyan University Press, 1978), 12.

30. MB to EG, January 13, 1931, February 27, 1931; Studio Films to AC, February 11, 1931, MBP.

31. MB to EG, January 13, 1931, February 27, 1931, MPB.

32. Scott MacDonald, "Ralph Steiner," *Lovers of Cinema: The First American Film Avant-Garde 1919–1945*, edited by Jan-Christopher Horak (Madison: University of Wisconsin Press, 1995), 213.

33. LL, "The Legacies of Schoenberg and Weill," *Aufbau* 65/25 (December 10, 1999): 14; LL to author, March 23, 2008.

34. AC to EG, March 19, 1931, March 27, 1931, MBP; Richard Hammond, "Pioneers of Movie Music," *MM* 8/3 (March–April 1931): 35–37; Olin Downes, "Concert of Music and Films," *NYT* (March 16, 1931); clippings, MBP.

35. Eric Beheim, "Surf's Up: Resurrecting a 1931 Avant-garde Film Score," unpublished manuscript, courtesy of the author.

36. MB to Berenice Skidelsky, October 31, 1929; MB, notes, MBP.

37. MB to Berenice Skidelsky, March 9, 1930, MBP.

38. Claire Reis to MB, March 27, 1931, March 31, 1931, May 11, 1931; MB to EG, April 1, 1931, MBP.

39. For the Hemingway story and vaudeville, see Ron Berman, "Vaudeville Philosophers: 'The Killers,'" *Twentieth Century Literature* 45/1 (Spring 1999): 79–93.

40. MB to EG, May 18, 1931, MBP; MB to Alexander Smallens, July 17, 1931, ASC.

41. Apollonius Rhodius, *The Argonautica* (Cambridge, MA: Harvard University Press, 1912), 115–137.

42. In an early draft, Blitzstein wrote "[Zeus will see that ye have always] plenty of work," changed subsequently in the libretto and his piano-vocal score to "plenty of do," and later corrected again in the latter to "plenty of work," suggesting some indecision on his part.

43. "3 Red 'Hunger' Riots Stir Only the Police," *NYT* (January 9, 1931); "The Harpies," Boosey & Hawkes promotional materials; GOR, 69.

44. MB to JD, September 6, 1932; MB to EG, January 27, 1935; EG, Journals, May 11, 1932, MBP.

45. Claire Reis to MB, November 15, 1931, MBP; Howard Taubman, "Blitzstein Opera Performed Here," *NYT*, and Francis D. Perkins, "Blitzstein's 'Harpies' Sung," *NYHT* (both May 26, 1953); R.S. [Robert Sabin], "New York Sees Premieres of Three One-Act Operas," *Musical America* 73/8 (June 1953): 7.

46. LEH, 198–199; Will Crutchfield, "Planning a Musical Pastiche By a Rarely Heard Master," *NYT* (September 12, 1988) ("as a sort"); Stephen Holden, "'Blitzstein Project' Gives a Taste of 30's Composer," *NYT* (September 26, 1988); MB, *The Harpies* (Premier Recordings 1009, 1991); John Rockwell, "Music: 2 Composers for the Theater," *NYT* (December 9, 1973).

47. MB, program notes, Piano Concerto, MBP.

48. Bernard Holland, "Music: Blitzstein at Meet the Moderns," *NYT* (January 28, 1986); BRA, 170.

49. Robert J. Dietz, "Record Reviews," *American Music* 8/3 (Fall 1990): 381–382.

50. MB to Serge Koussevitzky, November 16, 1931; Olga Naoumoff to MB, November 23, 1931, Serge Koussevitky Collection, LC; Leopold Stokowski to MB, March 21, 1932; Eugene Goossens to MB, May 10, 1932, MBP; GOR, 73, 554 n34; Colin McPhee, "New York's Spring Season, 1936," *MM* 13/4 (May–June 1936): 39–42.

51. MB, Piano Concerto (CRI CD 554, 1988); Michael Barrett, interview with author, April 18, 2008.

52. Barrett; Peter G. Davis, "Music," *New York* (February 10, 1986): 65; Tim Page, liner notes, MB, Piano Concerto; Paul Moor, "Recordings in Review," *Musical America* 110/1 (January 1990): 60.

53. JoAnn Falletta to author, November 1, 2011; Sara Davis Buechner to author, October 20, 2011.

Chapter 6

1. MB to JD, September 1932, September 6, 1932, MBP.

2. MB to Carl Engel, January 12, 1933, Carl Engel Collection, LC.

3. EG, Journals, February 14, 1933, MBP; Irma and Mordecai Bauman, *From Our Angle of Repose: A Memoir* (New York: privately printed, 2006), 139; Edwin H. Schloss, "Blitzstein Appears in Critical Recital," *Philadelphia Record* (April 22, 1933).

4. HAL; EG, Journals, April 25, 1932; EG to Lina Abarbanell, August 26, 1935, MBP.

5. Victor Bonham-Carter, *Dartington Hall: The Formative Years: 1925–1957* (Dulverton: Exmoor, 1958, 1970); Michael Young, *The Elmhirsts of Dartington: The Creation of an Utopian Community* (Boston: Routledge & Kegan Paul, 1982); Dartington Hall brochure, March 13, 1934, MBP.

6. Dorothy Elmhirst to David Morris, January 11, 1935, Dartington Hall Trust Archive; EG, Journals, April 12, 1934, MBP.

7. EG to Dorothy and Leonard Elmhirst, April 15, 1934, Dartington Hall Trust Archive.

8. MB, "Talk-Music-Dance; New York, 1933," *MM* 11/1 (November–December 1933): 39.

9. MB to Kathleen Hull-Brown, November 4, 1934, Dartington Hall Trust Archive; EG, "Brussels Letter," November 1934; EG to Lina Abarbanell, November 6, 1934, MBP.

10. Principal sources for this incident include MB to Dorothy and Leonard Elmhirst, November 19, 1934, Dartington Hall Trust Archive; MB to JD, November 29, 1934; EG to Lina Abarbanell, December 1, 1934, MBP.

11. MB to Dorothy and Leonard Elmhirst, November 19, 1934.

12. Dorothy Elmhirst to MB, December 6, 1934, Dartington Hall Trust Archive.

13. GOR, 95.

14. MB, "Theatre-Music in Paris," *MM* 12/3 (March–April 1935): 132–133; Kurt Weill to Rudolf Kommer, January 15, 1935, KWF ("so wenig," "Er scheint mehr Musikschriftsteller als Musiker zu sein"); Kim H. Kowalke, "The Threepenny Opera: The Score Adapted," *Die Dreigroschenoper: A Facsimile of the Holograph Full Score*, edited by Edward Harsh (New York: Kurt Weill Foundation for Music, 1996), 12.

15. MB to Dorothy and Leonard Elmhirst, November 21, 1934, Dartington Hall Trust Archive; MB to JD, November 20, 1934, MBP.

16. EG to her parents, October 11, 1932; MB to EG, September 29, 1932, MBP.

17. EG, Journals, December 31, 1934 ("light"), January 2, 1935, MBP.

18. MB to EG, January 22, 1935, January 23, 1935, January 24, 1935, January 27, 1935, MBP.

19. *Thirty Years of Treason: Excerpts from Hearings before the House Committee on Un-American Activities, 1938–1968*, edited by Eric Bentley (New York: Viking Press, 1971), 73.

20. EG, Journals, March 4, 1935, MBP.

21. "By-laws," Composers' Collective of New York, 1935, MBP; David K. Dunaway, "Unsung Songs of Protest: The Composers Collective of New York," *New York Folklore* 5/1–2 (1979): 1–19; David K. Dunaway, "Charles Seeger and Carl Sands: The Composers' Collective Years," *Ethnomusicology* 24/2 (May 1980): 159–168; Carol J. Oja, "Marc Blitzstein's 'The Cradle Will Rock' and Mass-Song Styles of the 1930s," *Musical Quarterly* 73/4 (1989): 445–475; Ann M. Pescatello, *Charles Seeger: A Life in American Music* (Pittsburgh: University of Pittsburgh Press, 1992); Judith Tick, *Ruth Crawford Seeger: A Composer's Search for American Music* (New York: Oxford University Press, 1997). For a view of related Soviet developments that probably helped shape the collective's thinking, see Alfred Schlee, "Under the Red Flag," *MM* 9/3 (March–April 1932): 108–113.

22. Dunaway, "Charles Seeger," 164.

23. Dunaway, "Unsung Songs of Protest," 1–19; *Songs of the People* (New York: Workers Library, 1937).

24. Charles Seeger, "On Proletarian Music," *MM* 11/3 (March–April 1934): 121–127; Elie Siegmeister, *Music and Society* (New York: Critics Group Press, 1938); see also Leonora Saavedra, "The American Composer in the 1930s: The Social Thought of Seeger and Chávez," and Robert R. Grimes, "Form, Content, and Value: Seeger and Criticism to 1940," both in *Understanding Charles Seeger: Pioneer in American Musicology*, edited by Bell Yung and Helen Rees (Urbana: University of Illinois Press, 1999).

25. Dunaway, "Unsung Songs," 5.

26. Charles Seeger to MB, July 18, 1934, MBP.

27. MB, "Idiom of Prol[etarian] Music," MBP, courtesy of Maria Cristina Fava.

28. Irwin Heilner to Charles Seeger, April 27, 1935, MBP.

29. MB to Virgil Thomson, February 10, 1936, March 12, 1936, and Ashley Pettis to Elie
    Siegmeister, January 24, 1936, Virgil Thomson Collection, Yale University; MB to Lazare
    Saminsky, February 10, 1936; Virgil Thomson to MB, February 20, 1936, March 16,
    1936, MBP; GOR, 117.

30. Carl Sands [Charles Seeger], "World of Music," *Daily Worker* (March 6, 1935); Albrecht
    Betz, *Hanns Eisler: Political Musician*, trans. by Bill Hopkins (New York: Cambridge Uni-
    versity Press, 1976, 1982); see also Sally M. A. Bick, "Eisler's Notes on Hollywood and the
    Film Music Project, 1935–42," *Current Musicology* 86 (Fall 2008): 7–39.

31. Blitzstein called the Mecca Temple concert "a fiasco" in a review of the Eisler farewell
    concert, MBP; see also Sands, "World of Music," regarding this "set-back"; *Hanns Eisler:
    A Rebel in Music*, trans. by Marjorie Meyer and edited by Manfred Grabs (New York: In-
    ternational, 1978), 88.

32. Grabs, 87, 95–96; Hanns Eisler, confidential report on MB, received November 16, 1935,
    GMF; Ronald D. Cohen and Dave Samuelson, *Songs for Political Action* (Hambergen,
    Germany: Bear Family Records BCD 15 720 JL, 1996), 59.

33. HAL; James K. Lyon, *Bertolt Brecht in America* (Princeton, NJ: Princeton University
    Press, 1980) (Lyon states that Jerome introduced Brecht to Blitzstein, but HAL quotes
    the latter as claiming to have first met Brecht and Eisler "a few years back while studying
    abroad"); David Drew, *Kurt Weill: A Handbook* (Berkeley: University of California Press,
    1987), 61; *Vom Kurfürstendamm zum Broadway: Kurt Weill (1900–1950)*, edited by Bernd
    Kortländer, Winrich Meiszies, and David Farneth (Düsseldorf: Droste, 1990), 154.

34. Bert[olt] Brecht, "The German Drama: Pre-Hitler," *NYT* (November 24, 1935); EG,
    "Principles of 'Educational' Theater," *New Masses* 18/1 (December 31, 1935): 27–28;
    Lyon, 17–18.

35. *Bertolt Brecht Letters*, trans. by Ralph Manheim and edited by John Willett (London:
    Methuen, 1990), 228 ("intelligent"); Berthold Brecht, "How the Carpet Weavers of
    Kujan-Bulak Honored Lenin," trans. by EG, *Daily Worker* (January 21, 1936); EG to
    V. J. Jerome, February 13, 1936, March 12, 1936, MBP; Lyon, 17–18; for an overview of
    Eva's involvement with Brecht, see Sally Lou Todd and LL, "Bert Brecht and Marc Blitz-
    stein," unpublished paper, Sally Todd Collection, WHS (also at KWF), 8–9.

36. Charles Seeger to MB, April 21, 1936, MBP; *Unison: Organ of the American Music League*
    1/1 (May 1936).

37. Charles Seeger, *Reminiscences of an American Musicologist* (Los Angeles: UCLA Oral His-
    tory Program, 1972), 212; Dunaway, "Carl Seeger," 166, 168.

38. Pescatello, 117, 118.

39. MB, "Composers as Lecturers and in Concerts," *MM* 13/1 (November–December 1935):
    45–46.

40. Downtown Music School brochure, Winter Term, January 6–March 27, 1936, MBP.

41. MB to EG, September 20, 1935, MBP; Earl Robinson with Eric A. Gordon, *Ballad of an
    American: The Autobiography of Earl Robinson* (Lanham, MD: Scarecrow, 1998), 67;
    GOR, 106–107; "Music Notes," *NYT* (April 20, 1940).

42. EG, Journals, February 5, 1932, April 14, 1932, MBP.

43. EG to her parents, October 11, 1932; MB to JD, October 3, 1932, October 16, 1932, MBP.

44. EG, Journals, March 1, 1933, MBP; "Composer Weds Writer," *Philadelphia Evening Led-
    ger*, March 6, 1933.

45. EG to MB [winter of 1933–34]; EG, Journals, June 29, 1933; MB to EG, January 23, 1935,
    MBP.

46. EG, Journals, December 31, 1934, January 1, 1935, January 14, 1935; EG to Lina Abar-
    banell, August 26, 1935, MBP.

47. EG, Journals, April 12, 1932, May 29, 1933; MB, notes, MBP.

48. EG to Lina Abarbanell, August 17, 1934, November 6, 1934, September 5, 1935; Alexandre Bruno to EG, September 22, 1934; MB to Lina Abarbanell, September 6, 1935; EG, memo, October 3, 1935, MBP.

49. MB to EG, September 20, 1935; EG to Lina Abarbanell, September 19, 1935; EG, notes, MBP.

50. EG to Henry Murray, March 3, 1936, March 29, 1936; MB to Henry Murray [late March 1936], MBP.

51. *"In Old Friendship": The Correspondence of Lewis Mumford and Henry A. Murray, 1928–1981*, edited by Frank G. Novak Jr. (Syracuse, NY: Syracuse University Press, 2007), 112–113; Joan Jacobs Brumberg, *Fasting Girls: The Emergence of Anorexia Nervosa as a Modern Disease* (Cambridge, MA: Harvard University Press, 1988), 217.

52. EG to MB, May 7, 1936, MBP.

53. Henry A. Murray, interview with Forrest Robinson, July 24, 1970, transcript, Henry Murray Collection, Harvard University; *"In Old Friendship,"* 111–115; EG to MB, May 22, 1936; Henry Murray to EG, May 25, 1936, MBP.

54. *"In Old Friendship,"* 114–115; Lewis Mumford, interview with Forrest Robinson, July 15, 1970, transcript, Henry Murray Collection, Harvard University.

55. Murray, interview; Eric Gordon reports that Blitzstein found Eva dead in her hospital room, GOR, 121.

56. MB to Lina Abarbanell, May 26, 1936; Incident no. 12397, Office of the Superintendent of the Cemetery of Mount Auburn, May 28, 1936; EG, Journals, January 10, 1927, MBP.

57. GOR, 124.

58. MB to MC, September 26, 1951, MCC.

59. MB to JD, May 5, 1944, MBP.

Chapter 7

1. MB, "New York Chronicle of New Music," *MM* 8/2 (January–February 1931): 39–42; "Music and the Machine: Dancers of the Seasons," *MM* 8/3 (March–April 1931): 38–42; "Spring Season in the East," *MM* 8/4 (May–June 1931): 33–39; "Tame Season in New York," *MM* 9/2 (January–February 1932): 79–85; "Premieres and Experiments—1932," *MM* 9/3 (March–April 1932): 121–127; "Music and Theatre—1932," *MM* 9/4 (May–June 1932): 164–168; "Popular Music—An Invasion: 1923–1933," *MM* 10/2 (January–February 1933): 96–102; "Talk-Music-Dance; New York, 1933," *MM* 11/1 (November–December 1933): 34–40; "Mid-Season in New York," *MM* 11/2 (January–February 1934): 99–103; "Towards a New Form," *Musical Quarterly* 20/2 (April 1934): 213–218; "Theatre-Music in Paris," *MM* 12/3 (March–April 1935): 128–134; "Second Workers' Song Book," *Daily Worker* (June 12, 1935), 5; "The Phenomenon of Stravinsky," *Musical Quarterly* 21/3 (July 1935): 330–347; "Composers as Lecturers and in Concerts," *MM* 13/1 (November–December 1935): 47–50; "Walter Piston in a One-Man Exhibition," *Boston Evening Transcript* (December 9, 1935); "New York Medley, Winter, 1935," *MM* 13/2 (January–February 1936): 34–40; "Les Jeunes Américains Dans La Musique," *Revue musicale* 17/163 (February 1936): 145–148; "Etats-Unis," *Revue musicale* 17/165 (April 1936): 314–315; "Coming—The Mass Audience!" *MM* 13/4 (May–June 1936): 23–29; "Music Manifesto," *New Masses* 19/13 (June 23, 1936): 28; "The Case for Modern Music," *New Masses* 20/3 (July 14, 1936): 27; "The Case for Modern Music: II—The Second Generation," *New Masses* 20/4 (July 21, 1936): 28; "The Case for Modern Music: III—Technique and Temper," *New Masses* 20/5 (July 28, 1936): 28.

2. Aaron Copland, "In Memory of Marc Blitzstein (1905–1964)," *Perspectives of New Music* 2/2 (Spring–Summer 1964): 6; ROR, 200.

3. MB, "New York Chronicle," 41 ("Pain"); "Spring Season," 37 ("The effect"); "Theatre-Music," 131 ("I think"); "Premieres and Experiments," 124 ("lovely"); "Composers as

Lecturers," 48 ("The substance"); LED, 22 ("brilliant"); however, in "Some American Composers," *Vogue* 109/3 (February 1, 1947): 232, Lederman deemed Blitzstein's "feeling for language," although "entirely his own," "not so distinguished as Thomson's."

4. MB, "New York Chronicle," 40 ("pseudo"); "Theatre-Music," 131 ("but a rank"); "Soviet Composers," MBP.

5. MB, "The Phenomenon" ("Stravinsky's").

6. MB, outline, *Music for Us*, MBP.

7. MB, "New York Medley," 39.

8. MB, "Masterworks of Modern Music" unpublished lectures, MBP (Blitzstein originally wrote "Jewish philosophers," later replacing "Jewish" with what looks like "medieval").

9. MB, "Spring Season," 34 ("constitute"); "Towards a New Form," 215 ("is stuck"); "Mid-Season," 100 ("The diagnosis"); "Walter Piston."

10. MB, "Masterworks" ("hysteria"); unpublished essay on Berg's Piano Sonata, MBP; "Spring Season," 36–37 ("for the most part").

11. MB, "Mid-Season," 101 ("offensive," "The careers"); "Phenomenon."

12. MB, "Composers as Lecturers," 47–48 ("really"); "Phenomenon," 347 ("juxtaposed").

13. MB, "Towards a New Form" ("self-defeating"); "Les Jeunes," 146 ("un Jehovah implacable"); "Aaron Copland and the *Piano Variations*," unpublished lecture, MBP.

14. MB, "Tame Season," 82 ("Surely"); "New York Medley," 38 ("The servility"); "Walter Piston" ("It is"); "Composers as Lecturers," 49 ("a good").

15. MB, "Masterworks"; "Popular Music."

16. MB, "Masterworks"; "The Case for Modern Music: II" ("He saw"); see also "Coming," "The Case for Modern Music: III."

17. MB, "The Case for Modern Music: II"; "Coming," 28 ("When we"); see also "Popular Music," "Masterworks."

18. MB, "Talk-Music," 38; "Towards a New Form," 217; "Les Jeunes" [dated December 1934], 148 ("une indication important des préoccupations actuelles"); "Second Workers."

19. MB, "Music Manifesto" ("masterworks," "possibly," "By his"); "Masterworks" ("one lamentable"); review of the Eisler farewell concert, MBP ("gets caught").

20. MB, "New York Medley," 36–37; EG, marginalia, all-Weill concert program (December 17, 1935), MBP; "Second Workers."

21. MB, "New York Medley," 34; "Reds Bar Composer," MBP ("Leftist"); Harold Denny, "Soviet Denounces 'Leftism' in Music," *NYT* (February 15, 1936), MBP.

22. MB, "Tame Season," 83–85 ("lacks chiefly," "with too many," "a fundamental discrepancy"); "Music and Theatre," 165 ("episodes"); "Premieres and Experiments," 122 ("the same"); in "Premieres and Experiments," he also writes that Chávez "has not yet found a form which will enable him to grow, or it is not the sort of music which is meant to grow" (124).

23. MB, "The Phenomenon," 331 ("Hence the"); "Premieres and Experiments," 123 ("Harris"); "Walter Piston."

24. MB, "The Case for Modern Music."

25. MB, "Music Manifesto" ("the tool"); "The Case for Modern Music: II" ("They sing"); "The Phenomenon" ("luxury-products," "In Stravinsky"), 346–347; "The Case for Modern Music: III" ("In a world").

26. MB, "New York Medley," 40 ("It is clear"); "The Case for Modern Music: II" ("wants culture," "towards the brink"); "Coming," 23–29 ("a cataclysmic").

27. "Composers' Conference—Yaddo," transcript, May 2 and 3, 1932, MBP; see also Rudy Shackelford, "The Yaddo Festivals of American Music, 1932–1952," *Perspectives of New Music* 17/1 (Fall–Winter 1978): 92–125.

28. "Composers' Conference"; COP, 141 ("concern with structure").

29. MB, "New York Chronicle," 41–42; EG, Journals, May 1, 1932 (for MB's having "come around" to the *Variations*); "Aaron Copland and the *Piano Variations*" ("masterpiece"); "New Music: A Thumbnail History," unpublished lecture ("The large-scale"); "Form: The

Modern Era," unpublished lecture (for *Oedipus* as the "first new *form*"); "Music in the Theatre," unpublished lecture ("From music's"), MBP.

30. MB, "Towards a New Form," 218; "New Music: A Thumbnail History"; "Revaluations and Trends of Tomorrow," unpublished lecture (for Blitzstein's Piano Sonata), MBP.
31. "The Case for Modern Music: III."
32. MB, "Weill Scores for *Johnny Johnson*," *MM* 14/1 (November–December 1936): 44–46.
33. MB, "On Writing Music for the Theatre," *MM* 15/2 (January–February 1938): 81–85.
34. MB, "Scenery or No Scenery?" *Theatre Workshop* 2/1 (April–June 1938): 10–12.
35. MB, "Theatre Music," *MM* 17/3 (March–April 1940): 181–184.
36. MB, "Music and the People's Front," *Daily Worker* (April 13, 1938).
37. MB, "Books," *TAC* 1/8 (March 1939): 18.
38. LED, 22.

Chapter 8

1. The main theme of the first movement initially appears at measure 3; the two themes of the second movement, at measure 1 and one measure before rehearsal 14, respectively; and the three themes of the finale at, it seems, measure 1, one measure before rehearsal 24, and three measures after rehearsal 25, respectively.
2. EG, Journals, January 4, 1932 ("I had no idea"), January 18,1932 ("It is very"), January 22, 1932 ("the feeling," "It is no longer"), January 28, 1932 ("the sense"), MBP.
3. "Doch alles, was uns anrührt, dich und mich,/nimmt uns zusammen wie ein Bogen-strich,/der aus zwei Saiten eine Stimme zieht./Auf welches Instrument sind wir ges-pannt?/Und welcher Spieler hat uns in der Hand? O süsses Lied," flyleaf, *Serenade*, MBP.
4. EG, Journals, April 14, 1932, MBP.
5. EG, Journals, April 30, 1932, MBP.
6. EG, Journals, April 30, 1932, May 1, 1932, MBP.
7. LEH, 201; GOR, 75; Aaron Copland and Vivian Perlis, *Copland: 1900 Through 1942* (Boston: Faber and Faber, 1984), 193; Oscar Levant, *A Smattering of Ignorance* (New York: Doubleday, Doran, 1940), 224–225 (Levant writes, "I was delighted to discover that Copland was sufficiently human to put his own 'Variations' last on this program," whereas in fact, the work, a substitute for some Antheil piano music, appeared second-to-last); MB, "Pierrot Lunaire in Lindy's," *MM* 17/3 (March–April 1940): 196–197.
8. Levant, 243–246; MB to DD, February 17, 1942, DDC.
9. EG, Journals, May 2, 1932; "Composers' Conference—Yaddo," transcript, May 2 and 3, 1932, MBP; "Critics of Music Are Denounced By Composers," *New York Tribune* (May 2, 1932); Alfred H. Meyer, "Yaddo—A May Festival," *MM* 9/4 (May–June 1932): 172–176.
10. AC to MB, May 18, 1932; EG, Journals, March 25, 1932, MBP.
11. James M. Keller, "Americans in Paris," *Chamber Music* 26/5 (September–October 2009): 78–82.
12. Felix Frankfurter, *The Case of Sacco and Vanzetti: A Critical Analysis for Lawyers and Laymen* (New York: Grosset and Dunlap, 1927); *The Letters of Sacco and Vanzetti*, edited by Marion Denman Frankfurter and Gardner Jackson (New York: Viking, 1928; Penguin, 2007); Herbert B. Ehrmann, *The Untried Case: The Sacco-Vanzetti Case and the Morelli Gang* (New York: Vanguard, 1933); *The Sacco-Vanzetti Case. Transcript of the Record of the Trial of Nicola Sacco and Bartolomeo Vanzetti in the Courts of Massachusetts and Subsequent Proceedings 1920–7*, prefatory essay by William O. Douglas (Mama-roneck, NY: Paul P. Appel, 1969); William Young and David E. Kaiser, *Postmortem: New Evidence in the Case of Sacco and Vanzetti* (Amherst: University of Massachusetts Press, 1985); Francis Russell, *Sacco and Vanzetti: The Case Resolved* (New York: Harper & Row, 1986); Paul Avrich, *Sacco and Vanzetti: The Anarchist Background* (Princeton, NJ: Princeton University Press, 1991); *The Matter of Sacco and Vanzetti 1920–1927: testi-mony, motion and affidavits, the appeal, the committee and conclusion* (Minnetonka, MN: Professional Education Group, 1992); Michael M. Topp, *The Sacco and Vanzetti Case: A*

Brief History with Documents (New York: Palgrave Macmillan, 2005); Bruce Watson, *Sacco and Vanzetti: The Men, the Murders, and the Judgment of Mankind* (New York: Viking, 2007).

13. Malcolm Cowley, "Echoes of a Crime," *New Republic* 84/1082 (August 28, 1935): 79; G. Louis Joughin and Edmund M. Morgan, *The Legacy of Sacco and Vanzetti* (New York: Harcourt, Brace, 1948); Murray Kempton, *Part of Our Time: Some Ruins and Monuments of the Thirties* (New York: Simon & Schuster, 1955); John Dos Passos, *The Theme Is Freedom* (New York: Dodd, Mead, 1956); David Felix, *Protest: Sacco-Vanzetti and the Intellectuals* (Bloomington: Indiana University Press, 1965); Carolyn West Pace, *Sacco and Vanzetti in American Art and Music* (Ph.D. dissertation, Syracuse University, 1997); Moshik Temkin, *The Sacco-Vanzetti Affair: America on Trial* (New Haven, CT: Yale University Press, 2009).

14. BLI ("for farce"); for a complete list of Blitzstein's revolutionaries and martyrs, including original misspellings, see LEH, 202.

15. MB to JD, August 8–14, 1931, MBP ("variation"); BLI ("was influenced"); see also statements by Blitzstein that he "based" the work on Sacco and Vanzetti, "Who's Who in the Cast," *Playbill: The Cradle Will Rock* (March 28, 1938), MBP, and Robert James Dietz, *The Operatic Style of Marc Blitzstein in the American "Agit-Prop" Era* (Ph.D. dissertation, University of Iowa, 1970). 44; EG, Journals, November 28, 1932, MBP (for dedication).

16. "Respighi and D'Annunzio," unidentified clipping (March 13, 1932), MBP.

17. Pace, 104.

18. EG, Journals, September 14, 1932, MBP.

19. EG, Journals, April 18, 1932, MBP.

20. MB, "Notes on Production of *The Condemned*," MBP.

21. EG, Journals, July 1, 1932 ("hair-raising"), August 12, 1932 ("breath-taking"), November 1, 1932 ("I feel"); EG to her parents, October 11, 1932; EG, essay on Marc Blitzstein's music, 1933, MBP, an important document, might be excerpted more fully, as follows:

> The significance and intrinsic originality of Marc Blitzstein's music come primarily from the fact that its basic, and also most striking, characteristics are two qualities rarely combined: a radical mind and a very unusual gift for dramatic expression. . . . this fusion [of "intellectuality and the dramatic instinct"] . . . seems to take place so naturally because of another quality, which, both an inborn trait and a conscious goal, pervades all of Blitzstein's work: objectivity. This quality . . . means that the composer is more interested in fulfilling the requirements of a creation than he is in expressing himself. It means that he is not a romantic composer . . . although his interest in theatre music, in view of tradition, might lead one to think he would be; and it means that he is not, except incidentally, an introspective composer, although his concern with spiritual qualities might lead one to suppose he would be. . . . This objectivity is one reason why text and music are a compelling unity in Blitzstein's works for the theatre. . . . He does not comment on it [a dramatic situation], as a subjective composer might, but recreates it in music. . . . Blitzstein's spirit, however, . . . is completely lacking in academicism. It is intuitively of this age. . . . The closeness to our age comes home to the listener in an impression of asymmetry, that seems to reside subtly in the lines and more strikingly, more hauntingly too, in the harmonic color of Blitzstein's music. . . . Blitzstein may be called a "neo-classic" composer not only because he partakes of what we call the classical ideal and makes use of some classic procedures, but because his music makes us feel that it will be regarded as we regard the classics by future generations. . . . His melodic gift, the least prominent factor in his natural endowment, is just beginning to be developed out of a certain rigor which may have been a fear of too much expressiveness—a danger of the intent on objectivity. And the contrapuntal procedure . . . seems at times too unrelieved. . . . lyric warmth . . . is still largely missing from Blitzstein's music. . . . Radical musical departures . . . and a greater emotional range seem forecast in his work to complete its scope. . . . The characteristic

greatness of Blitzstein's music is there [in *The Condemned*]: its universally available combination of monumentality and drama; its individual statement of human elements; its purity, depth, and concentration of spirit; above all, its complete musicality. . . . at some time Blitzstein will write a great comic work in music stemming directly out of this great tragic work.

22. Nadia Boulanger to MB, July 21, 1932; MB to JD, September 6, 1932; MB to JD, October 29, 1932, MBP.
23. GOR, 80.
24. EG, Journals, September 21, 1932, September 29, 1932; EG to JD, September 20, 1932 ("I trust"); MB to JD, October 3, 1932; EG to her parents, October 11, 1932, MBP; Madelon Coates to Henry Allen Moe, December 19, 1932, GMF.
25. MB to JD, October 3, 1932, October 16, 1932 ("audition"); MB to Albert Coates, November 22, 1932; MB to EG, December 27, 1932; EG, Journals, January 9, 1933, MBP.
26. G. M. Beckett to MB, January 11, 1935; internal memos about *The Condemned*, the second dated May 31, 1935, and signed AB [Aylmer Buesst], both approved by OM [Owen Mase], BBC Written Archives Centre.
27. EG, Journals, August 1, 1935, MBP.
28. BRA, 172.
29. Charles Seeger, "On Dissonant Counterpoint," *MM* 7/4 (June–July 1930): 25–31; Mark D. Nelson, "In Pursuit of Charles Seeger's Heterophonic Ideal: Three Palindromic Works by Ruth Crawford," *Musical Quarterly* 72/4 (1986): 458–475; John D. Spilker, "The Origins of 'Dissonant Counterpoint': Henry Cowell's Unpublished Notebook," *Journal of the Society for American Music* 5/4 (November 2011): 481–533.
30. Elliott Carter, "Expressionism and American Music," *Perspectives of New Music* 4/1 (Fall–Winter 1965): 1–13; David Schiff, *The Music of Elliott Carter* (New York: Da Capo Press, 1986); Elliott Carter to EG, June 3, 1935, Elliott Carter Collection, Paul Sacher Foundation; Felix Meyer to author, August 6, 2008; MB to DD, July 17, 1942, DDC.
31. MB to JD, August 16, 1933, MBP.
32. EG, Journals, August 20, 1933, MBP.
33. "Modern Music Gay In Premiere Spree" (February 6, 1934), Urban Archives, Temple University Paley Library; EG, Journals, March 16, 1934, MBP.
34. EG to Lina Abarbanell, May 13, 1934; MB to EG [1934], MBP; GOR, 552 n32, noting the dedication "For Gene" in the orchestral score, also writes that Blitzstein seems at one point to have submitted the manuscript under the name Martin Eastman: "If so, then 'Gene' might have been substituted for Eva, as this was the protagonist's name in one of her autobiographical novels."
35. GOR, 90.
36. Susan Elliott, "A Commitment to Causes," *NYT* (October 9, 1988).
37. Elliott.
38. MB to EG, September 20, 1935, MBP; MB to Nicolas Slonimsky, December 16, 1935, Nicolas Slonimsky Collection, LC; program notes, *Orchestra Variations*, American Composers Orchestra (October 9, 1988), courtesy of the American Composers Orchestra.
39. Allan Kozinn, "Classical Music Meets Pop Culture In New Renditions and Revivals," *NYT* (October 7, 1988); reviews of the *Orchestra Variations* by Tim Page, *Newsday* ("dull," "entirely"), and Will Crutchfield, *NYT* ("purely") (both October 12, 1988); Peter G. Davis, *New York* (October 24, 1988) ("arid," "hopelessly"); Bill Zakariasen, *Daily News* (October 11, 1988).
40. Charles Seeger to MB, July 18, 1934, MBP.
41. Some drafts of these texts are catalogued in box 9/folder 1, MBP, that is, in a poetry file, rather than among the *Children's Cantata* material.
42. For communist-related books and pamphlets, see "Blitzstein Separations," MBP.

43. Carol J. Oja, "Marc Blitzstein's 'The Cradle Will Rock' and Mass-Song Styles of the 1930s," *Musical Quarterly* 73/4 (1989): 455; GOR, 92.

44. Minutes, Meeting of the Program Committee of the Composers' Collective, March 28, 1935, MBP; Louis Biancolli, "Young Composer Plays Own Work," *World-Telegram* (April 16, 1936).

45. Bennet Zurofsky, interview with author, August 18, 2008.

46. GOR, 227, 228.

47. MB, 1936 Guggenheim Fellowship Application Form, GMF; EG, Journals, March 4, 1935, August 1, 1935; AC to MB, August 23, 1935 (Blitzstein never destroyed this letter, as Copland requested); EG, Journals, August 30, 1935; Rutheda L. Pretzel to MB, August 20, 1935; Ruth Page to MB, September 27, 1935, undated; MB to Ruth Page, August 25, 1935, MBP.

48. Ruth Page, "American Woman," MBP.

49. EG, Journals, August 30, 1935; EG to Lina Abarbanell, August 26, 1935; Ruth Page to MB, September 27, 1935, MBP.

50. "The Chesapeake Bay Retriever," press release, Pedigreed Pictures, MBP.

51. Ashley Pettis, "The WPA and the American Composer," *Musical Quarterly* 26/1 (January 1940): 101–112; Melissa J. de Graaf, "The Records of the New York Composers' Forum: The Documentary Motive and Music in the 1930s," *Notes* 64/4 (June 2008): 688–701.

52. Biancolli; Colin McPhee, "New York's Spring Season, 1936," *MM* 13/4 (May–June 1936): 39–42.

53. Aaron Copland, "Our Younger Generation: Ten Years Later," *MM* 13/4 (May–June 1936): 3–11.

54. COP, 139–140.

Chapter 9

1. GOR, 59 (MB referred to "Looking for Love," the title in his sketches, as "Start in Lookin'" in his letter to Simon).

2. GOR, 59, 67; LEH, 186.

3. MB to EG, January 13, 1931; MB to EG, April 1, 1931, MBP.

4. Morgan Y. Himelstein, *Drama Was a Weapon: The Left-Wing Theatre in New York 1929–1941* (New Brunswick, NJ: Rutgers University Press, 1963); Gerald Rabkin, *Drama and Commitment: Politics in the American Theatre of the Thirties* (Bloomington: Indiana University Press, 1964); Malcolm Goldstein, *The Political Stage: American Drama and Theater of the Great Depression* (New York: Oxford University Press, 1974); Ira A. Levine, *Left-Wing Dramatic Theory in the American Theatre* (Ann Arbor: University of Michigan Press, 1980); R. C. Reynolds, *Stage Left: The Development of the American Social Drama in the Thirties* (Troy, NY: Whitston, 1986); Ilka Saal, *New Deal Theater: The Vernacular Tradition in American Political Theater* (New York: Palgrave Macmillan, 2007), 89.

5. Edwin F. Melvin, "Song, Dance Satire and Jimmy Savo," *Boston Evening Transcript* (May 7, 1935).

6. EG to MB, January 24, 1935, MBP.

7. Nathaniel Buchwald, "World of the Theatre," *Daily Worker* (May 25, 1935); Elliot Norton, "Jimmy Savo Proves a Hit at Colonial," *Boston Post* (May 7, 1935); Ethan Mordden, *Sing for Your Supper* (New York: Palgrave Macmillan, 2004), 184.

8. Eve Arden, *Three Phases of Eve: An Autobiography* (New York: St. Martin's Press, 1985), 34; "Send for the Militia," orchestral score, courtesy of Susanna Moross Tarjan.

9. Carol J. Oja, "Marc Blitzstein's 'The Cradle Will Rock' and Mass-Song Styles of the 1930s," *Musical Quarterly* 73/4 (1989): 445–475.

10. "Chronology of Activities, Compositions, and Writings of Marc Blitzstein from 1905 to 1942," MBP.

11. EG to Lina Abarbanell, May 23, 1935, May 31, 1935, August 26, 1935; EG, Journals, August 1, 1935 ("on the"), August 4, 1935 ("I think"), MBP.

12. "Stay in My Arms," lyric sheet, MBP; David Jenness and Don Velsey, *Classic American Popular Song: The Second Half-Century, 1950–2000* (New York: Routledge, 2006), 129.

13. Albert Maltz, "Man on a Road," *New Masses* 14/2 (January 8, 1935): 19–21.

14. "Domestic Disturbances," *Basic Field Manual*, Vol. 7, Part 3 (U.S. War Department: 1935), 12–29.

15. M.M., "Music: The Composers' Collective of New York," *Daily Worker* (March 5, 1936).

16. "Bolsheviki Held Eitingon Family," *NYT* (May 25, 1919); "Furs: End of the Boom," *Time* (December 30, 1946): 74, 79; "Motty Eitingon, Dealer in Furs," *NYT* (August 1, 1956); Lee E. Thompson (daughter of Motty by his first wife) to author, September 1, 2008; Philip S. Foner, *The Fur and Leather Workers Union: A Story Of Dramatic Struggles and Achievement* (Newark, NJ: Nordan Press, 1950), 102, 197, 200–203, 506.

17. MB to EG, September 18, 1935, September 20, 1935, MBP.

18. MB, "New York Medley, Winter, 1935," *MM* 13/2 (January–February 1936): 36.

19. GOR, 125; Kurt Weill, "Music in the Theatre," transcriptions and notes, courtesy of KWF; see also Elisabeth Schwind, "'Weill hasn't changed, I have': Zur Ästhetik des Komponisten Marc Blitzstein," *Kurt Weill-Studien*, Vol. 1, edited by Nils Grosch, Joachim Lucchesi, and Jürgen Schebera (Stuttgart: J. B. Metzler, 1996).

20. David Farneth, *Lenya: The Legend* (New York: Overlook Press, 1998), 96; see also LL, "*Few Little English*: A Forgotten Song by Marc Blitzstein for Lenya," *Kurt Weill Newsletter* 15/2 (Fall 1997): 8–12.

21. MB to Kurt Weill, June 22, 1936, KWF; MB, "Weill Scores for *Johnny Johnson*," *MM* 14/1 (November–December 1936): 44–46.

22. Farneth, 96; *Speak Low (When You Speak Love): The Letters of Kurt Weill and Lotte Lenya*, trans. and edited by Lys Symonette and Kim H. Kowalke (Berkeley: University of California Press, 1996), 257, 267, 357 ("I would").

23. BLI ("Why don't"); Arthur Pollock, "Man Floating at Majorca Comes Out With 'Regina,'" *The Sunday Compass* (October 30, 1949); HAL; LED. In 1964, Lederman recalled that Blitzstein played "Nickel Under the Foot" for Brecht (LED), but Blitzstein clearly stated in 1962 that Brecht "listened to a sketch to music I had written involving a prostitute, a cop and a gent" (BLI). *Sketch No. 1* also fits more assuredly both in terms of chronology— Blitzstein wrote the *Sketch* in the fall of 1935—and in terms of varied references to the theme of "prostitution." That "Nickel Under the Foot" has an introduction that recapitulates the opening of the *Sketch* might have contributed to this misremembrance on Lederman's part.

24. MB to John Houseman, November 12, 1959, MBP; Robert Reinhart, "Borscht Alumni's Clicks," *Variety* (December 8, 1937); Irving Bassow, "City College Presents 'Cradle Will Rock' Tonight," *Daily Worker* (November 29, 1940); MB, "Of 'No For An Answer,'" *NYT* (January 5, 1941).

25. Gus's dialogue and music suggest that he might be Jewish as well as Polish; David T. Little, *The Critical Composer: Political Music During and After "The Revolution"* (Ph.D. dissertation, Princeton, 2011), 66–67, argues that Harry Druggist, to judge from his music, his reference to King Solomon, and John Houseman's conception of the part for the 1983 revival of the opera by the Acting Company, might be nonnative or Jewish as well, adding, "if Druggist *is* in fact of Eastern European decent [sic] like Gus Polock, then [t]he scene becomes even more tragic and politically charged, as one immigrant turns against another for a shot at the so-called American Dream."

26. Philip S. Klein and Ari Hoogenboom, *A History of Pennsylvania* (University Park: Pennsylvania State University Press, 1980), 462.

27. GOR, 131.

28. MB, *The Cradle Will Rock: A Play in Music* (New York: Random House, 1938), 148–149; *The Cradle Will Rock* (piano-conductor score) (New York: Tams-Witmark, 1938), 178 ("all the").

29. George Wolfskill, *The Revolt of the Conservatives: A History of the American Liberty League, 1934–1940* (Westport, CT: Greenwood Press, 1974); "Many Deaths Laid To 'Black Legion'; Klan Link Charged," *NYT* (May 24, 1936); "Black Legion Oath Has Pledge to Kill," *NYT* (May 26, 1936); John N. Ingham, *Biographical Dictionary of American Business Leaders A–G* (Westport, CT: Greenwood Press, 1983), 466.

30. Stephen H. Norwood, *Strikebreaking and Intimidation: Mercenaries and Masculinity in Twentieth-Century America* (Chapel Hill: University of North Carolina Press, 2002), 15–33; Walter P. Metzger, *Academic Freedom in the Age of the University* (New York: Columbia University Press, 1955); GOR, 132.

31. MB, "On Writing Music for the Theatre," *MM* 15/2 (January–February 1938): 81–85; Arthur Bronson, "Blitzstein To Rock The Cradle Again," *Philadelphia Record* (February 16, 1941).

32. MB, "Author of 'The Cradle' Discusses Broadway Hit," *Daily Worker* (January 3, 1938); HAL; MB, *The Cradle (A Play)*, 106–107; "Steel and the Middle Class," *New Masses* 20/4 (July 21, 1936): 3.

33. MB, "Lines on 'The Cradle,'" *NYT* (January 2, 1938); MB, "On Writing."

34. MB, "Author"; MB, "On Writing."

35. Henry Cowell, "In Time of Bitter War," *MM* 19/2 (January–February 1942): 84; Lynn Mally, "Inside a Communist Front: A Post-Cold War Analysis of the New Theatre League," *American Communist History* 6/1 (2007): 65–95; Lynn Mally, "The Americanization of the Soviet Living Newspaper," *Carl Beck Papers* no. 1903 (February 2008): 1–40.

36. BLI ("the first"); LED, 21 ("Have you"); see also LL, letter to the editor, *Kurt Weill Newsletter* 8/1 (Spring 1990): 6.

37. TAL, 43; John D. Shout, "The Musical Theater of Marc Blitzstein," *American Music* 3/4 (Winter 1985): 418; Saal, 111–123.

38. COP, 141; LEH, 212; LL to author, February 18, 2011, points in particular to the connection between the opening phrase of Moross's verse, "I'm sick and tired of living this way," and the phrase "Mobs develop from crowds" from "War Department Manual," and "Oh, you can live like Hearts-and-Flowers" from "Nickel Under the Foot."

39. John Gruen, *Close-Up* (New York: Viking Press, 1968), 169–170 (and Gruen, "Conversation with Marc Blitzstein," a slight variant, LHC).

40. BLI.

41. Little, 72–74.

42. MB, *The Cradle (A Play)*, 46, 71, 73; for Blitzstein's working method, see "Marc Blitzstein's 'The Guests' To Premiere This Thursday," *New York Star* (January 17, 1949), and MB, *Marc Blitzstein and his Theatre Compositions* (Westminster Spoken Arts 717, 1956).

43. The day after the work's premiere, Julian Seaman, "Music," *Daily Mirror* (June 17, 1937), reported that Blitzstein planned to use a Hammond organ for the presumed upcoming run of *The Cradle*; for Blitzstein's thoughts on the accordion, see Elsie M. Bennett, "An Interview with Marc Blitzstein," *A.A.A. News* 3/3 (July 1952): 3–4.

44. HAL; MB, "Lines On"; Eric Salzman, "No Longer Bare," *NYT* (February 7, 1960).

45. MB, "Lines On."

Chapter 10

1. Some of the more important sources concerning the first production of *The Cradle Will Rock* include Wilella Waldorf, "'The Cradle Will Rock' a Fugitive From the WPA," *New York Evening Post* (June 22, 1937); Wolfe Kaufman, "Actors and Audiences All Mixed Up As WPA Opera Goes Commercial," *Variety* (June 23, 1937); "So This Is Broadway," *World-Telegram* (June 25, 1937); Philip Barr, "Opera in the Vernacular," *Magazine of Art* 32/6 (June 1939): 356–357, 382–383; Hallie Flanagan, *Arena: The History of the Federal Theatre* (New York: Benjamin Blom, 1940, 1965); Hallie Flanagan Davis to MB, March 5, 1947,

MBP; MB, *Marc Blitzstein and his Theatre Compositions* (Westminster Spoken Arts 717, 1956); MB to John Houseman, November 12, 1959, MBP; MB, "Out of the Cradle," *Opera News* 24/15 (February 13, 1960): 10–11, 29; MB, "As He Remembered It," *NYT* (April 12, 1964, adapted from *Marc Blitzstein and his Theatre Compositions*); Robert James Dietz, *The Operatic Style of Marc Blitzstein in the American "Agit-Prop" Era* (Ph.D. dissertation, University of Iowa, 1970); John Houseman, *Run-Through: A Memoir* (New York: Simon & Schuster, 1972); Lehman Engel, *This Bright Day: An Autobiography* (New York: Macmillan, 1974); J. E. Vacha, "The Case of the Runaway Opera: The Federal Theatre and Marc Blitzstein's *The Cradle Will Rock*," *New York History* 62/2 (April 1981): 133–152; Barbara Leaming, *Orson Welles: A Biography* (New York: Viking, 1983); GOR; Barry B. Witham, "Backstage at *The Cradle Will Rock*," *Theatre History Studies* 12 (1992): 213–219; Simon Callow, *Orson Welles: The Road to Xanadu* (London: Jonathan Cape, 1995). These and many other sources contain numerous inconsistences, in large part because the seminal accounts by Blitzstein and John Houseman differ in many of their details. Neglected contemporary newspaper accounts help resolve some of these inconsistencies, but many remain.

2. MB, "Out of," 10; Houseman, 245.

3. Flanagan, 194–195; William Morrison, *Broadway Theatres: History & Architecture* (Mineola, NY: Dover, 1999) (the principal source for the number of seats in Broadway theaters cited in this book); Norman Lloyd, interview with Gary Rutkowski, September 7, 2000 (Archive of American Television, online video removed by the user).

4. Flanagan, 201; MB to JD, March 1, 1937, MBP.

5. Houseman, 175.

6. MB to JD, March 26, 1937, March 27, 1937, MBP; Houseman, 247.

7. MB to JD, February 26, 1937; MB to John Houseman, November 12, 1959; Houseman put the orchestra personnel at twenty-eight, Houseman, 254, 274.

8. Engel, 81; photographs of rehearsals of *The Cradle*, Federal Theatre Project Collection, Music Division, LC (for Yates); for MB's weekly salary, GOR, 138, reports $23.86, MB, "As He Remembered," $28; Michael Tilson Thomas claimed that his father helped bring the opera to Welles's attention, Royal S. Brown, "An Interview with Michael Tilson Thomas," *Fanfare* 19/4 (March–April 1996): 34, although Blitzstein had other shared contacts, including Copland, Thomson, and Edwin Denby; Leaming simply reports that Blitzstein went backstage after a performance of *Horse Eats Hat* to show Welles his score (130).

9. Leaming, 130, 132, 133.

10. Orson Welles, *The Cradle Will Rock: An Original Screenplay*, edited by James Pepper, with an afterword by Jonathan Rosenbaum (Santa Barbara, CA: Saint Teresa Press, 1994), 18, 112, 121.

11. Studs Terkel, *Hard Times: An Oral History of the Great Depression* (New York: Pantheon, 1970) ("We worked"), 365.

12. Houseman, 248; Leaming, 132; for some of Schruers's stage designs, see "Scenic Sketches for *The Cradle Will Rock*," *MM* 14/4 (May–June 1937): 229 (note misspelled name).

13. MB to JD, June 2, 1937, MBP; Flanagan, 202; Hallie Davis to MB, March 5, 1947.

14. "Steel Strike Opera Is Put Off By WPA," *NYT* (June 17, 1937); Hallie Davis to MB, March 5, 1947.

15. Charles E. Dexter, "New Rule Stops Production Of WPA Shows and Musicals," *Daily Worker* (June 17, 1937); MB, "Out of," 10.

16. Houseman, 255–256 ("demons"); Vacha ("equally," "If"), 139–140.

17. Waldorf lists theaters that had to be ruled out because they were nonunion, closed for the summer, in disrepair, or too expensive; Houseman, 259, mentions the difficulty of reaching theater owners as well as the unwillingness of theater owners to open a house for so brief an engagement; MB, "As He Remembered"; Houseman, 260.

18. Jean Rosenthal remembered little aside from riding "round and round it [the garment district] on that truck, waiting for Orson majestically to solve everything," Rosenthal and Lael Wertenbaker, *The Magic of Light* (Boston: Little, Brown, 1972), 18; Engel, 81,

claimed that Blitzstein's own piano was procured for the performance; contemporary accounts mention five firemen, but Houseman and later commentators say four.

19. Houseman, 263–265; MB, "Out of," 11.

20. Engel, 84; MB, "Out of," 11; Terkel, 366, quotes Sherman as saying, "You couldn't find them [fellow actors]. We were in different parts of the house."

21. Houseman, 268–269 (Houseman, 266, puts the curtain time at 9:05, but newspaper accounts say 9:45); MB remembered the evening as a "hot night," and it might have felt that way on stage, but the temperature that day had reached a high of only 78 degrees Fahrenheit.

22. MB, "As He Remembered"; Barr ("There is"); MB, "Out of" ("Not a hitch"); GOR, 144; Herbert Drake, "The Stage," *Cue* (June 26, 1937): 14 (for piccolo); Kaufman.

23. Houseman, 273–274; MB, "As He Remembered."

24. MB, *Marc Blitzstein and his Theatre Compositions* (Houseman, 272, says that MacLeish spoke during intermission); Archibald MacLeish, "Behind the Fourth Wall," *Stage* 15/4 (January 1938): 68–69; MacLeish, "Foreword," *The Cradle Will Rock* (New York: Random House, 1938): 5–11; for a rebuttal, see Deems Taylor, "The Audience *is* the Fourth Wall," *Stage* 15/5 (February 1938): 46–47; Welles, 111.

25. Virgil Thomson, "In the Theatre," *MM* 14/4 (May–June 1937): 237; Charles E. Dexter, "Does 'Cradle Will Rock' Ban Mean WPA Censorship," *Daily Worker* (June 18, 1937); Kaufman.

26. Witham.

27. Houseman, 266; Waldorf; WEVD broadcast the opera on June 26 and 27, and July 3, 1937.

28. "Show Goes On," [Pontiac, MI] *Press* (June 21, 1937) ("There has"); MB, "Scenery or No Scenery?" *Theatre Workshop* 2/1 (April–June 1938): 12.

29. John Harkins, "'Cradle Will Rock' Goes Big As U.S. Project 'Rebel' Play," *New York American* (June 22, 1937); Waldorf.

30. Houseman, 276; Howard Rushmore, "Our Show Will Go On, This Cast Tells Public," *Daily Worker* (June 30, 1937).

31. Hallie Davis to MB, March 5, 1947.

32. "W.P.A. Troupe Gives Opera at C.I.O. Picnic," *NYHT* (July 11, 1937); Louise Mitchell, "'Cradle Will Rock' Company Shows Play to Steel Workers," *Daily Worker* (July 14, 1937) ("We all"); Hiram Sherman offered an entirely different and presumably less reliable account of the Bethlehem performance from a distance of many years, Terkel, 366–367.

33. Most sources report a total run of 104 performances, which seems accurate given the opera's thirteen-week run from January 3 onward, although "News of the Stage," *NYT* (April 2, 1938) reported the total as 123, a discrepancy apparently due to the inclusion of pre-Windsor performances.

34. Leonard Lyons, "Lyons Den," *Post* (March 30, 1938); Robert Sylvester, "Six B'way Showmen Fight to Rock the 'Cradle' for Cash," *Daily News* (November 12, 1947), also puts the number of musicians at ten, although Houseman, 335–336, says that the Windsor needed to hire twelve musicians and a conductor.

35. Virgil Thomson, "In the Theatre," *MM* 15/2 (January–February 1938): 112–114; "He Was Six Men And Still Prefers To Be Blitzstein," *NYHT* (March 5, 1938); Houseman, 335.

36. Reviews of *The Cradle Will Rock* by Brooks Atkinson, *NYT*; John Mason Brown, *Post*; Burns Mantle, *Daily News* (all December 6, 1937); *Time* (December 13, 1937); Richard Watts Jr., *NYHT* (December 19, 1937); R. D. Darrell, *New Masses* (December 28, 1937); John W. Gassner, *One Act Play Magazine* (December 1937); Leonard Liebling, *Musical Courier* (January 1, 1938); Eleanor Flexner, *New Masses* (January 18, 1938); Stark Young, *New Republic* (January 19, 1938); Edith J. R. Isaacs, *Theatre Arts Monthly* (February 1938); Euphemia Wyatt, *Catholic World* (February 1938); Paul Rosenfeld, *MM* (March–April 1938); Irving Kolodin, *Theatre Arts Monthly* (October 1938); Barr; see also LEH, 230–249.

37. Rosenfeld; Thomson (1937); Barr; Alistair Cooke, transcript of his January 12, 1938, WEAF broadcast, MBP; Morgan Y. Himelstein, *Drama Was a Weapon: The Left-Wing Theatre in New York 1929–1941* (New Brunswick, NJ: Rutgers University Press, 1963), 117–118.

38. Thomson (1938); Liebling.

39. George Jean Nathan, "Labor Pains," *New York City News-Week* (January 3, 1938); Nathan, "Theater," *Scribner's* 103 (March 1938): 70–71 ("little more"); Mary McCarthy, *Mary McCarthy's Theatre Chronicles 1937–1962* (New York: Noonday Press, 1956), 23–26.

40. Samuel Lipman, *Arguing for Music/Arguing for Culture* (Boston: David R. Godine, 1990), 157–163; Barbara Rumney, "The Cradle Will Rock," [Sarah Lawrence] *Campus* (November 4, 1937); Virginia Kleitz, "Blitzstein's Coming Play Concerned With Students," *Campus* (March 14, 1938); Sybil Graham [Goldsmith], "Poison in the Theater," and also Barbara Rumney and Graham, "On the Fence," *Campus* (March 21, 1938); COP, 142–143; *The Collected Works of Harold Clurman*, edited by Marjorie Loggia and Glenn Young (New York: Applause, 1994), 103.

41. Aaron Copland, "Scores and Records," *MM* 15/3 (March–April 1938): 180.

42. *The Cradle Will Rock* (Musicraft Records BM 321-GM334, 1938), reissued as *Marc Blitzstein's The Cradle Will Rock* (American Legacy Records T 1001, 1964) and *Marc Blitzstein: Musical Theatre Premières* (Pearl/Pavilion Records GEMS 0009, 1998); Roy Gregg, "The Phonograph Rocks the Cradle," *New Masses* 27/9 (May 24, 1938): 29–31.

43. MB, "Income Tax Return—1938," MBP, indicating $7,380.46 income and $3,025.04 total expenses, leaving about $4,000.

44. BAL (only scenes from *The Cradle Will Rock* seem to have been presented on the Labor Stage in early 1939, "The Week's Opening," *NYT* [February 5, 1939]); LB, remarks, "Composers' Showcase: A Marc Blitzstein Tribute In Honor of His Eightieth Birthday," archival tape (April 28, 1985), courtesy of Brent Oldham; Drew Massey, "Leonard Bernstein and the Harvard Student Union: In Search of Political Origins," *Journal of the Society for American Music* 3/1 (February 2009): 67–84; LB presumably presented at most an abbreviated faculty room scene, as the program credits a Professor Scoot, but no Mamie or Trixie, unless LB assumed those parts himself.

45. "City Councilman Sullivan Asks For Police Investigation of Play," *Harvard Crimson* (June 9, 1939); reviews of *The Cradle Will Rock* by Elliot Norton, *Boston Post* (May 28, 1939), and Moses Smith, *Boston Evening Transcript* (May 29, 1939).

46. LB, "Tribute to Marc Blitzstein," *Findings* (New York: Simon & Schuster, 1982), 223–224 (see also LB, "Marc Blitzstein Remembered," program, Marc Blitzstein Memorial Concert [April 19, 1964], LBC); LB, remarks; MB to LB, June 2, 1939, MBP.

47. MB to MC, July 12, 1951, MCC; Helga Dudman, "Sacco and Vanzetti at Beit Yannai," *Jerusalem Post* (August 26, 1962) ("We are"); MB to DD, March 20, 1952, DDC; Burton Bernstein and Barbara B. Haws, *Leonard Bernstein: American Original* (New York: Collins, 2008), 153–154; MB, marginalia, *Trouble in Tahiti*, MBP; Vivian Perlis, interview with LB, 1983, Oral History of American Music, Yale University (MB mentions only an "American folk-tune," but LB sings the jarabe melody in 5/8, which fits the names); see also LEH, 19, and GOR, 421.

48. LEH, 19 ("We were"), 556; MB to DD, March 20, 1952, DDC; MB to LB, August 15, 1952, August 31, 1954, LBC; *Readings on* West Side Story, edited by Mary E. Williams (San Diego: Greenhaven Press, 2001), 42.

49. Eric Gordon, interview with LB, August 18, 1981, LBC ("very happy," "the most"); MB to MC, August 24, 1951, MCC.

50. MB to LB, August 31, 1954, LBC; MB, "American Opera Today," unpublished draft, MBP; MB to DD, March 20, 1952, July 29, 1956, DDC; MB to MC, March 27, 1952, February 24, 1953, MCC.

51. LB, tribute to MB, *Proceedings*, second series, 15 (New York: American Academy of Arts and Letters and the National Institute of Arts and Letters, 1965), 479–480; *Findings*, 224–226; Eric Gordon, interview with LB, April 24, 1987, LBC.

52. BAL; Wallingford Riegger, "'The Airborne,'" *New Masses* (April 16, 1946): 26–27; for more on borrowings from Blitzstein, see GOR, 364, 431, and Jack Gottlieb, *Working with Bernstein: A Memoir* (New York: Amadeus, 2010), 137, 399.

53. MEL, 414–437; David Jenness and Don Velsey, *Classic American Popular Song: The Second Half-Century, 1950–2000* (New York: Routledge, 2006), 130; ROR, 205.

54. Arthur Bronson, "Paul Robeson Sings at Academy," *Philadelphia Record* (March 8, 1941); GOR, 415.

55. Arthur Bronson, "'Cradle' Scores Again As Done by Bernstein And N.Y. City Symp," *Variety* (November 26, 1947), mentioned an orchestra of twenty-four, but "The Cradle Still Rocks," *Newsweek* (December 8, 1947): 78, put the figure at twenty-eight; see also MB, "Opera's History," *NYT* (November 23, 1947).

56. Thomson, "In the Theatre" (1937); reviews of *The Cradle Will Rock* by Louis Biancolli, *World-Telegram*; John Briggs, *Post*; Olin Downes, *NYT*; Irving Kolodin, *Sun*; Virgil Thomson, *NYHT*; Douglas Watt, *Daily News* (all November 25, 1947); Robert A. Hague, *PM* (November 26, 1947); Robert A. Simon, *New Yorker* (December 6, 1947); R. S. [Robert Sabin], *Musical America* (December 15, 1947); Cecil Smith, *New Republic* (December 22, 1947); see also LEH, 259–261.

57. Louis Calta, "'Cradle Will Rock' May Resolve Row," *NYT* (December 2, 1947); Louis Calta, "'Cradle' Sponsors Arrive At Accord," *NYT* (December 4, 1947); Sam Zolotow, "Mansfield To Get 'Cradle Will Rock,'" *NYT* (December 26, 1947) ("political friends").

58. Reviews of *The Cradle Will Rock* by Brooks Atkinson, *NYT*; Ward Morehouse, *Sun*; Robert Sylvester, *Daily News*; Richard Watts Jr., *Post* (all December 27, 1947); George Freedley, *Morning Telegraph*, and Howard Barnes, *NYHT* (both December 29, 1947); O. V. Clyde, *Daily Worker* (December 30, 1947); John Chapman, *Daily News* (January 1, 1948); Wolcott Gibbs, *New Yorker* (January 10, 1948); George Jean Nathan, *Journal-American* (January 12, 1948); John Mason Brown, *Saturday Review* (January 17, 1948); Harold Schonberg, *Musical Digest* (March 1948); see also LEH, 262–266.

59. Bert McCord, "News of the Theater," *NYHT* (December 30, 1947).

60. Elliott J. Pleze, "'The Cradle Will Rock' Thrills Large Audience," *Miami Times* (June 3, 1950); H. G. Sear, "Driving it Home," *Daily Worker* (July 3, 1951); R. S., "'The Cradle Will Rock' (Unity Theatre)," *Hatfield and Potters Bar Gazette* (June 29, 1951); see also LEH, 266–268.

61. GOR, 465; Eric Salzman, "No Longer Bare," *NYT* (February 7, 1960).

62. Reviews of *The Cradle Will Rock* by Harriett Johnson, *Post*; Miles Kastendieck, *Journal-American*; Paul Henry Lang, *NYHT*; Howard Taubman, *NYT*; Douglas Watt, *Post* (all February 12, 1960), Goth., *Variety* (February 17, 1960), Winthrop Sargeant, *New Yorker* (February 20, 1960); C.E.R. [Curtis E. Rice], *Musical Courier* (March 1960); R. E. [Richard Eyer], *Musical America* (March 1960); F.M. [Frank Merkling], *Opera News*, and Harold Clurman, *Nation* (both March 12, 1960); Richard RePass, *Opera* (May 1960); see also Howard Taubman, "Embattled Period," *NYT* (February 21, 1960), and Paul Henry Lang, "Naturalistic Opera And Its Problems," *NYHT* (April 3, 1960); Harold Prince to MB, February 21, 1960; MB to George Freedley, February 19, 1960, George Freedley Collection, NYPL.

63. Clurman.

64. LEH, 278–302.

65. Robert Leiter, "A New Look at The 'Cradle' That Rocked Broadway," *NYT* (May 1, 1983).

66. Reviews of *The Cradle Will Rock* by Herbert Hupferberg, *NYHT*, and Lewis Funke, *NYT* (both November 9, 1964); Andrew Porter, *New Yorker* (May 29, 1978); Edith Oliver, *New Yorker* (May 23, 1983); Irving Wardle, *London Times* (August 15, 1985); Anthony Tommasini, *NYT* (February 10, 2009); Lipman; see also Eric Bentley, "Comedy and the Comic Spirit in America," *The American Theater Today*, edited by Alan S. Downer (New York: Basic Books, 1967), 50–59, and Andrew Porter, "Thalia," *New Yorker* (June 6, 1983): 112.

67. BAL; *The Cradle Will Rock* [Theater Four] (MGM E 4289–2 OC, 1965, reissued, CRI SD 266, 1972); *The Cradle Will Rock* [The Acting Company] (Jay Records CDJAY 1300, 1985, 1999); *The Cradle Will Rock* [Blank Theatre Company] (Lockett Palmer Recordings

LPR 940411, 1994, 1995); *Marc Blitzstein and his Theatre Compositions*; John S. Wilson, "'Cradle' Wins Again," *NYT* (March 28, 1965).

68. Leaming, 512–514; Richard Trainor, "O'Connor, Lowry, Huston and Welles," *Sight and Sound* 54/1 (Winter 1984): 31–33; Welles; Jonathan Rosenbaum, *Discovering Orson Welles* (Berkeley: University of California Press, 2007), 84–85, 188–200; David C. Paul, "Censorship and the Politics of Reception: The Filmic Afterlife of Marc Blitzstein's *The Cradle Will Rock*," *The Oxford Handbook of Music and Censorship*, edited by Patricia Hall (New York: Oxford University Press, forthcoming), and notes about the Lardner screenplay, both courtesy of David Paul.

69. Tim Robbins, *Cradle Will Rock: The Movie and The Moment* (New York: Newmarket, 2000), 133; Ted Stanton, "The True 'Toddy,'" *NYT* (December 26, 1999); Ted Stanton, interview with author, January 23, 2009; Olive Stanton, "Householder," *New Yorker* (November 21, 1936); Janet Maslin, "Panoramic Passions On a Playbill from the 30's," *NYT* (December 8, 1999); Jason Sherman, "Playwright's Notes," *It's All True* (Toronto: Playwrights Canada Press, 2000), n.p.

70. Michael Denning, *The Cultural Front: The Laboring of American Culture in the Twentieth Century* (New York: Verso, 1996), 285; Joseph P. Swain, *The Broadway Musical: A Critical and Musical Survey* (New York: Oxford University Press, 1990), 12; Ethan Mordden, *Sing For Your Supper* (New York: Palgrave Macmillan, 2005), 180; Gerald Weales, "The Cradle Still Rocks," *The Reporter* 30/11 (May 21, 1964): 46, 48–50; BAL (for Da Silva and Copland); H. Wiley Hitchcock, *Music in the United States: A Historical Introduction*, third edition (Englewood Cliffs, NJ: Prentice Hall, 1969, 1988), 227; Geoffrey Block, *Enchanted Evenings: The Broadway Musical from* Show Boat *to* Sondheim (New York: Oxford University Press, 1997), 132. Chris Hedges, *Death of the Liberal Class* (New York: Nation Books, 2010); Erin Scialabba, "Clash of The Classes," [Syracuse University] *Daily Orange* (October 4, 2011).

71. Howard Da Silva (BAL) and Lehman Engel (Engel, 85), both of whom knew the original FTP production, expressed a preference for unadorned stagings, a line of thought picked up by Callow, who reported on negative reactions of the cast to the original sets (294) and concluded, "*The Cradle Will Rock* is too slight a piece to have survived all the genius Welles was eager to lavish upon it" (302); on the other hand, Charles Dexter (June 18, 1937), virtually the only critic to actually review the FTP dress rehearsal, thought the production the best thing about the show.

Chapter 11

1. Joris Ivens to Contemporary Historians, July 15, 1937, European Foundation Joris Ivens; premiere program, *The Spanish Earth* (August 20, 1937), MBP; Stanley Weintraub, *The Last Great Cause: The Intellectuals and the Spanish Civil War* (New York: Weybright and Talley, 1968); Joris Ivens, *The Camera and I* (New York: International, 1969); William Alexander, *Film on the Left: American Documentary Film From 1931 to 1942* (Princeton, NJ: Princeton University Press, 1981); Hans Schoots, *Living Dangerously: A Biography of Joris Ivens* (Amsterdam: Amsterdam University Press, 2000).

2. Ivens, 104–106 (for original scenario), 131, 136 ("My only").

3. Virgil Thomson, *Virgil Thomson* (New York: Da Capo Press, 1966), 254.

4. Ivens, 125, 129; Thomson, 274; William Washabaugh, *Flamenco: Passion, Politics and Popular Culture* (Washington, D.C.: Berg, 1996) 27n3, 46.

5. Thomson, 274; George Antheil, "On the Hollywood Front," *MM* 15/4 (May–June 1938): 251–254.

6. Ivens, 126, 129 (the text reads "phases" [126] as opposed to "phrases"); Ivens also stated that Blitzstein selected the recordings "with the assistance of Virgil Thomson," 129.

7. Carol A. Hess, "Competing Utopias? Musical Ideologies in the 1930s and Two Spanish Civil War Films," *Journal of the Society for American Music* 2/3 (August 2008): 319–354; "Air Raid Siren Halts Showing of War Film," *NYT* (April 25, 1938).

8. Ivens, 129, 131n.

9. Reviews of *The Spanish Earth* by David Platt, *Daily Worker* (August 20, 1937); Howard Barnes, *NYHT* (August 21, 1937); Peter Ellis, *New Masses* (August 24, 1937); see also Ivens, 132–137.

10. Alexander, 158; Ivens, 135.

11. Noel Straus, "Composers Unite," *NYT* (September 22, 1940) (for Arrow Press); Susan Richardson, *Defining a Place for Composers: The Early Histories of the American Composers Alliance and the American Music Center, 1937–1950* (Ph.D. dissertation, University of Indiana, 1997).

12. Contract between MB and Columbia Artists, August 12, 1937, MBP.

13. Davidson Taylor, "Why Not the Air?" *MM* 15/2 (January–February 1938): 86–91; Bradley Howard Short, *American Radio Opera: 1928–1971* (M.A. thesis, University of North Carolina at Chapel Hill, 1986); Margaret Susan Key, *"Sweet Melody Over Silent Wave": Depression-Era Radio and the American Composer* (Ph.D. dissertation, University of Maryland, 1995).

14. Paul Bowles, *Without Stopping* (New York: Putnam, 1972), 190 (Leonard Lyons remembered the event somewhat differently, undated article, MPB); Paul Rosenfeld, "Thanks to the International Guild: A Musical Chronicle," *By Way of Art* (New York: Coward-McCann, 1928), 14 (for chicken salad).

15. MB, "On Writing Music for the Theatre," *MM* 15/2 (January–February 1938): 82.

16. Norman Lloyd, interviewed by Francine Parker, *Stages: Norman Lloyd* (Metuchen, NJ: Scarecrow, 1990), 52; "Radio Programs Scheduled for Broadcast This Week," *NYT* (October 24, 1937); reviews of *I've Got the Tune* by Ben Gross, *Daily News*, and Irving Kolodin, *The Sun* (both October 25, 1937); *Radio Daily* (October 27, 1937); Robert Reinhart, *Variety* (October 27, 1937); *Time* (November 1, 1937); R. D. Darrell, *New Masses* (November 9, 1937, and November 30, 1937); Aaron Copland, *MM* (November–December 1938); Richard Gilbert, *Scribner's* 103 (January 1938), MBP.

17. Darrell (November 9, 1937); Gilbert; Copland.

18. Martin McCall, "Concert of Contemporary Music Proves Huge Success," *Daily Worker* (February 10, 1938); Howard Taubman, "Music in Review," *NYT* (February 7, 1938); "New Theatre League," *Variety* (February 23, 1938).

19. *The Marc Blitzstein Centennial Concert CD* (Original Cast Records OC 6127, 2005).

20. Harry Goldman, "When Social Significance Hit Broadway," *Theatre Quarterly* 7/28 (1977): 25–42; MB, "Theatre Music," *MM* 17/3 (March–April 1940): 181–184; Virgil Thomson, "In the Theatre," *MM* 15/2 (January–February 1938): 14.

21. Goldman; N.C., "Somebody had Given the Revised 'Pins' the Needles," *Daily Worker* (November 30, 1939); Michael Denning, *The Cultural Front: The Laboring of American Culture in the Twentieth Century* (New York: Verso, 1996), 295–309; Ilka Saal, *New Deal Theater: The Vernacular Tradition in American Political Theater* (New York: Palgrave Macmillan, 2007), 136–149.

22. MB, "Federal Theatre Project Plowed Under," courtesy of Eric Gordon; see also ILGWU Collection, Kheel Center for Labor Management Documentation and Archives, Cornell University.

23. John Mason Brown, "An Exciting Week-End for Propagandist Drama," *Post* (December 6, 1937); Heywood Broun, "It Seems to Me," *World-Telegram* (January 6, 1938, February 17, 1938); "Theatre: Two-a-Night," *Time* (March 14, 1938): 32 (for Roosevelt).

24. "20,000 Pack Garden to Salute Soviet," *NYT* (November 14, 1937).

25. "20,000."

26. Program, *One-Sixth of the Earth* (November 13, 1937), MBP; "Communist Group to Give Play," *NYT* (October 17, 1937); "Local news," *Post* (October 15, 1937), MBP; MB, "Moscow Metro," MBP (catalogued with music from *Regina*).

27. Virginia Kleitz, "Blitzstein's Coming Play Concerned With Students," [Sarah Lawrence] *Campus* (March 14, 1938); *Red Channels: The Report of Communist Influence in Radio and Television* (New York: American Business Consultants, 1950), 20 (for Browder);

"Hearings before the Committee on Un-American Activities" (May 8, 1958), and other documents, MBH.

28. Max Shachtman, "The Stalinist Convention," *New International* 4/7 (July 1938): 202–205; "Communists Show Bourgeois Tastes," *NYT* (June 2, 1938).

29. "Hearings."

30. "Hearings"; *Red Channels*, 20–23.

31. Eugene Lyons, *The Red Decade: The Stalinist Penetration of America* (New York: Bobbs-Merrill, 1941), 245–250; "Leading Artists, Educators Support Soviet Trial Verdict," *Daily Worker* (April 28, 1938).

32. Eugene Lyons, 246–250; "Back USSR Peace Stand, Say 400 U.S. Notables," *Daily Worker* (August 14, 1939); see also "To All Active Supporters of Democracy and Peace," *Soviet Russia Today* 8/5 (September 1939): 24–25, 28.

33. Harold Denny, "Wide Plot Shown By Moscow Trials," *NYT* (March 14, 1938); Joseph E. Davies, *Mission to Moscow* (New York: Simon & Schuster, 1941), 137; Frank A. Warren III, *Liberals and Communism: The "Red Decade" Revisited* (Bloomington: Indiana University Press, 1966), 163–192; see also Victor S. Navasky, *Naming Names* (New York: Viking Press, 1980), 296.

34. Leonard Lyons, "Lyon's Den," *Post* (ca. July 1937, October 9, 1937), MBP; Robert Coleman, "Blitzstein Finds Music Wedded to Drama," *Daily Mirror* (October 29, 1937).

35. Jack Gould, "News Notes of the Night Clubs," *NYT* (January 30, 1938); George Ross, "So This Is Broadway," *World-Telegram* (March 21, 1938) (Ross described the number as one "which takes a few of Hollywood glamor girls over the hurdles," but the surviving text suggests a male protagonist); "Gregory Ratoff, Actor, Director," *NYT* (December 14, 1960); George Ross, "So This Is Broadway," *World-Telegram* (ca. December 1940), MBP.

36. DD, Journals, April 22, 1941, DDC.

37. Virginia Spencer Carr, *Paul Bowles: A Life* (New York: Scribner, 2004), 131.

38. Malcolm Goldstein, *The Political Stage: American Drama and Theater of the Great Depression* (New York: Oxford University Press, 1974), 198–212; MB, "Comments...," *TAC* 1/1 (July 1938): 3; Theodore Strauss, "News of Night Clubs," *NYT* (April 30, 1939).

39. MB, "Wish," *TAC* 1/7 (February 1939): 25; "Books," *TAC* 1/8 (March 1939): 18; Theodore Strauss, "News of Night Clubs," *NYT* (April 30, 1939).

40. Denning, 326, and LEH, 554, presume that the sketch was performed by or written for Cabaret TAC, a real possibility, but their source, GOR, 176, does not actually make that claim.

41. John Houseman, *Run-Through: A Memoir* (New York: Simon & Schuster, 1972); Richard France, *The Theatre of Orson Welles* (Lewisburg, PA: Bucknell University Press, 1977); Barbara Leaming, *Orson Welles: A Biography* (New York: Viking, 1983); Frank Brady, *Citizen Welles: A Biography of Orson Welles* (New York: Scribner, 1989); *Orson Welles on Shakespeare: The W. P. A. and Mercury Theatre Playscripts*, edited with an introduction by Richard France (New York: Greenwood Press, 1990).

42. Leaming, 140–141.

43. George Jean Nathan, "Theater," *Scribner's* 103 (March 1938): 70–71; *Orson Welles on Shakespeare*, 105–106; although a few critics, such as Stark Young, "Three Stage Versions," *New Republic* 93/1200 (December 1, 1937): 101, spoke of the Cinna episode as one of "gripping sarcasm and horror," the scene must have featured a sort of black humor, hence, the description of the scene by Brooks Atkinson, "The Play," *NYT* (November 12, 1937), as "humorous," and the reference to Lloyd's portrayal of Cinna by John Mason Brown, *Post* (November 12, 1937), as "humorous yet deeply affecting."

44. Elliott Carter, "In the Theatre," *MM* 15/1 (November–December 1937): 52.

45. MB, "On Writing Music for the Theatre," *MM* 15/2 (January–February 1938): 83–84; Norman Lloyd, interview with Gary Rutkowski, September 7, 2000 (Archive of American Television, online video removed by the user), recalled Blitzstein using the Italian hymn "Giovinezza," but very likely confused, after a distance of years, that music with the composer's fascist march.

46. Houseman, 344–345 (Houseman erroneously remembered Anderson as thirteen years old at the time); Arthur Anderson, interview with author, December 20, 2008.

47. Houseman, 310, 312 (Blitzstein's rhythmicized treatment of Shakespeare's words survives among his sketches); see also Lloyd, *Stages*, 44–49.

48. "Shakespeare B'way's In-'n'-Outer; 'Caesar' Clicks, 'Cleo,' 'Like' Fold," *Variety* (November 17, 1937); Carter, 52; Thomson, 114.

49. George Ross, "So This Is Broadway," *World-Telegram* (December 9, 1937); Houseman, 306–307.

50. Anderson, interview; the Mercury's two *Julius Caesar* recordings (from March and the summer) have been reissued by Pavilion Records as Pearl Gems 0020 and 0015, respectively.

51. Thomson, 281; "Gossip of the Rialto," *NYT* (April 10, 1938); Orson Welles and John Houseman, "The Summing Up," *NYT* (June 12, 1938); Michael Anderegg, *Orson Welles, Shakespeare, and Popular Culture* (New York: Columbia University Press, 1999), 46, 48.

52. *The Mercury Shakespeare*, edited by Orson Welles and Roger Hill (New York: Harper, 1934, 1939) (Welles's punctuation used).

53. GOR, 171; MB to AC, August 17, 1938, ACC; "Metro-Goldwyn-Mercury," *Stage* 15/12 (September 1938): 30–31; Brady, 147–151.

54. Houseman, 376

55. Houseman, 378–379.

56. Blitzstein's manuscript for "Ode to Reason" states "words by Georg Büchner," but the text remains unidentified, Gerhard P. Knapp to author, February 18, 2009; [MB?], liner notes, *Marc Blitzstein: Songs of the Theater* (Concert Hall CHC 24).

57. MB's translation of "La Marseillaise" reads in its entirety, "Arise ye children of the nation!/The day of glory is at hand!/See the tyrant's foul bloody banners!/Lifted brazenly in our land!/Lifted brazenly in our land!/Do you not hear the mad imprecation/of the horde laying waste as it roams./They force their way into our homes!/They assault our sons and our comrades!/To arms, everyone!/Advance with steel and guns!/March on/March on pure in our faith/in Liberty or death!"

58. Houseman, 384–385; Manngreen, "Left on Broadway," *Daily Worker* (October 20, 1938).

59. Houseman, 385.

60. Brooks Atkinson, "The Play," *NYT* (November 3, 1938); "Gotham Hobgoblin," *NYT* (November 13, 1938) ("raffish"); John Gutman, "In the Theatre," *MM* 16/1 (November–December 1938): 54–58; Ruth McKenney, "Big Themes in the Theater," *New Masses* (November 15, 1938): 28–29; see other excerpted reviews in "Plays. . . . Possibilities," *Box Office* (November 12, 1938): 82.

61. Michael J. McEvoy, interview with author, January 20, 2010.

Chapter 12

1. MB, 1937 Guggenheim Fellowship Application Form, GMF.

2. MB, 1938 Guggenheim Fellowship Application Form, GMF; Herbert Drake, "The Playbill: Aftermath of a Hit," *NYHT* (December 12, 1937); "News of the Stage," *NYT* (February 24, 1938).

3. MB, "Of No for an Answer," *NYT* (January 5, 1941); GOR, 179, 198.

4. "Gossip of the Rialto," *NYT* (August 14, 1938); MB to DD, postmarked December 20, 1939, DDC (for news that the opera "at last is done"); "News of the Rialto," *NYT* (January 14, 1940); Minna Lederman to MB, January 9, 1940, MBP (this letter relates Lederman's reaction to what appears to have been a play-through of a four-act version of the piece).

5. MB to DD, August 22, 1939, DDC; MB to MC, July 8, 1948; [MC to John Houseman, ca. November 1949], courtesy of SD; MC, "In Memory of Marc Blitzstein," MCC.

6. GOR, 179; DD, Journals, September 10, 1939, September 21–22, 1939, October 1–3, 1939 ("grossly"), DDC; DD, unpublished memoir, courtesy of Samuel Elliott.

7. DD, unpublished memoir.

8. DD, Journals, July 10–11, 1939 ("type"), June 15, 1941 ("Marc revolted"), July 6, 1945, April 25, 1946 ("like"), DDC; MB to DD, June 16, 1941, DDC ("threesome").

9. MB to DD [late 1939], June 16, 1941, November 9, 1957, DDC.

10. MB to DD, May 25, 1943, June 29, 1959; DD, Journals, August 15, 1956, January 23, 1964, DDC.

11. DD, Journals, April 1, 1946, October 29, 1946 ("effective"), April 29, 1953 ("headlong"), July 20, 1953, January 17, 1957 ("power"), DDC.

12. MB to DD, January 8, 1943; DD, Journals, November 2, 1961, DDC.

13. MB, sketches, *No for an Answer*, MBP; MB to MC, July 19, 1939, MCC; MB to DD, August 15, 1939, August 22, 1939, DDC.

14. MB, "Of No for an Answer"; Marion Bussang, "Blitzstein Sings a New Song of Social Significance," *Post* (January 2, 1941).

15. This discussion of the opera draws primarily on the completed piano-vocal score, but also a final script, including some annotations in MB's hand; in addition, references to Nick's luncheonette as a "roadside shack," Paul as one of Princeton's "campus radicals," and Jimmy and Bobbie as "stranded vaudevillians" derive from a four-page "Narration," MBP, written by MB after he had completed the opera; note that the scene division of the synopsis given here matches the work's presentation as at the premiere, which conflated scenes nine and ten of the vocal score's eleven-scene first act into a single scene (hence, a total of ten scenes for the first act). For a sketch for the opera's principal mise-en-scène, see Howard Bay, "Project for Marc Blitzstein's Opera," *MM* 18/2 (January–February 1941): 70.

16. GOR, 192.

17. "Historic People's Peace Meeting Opens Today" [April 5, 1941], MBP; "Anti-War Rally Here Washed Out By Rain," *NYT* (April 6, 1941).

18. Bussang.

19. TAL, 157.

20. GOR, 197–198; TAL, 160–169.

21. Beverly Popper to author, March 3, 2011 (for Blitzstein's smoking "a couple of joints" in the early 1960s in order to overcome, apparently in vain, "a small block"); GOR, 192, 194; V. J. Jerome, *Intellectuals and the War* (New York: Workers Library [1940]).

22. TAL, 165 ("Somewhere"); Lederman; Virgil Thomson, "Blitzstein's Operas," *NYHT* (January 12, 1941).

23. John Houseman, *Run-Through: A Memoir* (New York: Simon & Schuster, 1972), 372; Virginia Spencer Carr, *Paul Bowles: A Life* (New York: Scribner, 2004), 131.

24. James Morison, "No for an Answer," *New Masses* 38/4 (January 14, 1941): 28.

25. MB, liner notes, *No for an Answer* (Keynote Album No. 105, 1941), MBP.

26. Robert A. Simon, "Musical Events," *New Yorker* (January 11, 1941): 49.

27. MB, "On Collaborating With One's Self," *NYHT* (January 12, 1941); MB, *Marc Blitzstein and his Theatre Compositions* (Westminster Spoken Arts 717, 1956).

28. Michael Tilson Thomas, "Musical," program book, *No for an Answer* (American Conservatory Theater, 2001), 6.

29. James Whittaker, "'No for an Answer' Has Premiere," *Daily Mirror* (January 6, 1941); COP, 142.

30. James Geller to William Morris, March 1, 1940, MBP; Alice Evans to Ben Irwin, undated, New Theatre League Collection, NYPL (for Draper); "Rialto Gossip," *NYT* (February 18, 1940); GOR, 203 (for the planned instrumentation); MB to Harold Spivacke, November 27, 1939, December 11, 1939, December 23, 1939; Spivacke to MB, December 8, 1939, December 15, 1939, Harold Spivacke Collection, LC.

31. Brooks Atkinson, "Defense of the Arts," *NYT* (January 26, 1941) (Atkinson, however, mistakenly referred to a $2.20 top, whereas the top ticket was $3.30).

32. Actor Robert (F.) Simon is not to be confused with writer-critic Robert A. Simon.

33. "News of the Stage," *NYT* (January 14, 1939); Carol Channing, *Just Lucky I Guess: A Memoir of Sorts* (New York: Simon & Schuster, 2002), 39–42.

34. "Hearings before the Committee on Un-American Activities" (May 8, 1958), MBH; Channing, 42.

35. Reviews of *No for an Answer* by Brooks Atkinson, *NYT*; John Briggs, *Post*; Irving Kolodin, *Sun*; Louis Kronenberger, *PM*; Arthur Pollock, *Brooklyn Eagle*; George Ross, *World-Telegram*; Robert Sylvester, *Daily News*; Virgil Thomson, *NYHT*; Whittaker (all January 6, 1941); George Freedley, *Morning Telegraph*, and Ralph Warner, *Daily Worker* (both January 7, 1941); M. W. M., *Wall Street Journal* (January 10, 1941); Robert A. Simon, *New Yorker* (January 11, 1941); Virgil Thomson, *NYHT*, and Ira Wolfert, *Cleveland Plain Dealer* (both January 12, 1941); *Opera News* and *Time* (both January 13, 1941); James Morison, *New Masses* (January 14, 1941); Naka, *Variety* (January 15, 1941); Kelcey Allen, *News Record* (January 17, 1941); Ralph Warner, *Sunday Worker* (January 19, 1941); Lou Cooper, *New Masses* (January 21, 1941); Nina Naguid, *Musical Leader* (January 25, 1941); Samuel L. M. Barlow, *MM* (January–February 1941).

36. Atkinson; Thomson (January 6, 1941, and January 12, 1941); Barlow; Cooper; Wolfert; Virgil Thomson, "George Gershwin," *MM* 13/1 (November–December 1935): 13–19; Naguid.

37. Atkinson; Barlow; Warner (January 7, 1941, and January 19, 1941); Morison.

38. "Blitzstein Asserts Moss Seeks to Censor Opera," *NYHT* ("I have no"); "Blitzstein Defied License Ban," *PM*; "Blitzstein Opera in a Censor Row," *NYT* (all January 10, 1941); "Leaders of Theatre World Protest Ban on 'No for an Answer,'" *Sunday Worker* (January 19, 1941); GOR, 203; Arthur Bronson, "Blitzstein to Rock the Cradle Again," *Philadelphia Record* (February 16, 1941) ("You tell me").

39. Shirley A. Wiegand and Wayne A. Wiegand, *Books on Trial: Red Scare in the Heartland* (Norman: University of Oklahoma Press, 2007), 121, 207.

40. "We saw 'No for an Answer,'" brochure, MBP.

41. "A Letter to Ten Thousand People," brochure, MBP; "'Solitaire' Placed on Fall Schedule," *NYT* (April 14, 1941).

42. *Marc Blitzstein: Musical Theatre Premières* (Pearl/Pavilion Records GEMS 0009, 1998); Leonard Lyons, "The Lyons Den," *Post* (April 16, 1941); Howard Taubman, "Excerpts From His Opera, 'No for An Answer,'" *NYT* (April 27, 1941); Colin McPhee, "Records and Scores," *MM* 18/4 (May–June 1941): 267; "Fourth American Writers' Congress," *The Clipper* 11/4 (June 1941): 3.

43. "News of the Stage," *NYT* (June 20, 1941); MB to DD, postmarked June 21, 1941, July 11, 1941, DDC.

44. "News and Gossip of the Rialto," *NYT* (October 5, 1941); MB, "In the Drama Mailbag," *NYT* (October 19, 1941, letter signed October 9); MB to DD, July 11, 1941, DDC ("went overboard," "The tide of war").

45. Ann Holmes (of Philadelphia) to Toby Cole (of the New Theatre League), ca. 1941, New Theatre League Collection, NYPL, courtesy of Lynn Mally; Philip Barr to MB, April 20, 1960, MBP.

46. Reviews of *No for an Answer* by Howard Taubman, *NYT* (April 19, 1960); L.T. [Lester Trimble], *NYHT* (April 19, 1960); Leonard Altman, *Villager* (April 21, 1960); Nancy K. Siff, *Village Voice* (April 27, 1960); J.W.F. [John W. Freeman], *Opera News* (November 19, 1960).

47. Howard Taubman, "Records: Robeson," *NYT* (February 28, 1943); LEH, 333–334; Martin Bauml Duberman, *Paul Robeson* (New York: Knopf, 1988), 421.

48. Robbie Lieberman, *"My Song Is My Weapon": People's Songs, American Communism, and the Politics of Culture 1930–1950* (Urbana: University of Illinois Press, 1989), 91; MB, "The Purest Kind of a Guy," *Bulletin of People's Songs* 2 (July–August 1947), 7; MB, "The Purest Kind of a Guy," *Sing Out!* 27/2 (July–August 1978): 26–27; Anthony Tommasini, "For Song Festival, a Program of Personal Significance," *NYT* (December 2, 2010).

49. *Charlotte Rae sings Songs I Taught My Mother* (PS Classics PS-644, 1955, 2006); in performances of "In the Clear," pianists sometimes misplay the right hand's second E in the first measure as $E^\natural$ rather than $E^\flat$.

50. Douglas Moore to MB, January 30, 1963, MBP; MB to Tennessee [Williams], January 23, 1963, Douglas Moore Collection, Columbia University.

51. Wilfrid Mellers to MB, June 7, 1941, MBP; Mellers, "The Language and Function in American Music," *Scrutiny* 10/4 (April 1942): 346–357; Mellers, "New Trends in Britain: A Note on Rubbra and Tippett," *MM* 21/4 (May–June 1944): 215; MEL, 420–421.

52. TAL, 160, 169; John D. Shout, "The Musical Theater of Marc Blitzstein," *American Music* 3/4 (Winter 1985): 420–421; David Z. Kushner, "Marc Blitzstein: Musical Propagandist," *Opera Journal* 26/2 (1993): 13–14.

53. Peter Maleitzke, interview with author, February 26, 2007.

54. Robert Hurwitt, "New Deal-era 'Answer' full of revelations," *San Francisco Chronicle* (October 29, 1929); *No for an Answer* (videotape), Allen Fletcher Library, American Conservatory Theater.

Chapter 13

1. MB to Henry Allen Moe, September 25, 1939, March 28, 1940; Moe to MB, March 27, 1940, MBP; in his March 28 letter to Moe, MB wrote, "May I thank you personally for advising me not to be discouraged by eight rejections? The ninth did it!" but in fact he applied a total of seven times, namely, in the competitions of 1929, 1930, 1933, 1936, 1937, 1938, and 1940; MB actually had proposed "an extended study of all forms of musical theatre from earliest to most recent times" as well as "the creation of a work for the musical stage," MB, 1938, 1939, and 1940 Guggenheim Fellowship Application Forms, GMF; Leonard Lyons, "Lyons Den," *Post* (ca. December 1937), MBP; John Dos Passos, confidential report on MB, received November 16, 1937, GMF.

2. MB to Henry Allen Moe, May 19, 1940; E. W. Cobb to Moe, July 24, 1940, GMF.

3. David Farber, *Sloan Rules: Alfred P. Sloan and the Triumph of General Motors* (Chicago: University of Chicago Press, 2002), 210.

4. Harrison Engle, "Thirty Years of Social Inquiry," *Film Comment* 3/2 (Spring 1965): 24–37.

5. Willard Van Dyke, "Valley Town, How It Was Made," *U.S. Camera* 1/13 (December 1940): 98–109, 116, courtesy of the Center for Creative Photography (Tucson, Arizona); Harold J. and Stanley Ruttenberg, "War and the Steel Ghost Towns," *Harper's* 180 (January 1940): 147–155 (also in Rick Prelinger, *Our Secret Century*, Vol. 2 [Los Angeles: Voyager, 1996]).

6. Van Dyke, 102, 104.

7. Van Dyke; James Blue, interview with Willard Van Dyke (August 2, 1973), in Prelinger.

8. Engle, 27.

9. Ruttenberg.

10. GOR, 186.

11. William Alexander, *Film on the Left: American Documentary Film From 1931 to 1942* (Princeton, NJ: Princeton University Press, 1981), 264–266; "Educational Film Institute," *Film News* 1/7 (July 1940): 1–2.

12. Alexander, 266, and GOR, 187, suggest that the editors also redubbed the actress playing the wife, but the same actress seems to have been used in both the director's cut and the edited version.

13. Alexander, 259, 266, 269; Blue.

14. Howard Taubman, "Composers Hear Their Film Music," *NYT* (January 13, 1941).

15. Paul Bowles, "On the Film Front," *MM* 18/1 (November–December 1940): 58–61; B. H. Haggin, "Music," *Nation* 152/7 (February 15, 1941): 194; Blue; Alexander, 261; Richard M. Barsam, *Nonfiction Film: A Critical History*, revised and expanded (Bloomington: Indiana University Press, 1973, 1992), 169.

16. Theodore Strauss, "Homesteading Our 'Native Land,'" *NYT* (May 3, 1942); Irene Thirer, "Paul Strand and Leo Hurwitz Offer Data on 'Native Land,'" *Post* (May 9, 1942); Michael

and Jill Klein, "*Native Land*: An Interview with Leo Hurwitz," *Cinéaste* 6/3 (1974): 3–7; Alexander; Martin Bauml Duberman, *Paul Robeson* (New York: Knopf, 1988), 261.

17. Thirer; Alexander, 213.

18. Leo Huberman, *The Labor Spy Racket* (New York: Monthly Review Press, 1937).

19. Klein, 7; Thirer.

20. Wyn Craig Wade, *The Fiery Cross: The Ku Klux Klan in America* (New York: Simon & Schuster, 1987), 261; Herbert Shapiro, *White Violence and Black Response: From Reconstruction to Montgomery* (Amherst: University of Massachusetts Press, 1988), 243–250; for more on *Native Land*, see Alexander and Richard M. Barsam, *Nonfiction Film: A Critical History* (Bloomington: Indiana University Press, 1973, 1992), 149–151; Michael Klein, "*Native Land*: Praised Then Forgotten," *Velvet Light Trip* 14 (Winter 1975): 12–16; and Peter C. Rollins, "Ideology and Film Rhetoric: Three Documentaries of the New Deal Era (1936–1941)," *Hollywood as Historian: American Film in a Cultural Context*, edited by Peter C. Rollins (Lexington: University Press of Kentucky, 1983), 43–48.

21. Alexander, 236, 241.

22. Klein, "*Native Land*: An Interview," 6; David Platt, "'Native Land' is Powerful Expose of America's 'Little Hitlers,'" *Daily Worker* (May 12, 1942); for an earlier draft of this epilogue, see Leo Hurwitz to Charles Frazier, February 23, 1942, MBP.

23. MB, "Composers Doing Their Stuff," *NYT* (May 3, 1942); program, "Music at Work" (May 10, 1942), MBP; Virgil Thomson, "Music," *NYHT* (May 11, 1942); Blitzstein asked Irving Berlin to suggest "one of your numbers which you cherish yet has not had smash popularity," MB to Irving Berlin, March 20, 1942, Irving Berlin Collection, LC.

24. MB, "The Other Side," *NYT* (December 7, 1941); Artur Schnabel and Roger Sessions, "One Point of View," *NYT* (November 30, 1941).

25. Reviews of *Native Land* by William Boehnel, *World-Telegram*; Bosley Crowther, *NYT*; Dorothy Masters, *Daily News*; John McManus, *PM*; David Platt, *Daily Worker*; Wear., *Variety*; Archer Winston, *Post* (all May 12, 1942); E. G., *NYHT* (May 13, 1942); Herbert Cohn, *Brooklyn Eagle* (May 16, 1942); Virgil Thomson, *NYHT* (May 31, 1942); Léon Kochnitzky, *MM* (May–June 1942); Ralph Ellison, *New Masses* (June 2, 1942).

26. Pete Seeger to MB, May 25, 1942, MBP; Kochnitzky; Thomson.

27. "Begin Showing Of 'Native Land,'" MBP; Wauhillau La Hay, "'Native Land' Beautifully Directed and Produced," *Chicago Sun* (February 1, 1943); Klein, "*Native Land*: An Interview," 6.

28. John Briggs, "New Blitzstein Poured Into an Ancient Mold," *Post* (July 11, 1946); Louis Biancolli, "Marc Blitzstein's Film Score Good Symphonic Work," *World-Telegram* (July 11, 1946); GOR, 443–444; program notes, *Native Land* Suite, New York Philharmonic (July 29, 1958), MBP, perplexingly state that Blitzstein "deleted five sections from the original Suite and added three other episodes from the film score to constitute the present definitive work for symphonic repertoire"; meanwhile, the MBP contains the outline of a slightly different eight-movement suite that most likely predates the Halasz premiere.

29. MB to DD, February 17, 1942, DDC.

30. Kate Smith and Danny Kaye, inscriptions, MBP; MB, "Composers Doing"; GOR, 216; a telegram to Blitzstein from Robert W. Horton, director of the Division of Information of the Office for Emergency Management, dated February 4, 1942, states, "Unexpected developments necessitate cancelling Night Shift plans. Thanks for your willingness to help," although Blitzstein and others apparently continued working on the film past this date.

31. BRA, 175.

32. MB to Richard Griffith, December 25, 1940, ACC; MB, notes, February 25, 1943, MBP.

33. William G. King, "Music and Musicians: About Marc Blitzstein," *Sun* (October 19, 1940). Arthur Bronson, "Blitzstein To Rock The Cradle Again," *Philadelphia Record* (February 16, 1941); "News of the Stage" *NYT* (June 20, 1941); "Gossip of the Rialto," *NYT* (May

17, 1942); MB to Claire Reis, June 14, 1941, December 3, 1941, December 2, 1942, Claire Reis Collection, NYPL; GOR, 208–209.

34. MB, "Singing Country," *MM* 19/2 (January–February 1942): 139–140; John A. Lomax to MB, May 6, 1942, MBP.

35. Elizabeth Fones-Wolf and Nathan Godfried, "Regulating Class Conflict on the Air: NBC's Relationship with Business and Organized Labor," *NBC: America's Network*, edited by Michele Hilmes (Berkeley: University of California Press, 2007), 73–75.

36. Attributions as found in the NBC and Peter Lyon archives, WHS; the July 4 script, "There is Strength," survives in the NBC archives.

37. GOR, 222.

38. GOR, 222, 558 n16; "Browder Demands Aid for Roosevelt," *NYT* (January 12, 1943); Lewis Nichols, "'Lunchtime Follies,'" *NYT* (June 13, 1943); Arlene Wolf, "Lunchtime Follies, S.R.O.," *NYT* (July 11, 1943); MB, "The Quiet Girl," *Sing America*, compiled and edited by Anne Allan (New York: Workers Bookshop, 1944); MBS2.

Chapter 14

1. Lieutenant W. E. Blackman to MB, August 22, 1942, MBP; MB to DD, August 23, 1942, DDC.

2. MB to LB, August 30, 1942, LBC.

3. MBH; MB, FBI file, November 8, 1940, May 23, 1941, January 5, 1942, January 28, 1942; see also Maurice Isserman, *Which Side Were You On? The American Communist Party during the Second World War* (Middletown, CT: Wesleyan University Press, 1982), 180–184.

4. Jan Herman, *A Talent for Trouble: The Life of Hollywood's Most Acclaimed Director, William Wyler* (New York: Putnam, 1995), 244–245; MB to MC, September 8, 1942, MCC; MB to JD, September 13, 1942, MBP.

5. MB, "A Musician's War Diary," *New Masses* 50/7 (August 13, 1946): 3–6; MB to JD, August 27, 1942; MB to Samuel and Madelin Blitzstein, October 8, 1942, MBP.

6. MB to SD, November 5, 1942, MBP.

7. Herman, 249; MB to his family, December 5–9, 1942 [catalogued as 1943], MBP.

8. Herman, 250; MB to JD, December 13, 1942, January 10, 1943; Anatole Litvak, letter of recommendation for MB, January 9, 1943, MBP.

9. MB to JD, December 18, 1942 (MB had met with Lay on December 17), December 25, 1942, MBP.

10. MB to JD, January 25, 1943, MBP; MB to Anna Levy, February 25, 1943, courtesy of SD ("full of"); James Dugan to JD, July 9, 1965; MB to JD, October 14, 1943, MBP.

11. Richard Wilbur, "Negro GIs Making Musical History," *Stars and Stripes* (September 17, 1943); "Negro Chorus Concert to Be Broadcast Here and in U.S.," *Stars and Stripes* (September 28, 1943).

12. MB, "A Musician's," 4–5; MB to JD, August 31, 1943, September 30, 1943, MBP; MB, "Mr. Blitzstein Reports," *NYT* (October 3, 1943).

13. MB, "A Musician's," 4; *I Can Tell The World 1943–1944*, edited by Alexander B. Jordan ([Ipswich, Suffolk?] U.S. Army Negro Chorus, 1944), 16; Wilbur.

14. MB, notes, MBP; MB, "A Musician's," 5.

15. MB to DD, December 14, 1943, DDC; MB to JD, October 14, 1943, MBP; GOR, 248.

16. MB, "A Musician's," 5; MB, "Mr. Blitzstein"; GOR, 240–242; F[erruccio] Bonavia, "U. S. Army Choir Heard in London," *NYT* (October 31, 1943); "Negro Chorus Concert" (for changed lyrics); "Allied Soldiers Cheer Chorus," *Stars and Stripes* (September 30, 1943) (for Devers and Lee).

17. MB, "A Musician's," 6; MB, "Mr. Blitzstein."

18. MB to Samuel and Madelin Blitzstein, November 1, 1943, MBP; MB to DD, May 25, 1943, DDC; MB to AC, July 9, 1943, ACC.

19. MB to JD, November 26, 1943, MBP.
20. MB to Samuel and Madelin Blitzstein, February 24, 1944; MB to JC, April 1, 1944, MBP.
21. MB, "A Musician's War Diary, Part II," *New Masses* 50/8 (August 20, 1946): 6–8; MB, "Interchange of Popular Music," *Musicology* 1/2 (Spring 1946): 193–196; MB to Samuel and Madelin Blitzstein, April 30, 1944, MBP.
22. MB to JD, May 26, 1944, MBP ("sounding"); MB, "Blitzstein on Toscanini," *NYT* (April 14, 1946).
23. GOR, 248; "Interval Talk" (broadcast June 21, 1943), "Answering You" (recorded August 2, 1943), "Television Was Fun" (recorded June 3 and 4, 1944), transcripts, BBC Written Archives Centre.
24. MB to Samuel Blitzstein, August 31, 1944; MB to JD, September 7, 1943, October 17, 1944, MBP.
25. MB to Samuel and Madelin Blitzstein, March 24, 1943, April 2, 1943; MB to JD, September 7, 1944, September 13, 1944, MBP.
26. MB [to his family], December 4, 1944, MBP; MB, "Major & Minor," *Philadelphia Record* (December 2, 1945); MB, "A Musician's, II" (according to this source, he arrived in Paris on October 29, but according to the December letter, October 30).
27. MB, "A Musician's War Diary, Part III," *New Masses* 50/9 (August 27, 1946): 10–11; MB, "Major."
28. MB, "A Musician's, III," 11–12 (MB refers to Marraine as "Henriette Henry" but her surname apparently was Bayeux); MB, "Major"; MB [to his family], December 4, 1944; MB to Anna Levy, December 13, 1944, MBP.
29. Annegret Fauser, "'War's New Weapon': Music, Propaganda, and the OWI during World War II," courtesy of the author; MB to JD, February 8, 1945, MBP; MB to AC, February 15, 1945, ACC; MB to JD, March 1, 1945, MBP.
30. MB to JD, January 7, 1945, February 8, 1945; MB to Anna Levy, February 14, 1945; MB to Samuel and Madelin Blitzstein, March 27, 1945 ("the changing"), April 17, 1945, MBP; James Chapman, "'The Yanks Are Shown to Such Advantage': Anglo-American rivalry in the production of 'The True Glory' (1945)," *Historical Journal of Film, Radio and Television* 16/4 (October 1996): 533–554; GOR, 262; Blitzstein later recalled doing only "research for the music" for *True Glory*, Dorothy Norman, "Such Wondering Things Happening to Music," *Post* (April 1, 1946).
31. Madelin Blitzstein to MB, April 22, 1945; JD to MB, April 29, 1945, MBP.
32. MB to JD and Madelin Blitzstein, May 5, 1945, MBP.
33. MB to JD, December 6, 1943, MBP; GOR, 234.
34. MB to JD, October 17, 1944, October 26, 1944, MBP.
35. MB to JD, October 8, 1942 ("deeper"), November 22, 1942 (Olivier); MB, "Mr. Blitzstein," MBP ("They know"); MB, "A Musician's, III," 12 ("bigwigs"); MB to Samuel and Madelin Blitzstein, April 17, 1945 ("Tory"); MB to JD, March 5, 1944 ("new"), December 14, 1944 ("great"), MBP.
36. MB, "A Musician's," 3; MB to JD, September 7, 1944 ("unpleasanter"); MB [to his family], December 4, 1944 ("In Grenoble"); MB to JD, December 14, 1944 ("When"); MB to Anna Levy, April 22, 1945, MBP.
37. MB to Samuel and Madelin Blitzstein, March 10, 1943, MBP (for Marx); MB, "A Musician's, III," 12.
38. MB to DD, December 14, 1943, DDC.
39. MB to Samuel and Madelin Blitzstein, November 1, 1942, MBP; MB to AC, January 22, 1943, ACC ("dull"); MB, "London: Fourth Winter of the Blackout," *MM* 20/2 (January–February 1943): 117–120.
40. MB to Anna Levy, February 14, 1944, MBP; MB, "London," 119; MB to AC, April 5, 1943, ACC.
41. *Letters from a Life: The Selected Letters and Diaries of Benjamin Britten 1913–1976*, Vol. 2, edited by Donald Mitchell and Philip Reed (Berkeley: University of California Press, 1991), 915, 917; MB to AC [fall 1942], MBP ("super-kind"); MB to DD, May 25, 1943, DDC; MB to AC, April 17, 1944, ACC.

42. MB to AC, January 22, 1943, April 5, 1943, April 17, 1944, ACC.

43. MB, "London," 120; MB to Anna Levy, November 26, 1943, MBP.

44. MB, "London," 119–120; MB to Madelin Blitzstein, July 29, 1943, MBP ("All in all"); MB to DD, December 14, 1943, DDC ("stonily"); MB to JD, September 13, 1944, MBP ("the best"); MB to Anna Levy, January 29, 1943, courtesy of SD ("had a glimpse"); MB, "Major" ("pretty good").

45. MB to Samuel and Madelin Blitzstein, November 1, 1942; MB [to his family], December 4, 1944, MBP; MB, "London," 118–119.

46. MB to AC, April 5, 1943, ACC; MB to JD, May 5, 1944, MBP ("so much"); MB to DD, December 21, 1942, DDC ("a great"); MB to JD, March 9, 1944 ("decenter," "It isn't"); MB to Samuel and Madelin Blitzstein, October 21, 1944 ("got on"), MBP.

47. MB to AC, January 22, 1943, April 5, 1943, ACC; AC to DD, postmarked January 13, 1943, DDC.

48. MB to DD, April 28, 1943, DDC; MB, "A Musician's," 4; MB to JD, February 3, 1943, MBP.

49. MB to Samuel and Madelin Blitzstein, October 21, 1944, MBP.

50. MB to JD, December 26, 1944, January 7, 1945, February 21, 1945, MBP.

51. Bill Hewitt to MB, April 20, 1945; JD to MB, April 27, 1945, MBP.

52. Ian Johnson, *William Alwyn: The Art of Film Music* (Rochester, NY: Boydell Press, 2005), 120–122 (Johnson mistakenly writes that Alwyn "was called in when ... Blitzstein, fell ill").

53. Brochure, Samuel Blitzstein Memorial Fund, MBP; MB, "A Musician's, III," 12.

Chapter 15

1. Dorothy Parker, "War Song," *New Yorker* (March 4, 1944): 22; GOR, 253.

2. MB to Ned Rorem, February 24, 1960, Ned Rorem Collection, LC; ROR, 200.

3. Charlotte Rae, liner notes, *Charlotte Rae sings Songs I Taught My Mother* (PS Classics PS-644, 1955, 2006), recalled the number as banned by the "Lord Constable," presumably meaning the Lord Chamberlain; the revised final line as found in Rae's recording and transcribed here differs slightly from a rewrite found among Blitzstein's papers: "And wondering how to get this rampant little maid allayed"; LEH, 380; GOR, 393, states, based on his interview with Rae, that she sang the song in Ben Bagley's *The Littlest Revue* (1956), but none of three surviving programs mentions the song, Richard Norton to author, December 28, 2010; review of *Songs I Taught My Mother, Playboy* (March 1956): 9; *A Blitzstein Cabaret* (Premier Recordings PRCD 1005, 1990); for the song's debut 1999 publication, LL drew on both the original and the revised lyrics, and made some minor musical changes as well.

4. LB, remarks, "Composers' Showcase: A Marc Blitzstein Tribute In Honor of His Eightieth Birthday," archival tape (April 28, 1985), courtesy of Brent Oldham.

5. ROR, 196–197; Ned Rorem, *Knowing When to Stop: A Memoir* (New York: Simon & Schuster, 1994), 296; Jack Gottlieb, *Funny, It Doesn't Sound Jewish: How Yiddish Songs and Synagogue Melodies Influenced Tin Pan Alley, Broadway, and Hollywood* (Albany: State University of New York in association with the Library of Congress, 2004) (includes LB's ca. 1965 rendition); LB, remarks; BAL.

6. GOR, 272; Gottlieb, 217–218; see also Allan Kozinn, "Jewish Works (Though Not 'White Christmas')," *NYT* (November 21, 1997).

7. "Negro Chorus Scores Hit In London With '76 Theme," *Philadelphia Inquirer* (September 30, 1943); MB, "Mr. Blitzstein Reports," *NYT* (October 3, 1943); "Negro Chorus Concert to Be Broadcast Here and in U.S.," *Stars and Stripes* (September 28, 1943); see also chapter 14, 264.

8. For the use of the word "freedom" in coeval compositions, see GOR, 239.

9. MB to JD, May 5, 1944, MBP; program notes, *Freedom Morning*, Philadelphia Orchestra (April 14, 1944) and New York Philharmonic (August 4, 1944).

10. *I Can Tell The World 1943–1944*, edited by Alexander B. Jordan ([Ipswich, Suffolk?] U.S. Army Negro Chorus, 1944), 17; Gail Kubik, "London Letter," *MM* 21/4 (May–June 1944): 240–243; MB, "A Musician's War Diary," *New Masses* 50/7 (August 13, 1946): 5; MB to AC, April 17, 1944, ACC; MB to JD, May 26, 1944, MBP.

11. Reviews of *Freedom Morning* by Linton Martin, *Philadelphia Inquirer*; Edwin H. Schloss, *Philadelphia Record*; Elizabeth Emerson Stine, *Philadelphia Evening Bulletin* (all April 15, 1944); Vincent Persichetti, *MM* (May–June 1944); unidentified, *Sun*, and Paul Bowles, *NYHT* (both August 5, 1944); MB to JD, September 7, 1944, MBP.

12. MB to Samuel and Madelin Blitzstein, April 30, 1944; MB to JD, May 5, 1944; MB to Samuel Blitzstein, August 31, 1944, MBP.

13. BRA, 175.

14. MB [to JD?], December 18, 1942; MB to JD, December 25, 1942; MB to his family, February 16, 1943, MBP; Barbara B. Heyman, *Samuel Barber: The Composer and His Music* (New York: Oxford University Press, 1992), 216.

15. MB to JD, August 6, 1943, MBP; MB to AC, July 9, 1943, ACC.

16. MB to JD, October 14, 1943, November 26, 1943, MBP; MB to AC, April 17, 1944, ACC; Robert Musel, "Marc Blitzstein Honors Airmen In New War Ballad Symphony" [spring 1944], MBP.

17. "It Happens In Music," *NYT* (March 24, 1946); Dorothy Norman, "Such Wondering Things Happening to Music," *Post* (April 1, 1946).

18. GOR, 277.

19. MBP holds two separate orchestral scores (one incomplete) of "Theory of Flight," but only one orchestral score of the entire work, suggesting that the earlier London version of the work does not survive.

20. MB, notes, MBP; MB, program notes, *Airborne Symphony*, New York City Symphony (April 1, 1946) ("because," "negro"); MB to JD, December 1, 1943, December 6, 1943, MBP; MB to Alexander Smallens, February 5, 1945, ASC.

21. MB, notes, MBP; Irving Kolodin, "Air Symphony To Be Offered," *Sun* (March 27, 1946); MB, program notes; MB [to JD?], October 25, 1946, MBP.

22. MB to his family, November 30, 1942; MB, notes, MBP; MB, "London: Fourth Winter of the Blackout," *MM* 20/2 (January–February 1943): 118.

23. MB, notes; MB to JD, August 6, 1943, MBP; MB, "London,"118.

24. MB, program notes; MB, notes, MBP.

25. Robert A. Brady, *The Spirit and Structure of German Fascism* (New York: Howard Fertig, 1937, 1969), 196–197, 200; Seymour Peck, "Blitzstein Tells of 'Airborne,'" *PM* (March 29, 1947).

26. MB, notes, March 30, 1943, MBP.

27. Peck; GOR, 273.

28. MB, notes, January 21, 1943, January 31, 1943, MBP; Charles Osborne, *W. H. Auden: The Life of a Poet* (New York: Harcourt Brace Jovanovich, 1979), 318; MB to AC, July 9, 1943, ACC; Virgil Thomson, "Music," *NYHT* (April 2, 1946); Donald Fuller, "Airborne Over New York: Spring 1946," *MM* 23/2 (Spring 1946): 116–123; Norman Corwin, "'On a Note of Triumph': Norman Corwin's Radio Classic, 60 Years Later," National Public Radio (May 26, 2005); Norman Corwin to JD, November 9, 1942, MBP.

29. MB to JD, October 27, 1942 ("air-force songs"), September 30, 1943 (for "second front number"), MBP.

30. MB to Serge Koussevitzky, June 10, 1949, June 23, 1949, Serge Koussevitzky Collection, LC.

31. Reviews of the *Airborne Symphony* by Grena Bennett, *Journal-American*; Louis Biancolli, *New York Telegram and Sun*; Olin Downes, *NYT*; Harriett Johnson, *Post*; Irving Kolodin, *Sun*; Thomson (all April 2, 1946); Bron. [Arthur Bronson], *Variety*, and Robert Hague, *PM* (both April 3, 1946); Louis Harap, *Daily Worker* (April 4, 1946); E., *Musical America* (April 10, 1946); Robert A. Simon, *New Yorker* (April 13, 1946); *Newsweek*,

Time, and H.W.L, *Musical Courier* (all April 15, 1946); Wallingford Riegger, *New Masses* (April 16, 1946); Fuller; Harold Clurman, *Tomorrow* (June 1946).

32. Thomson; MB to Orson Welles, April 3, 1946, Orson Welles Collection, Lilly Library, Indiana University.

33. Riegger; Clurman.

34. E., *Musical America*.

35. May B. Schamberg to MB, April 2, 1946; Trude Rittman to MB, April 2, 1946, MBP; Lee Hays, *"Sing Out, Warning! Sing Out, Love!" The Writings of Lee Hays*, edited by Robert S. Koppelman (Amherst: University of Massachusetts Press, 2003), 83; LEH, 374.

36. Bernard Rogers to MB, May 28, 1946, MBP; MB, "Notes on the 'Airborne' Symphony," *RCA Victor Record Review* 10/2 (June 1947): 5, 11.

37. "28 Page One Awards," *NYT* (November 7, 1946); Edward Hunter, letter to the editor, *NYT* (November 15, 1946); John T. McManus, letter to the editor, *NYT* (November 25, 1946).

38. *Radio's Best Plays*, selected and edited by Joseph Liss (New York: Greenberg, 1947).

39. Skitch Henderson, program notes, *Airborne Symphony*, New York Pops (November 11, 2005); R.P. [Ross Parmenter], "Pops Series Begins At Carnegie Hall," *NYT* (May 5, 1953); *Skitch Henderson at 80: A Man and His Music* (New York: New York Pops, 1998).

40. Irving Kolodin, "Blitzstein's 'Airborne,' Mozart's 'Flute,'" *Saturday Review* 49/44 (October 29, 1966): 50–51.

41. Donal Henahan, "A 'Ruptured Duck' That Just Will Not Fly," *NYT* (August 15, 1976); Ned Rorem, *Knowing When to Stop: A Memoir* (New York: Simon & Schuster, 1994), 314 (and ROR, 196); Bernard Holland, "3 Works From 3 Countries at a War's End," *NYT* (May 2, 1995); Robert Cushman, liner notes, *Marc Blitzstein: Musical Theatre Premières* (Pearl/Pavilion Records GEMS 0009, 1998); Nicholas Tawa, *The Great American Symphony: Music, the Depression, and War* (Bloomington: Indiana University Press, 2009), 137–146; Steve Schwartz, review of *American Masters 2*, *Classical Review Net* (2005): http://www.classical.net/music/recs/reviews/s/sny61849b.php.

42. Holland; K. Robert Schwarz, "Grandiose Patriotic Fervor Soaked in Jazz, Blues and Pop," *NYT* (April 30, 1995) ("jingoistic").

43. Schwarz ("the boundless").

Chapter 16

1. Bill Hewitt to MB, undated, MBP.

2. MB to MC, April 5, 1948 ("alone"), MBP; CD to author, February 23, 2011; in his novel *A Kind of Darkness* (London: Rupert Hart-Davis, 1962), CD also depicted a character modeled after Hewitt, Frank Walton, as alcoholic and pugnacious, but also "energetic, attentive, interested" (23); DD, Journals, March 15, 1946, February 23, 1950, DDC.

3. MB to MC, September 18, 1952, MBP; CD, February 23, 2011.

4. GOR, 255, 276, 300; Eric Gordon to author, June 1, 2009; Arthur Lynch, interview with author, June 13, 2009.

5. "Army Used 'Reds' House Group Told," *NYT* (July 19, 1945); "Fear Red Spies Beat Army Ban to Atom Facts," *Journal-American* (March 10, 1946).

6. "Thousand Artists, Writers Back Davis," *Daily Worker* (September 25, 1945); "Wheeler to Take Frank Fay's Role," *NYT* (June 1, 1946); "Leaders in Arts, Sciences Hit Pix Purge," *Daily Worker* (December 1, 1947); *Red Channels: The Report of Communist Influence in Radio and Television* (New York: American Business Consultants, 1950), 20–23; MB, FBI file, April 22, 1949.

7. "Panel on Soviet Music: A Transcript," *Musicology* 1/2 (Spring 1946): 169–196 (MB, "Interchange of Popular Music," 193–196).

8. GOR, 289, 309; *American-Soviet Music Review* 1 (Fall 1946).

9. Howard Taubman, "Music of 2 Lands Is Theme of Show," *NYT* (May 13, 1947); Miles Kastendieck, *Journal-American* (May 13, 1947).

10. MB, "An Analysis of Prokofiev," *Soviet Russia Today* 15/7 (1946): 23.

11. William Saroyan, "Formula for the Theatre—By Saroyan," *NYT* (October 10, 1948); MB, notes, October 10, 1948, MBP.

12. "'Show-Time for Wallace' Cabaret at Cafe Society T'nite," *Daily Worker* (April 5, 1948); "500 Leaders in Arts and Sciences Back Wallace," *Daily Worker* (October 19, 1948); MB to MC, April 17, 1948, MCC.

13. "Moscow Says 32 Artists in U.S. Join in Soviet Fight on Our Policy," *NYT* (May 3, 1948); "Soviet Magazine Quotes 32 in U.S. As Siding with Russian Policy," *PM* (May 3, 1948); "32 'Artists' Vs. Uncle Sam," *Daily News* (May 4, 1948); 12 Soviet writers, "Why Are You Silent?" *New Masses* 66/3 (January 13, 1948): 10–12; MB and 31 others, "American Message: A Reply to an Open Letter of Soviet Writers," *Masses & Mainstream* 1/3 (May 1948): 3–6; Norman Cazden, "What's Happening in Soviet Music?" *Masses & Mainstream* 1/2 (April 1948): 11–24; MB to MC, May 5, 1948, MCC.

14. MB and 31 others, letter to the editor, *NYT* (May 24, 1948); draft of letter, May 12, 1948, MBP.

15. "Sponsors of the World Peace Conference," *NYT* (March 24, 1949); "Our Way Defended to 2,000 Opening 'Culture' Meeting," *NYT* (March 26, 1949); see also *Review of the Scientific and Cultural Conference for World Peace* (Washington, D.C.: Committee on Un-American Activities, April 19, 1949).

16. GOR, 326–327 (including a quote by MB to Bill Hewitt, March 31, 1948); according to GOR, Konstantin Simonov and Ilya Ehrenburg also attended this mixer, but Hewitt, the source for this information, apparently conflated a possible get-together in 1946, when Simonov and Ehrenburg visited the United States, with this one in 1948.

17. "Panel Discussions of the Cultural Conference Delegates Cover a Wide Range of Subjects," *NYT* (March 27, 1949); "Shostakovich Bids All Artists Lead War on New 'Fascists,'" *NYT* (March 28, 1949); GOR, 326; Elizabeth Wilson, *Shostakovich: A Life Remembered*, 2nd ed. (Princeton, NJ: Princeton University Press, 1994, 2006), 272–276; Laurel E. Fay, *Shostakovich: A Life* (New York: Oxford University Press, 2000), 172–174; Howard Pollack, *Aaron Copland: The Life and Work of an Uncommon Man* (New York: Henry Holt, 1999), 70, 282–284; *The Selected Correspondence of Aaron Copland*, edited by Elizabeth B. Crist and Wayne Shirley (New Haven, CT: Yale University Press, 2006), 196–197.

18. Irma Bauman, interview with author, June 21, 2007; Blitzstein signed a June 5, 1949, telegram on behalf of John Gates, Henry Winston, and Gus Hall, MB, FBI file, June 14, 1955; "200 Notables Ask Gov't to Halt Contempt Persecution," *Daily Worker* (February 19, 1951); "Hearings before the Committee on Un-American Activities" (May 8, 1958), MBH.

19. *Red Channels*, 9; Merle Miller, *The Judges and the Judged* (Garden City, NY: Doubleday, 1952); John Cogley, *Report on Blacklisting*, Vol. 2 (New York: Fund for the Republic, 1956); David Everitt, *A Shadow of Red: Communism and the Blacklist in Radio and Television* (Chicago: Ivan R. Dee, 2007).

20. *Red Channels*, 20–23; K. Kevyne Baar, *Investigating Broadway: The House Committee on Un-American Activities Meets Members of the New York Theatre Community at the Foley Square Courthouse, August 15–18, 1955* (Ph.D. dissertation, Saybrook Graduate School and Research Center, 2006).

21. MB, FBI file, January 13, 1947, February 24, 1947, December 10, 1948, April 22, 1949, June 13, 1949, May 13, 1950, August 8, 1950, August 17, 1955, September 6, 1955.

22. MB, notes for a *NYT* article, MBP; MB, "Interchange" ("a really integral"); Max de Schauensee, "Blitzstein Describes Function of Music in Lecture Here," *Philadelphia Evening Bulletin* (October 23, 1946); Charles Sinnickson Jr., "Blitzstein Gives Lecture-Recital," *Philadelphia Record* (October 23, 1946); MB, "Toward a Lyric Theatre," *NYT* (May 11, 1947).

23. MB, "Interchange."

24. "Gossip of the Rialto," *NYT* (August 26, 1945); on September 5, 1945, Blitzstein signed a contract with James Proctor and the New Opera Company for a work, "Wait For Me," presumably the same piece as *Goloopchik*.

25. [MB?], liner notes, *Marc Blitzstein: Songs of the Theater* (Concert Hall Society, CHC 24).

26. [MB?], liner notes.

27. Robert A. Simon, "Musical Events," *New Yorker* (May 11, 1946): 81–82; Noel Strauss, "Cooper's Cantata in Premiere Here," *NYT* (May 3, 1946).

28. MBS1 and MBS2.

29. MB, "On Top of Old Smoky," *The People's Songbook*, edited by Waldemar Hille (New York: Boni and Gaer, 1948), 33; MB to Mordecai Bauman, January 7, 1948, Mordecai Bauman Papers, Tamiment Library, NYU (for the date for "Dublin Street Song").

30. Max Allentuck to MB, October 18, 1946, MBP.

31. MB, notes; LH, *Another Part of the Forest*, working script, MBP ("have to coincide"); *Another Part of the Forest* (New York: Viking Press, 1946, 1947), 47, 48, 56; in his notes, Blitzstein writes, "use Divertimento (D major?) for Violin, Viola, Cello—Leopold Mozart," but the latter never wrote a divertimento for that combination; perhaps Blitzstein meant one of Leopold's divertimentos for two violins and cello, one of which is in D major; this also would fit better given the play's depiction of Marcus and Jugger as both handling violins.

32. Brooks Atkinson, "The Play in Review," *NYT* (November 21, 1946) ("lurid"); for more reviews, see Barbara Lee Horn, *Lillian Hellman: A Research and Production Sourcebook* (Westport, CT: Greenwood Press, 1998), 80–83; Katherine Lederer, *Lillian Hellman* (Boston: Twayne, 1979), 71.

33. Cheryl Crawford to MB, September 17, 1946, MBP.

34. The page numbers of Blitzstein's cues conform to G. B. Shaw, *Androcles and the Lion* (New York: Brentano's, 1916); Brooks Atkinson, "The Play in Review," *NYT* (December 20, 1946); Jack O'Brien, "Shaw Comedy Is Delightful, Says Critic," *Richmond News Leader* (December 21, 1946); Howard Barnes, "'Androcles and the Lion' A Triumph of Direction," *NYHT* (December 29, 1946).

35. Atkinson; O'Brien; Barnes; Robert Garland, "The Drama," *Journal-American* (December 29, 1946).

36. Amanda Vaill, *Somewhere: The Life of Jerome Robbins* (New York: Broadway Books, 2006), 91.

37. MB, notes, MBP.

38. MB, notes, MBP.

39. MB, notes, MBP.

40. *American Composers at the Piano* (Concert Hall B-9, 1947); Milton Widder, "Notes and Sketches," *Cleveland Press* (January 17, 1948).

41. Martin Duberman, *The Worlds of Lincoln Kirstein* (New York: Knopf, 2007), 443; see also Nancy Reynolds, *Repertory in Review: 40 Years of the New York City Ballet* (New York: Dial Press, 1977); Deborah Jowitt, *Jerome Robbins: His Life, His Theater, His Dance* (New York: Simon & Schuster, 2004); Vaill; John Houseman, *Final Dress* (New York: Simon & Schuster, 1983), 23 (for Mina and Lincoln).

42. MB, "Marc Blitzstein's 'The Guests' To Premiere This Thursday," *New York Star* (January 17, 1949).

43. George Balanchine, *Balanchine's New Complete Stories of the Great Ballets*, edited by Francis Mason (Garden City, NY: Doubleday, 1954), 194–195.

44. Balanchine, 194–195.

45. [MB?], notes for *The Guests*, Jerome Robbins Collection, NYPL (these notes appear with others written by MB).

46. [MB?], notes.

47. Betty Cage to Chappell and Co., June 2, 1949; Betty Cage to MB, July 6, 1949, archives, New York City Ballet, courtesy of Laura Raucher; MB to Lincoln Kirstein, January 20, 1949, Lincoln Kirstein Collection, NYPL.

48. Reynolds, 94; Maria Tallchief with Larry Kaplan, *Maria Tallchief: America's Prima Ballerina* (New York: Henry Holt, 1997), 109–110.

49. Harriett Johnson, "The Guests' Premiere By N. Y. City Ballet Co.," *Post* (January 21, 1949).

50. Reviews of *The Guests* by L.B., *World-Telegram*; Johnson; Miles Kastendieck, *Journal-American*; John Martin, *NYT*; H.C.S. [Harold C. Schonberg], *Sun*; Robert Sylvester, *Daily News*; Walter Terry, *NYHT* (all January 21, 1949); Bron. [Arthur Bronson], *Variety* (January 26, 1949); Cecil Smith, *Musical America* (February 1949); Doris Hering, *Dance Magazine* (March 1949).

51. Bron. ("much the"); Hering ("ideally"); Sylvester; Smith.

52. Henry Cowell, "Current Chronicle," *Musical Quarterly* 35/2 (April 1949): 293–296.

53. MB to MC, February 20, 1949, MBP.

54. MB to Lincoln Kirstein, June 24, 1949; Betty Cage to MB, July 6, 1949; Lincoln Kirstein to MB, June 23, 1949, August 29, 1949, archives, New York City Ballet; MB to MC, April 4, 1953, MCC; MB to DD, January 8, 1954, DDC.

55. Walter Terry, "The Ballet," *NYHT* (November 26, 1949); John Martin, "Robbins Does Lead in His Own Ballet," *NYT* (November 26, 1949); Walter Terry, "The Ballet," *NYHT* (February 22, 1950); John Martin, "City Ballet Group Offers 'Firebird,'" *NYT* (February 22, 1950).

56. Reviews of *The Guests* by Cyril Beaumont, *London Times*, and Richard Buckle, *Observer* (both August 6, 1950); L. J. H. Bradley, *Ballet* (September–October 1950); unidentified, *Scotsman* (August 2, 1950); *Letters from a Life: The Selected Letters and Diaries of Benjamin Britten 1913–1976*, Vol. 3, edited by Donald Mitchell, Philip Reed, and Mervyn Cooke (Berkeley: University of California Press, 2004), 601.

57. John Martin, "Ballet: 'Allegro Brillante,'" *NYT* (March 2, 1956); Tallchief, 211.

58. MB to Lincoln Kirstein, August 30, 1950, Lincoln Kirstein Collection, NYPL.

59. Jowitt; Vaill; *Thirty Years of Treason: Excerpts from Hearings before the House Committee on Un-American Activities, 1938–1968*, edited by Eric Bentley (New York: Viking Press, 1971), 625–634; MB to MC, May 7, 1953, MCC; GOR, 343; MB to LB, December 30, 1955, LBC.

60. Bentley, 634.

61. Jowitt, 153–154; LB, "Excerpts from a West Side Log," *Playbill: West Side Story* (September 26, 1957): 43; Humphrey Burton, *Leonard Bernstein* (New York: Doubleday, 1994), 187, questions the accuracy of this "log," but a contract dated February 8, 1949, in the LBC (courtesy of Mark Horowitz) reveals that LB had been working on a Romeo and Juliet theater piece as early as this.

62. Bennett Lerner, "Three Musical Discoveries," *Keyboard Classics* 6/4 (July–August 1986): 4–7, 23; Bennett Lerner, *Piano Pieces by Roy Harris, Marc Blitzstein, Paul Bowles and Irving Fine: A Performing Edition* (DMA thesis, City University of New York, 2001), 42–69, 121–137.

63. Greg Lawrence, *Dance with Demons: The Life of Jerome Robbins* (New York: Putnam, 2001), 140.

Chapter 17

1. Margaret Grant to MB, May 11, 1946, MBP.

2. William Wright, *Lillian Hellman: the image, the woman* (New York: Simon & Schuster, 1986); Carl Rollyson, *Lillian Hellman: Her Legend and Her Legacy* (New York: St. Martin's Press, 1988); Deborah Martinson, *Lillian Hellman: A Life with Foxes and Scoundrels* (New York: Counterpoint, 2005).

3. LH, *The Little Foxes* (New York: Viking Press, 1939), 1–6, 66.

4. LH, 49.

5. LH, 100.

6. LH, 153.

7. LH, 86, 148; Karl Marx and Friedrich Engels, *The Communist Manifesto* (New York: Penguin Books, 1888, 1967), 82.

8. LH, 32, 100, 153.

9. Elise K. Kirk, *American Opera* (Urbana: University of Illinois Press, 2001), 267.

10. Gordon Allison, "How 'The Little Foxes' Was Set to Music," *NYHT* (October 30, 1949); MB, notes, MBP.

11. Allison.

12. LH, confidential report on MB, received December 14, 1939, GMF; Allison; "Lillian Hellman–Marc Blitzstein Contract," July 7, 1947, MBP.

13. MB to MC, April 17, 1948, MCC; see also Christopher Emile Mehrens, *The Genesis of Marc Blitzstein's Opera* Regina (M.A. thesis, University of North Carolina, 1987).

14. LH to MB, June 27, 1947, September 8, 1948, LHC; MB, notes, MBP ("for Marshall's sake," "soft-soap").

15. MB, *Regina: An Opera in Three Acts* (New York: Chappell, 1953); MB, *Regina: An Opera* (New York: Chappell, 1954); MB, *Regina* (Columbia Records 03S 20, 1959); MB, *Regina* [Scottish Opera version], restored by Tommy Krasker and John Mauceri (New York: Tams-Witmark, 1991); MB, *Regina* (London Records 433 812-2, 1992); *Regina: An Opera in three acts in English by Marc Blitzstein* (Chicago: Lyric Opera, 2003).

16. MB, notes, MBP.

17. LH to MB, June 27, 1947.

18. MB, notes, MBP.

19. Patrick Burke, *Come In and Hear the Truth: Jazz and Race on 52nd Street* (Chicago: University of Chicago Press, 2008), 194.

20. MB, notes; MB, *Regina*, "script, first draft," MBP.

21. MB, *Regina*, "script."

22. LH to MB, June 27, 1947, September 8, 1948.

23. MB, notes, MBP; Brenda Lewis, interview with author, September 30, 2009; MB, *Regina*, "script, n.d.," 1-2-25/26, MBP; MB, *Regina* (1953), 21.

24. Klaus-Dieter Gross, "McCarthyism and American Opera," *Revue LISA/LISA e-journal* 2/3 (2004): 164–187.

25. MB, notes, July 17, 1946, MBP.

26. Brenda Lewis, interview; LB, "Prelude to a Musical," *NYT* (October 30, 1949).

27. Anne Bill Foradori, *Marc Blitzstein's* Regina: *A Pivotal Work in American Musical Theatre* (DMA thesis, Ohio State University, 1994), 48.

28. MB, notes; MB, "Gist of Lillian's Telephone Call," June 21, 1949, MBP; for Brechtian elements in *The Little Foxes*, see Timothy J. Wiles, "Lillian Hellman's American Political Theater: The Thirties and Beyond," *Critical Essays on Lillian Hellman*, edited by Mark W. Estrin (Boston: G. K. Hall and Co., 1989), 90–112; for more on Brechtian elements in *Regina*, see TAL, 232–248.

29. Sam Zolotow, "Dumont Television Leases Mansfield," *NYT* (August 19, 1949).

30. Cheryl Crawford to MB, November 11, 1948; Seymour Peck, "Blitzstein Tells of 'Airborne,'" *PM* (March 29, 1947).

Chapter 18

1. Cheryl Crawford, *One Naked Individual: My Fifty Years in the Theatre* (New York: Bobbs-Merrill, 1977), 172; MB to Serge Koussevitzky, February 8, 1947, April 3, 1947, April 19, 1949; Koussevitzky to MB, April 1, 1947, April 21, 1949, Serge Koussevitzky Collection, LC; MB to MC, April 17, 1948, May 5, 1948, MCC.

2. MB to MC, February 20, 1949, MCC; Sam Zolotow, "'Regina' Musical, Will Open Tonight," *NYT* (October 31, 1949).

3. William Warfield with Alton Miller, *William Warfield: My Music & My Life* (Champaign, IL: Sagamore, 1991), 97–98; Arthur Berger, "City Opera's Spring Season Is Opening Thursday," *NYHT* (March 15, 1953).

4. Harriet Van Horne, "Big Pickens Sister," *Collier's* 124/12 (September 17, 1949): 25, 76; Robert Lewis, *Slings and Arrows: Theater in my Life* (New York: Stein and Day, 1984), 201.

5. Earl Wilson, "Warmer Jane Pickens Thaws Public," *Wheeling News-Register* (November 23, 1949); Lewis, 201 ("settled"), 208 ("appearing"); Robert Wilder Blue, "Brenda Lewis Recalls Marc Blitzstein and *Regina*," USOperaWeb (Winter 2002); DD, Journals, November 4, 1949, DDC; reviews of *Regina* in New Haven by F.R.J., *New Haven Journal*, and Fred H. Russell, *Bridgeport Post* (both October 7, 1949); Bone., *Variety* (October 12, 1949); Sidney Golly, *Billboard* (October 15, 1949); in Boston by Peggy Doyle, *Boston American*; Cyrus Durgin, *Boston Globe*; Helen Eager, *Boston Traveler*; Elinor Hughes, *Boston Herald*; Elliot Norton, *Boston Post*; L. A. Sloper, *Christian Science Monitor* (all October 12, 1949); L. G. Gaffney, *Boston Record* (October 13, 1949); Herbert P. Gleason, *Harvard Crimson* (October 15, 1949); Warren Storey Smith, *Boston Post* (October 16, 1949); in New York by Brooks Atkinson, *NYT*; Howard Barnes, *NYHT*; Mark Barron, *Norfolk Ledger-Dispatch*; John Chapman, *Daily News*; Robert Coleman, *Daily Mirror*; George Currie, *Brooklyn Eagle*; Thomas R. Dash, *Women's Wear Daily*; Rowland Field, *Newark News*; Robert Garland, *Journal-American*; William Hawkins, *World-Telegram*; Irving Hoffman, *Hollywood Reporter*; Harriett Johnson, *New York Post and the Home News*; Ward Morehouse, *Sun*; Arthur Pollock, *Daily Compass*; Virgil Thomson, *NYHT*; Richard Watts Jr., *Post* (all November 1, 1949); Whitney Bolton, *Morning Telegraph*; Arthur Bronson, *Variety*; Richard P. Cooke, *Wall Street Journal*; Hal Eaton, *Newark Star-Ledger*; Russell Rhodes, *Journal of Commerce* (all November 2, 1949); Margaret Baker, *Englewood Press-Journal* (November 3, 1949); Paul Affelder, *Brooklyn Eagle* (November 6, 1949); Barnard Rubin, *Daily Worker*, and Harold Stern, *Jewish Daily* (both November 8, 1949); Gabriel Gilbert, *Cue*; Wolcott Gibbs, *New Yorker*; Margaret Marshall, *Nation* (all November 12, 1949); Frank M. Lachmann, *Heights Daily News*; George Jean Nathan, *Journal-American*; *Newsweek*; *Time* (all November 14, 1949); John Mason Brown, *Saturday Review* (November 19, 1949); Jack Gaver, *Columbus Citizen* (November 27, 1949); Harold Clurman, *New Republic* (December 5, 1949); *Theatre Arts* (January 1950); see also Elliot Norton, "'Regina' Imperfect but Impressive," *Boston Post* (October 16, 1949); William Hawkins, "Stature of 'Regina' Grows on Spectator," *World-Telegram* (November 9, 1949); Brooks Atkinson, "Musical Experiment," *NYT*, and Arthur Pollock, "Blitzstein Weds Music To Drama in His 'Regina,'" *Sunday Compass* (both November 13, 1949); Herbert Kupferberg, "'Regina': Is It Bringing Broadway and Opera Closer?" *NYHT* (December 4, 1949); Howard Taubman, "Good Opera Need Not Be Grand Opera," *NYT* (December 11, 1949); Virgil Thomson, "Music in Review," *NYHT* (December 13, 1949); Thomas R. Dash, "'Regina' Deserves Better Fate," *Women's Wear Daily* (December 16, 1949).

6. Van Horne; "Jane Pickens Picked Role; Tomorrow She Will Sing It," *Brooklyn Eagle* (October 30, 1949); Robert Lewis, "'Regina' New Kind of Musical," *Boston Post* (October 19, 1949); Douglas Watt, "Bolger to Take Rest Pre-Christmas Week," *Daily News* (October 13, 1949) ("By that time"); Lewis, *Slings*, 202–204 ("I always"); Blue; Atkinson (November 13, 1949); Dash (November 1, 1949).

7. Berger.

8. Bone.; Norton (October 12, 1949, and October 16, 1949; Norton also mentions that someone had forgotten to turn on the stage microphones for the first act, but Brenda Lewis, interview with author, September 30, 2009, insists that the production never made use of microphones).

9. Vernon Rice, "Theatre," *Post* (October 29, 1949) ("arty").

10. LB, "Prelude to a Musical," *NYT* (October 30, 1949).

11. Bert McCord, "News of the Theater," *NYHT* (October 29, 1949); Elinor Hughes, "'Regina' Cherished Project of Composer Marc Blitzstein," *Boston Herald* (October 19, 1949) ("I think"); Arthur Pollock, "Man Floating at Majorca Comes Out With 'Regina,'" *Sunday Compass* (October 20, 1949) ("I call"); Atkinson (November 13, 1949); Gordon Allison, "How 'The Little Foxes' Was Set to Music," *NYHT* (October 30, 1949).

12. Leonard Lyons, "The Lyons Den," *Post* (November 2, 1949); Golly; Hughes (October 12, 1949) ("stunning"); Atkinson (November 1, 1949).

13. Sloper; Hawkins (November 1, 1949); Gaver; Gaffney; Hoffman.

14. Garland; Atkinson (November 1, 1949); Barnes; Brown; Dash (December 16, 1949).

15. Affelder ("master"); Hawkins (November 1, 1949) ("twice"); Barnes ("strange"); Rubin; Ward Morehouse, "Broadway After Dark," *Sun* (December 16, 1949).

16. Taubman; Rubin; for more on Blitzstein and the CPUSA at this time, see GOR, 337.

17. Thomson (November 1, 1949, and November 13, 1949); Nathan.

18. Oscar Hammerstein II and Richard Rodgers, "An Optimistic Appraisal of Our Theatre," *NYT* (January 1, 1950); GOR, 339; Frank Loesser, "About 'Regina,'" *Regina* (Columbia Records 03S 20, 1959).

19. COP, 144.

20. "Tele Follow-Up Comment," *Variety* (November 16, 1949).

21. Taubman; Howard Taubman, "A Living Memorial," *NYT* (May 18, 1952) ("one of"); Warfield, 97; BAL ("It was"); Douglas Watt, "Musical Events," *New Yorker* (June 14, 1952): 103–105.

22. "We Saw Regina," *NYT* (December 13, 1949); Lewis, *Slings*, 106, 206; GOR, 339; Paul Moor, "Tradition of Turbulence," *Theatre Arts* 34/3 (March 1950): 36–38; Lewis Funke, "Rialto Gossip," *NYT* (December 25, 1949); Crawford, 173–174.

23. Robert Coleman, "Book for Runyan Musical Set, Casting to Start," *Daily Mirror* (November 19, 1949).

24. Both the LHC and MBP contain drafts of LH's narration; Lewis, *Slings*, 206.

25. Lewis, *Slings*, 206.

26. "Lillian Hellman Balks House Unit," *NYT* (May 22, 1952); LH, *Scoundrel Time* (New York: Little, Brown, 1976), 123–126; Lewis, *Slings*, 206.

27. Reviews of *Regina* by William Hawkins, *World-Telegram and Sun*; Ross Parmenter, *NYT*; Francis D. Perkins, *NYHT*; Vernon Rice, *Post*; Douglas Watt, *Daily News* (all June 2, 1952); Arthur Bronson, *Variety* (June 4, 1952); Watt (June 14, 1952); Raymond Ericson, *Musical America* (June 1952) ("loudly").

28. Arthur Berger, "City Opera's Spring Season Is Opening Thursday," *NYHT* (March 15, 1953); Henry Hewes, "Broadway Postscript," *Saturday Review* 36/14 (April 4, 1953): 41–42; MB, *Regina: An Opera in Three Acts* (New York: Chappell, 1953), 47; Lewis, *Slings*, 207.

29. Reviews of *Regina* by Robert Bagar, *World-Telegram and Sun*; Arthur Berger, *NYHT*; Howard Taubman, *NYT*; Douglas Watt, *Daily News* (all April 3, 1953); Arthur Bronson, *Variety* (April 8, 1953); *Newsweek* and *Time* (both April 13, 1953); Irving Kolodin, *Saturday Review* (April 18, 1953); Richard RePass, *Music Review* (August 1953); Richard RePass, *Canon* (December 1953); LEH, 416–418; DD, Journals, April 29, 1953, DDC.

30. Review of *Regina*, *Newsweek* (April 13, "This is where"); MB to MC, March 8, 1953, MCC; MB to DD, January 8, 1954, DDC.

31. MB to Antonio Ghiringhelli [May 9, 1954]; Ghiringhelli to MB, May 15, 1954; Gian Carlo Menotti to MB, June 1, 1954; Ghiringhelli to LB, November 9, 1954, MBP.

32. MB to LB, March 15, 1955, LBC; LB to MB, March 20, 1955; MB to LB, March 23, 1955, MBP.

33. Victor de Sabata to MB, March 27, 1955; LB to MB, March 28, 1955; MB to LB, April 5, 1955, MBP.

34. Julius Rudel, interview with author, September 29, 2009; reviews of *Regina* by Paul Affelder, *Brooklyn Eagle*; Frank Aston, *World-Telegram and Sun*; Robert Coleman, *Daily Mirror*; Thomas R. Dash, *Women's Wear Daily*; Harriett Johnson, *Post*; Miles Kastendieck,

Journal-American; Francis D. Perkins, *NYHT*; Howard Taubman, *NYT*; Douglas Watt, *Daily News* (all April 18, 1958); Winthrop Sargeant, *New Yorker* (April 26, 1958); Lester Trimble, *Nation* (May 3, 1958); see also Howard Taubman, "Worth Doing," *NYT* (May 4, 1958); F.M. [Frank Merkling], "Americana at the Center," *Opera News* 23/2 (October 27, 1958): 8.

35. Taubman (April 18, 1958, "some wonderful"); Johnson (April 18, 1958); Taubman, "Worth Doing"; GOR, 435; LH, "An American Opera," *Regina* (Columbia); Claire Reis to MB [April 17, 1958], MBP; Rudel; Robert Russell Bennett to MB, May 2, 1959, MBP. In this same letter, Bennett also made a rather oblique criticism of *Regina*, which he deemed "powerful and beautiful," by way of the "slight suggestion" that as Blitzstein moved on to write "the great American opera," he remember that "very important dramatic phrases and words punctuated by very important orchestral music may load the ear with too much to carry. There are very few such moments in Regina. They are hard to avoid."

36. Blue.

37. Eric Salzman, "Baby Doe and Regina," *NYT* (November 8, 1959); Virgil Thomson, "From 'Regina' to 'Juno,'" *Saturday Review* 42/20 (May 16, 1959): 82–83; Eric Myers, "Recordings," *Opera News* 75/7 (January 2011): 67–68.

38. MB, Journals, July 6, 1959, July 11, 1959, July 16, 1959; LB to MB, April 17, 1955 (for Diamond), MBP; MB to DD, November 19, 1957, DDC (for Guerrieri); Friedelind Wagner to Lina Abarbanell, September 29, 1959, MBP.

39. LH to Julius Rudel, March 18, 1964, LHC; Alan Rich, "At Philharmonic Hall, Loving Tribute To the Memory of Marc Blitzstein," *NYHT* (April 20, 1964); Harold C. Schonberg, "Music: Marc Blitzstein," *NYT* (April 20, 1964).

40. Jamie James, "How Many Great American Operas? One for Sure," *NYT* (October 4, 1992).

41. Irene Diamond to LB, October 2, 1972, LBC; MB, *Regina* [Scottish Opera version], restored by Tommy Krasker and John Mauceri (New York: Tams-Witmark, 1991); MB, *Regina* (London Records 433 812–2, 1992), including Tommy Krasker, "Regina Restored," and John Mauceri, "A Note by the Conductor"; *Regina: An Opera in three acts in English by Marc Blitzstein* (Chicago: Lyric Opera, 2003); John Mauceri, interview with author, October 3, 2009; Harry Kraut to LH, March 27, 1980; LH to Kraut, April 9, 1980, LHC.

42. The added material includes portions of the first scene (later prologue) that highlight the spiritual-versus-jazz theme; that part of "Small Talk" that includes some discussion of "colored" bands; that section in "Big Rich" in which Birdie requests that Oscar not hunt for sport; some of "My, My"; Ben's "Thirty Years I Tried," which reveals his corrupt business practices and Horace's disdain for them; the transition to the party scene, in which Regina comments on the arriving guests; some portions of "Chinkypin"; Birdie's vocal line in "Blues"; and the instrumental interlude, derived from "Gallantry," in "Regina's Waltz." Mauceri and Krasker also removed a jazz strain from the prologue (at rehearsal T in the published 1954 score), adapted some of the discarded "Polka" in lieu of some underscoring derived from "Sing Hubbard," and thinned out the scoring for "Galop."

43. Reviews of *Regina* by Patrick O'Connor, *London Times Literary Supplement* (May 24, 1991); Wilfrid Mellers, *Musical Times* (July 1991); Raymond Monelle, *Opera* (July 1991); P.J.S. [Patrick J. Smith], *Opera News* (January 30, 1993); David E. Anderson, *Opera Quarterly* (Spring 1997).

44. Archival recordings of productions by the Houston Grand Opera (courtesy of Brent Oldham) and Bard (courtesy of Irene Zedlacher); Michael Egel, interview with author, September 29, 2009; Carl Joseph Ratner, *Chicago Opera Theater: Standard Bearer for American Opera, 1976–2001* (DMA thesis, Northwestern University, 2005), 95–98; Olin Chism, "'Regina' Does Out Drama But Falters Musically," *Dallas Morning News* (October 2, 2003).

45. Bernard Holland, "'Regina' With Music Restored," *NYT* (October 21, 2003); Edward Rothstein, "Those Greedy Little Foxes, in Music by Blitzstein," *NYT* (October 12, 1992);

Anne Midgette, "That Frightening Regina, Her Breeding and Rage," *NYT* (August 1, 2005); Joseph Horowitz, "On Copland, Blitzstein, and Gershwin," *Times Literary Supplement* (September 16, 2005).

46. Christopher Emile Mehrens, *The Genesis of Marc Blitzstein's Opera* Regina (M.A. thesis, University of North Carolina, 1987); Larry Phillip Fox, *A Comparative Analysis of Selected Dramatic Works and Their Twentieth Century Operatic Adaptations* (Ph.D. dissertation, University of South Carolina, 1992); Anne Bill Foradori, *Marc Blitzstein's* Regina: *A Pivotal Work in American Musical Theatre* (DMA thesis, Ohio State University, 1994); Ratner; MEL, 421–428; Blue.

Chapter 19

1. MB to LB, April 16, 1950, May 19, 1950, LBC (Blitzstein's revisions remain unaccounted for).
2. Elinor Hughes, "Blitzstein Turns Director Fro [sic] Britten Opera, Loves It," *Boston Herald* (November 27, 1950).
3. Eric Crozier, *Let's Make An Opera!* (New York: Boosey & Hawkes, 1949); MB, *Let's Make an Opera*, script, MBP; *Letters from a Life: The Selected Letters of Benjamin Britten 1913–1976*, Vol. 3, edited by Donald Mitchell, Philip Reed, and Mervyn Cooke (London: Faber and Faber, 2004), 606; Benjamin Britten, *The Little Sweep* (London: Boosey & Hawkes, 1950), 2, 4, 54, 105 (annotated by MB, MBP).
4. MB to MC, December 15, 1950, MCC.
5. Reviews of *Let's Make an Opera* by Peggy Doyle, *Boston Evening American*; Cyrus Durgin, *Boston Daily Globe*; Helen Eager, *Boston Traveler*; Elinor Hughes, *Boston Herald*; Elliot Norton, *Boston Post*; Harold Rogers, *Christian Science Monitor* (all November 28, 1950); Bone., *Variety*, and L. G. Gaffney, *Boston Daily Record* (both November 29, 1950); Brooks Atkinson, *NYT*; Howard Barnes, *NYHT*; Robert Coleman, *Daily Mirror*; Thomas R. Dash, *Women's Wear Daily*; William Hawkins, *World-Telegram and Sun*; John McClain, *Journal-American*; Arthur Pollock, *Daily Compass*; Richard Watts Jr., *Post* (all December 14, 1950); John Chapman, "Let's Make an Audience," *New York Sunday News* (December 24, 1950).
6. Dash ("zest"); Doyle ("know-how"); MB to MC, December 15, 1950; Mitchell, 628–629.
7. MB, "Review of Records," *Musical Quarterly* 40/3 (July 1954): 454–456; MB, "On The Threepenny Opera," *Musical Show* (October 1962): 2.
8. MB, "'Threepenny Opera' Is Back," *NYHT* (March 7, 1954); Kim H. Kowalke, "'The Threepenny Opera' in America," *Kurt Weill: The Threepenny Opera*, edited by Stephen Hinton (New York: Cambridge University Press, 1990), 78–119; Kim H. Kowalke, "*The Threepenny Opera*: The Score Adapted," *Die Dreigroschenoper: A Facsimile of the Holograph Full Score*, edited by Edward Harsh (New York: Kurt Weill Foundation for Music, 1996), 11–15; Cheryl Crawford, *One Naked Individual: My Fifty Years in the Theatre* (New York: Bobbs-Merrill, 1977), 213.
9. Bertolt Brecht, *The Threepenny Opera*, trans. by Desmond Vesey and Eric Bentley, *From the Modern Repertoire: Series One*, edited by Eric Bentley (Denver: University of Denver Press, 1949); Lotte Lenya to Alfred Kalmus, September 3, 1954, KWF.
10. MB, "'Threepenny Opera' Is Back"; Donald Spoto and Lys Symonette, "An Oral History Interview with Maurice Abravanel" [1985?], KWF, 4–6; MB, telegrams to Kurt Weill, November 19, 1936, January 9, 1947, October 30, 1949, Kurt Weill Collection, Yale University; Crawford, 213.
11. MB, "'Threepenny Opera' Is Back"; MB to LB, April 16, 1950, LBC; MB to MC, July 4, 1950, MCC.
12. MB, "Prize 'Dreigroschen,'" *Saturday Review* 41/43 (October 25, 1958): 64–65; Stephen Giles, "Rewriting Brecht: *Die Dreigroschenoper* 1928–1931," *Literaturwissenschaftliches Jahrbuch* 30 (1989): 249–279 ("explicitly Marxist," 266); Blitzstein's scripts include three prepared in the period 1950–52 (microfilm 62/185–590, MBP); five associated with the

off-Broadway production (62/591–962; 63/106–184); and one associated with the 1956 London production (63/1–105); all English song titles are Blitzstein's.

13. Brecht, *Threepenny*, 227; Blitzstein presumably consulted this Vesey-Bentley 1949 translation as well as a somewhat different typescript version of the work by the same two translators found among his papers.

14. MB to Sam Wanamaker, January 18, 1956, MBP; Lotte Lenya, *Lenya: The Legend*, edited by David Farneth (New York: Overlook Press, 1998), 132.

15. Lenya to Kalmus; see also Emory Lewis, "Musicals Off Beat," *Cue* (April 3, 1954): 16; Eric Bentley to MB, November 9, 1951; Leon Kellman to Peter Suhrkamp, November 11, 1953; Bertolt Brecht to MB, June 14, 1955, MBP ("grossartig").

16. "City Troupe to Give New Productions," *NYT* (January 18, 1952); Kurt List, "A Musical Brief for Gangsterism," *New Leader* 35/5 (February 4, 1952): 26; Dwight Macdonald, letter to the editor, *New Leader* 35/9 (March 3, 1952): 27; "Weill Opera Put Off Until Fall," *NYT* (February 7, 1952); MB to Irma Bauman, February 7, 1952, January 26, 1957 ("arch-worm"), Mordecai Bauman Papers, Tamiment Library, NYU; MB to MC, January 22, 1952, February 9, 1952, MCC.

17. LB to Helen Coates, January 21, 1952, LBC.

18. *The Threepenny Opera*, June 14, 1952, archival recording, KWF; reviews of *The Threepenny Opera* by Harold Rogers, *Christian Science Monitor*, and Howard Taubman, *NYT* (both June 16, 1952); Billy Rose to MB, December 3, 1952, MBP; Crawford, 213.

19. Donald Spoto, "Stanley Chase: An Oral History Interview," March 24, 1987, KWF.

20. Donald Spoto, "An Oral History Interview with Carmen Capalbo," March 7, 1986, KWF; Spoto, "Chase."

21. Sam Wanamaker to MB, January 6, 1956; MB to Wanamaker, January 10, 1956, MBP.

22. Spoto, "Chase"; David Farneth and Peggy Meyer Sherry, "An Oral History Interview with Saul Bolasni," April 18, 1991, KWF; GOR, 375.

23. David Farneth, "Transcript of Interview with Scott Merrill," November 2, 1998, KWF.

24. The assertion that Blitzstein "romanticized the 'Love Song' as a harmonized duet," David Farneth's assertion that Blitzstein "romanticized the 'Love Song' as a harmonized duet," in liner notes (12), *The Threepenny Opera* (Decca 012 159 463-2, 2000), accordingly seems overstated; at Brandeis, David Brooks sang the duet in unison with Jo Sullivan.

25. Charles Russo, interview with author, November 22, 2009.

26. Farneth, "Bolasni"; Spoto, "Capalbo"; Farneth, "Merrill."

27. Spoto, "Capalbo"; Sam Zolotow, "Blitzstein Work Due Here March 2," *NYT* (January 4, 1954); GOR, 375; Spoto, "Abravanel"; Foster Hirsch, *Kurt Weill on Stage: From Berlin to Broadway* (New York: Knopf, 2002), 328; Capalbo, interview with author, February 16, 2010.

28. Spoto, "Capalbo."

29. Reviews of *The Threepenny Opera* by John Chapman, *Daily News*; Robert Coleman, *Daily Mirror*; L.F. [Lewis Funke], *NYT*; Jay S. Harrison, *NYHT*; William Hawkins, *World-Telegram and Sun*; John McClain, *Journal-American*; Louis Sheaffer, *Brooklyn Eagle*; Richard Watts Jr., *Post* (all March 11, 1954); Jess., *Variety* (March 17, 1954); Brooks Atkinson, *NYT*, and Virgil Thomson, *NYHT* (both March 21, 1954); Harold Clurman, *Nation*, and Henry Hewes, *Saturday Review* (both March 27, 1954); Olin Downes, *NYT* (April 4, 1954); William Becker, *Hudson Review* (Summer 1954).

30. Thomson; Arthur Berger, "Opera Translation Involves More Than Word Meanings," *NYHT* (December 14, 1952); Jack Beeson, "American Opera: Curtains and Overtures," *Columbia University Forum* 3/4 (Fall 1960): 20–26.

31. Becker, 268; Lenya to Kalmus; Eric Bentley, "Theatre," *New Republic* 130/14 (April 5, 1954): 21; Eric Bentley, *Bentley on Brecht* (Evanston, IL: Northwestern University Press, 1981, 2008), 442 ("excessively"); Eric Bentley, "How Free Is Too Free?" *American Theatre* 2/8 (November 1985): 10–13 ("very free," "Blitzstein and I").

32. MB to DD, April 24, 1954, September 14, 1963 ("superb"), DDC; MB, "Prize"; Meryle Secrest, "He Doesn't Mind Being in Shadow," *Washington Post* (May 14, 1963).

33. Spoto, "Capalbo."

34. MB to Sam Wanamaker, December 18, 1955, MBP.

35. Wilder Hobson, "Pleasures of High Summer," *Saturday Review* 37/31 (July 31, 1954): 59; "Year's Best Records Listed Categorically," *NYHT* (December 5, 1954); although the received wisdom states that *The Threepenny Opera* was the first recorded off-Broadway show, Tikva Records recorded Arnold Perl's *The World of Sholom Aleichem* in 1953.

36. "Solomon Song" and "Mack the Knife," archival audio of the *Polly and Jerry* episode, KWF (the "Mack the Knife" included as a bonus track with *The Threepenny Opera*, Decca 012 159 463-2, 2000); Blitzstein also accompanied Lenya singing "Surabaya-Johnny" in German on television, possibly for the same show, *Lenya* (Hambergen, Germany: Bear Family Records BCD 16 019 KL, 1998).

37. Brooks Atkinson, "'Homeward Look' Opens in the Village," *NYT* (June 4, 1954); "Theatre: Off-Broadway," *NYT* (September 15, 1954).

38. Reviews of *The Threepenny Opera* by Thomas R. Dash, *Women's Wear Daily*; L.F. [Lewis Funke], *NYT*; Miles Kastendieck, *Journal-American*; Walter F. Kerr, *NYHT*; Richard Watts Jr., *Post* (all September 21, 1955).

39. "Sue Over 'Opera'; Show Continues," *Variety* (December 21, 1955); MB to DD, February 28, 1956, DDC.

40. Oscar Lewenstein to MB, November 30, 1955; Sam Wanamaker to MB, December 7, 1955 ("hates"), December 12, 1955 ("hamburgers"); MB to Wanamaker, November 21, 1955, MBP.

41. Reviews of *The Threepenny Opera* by John Barber, *Daily Express*; Martin Cooper, *Daily Telegraph* ("unambiguously"); Alan Dent, *News Chronicle*; Philip Hope-Wallace, *Manchester Guardian* ("American-Jewish"); Andrew Porter, *Financial Times*; Milton Shulman, *Evening Standard*; Stephen Williams, *Evening News*; Cecil Wilson, *Daily Mail* (all February 10, 1956); Harold Hobson, *Sunday Times*, and Kenneth Tynan, *Observer* (both February 12, 1956); Myro., *Variety* (February 22, 1956).

42. Will Friedwald, *Stardust Melodies: The Biography of Twelve of America's Most Popular Songs* (New York: Pantheon Books, 2002), 77–103; "George Avakian . . . In Conversation with David Farneth and Lauriejean Reinhardt," *Lenya* (Bear Family), 178–186 (accompanying book to an 11-CD collection that includes some of these tracks, including an extended rehearsal segment with Lenya and Louis Armstrong); Jim Goggin, *Turk Murphy: Just For The Record* (San Leandro, CA: San Francisco Traditional Jazz Foundation, 1982).

43. MB to Sam Wanamaker, December 13, 1955, MBP; MB, "On The Threepenny Opera."

44. John Lewis Carver, "Exposed! The Hit Song That Makes $$$ For The Reds!" *Top Secret* (June 1956): 24–25, 49–51; Harold C. Schonberg, "Kurt Weill Program Heard at Stadium," *NYT* (August 2, 1958).

45. Sam Zolotow, "Long Run to End for 'Threepenny,'" *NYT* (December 6, 1961); Peter Hamill, "The Curtain Falls on 'Threepenny Opera,'" *Post* (December 18, 1961); Farneth, "Merrill"; Farneth, "Bolasni"; Russo.

46. Reviews of *The Threepenny Opera* by both Emilia Hodel and Jack Loughner, *San Francisco News-Call Bulletin*, and Martin Russell, *San Francisco Examiner* (all September 14, 1960); Stef., *Variety* (September 28, 1960); Farneth, "Merrill."

47. Stefan Brecht to Leon Kellman, November 18, 1956, MBP; Capalbo, interview with author; MB, "On the Threepenny Opera"; MB to Natalie P. Kissel, March 8, 1956, MBP; 1956 income based on a list compiled by the composer of "income" ($12,660.56) minus his ASCAP dues and William Morris commissions ($1,099.97); he approximated his 1962 gross income as $22,000, David J. Algase (MB's accountant) to MB, November 21, 1962, MBP.

48. Spoto, "Chase"; Hirsch, 332–333; Kowalke, "'The Threepenny Opera' in America," 114–115; "George Avakian," 179; MB, "On the Threepenny Opera."

49. Kim Kowalke, interview with author, November 20, 2009, to author, November 23, 2009.

50. "Rose Confirms Plans to 'Lease' Theatre," *NYT* (November 18, 1952); MB to MC, December 16, 1952, MCC; MB, notes, MBP ("passion").

51. MB, notes, MBP; programs, *The Threepenny Opera*, MBP; John Gutman to MB, November 17, 1954, November 25, 1954 ("a very"); MB to Gutman, November 22, 1954, MBP.

52. Giuseppe Verdi and Francesco Maria Piave, *La Traviata* (New York: G. Schirmer, 1899, 1926), trans. by Natalia Macfarren (New York: G. Schirmer, 1899, 1926), 40; Blitzstein's translation, one of several variants, from his annotated vocal score of the same.

53. MB, notes, October 26, 1952, MBP; MB to MC, October 27, 1952, MCC.

54. Ubiquitous, "Along 57th Street," *Musical Courier* 152/6 (April 1955): 5; H.W.L. [Henry W. Levinger], "Jennie Tourel, soprano," *Musical Courier* 152/6 (April 1955): 23; Ned Rorem, *Wings of Friendship: Selected Letters, 1944–2005* ([Washington, D.C.] Shoemaker & Hoard, 2005), 117.

55. LEH, 580.

56. MB, "On 'Mahagonny,'" *Saturday Review* 41/22 (May 31, 1958): 40, 47; reprinted in *Score* 23 (July 1958): 11–13.

57. MB, "On 'Mahagonny,'" 47; "Two Great Resorts—A Candid Look," *Life* (January 20, 1958): 87–94.

58. MB, "On 'Mahagonny,'" 40, 47; MB, "New York Medley, Winter, 1935," *MM* 13/2 (January–February 1936): 36; GOR, 305.

59. Bertolt Brecht, *Aufstieg und Fall der Stadt Mahagonny* (Berlin: Suhrkamp, 1955); MB to DD, January 8, 1954, DDC ("dream-studio"); Kurt Weill, *Aufstieg und Fall der Stadt Mahagonny* (Vienna: Universal, 1929).

60. Donald Spoto, "An Oral History with Carmen Capalbo (II)," April 23, 1986, KWF; Capalbo, interview with author ("rough draft," as opposed to "the entire thing," as stated in the "Oral History"); Stefan Brecht to Leon Kellman, February 17, 1958; MB to Stefan Brecht, February 19, 1958, MBP; MB, "On 'Mahagonny,'" 40.

61. Stefan Brecht to MB, March 27, 1959; MB to Helene Weigel, May 24, 1959; MB, Journals, July 8–13, 1959, MBP.

62. MB, "Primer on Brecht," *Nation* 189/7 (September 12, 1959): 137–139.

63. Spoto, "Capalbo (II)"; Lotte Lenya to Charles Seton, March 30, 1960, KWF; Bertolt Brecht, *The Rise and Fall of the City of Mahagonny* and *The Seven Deadly Sins of the Petty Bourgeoisie*, trans. by W. H. Auden and Chester Kallman and edited by John Willett and Ralph Manheim (New York: Arcade, 1996), 12 (this published version of the song exactly matches the 1960 typescript, Dave Stein to author, December 18, 2009); MB, "Jenny" ["Havana Song"], undated, similar to other drafts dating from July 1956, but presumably later, very possibly 1958; Blitzstein placed an exclamation point beside a news item reported by Dorothy Kilgallen in a September 11, 1960, article in the *Journal-American* stating that he had run into problems with Lenya "over production plans" regarding *Mahagonny*, MBP.

64. Spoto, "Capalbo (II)"; Stephen Sondheim, interview with author, June 12, 2011; GOR, 512; Clive Barnes, "'Mahagonny,' Brecht-Weill Lyric Opera, Here at Last," *NYT* (April 29, 1970).

65. MB to DD, October 9, 1957, DDC.

66. Peter Thomson, *Brecht: Mother Courage and Her Children* (New York: Cambridge University Press, 1998), 35; MB to DD, October 9, 1957 ("not sensationally").

67. Bertolt Brecht, *Mutter Courage* (Berlin: Suhrkamp, 1955); *The Modern Theatre*, Vol. 2, edited by Eric Bentley (Garden City, NY: Doubleday, 1955); MB to DD, October 9, 1957 ("as usual"); Paul Dessau to MB, January 8, 1958, January 29, 1958; MB to Lina Abarbanell, July 1, 1960, MBP; for more on the Dessau score, see *The Modern Theatre*, 325.

68. MB to Stuart Scheftel, November 8, 1957, MBP; Arthur Gelb, "Welles To Stage Satire By Brecht," *NYT* (September 23, 1957); MB to DD, March 4, 1958, DDC; Sam Zolotow, "Siobhan M'Kenna Eyes Brecht Play," *NYT* (March 27, 1959) ("struck"); Tony Richardson to MB, September 8, 1958, September 29, 1958; John Willett to MB, September 9, 1958, MBP.

69. Zolotow, "Siobhan"; Stefan Brecht to MB, March 27, 1959, MBP; Sam Zolotow, "Playwrights Set 2 Play Premieres," *NYT* (June 12, 1959); Sam Zolotow, "Broadway Debut for Lucille Ball," *NYT* (October 27, 1959); Milton Esterow, "Tangled Rights," *NYT* (February 25, 1962); Amanda Vaill, *Somewhere: The Life of Jerome Robbins* (New York: Broadway Books, 2006), 350; Eric Bentley to author, January 24, 2010, claims that Blitzstein felt "betrayed" after Crawford selected Bentley's version of the play over his own.

70. Bertolt Brecht, *Mother Courage and Her Children*, trans. by Eric Bentley (New York: Grove Press, 1961).

71. Reviews of *Mother Courage* by Barbara and Scott Siegel, *TheaterMania.com* (September 6, 2005); Alexis Soloski, *Village Voice* (September 13, 2005); Terry Teachout, *Wall Street Journal* (September 16, 2005); Wilborn Hampton, *NYT* (September 17, 2005); Brad Bradley, *CurtainUp.com* (2005); David Fuller, interview with author, December 21, 2009; Estelle Parsons, interview with author, February 15, 2011; Richard Block, interview with author, February 26, 2011 ("certainly").

72. Bob Dylan, *Chronicles*, Vol. 1 (New York: Simon & Schuster, 2004), 272–276; Jason Zinoman, "When Bobby Met Bertolt, Times Changed," *NYT* (October 8, 2006); Sean Wilentz, *Bob Dylan in America* (New York: Doubleday, 2010), 43.

73. MB, "On 'Mahagonny,'" 40; MB to DD, August 24, 1956, DDC; MB to LB, August 26, 1956, LBC.

Chapter 20

1. MB to LB, April 16, 1950, LBC; Lewis Funke, "News and Gossip Gathered on the Rialto," *NYT* (May 21, 1950); Sam Zolotow, "Grace to Sponsor Irish Comedy Here," *NYT* (August 25, 1950); MB to MC, August 31, 1952, January 6, 1953, MCC.

2. MB to MC, November 21, 1951, November 29, 1951, December 5, 1951, December 10, 1951, MCC.

3. MB to DD, July 30, 1953, DDC; MB to LB, November 1, 1953, LBC; MB to MC, August 5, 1954, MCC; Leon Kellman to MB, August 6, 1953, MBP.

4. The title page of one of his scores gives the breakdown of strings alternately as 5-4-2-4-1 and 3-2-2-2-1.

5. MB, notes, February 5, 1950, March 16, 1950, July 19, 1950, MBP; MB to MC, February 17, 1953, MCC.

6. MB, notes, MBP; MB to LB, April 27, 1951, LBC.

7. MB, notes, including December 31, 1950 ("hard-boiled"), January 27, 1951 ("Listening"), July 2, 1953 ("it stays"), MBP.

8. MB, "Notes on the Musical Theatre," *Theatre Arts* 34/6 (June 1950): 30–31; MB, "American Opera Today," "The Consul," "Don't Ever Call It Opera," "Opera in America" ("opera"), "What Can Be Sung," and other unpublished drafts, MBP.

9. MB, "Notes on the Musical Theatre."

10. MB, "Gian-Carlo Menotti, *The Saint of Bleecker Street*," *Notes* 13/3 (June 1956): 521–523; MB, "American Opera Today."

11. MB, "Richard Mohaupt: *Double-Trouble*," *Notes* 12/2 (March 1955): 319; MB to DD, February 15, 1955, DDC.

12. MB, notes, August 24, 1951 ("comic-tragic"), October 18, 1951 ("comedy which"), MBP.

13. MB, notes, MBP.

14. MB, notes, including March 31, 1950 ("psychically"), January 4, 1951, September 23, 1951 ("enthralled"), August 6, 1952 ("I wish"), MBP; Louis Berg, *The Human Personality* (New York: Prentice Hall, 1933), 265–266; in his finished libretto, Blitzstein omitted Reuben's response, "Circus trapeze," to Nina's question, "Your father jumped off a bridge?" leaving the impression that Pop killed himself by jumping off a bridge.

15. MB, notes, including March 31, 1950, and April 2, 1950 (for Selznick), August 15, 1951 ("pure-in-heart"), February 5, 1952 ("becomes"), MBP.

16. MB, notes, including April 16, 1951 ("natural"), October 1, 1951 ("whole"), August 14, 1952 ("the terror"), June 27, 1953 (for Nina and the police), MBP; GOR, 353–354, 383 (drawing on earlier drafts, GOR cites Nina's new job as that of a "chorus girl").

17. Herbert Asbury, *The Gangs of New York: An Informal History of the Underworld* (Garden City, NY: Garden City Publishing, 1927) (MB cites p. 190, from which he borrowed the idea of Bart as a "king," and which also includes this sentence regarding Billy McGlory's saloon: "There is beastliness and depravity under his roof compared with which no chapter in the world's history is equal"); Blitzstein possibly derived the name Malatesta (in Italian, more or less, "headache") from a character in Donizetti's *Don Pasquale* or perhaps from the sixteenth-century tyrant Sigismondo Malatesta, the subject of some of Ezra Pound's cantos; MB, notes, including September 30, 1951 ("vamp"), June 23, 1953 ("on the realistic"), September 6, 1953 ("Never"), MBP.

18. Blitzstein wrote several numbers, including "Ever So Gently," "Talk to Me," "Two Little Girls," "You Will Take a Long Journey," and the instrumental "Scat-Dance," that never made it into this pre-Boston version.

19. Correlating the names of the four Barflies with their designations in various scripts and scores as Barfly I, II, III, and IV remains difficult because of inconsistencies among the sources; in one such source, Blitzstein distinguishes the four Barflies, all involved in rackets themselves, as follows: "I (bass), little, spidery; II (bass), broad and husky; III (tenor), fat and intense; IV (tenor), lean and long, optimistic."

20. MB, notes, MBP.

21. MB, notes, including January 4, 1951 ("which"), August 28, 1952 ("Bart"), MBP.

22. MB, notes, including August 14, 1951 ("No need"), August 11, 1953 ("from alarm"), February 21, 1955 ("nauseating") (the shootout with the gunman, August Robles, took place on February 20, 1955), MBP.

23. Christopher Bigsby, *Arthur Miller* (Cambridge, MA: Harvard University Press, 2009), 114; thinking of *Regina*, Klaus-Dieter Gross, "McCarthyism and American Opera," *Revue LISA/LISA e-journal* 2/3 (2004): 164–187, writes "In Blitzstein's and [Earl] Robinson's socialist operas McCarthyism is present in defiance, through neglect," but Blitzstein conceived *Regina*, based largely on a 1939 play, in the immediate postwar years, whereas he wrote *Reuben Reuben*, not considered by Gross, at the height of the Red Scare of the 1950s.

24. MB, notes, MBP.

25. MB, notes, December 24, 1950, MBP; MB to LB, November 1, 1953, LBC.

26. Cheryl Crawford to Marlon Brando, July 27, 1953; Crawford to Sam Jaffe, September 29, 1954; Crawford to Michael Kidd, November 11, 1954; Crawford to Richard Rodgers and Oscar Hammerstein, January 21, 1955, Cheryl Crawford Collection, NYPL.

27. MB to MC, July 1, 1954, October 17, 1954, MBP; "'Seventh Heaven' Due as a Musical," *NYT* (November 15, 1954); MB to DD, September 29, 1954, DDC; MB to LB, March 23, 1955, LBC.

28. MB to DD, April 24, 1954, DDC; Louis Calta, "Patrice Munsel Ponders Musical," *NYT* (May 4, 1954); Cheryl Crawford to MB, June 2, 1954, Cheryl Crawford Collection, NYPL; "Lewis Wondering About 3 Musicals," *NYT* (June 21, 1954).

29. Grace Davidson, "Cheryl Makes Discovery," *Boston Post* (October 10, 1955); MB to MC, July 1, 1954, MCC ("natural"); MB to DD, September 29, 1954, DDC.

30. MB to LB, April 21, 1955, LBC ("very able"); MB to MC, September 3, 1955, MCC ("beautiful"); Andrew B. Harris, *The Performing Set: The Broadway Designs of William and Jean Eckart* (Denton: University of North Texas Press, 2006), 59–64.

31. *Reuben Reuben*, archival tape (October 1955), MBP.

32. Alan Frazer, "We Want a Hit!" *Boston American* (October 12, 1955); Cheryl Crawford, *One Naked Individual: My Fifty Years in the Theatre* (New York: Bobbs-Merrill, 1977), 178–179; MB to MC, October 20, 1955, MBP; reviews of *Reuben Reuben* by Peggy Doyle, *Daily News*; Alta Maloney, *Boston Traveler*; Elliot Norton, *Boston Post* (all October 11, 1955); Cyrus Durgin, *Boston Globe*; L. G. Gaffney, *Boston Record*; Guy, *Hollywood Daily Variety*; Guy, *Variety*; Elinor Hughes, *Boston Herald* (all October 12, 1955); George E. Ryan, *Boston Pilot* (October 15, 1955); Dewar., *Billboard* (October 22, 1955); see also second thoughts by Cyrus Durgin, *Boston Globe*, and Elliot Norton, *Boston Post* (both October 16, 1955).

33. Durgin (October 12, 1955); Norton (October 11, 1955, and October 16, 1955); Maloney; Ryan; Guy, *Variety*.

34. John Pasbur to MB, October 12, 1955 ("very"); A[braham] Levin to MB, October 20, 1955; Victor Yellin to MB, October 14, 1955; Leonard Burkat to MB, October 24, 1955; Seymour Bluhm to Cyrus Durgin, October 28, 1955, MBP.

35. Mary X. Sullivan, "Producer Has Big Hopes for 'Reuben,'" *Boston Advertiser* (October 16, 1955) ("We," based on an interview conducted October 12); "Anderson, Nash 'Doctor' 'Reuben Reuben'" *Post* (October 16, 1955); Robert Anderson to Cheryl Crawford, MB, and Robert Lewis, October 13, 1955; MB, notes, October 14, 1955, MBP.

36. Elinor Hughes, "'Reuben Reuben' to Close Here; Other Theater News," *Boston Herald* (October 18, 1955); Hal Eaton, "Producer of $200,000 Flop to Repay Backers," *Long Island City Star Journal* (October 29, 1955); Crawford, 179.

37. William Eckart, "The Original Whistle: 'Gems Search for a Setting,'" *Sondheim Review* 2/1 (Summer 1995): 20–21; Harris, 64.

38. Sam Zolotow, "Plans for 'Reuben, Reuben,'" *NYT* (October 17, 1955); MB to Robert Lewis, October 18, 1955; Lewis to MB, October 20, 1955, MBP.

39. MB to Robert Lewis, October 21, 1955; Lewis to MB, October 22, 1955, MBP.

40. "'Reuben' Folding For 250G Loss," *Variety* (October 19, 1955); George Clarke, "Miss Crawford Accepts Inevitable, Closes Play," *Boston Record* (October 19, 1955) ("one of"); Walter Winchell, "Memos of a Girl Friday," *Daily Mirror* (October 21, 1955); Dorothy Kilgallen, "Fingers Pointed After a Flop," *Journal-American* (October 21, 1955).

41. MB to MC, October 20, 1955, MCC.

42. MB, notes, November 10, 1955, MBP.

43. MB to DD, February 28, 1956, October 9, 1957, DDC.

44. Walt Kelly, undated *Pogo* comic strip, MBP.

45. LB to DD, January 24, 1956, DDC; CD to author, April 12, 2010; MB to MC, June 30, 1956, MCC.

46. Wilfrid Mellers, "Music, Theatre and Commerce: a note on Gershwin, Menotti and Marc Blitzstein," *Score* 12 (June 1955): 76; GOR, 381–390 (the observation, "While less operatic than *Regina*, it is also less tied to standard commercial forms than the songs of *Cradle*," 389, borrows from Mellers).

47. Ken Mandelbaum, *Not Since Carrie: Forty Years of Broadway Musical Flops* (New York: St. Martin's Press, 1991), 123–125; Ethan Mordden, *Coming Up Roses: The Broadway Musical in the 1950s* (New York: Oxford University Press, 1998), 136–137.

48. LB, remarks, "Composers' Showcase: A Marc Blitzstein Tribute In Honor of His Eightieth Birthday," archival tape (April 28, 1985), courtesy of Brent Oldham.

49. Tommy Krasker, liner notes, *I Wish It So* (Elektra Nonesuch 9 79345-2, 1994); Jamie James, "How Many Great American Operas? One for Sure," *NYT* (October 4, 1992); Stephen Sondheim, interview with author, June 12, 2011, to author, June 14, 2011 (with respect to Bernstein, Sondheim intriguingly contended that Paul Bowles exerted a far more decisive influence).

50. "Brotherhood of All Mankind Is Stressed At Meeting of the Interracial Fellowship," *NYT* (April 8, 1946); John Briggs, "All Races and Faiths: Interracial Fellowship Chorus Rounds Out Ten Years of Devoted Activity," *NYT* (April 28, 1957); "The Interracial Fellowship Chorus," *Crisis* 64/5 (May 1957): 309, 318.

51. GOR, 417.

52. MB to MC, September 28, 1956 ("a dream"), September 29, 1956 ("indefinitely"), October 12, 1956 ("an immense"), MCC; MB to DD, September 15, 1956 ("I had forgotten," "I am surrounded"), DDC.

53. DD, Journals, January 17, 1957 (for pneumonia), DDC; GOR, 420, also mentions a hernia operation.

54. MB, program notes, *This Is the Garden* (May 5, 1957), MBP; MB to DD, September 15, 1956, DDC.

55. MB, notes, including June 9, 1956, July 27, 1956, July 29, 1956, MBP.

56. Justin Smith, "Grand Oratorio with a Social Conscience: Marc Blitzstein's *This Is the Garden* (1957)," *Choral Journal* 49/8 (February 2009): 32–47; Eric Gordon, "Marc Blitzstein at 100," *Jewish Currents* 59/1 (January–February 2005): 28–29.

57. Smith, 40–41; LEH, 462 (for LB's response to the cantata, according to DD); MB to DD, October 9, 1957, DDC.

58. MB, notes, July 29, 1956, MBP.

59. Briggs.

60. Reviews of *This Is the Garden* by Jay S. Harrison, *NYHT*; Harriett Johnson, *Post*; Howard Taubman, *NYT* (all May 6, 1957); MB to DD, October 9, 1957, DDC.

61. R.S. [Robert Sabin], "Marc Blitzstein Writes Cantata," *Musical America* 78/9 (August 1958): 26; COP, 143–144.

62. Dan Perkins to author, May 11, 2010; JoAnn Rice, interview with author, July 4, 2010; Smith, 34.

Chapter 21

1. John Houseman, *Front and Center* (New York: Simon & Schuster, 1979), 330; MC intimated to Houseman in 1949 that MB had not liked his work on the 1946 musical *Lute Song* [MC to John Houseman, ca. November 1949], courtesy of SD.

2. Michael Anderegg, *Orson Welles, Shakespeare, and Popular Culture* (New York: Columbia University Press, 1999), 35; Jacob Gordin, *The Jewish King Lear: A Comedy in America* (New Haven, CT: Yale University Press, 2007); Houseman, 328.

3. MB to MC, August 2, 1950, MCC.

4. MB to John Houseman, August 25, 1950; Houseman to MB [1950], MBP.

5. MB to John Houseman, August 25, 1950.

6. Houseman, *Front*, 343.

7. Reviews of *King Lear* by Brooks Atkinson, *NYT*; Howard Barnes, *NYHT*; John Chapman, *Daily News*; Robert Coleman, *Daily Mirror*; Thomas R. Dash, *Women's Wear Daily*; John McClain, *Journal-American*; Arthur Pollock, *Daily Compass* (all December 26, 1950); Bron. [Arthur Bronson], *Variety* (December 27, 1950); Wolcott Gibbs, *New Yorker*, and *Cue* (both January 6, 1951); *Newsweek* (January 8, 1951); John Mason Brown, *Saturday Review* (January 20, 1951); Harold Clurman, *New Republic* (January 22, 1951).

8. MB to MC, December 15, 1950, MBP.

9. Margaret Harford, "Stirring 'King Lear' Presented at UCLA," *Los Angeles Times* (June 9, 1964); "Mathis, Folk Singers Billed at Greek Theater," *Los Angeles Times* (July 19, 1964); reviews of *King Lear* by Clive Barnes, *Post*, and Leo Seligson, *Newsday* (both April 10, 1978).

10. Barbara Leaming, *Orson Welles: A Biography* (New York: Viking, 1983); Frank Brady, *Citizen Welles: A Biography of Orson Welles* (New York: Scribner, 1989); Anderegg.

11. MB, "Volpone" and "King Lear" (both dated October 30 [1955]), MBP.

12. Orson Welles to MB, November 8, 1955, December 4, 1955, MBP; Louis Calta, "Welles to Star for City Center," *NYT* (November 22, 1955); Bert McCord, "Welles and Gleason Will Co-Star in 'Volpone,'" *NYHT* (December 1, 1955) (the notion of *Twelfth Night* as a second bill also came to naught); "A Streamlined 'Lear,'" *NYHT* (December 6, 1955); Louis Calta, "Orson Welles Drops 'Volpone,'" *NYT* (December 8, 1955).

13. Orson Welles to MB, April 12, 1956, MBP; "Welles to Make Television Films," *NYT* (April 9, 1956).

14. Otto Luening, *The Odyssey of an American Composer: The Autobiography of Otto Luening* (New York: Scribner, 1980), 549–561; MB to Bruce Becker, November 24, 1955, MBP.

15. Reviews of *King Lear* by Brooks Atkinson, *NYT*; John Chapman, *Daily News*; William Hawkins, *World-Telegram and Sun*; Walter F. Kerr, *NYHT*; John McClain, *Journal-American*; Richard Watts Jr., *Post* (all January 13, 1956); Land., *Variety* (January 18, 1956); Wolcott

Gibbs, *New Yorker* (January 21, 1956); *Newsweek* and *Time* (both January 23, 1956); Henry Cowell, *Musical Quarterly* (April 1956).

16. Mel Gussow, "'Lear' Presented By Acting Company," *NYT* (April 10, 1978); Luening, 551; Lewis Funke, "Welles' Injuries Hurt City Center," *NYT* (February 1, 1956).

17. Ross Parmenter, "The World of Music: For the Star Singers," *NYT* (March 4, 1956).

18. [Irving Kolodin], program notes, *Lear: A Study*, New York Philharmonic (February 28, 1958); MB, "On 'Lear: A Study,'" MBP.

19. MB to MC, December 15, 1950, MBP; MB to DD, December 26, 1957, DDC; MB, "On 'Lear.'"

20. MB to DD, March 4, 1958, DDC; reviews of *Lear: A Study* by Jay S. Harrison, *NYHT*, and H.C.S. [Harold C. Schonberg], *NYT* (both February 28, 1958); Harriett Johnson, *Post* (March 2, 1958).

21. ROR, 193–207 (Rorem misremembered the "filched" gesture as involving a falling minor as opposed to a major third); see also a revised version of this essay in Ned Rorem, *Knowing When to Stop: A Memoir* (New York: Simon & Schuster, 1994), 312–323; Ned Rorem, interview with author, January 18, 2010.

22. MB to Ned Rorem, February 22, 1962, Ned Rorem Collection, LC; ROR, 193–207 (Rorem mistakenly writes "arty-farty," 201); MB, "On Two Young Composers," MBP; William Flanagan Jr., "The Riotous Garden of American Opera," *High Fidelity* 6/11 (November 1958): 44.

23. CD to author, January 13, 2010, January 15, 2010; LEH, 460.

24. John Houseman, *Final Dress* (New York: Simon & Schuster, 1983).

25. "Stage and Television Director Is Slain in Apartment in Boston," *NYT* (March 17, 1967).

26. Roberta Krensky Cooper, *The American Shakespeare Theatre: Stratford, 1955–1985* (Washington, D.C.: Folger Books, 1986), 54–55; reviews of *A Midsummer Night's Dream* by Brooks Atkinson, *NYT*; John Chapman, *Daily News*; Frances Herridge, *Post*, Miles Kastendieck, *Journal-American*, Herbert Whittaker, *NYHT* ("gay, amusing") (all June 23, 1958); Harold Clurman, *Nation* (July 5, 1958); Harriett Johnson, "Blitzstein's Music In 'Dream' Proves 'Such Sweet Thunder,'" *Post* (August 13, 1958); see also Stratford publicity material, MBP.

27. MB to AC, July 10, 1958, ACC; MB to DD, July 20, 1958, DDC; MB to A[rnold Arnstein], June 26, 1958, MBP; Houseman, *Final*, 140.

28. MB, notes, MBP.

29. Earle Hyman, interview with author, February 2, 2010; Barbara Barrie, interview with author, February 26, 2011.

30. Reviews of *The Winter's Tale* by Frank Aston, *World-Telegram and Sun*; Brooks Atkinson, *NYT*; Mark Barron, *Journal-American*; Frances Herridge, *Post*; Walter Kerr, *NYHT* (all July 21, 1958); Elem., *Variety* (July 23, 1958); Louis Calta, "Stage Designer Buys Two Plays," *NYT* (August 31, 1960).

31. For more on these songs, see William R. Diehl, *A Recital and Study of Eighteen Songs Based on Literature From Ten Plays of William Shakespeare as Set to Music by Selected Composers of Five Periods of Music History* (Ed.D. thesis, Columbia University, 1967).

32. New Music New York gave what it called the "world premiere" of the "Trio" on May 1, 2007, at Saint Peter's Church in New York, although according to Hyman and Barrie (interviews with author), the trio was performed at Stratford.

Chapter 22

1. MBH.

2. Walter Goodman, *The Committee: The Extraordinary Career of the House Committee on Un-American Activities* (New York: Farrar, Straus and Giroux, 1964); Richard M. Fried, *Nightmare in Red: The McCarthy Era in Perspective* (New York: Oxford University Press, 1990).

3. Sarah B. McCall, *The Musical Fallout of Political Activism: Government Investigations of Musicians in the United States, 1930–1960* (Ph.D. dissertation, University of North Texas, 1993), 92.

4. MBH; Dolores Scotti to Richard Arens, November 21, 1956, April 24, 1958, MBH.

5. Goodman; Fried; McCall; *Thirty Years of Treason: Excerpts from Hearings before the House Committee on Un-American Activities, 1938–1968*, edited by Eric Bentley (New York: Viking Press, 1971); K. Kevyne Baar, *Investigating Broadway: The House Committee on Un-American Activities Meets Members of the New York Theatre Community at the Foley Square Courthouse, August 15–18, 1955* (Ph.D. dissertation, Saybrook Graduate School and Research Center, 2006).

6. "Hearings before the Committee on Un-American Activities" (May 8, 1958), MBH.

7. CD to author, December 28, 2007 (for Soviet invasion); "Hearings."

8. Telford Taylor to Frances E. Walter, May 29, 1958; Walter to Taylor, June 3, 1958, MBH; MB, "Music and the People's Front," *Daily Worker* (April 13, 1938); John Houseman, *Final Dress* (New York: Simon & Schuster, 1983), 138–140.

9. MB to DD, July 20, 1958, DDC.

10. MB, FBI file, February 25, 1959, March 27, 1959, July 21, 1959, August 12, 1960, April 8, 1963, February 25, 1964.

11. Gregory Bossler, "Writers and Their Work: Joseph Stein," *Dramatist* 8/3 (January–February 2006): 6–11.

12. Joseph Stein, talkback (transcribed by author), *Encores!* (March 29, 2008) ("overwhelmed"); Joseph Stein to author, June 2, 2010 ("The earthiness"); Joseph Stein, "Notes on the Musical 'Juno,'" program book, *Juno*, MBP, also quoted in Elliot Norton, "O'Casey OK'd 'Juno' As American Musical," *Boston Daily Record* (January 6, 1959); Bossler.

13. Stein, "Notes"; Stein, talkback.

14. Stein, "Notes"; Stein, talkback; *The Letters of Sean O'Casey 1955–58*, Vol. 3, edited by David Krause (Washington, D.C.: Catholic University of America Press, 1989), 326, 331, 334 ("I know"); *The Letters of Sean O'Casey 1959–64*, Vol. 4, edited by David Krause (Washington, D.C.: Catholic University of America Press, 1992), 23 ("chance"), 27–28 ("very charming").

15. David Krause, *Sean O'Casey: The Man and His Work* (New York: Macmillan, 1960, 1975); Christopher Murray, *Sean O'Casey* (New York: Faber and Faber, 2000); Christopher Murray, *Seán O'Casey: Writer at Work: A Biography* (Ithaca, NY: McGill–Queen's University Press, 2004).

16. Sean O'Casey, *Juno and the Paycock*, in *Three Dublin Plays* (New York: Faber and Faber, 1998), 148.

17. O'Casey, 145–146.

18. Stein, talkback ("consummate"); Stein, "Notes" ("fascinated"); Stein, June 2, 2010; ("When"), in which the author states, at a distance of over fifty years, that he "talked to Marc well before I went" to England, although most sources of the time suggest otherwise, the April 1957 date provided by Blitzstein in Murray Schumach, "Enter: O'Casey's Juno, Singing," *NYT* (March 1, 1959).

19. MB to DD, October 9, 1957; MB to DD, August 24, 1956, DDC; "Hearings."

20. Sam Zolotow, "Glickman Is Out As 'Juno' Adapter," *NYT* (May 17, 1957); Stein, June 2, 2010; GOR, 426.

21. Joseph Stein and MB, *Juno*, original script (August 6, 1957, and August 11, 1957); Stein, "Notes"; MB to DD, October 9, 1957; MB to [James] Cagney, September 11, 1957, MBP.

22. Joseph Stein to Sean O'Casey, July 24, 1957, MBP; O'Casey, 117; Krause, *Letters*, Vol. 3, 601, 605; in this early script, Juno is a housewife rather than a working woman, and Mary no longer a striking worker but rather a shop employee, but Stein came back to O'Casey for the final script.

23. Stein and MB, 1-3-27.

24. MB, notes, MBP; Stein and MB, 1-2-11a, 2-5-35a.

25. O'Casey, 69, 81, 82, 119–120; O'Casey, lyrics, MBP; Krause, *Letters*, Vol. 3, 311–313; Stein and MB, 1-2-19a, 1-3-26a, 1-2-22c, 2-2b-14 (Blitzstein later revised some of these lyrics).

26. MB, notes, MBP.

27. MB, notes, MBP; Stein and MB, 2-2a-8c.

28. S.G. [Stanley Green], review of *Juno* original cast recording, *HiFi Review* 3/1 (July 1959): 72.

29. *Original Demo Sung and Played by Marc Blitzstein* (Box Office JJA 19772, 1982).

30. Krause, *Letters*, Vol. 3, 605, 629–630; *Letters*, Vol. 4, 23.

31. John F. Wharton, *Life Among the Playwrights: Being Mostly the Story of The Playwrights Producing Company, Inc.* (New York: Quadrangle, 1974); Schumach.

32. Krause, *Letters*, Vol. 3, 600.

33. MB, notes, August 4, 1958, MBP; Tony Richardson to MB, October 22, 1958, MBP; "Kober Completes Play Begun In '31," *NYT* (October 27, 1958); MB to Lina Abarbanell, January 8, 1961, MBP.

34. For a breakdown of orchestration responsibilities and fees, see Steven Suskin, *The Sound of Broadway Music: A Book of Orchestrators and Orchestrations* (New York: Oxford University Press, 2009), 447, which, in light of materials in the MBP, further would suggest that Bennett perhaps contracted his friend Philip J. Lang for help on three songs, two of which never made it to Broadway; MB's notes specify the strings as 5-3-2-2-1.

35. Krause, *Letters*, Vol. 3, 629–630, 651.

36. Regarding "My True Heart," by the time of the final script, Blitzstein changed Mary's line, in a coda not included in the Chappell edition of the song, "If you want me, take me now. I give you my true heart," to the less provocative "Now I've told you all I feel, I give you my true heart," as found in the cast album, with the much later Boosey & Hawkes edition restoring the original text.

37. Reviews of *Juno* by Richard L. Coe, *Washington Post and Times Herald* (January 18, 1959); Jay Carmody, *Washington Evening Star*, and Tom Donnelly, *Washington Daily News* (both January 19, 1959); Liz., *Variety* (January 21, 1959); GOR, 448–449; MB, "Notes from L. Hellman, advisor to Kings," MBP; see also Jay Carmody, "'Juno's' Big Need 'J.B.'s' Patience," *Washington Evening Star* (January 25, 1959).

38. Jo Sullivan Loesser, interview with author, June 13, 2011; reviews of *Juno* by Peggy Doyle, *Boston Evening American*; Cyrus Durgin, *Boston Daily Globe*; Elinor Hughes, *Boston Herald*; Melvin Maddocks, *Christian Science Monitor*; Elliot Norton, *Boston Daily Record* (all February 5, 1959); see also Cyrus Durgin, "Show Business Treatment Lavished on Irish Classic," *Boston Globe* (February 8, 1959), and Elinor Hughes, "'Juno' Holding at Shubert," *Boston Herald* (both February 15, 1959).

39. Arthur Gelb, "Circle in Square Lists 'Our Town,'" *NYT* (February 9, 1959); Sam Zolotow, "2 Producers Seek Star for Comedy," *NYT* (February 10, 1959); MB to MC, March 9, 1959, MCC.

40. Melvyn Douglas and Tom Arthur, *See You at the Movies: The Autobiography of Melvyn Douglas* (Lanham, MD: University Press of America, 1986), 104–105; Carol Easton, *No Intermissions: The Life of Agnes de Mille* (New York: Little, Brown, 1996), 365–367 ("difficult," "small"); MB to MC, March 9, 1959 ("inert," "bitch"), March 15, 1959 ("horror," "I met," "The last"), MCC; Trude Rittman, note, "First Sketch Dublin Night," and MB and Rittman, "Ballet" (February 18, 1959), Trude Rittman Collection, NYPL, courtesy of Daniel Batchelder.

41. Patrick Galvin, *Irish Songs of Resistance (1169–1923)* (New York: Folklore Press, 1956), 27; Sean O'Casey, *Collected Plays*, Vol. 2 (London: Macmillan, 1949), 235; Alfred Perceval Graves and Charles Wood, *Irish Folk-Songs* (London: Boosey, 1897), 67–71.

42. O'Casey, *Juno*, 146; Stein and MB, *Juno*, "final revised script," 2-5-31, MBP; program book, *Juno*.

43. Reviews of *Juno* by Frank Aston, *World-Telegram and Sun*; Brooks Atkinson, *NYT*; John Chapman, *Daily News*; Thomas R. Dash, *Women's Wear Daily*; Walter Kerr, *NYHT*; John McClain, *Journal-American*; Richard Watts Jr., *Post* (all March 10, 1959); Hobe., *Variety* (March 11, 1959); Kenneth Tynan, *New Yorker* (March 21, 1959); *Time* (March 23, 1959);

MB to MC, March 15, 1959, MCC. As presented on Broadway, the musical, set in Dublin in 1921, had a prologue and nine scenes in the first act, seven scenes in the second: Prologue. The street in front of the Boyle home. Early evening in summer. A group of Dubliners witness the murder of Robbie Tancred by British troops ("We're Alive"). Scene one. The Boyle home. Johnny Boyle, who has lost an arm in the struggle for independence, expresses anxiety over Robbie's death, while his sister Mary, a striking employee, expresses her hopes to her mother Juno ("I Wish It So"). Juno, a working woman, muses on a mother's lot ("Song of the Ma"). Scene two. Another street. Thinking Charlie Bentham a bill collector, four neighbors—Mrs. Brady, Mrs. Coyne, Mrs. Madigan, and Miss Quinn—steer him away from the Boyle home. Scene three. The street and Foley's bar. Some drinking companions sing a patriotic anthem ("We Can Be Proud"). Jack Boyle, an unemployed laborer, struts before his crony Joxer Daly and the other men at the pub ("Daarlin' Man"). Scene four. A park square. Jerry Divine, a union leader, pleads for the affection of Mary, his former girlfriend ("One Kind Word"). Scene five. The Boyle home. Juno and the shiftless Boyle bicker ("Old Sayin's"). Boyle reminisces about his fictitious sailor days with Joxer ("What Is the Stars?"). Bentham, a young attorney, informs the Boyle family that they are due to inherit a fortune, and Juno and Boyle look forward to a new life ("Old Sayin's," reprise). Scene six. Another street. The four gossips vent their problems ("You Poor Thing"). Scene seven. A square in the city. Johnny takes an evening stroll ("Dublin Night"). Scene eight. A park square. Evening, a few days later. Mary and Bentham express their love ("My True Heart"). Scene nine. The street. The Boyles celebrate their good fortune with their neighbors ("On a Day Like This").

Act II. Scene one. The Boyle home. Evening, a few days later. Juno and Mary entertain Boyle, Joxer, Bentham, and Jerry with a duet ("Bird Upon the Tree"). Scene two. A yard behind the house. Mrs. Madigan and other guests, including the tailor "Needle" Nugent, arrive for a party at which Boyle shows off his new gramophone ("Music in the House," including "It's Not Irish" and "The Liffey Waltz"). Mrs. Tancred passes by on her way to her son's funeral ("Hymn"). A member of the Irish Republican Army (IRA) commands Johnny's presence at a meeting the following evening, and Johnny vents his despair ("Johnny"). Scene three. A street. The four gossips note that Bentham seems to have deserted Mary and that the Boyles have not yet received their inheritance ("You Poor Thing," reprise). Scene four. The Boyle home. As Juno takes Mary to the doctor, Nugent and Mrs. Madigan come to collect their debts, and Boyle and Joxer quarrel. Juno tells Boyle that Mary is pregnant and that the child's father, Bentham, has fled, and Boyle informs Juno that Bentham mishandled the will and, moreover, that Mary is not to come home. Left alone with the furniture men who have come to reclaim the Boyles' furnishings, Johnny confronts two IRA men, who drag him away. Scene five. A park square. Mary reflects on her situation ("For Love"). Jerry offers Mary his love until he hears she is to have a baby ("One Kind Word," reprise; "For Love," reprise). Scene six. The Boyle home. Juno learns that Johnny's been killed ("Where?"). Juno and Mary prepare to leave for Juno's sister's farm ("Bird Upon the Tree," reprise). Scene six. The street and Foley's bar. As Juno and Mary depart, Boyle and Joxer carouse in a local pub ("Finale Act II," including "Daarlin' Man," reprise).

Some uncertainty exists with respect to both the first-act and second-act finales. In the original script, as the first act concludes, Johnny, unnerved by some diehards, rushes into the house, followed by Juno, but the final revised script gives no indication of any exits. Similarly, according to both the final revised script and the score reconstructed from original parts, the second act concludes without any reprise of "We're Alive" (although used, according to the score, for curtain calls), but the cast album reprises "We're Alive" at the show's conclusion, and Stein, June 2, 2010, recalled, although at a distance of more than fifty years, that the second-act finale included "We're Alive."

44. *"The Broadway Sound": The Autobiography and Selected Essays of Robert Russell Bennett*, edited by George J. Ferencz (Rochester, NY: University of Rochester Press, 1999), 234; MB to MC, March 15, 1959.

45. Krause, *Letters*, Vol. 4, 23–24, 27–28, 39, 52.

46. Robert Dolan to MB, March 28, 1959, MBP; *Hugo Friedhofer: The Best Years of His Life*, edited by Linda Danly (Lanham, MD: Scarecrow Press, 1999), 86; Oliver Rea to Lina Abarbanell, March 19, 1959, Lina Abarbanell Collection, NYPL.

47. *Juno* (Columbia Records OS 2013, 1959); S.G. [Stanley Green]; Virgil Thomson, "From 'Regina' to 'Juno,'" *Saturday Review* 42/20 (May 16, 1959): 82.

48. MB, Journals, July 16, 1959, July 22, 1959, MBP.

49. MB, Journals, July 17, 1959, MBP.

50. Lewis Funke, "'Fiddler's' Men at Work," *NYT* (December 13, 1964); Mel Gussow, "O'Casey's Juno Sings," *NYT* (May 21, 1976); Ken Mandelbaum, *Not Since Carrie: Forty Years of Broadway Musical Flops* (New York: St. Martin's Press, 1991), 313.

51. Joseph C. Koenenn, "Vineyard Stages a Love Affair," *Newsday* (September 19, 1991); reviews of *Juno* by Mel Gussow, *NYT* (October 31, 1992); Stephen Holden, *NYT* (November 6, 1992); LL, *Opera Monthly* (January 1993).

52. Mandelbaum, 312; Ethan Mordden, *Coming Up Roses: The Broadway Musical in the 1950s* (New York: Oxford University Press, 1998), 222; Marc Miller, "Pure Columbian Gold," *TheaterMania.com* (April 12, 2002); see also Sally Lou Todd, "*Juno*: A Study of the Nature of a Pre-Mature Revolution," unpublished essay (June 3, 1975), MBP.

53. Easton, 369, 454–457; Martha Johnson, interview with author, July 3, 2010; John Gruen, "Agnes de Mille: Eager as Ever," *NYT* (May 8, 1988).

54. Anna Kisselgoff, "De Mille's 'Informer': Of Love and Ireland's Pain," *NYT* (May 12, 1988); Lynn Garafola, *Legacies of Twentieth-Century Dance* (Middletown, CT: Wesleyan University Press, 2005), 396.

55. Jack Viertel to LL, May 22, 2007, December 27, 2007, December 28, 2007, January 16, 2008; Warren Carlyle to author, July 20, 2010.

56. Reviews of *Juno* by David Finkle, *TheaterMania.com* (March 28, 2008); Ben Brantley, *NYT* (March 29, 2008); Everett Evans, *Houston Chronicle* (April 6, 2008).

57. Mordden, 223.

Chapter 23

1. MB to MC, March 9, 1959, MCC.

2. MB to MC, March 15, 1959, MCC; MB to DD, May 20, 1959, DDC; Kathy Kienholz to author, August 19, 2010.

3. Aaron Copland and Vivian Perlis, *Copland Since 1943* (New York: St. Martin's Press, 1989), 281.

4. Patricia Bosworth, "Rebel with a Purse," *Vanity Fair* 484 (December 2000): 250–266.

5. MB to Anna Blitzstein, June 15, 1959, MBP ("dream"); MB to DD, June 29, 1959, DDC ("the great"); MB, Journals, MBP ("so"); GOR, 459, claims that Blitzstein "boiled down the purpose of his trip to these motivations: '1) Make money, 2) Try to be your wish-fulfillment homosexual self, 3) Combine the two,'" but this undated note scribbled in his journals (which includes a fourth, somewhat undecipherable comment), appears among jottings made during his trip to the Venice Biennale in 1961; moreover, heading these jottings "Motivations of?" he left no clear context for these remarks, although the words "Rocco e i suoi fratelli," written above these notes, suggests that he might have had in mind with respect to them Luchino Visconti's 1960 film of that name.

6. MB, Journals, MBP; MB to Morris Golde [summer 1959], MB–Morris Golde Correspondence, Music Division, LC ("poor, coy," "adorable").

7. MB to Ned Rorem, August 6, 1959, Ned Rorem Collection, LC; MB to DD, September 30, 1960, DDC; Augustin Souchy, *Sacco und Vanzetti: Zwei Opfer Amerikanischer Dollarjustiz* (Berlin: Der Syndikalist, 1927), MBP ("au souvenir de notre premiere rencontre, June, 1959").

8. MB, notes for *Horizon* and *Saturday Evening Post*, articles [1959], MBP.

9. MB, "Music's Other Boulanger," *Saturday Review* 43/22 (May 28, 1960): 60.

10. BLI; MB to JD, April 4, 1962, MBP.

11. MB, "On The Threepenny Opera," *Musical Show* (October 1962): 2.

12. John Gruen, *Close-Up* (New York: Viking Press, 1968), 167–168 (and Gruen, "Conversation with Marc Blitzstein," a slight variant, LHC) ("because of their," "I would").

13. MB, notes, October 26, 1959, MBP; Mary Rodgers, interview with author, July 24, 2010.

14. Rodgers, interview.

15. Seymour Peck, "Lillian Hellman Talks of Love and 'Toys,'" *NYT* (February 21, 1960); Lillian Hellman, *Toys in the Attic* (New York: Random House, 1959, 1960), 62.

16. Hellman, 8, 11, 43, 85–86, 104.

17. *Bayou Ballads: Twelve Folk-Songs From Louisiana*, texts and music collected by Mina Monroe and edited with the collaboration of Kurt Schindler (New York: G. Schirmer, 1921).

18. Reviews of *Toys in the Attic* by Frank Ashton, *World-Telegram and Sun*; Brooks Atkinson, *NYT*; Walter Kerr, *NYHT*; John McClain, *Journal-American*; Robert Coleman, *Daily Mirror*; Richard Watts Jr., *Post* (all February 26, 1960); Kenneth Tynan, *New Yorker* (March 5, 1960); Robert Brustein, *New Republic* (March 14, 1960); Harold Clurman, *Nation* (March 19, 1960); Bruce Bohle, *Theatre Arts* (May 1960).

19. Ross Parmenter, "The World of Music," *NYT* (December 13, 1959).

20. MB, Journals, February 11, 1960, MBP; MB to DD, September 30, 1960, DDC.

21. Don Ross, "Opera Being Done on Sacco-Vanzetti," *NYHT* (February 26, 1960); "Opera—Strange Venture," *Newsweek*, and "A Hell of a Noble Story," *Time* (both March 7, 1960); MB, "The Sacco-Vanzetti Opera Commission" (letter to the editor), *NYHT* (March 9, 1960).

22. Constance Askew to MB, February 1960; Mary Weaver to MB, March 1, 1960; Gardner Jackson to MB, March 16, 1960, MBP.

23. [William F. Buckley Jr.], "The Week," *National Review* 8/11 (March 12, 1960): 157–158; George E. Sokolsky, "'Sacco and Vanzetti' On the Met Stage?" *Journal-American* (March 30, 1960); Edward B. Simmons, "Composer Long Tied to Red Fronts," *New Bedford Standard-Times* (March 29, 1960); George E. Sokolsky, "These Days," *Daily Kennebec Journal* (April 23, 1960); Athan G. Theoharis, "FBI Files, The National Archives, and the Issue of Access," *Government Publications Review* 9/1 (January–February 1982): 30–31; see also Maria Cristina Fava, *Marc Blitzstein's* Sacco and Vanzetti *and the Rhetoric of McCarthyism* (M.A. thesis, Bowling Green, 2002).

24. "Sacco-Vanzetti Case: New Interest in an Old Issue," *U.S. News and World Report* 49/4 (July 25, 1960): 79–81; "Music Unit Attacks Opera by Blitzstein," *NYT* (September 2, 1960) ("Mr. Blitzstein avows"); "Soapbox Opera," *Boston Herald* (September 8, 1960); Sokolsky, "These Days" ("whether or not"); MB, Journals, March 28, 1960, MBP; Anthony Bliss, quoted by B. A. Prince to Francis E. Walter, April 13, 1960, MBH ("We do not").

25. Ned Rorem, *Setting the Tone: Essays and a Diary* (New York: Coward-McCann, 1983), 230–231; David Stimer to MB, May 8, 1959, MBP; MB to DD, September 15, 1959, DDC; Alice Esty to MB, June 8, 1959, June 16, 1959, MBP.

26. Richard Wilbur to MB, June 4, 1959, MBP; Wilbur, interview with author, October 16, 2011.

27. MB to Alice Esty and David Stimer, August 19, 1960, MBP.

28. LB, "Marc Blitzstein Remembered," program, Marc Blitzstein Memorial Concert (April 19, 1964), LBC; MB, notes, May 28, 1960, MBP.

29. Eric Salzman, "Alice Esty Offers Song Recital Here," *NYT* (March 14, 1961); Martin Bernheimer, "Alice Esty Sings at Carnegie Recital Hall," *NYHT* (March 14, 1961).

30. DD, Journals, November 8–9, 1960, DDC; ROR, 200.

31. MB to Anna Blitzstein, November 20, 1960, MBP; MB to AC, December 11, 1960, ACC; MB to JD, December 2, 1960, MBP.

32. "Symposium on the Marc Blitzstein/Leonard Lehrman *Sacco and Vanzetti*" (August 18, 2001): http://www.ljlehrman.artists-in-residence.com/articles/operajournal2.html ("My major").

33. MB to Anna Blitzstein, December 6, 1960 ("so theatrical"); MB to MC, January 12, 1961 ("dull"), MBP; MB to DD, February 11, 1961, March 7, 1961, DDC.

34. MB to Lina Abarbanell, December 20, 1960 ("good"); MB, Journals, January 5, 1961 ("stood"), MBP; MB to MC, January 12, 1961, MCC; MB to LB [late November 1960], LBC; MB to DD, April 25, 1961, DDC.

35. MB to JD, April 17, 1961, MBP ("bust"); MB to DD, April 25, 1961, DDC.

36. MB to JD, January 20, 1961 ("So THAT"), January 14, 1961 ("so students"), February 18, 1961 ("The same," "much either"); MB to Anna Blitzstein, January 22, 1961, MBP.

37. Ned Rorem, *Facing the Night: A Diary (1999–2005) and Musical Writings* (New York: Counterpoint, 2006), 160–161; "Ned's World," *Out* 9/5 (November 2000): 114.

38. MB to Morris Golde, April 27, 1961, May 12, 1961, May 20, 1961, MB–Morris Golde Correspondence, Music Division, LC; MB, Journals, May 19, 1961, MBP.

Chapter 24

1. MB to Adolfo Valletri [November 1961], MBP ("Italiano atroce") (only English and Italian drafts of this letter, presumably sent, survive).

2. Richard A. Kimball to MB, May 25, 1961; MB, Journals, October 9, 1961; Edward F. D'Arms to MB, November 7, 1961; MB to D'Arms, November 8, 1961, MBP.

3. Elizabeth Ames to MB, November 10, 1961, November 20, 1961; MB to JD, April 4, 1962, MBP; Wallace Fowlie, *Sites: A Third Memoir* (Durham, NC: Duke University Press, 1987), 93–94.

4. Tino Balio, "Wisconsin Center for Film and Theater Research," *Special Collections* 1/1 (Fall 1982): 65–74; Robert H. Hethmon to MB, March 17, 1961, WHS.

5. Robert H. Hethmon, "Field Report," October 15–23, 1961; Hethmon to Fred H. Harrington, October 25, 1961, WHS.

6. Robert H. Hethmon to Fred H. Harrington, April 2, 1962, WHS; MB to MC, February 7, 1962, MCC.

7. Robert James Dietz, *The Operatic Style of Marc Blitzstein in the American "Agit-Prop" Era* (Ph.D. dissertation, University of Iowa, 1970); TAL.

8. "An Exchange of Ideas" and David Ben-Gurion, "Dialogue IV: The New Challenge," *Congress Bi-Weekly* 29/12 (September 24, 1962): 3, 43–51; Douglas Little, "The Making of a Special Relationship: The United States and Israel, 1957–1968," *International Journal of Middle East Studies* 25/4 (November 1993): 563–585; "U. S. Jews Dispute Ben-Gurion on Israeli Ties," *NYT* (June 15, 1962).

9. MB, Journals, MBP.

10. "Dialogue III: Jews in the Creative Arts," *Congress Bi-Weekly* 29/12 (September 24, 1962): 32–43.

11. "Dialogue III," 37–38; as sometimes the case with certain proper names, Blitzstein in his personal papers often chose not to capitalize "Jew" and "Jewish."

12. MB, Journals, MBP; A. Mann, "Hamifletset haksumah hazrah lithiyah," *D'var Hashavuah* (August 3, 1962), MBP (Blitzstein apparently referred to himself as having "political socialist ideas" ["deotav hapolitiyot hasozialistiyot"]).

13. MB, Journals, MBP.

14. MB to JD, June 18, 1962, MBP; Helga Dudman, "Sacco and Vanzetti at Beit Yannai," *Jerusalem Post* (August 26, 1962).

15. Meyer Weisgal to MB, July 4, 1962; Dudman; MB to JD, July 17, 1962 ("joined"), July 26, 1962 ("practically cried," "I feel"), August 7, 1962 ("the most"); MB to Anna Blitzstein, July 26, 1962, MBP.

16. MB to JD, June 2 [possibly 22], 1962 ("dreadful," "dream"), June 18, 1962 ("beyond," "stupendous"); MB, Journals, August 12, 1962, MBP.

17. MB to JD, June 18, 1962, MBP; MB to Morris Golde, August 9, 1962, MB–Morris Golde Correspondence, Music Division, LC.

18. MB to JD, June 18, 1962 ("of course"), June [possibly July] 11, 1962 ("everyone"), MBP; MB to MC, July 1, 1962, MCC ("Nobody").

19. William C. Fels to MB, February 14, 1962; Harry W. Pearson to MB, May 11, 1962, MBP.

20. MB, notes, MBP; Sheilah Marlowe, "Marc Blitzstein of Philadelphia: Bennington's Playwright-in-Residence," *Bennington Banner* (October 11, 1962).

21. MB, notes, instructors' midterm and final reports; MB, memo, October 10, 1963, MBP.

22. MB, memo; Meryle Secrest, "He Doesn't Mind Being in Shadow," *Washington Post* (May 14, 1963); Reed Wolcott to MB, May 4, 1963, October 7, 1963, MBP; Laurence Hyman, "Death of a Genius," *Berkshire Eagle* (February 1, 1964).

23. Janna Malamud Smith, *My Father is a Book: A Memoir of Bernard Malamud* (New York: Houghton Mifflin, 2006), 181–182.

24. MB to DD, January 11, 1963; Alden Nash to LH, February 14, 1964, MBP.

25. MB, marginalia, ISCM program (January 25, 1963), MBP.

26. MB to DD, December 3, 1962, September 14, 1963, DDC; Jean Dalrymple to MB, May 3, 1963; Wilfrid Mellers to MB, July 2, 1963, MBP.

27. Harry K. Mansfield to MB, February 14, 1963, February 19, 1963; MB to Mansfield, March 3, 1963, Chapelbrook Foundation Records, Five Colleges Libraries.

28. MB to Morris Golde, November 17, 1963, MB–Morris Golde Correspondence, Music Division, LC; MB to DD, September 14, 1963, DDC; Dudman ("The world"); see also Caryn Levy, "College Program to Honor Late Teacher Marc Blitzstein," *Bennington Banner* (June 3, 1964).

29. MB to DD, November 5, 1963, DDC ("beautiful"); MB to JD, November 9, 1963 ("shenanigans"); MB to his family, November 22, 1963 ("cushy"), MBP.

30. MB to JD, December 3, 1963 ("atavistic," "personal"), December 11, 1963 ("who smokes"), December 13, 1963 ("intellectually"); MB to Anna Blitzstein, December 5, 1963 ("As to"), December 12, 1963, MBP; Bernard Malamud, tribute to MB, *Proceedings*, second series, 15 (New York: American Academy of Arts and Letters and the National Institute of Arts and Letters, 1965), 457; GOR, 523 ("despondent").

31. MB to LB, December 19, 1963, LBC; Deborah Martinson to author, August 25, 2010. Here is the dream in its entirety:

DREAM. (December 19, 1963, 6.15 A.M., just before awakening). It seemed to be the "new" Philadelphia, in time of a great convention or something: people milling about, doing silly convention-like things. I remember thinking this wouldn't after all be a bad place to live *now*, with the combination of new boulevards and old Georgian architecture. Lillian [Hellman] came by, and rescued me from the crowd in her limousine—with chauffeur. We landed in my bedroom suite at some posh hotel. Arthur Kober appeared; and the two of them went into a long, presumably comic (distasteful to me, I recall) session of making-fun-of-luxury-while-enjoying-it; other subjects were touched on (can't remember), all sardonic, some spiteful. The bedroom door opened (by this time Lillian was stretched out on the bed, fully clothed, resting). In came what seemed to be Lil's "duenna"—a youngish girl in red, hair parted in the middle; mousy, complaisant; and a huge beautiful thirty-year-old negress. The latter came directly to Lillian, sat on the bed beside her, and started to smooch, rubbing her nose, mouth and chin over L.'s face. The mood abruptly changed; I heard gasps, cries and saw a kind of battling-fumbling; I thought they were quarreling. But it was L. who had taken the initiative, and over the protests of the negress, she began to draw out the woman's right breast from her brassière, the woman saying "no no" all the time. Finally the breast was out and exposed; the woman near to tears. Lillian: "But it's *wonderful*, Jerry; I *like* it!" Then she said something (words garbled here) about the nipple resembling a man's "thing." And as I looked, I saw that indeed it was like a tiny circumcized prick; dark of course, but with a blond-flesh tip.* Arthur Kober and the other girl had been silent, out of the picture, all this time. Then they all left; and as the girl in red went out the door, I said something reassuring to her, such as she must be used to this kind of thing, and would recover as always. I closed the door behind them;

and woke up. *This part is the most obviously autobiographical; but then I guess all of it is. Lillian for example is probably someone else. The negress resembled Mme. Calvert, here at Fort-de-France's Office de Tourisme; but much comelier, and not so fat.

32. Beth Martin, interview with author, June 12, 2011; Edward Applebaum, interview with author, June 12, 2011.

33. Irene Diamond to MB, December 5, 1963, December 31, 1963, courtesy of Carolyn Erskine (MB's grandniece); MB to Rudolf Bing and John Gutman (undated draft, catalogued with *Sacco and Vanzetti* materials); Gutman to MB, January 4, 1964, MBP.

34. MB to Anna Blitzstein, January 12, 1964, January 18, 1964, MBP.

35. GOR, 526, states that MB was found between three and four in the morning, although the local press, "Agression nocture à Ste-Thérèse," [Martinique] *L'information* (January 23, 1964), reported the time of discovery as 6:30 A.M.; see also "A la suite d'une agression le compositeur américain Marc Blitzstein décède à l'hôpital," *L'information* (January 28, 1964).

36. GOR, 526–527; William B. Milam, interview with author, October 1, 2010.

37. William B. Milam to JD, January 22, 1964, MBP; "3 Sailors Arrested in Death of Composer Marc Blitzstein," *Philadelphia Evening Bulletin* (January 25, 1964).

38. GOR, 155; David A. B. Murray, "Homosexuality, Society, and the State: an Ethnography of Sublime Resistance in Martinique," *Identities* 2/3 (January 1996): 252, 269.

39. Ned Rorem, *Knowing When to Stop: A Memoir* (New York: Simon & Schuster, 1994), 313; GOR, 527. Researching *Reuben Reuben* and *The Threepenny Opera*, Blitzstein ostensibly read a passage about a notorious nineteenth-century New York saloon, McGlory's, that uncannily prefigured his own demise, its author stating that "it was not unusual to see a drugged and drunken reveller, his pockets turned inside out by the harpies who had fawned upon him but a few minutes before, dragged from a table by one of McGlory's capable bouncers and lugged into the street, where his pockets were searched anew by the lush workers. Frequently the latter stripped the victim of his clothing and left him naked in the gutter," Herbert Asbury, *The Gangs of New York: An Informal History of the Underworld* (Garden City, NY: Garden City Publishing, 1927), 187.

40. Eric Salzman, "Varese's Prophetic 'Deserts,'" *NYHT* (January 24, 1964).

41. "Marc Blitzstein, Composer, 58, Killed in Automobile Accident," *NYT* (January 24, 1964); Ross Parmenter, "Gift of Characterization," *NYT* (January 24, 1964).

42. "3 Sailors Accused of Killing Blitzstein," *NYT* (January 25, 1964).

43. Burton Lane to JD, January 24, 1964; I. F. Stone to JD, January 28, 1964; Bernard Malamud to JD, January 28, 1964; DD to JD, January 30, 1964; Helen Rosen to JD, January 29, 1964; Lollie and George Peckham to JD, January 29, 1964; Elizabeth Pond to JD, February 8, 1964, MBP.

44. "120 Attend Service Honoring Blitzstein," *NYT* (February 1, 1964); LH, notes, LHC; LH, "Marc Blitzstein Remembered," *NYT* (February 2, 1964); "Marc Blitzstein Remembered," program, Marc Blitzstein Memorial Concert (April 19, 1964), LBC.

45. Alan Rich, "At Philharmonic Hall, Loving Tribute to the Memory of Marc Blitzstein," *NYHT* (April 20, 1964).

46. Reviews of the Marc Blitzstein memorial concert by Harriett Johnson, *Post*, and Harold C. Schonberg, *NYT* (both April 20, 1964); Leighton Kerner, *Village Voice* (April 30, 1964); Irving Kolodin, *Saturday Review* (May 2, 1964).

47. JD, "1964 Soviet-American Women's Conference," *Four Lights* 24/6 (June 1964): 1; CD to author, August 30, 2010; DD to JD, May 5, 1965, DDC; JD to LB, March 28, 1965, MBP.

48. "Marc Blitzstein Remembered," program, Marc Blitzstein Memorial Concert (April 19, 1964), LBC; Aaron Copland, "In Memory of Marc Blitzstein (1905–1964)," *Perspectives of New Music* 2/2 (Spring–Summer 1964): 6–7; LED; LB, *Findings* (New York: Simon & Schuster, 1982), 223–224.

49. Theodore Strongin, "A Missing Opera by Blitzstein Reported Found in Car Trunk," *NYT* (May 12, 1964); "Blitzstein Score in Auto 5 Months," *NYT* (May 13, 1964).

50. Levy; Smith, 182–183.

51. LB, tribute to MB, *Proceedings*, second series, 15 (New York: American Academy of Arts and Letters and the National Institute of Arts and Letters, 1965), 479–480; LB, *Findings*, 224–226; LB to NB, November 29, 1964, Nadia Boulanger Collection, Bibliothèque nationale de France, courtesy of Matthew Mugmon; Malamud, tribute.

52. "3 Convicted in Fatal Assault on Musician Marc Blitzstein," *Philadelphia Evening Bulletin* (April 1, 1965); GOR, 533; Milam, interview; CD, August 30, 2010; Blitzstein's death figured prominently in Truman Capote's story "Music for Chameleons," *Music for Chameleons* (New York: Random House, 1975, 1980), 3–12.

Chapter 25

1. John Gruen, *Close-Up* (New York: Viking Press, 1968), 166–167 (and Gruen, "Conversation with Marc Blitzstein," a slight variant, LHC); MB, notes, September 22, 1959, MBP.

2. MB, notes, including January 27, 1960, MBP.

3. Tom O'Connor, inscription, "Hearing before Judiciary Committee of Massachusetts Legislature on the Sacco-Vanzetti Case," MBP.

4. Robert H. Montgomery, *Sacco-Vanzetti: The Murder and the Myth* (New York: Devin-Adair, 1960); James Grossman, "The Sacco-Vanzetti Case Reconsidered," *Commentary* 33/1 (January 1962): 31–44; Francis Russell, *Tragedy in Dedham: The Story of the Sacco-Vanzetti Case* (New York: McGraw-Hill, 1962).

5. Lisa McGirr, "The Passion of Sacco and Vanzetti," *Journal of American History* 93/4 (March 2007): 1113, 1115; Robert J. Clements, "Letter from Rome: The Triumph of Sacco and Vanzetti," *Columbia University Forum* 4/4 (Fall 1961): 32–37; MB, notes, MBP; this period also witnessed, perhaps not coincidentally, renewed interest in other sensational cases from the 1920s, as suggested by the films *Compulsion* (1959), about Leopold and Loeb, and *Inherit the Wind* (1960), about the Scopes trial.

6. MB, notes, MBP.

7. LB, remarks, Marc Blitzstein Memorial Concert, archival tape (April 19, 1964), courtesy of Brent Oldham; MB, notes, January 6, 1961, MBP.

8. LEH, 493, 500; MB, notes, July 3, 1960 ("You know"); MB, marginalia, Ralph Colp Jr., "Sacco's Struggle for Sanity," *Nation* 187/4 (August 16, 1958): 65–70.

9. MB, notes, MBP; see also MB, *Marc Blitzstein and his Theatre Compositions* (Westminster Spoken Arts 717, 1956) (for being in Ben Shahn's "camp").

10. MB to Ned Rorem, June 29, 1960, Ned Rorem Collection, LC; MB to MC, May 29, 1960, MCC.

11. MB to Mordecai and Irma Bauman, January 29, 1961; MB to Irma Bauman, January 5, 1962 ("turning-point"), Mordecai Bauman Papers, Tamiment Library, NYU; MB to Lina Abarbanell, February 17, 1961, MBP; MB to DD, May 4, 1961, DDC; MB, notes, December 25, 1961, MBP ("break-through").

12. MB to LB, December 27, 1961, LBC; LED, 23; GOR, 485; Ann Thorne, interview with author, August 12, 2010.

13. Robert Leiter, "Mr. Vivid," *Pennsylvania Gazette* 82/5 (March 1984): 21–25 ("Marc couldn't"); John D. Shout, "The Musical Theater of Marc Blitzstein," *American Music* 3/4 (Winter 1985): 426; Maria Cristina Fava, *Marc Blitzstein's Sacco and Vanzetti and the Rhetoric of McCarthyism* (M.A. thesis, Bowling Green, 2002), 92–93; MB, notes, January 7, 1962 (for Grossman), February 8, 1963 (for Sinclair), MBP; MB to Michael Musmanno, June 24, 1963, Michael Musmanno Collection, Duquesne University; MB to MC, July 2, 1960, MCC ("down to").

14. MB to DD, September 14, 1963, DDC (for his plans to continue work on the opera).

15. MB, notes, June 18, 1960, MBP.

16. MB, "Notes on Characters," June 2, 1960, MBP; GOR, 499.

17. MB, notes, January 16, 1961, MBP ("balked").

18. MB, notes, February 14, 1963, March 2, 1963, MPB.

19. MB, notes, September 16 [1959] ("force"), June 20, 1960 ("were unequipped"), June 21, 1960 ("condone"), MBP; *The Letters of Sacco and Vanzetti*, edited by Marion Denman Frankfurter and Gardner Jackson (New York: Viking Press, 1928, 1930), 121, underlined by MB; for Sacco's and Vanzetti's relations to the Galleanists, see especially Paul Avrich, *Sacco and Vanzetti: The Anarchist Background* (Princeton, NJ: Princeton University Press, 1991).

20. MB, notes, December 6, 1961, MBP ("magnificent"); *Letters of Sacco*, 65.

21. MB, notes, September 1, 1960, MBP.

22. MB, notes, MBP.

23. "Transcript of the Symposium on Marc Blitzstein's Unfinished Opera *Sacco and Vanzetti*," *Opera Journal* 29/1 (March 1996): 30, 45; MB, notes, October 9, 1961, MBP.

24. BLI; Gruen, 170.

25. William Schuman to LB, January 27, 1964, William Schuman Papers, NYPL; LB, marginalia, S. H. M. Clinton to LB, March 18, 1980, LBC ("good deal"); LB, *Findings*, 224–226; Gruen, 171; Daron Hagen, interview with author, November 13, 2010; "Symposium on the Marc Blitzstein/Leonard Lehrman *Sacco and Vanzetti*" (August 18, 2001): http://www.ljlehrman.artists-in-residence.com/articles/operajournal2.html; LL, "Unifying the Cultural Left: Edith Segal, Emma Goldman, and the Completion of Marc Blitzstein's *Sacco and Vanzetti*," *Representing Sacco and Vanzetti*, edited by Jerome H. Delamater and Mary Anne Trasciatti (New York: Palgrave Macmillan, 2005), 91–100.

26. The manuscript copy of "With a Woman To Be" sent to the Metropolitan Opera seems to have disappeared, but the text as sung by Luigi Alva at the memorial concert incorporates some changes made in a very late surviving manuscript dated December 15, 1963, but not reflected in the published version, changes that perhaps make the aria even stronger: "apartament" instead of "apartment" (requiring a quarter and an eighth-note in lieu of a dotted quarter); "Then she stand up" instead of "She ask me in"; "Open up your mouth" instead of "Open up my mouth"; "You say you don't know,/You need time,/You must think" instead of "She say she don't know,/She need time,/She must think."

27. Joseph R. Pehrson, "Musical Clones?" and B.L.C. [Barry L. Cohen], "Whose Opera Is It Anyway?: Another Opinion," *New Music Connoisseur* 9/4 (August 17, 2001): 9–10; Melissa J. de Graaf, "*Sacco and Vanzetti* Resurrected: The Completion of Marc Blitzstein's Political Opera," courtesy of the author.

28. "Symposium" (for Lewis); Cohen; Pehrson; LEH, 519–520; see also YouTube for a posted videotape of the August 19, 2001, performance of *Sacco and Vanzetti*.

29. Joel Honig, "Dead Man Writing," *Opera News* 66/5 (November 2001): 88; "Storm of Protest" (letters to the editor), *Opera News* 66/8 (February 2002): 6, 8–9; LL, letter to the *New Music Connoisseur* 10/1 (Spring 2001): http://ljlehrman.artists-in-residence.com/NMCv10no1ltr.html.

30. "Storm of Protest," 8–9.

31. Jay S. Harrison, "Jay S. Harrison Covers the New York Music Scene," *Musical America* 84/5 (May 1964): 33–34.

32. MB to DD, September 14, 1963, DDC ("breather").

33. *Bernard Malamud: A Collection of Critical Essays*, edited by Leslie A. Field and Joyce W. Field (Englewood Cliffs, NJ: Prenctice-Hall, 1975), 10.

34. MB, notes, November 12, 1962 ("parable"), undated ("full"), MBP.

35. MB to LB, September 7, 1963, LBC.

36. Blitzstein used the text of "Idiots First" as originally published in *Commentary* 32/6 (December 1961): 491–496, and republished by the *Bennington College Bulletin* 30/4 (May 1962): 7–10, a version slightly different from the one published by Malamud in his collection *Idiots First* (New York: Farrar, Straus, 1963); in the earlier version, Ginzberg says, "That's how it goes," not as in the later publication, "That's how it goes in this country," as used by LL in his completion of the opera; note also that Blitzstein standardizes Mendel's "You bastard, don't you understand what it means human?" by adding "to be [human]."

37. MB, sketches and reduced score, *Idiots First*, MBP.

38. Malamud, "Idiots First," *Bulletin*, 10; MB, sketches, August 24, 1963, November 10, 1963. MBP.

39. TAL, 364.

40. LL, *A Musical Analysis of* Idiots First (M.A. thesis, Part II, Cornell University, 1975).

41. LL, *Musical*, 10.

42. MB to Anna Blitzstein, December 23, 1963, MBP; LB, remarks.

43. Harold C. Schonberg, "Music: Marc Blitzstein," *NYT* (April 20, 1964). For the edition of "Then" in MBS1, LL added a five-measure introduction derived from the song's final measures; and for "How I Met," he added an ending of a single staccato note along the lines of the 1964 concert premiere, whereas the song proper could be said to end some six measures earlier, at the fermata just before the "Lo stesso."

44. LB, *Findings*, 225.

45. LL to author, March 18, 2011 (for approval by family and friends).

46. See also YouTube for a posted videotape of a March 21, 1992, performance of *Idiots First* at New York University.

47. Reviews of *Idiots First* by David Sykes, *Ithaca New Times* (August 18, 1974); William A. Storrer, both *Opera News* (June 1976) and *Opera* (July 1976); Bill Zakariasen, *Daily News* (January 16, 1978); Peter G. Davis *NYT* (January 18, 1978); Leighton Kerner, *Village Voice* (January 30, 1978); Bernard Holland, *NYT* (March 21, 1992); Arlo McKinnon Jr., *Opera News* (June 1992); Michael Kowal, *Congress Monthly* (September–October 1992); Leighton Kerner, "The First Annual 'Village Voice' Obopies," *Village Voice* (June 19, 1978); ROR, 202–203.

48. Irving Kolodin, "In Memory of Blitzstein—Martinon," *Saturday Review* 47/18 (May 2, 1964): 25; for more on the thematic concerns of the late librettos, see TAL.

Conclusion

1. Dan Sullivan, "Theater: Blitzstein Words and Music," *NYT* (December 1, 1966); Gilbert Chase, *America's Music: From the Pilgrims to the Present* (New York: McGraw-Hill, 1955); MEL; H. Wiley Hitchcock, *Music in the United States: A Historical Introduction*, third edition (Englewood Cliffs, NJ: Prentice Hall, 1969, 1988); Charles Hamm, *Music in the New World* (New York: W. W. Norton, 1983); COP, 143–144.

2. BAL.

3. Susan Elliott, "A Commitment to Causes," *NYT* (October 9, 1988).

4. Eric Gordon, interview with author, September 12, 2010; Eric A. Gordon, "Marc Blitzstein at 100: A Renewal of Interest in a Dark Time," *Jewish Currents* 59/1 (January–February 2005): 28–29.

5. Reviews of Eric A. Gordon's *Mark the Music* by Don Shewey, *NYT* (July 16, 1989); Richard Dyer, *Boston Globe* (August 30, 1989); Brian Byrnes, *Kurt Weill Newsletter* (Fall 1989); Brian E. Drake, *Opera Monthly* (February 1990); Robert L. Kendrick, *Notes* (March 1990); LL, *Jewish Affairs* (March–April 1990); Arlo McKinnon Jr., *Opera News* (September 1990); Lawrence D. Mass, *Journal of Homosexuality* (1991); see also Gordon and LL, "Response and Rejoinder," *Jewish Affairs* 20/3 (May–June 1990): 2, 15, 19, 21.

6. Mass; Kendrick; for Jewish stylistic traits, see Jack Gottlieb, *Funny, It Doesn't Sound Jewish: How Yiddish Songs and Synagogue Melodies Influenced Tin Pan Alley, Broadway, and Hollywood* (Albany: State University of New York in association with the Library of Congress, 2004), 217–218; for alleged gay traits, see Nadine Hubbs, *The Queer Composition of America's Sound: Gay Modernists, American Music, and National Identity* (Berkeley: University of California Press, 2004), 155, which places Blitzstein among other mid-twentieth-century gay American composers who, the author asserts, cultivated "a tonal idiom self-consciously oriented to transparence, simplicity, and other perceived 'Frenchisms,'" an argument supported, in Blitzstein's case, by his admiration for Satie and Milhaud but

qualified by his closeness to such composers as Stravinsky, Prokofiev, Hindemith, Eisler, Weill, and Shostakovich.

7. John Warthen Struble, *The History of American Classical Music: MacDowell through Minimalism* (New York: Facts On File, 1995); Elise K. Kirk, *American Opera* (Urbana: University of Illinois Press, 2001); Joseph Horowitz, *Classical Music in America: A History of its Rise and Fall* (New York: Norton, 2005).

8. Peter Sculthorpe, "Some Thoughts about Marc Blitzstein," email to author, June 8, 2011.

9. John Jansson to author, April 30, 2011; Dori Parnes to author, March 27, 2011, April 8, 2011; Paul A. J. Oomens to author, March 27, 2011 ("superb"), March 29, 2011 ("economic crisis").

10. Virgil Thomson, "Not Quite an Opera," *NYHT* (November 1, 1949).

11. COP, 141–142; Michael Denning, *The Cultural Front: The Laboring of American Culture in the Twentieth Century* (New York: Verso, 1996), 285, 291; Ilka Saal, *New Deal Theater: The Vernacular Tradition in American Political Theater* (New York: Palgrave Macmillan, 2007), 7, 37, 111, 115; Eric Winship Trumbull, *Musicals of the American Workers' Theatre Movement—1928-1941: Propaganda and Ritual in Documents of a Social Movement* (Ph.D. dissertation, University of Maryland, 1991).

12. BAL.

13. MB, *Marc Blitzstein and his Theatre Compositions* (Westminster Spoken Arts 717, 1956).

14. MEL, 416.

INDEX